THE WES PENRE PAPERS: THE FIRST LEVEL OF LEARNING (PART 1)

WES PENRE

The First Book in
The Wes Penre Chronicles Series

PREVIOUS BOOKS BY WES PENRE:

NON-FICTION

Spiritual Handbook for the Twenty-First Century *(2013)*
Synthetic Super Intelligence and the Transmutation of Humankind:
A Roadmap to the Singularity and Beyond *(2016)*

THE ORION BOOK DUOLOGY:
The ORION Book Volume 1 *(2023)*
The ORION Book Volume 2 *(2023)*

THE STORY OF ISIS AND THE WAR ON BLOODLINES (2024)
SIMULATIONS AND THE WHEELS OF TIME
IN THE DEVELOPING WORLDS (2024)

FICTION
THE ISMARIL'S JOURNEY TRILOGY:
The Book of Secrets *(2021)*
The Underworld *(2022)*
Ismaril's Sword *(2023)*

Acknowledgement

I want to dedicate this book to all my wonderful friends, patrons, and forum members who have supported me through the entire writing process. Your support has been a massive inspiration for me.

A special dedication to the Lady of Fire, who personally encouraged and aided me with such enthusiasm. You know who you are. Your commitment is very much appreciated and has greatly helped me through the process of editing the material for this book.

Contents

INTRODUCTION TO THE WES PENRE PAPERS

"Scientific Theory, more often than not, is born of bold assumptions, disparate bits of unconnected evidence, and educated leaps of faith."

-- John Brockman, editor

What We Believe but Cannot Prove: Today's leading thinkers on science in the age of certainty.

I found Brockman's statement in one of Dr. A.R. Bordon's and J.W. Barber's essays, *Catastrophism, Exopolitics, and the Return of NI.BI.RU.: A Case For The Long-Term Or Extended View of Exopolitics* (from the "Journal of End Time Studies" Series). Both Bordon and Barber are scientists, but in an unorthodox and highly innovative way, as we shall see in the following Science Papers.

John Brockman, editor and publisher of EDGE, an organization of science and technology intellectuals, asked the question, "What do you believe to be true though you cannot prove it?" to several scientists for his book, *What We Believe but Cannot Prove: Today's leading thinkers on science in the age of certainty* (2006). What's most interesting is perhaps not the answers Brockman received, but the fact that the question was asked in the first place.

I believe it's imperative that when we research; whether it's science, metaphysics, so-called "conspiracy theories", our human origins, our present and future challenges as a human species, or anything else that can sometimes be hard to physically prove due to the nature of the studies, we very much need to use our intuition, and trust our perceptions of what is true and what is not. Also, intuition is senior to belief.

Most humans perceive themselves as living in a very solid, physical reality, where they have forgotten who they are and where they come from. Often when we make a statement of a nature which is not within the norm of physicality or current belief systems, we are still required to put physical evidence on the table, until it fits in with current norms. If we can't, what we say is often dismissed from beginning to end due to "lack of evidence", although it's impossible since the phenomenon is not physical in nature. Evidence is sometimes cognitive, downloaded from our Higher Selves, and often free from the paradigms of non-working belief systems already existing. This is the level at which great minds have worked through history. Often, they were not prophets in their time, but instead ridiculed, ignored, or even killed for thinking differently. Eventually, the world caught up with them, embraced their work, and started acting as if it had always been true; it became self-evident.

Not until mankind has learned that we are spirits in a body/mind complex (which in new advanced physics is called *biomind*) can we start operating on a higher level. In the meantime, we can only do our best to connect the dots as they were and come to conclusions that work for us as individuals and interconnected biominds, based on a combination of physical evidence and intuition, which in a true way can be said to be communication with the Highest Source[1].

Although we are all on an individual path in a Multiverse where everything is connected on a subquantum level, we are at the same time contributing our personal experiences to the collective consciousness and awareness as a human species on Planet Earth, and what one experiences affects the collective. In a broader perspective, humankind as a *collective experience* affects the rest of the Multiverse because everything is interconnected.

However, for an entire species, connected via a common genetic template, and through a collective, interacting *super-mind*, or Oversoul, to evolve into a higher state of consciousness, we need to be both teachers and students at the same time. There are many ways to share what we learn; one way, of course, is to share it with as many people we can through books like this, and another is to just use our increasing state of consciousness to affect our environment positively by just being ourselves. People around us will feel the change and eventually follow; perhaps slowly in the beginning, but faster as we go along. They, in their turn, will continue doing the same thing, with quicker results as we all progress. A third alternative is to do both the one and the two above. I have chosen to do the latter for the time being, knowing there will be a time, perhaps sooner than later, when alternative two will be my sole preference.

So, what has all this to do with science?

Actually, quite a bit. Maybe not so much with traditional science, but with the *New Very Advanced Science* that has developed over the last few decades; science that goes beyond quantum physics and takes us closer to the core of existence, which includes the soul/spirit, and acknowledges the

---

[1] More about the *Highest Source* in upcoming books in this series.

fact that we all are ONE, connected on a subatomic level with All That Is, which is the true nature of the Divine Creator.

The reader will notice that as a common thread through all the papers (at least in this first book in the series) is the alien presence on Earth today and in the past. I will also bring up the ET issue in detail when comes to those who hover in the near Earth space; why they are here, and what we should do with the disclosure issue. We will see that cutting edge science of today and the ET presence go hand in hand; they are quite interwoven.

I have chosen to present one specific scientific group I have connected with, which has opened up new avenues in the field of science; not only because they acknowledge the presence of a Prime Creator of our universe, but also because the reason they could study the higher realms of the universe and the Multiverse was *because* of the alien presence; these beings actually helped them develop this New Very Advanced Science, which they call *Life Physics*, resulting in *The Working Model* as opposed to the mainstream scientific *Standard Model.* Mind you, having help from extraterrestrials is nothing new. There are metaphysical sources, like the Pleiadians, the Ra Collective, and others, who claim that both Einstein and Nikola Tesla had help from those "not from here" in their research. The main difference is that the group I have connected with openly admits that ETs had more than a few fingers in what developed into the Working Model—a giant leap from Einstein's Theory of Relativity and David Böhm's quantum physics.

The sequel of Science Papers that are opening this website is going to be a big leap for many readers, but a necessary one. You will be taken on an amazing journey through a Multiverse which has been explored by rogue scientists for as little as 10-15 years or so[2]. It's probably going to be a very different experience from earlier experiences you may have had in your life; even if you have previously studied quantum mechanics, metaphysics, ufology, the Power Elite, the history of planet Earth, the Mystery Schools, or all of the above; this is still going to be new for you.

These Science Papers are introducing a new, very advanced physics, here presented in plain, intelligible English, or as close to it as possible. The Life Physics Group in California (LPG-C)[3] has, through something they call *ENS* (*Extension Neurosensing*), been able to map out the universe, its seven superdomains, with 11 dimensions. ENS is a new, advanced form of remote viewing, and how it works will be explained in more detail. Later in this first book, I will also show LPG-C's version of how this Universe was created, who created it, and possibly why.

We can't study science without bringing up the ET issue (extra-

---

[2] As of 2010, when this was written.
[3] https://www.facebook.com/LifePhysicsGroup/

terrestrials). We need to understand that not only do they exist (of course they do), but moreover, they are not only "out there" somewhere in the vast universe, *but they are also here now!* There are at least 118-120 alien species in near Earth space today that we know of, LPG-C claims, and many of them are living among us here on our very planet.

So, are they friendly? The answer is, of course, yes and no. We are all individuals, and all of us are both friendly and unfriendly at the same time. ETs are not different from us in that respect. We need, once and for all, to get rid of the labels "good" and "bad" aliens. There are no such things, only different imperatives. All species want to survive as a biokind (physical body) and biomind (body/mind) if they are physical beings; however, as a group they may have imperatives that are counter-survival to our own human collective, and we call that "bad" or "evil", but from their point of view it may be a way to survive, even if that means sometimes putting the human soul group in jeopardy. And in all species, except for those in the "hive mind" category, there are good and bad people. Before we learn more about ETs, there is the basic thing to understand: Most of them are just like us, only more intelligent and further advanced, technologically. Many of them even look like us.

In more than one way, ETs have saved us from extinction. As much as some of them have tampered with our DNA for their own reasons (which we will go into later), others have saved us from natural catastrophes, and we are not even aware of that these ETs exist. They have been silently working in the background. Of course, they are not here, doing this for us, just to be nice; they all have their reasons, which differ from species to species, but no matter imperatives, *most* ETs out there get along fairly well, and even trade on a galactic level, just like we do between countries here on Earth.

Contact with these near Earth space ET groups has already been made on a grand scale by LPG-C. They have communicated with ambassadors for different alien species, respectively, being temporarily stationed here close to Earth to, among other things, study our development. The representatives from all the ET races LPG-C are meeting with are "non-gov", meaning they are not represented by their own government, but are supposedly just "concerned members" of their particular species. This team of human scientists have listened to them, addressed the concerns we have as a human species, and the help we eventually may need to solve them.

Perhaps the most urgent matter in our time is to protect our biokind and claim sovereignty as a species. It is important to emphasize I am *not* a scientist or a member of the LPG-C, and I may not agree with all they have concluded, but their group is certainly interesting enough to look deeper into. One thing I have in common with them is that we both realize that humankind has been seeded by an outside intelligence, and genetically

4

engineered and tampered with by different alien races, in these papers called "creator gods" with a small "g", due to that they are not Gods at all, but very advanced ETs, although some of them have showed themselves off as Gods to the early humans, and others were worshipped as such although that was not their purpose. In the extension, we were genetically manipulated to become today's homo sapiens sapiens (the thinking man) by an ET race ages ago to be used as workers, or slaves, rather. They mixed their own mRNA/DNA with our previously existing one, and in certain terms, they have claimed ownership of us ever since.

Now, says Dr. A.R. Bordon, chief scientist of LPG-C, is the time for us to grow from adolescence to adulthood. To be able to do this, however, we need to understand the dynamics of what is happening around us right now, and who oversees our reality, how we are manipulated, and why. We need to become aware of who we are and claim ownership of our biominds.

One thing is certain: We need to grow up fast, and we're not doing it only by watching football and soap operas on TV.

According to Dr. Bordon, if we can get at least 3% of the world population to join in mind with common imperatives of what we want as a species, the ETs will take us seriously and give us what we ask for; sovereignty over our biominds, and ownership of Earth. This is what has come out from the discussions between LPG-C and ETs of the *LINK*, the contact group LPG-C are members of and who meet annually here on Earth, and sometimes off-planet.

I am not totally in line with what Dr. Bordon's group is suggesting when comes to the ET subject, either, as will be better conveyed in the following Levels of Learning. I think the view on the Multiverse by this rogue science group is very interesting and well worth the reader's consideration. Their so-called Working Model, presented in Chapters 1 & 2, is a huge expansion of the Standard Model.

So, let's start this book by looking at what LPG-C has to offer.

(**Disclaimer**: A final note before we start: The entire series of papers, from the *First Level of Learning* through the *Fifth Level of Learning* are my progressive work, built on my research between 2010 to 2015. Therefore, the reader must appreciate that they are following my personal "journey through the Multiverse," where one paper builds on the next, all the way through the last paper of The Fifth Level of Learning. Thus, the reader will find that the narrative content sometimes either change slightly over time or evolve into a higher level of learning. Wes Penre 2024)

PAPER 1:
EXPLORING THE UNUM, THE BUILDING BLOCKS OF THE MULTIVERSE
Wednesday, February 16, 2011 @ 11:50 AM

ENS (Extension Neurosensing)—A New, Advanced Form of Remote Viewing

For thousands of year mankind has been wondering about the Universe and what is "up there", or "out there". Just like us, our ancient ancestors did the same thing; they looked at the Sun, the moon, the stars, and the vast space, wondering, what is the purpose? In fact, the ancients probably knew more about this than the average person does today, which will be obvious to the reader after finishing this series of papers, but they still didn't know exactly how the Universe is constructed, how it started (except through myth), and what it would look like if we had the chance to view it from "outside" itself, through an "avatar".

The breath-taking truth is that now we can do this, thanks to Extension Neurosensing (ENS), which is an advanced form of Remote Viewing (RV).

RV is nothing new; it has been used by the Military and the Government for decades. Even private people are using it. The most well-known people in this field were members of the Church of Scientology, such as late Ingo Swann[4], Harold Puthoff[5], and Ed Dames[6] who most likely was a scientologist as well. I was myself a member of the church in the late 1980s[7], so I am a witness to that RV was used within Scientology with various success, although it wasn't officially called remote viewing; it

---

[4] http://en.wikipedia.org/wiki/Ingo_Swann
[5] http://en.wikipedia.org/wiki/Harold_Puthoff
[6] http://www.eddamesremoteviewing.com/
[7] I defected from the Church of Scientology in the early 1990s, due to disagreements with the new Church Management after the departure of L. Ron Hubbard, and haven't practiced Scientology since. However, the Church was a catalyst for me and a necessity and a springboard for me to start my own research. As always, when looking into a subject as large as Scientology, one needs to use discernment when picking out the diamonds from mundane, glimmering stones.

was called "exteriorization". The Military took the technology used in the church and brought it to yet another level.

However, aside from all that research, Life Physics Group in California (LPG-C), independently and without claiming any connection with any Military, religion, or Government bodies, has given a whole new meaning to RV. From having practiced this new science, they have mapped the Universe in a way that has never been done before, down to the lowest sub-quantum levels they can reach, through the dimensions, and are now even aware of what exists outside the 4 Dimensional space/time. It is fascinating because previously some of this information has only been available through metaphysical entities, channeled by, or otherwise connected with, human instruments/vehicles/bodies. Now, pioneers in modern science have discovered the same thing and expanded upon it to give us a more holistic picture of the Multiverse and its different levels of manifestation (LOMs).

In the first paragraph, I am using the word "outside" for simplicity, although there is no "inside" or "outside". In fact, the scientists at LPG-C have scientifically managed to prove that everything in the Multiverse (which is an infinite number of serial and parallel realities, originating in thoughts) is connected, and thus we can be (and are) in different places at the same time, while still staying put in what we perceive as our current bodies; our *home station*, if you will. Basically, we are living different lives, independent of each other, simultaneously, in different time periods on Earth, and even on other, different planets. Their research has also shown that we can make a replica of our mRNA/DNA setup and "teleport it" to another place in time while at the same time remaining where we started, e.g. in our home. This, as I will show later, will be extremely helpful in the not-so-far future when we start traveling over the Universe.

Sounds like science fiction? It sure does, but not only has LPG-C# known about this for years, but just recently, on January 31, 2011, *TechWorld* posted an article about Nobel Prize nominee, Dr. Luc Montagnier, who says that he and his team of scientists have discovered how to successfully teleport DNA from one place to another. Not only did it transport, but also made a replica of itself, so that the same DNA mockup existed simultaneously in two places[8]. This is a major breakthrough for human science, and the discovery also verifies what I have been told, that many alien races use this technique to travel through space and time; something we will discuss in a later paper.

---

[8] http://news.techworld.com/personal-tech/3256631/dna-molecules-can-teleport-nobel-prize-winner-claims/

Figure 1.1: Dr. Luc Montagnier

We live in extraordinary times. So much is happening so quickly. Not only have we advanced technologically, but time is also speeding up on personal, spiritual levels; we are quickly becoming more aware as human beings. Science and spirit are beginning to merge for the first time in eons; in the minds of men, they have been two separate things. But now, more and more people start to realize that everything is connected on a subquantum (sub-atomic) level. I am you; you are me; Earth is us, and so is the entire Universe. We are all ONE on the highest level. Not until science acknowledges the spirit, and the two are integrated to the extent that it becomes "common knowledge" can we really take a quantum leap into the future. This sounds like an impossible goal, but it is achievable.

In a nutshell, ENS works as follows (without going into the complex scientific jargons around it): A human being, applying this technique, lies relaxed in a resonance-inducing sarcophagus, while his vital energy thresholds are monitored. A *photonic body* (an avatar) is induced and through advanced technology and the person's own mental abilities, he is capable of neurologically "extending himself" wherever he wants; nearby, to the edge of the physical universe, or even beyond![9] Hence, the Physics Group has been able to open the doors of perception to explore nature and the universe in a manner that has never been possible before, or even been perceived as a possibility. By expanding on the research of scientists such as Albert Einstein and David Böhm[10], they have been able to accomplish getting astonishing results from this technique.

It has not been an easy task to get to the point where they have been

---

[9] A much more complex and detailed scientific description of how this works, including mathematical formulas, can be studied in *FOUNDATION REPORTS IN LIFE PHYSICS--Vol 1 No 1--COMPLETE* – *Review, January-June 2004* by Dr. A.R. Bordon, pp. 26..

[10] http://en.wikipedia.org/wiki/David_Bohm

able to decode and decipher their ENS experiences into a comprehensible and emergent picture. Now they have managed to do just that, and it has turned into something they call the Working Model. For them, it has been a rollercoaster ride of failure and success, lots of hard work, but for us, now presented with this model, it is like an exciting journey through the Multiverse, or the *Unum*, as they call it. When I was introduced to it, it certainly blew my mind, and I am confident it will be yours, too.

I wouldn't have been too thrilled if this technique was merely dependent upon technology and machines to work, because a machine is designed to do a certain task, and that's what it does. It doesn't do anything outside of what it is designed to do, is thus limited in its application, and can even be misleading. However, in this case, technology is only used to get the process started; it's the human being who does the job. It's nothing less but fascinating, as we shall see.

First comment that comes to mind regarding ENS is that if a human being extends himself/herself and starts experiencing things, it's a very subjective experience and not necessarily reliable. Because like Dr. Bordon of LPG-C# said, much of what they "see" or "perceive" on their journey in the Multiverse is hard to decode with the human mind; we are not yet set up to do that. This is why they have more than one neurosensor. When all neurosensors have gone on the same expedition, they write down their experiences without telling the others, and then they compare notes afterwards. Apparently, most of the time their experiences match quite well and sometimes they don't. But this is how their research moves forward, and eventually they can build some structure to it.

I would imagine they must be aware of the following: After having used different people to explore, it's still not 100% reliable, even if they all decode things similarly. They decode it as a biomind would decode something it doesn't totally comprehend, and that could be similar for all the human species, and still not be accurate. Also, after a while, the neurosensors start knowing each other and each other's interpretations, and this too colors the result; especially as the science group itself consists of a small clique of members. Despite this (and again, I can hardly even call myself a layman in the field), I believe that at least the majority of the Working Model is working. Dr. Bordon has also told me that this model has been confirmed by some alien species, while others have shown interest in learning more from us. Dr. Bordon is excited about that, because it shows, as he says, that we humans have something to contribute to the cosmic community and not just the other way around. I agree that we should be excited, albeit we have more to contribute to the cosmic society than even LPG-C is aware of, as we shall see much later on, in another paper. It's called the "Living Library". Also, it's my understanding that ENS and some of the principals of the Working Model were presented by ETs.

As I said in the *"Introduction to the Wes Penre Papers"*, science and religion need to merge. LPG-C is very aware of this, and that is exactly what they are doing with the Working Model. This is science which not only takes the existence of a higher consciousness into the equation but *bases it* upon its existence. This is the reason I got interested in their work, initially, but once I had dug into their material, I found that there was so much more to it, and I still have so much to learn about it, even on a layman's level.

I wouldn't even bother to write this paper if LPG-C didn't include "God", or "Source", or "All That Is", or the "Prime Creator" (many names for the same thing), in their equations. For the first time in eons, a group of alternatives, brilliant scientists have been willing to look at science as a combination of matter and spirit, realizing they are one and the same.

It should be mentioned as well that there are a few more alternative science groups out there who are doing a good job decoding reality, but I have decided to focus on our Californian group this time. Just recently, rogue scientist, Steven J. Smith, was most likely murdered due to what he was involved in (he was sporadically in contact with me close to his death, and he knew he was in danger; he actually told me that) (http://battleofearth.wordpress.com/2010/11/14/rogue-scientist-steven-j-smith-murdered/). So not everybody in high places, being it in the mainstream science community or the government, is thrilled over the new paradigms these alternative scientists come up with.

The Unum/Multiverse is ever-changing: In a fluid Multiverse, where everything is in motion and nothing forever remains solid, what is true today may not be true tomorrow.

The Idiomaterial Multiverse

I have here done my best to simplify LPG-C Working Model so people hopefully can understand it. I know the result is not perfect because when we are dealing with new concepts, we sometimes lack words and terms, and it's hard to know how to express them in writing. It's all explained in great details on their Facebook page (see footnote in the Introduction section earlier in this book), but its scientific language is impossible to understand for the layman; even highly educated people in other fields of learning can't understand it; even those with doctor's degrees.

However, Kurt Strzyzewski at the University of Wisconsin-Milwaukee[11] did a great job narrowing down all the science behind the Working Model to just a short essay, making it comprehensible for the common man, but it's still fairly complex. I am mainly going to use Strzyzewski's summary as

---

[11] http://www4.uwm.edu/search/whitepages/

a base for my own Science Papers and do my best to simplify the language even more. The reader may judge whether I succeed or not, so here we go:

> LPG-C uses the word Unum for Multiverse, and who knows, this may be the term we will use for the Multiverse in general in the future.

> All of creation is idiomaterial non-physical and physical thought/matter, life is organized by overfunctions, and the universe is one of seven superdomains.[12]

The above quote by Dr. A.R. Bordon of LPG-C describes the Working Model in just two sentences. If the reader afterwards wants to study the original essays (which is my advice; read the end notes for references in the following subsections), I strongly advise to first read this peeled-off version for better comprehension, because otherwise, this *is* a highly scientific subject and very complex. The Working Model tells us that the Unum is a natural, living system in itself and contains what we call the known 4 Dimensional Universe (length, width, height, depth and time), but is so much more than that. When a neurosensor is out of his/her body, exploring, they can expand beyond the physical universe and experience what is there without interfering with what is going on. Beyond the physical realms are six other domains, which can be classified as the realms of "ultimate causation", consisting of vacuum and plenum[13], quantum and sub-quantum[14],[15]. In the Working Model these 7 domains are all together called the 7 Superdomains, not to be confused with the 7 superuniverses in texts such as the Urantia Papers[16]. The dominating characteristic of the Superdomains is form giving, and thus the term Idiomaterial Universe was born. And us being mind/body, we are idiomaterial ourselves; thought creates matter, and there is no way to tell matter and thought apart.

Idiomaterial Life Physics not only has as its goal to describe the fundamentals of life through science but is also a guide for any body/mind/spirits encoded to do so; to explore the purpose of the Multiverse, experience its endless potentials and come to the realization

---

[12] © 2009, Dr. A.R. Bordon: *"ULTIMATE THOUGHT: Life in a Bicausal Universe"*, http://www.lifephysicsgroup.org/foundation-books02.html

[13] Plenum: "4. the whole of space regarded as being filled with matter (opposed to vacuum)." Ref: http://dictionary.reference.com/browse/plenum

[14] Quantum is equivalent to the atomic level of reality, while sub-quantum is the sub-atomic level. See Wikipedia for more detailed definitions.

[15] Much of the description of the Unum presented in this section is a simplified version of Dr. Kurt Strzyzewski's essay, *Introduction to Idiomaterial Life Physics*, June 2010. A copy can be ordered by contacting Wes Penre at wespenre2@gmail.com.

[16] Urantia Papers online: http://urantiabook.org/newbook/

that we all are connected. This goes for all body/mind/spirit complexes, who can access information containing such thought form. This thought form, we as biokind (biological entities) and biomind (biological entities, including mind/spirit), are accessed through something which in Life Physics is called the *T-Boundary*, short for Thought-Boundary. This is a superdomain of its own, providing us with the purpose to accomplish the above. I should add that not all life forms in the Unum are physical in nature; there are those who don't have bodies, or can create them as they go along, by accessing different dimensions, and these entities are of course also a part of the above encoding.

Now, let us start with explaining what happens when a baby is born here on Earth:

One of the first things which occurs is that we experience sensory input into the cortical brain and its comprehension of the *"Earth Model"* becomes natural. This set up model makes it possible for us to differentiate between different 4-space/time places and objects, and we can, over a short span of time, more easily grasp our earth reality. The ability to grasp our reality is based on our ability to process thoughts, which are manifested in the hologram experienced as earth reality, to which we now claim ownership and observership. Perhaps we can compare it with plugging into a new computer and starting it for the first time. Once it's booted up, files need to be indexed and installed, and browsers; necessary software needs to be installed as well, and certain downloads must be done before we can truly explore the computer world. However, once this is done, we're hooked up with everybody else who has a computer in the global network we call the Internet (Earth in our metaphor).

However, if we still use the above metaphor, someone who has not been indexed here on Earth will have different "software" and programs installed, on thought- and holographic levels, which do not correspond exactly with Earth index, and the thinking process may not be the same as if s/he was indexed on this planet. Therefore, reality in the Multiverse is highly subjective and always subject to change.

Seven Levels of Manifestation (LOMs)

Before we take the Grand Tour through the Unum/Multiverse, I will let Dr. Kurt Strzyzewski start us off:

> In 2001 the exploration of the Unum began at LPG through the use of extension neurosensing (ENS) technology. This technology allows for a human biomind to gather data and information and store it into the enteric brain[17], where it can then be properly

decoded and deciphered into sensorially intelligible information. A team of seven extension neurosensors led by Dr. A.R. Bordon began the arduous task of detecting, decoding and deciphering information into a comprehensible and emergent picture; the Working Model. It was realized early on that the human being's living matrix made it an ideal candidate for "tuning in" and directly accessing any aspect of a targeted natural process within the construct of the Unum. This detection process in which information in the memory of the Unum was directly accessed proved to be much easier than the laborious task of translating all accessed data and information into an accurate Working Model.

It therefore became necessary to not only blindly gather information but to use intellectual, critical and analytical reasoning to assign meaning to all gathered information...[18]

The Multiverse, says Dr. Strzyzewski, is in itself intelligent, seamless and completely connected on a sub-quantum level, something that's been taught in metaphysics for a long time. However, to more easily catalogue and conceptualize the Unum, LPG-C has developed the mathematical and gnosive (communication mind-to-mind) concept of "levels of manifestation" (LOM), which works in a downward order, from implication at its top to explication further down. This turns Nature into a seemingly endless range, where all LOMs coexist and interact on every level to form the Whole.

The LOM can be illustrated in a very simplistic form like here below:

---

[17] The enteric brain is buried around our gut, or the digestive system. Read more here: *"Enteric Brain Technique"*,
http://evolutionaryhealinginstitute.com/index.php?option=com_content&view=article&id=3&Itemid=15

[18] Dr. Kurt Strzyzewski: *Introduction to Idiomaterial Life Physics, p.2,* June 2010

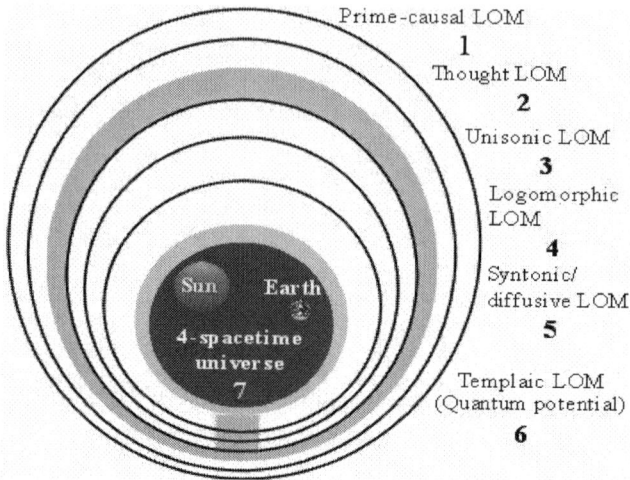

Figure 1.2: The 7 Levels of Manifestation (LOMs)

Although Einstein's Theory of Relativity became the way of looking at things throughout the 20th Century and taught in school, it doesn't mean we learned how it works on its highest scientific level, including all the abstract math involved, but in a way most of us could understand. Those who want to continue studying physics will sooner or later run into this complex mathematical world, but that is by choice. The rest of us only understand the basics. The Matrix we live in, the frequency of visible light, is literally based on mathematics, for thus is the mindset of the Architect (think *Matrix series*).

In its simplest sense it is a ratio of time/space, which is specifiable, within which idiomaterial (spirit/material) manifestations of all possibilities take place; we are talking about manifestations as small as the tiniest cell, or atom, to that of the entire Multiverse. Everything is intelligent and has infinite potential.

Interestingly enough, when a neurosensor enters any given LOM "outside" 4 space/time (see *figure 1.2*), things gets pretty challenging. Each LOM shows to hold all outcome probabilities possible in all levels of manifestation, and we're talking forming literal histories; each LOM as time/space ratio contains timelines which include the 5 infinites:

1. Past time-like
2. Future time-like
3. Space-like
4. Past null
5. Future null infinities

Continuous research indicated that it was imperative to learn more about the boundaries of all the 7 LOMs to understand the common superfunctions of the Unum; something the Working Model refers to as Superdomains.

The 7 Superdomains

The Unum consists of 7 Superdomains in total, formed from within the T-Boundary (Thought Boundary), which is the term for thought implication on top, moving "downward" through the LOMs and Superdomains to manifest in explication in form and matter. The T-Boundary can be depicted as a fuzzy "shield" around the egg-shaped Unum. Each of the Superdomains has its own ratio of space and time, and now we must stretch our imagination:

The various Superdomains have different ratios depending on *when* and *where* you are located. Each of the seven domains are completely interconnected, but at the same time work as unique superdomains in and of themselves. To explain this in simpler terms, it can be compared to us humans, who are also connected with each other and everything else in the Multiverse, but depending on where and when we are, we experience ourselves as separate beings at the same time as we are ONE.

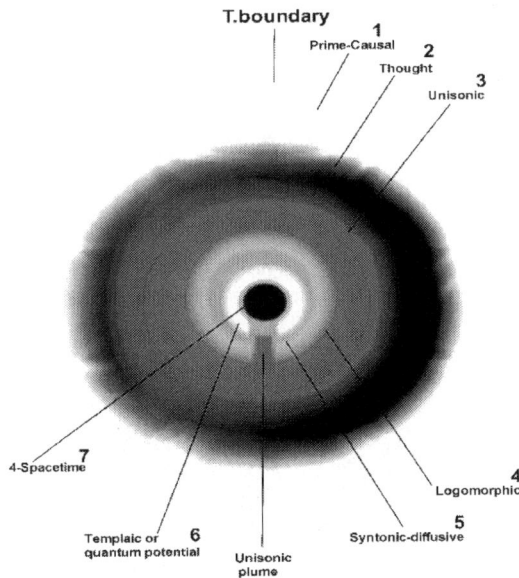

Figure 1.3: Organization of the Unum superdomains as an ovoid-shaped metastructure presented here as a 2-dimensional image of a superdomain 8-dimensional continuum.

The Unum, as depicted in *Figure 1.3*, has an ovoid (egg-like) shape with an

15

onion-like, layered metastructure with fuzzy boundaries, separating the domains. The entire Unum is a limitless plenum (the combination of space spirit/ether, including matter) of energetics organized as a super-continuum. Thought, as energy and infinite potential, can via emotion (which is a form of energy as well) and intention work itself in interconnectivity and, in singularity or in unison respectively, manifest in matter. The denser the energy, the more work to make it manifest. On certain levels, you create what you want with your thoughts, emotions and intentions only, while in our dense reality here on Earth, we often need to take additional steps to make things manifest in the physical.

To understand how the Unum works, we need to take a tour into each of the 7 superdomains, one by one, to see what is there and what is its function. This has been done via ENS, and with help from certain extraterrestrial beings, and the following are the conclusions made by the scientists involved. These experiences, more often than not, show to be very coherent with each other, and if six to seven people perceive and experience the same, or similar things, the evidence after a while will be considered quite solid:

The Prime-Causal Superdomain

This superdomain is the outer shell of the Unum *(fig. 1.3)*, and its function is the creation of thought, with two other additional functions:

- Manifestation of thought-matrices
- Transform downward-causal chain

Thought-Boundary (T-Boundary) information is thus sent through a downward cascading effect, which is applied equally in the next 5 "lower" superdomains in the following order (each of them will be looked into separately in sequence as well):

- Thought (B)
- Unisonic (C)
- Logomorphic (D)
- Syntonicdiffusive (E)
- Templaic (F)

Figure 1.4 (below) shows what a *thought-matrix* would look like at its inception point and the result and *thought-essence* it is producing at the time. The effect is instantaneous, and will be explained in more details in the next two sub-sections:

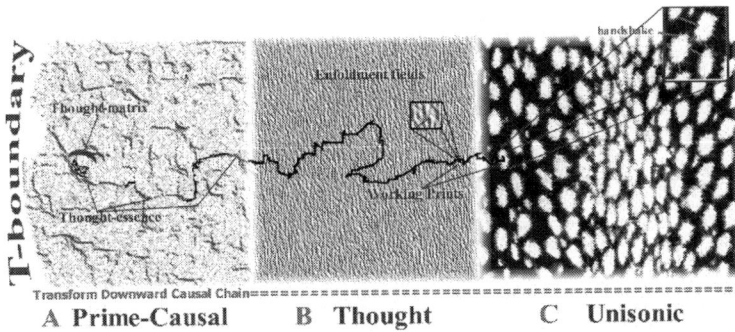

FIGURE 3 -- Instantaneous transformation of creative impulses into superdomain specific transforms

Figure 4 A, B, and C: Thought-Matrix at inception point and its result in the two next Superdomains "below."

Thought Superdomain

The Prime-Causal and the Thought Superdomains work in unison to creative impulses which become thought-essences and thought-matrices simultaneously, in parallel. The two primary functions of the Thought Superdomain are:

- Take an accurate "photo" of the thought.
- Record sound associated with the thought.

This Superdomain also has as its function to invest in "creative impulses", originated at the Prime-Causal or 4-space/time superdomains. This creative impulse investment has the quality of making a distinguishable and coherent "whole", so that it can be understandable as a concept. In simpler words, this means that a thought is sent down to the 4-space/time, for example, being processed there, and sent back up to be processed. Once an accurate "photo" is taken of the original thought, the second primary function kicks in automatically. Then the thought is instantly moved forth to the Logomorphic (morphic meaning transforming) and Syntonicdiffusive (syntonic = adjusted to the same, or a particular frequency) Superdomains19.

Fig. 4-B above illustrates how the enfoldment fields of the thought domain appears as a plain surface with no major characteristics other than the marking of the thought essence that can be seen as a line through the

---

[19] Dr. A.R. Bordon: *"Foundation Report in Life Physics, Vol. 1, No. 1, Jan-Sep 2004", p.13.*

Prime-Causal and Thought Superdomains. In general, this process can be likened to a computer hard drive, recording a file onto a disk.

So, in summary, as we can see, not only do the superdomains work themselves in a downward fashion, but the thought, as it's being processed through the domains, are then manifesting in its lowest Superdomain (4-space/time) and is sent back up the domains again after having been processed, manifested and acted upon. Hence, one single thought eventually becomes experience, and this experience is being part of, shared, and accessible to any entity evolved enough to receive the information (in *any* of the 7 Superdomains, not only 4-space/time). Metaphysically speaking here, if I may, it means one has to be on the same frequency or above, to be able to receive and interpret the thought.

Another important role of this superdomain is to function as **the ultimate "back up" domain**. Any thought that has ever been thought, and every action that has even been taken, is stored here, like in **a super-giant Akashic Record**. Here is the story of the Unum, preserved forever, way after a 4-dimensional Universe dies, and anyone living in the Unum (or potentially elsewhere) has access to this ultimate "library" if they have evolved enough. We are using it daily without knowing about it, but as we evolve, we can more consciously access it and "visit" it[20]. Then, in a downward fashion, each planetary body has its own "Akashic Records", which includes any and every thought and action made within that planetary body. More about that later…

Unisonic Superdomain

This Superdomain is apparently the one that has been the hardest to decipher by the neurosensors. Its main function is to bring the information on the "disk" (the thought/sound signature complex) and propel it forward (or downward) on its way to becoming a 4-space/time object or form, making the refinements required; almost like adjusting the quality of the contents of the disk before bringing it forward to the next step in the process of getting the "final product".

In *Figure 4-C* above, we are shown how the new arriving thought-essences are joined together (red) in a handshake-like effect that interconnects with all other sound walls in the superdomain.

Note aside, already as a young adolescent, I intuitively "knew" that the Universe was music in its purest form, and that it was held together by frequency. When I looked at pictures of the Universe and the giant galaxies, the stars, and the planets, I could hear in my head that each heavenly body was playing its own instruments, had its own sound and

---

[20] Penre/Bordon Correspondence, January 2011.

contributed to a larger symphony, which was that which was played by the entire galaxy. Other galaxies play other symphonies, and I could imagine how the whole Universe was one big super-symphony where everything is playing its part on the Divine's complex, but yet so simple, musical sheet.

Although there is much more to it than that, the feeling I got from experiencing this phenomenon just by looking at high resolution pictures was almost overwhelming. I also realized that music is universal, and those of us who are able to create our own music are basically "downloading" bits and pieces from the galactic symphony, creating something unique and personal from it with the purpose of having an emotional experience/impact on self and other-selves, and then add this minor composition to the already existing giant overall symphony of the Milky Way and the Universe as Infinite Potential and thus change the super-symphony with a few notes; or rather, add to it. That is creation. How successful we are depends on how much "in tune" we are with the Multiverse. Thus, we can compare classical composers like Mozart, Beethoven, Bach etc., with a "death metal" and low frequency music composer. Who is most in tune with the Harmonic Multiverse; who of the two is more in tune with Source?

I also realized that each one of us is playing his/her own melody constantly, but mostly unconsciously, by just being a body/mind/spirit complex (biomind). If we can perceive this, we can recognize each other merely from the unique "song" we are constantly "playing" for our environment. This "song" is ever-changing as our frequencies change; it's even changing from day to day, hour to hour, minute to minute. Each of us is not only one frequency, but we exist in harmonics of different frequencies. The more balanced we are, and the more evolved, the more "beautiful" the harmonics we emit are perceived by the Multiverse around us, and we are perceived as more "pleasant" by people in our environment. Consequently, the more in harmony and in balance the inhabitants of a certain galaxy are as a whole, the more harmonic and pleasant is the overall symphony of the galaxy. So potentially, by becoming more aware of being multi-dimensional and being able to consciously experience that we exist in many places in space/time and time/space simultaneously, we can also "feel out" a certain galaxy before entering it. How harmonic and pleasant is the symphony played by that certain galaxy? Not so pleasant? Well, if I enter, I'd be more alert than if the symphony is perceived as more pleasant to our sensors. The same thing would go for feeling out a particular planet. This kind of thinking, of course, is limited to one perception only (sound frequency), when the Multiverse can, and should be, perceived multi-perceptional, but the thought is fascinating and mind-boggling.

Logomorphic and Syntonic-Diffusive Superdomains

The Logomorphic Superdomain has as its function to install "rules of operation" and "rules of manifestation" when comes to thought, to prepare for entering 4-space/time. The Syntonic-Diffusive Superdomain is actively assisting in the creative impulses from the T-Boundary of the former superdomain (in the same "downward" fashion as described earlier). Its primary task is maintenance of functionality; to keep the thoughts stable on their way down the Superdomains. It has an "indexing function", which can be compared with registering property with the Library of Congress or similar.

But the Syntonic-Diffusive Superdomain also has another different function, which can be likened with branding livestock, perhaps. It established a "homing" function to know where it came from and where it needed to return to once its function(s) were fulfilled at its intended destination[20].

A false-color facsimile of a neurosensor's holonomic experience in the Syntonic-diffusive superdomain

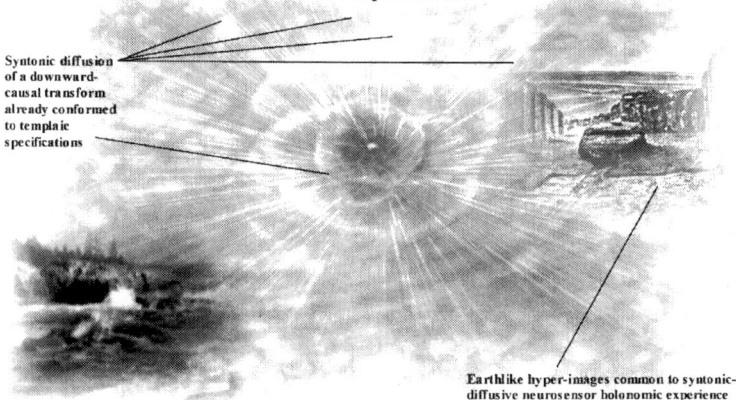

Syntonic diffusion of a downward-causal transform already conformed to templaic specifications

Earthlike hyper-images common to syntonic-diffusive neurosensor holonomic experience

Figure 1.5: A false-color facsimile of a neurocensor's holonomic experience in the Syntonic-diffusive superdomain click on the image for enlargement

As we can see in *Figure 1.5*, the further down the superdomains the thoughts move, the more they manifest as shape and form. Intelligent artificial structure is now visible to the neuro-sensor. Also visible are the downward causal transforms which have already been conformed to a templaic specification.

Templaic/Quantum Potential Superdomain

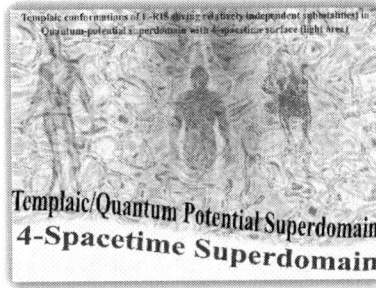

Templaic conformations of 1-k18 during relatively independent [illegible] in Quantum-potential superdomain with depinactive surface (light area)

Templaic/Quantum Potential Superdomain
4-Spacetime Superdomain

Figure 1.6:   Human form visible in the Templaic/Quantum Potential Superdomain.

Much of life physics lies in phenomena between 4-space/time and the Templaic Superdomain, or what is now referred to as the subquantum or the vacuum. Here is where all creative impulses take form before they enter 4-space/time, where we perceive ourselves to be.

All quanta, in whatever role or conformational function they may be, know all 4-space/time rules and have access to all 4-space/time points.

The existence of 4-space/time rules are predicated on the existence of its *mirror template* and quanta support ranges in the Templaic Superdomain.

4-Space/Time Superdomain

Figure 1.7: Satellite image of a Galaxy; a massive, gravitationally bound system that consists of stars and stellar remnants, an interstellar medium of gas and dust, and an important but poorly understood component tentatively dubbed dark matter[21].

This last superdomain is the innermost of them all in the Unum, as we can see in *Figures 1.2 and 1.3*. The first six superdomains have as one of their common functions to project, foster, promote, and support the "lowest" of the superdomains. It is here where all creative impulses, originating in the Prime-Causal Domain, move through an instantaneous process to become a templaic conformation, and ultimately an object or a "thing." We often refer to these objects as matter, which in certain terms is a bit misleading, as matter in itself does not truly exist, and in reality matter is just a range of energetic frequencies which our senses interpret as being more or less solid.

There are numbers of "natural" phenomena manifesting in 4-space/time, including Astronomical, Astrophysical, and Cosmological. Astronomy is concerned about celestial bodies, such as galaxies, stars, planets, comets, nebulae and so on, while astrophysics is dealing with the physics of the universe, like luminosity, temperature, density and chemical composition of celestial objects. Cosmology is more directed toward the study of the universe as a whole as it is *now*, including humanity's role in it. These three areas form the natural basis for 4-space/time as one superdomain of the Unum. Important to realize is that objects in 4-space/time are actually macro-quantum objects, and therefore available to the biomind by their "quantum-numbers.[22]" This plays an important role for the biomind; in fact, any biomind has access to *any* object's quantum

[21] Sparke, L. S.; Gallagher III, J. S. (2000). Galaxies in the Universe: An Introduction. Cambridge: Cambridge University Press.

[22] A. R. BORDON, E. M. WIENZ, J.A. SANCHEZ C.J. Colossimi-Jaime; *"Essay 2: Factors Affecting the Internal Phychophysiology of MPO-LERM"*

number as it exists in the Thoughts Superdomain as an *upward* chain from causality (from here to Source or T-Boundary). Hence, you basically know everything about everything instantly.

The T-Boundary

The T-Boundary (or Thought-Boundary) is the boundless region which is the source of simultaneous manifestation of all superdomains within the Unum. To an outside observer, the T-Boundary would appear as an extremely bright point; much like the opposite end of a black hole, but without the rotating, familiar whirl that goes with it, when viewed from inside the Prime-Causal Superdomain *(Figure 1.8).*

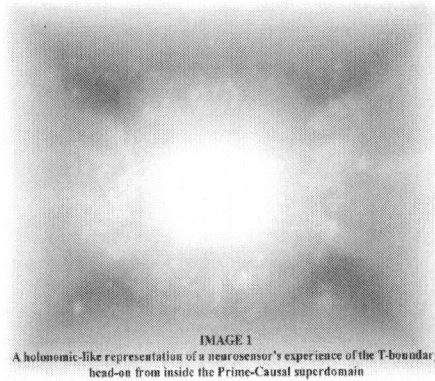

IMAGE 1
A holonomic-like representation of a neurosensor's experience of the T-boundary
head-on from inside the Prime-Causal superdomain

Figure 1. 8: Holonomic-like representation of a neurosensor's experience of the T-boundary head-on from inside the Prime-Causal superdomain

It's the T-Boundary that allows manifestation and de-manifestation to flourish. There is no primary function of the T-Boundary beside its "instinct" alone, which makes it uniquely important for the creation and manifestation of the Unum.

Regions of the Unum

Located inside this enormous Thought Superdomain, is the Condensate region, which is separated from the Thought-substance region by a Unisonic harmonic zone, not semitransparent but rather contains a diverse and rich assortment of colors and rings. These Logomorphic rings are the result of a toroidal field (a surface generated by rotating a closed plane curve about a coplanar in the same plane line that does not intersect the curve) that encompasses our Universe, the quantum-vacuum and space/time.

23

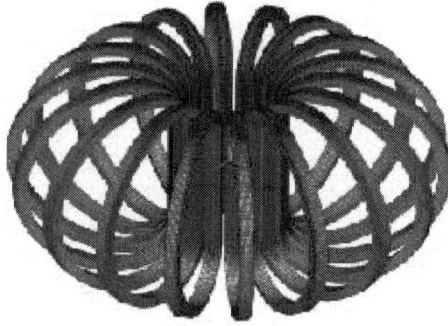

Figure 1.9: Logomorphic rings produced by Toroidal field located inside the Condensate region of the Unum.

The Condensate and Thought-substance regions are very important in the development of the formation of life. Life as physical information starts as thought-substance information, in the Thought-substance region of the Unum. The conformation of life, which tells us how life information begins and ultimately gets matches into a biological life form in space/time is realized in the Condensate region of the Unum. The sub-quantum vacuum-plenum plays a very important role in the latter, as we shall see.

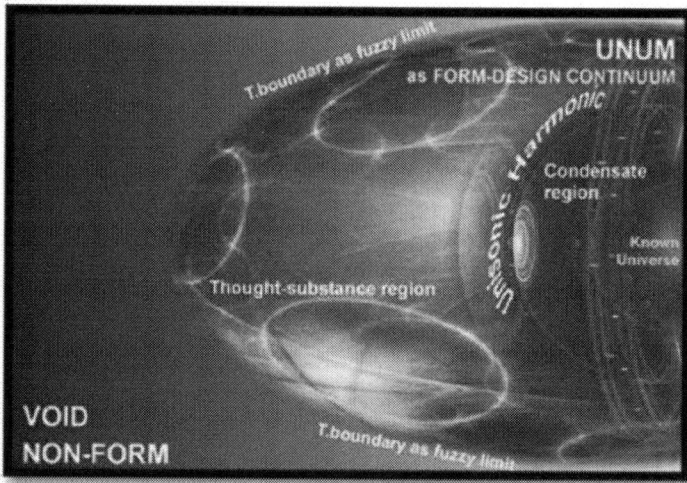

Figure 1.10: 2-dimensional representation of the two primary regions of the UNUM. Almost gives the impression of a gigantic, "consciously aware" spaceship on a journey through the VOID.

Subquantum Vacuum-Plenum

Looking at *Figure 1.10*, we can see that beyond the major regions of the Unum lies something which Life Physics calls The Void. This is the ultimate vacuum, the Subquantum which are the fundamental building blocks that defines not only space and time, but also conforms life information that exist in space/time, making this vacuum a remarkable medium with the following characteristics:

- It has access to all physical matter, including all living things.
- It displays the properties of a superfluid medium.
- It doesn't offer resistance to a physical object or structure.
- It generates displacements in dual transformations, such as simultaneously generated electric into magnetic fields, and vice versa.
- It does not have a density in the same way a physical object does

By further studying the above, LPG-C started researching the composition of the subquantum vacuum-plenum, its electromagnetic properties, interactions with matter, and behavior of waves in the medium. It was then realized that it was the subquantum vacuum-plenum that was the interconnected region, accessing the quantum potential, syntonic-diffusive, logomorphic, and unisonic intersuperdomain sets.

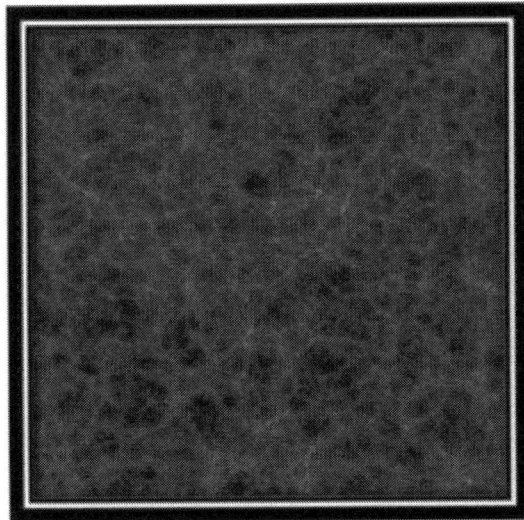

Figure 1.11. Vacuum-plenum in dark matter medium manifesting in space/time

In Astronomy it's suggested that most of the mass in the Universe is dark matter, and it has been a mystery to scientists over the years; most of the energy in the universe is even in a more mysterious form, called dark energy *(fig. 1.11)*. However, we are going to discuss the dark universe to a great extent in The Second, Fourth, and Fifth Levels of Learning. Although science may not yet have any good theory for what it is, there is much evidence to what it is and to what it contains.

Further investigation showed that there is an interconnection of all 4-space/time energy (as quanta and elementary particles) with the subquantum vacuum-plenum (the Void) through a process of cooperative sustainability. In simpler terms, everything is interconnected on a subquantum level, which ultimately makes everything in existence ONE; there is no separation! This ONE-ness is "All That Is", the ultimate definition of "God", and so it has proven to be in the Working Model.

The Overfunction and the Akashic Records

The term "Overfunction" used in Life Physics can perhaps be compared to what in metaphysics is called the Oversoul. According to the Physics Group, there are 12,960,000 degrees of Infinites in interconnectivity between the Thought Superdomain and 4-space/time. It's a mind-boggling concept, which to some extent can be illustrated in the diagram below:

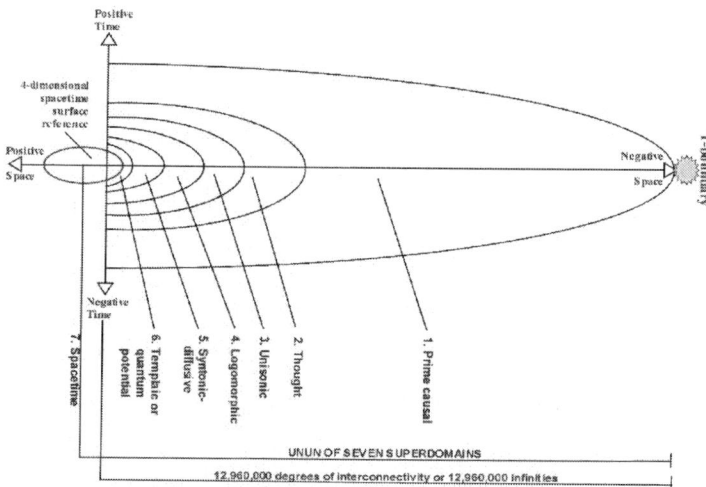

Figure 1.12 - The 12,960,000 Infinite Interconnectivity degrees and negative and positive space click to enlarge

Like we mentioned above, the T-Boundary is a respiratory of the biokind's memories (biokind being the term for biological entities like ourselves). It's the ultimate Akasha Record, if you will. It records all our memories, experiences, knowledge and technologies; actually every single thought we've ever had. And it's stored for Eternity. One can say that the biokind as a "biomind" (the mind/spirit of a biokind) becomes the sum total of its membership as one metastructure of minds sharing the same software and the same operator.

Further research showed that all complex oscillating biological entities (COBEs), are eligible to access information contained within the biokind repository of information. In other words, if a COBE is advanced enough, they could develop their own Overfunction/Oversoul by taking advantage of this inherited property as a prerequisite for further evolution and evolvement.

This means that the biominds of a certain biokind, through levels of self-realization, are putting the puzzle pieces of life together. They start understanding the fact that they are not one-of-a-kind, but we are all ONE. Firstly, all members of a certain biokind are ONE, both in biokind and biomind, and secondly, they are one with everything in the Unum on a subquantum level. Thirdly, by realizing the first two, the conclusion can only be that God is in everything, and everything is in God, and thus, each of us is God.

This leads us to the very metafunction of the T-Boundary. Dr. Strzyzewski says:

> The T-boundary's "wish" is for COBESs *sic* to know and realize that the purpose of what at this stage of human development we refer to as "science" is to detect, decode, and decipher the cumulus available as the Working Model which, by the way, is also indicated to be available to all COBE life forms capable of interfacing with thought-forms containing such information." *Therefore, the Overfunction itself becomes the Unum for the idiomaterial biomind, allowing for the biomind to experience itself in the Unum and at the same time, become the Unum* emphasis not in original.[23]

The "Big Bang" Theory Revisited

The theory in mainstream science is still that the Universe was created through a "Big Bang" and has been expanding ever since. It's also been postulated that before this universe was created through the Big Bang, nothing existed. This has been reevaluated by LPG-C.

The neurosensors have found out, much to their astonishment, from using ENS and from having had contact with ETs in near space, that the universe (4-space/time) we are currently experiencing is the 4th or 5th of

---

[23] Ref: Dr. Kurt Strzyzewski: *"Introduction to the Overfunction"* (undated)

its kind; our Universe is on its 4th or 5th cycle![24] It is known that the previous universe was destroyed (or imploded) due to that we misused dark energy to such a degree that the light of the galaxies in the old universe literally went out.[25] They became "dead galaxies" and were thus depleted from life forms. Therefore, it was destroyed, and this new universe was created around 13.7 billion years ago and is teeming with life. Hopefully, we have learned our lessons from last time and will not repeat the same mistake in this universe. On the other hand, if we do, it's obvious that life starts all over again. Mind you, that it is only 4-space/time that recycles; the other superdomains seem to stay intact; at least this is my understanding.

Also, there are also other universes (4-space/times), besides our own, existing in parallel with this one, and they are all in different stages of development. A succeeding universe, in my comprehension, which has learnt what it was set up to experience, will return to Source as a "mission completed" and a new universe will be created, built on the experience from the previous. In a sense, this could very well be the base for the reasoning by the Ra Collective,[26] channeled in the early 1980's by Carla Rueckert, where these entities were talking about ascending in octaves. There is, however, nothing in Life Physics which indicates that anything cycles in octaves, but there is still a lapse in acceptance between science and metaphysics. Metaphysical entities are often more than willing to merge the two, but science has always been much more reluctant. I hope that will change soon.

Until recently, most humans on Planet Earth have only known of species native to this planet. The question whether ETs exist or not has never really left the discussion table, and the real knowledge and the evidence of the existence of extraterrestrial beings has been suppressed and intentionally kept on a level of pure speculation when the evidence of their existence is overwhelming. Not only do they exist in abundance throughout the Multiverse, in many different shapes and forms, but some of them are already here on Earth, walking among us, and we don't even notice.

Let's take a look at this subject in the next chapter.

---

[24] *ibid. op. cit., p. 2.*

[25] A.R. Bordon undated: *"Life Physics of Ultimate Causation: A Research Program Using Bioelectronic Applied Mental Interfacing in 4-Spacetime by an Integrated Human Biomind/Biotuner"*.

[26] Bordon 2007: "The Link", Chapter 9.

PAPER 2:
KNOWN LIFE FORMS WITHIN THE MILKY WAY AND BEYOND
Tuesday, February 25, 2011

Idiomaterial Life Forms and the Merkaba

In physics, interaction between the simplest particles in the universe is the fundamental way of looking at things. The atoms in our bodies obey to these fundamental interactions, but the Information Cloud (what we usually call the Spirit or soul) is not limited by them. It is this information cloud that is the real us; the bodies are only the vehicles which we need to be able to function in the physical universe (4-space/time). The body is just hosting the Information Cloud. However, contrary to some New Age ideas, the body is necessary for us to be able to have the appropriate experiences, and not something we should try to abandon in the process. It's here, in the physical, that the "game" is mainly being played out. Even when we get more evolved, we will need our bodies to travel in space and time.

Since ancient times, the Information Cloud has been called by many names, such as "light body" and "Merkaba", acting as a divine light vehicle, supposedly used by Ascended Masters to communicate with those who can tune into these higher realms. In fact, according to the Life Physics Group, the Mer-Ka-Ba refers to the spirit/body surrounded by counter-rotating fields of light, which transfers the spirit-body (the biomind) from one dimension to another[27]. In *Fig. 2.1,* we the rotating field unit can be described as an electromagnetic double cardioidal spin[28], or rotating magnetic field.

It's inside the subquantum vacuum-plenum where we see the

---

[27] http://www.crystalinks.com/merkaba.htm
[28] def: "Cardioid can be defined as the trace of a point on a circle that rolls around a fixed circle of the same size without slipping." ref: http://xahlee.org/SpecialPlaneCurves_dir/Cardioid_dir/cardioid.html

Information Cloud begin to take shape. The vacuum-plenum *is* the Merkaba and manifests throughout the living matrix of the biomind. Through the Information Cloud, thought literally becomes reality, according to LPG-C and their Working Model.

LPG-C teaches us further: The human biomind, as thought/matter in a bioelectronic matrix, expresses a hologrammic form as a "fundamental" body (the one you perceive yourself to be in now), but can also express several different "resonant harmonic" bodies, which can take the form of avatars. An avatar is just another body conformed out of the same energy of which our 4-space/time bodies are, only this new body is somewhere and somewhen else, wherever and whenever we wish to go; whether it is to the future, the past, some planet in a distant galaxy, or to Source. When a neurosensor practices ENS, he extends a point-of-view away from the *fundamental body* (but still linked to it), as a *resonant harmonic* avatar, described above. He can then extend himself space-wise and time-wise, using his living matrix as the vehicle. This is nothing exclusive, except for us here on Earth; it's done all the time by beings from the stars, and pure energetic entities as well.

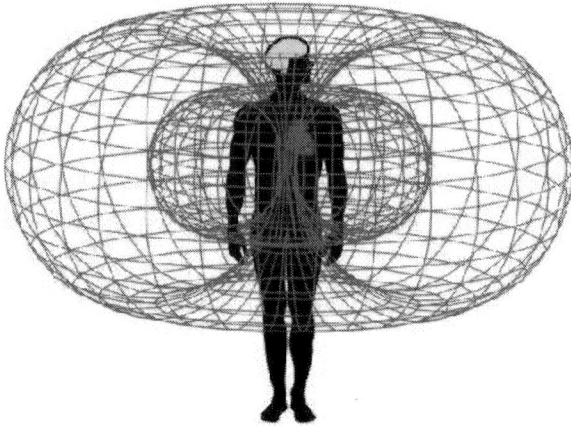

Figure 2.1: The Information Cloud which makes up the body's Spirit, soul and mind.

My own thought on this, which will be brought up later, is that this will be a very common way for us humans in the near future to travel through space and time in the Multiverse. It can be done with or without technology, and when technology is used, it's sparse; and no rocket ships or other spacecraft are needed.

Different Life Forms in 4-Space/Time

The life forms in the Unum have been catalogued by the LPG-C under 2 categories. They have found that life out there is either ontobiological or ontocyberenergetic. These two terms can be broken down into their prefixes and we can begin to see why there are two main types of life forms in the 4-space/time.

Onto: refers to the element of existence and life form

Bio: refers to the biology of the life form in question. So therefore:

Ontobiological = biological life forms

Energetic: refers to the infrastructural medium which holds the soul, or as Advanced Physics calls it, the *Information Cloud.*

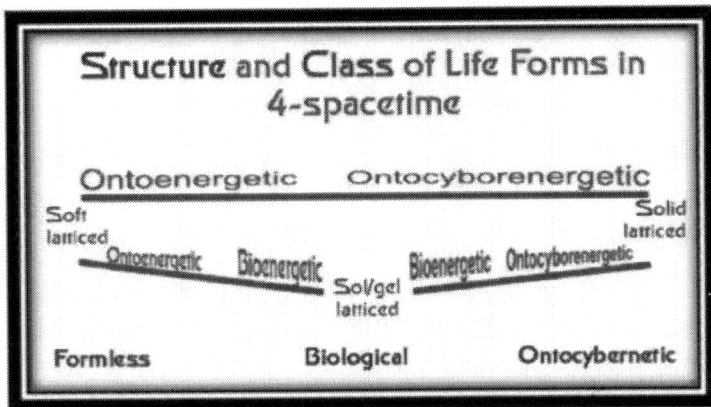

Figure 2.2: Structure and class of various 4-space/time life forms

Ontobioenergetic: Extraterrestrials with a physical, biological body, such as us humans. The term biokind is used to describe biological species anchored in the same kind of DNA set which is common to all life in our galaxy but manifested differently depending on evolutionary circumstances and interfering hybridization by outside races[29].

Here are some examples as experienced by a neurosensor:

The first class was made of groups of **humanoids** *(fig. 2.3.1 below)*, just like us. In fact, the only variance we detected was height and weight. Our best estimate is that these people, males and females, are anywhere between five

---

[29] ©2007. A.R. Bordon: *"THE LINK---EXTRATERRESTRIALS IN NEAR EARTH SPACE AND CONTACT ON THE GROUND" p. 78.* http://battleofearth.wordpress.com/2010/04/17/the-link-extraterrestrials-near-earth-space-and-contact-on-the-ground/

and seven feet, and some even taller. In terms of other physical characteristics, skin color ranged from very light to very tan, almost black but without Negroid features. Others displayed Negroid features but were relatively light skinned and hair straight and brown to dark brown. As nearly as could tell by mere gnosive observation (not examining the inside of their bodies to discern physiology and genotype), all of these appeared to be carbon based. The humanoids represented about 60 percent of our sample.

The second group was **sauroid**, or what the popular literature refers to as **lizard like or reptilian** *(fig. 2.3.2)*. These, too, offered wide variances in phenotype and genotype. They were humanoid-like with leathery hard skins, and they were extremely tall (seven feet by our estimate), or about the same height as us Earth humans (5.6 to 6 ft.); and a third subtype was about 5 feet tall at the most. All such forms were male-female typed. Then there was the **moth like**, very large and very tall, with what can best be described as wings or wing-like protrusions between what we could discern as arms and the trunk of the body. By very large, we mean seven feet and taller. No distinguishable male-female types were discerned. The third subcategory was the group referred to in the literature as "**the grays** *(fig. 2.3.3)*." Of these, there were at least a dozen variances—in height, body types (including eye size and construction), weight, skin color and means of reproduction. This class represented approximately 30 percent of our sample.

The third group was a small conglomerate of biokinds that looked humanoid, but their genotype and biology showed them to be **iron based** (for two humanoid **insectoid** blends *fig. 2.4*), one subgroup of **magnesium based** (circulatory system) make up, a third subgroup of **silicon based** (sensoria and skeletal structure) sol/gel (soluble/gelatinous) silicon states, but the beige color skin looked rough, even harsh (like the unpolished surface of cement blocks)[30] *bold and italic parts not in original, editor's note.*

---

[30] Ibid. op. cit.

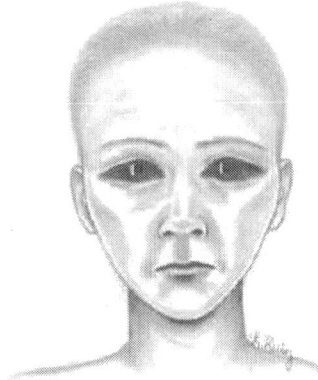

Figure 2.3a - :A male "Tall White" humanoid

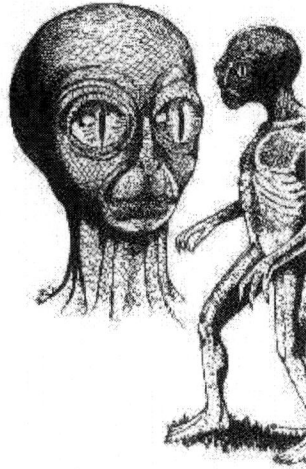

Figure 2b - Sauroid/Reptilian

Figure 2.3c - Gray

Figure 2.3d - Insectoid

Ontocyboenergetic (**onto** = life form; **cybo** = artificial; **energetic** = soul carrier): This life form has both artificial and natural systems, also known as a cybernetic organism *(Fig. 2.4.1)*. They often have living tissue over a metal or ceramic-like endoskeleton. Ontocyboenergetic means they are intelligent, cybernetic organisms dressed by organic tissue. They are hominid, and with a larger head than the trunk head human proportions, and their height is almost 7 feet. This group of beings has not been examined closely by the LPG-C yet. What is known is that there are several groups in this class, some not from our galaxy[31].

---

[31] A.R. Bordon and E.M. Wienz: *"A NEW AND VERY ADVANCED PHYSICS: EXTENSION NEUROSENSING IN THE STUDY OF FUTURES*

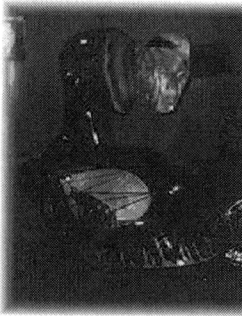

Figure 2.4a - Ontocyberenergetic entity

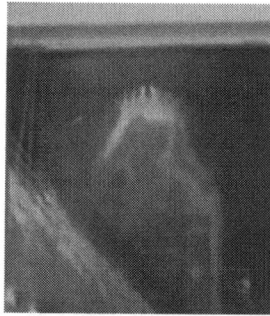

Figure 2.4b- Massless Ontoenergetic hyperversal

Different Life Forms beyond 4-Space/Time

All other life forms in the superdomains higher than 4-space/time are referred to as massless ontoenergetic entities (MOD):

Ontoenergetic (life forms/souls without a biological body): Transduce[32] life forms (transversals or hyperversals) are numerous throughout the universe, some with planets that have larger populations than Earth *(Fig. 2.4b)*. Transversals and hyperversals[33] in this context mean life forms that can transfer their consciousness through space and time with or without any technology, in pure energetic form, or in a transparent "light-body". These life forms have the impressive ability to move through the quantum superdomain from one position to another on a planet's surface. They are capable of thought-based technologies far beyond that of any ontobioenergetic beings, such as humans.

There are two different classes of ontoenergetic life forms:

Ontoenergetic one (OE1): capable of transporting themselves between LOMs with only their Information Cloud/soul. They can move both space-like and time-like through the different levels, between different points without using bodies.

Ontoenergetic Two (OE2): can transport themselves between LOMs in much the same way as the OE1, except that not only do they bring their Information Cloud, but they also bring an energetic body, having the same

---

SCENARIOS---A Preliminary Report" pp. 3.

[32] Def of 'transducer': "a device that receives a signal in the form of one type of energy and converts it to a signal in another form: A microphone is a transducer that converts acoustic energy into electrical impulses." *Ref: Dictionary.com.*

In the sense of transducer life forms, LPG-C means a life form that can transform itself from pure energy to something visible, like a transparent light body or similar.

[33] "Hyperversals: a New Category of Aliens?":
http://www.bibliotecapleyades.net/vida_alien/vidaalien_signtimes12.htm

properties as the first harmonic body of an extension neurosensor, as described in Section 1 above.

Early exploration of the Unum by extension neurosensors revealed earth-like landscapes even in the Syntonic-Diffusive, Logomorphic, and the Unisonic Superdomains. They also revealed humanoids with energetic bodies that were not only inhabiting these landscapes but were seemingly creating them using the combined minds of the humanoids living there— *massless ontoenergetic entities*. These beings are able to light-encode a reality matrix of their own choosing in a finite area of a LOM. A neurosensor entering one of these domains may find himself or herself in a very real manifestation of an earth-like environment, including trees, mountains, oceans and so on; all which are products of the collective ontoenergetic imagination.

Indexing of Planetary Bodies and the Reality of the "Ascension" Concept

According to the Working Model, once we are incarnated on a certain planet, we are working within a certain frequency range, which is specific for that planet. The same goes for other celestial bodies in the universe and it even pertains to life in higher LOMs. It is our "local space/time" and is what we have as long as we are living as biokinds/biominds on a particular planet, i.e. Earth, due to how we are constructed, and the way we grasp and process information about what is internal and external to our body/mind8.

Dr. Bordon is further telling me that what was to become the Working Model taught him and his group that all life forms are body/minds, including the so-called "lower" life forms, such as animals and plants. Mind, in this context, is a range of instantaneous connectivity with the "self"; one's own Information Cloud; the interconnectivity with the collective Information Clouds on the planet, and the super-connectivity with everything in the Unum. In the higher aspect of things, "spiritual", "physical", "living" and "life form" are quite vague concepts because they are all manifestations of the same thing and are all interconnected and equal in importance. Hence, when someone says, "I'm being spiritual", it only means that this person is focusing on that *one* aspect of life and is probably excluding the importance of the others, thus limiting his/her life view. Evolving as a person and as a species does not mean that we should only be "spiritual," but instead think in more holistic terms and therefore include all aspects of life; the "spiritual" part being only one.

The Working Model is teaching us this means that once we're born onto a certain planet (let's say Earth), we are "indexed" to the hologrammic frequency of that planet. Consequently, as soon as we start using our bodies after having attached our Information Cloud (soul) to it, we are beginning to view reality from the perspective of the collective consciousness of that planet. Earth, for example, is already indexed to a certain frequency range, so those incarnated here can have experiences within that particular range. This is also why we view things similarly, both when it comes to concepts and material things in our environment.

Being indexed only once to a certain planet, e.g. Earth, means that we don't come back to the same planet again.

Does this suggest we only incarnate here once, have never been here before, and will never be here again in the future? Is the life we're living now, in 2024, our only life on Earth? This is what Dr. Bordon told me in correspondence between the two of us (the emphasis is mine):

> We don't die... Never have, never will. No such thing as "death" in this or any other LOM. There is only information as energy. We refer to our "soul" and "spirit" as an information cloud, which is what it literally is. Albeit, one that is superposed upon a body. We do bring all "memories" from other incarnations with us - *but the catch is that we don't incarnate on the same planet sequentially, we incarnate on different planets in sequence.* It is physically impossible to return to the same planet, as one is already indexed to the overfunction of that planet and returning would be moving "backward" where life moves "forward." Forward here means moving through the Unum as experiencer of Life that contributes to understanding of creation by all information clouds indexed to all overfunctions in all planets and spacetime/LOMs (such as de Sitter spaces which contain life forms who "think up" (create) their own "heaven" or "place of rest" or "place of in-between") source: **Penre/Bordon Correspondence, Jan 26, 2011.**
>
> ...
>
> Your information cloud lives multiple lives in multiple ratios of space/time because as a living information cloud, we are theoretically a macro-quantum Hall fractional entity - meaning we can divide ourselves into many resonant forms of the original and go live somewhere, while say 3/5 stays put in, say, anyone of large numbers of de Sitter spaces we are capable of using to think up resting places for ourselves and ours.
>
> *...this does not mean your information cloud only lives one biological life at a time, if it did, it would be such a waste of life capacity.* Each information cloud is capable of setting up harmonic resonant aspects of itself - *this means an aspect-piece of the "source" cloud is harmonic to it while "existing" in another life form, say, as a verdant or as a Pleiadian, or any other biokind.*
>
> Oh, and there is a developmental curve to the existence of information clouds, once the T-boundary is able to create them in a unique downward creation causal chain. Examine what this means,

and it will blow you away. We go through all of these versions of the source we are in order to do what...? To learn for ourselves? No... We go through these experiences as primary and as harmonics to contribute to the overall LIFE management of Creation.

You see, we are on the fourth cycle/phase transition of universe version, three others prior having been failures for us as Life, as we managed to misuse dark energy such that there were "dead" galaxies where dark energy was depleted by the life forms which lived in them. The Universe as we know it is teeming with life, my brother. Teeming! Think of a phase transition as the equivalent of a big bang, but not one ending in a singularity or starting in one. ... Reincarnation? Well, again, we would represent a waste of life if we did not phase transitioned ourselves from one life form into a rest place into another life form, for many such transitions...**source: Penre/Bordon Correspondence, Jan 26, 2011.**

These are interesting concepts, but ponder what it is he is actually saying here. He is telling me that we all live again and again, but are only indexed once to each planet, and then we move on to live somewhere else. He is also saying that we live multiple lives simultaneously.

My own research, as it has progressed, has revealed something different. We may, as Dr. Bordon says, live lots of simultaneous lives, here and everywhere. However, *we do live more than one lifetime on one planet (such as Earth)*. My conviction (and I will show this in detail later as there is much evidence for this) is that we send soul fragments of ourselves (our Oversoul) down to Earth and somewhere else, simultaneously, to live several lives on the same planet, and those lives are only separated by time and line of focus. I am going over this in very simple terms now because I will make an effort later to be more detailed, but this means we live more than one lifetime on Earth. I agree with Dr. Bordon that once, we were meant to live *one* long life on Earth, and then move on. But there are alien forces who keep recycling us, which is not how it was *meant* to be to begin with.

Let's see what else Dr. Bordon has to say on this subject. It becomes interesting when he is revealing his sources:

Let's use modeling offered by the Working Model as well as gnosive evidence of teachings and work at then City-of-the-Sun-God (in pre-dynastic Egypt) by the Lord Ningishzidda (Anunnaki "god", also known as Thoth *Wes' comment*), prior to his exile to the Abzu by his brother Marduk. This would put this source at about 35,000 to 40,000 years ago.[34]

---

[34] This time frame seems correct and corresponds to other research, including Sitchin, which says Ningishzidda/Thoth was actively teaching humankind the higher

...

The next level of information up this ladder is what Ningishzidda taught his pupils was the KA or essence, not just physical, but also informational, more or less corresponding to the biomind (which, more than less corresponds to the corpoconscious entity of body information, bioinformational/auric/Meissner field).

The next level would correspond to the true KA or essence or what we here at the shop chose to call the "information cloud" or soul/spirit of an entity. Now, what happens here is that *every object in the world (including biological entities) have a light-cone which attaches them to the far future and far past, such that the object and its information cloud* (which is actually, really, subquantal but also indexed much higher ... and which places a most deterministic spin on what and how an object or living thing is to be. *This subquantal determinism is what makes literally impossible for an information cloud that decouples from a body and enters any one of myriad de Sitter spaces as a kind of interregnum to return to the previous coupling conformation; not because it is physically impossible, but because it is informationally impossible.* The subquantal information "arrow" of a living object cojoining templates (the one that, in the world, already exists of the person that is Joe or Mary or Max in a current life-phase in the subquantum as subquantal information cloud) points only to a conjoining to a physical mass that it superposes as glove to hand for the time period of that life-phase. Now, imagine the trouble Ningishzidda had in explaining this intricacy to his students! *Thus, the person who is Max or Joe or Mary in (let me use contemporary English terms) the current incarnation is indexed to its information cloud here which is indexed to its subquantal information cloud. So, the learning done by Max and Mary and Joe enriches their information cloud (which literally means feeding information to the Thought resonant harmonic of the T-boundary directly and constantly) is done vertically - meaning phase sequentially, not phase horizontally, in other words, staying on one universe location (e.g., planet Earth) and returning to the same location every life-phase in sequence. This would constitute a loop which the Working Model indicates would be physically impossible because it is informationally impossible. In other words, it is how the T-boundary builds the Unum/universe.* again, emphasis *not in original* source: Penre/Bordon Correspondence, Feb 14, 2011.

---

physics around 36,000 years ago.

So, what Dr. Bordon tells us: Because it is informationally impossible to live on Earth more than once, there is no such thing as past and future lives on *this* particular planet. Instead, the soul/information cloud brings with it the experience from that lifetime, collected in what he pictures as "vertical time", and thus contributes to the overall experience of the Earth consciousness.

Although I've come to realize that this may very well be correct to a certain degree, it's not the whole story. I have tried to discuss this further with Bordon, but he's not been very responsive on this subject. First, the evidence that we live more than one lifetime on each planet is overwhelming, which I will show the reader as we continue, and even if Thoth was correct about vertical time, our Oversoul (or as Bordon calls it, "subquantal information cloud") splits itself in several factions which are all spread out on Earth (and elsewhere) from vertical time into linear. Think of it as an almost endless wooden plank (linear time) with a past, present and a future. Then you drop hundreds of knives from above, simultaneously, so they stick and stand up from the plank in different places. The knives are different versions of you, hooking yourselves from vertical time into linear. Thus, you live many lifetimes on the same planet. Your line of focus, as you read this paper, is in the 21st Century lifetime (one of the knives), but you have a lot more lives, separated by time and space. This is *one* way of looking at it.

In this level of learning, we will talk a lot about the Anunnaki, and those who live on the planet Nibiru, so I will only briefly mention them now. Ningishzidda is En.ki's son, according to some, and is, as mentioned, equivalent to Thoth in Egypt. It is from this being Dr. Bordon and LPG-C have learnt the above. Then, of course, they have put that information in context with what else they have learnt about what they call the Unum, the "known universe," which is, as I see it, the Matrix, including the astral. The UNUM (Matrix) is shaped like an egg, which I think is correct, and outside this egg is what LPG-C calls the Void. My research tells me this is correct, too, but it's more than that—it is also the Greater Universe, which is teaming with life. The UNUM is a closed construct.

Dr. Bordon continues:

> The second source is gnosive evidence my small ENS team and I have gathered concerning the work of a character we knew and called Lord Ningishzidda, an Earth-born Sa.A.Mi/Annunaki over the last 10 years from a cumulus (line of research heuristics initiated on 12 January 2001). This line begins in central Egypt at approximately 37,500 years from today using the 1945 timeline as common time start forward.

> The evidence suggests that Ningishzidda was a master instructor at a complex in central Egypt and also a master instructor at a delta location following the completion of some irrigation projects done

at that site. This is a time period that sequentially to 1945 would place it at roughly 37,500 years from today. The twin mounds (pyramids) were not in existence at the time, and the corps of Sa.A.Mi.s in the midst numbered in the 50s, with a concentration at about the site where Luxor is now. The event stream we followed to support the above contention comes from a time approximating the time of the appearance of the home planet Nibiru by Ur reading of the signs. In the event sequence in question, the Sa.A.Mi. in question was mastering initiates who were to minister the needs to the first and second divine pharaohs (namely Father Ptah and Father Ra to local priests) *Ptah being Ea/the En.ki and Ra being Marduk, editor's note.*

The specific instantiation of an information stream concerning instruction on and about the life-phase sequencing of a human being on Earth then begins with instructions on the management of the KA of a human being by energetic means. This involved instruction on and about the krist or consortium of KAs to which all living human KAs belonged. It also involved the use of management tools taught by the master on how to assist in the processing of a passing KA from Earth-phase to a new phase. We took that to mean the passage from Earth to interregnum back to a new location. He taught his pupils that the direction of the evolvement of the cloud (he used that term to refer to the KA) was two ways—to the enrichment of the KA and to the enrichment of the krist. That all men-groups (we translated that as nations, civilizations) were bound to the process of enrichment and that all who go through a phase return to the lessons left unfinished or undone in the previous phase to be taken up again in the new phase, and that this was akin to returning to one's homeland to make right all things done wrong by the law of the krist.

If you read this carefully, it does not indicate that return is to a "previous stations," but that the idea was inculcated through the use of a metaphor that indicated at least to us, and in particular to me then that the return to a post-rest station or what we now refer to as interregnum was not necessarily back to the homeland but to something else, some other place, other than the Earth. **source: Penre/Bordon Correspondence, Feb 14, 2011.**

I do not read into Ningishzidda's teaching the same thing Dr. Bordon does, if we stay in the framework of what was just discussed. *KA* is of course the information cloud (the soul) and the *krist* is the planetary mass consciousness. As I see it, the Anunnaki is saying that we have to face our karma, and we come back to do just that. Nowhere does he say that you necessarily go to another planet, but we stay here until our karma is paid off, which can potentially be a thousand lifetimes, figuratively speaking, or be an eternal task. My research has demonstrated to me that we are living many simultaneous lifetimes here on Earth and that we now, in the so-called "End Times" are healing ourselves along the lines of time by confronting "unhandled business" from other simultaneous lives as our own ancestors, whether they are in the perceived past or in the future.

The following is what I consider to be true, based both on research and experience: we simultaneously have one body here in the 21st Century, while we may inhabit other bodies in the 1500s, 700s, 800 BC, 50,000 BC etc.; we even have bodies in a probable future. We usually don't notice this, because our different simultaneous lives are separated by time, as we perceive it (in a linear fashion). This is why we are normally not aware of our parallel incarnations.

Vertical Time versus Linear Time *(how a soul can live several lifetimes at once in the Multiverse)*

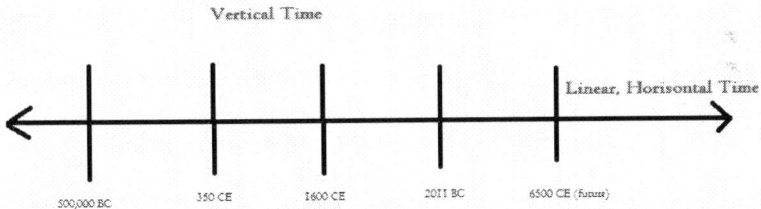

Vertical Time

Linear, Horizontal Time

500,000 BC   350 CE   1600 CE   2011 BC   6500 CE (future)

This simple diagram is showing how a person lives simultaneous lives, only separated by time. We, here on Earth, are in general perceiving time as being linear, and with this in mind, this diagram works. Different parts of our Information Cloud (soul) are incarnating on the same planet (in this case Earth), at different times to have different learning experiences.

In addition, we also incarnate on other planets in the same fashion. In reality, all time is simultaneous, albeit that's not how we perceive it, and this is per design. Through the existence of Vertical Time, we can choose different insert points where we want to incarnate to gain as rich experiences as possible on one particular planet.

Figure 2.5 - Linear vs. Vertical Time: How we live simultaneous lives

The diagram above explains how we are living several lives simultaneously. As you can see, I agree with LPG-C's concept of vertical time, but not about the details.

According to LPG-C, time is energy, and each planetary body has a time energy field surrounding it, determining the speed of time on a particular planet. I don't know to what extent that is true—I personally am convinced this planet is micromanaged by an alien invader force, and we also have Saturn as the timekeeper (more about that much later). Earth is revolving around the Sun as it is rotating around herself as well. If no one on the planet is paying attention to time, all that would happen would be that these beings experience day and night and all in between, plus different seasons, changing on a regular basis. The time we perceive in modern times is a fairly recent way of looking at time.

Then, if intelligent beings on the planet were determined to measure time, they could do so by locating themselves in cosmos, watching the stars and their constellations, and then recognize what the sun cycle is and when the seasons would change. That's all they needed to know. Eventually, a more linear concept could emerge, and we would have time measured similar to what we have today. So, I am not sure where this time energy field comes into the picture, but then again, I'm not a scientist.

I am convinced that at this point a lot of souls have incarnated here to experience the strong energies around the so-called "end times", in efforts to help raising the frequency of Planet Earth in order to raise ourselves about the frequency fence we are currently stuck in[35]. This may very well be another interpretation of what LPG-C is talking about regarding that being indexed to a certain planet means we stay in its frequency field.

Ascension (if we still want to use this term in the same sentence as the Working Model) would then be to grab information available to us anytime from the Akashic records, process it and learn from it, and bring it with us through our information cloud as experience into another reality and frequency band when we incarnate into another planet after body death on Earth. So, when we feel like we are "lifted up" spiritually and become more awake and aware, it is not an ascension process in the New Age way of viewing it, but instead a jump up the ladder to a new level of experience *within the frequency range available to us*, depending on what planet we live on. Then, after having learnt what we have learnt from the experiences we've had during a lifetime, we take this information with us and move on to another planet of a higher frequency band, or similar to Earth (depending on how much we learnt during a lifetime) and continue our experiences there.

Again, this is "ascension" in line with how the Working Model looks at it, but although I feel that much of what I've learned about the Working Model is correct, I have found evidence that the above is not correct. I agree that Earth is operating within a certain frequency band/range; however, I do *not* think this frequency band is natural, but is more of a frequency *fence*, set up by one or more ET races to be able to mentally and physically control us. It's a control system built in many layers, and it is quite complicated. I will discuss this later and show the reader what I base my ideas on, but I find my evidence solid. I will expand on it even more in the papers in *"Second Level of Learning"* and onward from there. Maybe LPG-C missed this, or misinterpreted it in their exploration of the Unum, or there are other factors involved (such as misinformation from the ET races they are in connection with). We can certainly leave the planet in our avatar (or harmonic body/light body), and explore the Unum without our 3-D body, but is what we see really what we think it is? Or is there a way to

---

[35] © 1992 Barbara Marciniak: *"Bringers of the Dawn"* and different lectures by Marciniak, channeling "The Pleiadians".

control what is being experienced by the ENS when out of the body and moving into time/space (the astral)?

What is Past Life Memories?

There are basically two kinds of past life memories: the genetic memories and soul memories.

If we start with the genetic memories, simply put, we inherit these memories from our ancestors on a cellular level. Thus, we can "remember" things our father and mother, our paternal grandparents, and their ancestors along the lines of time experienced; it's all transferred down to the children through bloodlines, apart from spiritual memories. Upon that, of course, we have two grandparents on each side of the family, and thus, the tree branches out. Then, in the next generation, there will be twice as many, and so on.

So, can we carry memories with us from 200 years ago? 5000 years ago? 500,000 years ago? Absolutely! We not only can, but we do. The only thing which separates us from each other is time and focus, as we look at it here on Earth. If all time was perceived as happening simultaneously (which is true on a subquantum level), we would be able to experience all different times and timelines at the same moment. However, this is not supposed to be the case, because that would limit our purpose to explore the lifetime, we're currently in on a certain planet.

Our genetic memories don't distinguish how much time has passed, in our terms of looking at time. When we remember the past lifetimes of our ancestors, it doesn't matter if an incident occurred 50 years ago or 100,000 years ago; the memories can be equally clear or nebulous. We also have the capability to recall several lifetimes at once, because everything our ancestors did and thought is stored in the memory bank on a cellular level, in our DNA[36].

Although I differ with the Working Model on the indexing subject, I will let the Working Model talk for itself, and we will discuss what I may suspect is discrepancies and false teachings later. I think it may be helpful for the reader to grasp the concept of the Working Model (at least the simplified version I'm presenting here), because it has everything to do with the alien present on Earth today.

Memories stored in the genetic memory bank is nothing new; it's been taught in many schools of learning over time. What may be considered new by many is that we, as spiritual beings, did not experience these lifetimes firsthand; our ancestors did. If the Information Cloud does not reincarnate on the same planet twice, connects with a biokind, e.g. here on

---

[36] "The Pleiadians", channeled by Barbara Marciniak, 2010.

Earth, and becomes a Spirit/mind/body complex, it immediately plugs into the indexed common experiences of that bloodline, and ultimately to all other bloodlines that have ever lived on that planet. It's like plugging into a computer system; once you're plugged in, you have access to the whole network. Those who watched the "Matrix movies" know what I'm talking about.

Figure 2.6 - Genetic past lives memories

Then, on the other hand, we have the soul memory. Some psychiatrists and researchers have started encountering some interesting things in their patients and volunteers for their research. Many people recall lifetimes as beings not from this Earth. They describe different worlds where they looked physically different from what we do here on this planet, and they remember alien cultures and customs.

This is the soul memory of genetic memories on other planets. Just as the physical body, on a cellular level, remembers everything that's happened in the past on that planet, the soul remembers everything that's happened in all lifetimes on all different planets it has experienced—ever. So, we bring everything with us, on all levels[37]. We also have an Oversoul in a higher frequency, and this Oversoul remembers everything that's happened to a single soul, whole soul group, and everything that's happened in the Multiverse because DNA is not just isolated to a physical body, it stretches from the Universe's lowest regions to its highest.

Observership and "Common Reality"

Observership is a very important part of the "game" in the Unum. This term is not limited to higher form of beings, or just bioenergetic entities; it is applicable to all forms of life, even animal and plant life. However, for

---

[37] Penre/Bordon correspondence, February 23, 2011.

the purpose of this paper, we are concentrating on the higher level functionality of observership with regards to higher mammals, including us homo sapiens-sapiens (the thinking human). It's the process of observership which allows for us to carry out the fundamental purpose of the T-Boundary; *to know itself in an extension of itself in form of Information Clouds.*

First, the observer is realized by anything in Nature; as everything that exists from here to the Source. The difference in the observer can make a tremendous difference in how we see things. The information-set viewed can be seen as chaotic as the picture to the left *(fig. 2.7.1)* or as a table to the right *(fig. 2.7.2)*, depending on who is viewing it and from where and when:

Figure 2.7 - A 4-D object seen from one's perspective and Figure 7:2 seen from another's.

These two different views of the same kind of object are for real; the object is just viewed from two different LOMs. The difference is being the observer and the observer's "index", meaning the index of a certain planet (e.g. Earth), which come together to form a hologrammic picture of reality, something we shall address soon.[38]

Secondly, the act of observing may affect the process being observed, resulting in a different outcome than if the object was unobserved. Since observership occurs in everything; both the observer and the observed will process the information even if they are consciously unaware of it. The observer and the observed are experiencing the process depending on their "index", i.e. which planet they are on/from and/or which LOM. If someone from another planet or LOM came to Earth and observed the bowl of fruit, they would be able to decode what they observed so that it will be perceived in the same way as it is perceived by those indexed to the Earth frequency.

Thirdly, the most important aspect of observership is the very act of

---

[38] As most of us know, insects also see the world differently than we do.

observation. Observation is a function of consciousness, and consciousness is the interconnection of all energy (as quanta and elementary particles) in a never-ending continuum. The effects of this can be seen both on the quantum/subquantum level as well as in 4-space/time. As we evolve, we will feel more connected with the T-Boundary. Once this connection occurs, we begin to see the role consciousness plays. It's the interconnection of energy which penetrates all life throughout the Unum.

In Life Physics there is a concept called **MPO·** or **M**anifest **P**roduction **O**bservership, which is a technical word for "common reality". It is the reality which is literally created (or fabricated) by all observers in the given space/time ration where it is manifest. The MPO is the ultimate hologram in which the observer exists.

Space/Time vs. Time/Space

Let us first define time. The Working Model explains that time is energy as well; "dark energy", which surrounds everything in the universe, including galaxies, stars and planets, and all intergalactic space in our universe. It is also perceived differently, depending on where and when you are. Just like each planet has an "index" as we discussed above, it is also surrounded by its own dark energy, which is its time, or planetary "clock" if you will[39]. We can think of the subquantal energetic medium of dark energies as the medium through which Earth moves, like through water; it's quite equally stable and equally dense. However, as our planet moves through seconds, minutes, hours, days, weeks, and months on its orbit around the sun, there are going to be small time varieties, not noticeable for us living here. Still, there are going to be minor spurts of time and other moments when time slows down. This is more noticeable on a planet with a much longer orbit, and in these cases, beings living on a such planet would experience more detectable time spurts.

Also, how beings perceive time is to some degree dependent on how far from the sun the planet is on which they live. Obviously, a year is going to be perceived as longer on a planet like Jupiter, which is farther away from the sun than Earth. The latter is completing a year (one orbit around the sun) faster than Jupiter. However, interestingly enough, longevity of a certain species is apparently also depending on the length of the orbit around the sun. If we, out of simplicity, say that a human lifespan is 100 years, and we have beings on a planet where it takes 4,000 years to orbit its sun, each member of this species lives approximately 4,000 times longer. Its lifespan would therefore be 400,000 years. This is approximate, of course, and varies slightly due to genetics, DNA and other factors, but in

---

[39] I would suggest Saturn is the "timekeeper" for our Matrix.

general this seems to be the case[40]. An interesting example of this are those beings, described in the work of late Zecharia Sitchin 1920-2010, called *The Anunnaki.*[41] It takes their planet around 3,600 years to orbit the sun, but they also live approximately 3,600 times longer than humans by default; 3,600 years for us being 1 year for them. We are going to talk a lot about this alien race later on.

Figure 2. 8 - The Ouroboros, the snake biting its own tail, here representing cyclic time

Moreover, time is not linear the way humans perceive time. Linear time, with a past, present and a future, is something we have developed here to be able to have these certain experiences which are unique to this planet. We have "forgotten" that we are multi-dimensional by default and live multiple lives simultaneously. On a subquantum level, however, all time is simultaneous in an ever-existing present.

Time is also cyclic in nature, with cycles within cycles or "wheels within wheels", as perceived in the Mystery Schools. There are small cycles of time and bigger cycles. A planet has its own cycle, divided into lesser ones as well. Some say a greater Earth cycle is about 26,000 years,[42] others say 75,000 years,[43] while I have also heard 500,000 years; it's all arbitrary, depending on our focus point. Whatever our focus point is, many now agree that we are closing in on the "end-times" as described both in the

---

[40] Penre/Bordon correspondence, February 1, 2011. This information was given to me by Dr. Bordon, with a side note that the Anunnaki, when still living on their home planet Nibiru, are more likely to live around 120,000 years. This doesn't add up, because most of the Anunnaki royalty, like the Enki, Enlil, and the other well-known characters in ancient myth and history, are still alive, and have been at least for the last 500,000 years. In the subsequent papers, "Learning Level II" I will discuss this subject. My research has revealed the answers to this question, but it's too much to include in the "Level I" papers.

[41] Zecharia Sitchin: *The Earth Chronicles.*

[42] see "The Pleiadians", channeled by Barbara Marciniak.

[43] see "The Ra Material".

47

Bible, the Mayan Calendar and elsewhere. There is a general concept that the year 2012 is the end of this current, Greater Cycle, and the world will end the way we know it. Although there are those who proclaim there is going to be a literal "end of the world", I think the majority of people who have looked into this are in agreement that it is a shift of consciousness, which will take on new forms and, in some terms, be perceived as a New Era. On Winter Solstice 2012, our solar system is also in perfect alignment with the Galactic Center and has completed a full cycle around the Milky Way galaxy, which only happens every 26,000 years. According to many metaphysical sources, this means a big leap in consciousness, because there is a lot of energy involved in this process, and energy is also information, particularly when transferred on gamma rays.

Simultaneously, the energy of our own Sun is changing, creating a boost in consciousness, something I believe many of us have experienced. In fact, according to The Pleiadians, the rise in consciousness has been an ongoing process since 1987. The time between 1987 and 2012 is what they call the *nano-second*, which is the time frame where the most intense boost will occur, and we will also over these 25 years' experience time speeding up and time as we know it collapsing. As a consequence, certain timelines are merging, and we become more aware of our multi-dimensionality. I can personally attest to that this has indeed been the case for me. My true awakening happened just before the nano-second started; in 1985-86, and I know there are a lot more people who experience a time spurt as well; I'm just one in a crowd.

In larger terms, even universes have their cycles. I can't say at this point how long it takes for a universe to complete a cycle; it quite possibly depends on how fast the universal consciousness evolves, but apparently, and according to the experience of LPG-C, universes do complete their cycles, implode, and start all over. It makes sense, of course, that our universe, spherical or egg-shaped, is orbiting something larger. This is evident, because everything in the known universe is orbiting something larger; it wouldn't stop with this single universe. Most likely, our universe orbits other universes in a cluster of universes. I am even going to be bold to suggest that each galaxy is a universe of its own. This is, coincidently, also the way the RA collective perceives universes.

Here is another good reference on time, which makes the concept quite comprehensible. It comes from the modern Bavarian Illuminati,[44] presently located mainly in the United Kingdom. Their Order has a lot of old, gnostic information available to them; information that's been kept hidden until recently, when they have released this information in increments to have mankind ponder new science and new concepts about the universe,

[44] http://armageddonconspiracy.co.uk/

time, the Spirit, God, and other important issues. Why are they releasing this information now? The Order has been opponents to the Powers That Be on this Earth, they claim, since the days of Solomon (perhaps even longer) but have had to go underground for their own safety and for their information to stay safe within the Order. They were the ones behind the Russian, French, and American Revolutions. They have fought behind the scenes against the Royal Families and the International Bankers, but now, as we are approaching big changes, the Order believe it is time to let people know how humanity has been deceived over the millennia. I have been in contact with this Order as well as LPG-C during my research for these papers (I was in contact with the Illuminati before LPG-C), and I reminded the Bavarian Illuminati of their bloody past. Their answer was that the Order is not engaged in war and violent resistance anymore and has realized the limitations of using these methods. This time around they want to use information; dissemination; education, and a peaceful resistance movement, which they have already started. They call it *The Movement*.[45] Personally, I haven't seen any Movements with a positive outcome. This is not because the members are not good-hearted and serious, but because movements, if they are a threat to the Power Establishment, are either taken out, being infiltrated, or discredited to such a degree that they lose most of their support.

Figure 2.9 - The Illuminati (http://armageddonconspiracy.co.uk/)

---

[45] https://the-movement.info/joomla/

Still, we need to keep in mind (and this is important) that groups that seem to be opposed to each other (like the Bavarian Illuminati and the Powers That Be, who are running the show behind the scenes in a fashion that is not benefiting mankind), may be two sides of the same coin, meaning they are playing out the common agenda against each other, when on a higher level they are controlled by the same forces, run by the same ETs, pretending to oppose each other to create conflict and war and ultimately keep humanity on a lower frequency. Then, of course, by having a person signing up for "movements" also means the "resistance" can be cataloged by the Powers That Be. Normally, the members of such groups, even on relatively high levels, are unaware of who is *really* pulling the strings. This doesn't mean we shouldn't investigate what they have to say. Sometimes, like in the case of the Bavarian Illuminati, we will be able to get some good information that way. Mind you, I am not saying it's one way or the other when comes to this group; I just want to make the reader aware of how things work behind the scenes.

The Bavarian Illuminati (which should not be confused with the "Illuminati" described on conspiracy sites as being the "bad guys" ruling the world) has narrowed down God and existence into one simple formula:

$$r >= 0$$

R (r) stands for "reality", which is the energetic universe, including living things in it, while 0 is God. The theory behind this is that Reality is greater than God because Reality is ever-expanding, but at the same time Reality *is* God, so when Reality expands, so does God. Therefore, Reality and God are also equal. Here they take this concept and explain it in terms of an analogy. For more information, I advise the reader to visit their website, http://armageddonconspiracy.co.uk.

> What does the universe look like from outside space and time? If everything is interconnected because there is no physical distance between any two things, how does that work? If no time ever passes, how can anything ever change? Isn't everything just eternally frozen? Isn't the universe outside space and time incomprehensible?
>
> Certainly, we cannot hope to describe it in the familiar terms of space and time since these do no sic apply. Still, it is useful to have some kind of image in our minds.
>
> The $r = 0$ cosmos is hard-wired to the $r > 0$ cosmos. The $r = 0$ domain is not in space and time, but is indissolubly linked to something that is (the $r > 0$ domain). So, the $r = 0$ DOES experience space and time, albeit at second hand. In particular, it

experiences it informationally, mentally. Consider a time-lapse film. You film traffic going over a bridge for a 24-hr period. You then speed up the film and compress the 24 hours into, say, 24 minutes. The speeded up film looks both familiar and very different. The compressed film is operating according to different rules of space and time compared with the original film. Now speed up the film to infinity. What happens? If something is travelling infinitely fast, it does not experience the passage of time. It gets anywhere in no time. Everything is instantaneous. The time-lapse film ends as soon as it begins. All of the information it contained is processed instantly.

...

How the brain interacts with the soul Imagine that you are the owner of a radio-controlled helicopter. There's a little silver pilot sitting in the cockpit. You start remotely flying the helicopter and you've never had so much fun. But then you think - this COULD be better. Specifically, it could be better if your consciousness was somehow transferred into the little pilot guy. For you, if the helicopter crashes, it's too bad. You'll need to get a new one. If your little pilot crashes, he's dead. The stakes are so much higher for him, hence the excitement is so much greater. Your hobby is transformed into a life and death struggle if you can switch your consciousness into the pilot.

So, imagine that your "soul" in the r = 0 domain is controlling a physical body, a human being, in the r > 0 domain. Well, it's quite a lot of fun having this remote-controlled "android" doing things at your behest. But the creature is disposable. You're not feeling what it's going through. Everything is taking place at a distance. You are experiencing second-level, second-hand emotions. Your mind needs to be inside that human being if your life is to become meaningful. What is a human brain? What's the point of it? If minds exist independently of matter, who needs a physical brain? The answer could not be simpler. The brain, with its countless brain cells and connections, is the means by which consciousness in the r = 0 domain gets transferred into the r > 0 domain. That's the amount of processing power a mind needs if its to change its perceptions from that of something outside space and time to something inside space and time. It needs to be able to process, via the physical senses, all of the signals coming from its environment. It needs to understand spatial and temporal pleasure and pain. It needs to feel emotion.[46]

How we perceive time is, as we can see, quite subjective. It's obvious that

---

[46] http://armageddonconspiracy.co.uk/Zero-and-Infinity%282129713%29.htm

when we are at work, for one person the day seems to fly by while for another it seems endless: subjective time. Interesting also is that a few hundred years ago, people weren't as linear in their perception of time compared to now. Most of us wear watches; clocks and watches are common things; on the computer in front of me, at work, on buildings while I'm driving, in stores; virtually everywhere. It's very important in our society to be "on time," or we can even lose our jobs. While doing certain data entry on the computer in some jobs, it's imminent that we don't spend more than a few seconds on each entry etc. In the industrial society, time is everything. It's all a race against time, because "time is money." Money is energy, and whomever controls money also controls time. That's how it works.

When I was listening to a Pleiadian CD the other day,[47] an engineer in the audience said we humans became more linear in our thinking after the railroads were built and the trains started rolling down the tracks. They had to be "on schedule" so people knew how long they could expect to wait at the station before the train arrived. Before that, we were more multi-dimensional in our thinking, and more open to ideas that did not involve linear time. There is truth to this.

Let's ponder the following scenario in relation to time: An alien race from another star system, let's say 50 light-years from Earth, wants to visit us in the year 2011. They are quite an advanced race, so they have no problems finding Earth on the star map; they know our coordination and can easily, by using wormholes, black/white holes, stargates and antigravity, travel to us fairly instantly. So, hypothetically, they take their hyper-dimensional spaceship and arrive at Earth in ... what time? Their own planet has a totally different orbit than ours and they don't count time as we do. Imagine that their days are 20 of our days and their years are 100 of ours. How do they know in what time period they arrive at Earth? They have no way of knowing that without using advanced mathematics. They need to know the coordinates.

Channeled transversals and hyperversals sometimes have the same problem. They, too, can easily tune into the earth's consciousness, but in what time period will they arrive? Due to our own catastrophic events, it's now easier for both benevolent and not so benevolent entities to enter our space/time because we left big rips and holes in space (and possibly in the Earth Grid) and opened portals and wormholes where they could come in when we dropped the atom bombs over Hiroshima and Nagasaki in 1945. By dropping these bombs, we were successfully advertising our existence to the Multiverse. That's when we got some real attention from beings all over the (star)map. Lots of alien entities could now enter our reality in

---

[47] Discussed during a Pleiadian lecture, 2010.

modern times, and this was perhaps not a good idea. After that we continued dropping a-bombs in remote places, and guess what? More entities came through as more portals were opened up.[48] This could also have been done intentionally to let certain ETs in.

Both in metaphysics and in mainstream physics there is a distinction between space/time and time/space. The best way to look at it is that space/time and time/space are ratios of each other. Space/time is thus the reality we experience as biominds in our 4D universe, while time/space is the reality we experience in the ether or the astral plane, e.g. "between lives." Time is perceived differently in the two because the latter is related to the dark energy which determines time in the astral.

Although ghosts (discarnate spirits) hovering in the frequency field close to ours, are rare, relatively speaking, they may stay around as "lost souls" for a long time, in our terms. The spirit itself may think it has only been around for minutes, or days. These spirits didn't "make it" to the rest area (Sitter space) between lives, and because of attachments to their previous life, they just can't let go. It could be because of a traumatic, sudden death, which puts the soul in a state of confusion, sometimes not even realizing that they are dead. Or it could be the separation from a loved one, or even the loss of material things dear to them. One or more of these examples in combination, without them having a clear picture of where they want to go, or whom they want to meet with after body death, is what makes some souls stay around, perceived by us biokinds as ghosts. However, sooner or later they usually realize where and who they are and move on. We all have guides helping us cross over, but if we're stuck in an incident or similar from our previous life and are ignorant of the fact that we are in a spiritual form after death, some people won't even notice that the guides are around or may not want to follow them. It's always important not to get attached to things in a compulsive way and think that it's more important than our progress. In the death moment, we need to let go of attachments. It's natural to feel a loss after we lose our body, but we just need to let go and move on. That's life and how it works, and it's how we progress.

Wormholes (Einstein-Rosen Bridges)

Something that has also been proven in the Working Model is the strange phenomenon of *wormholes*. The neurosensors found out firsthand that in the 4-space/time universe there are networks and webs of relatively stable *Einstein-Rosen bridges* (**ER bridges**)[49] *(Fig. 2.10)* which interconnect all stars

---

[48] *Ibid.*
[49]

in all galaxies, and even galaxies to each other. ER bridges can be seen through telescopes that capture images in the visible light range. An example of this is the energetic pipeline connecting NGC 1409 and NGC 1410 *(Fig. 2.10)*. Each star system of planets within a galaxy appears to also be plugged into a near universal web of such wormholes. The "Fifth Rule" applies to this phenomenon:

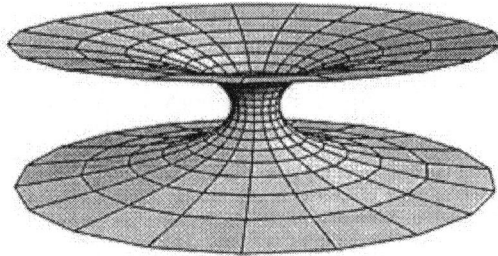

Figure 2.10 - Einstein-Rosen Bridge (Wormhole)

The fifth rule states that spacelike accessibility of one LOM# from another in spacetime is possible by life form translation from one LOM to the other through the induction of a spacetime origin singularity in the index (or origin) LOM to an LOM of choice by vector intention; or by life form transduction (or tunneling) by use of the naturally occurring stable intra- and intergalactic spiderweb of Einstein-Rosen bridges, or wormholes, such that time values in any two LOMs are time relationships between space/time addresses in the index and target LOMs.[50]

http://www.krioma.net/articles/Bridge%20Theory/Einstein%20Rosen%20Bridge.htm

[50] A.R. Bordon: "Foundation Report in Life Physics, Version 3, No. 1, Jan-June 2006" p. 27 *op. cit.*

Figure 2.11 - Energetic "pipelines" connecting galaxies NGC1409 and NGC1410

This, of course, makes space traveling fairly easy once a species has learnt how to use these wormholes to more or less instantly go from one place to another anywhere (and probably anywhen) in the 4-space/time universe. Wormholes can also, without breaking physical laws, be used as "time machines" after a few initial problems have been solved:

> If an advanced civilization could take one natural wormhole mouth as it begins to increase in mass and its twin (the end of the wormhole) will correspondingly be reduced in mass until it acquires a net negative mass, a relatively stable wormhole engineered to remain viable would then be possible. ... MT wormholes could also be made into time machines through time dilation, thus creating a time difference between one mouth and the other. ... what if the instability could be evaded, say, for small aperture wormholes (e.g., 340 feet in diameter) with mouths separated by extremely large distances, say, 40 million light years?[51]

These two Science Papers, explaining the absolute basics of the Working Model, I hope has given some interesting new perspective to the readers view on the latest in science.

---

[51] A.R. Bordon: "Foundation Report in Life Physics, Version 3, No. 1, Jan-June 2006", Note 13, *op. cit.*

PAPER 3:
THE PRIME CREATOR EXPERIENCING ITSELF
Thursday, February 17, 2011

From Nothingness to Somethingness

In the beginning there was Infinity, and Infinity was Nothingness or Infinite Void. There were no thoughts, no emotions, no light, no darkness, no sound, no material universe, only silence and Nothingness. Then this silence became Aware. It developed a Super Consciousness that is All That Is. From that Super Consciousness self-awareness and thought emerged. Out of self-awareness and thought came Infinite Potential. Infinite Potential is genderless and genders at the same time because it is All That Is.

Once, an eternity ago in human terms, Infinite Potential, which we may call Source, who knew everything there was to know, was "wondering" how it would be if there were things It didn't know. Of course, Source could experience anything and everything It wanted to, but *only* from Its own single point of view and regarding Its own Infinity. If It wanted to experience another Infinity, It had to create another unique self-aware unit of awareness, just like Itself, who could create *its* own Infinity.[52] Therefore, the way to expand Itself and create Infinite Universes from other viewpoints was to extend Itself to a lot of unique units of awareness, which It did; It went from Oneness to Separateness. It may also very well have been that this Source Awareness felt lonely.

So, Source created a game to play with Itself; It created the Unum/Multiverse (or many Unums) from Its own Infinite point of view and then populated it with an almost infinite number of awareness units; separate parts of Itself. Figuratively speaking, if we imagine Source being

---

[52] ©1993 William Bramley: "The Gods of Eden", Chapter 40.

an infinite ball of clay, It took a part of Itself and created a model, or a "landscape", which became what Life Physics Group California calls "The Unum"; then It extended Itself in consciousness into an indefinite amount of "nerve endings", which were "miniature" parts of Itself. It gave these extended awareness units unique personalities and traits, so each one of them could create their own universes within a First Source Unum (Construct), and bring back every thought, every move, and every experience back to Source.

The Unum we live in became the playground (or "clayground", according to our analogy) with its seven Levels of Manifestation. Being Infinite Potential and All That Is to begin with, Prime Creator, by using energy to create different densities and dimensions, could now, from completing the LOMs (levels of manifestations) put players on the stage. The way It did this was to let parts of Itself go into the Unum and start seeding and creating intelligent life forms of lower densities than that of the purest form of Source. The purpose and the idea were to have separated parts of Itself explore the Unum and bring back the unpredictable experiences to Itself, so Source could learn more about Itself. This game has been going on ever since and will probably go on for all eternity. And now, when Source started creating, IT became SHE, since creativeness starts with the feminine aspect as thought, imagination, and intention to create. This is an "inward" process. This inner creation is then manifested in the Void, appearing as something external. This "outward" motion is masculine in nature. So, the feminine comes first.[53]

Many have asked themselves throughout time whether 4-space/time is infinite, with an infinite number of galaxies, or not. The universe is both; it's Infinite Potential, and we who live in it are the ones creating it (and serial and parallel universes within the Universe itself, by creating probable realities) with our thoughts, emotions, and actions, each and every second of our existence. This means that the universe is potentially infinite and ever-expanding. If I were able to measure exactly how big the universe is at this exact second, it would be false the next second, or even the next nano-second,[54] because it would already have expanded way beyond the calculations.

The questions who God is and how everything started is of course, and should be, mind-boggling, and this is a subject for an endless series of papers itself, and it's not my purpose at this time to speculate too much about this; I will do that in the sequels to this First Level of Learning. There is evidence in quantum and subquantum physics, and in metaphysics, that there is a Prime Creator that includes everything there is,

---

[53] The concept of the Universe being feminine has been added to this book and is not in the online original version.

[54] Nano means *a billionth of something*.

but there is an even bigger question: if Prime Creator came out of a Nothingness and suddenly became aware, who made It aware, or how did It become aware? What came before "thought"? In other words, is there something even bigger than what we now call the Prime Creator?

A Hierarchy of Creator Gods

To have the game started, Prime Creator appointed separated part of Herself, so-called "creator gods", who were close to Herself in vibration and had the knowledge and capacity to create realities in the Unum; even galaxies, stars, nebulae, and planets, and seed them with life. She then told the parts of Herself which were the creator gods: *"Go out and create, and bring all things back to me! You go out and gift of yourselves freely, so that all that you create in this universe can understand its essence, my identity!*[55],[56]

---

[55] there is the idea that life might have been intentionally spread throughout space and seeded on the surface of other worlds by a guiding intelligence. A detailed version of this hypothesis was put forward in 1973 by the molecular biologists Francis Crick (co-discoverer of the structure of DNA) and Leslie Orgel (Crick & Orgel 1973). The chances of microorganisms being passively transported from world to world across interstellar distances, they felt, were small. The probability of successful seeding would be greatly increased, they pointed out, if the fertilization were carried out deliberately by an existing technological civilization. Their argument depended first upon demonstrating that it was possible for an advanced extraterrestrial civilization to have developed in the Galaxy before life first appeared on Earth.

This they were able to. As for the means of dispensation: The spaceship would carry large samples of a number of microorganisms, each having different but simple nutritional requirements, for example, blue-green algae, which could grow on CO_2 and water in "sunlight". A payload of 1,000 kg might be made up of 10 samples each containing 10^{16} microorganisms, or 100 samples of 10^{15} microorganisms.

Crick and Orgel further suggested that directed panspermia might help resolve one or two anomalies in the biochemistry of life forms on Earth. One of these was the puzzling dependence of biological systems on molybdenum. Many enzymes, for example, require this metal to act as a cofactor. Such a situation would be easier to understand if molybdenum were relatively abundant on Earth. However, its abundance is only 0.02% compared with 0.2% and 3.16%, respectively, for the metals chromium and nickel, which are chemically similar to molybdenum. Crick and Orgel commented:

If it could be shown that the elements represented in terrestrial living organisms correlate with those abundant in some types of star-molybdenum stars, for example-we might look more sympathetically on "infective" theories.

A second example they give concerns the genetic code:

Several orthodox explanations of the universality of the code can be suggested, but none is generally accepted to be completely convincing. It is a little surprising that organisms with somewhat different codes do not coexist. The universality of the code follows naturally from an "infective" theory of the origin of life. Life on Earth would represent a clone derived from a single set of organisms.

There might be a variety of reasons why an advanced civilization would wish to intentionally initiate life elsewhere: as an experiment in astrobiology using an entire

Some say that the original creator gods were 7 in numbers,[57] as 7 is the number of the Matrix/Unum, roaming in other dimensions, LOMs, of the Unum, and these 7 creator gods, after noticing that everything went per the plan, then created hierarchies of "lesser" creator gods, who went out and seeded planets in 4-space/time with lower density life forms.[58] These lesser gods, in addition, created their own hierarchy and so on. However, because all is ONE to begin with, there is really nothing that's greater or lesser than anything else, but in terms of creator gods, they were just assigned more or less complicated tasks because this was the way which seemed to work the best, and the fastest way to seed life into Source's Multiverse. These Greater Gods did not exist in time as we perceive it here on Earth, so a million years, or even billions of years, is nothing for these entities.[59]

The 7 original creator gods are known under different names here on Earth, but I will use the term the *Founders*. Then, the "lesser" gods right underneath them in the hierarchy, are The Family of Light[60] or *The Tribes of Light*.[61] (**Note:** I will from hereon use the term Tribes of Light *only* when we are discussing the WingMakers Material, otherwise I will use either Family of Light or specifically name the alien species in question). The Andromedans, who were channeled by Alex Collier, mentioned the Founders as well, calling them either the Paa Tal or The Founders.[62]

The Galactic Tributary Zone and the 7 Planetary Zones

The 4-space/time universe expands from the center and out in a spinning, spiral fashion; counter-clockwise, like the Merkaba. In the center of the universe there is something called a Tributary Zone. When the Founders

---

world as a laboratory; to prepare a planet for subsequent colonization (see terraforming); or, to disseminate the genetic material of the donor world to ensure its survival in the event a global catastrophe. A.R. Bordon & J.W. Barber: *"CATASTROPHISM, EXOPOLITICS AND THE RETURN OF NI.BI.RU.: A Case For The Long-Term Or Extended View of Exopolitics", Life Physics Group, California & Institute for End Time Studies, 2006, footnote #1*

[56] "ETANGLES The Pleiadians - Part 1", channeled lecture by Barbara J. Marciniak on Friday, November 15, 1990 at 7:30 PM - Terman Auditorium, Stanford, California, http://evolve.8.forumer.com/viewtopic.php?t=475

[57] This corresponds to the 7 Archons in the Gnostic Texts, who supposedly formed and manipulated the Unum/Matrix. *This footnote is an addition to the original texts online.*

[58] *ibid.* (See the sequels for a more expanded version of this concept.)

[59] *ibid.*

[60] *ibid.*

[61] http://wingmakers.com/ ; http://lyricus.org/ ; http://eventtemples.com/

[62] http://www.bibliotecapleyades.net/andromeda/andromedacom_galactichistory01.htm

create a galaxy, they export this zone from the center of the universe and place it in the center of the galaxy.[63] This zone is located on a planet close to the core (or Central Sun) of the galaxy, but "hidden" within a frequency that ordinary galactic and intergalactic beings can't enter, unless they are able to vibrate on that frequency. Or, as the *Lyricus Teaching Order* (originating from the Tribes of Light) puts it:

> Within the galaxy is a Tributary Zone, which is a synthetic "planet" that is designed to house the knowledge system appropriate for the species of that particular galaxy. Lyricus uses these Tributary Zones as research and training centers wherein its teachers can gather the information, translate it into the indigenous cultural or scientific formats of the species, and then export it to a specific planetary species.[64]

Figure 3.1 - Artist's perspective of a galaxy with its Central Sun, where the Tributary Zone is located.

The Lyricus Teaching Order members, in the WingMakers Story (http://wingmakers.com) are ambassadors to the Tribes of Light. The basic philosophy of the WingMakers and the Lyricus Teaching Order is that there are 7 superuniverses, just like we are taught when reading the Urantia Papers.[65] Each superuniverse has its own Tributary Zone; thus 7 Tributary Zones all together. These Tributary Zones exist as places of inquiry and

---

[63] http://wingmakers.com/jamesqa2.html

[64] *Lyricus Teachers and Methodologies, op. cit.,* http://lyricus.org/.

[65] The Urantia Book can be read free online: http://www.urantia.org/en/urantia-book-standardized/urantia-book-standardized .

knowledge dissemination, perhaps as another "nerve ending" of the Thought Superdomain, where the entire Akashic Records are contained. Then, according to the Lyricus Order, the zone placed in each galaxy would more specifically contain the Akashic Records of a particular galaxy, and everything that has happened within it from its creation to its fulfillment. It's like exporting a *part* of a gigantic library.

Figure 3.2 - Artist's vision of a galactic Tributary Zone (source: WingMakers.com)

Even the Tributary Zones work like a hierarchy. From the galactic Tributary Zone, the Tribe of Light is then exporting 7 zones to each life-bearing planet, and in the case of Planet Earth, there is one zone on each continent. Each planetary Tributary Zone is like a mini-library, each one specific to a certain field of knowledge, such as cosmology, metaphysics, science, religion etc.

Figure 3.3 - Global Positioning of WingMakers Tributary Zones

These 7 Tributary Zones are real locations, despite what has sometimes been said even on the WingMakers site, and they are apparently stationed where they are indicated in *fig. 3.3*, and these sites are supposed to be found and explored, one by one, decoded and revealed to humanity when we're ready. Thus far, only the site in New Mexico has been officially sited (see Wingmakers.com). The original purpose of the WingMakers site was for incarnated member of the Lyricus Teaching Order to help locating and decoding the material, which in its original form was exported from higher LOMs and not in a language known to any species in the galaxy. Each Tributary Zone, on each planet, needs to be decoded so it can be communicated in one or more languages spoken on the planet in question, according to both the WingMakers and LPG-C.

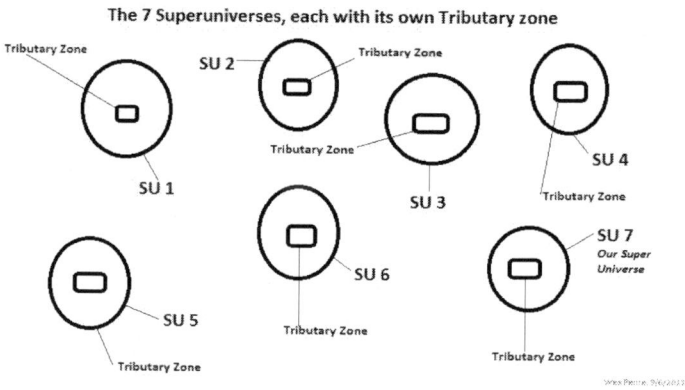

Diagram 3.4 - The 7 Tributary Zones in the center of the 7 superuniverses.

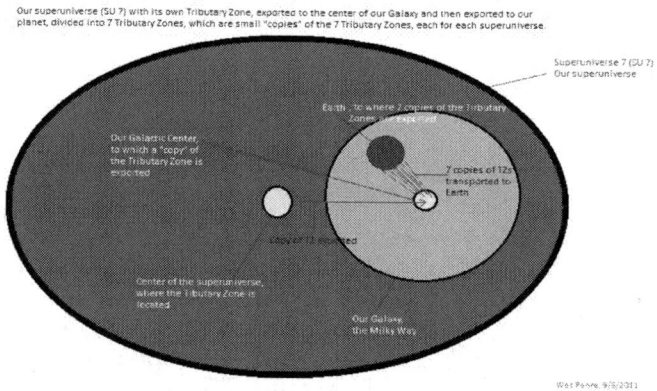

Diagram 3.5 - Distribution of the Tributary Zones in the center of our superuniverse.

My own research has shown that this issue with the Tributary Zones is very complicated and involves the focus of many different alien species, much more so than is indicated both by the Lyricus/WingMakers and LPG-C. But to understand this very important subject, we need to peel the onion, and this is where we start. In the papers of the *"Second Level of Learning"* I will extensively expand on this. As we shall see, there is a connection between the WingMakers Material (http://wingmakers.com) and LPG-C (Life Physics Group California) (http://lifephysicsgroup.org/).

In 1969 or 1970, I was on the Swedish island of Gotland, east of Stockholm, and between Sweden and Russia, where the Lummelunda Caves are located. They are deep tunnels and caves, extending into the Inner Earth. This is also where one of the Tributary Zones is supposedly located. They had guided tours there, and I was joining one. We walked downward into something that looked like taken from the Orc tunnels in *The Lord of the Rings* by J.R.R. Tolkien, with stalagmites and stalactites extending from floor and ceiling. However, we were only allowed to stride for about 20 minutes, after which there was a big sign blocking the ongoing tunnel. The sign said something to the effect, "Here, but no further." Since I read the WingMakers Material for the first time in the year 2000, I've always wondered if those who maintain these caves and tunnels stumbled upon the Tributary Zone farther down. Up to this day, I don't know. I only know the guided tours still end at that same place.[66]

From Lyricus Teaching Order:

Each galactic Tributary Zone is different in terms of the knowledge system that it houses. The leader of the cultural quarter of power – in this case, James Mahu – reviews the content contained within the Tributary Zone and aligns it with his knowledge of the species' belief systems and historical context, and then translates the content into human terms. This is done to establish the first exterial "footprint" of Lyricus on the planet.

The primary purpose of this initial facet of the knowledge system is to bring encoded sensory data streams to the species that can help individuals shift their consciousness from an individual, planetary-based set of objectives to a more cosmologically-based set of objectives for the species as a whole – namely the discovery of the Grand Portal. This is generally done without too much definition given to Lyricus.

...

> The knowledge system is brought to the species gradually and in a manner that the species assimilates it as its own. Complementary to the exterial unfolding of Lyricus is the unfolding of the inward process to implant certain aspects of the Lyricus knowledge system within the Genetic Mind of the species, thus making it accessible to all humanity. This process is conducted through the combined

---

[66] This part about the Lummelunda Caves is not in the online version of the papers.

efforts and technologies of the Lyricus team residing within the Tributary Zone.

What is being done on the planet and off the planet (the inner and outer work) is coordinated by the Lyricus leader of the religious quarter. This is the individual who is last to incarnate within the human species and is the one that will step forward in the final days just prior to, or directly after, the discovery of the Grand Portal. This is the individual who will unify the disparate beliefs of the species and anchor them on the science of multidimensional reality and the all-encompassing brotherhood of the individuated consciousness.[67]

The Grand Portal they are talking about is allegoric to the time when religion and science merge into one, and the human race realizes as ONE that we are spiritual beings inhabiting a body. When this happens, according to Lyricus and the WingMakers, we can become multi-dimensional as a species. Religion here does not imply the established religions here on Earth with their different dogmatic teachings, but rather religion as spiritual awareness. (As a side note the Pleiadians are using the 12 system[68] rather than the 7 system when dealing with humans, and so do the Guardians,[69] with whom A'shayana Deane is in contact. More about that later).

---

[67] "Lyricus Teachers and Methodologies", *op. cit.,* http://lyricus.org/.
[68] Marciniak, Barbara 1992: *"Bringers of the Dawn"*.
[69] Deane, A'shayana 2002: *"Voyagers I & II"*.

PAPER 4:
THE FLOW OF ENERGY IN DAILY LIFE
Friday, Feb. 18, 20211

The Law of Attraction

Some may say karma and the Law of Attraction are the same thing, but there is a difference. Both laws are in effect and are natural to the Multiverse.

Karma is a highly accepted part of Eastern Religion and philosophies and has carried over as a concept to the Western world as well. Unfortunately, here in the western hemisphere we have misunderstood the concept and are separating between "good" and "bad" karma.

There is no such separation.[70]

Karma

Karma is a universal law and is in effect to enhance the growth of the spirit, or so we've been taught. We live in a Freewill Universe where you are totally free to do and experience whatever you want, but what you do is coming back to you. This means that if you dedicate yourself to enhancing the spiritual growth of self and others, your karma will reflect that, and the universe pays your back in a currency that helps you grow. However, if you dedicate your life to theft, murder, lying, cheating, controlling others and whatnot, those kinds of energy are going to hit you back, and you will eventually, in the same lifetime, or in another, experience the other side of the coin, where someone steals from you, deceives you, and even kills you.

In the universe, everything is energy, and karma has everything to do with energy (and polarity).

---

[70] The "Karma" part has been removed from this paper but is still available in the online version. Karma is instead discussed in a much more accurate way in upcoming books in this series.

The Law of Attraction

The Law of Attraction is a causative law, and it works automatically to a certain degree, and can be worked on more consciously once a person becomes aware of how energies work.

Many people watched the video *The Secret*, which came out a few years ago, promoting the Law of Attraction, apparently released by members of the Rosicrucian Order. Another very good reference, which is in my opinion presenting a material easier to apply and not as vague as The Secret, is *The Teachings of Abraham*, which is channeled material by Esther and Jerry Hicks.[71] It gives you a whole list of exercises you can do on a daily basis to learn how to attract what you want, based on how you handle energy.

In a nutshell, the Law of Attraction works like a magnet: You attract what you give out. The Universe is not judgmental, so you can decide whatever you want to attract, whether it's hurting or helping others.

The Law of Attraction works the same on romantic relationships as it does in every corner of life. You attract what you give out. Some people may protest and say that they attract abusive boyfriends, one after the other, and that's not what they want, so therefore the Law of Attraction does not work. Well, it does, but the person who attracts abusive men (or women) has trauma to confront in this particular area of life. In almost all these cases, the person has had an abusive childhood in one way or another and needs to handle and take charge of that past situation before they can attract more positive people into their lives.

The Law of Attraction is very useful even to break karmic cycles. If you break patterns and start attracting what enhances your spiritual growth, the energies will adjust accordingly, and as we shall go into later, you can, and will, heal your previous lives.

If you, the reader, is interested in learning more about the Law of Attraction, I suggest you read the Abraham/Hicks material.[72]

---

[71] *Ask and It is Given* is the name of the website of Esther and Jerry Hicks, Esther being the channeler of the entity who calls himself "Abraham", and this is their online address: http://www.abraham-hicks.com/lawofattractionsource/index.php . A .pdf version of the material, including exercises, can be found here: http://user32012.websitewizard.com/files/unprotected/Abraham/Ask-and-It-isGiven---Abraham.pdf

[72]   http://user32012.websitewizard.com/files/unprotected/Abraham/Ask-and-It-isGiven---Abraham.pdf

Psychic Vampirism

As an important spin on the Law of Attraction I also want to bring up the subject of "psychic vampires." We all know the myth about the vampires who suck blood from their victims and make them into vampires as well. Although there is some truth to this myth, it can also be seen as a metaphor.

The worst vampires you can imagine are not necessarily those who suck your blood, but *those who suck your energy!*

We have all encountered them, and it's always traumatic when we do.

I have been aware of the existence of such people since I was young and used to avoid them when I could, after having had a few quite horrible encounters with them. They are not large in numbers--perhaps 5-8% of the whole population, but the damage they do to their environment is so devastating that it seems like they are larger in number.[73]

Michael Tsarion is an author, lecturer, and a researcher, and he once wrote quite a short, but very down-to-the-point article about psychic vampirism. When I have encountered people in my life lately, who seem to have a problem with one or more of these vampires, I always give them a copy of this article, and so far, it has always blown their minds and helped them in their process of turning a bad situation around. Once they have recognized it for what it is, most people are then willing to take steps to disconnect from such people, or if a family member, be able to come up with ideas to handle their own unique situation.

The article is so short that I am going to repost it here for the reader's convenience. I hope it will help some who are in this situation:

Vampirism

How much do you know about the people you think you know?

Do your emotional attachments to people blind you to their real natures, and if so, how much?

Person A - becomes dependent on others, under the name of love.

Person B - makes others dependent upon them, under the name of love.

Person C - does both.

Person D - does neither.

LISTEN UP...

---

[73] In 2024, when this editing is being done, psychologists tell us the number of narcissists in society is currently increasing rapidly, primarily because of social media.

There is no gadget or meter to know when a potential psychic or energy vamp is sucking you dry... The only way to tell you are under attack are...

Feel like shit for no reason

Life starts to suck, for no reason

Constant anxiety, for no reason

Health suffers, energy is down, for no reason

Your sic depressed and feelings of futility abound, for no reason

Bad dreams, for no reason

Bad attitude, for no reason

Attracting obstacles, for no reason

Getting suspicious, for no reason

Begin to doubt yourself, your god, your destiny, your fate, your sanity, for no reason

oh yes, and you think its ALL YOUR OWN FAULT...Well, maybe it is, and maybe there is something else to learn...

Yes, there is no physical meter with a dial that goes to the red when your being drained and dumped on by others... but there is one kind of meter that has been with us from the beginning... THE HUMAN INTUITION... backed up by arts like Vibrational Kinesiology, and with a healthy dose of REASON, and EMOTIONAL INTELLIGENCE... it may all start making sense.

It had better... cause they don't all live in Transylvania, and they don't all dress in black...

A few mainstream psychoanalysts have been getting rather frustrated with those clients who just cannot get better, and who seem to backslide, or whose issues seem vague and insurmountable... Yes, they have tried it all, going along with the traditional theories concerning Personal Responsibility, and that we create our own sickness, and all that.

These are important theories...but guess what?

After getting nowhere, a few smart psychologists have put down the textbooks and taken of sic their spectacles, and have asked those poor patients, the ones with their heads in their hands, questions like...

"So who is around you at this time..." or "So who are you hanging around with..." or "tell us about the people you love..."

Aaaah! - Answers at last. The light shines in at last...The red flags are waving and the mist clears...

Don't sic believe me? Well, I did not invent it...

Healing fails to occur because it is easier to harm another than heal oneself -
Vernon Howard

*Humanity must perforce prey on itself, like monsters from the deep -*William
Shakespeare

*Now the betrayer had given them a sign, saying, "The one I shall kiss is the
man; seize him -* Matt 26:48

*For Brutus, as you know, was Caesar's angel: Judge, O you gods! how dearly
Caesar loved him. This was the most unkindest cut of all; For when the noble
Caesar saw him stab, Ingratitude, more strong than traitors' arms, Quite
vanquish'd him: then burst his mighty heart...*William Shakespeare (Julius
Caesar)

*And the brother shall deliver up the brother to death, and the father the child:
and the children shall rise up against their parents, and cause them to be put to
death. And ye shall be hated of all men for my name's sake: but he that
endureth to the end shall be saved –*(Matt 10:21-22)

*And when his twelve disciples were called together, he gave to them power of
unclean spirits, to cast them out of men, and to heal every languor, and sickness
-* (Matt 10:1)

*They that are not as I am made themselves like me. They that are unworthy of
me made me angry. The wretches that belong not to the house of my father rose,
they took arms against me, they rose, they took arms against me, making war
with me, making war with me, fighting for my holy robe, for my enlightening
light, that it might lighten their darkness, for my sweet fragrance, that it might
sweeten their foulness, because of my brethren, the sons of light, that they might
give a peace to their land, because of my sister, the hour of light, that she might
be a strengthening of their building -* (The Manichean Psalms of Thomas)

*Their webs shall not become garments, neither shall they cover themselves with
their works: their works are works of iniquity, and the act of violence is in their
hands -* (Isaiah 59:6)

and the salvation?... That's easy...

---you there yet?[74]

The reason I'm bringing this subject up is because it is extremely
important that we have the knowledge of these people and entities, or it
will seriously halt our progress and can even be a threat to our immediate

---

[74] Ref: http://www.illuminati-news.com/0/vampirism.htm;
http://www.psychicvampirism.com/

lives. If nothing else, these vampires put deep scars in our souls that always need healing.

So, the bottom-line is: When you notice that someone you are connected with constantly makes you feel uncomfortable and tired for no apparent reason and things start to go wrong in your life, then take into consideration that this other person may be a psychic vampire. Sometimes the psychic vampire is not obvious, and it will take a while to stop them. Important, though, is to not go on a witch hunt and start accusing innocent people of being vampires; it doesn't help the situation. I am saying this, because when somebody has been drained of energy for a long time, they tend to become more or less paranoid, feeling like they are boxing shadows. The way to spot a vampire is to be aware of how you feel in the presence of a certain person. When you interact with them, do you feel empowered, neutral, *drained and/or depressed during the visit and/or afterwards*? Is there somebody you relate to who makes you feel intimidated, useless, ugly, or stupid? If so, that's your vampire.

Still, before you decide who it is, always notice how you feel every time you connect with him/her, and afterwards, how you feel when that person is *not* around for a few days or longer. Never judge somebody just because they happen to act like a vampire once or twice. That person could have a bad day or in their turn be in contact with a vampire. It's the recurrence that is the indicator!

It's often hard to get rid of such people; they tend to hang on like parasites and are experts in pushing your buttons. They may cry and beg for you to stay, or they'll tell you that you can't live without them; that you need them for your survival. Often, after a traumatic argument or violent incident, they bring flowers and cry at the door. Some fall for this, especially when they have had this connection for a long time. The positive person has been so dependent upon the dominant vampire that he or she thinks he or she can't live without him/her. This, of course, is not true, and because of that, the "victim" (although I don't like to use this word) is already weak from having had her or his energies pulled, thinks the vampire is correct and chooses to stay in the bad situation. They often also feel sorry for the vampire because these beings are experts in making you feel bad and not caring enough for them. They are also often super-jealous. To stay connected with a person like that can be fatal for many reasons. One being that when your life energy is sucked out, your immune system will become depleted and you're prone to getting seriously ill.

Why do vampires do this? Well, these people have a hard time creating their own energy because they don't know how to, so they need someone else (preferably someone with lots of positive energy) to feed their own energy. And they always feed out of fear. They create fear in the other person and that fear is their life energy. Vampires have forgotten how to genuinely give something "from their heart"; their heart chakra is hopelessly closed, they are disconnected from the Prime Creator, and when they choose to give, it's always with a *"what's in it for me?"* They are out of balance with their energy currents to the extreme. Many are also possessed by entities from the lower astral planes who use these human vehicles to feed off your fear. If they can feed from someone else, they feel strong and vital, but when the victim is too low on energy, they may walk away as destructively as possible and choose a new victim; or they have several victims whom they are working on at the same time (infidelity).

Whatever is the case, if such person should be exposed and no longer is able to pull life energy out of somebody else, they would collapse and eventually die, unless they start on building their own energy by being more positively oriented and thus more in balance, something psychology tells us they are unable to do.

In psychology, these people are called narcissists.

Schrödinger's Cat and Different Timelines

A good example of what the Multiverse is in relation to timelines can be studied in the theorem called "Schrödinger's Cat".[75] It is the paradox which was described by the Austrian Physicist, Erwin Schrödinger back in 1935. Although he doesn't use the word Multiverse in his research, he was still describing how the Multiverse works.

Figure 4.2 - Schrödinger's Cat

Schrödinger, in simple terms, is picturing a cat in a box. The person outside the box knows there is a cat inside but can't see it because the box is blocking the view of the animal. The question is if the cat inside the box is dead or alive. From this person's perspective, he will know when he opens the box, but from a quantum viewpoint, the cat is both dead and alive before the box is even opened. At the same moment as the person thinks the animal can be either way, both realities are initiated. In that instant, at least two timelines are created simultaneously, one as real as the

---

[75] http://en.wikipedia.org/wiki/Schrödinger%27s_cat

other.

It's a big leap in consciousness to go from a belief system where we think there is only one Universe to the concept of a Multiverse and Infinite Potential; especially when we realize that we may exist in many of them at the same time, often unaware of our other-selves. We are bound to the laws of time we to some degrees have made up here and are from this aspect dependent upon the cycles of the stars, planets, and galaxies.

Who can imagine what would happen if all these potential realities became known to us in an instant? The charge would be so great that we would probably literally explode. No one could handle the complexity of that when brought up to a conscious level. Insanity is not even the word to start describing it. We may get a glimpse of this if we look at a schizophrenic person talking to themselves; they have all these voices in their head, talking to them, and with each other, simultaneously. But are the schizophrenics just delusional? I would say, no. Whether it's from trauma or otherwise, these people have opened themselves to the Multiverse to an extent that they are totally overwhelmed. It's too much download and inter-connection at once. In this sense, schizophrenic people are more multi-dimensional than the average person, but they have no idea what they are experiencing, and they get a big chunk of it at once, which overloads the system.

Fortunately for the big majority, this is not how it's going to pan out. We are experiencing a gradual awakening, so we can handle the increase of information. That's the normal evolution of the biomind. Also, becoming multi-dimensional is a learning process, and there are tools we can use to accomplish the task quicker. How this works will be discussed later.

PAPER 5:
THE MISCONCEPTION OF THE ASCENSION PROCESS AND THE NATURE OF CHANNELING
Friday, February 18, 2011

The Ascension Fraud

It may feel like the rug is being swept away beneath the feet of those who believe in Ascended Masters who will come and save us, and ascension processes that just happen out of the blue. I don't want to put the whole New Age movement under one umbrella, but we need to realize (the sooner, the better) that there will be no sudden shift of consciousness that is magically going to lift those who are "enlightened" to the 4th or 5th Dimensions. There are no Ascended Masters who will come down and call upon those who are "worthy" to ascend. I am not saying the there are no "Ascended Masters," but if they are worthy of their title, they are not going to interfere with our development as individuals, or as a species. If someone is landing in big spaceships, saying they are here to save you, run the other way.

The Ascended Masters, whom some people channel, are not working in humanity's favor, so buyers beware! Those who show themselves off as either gods or superior beings are frauds or saying they are someone they are not. There is a checklist you can use if you're into channeled material and trying to discern who is who; who's the "good guy" and who's the "bad guy" and we are getting to that soon.

The same thing if you tune into the "love and light" movement, where they say that if you see and hear no evil, there will be no evil. In a sense that is true, because we create our own reality, but we are also interacting with other people and with different organizations every day, and the sequence is that light comes before love. Light is information, and unconditional love is God or Source in Its pure essence. Therefore, we need the knowledge *before* we can understand what to do with it.

Another thing to beware of are those channelers who say that the

Global Elite has the power, and you have to fight them. Again, run!

There is not much of a difference between Christians, who think that there will be a rapture; those who are "Born Again" will be "beamed up" by God, while the more unfortunate, who may be great people, but are not baptized, will be left to burn in the eternal fire, and the New Age movement where they say that you will be "beamed up" to Paradise in the 4th and 5th Dimensions.

So, am I saying that there is no ascension? No, there will be an ascension, but although the ascension process is a natural thing which happens in cycles, it doesn't come for free. We need to know the dynamics of the process and we also need to be aware of what is happening in our own reality before we can go to the next. In other words, we must know what we're doing. Too many people are just reading and listening to channeled material and other metaphysical information, feeling good about it and then go on with their lives like if nothing has happened, certain of that now when you "know," the ascension will come automatically because they know more than other people. This will not do much for a person's ascension other than that they have some valuable information. The "secret" to *real* ascension is to learn about life and then *live what we learn!* Anyone can listen and read, but it requires some courage to change your ways and start walking the talk.

Still, when push comes to shove, the real thing is so much better and more exciting than the illusion (read *de*lusion).

In the next subsection, I want to bring up the concept of channeling and some valuable leads on how to discern helpful material from not so helpful. I have personally listened to quite a few sources and read more than a few books on the subject, and after a while it becomes clearer what is good channeling and what's not.

We humans have lived generation after generation in fear. There has always been this "invisible authority" present, which we can't really pinpoint down, controlling our lives, belief systems and thinking in general. Those who speak up are usually, in one way or another, made examples of. This induces fear in others, who want to, but then dare not, speak *their* truth. "If I speak up, I will lose my job"; "If I tell them what I believe, they will think I'm crazy and stop talking to me"; "What will my family say?" We all recognize these thoughts, but they are all based on fear. It's "easier" to be quiet and not speak up, but still, if we don't, we will not evolve, and we will not help others see a bigger picture, whether it has to do with our job or spiritual beliefs. We will also not feel good about ourselves.

The same cabal is still in charge after thousands of years of overt and covert tyranny (see http://illuminati-news.com/moriah.htm). The Internet has helped humans to connect all over the globe in a way that has not been possible before (at least not since Atlantis, if even then), and there is of course little the Powers That Be, PTB, can do to stop that, other than turning on the "kill switch" and shut down the Internet. In China, certain websites are not accessible due to strict censorship, but here in the west we're pretty much free to communicate whatever we want. There is an ulterior reason for this, or course, which is to collect data and information on the human soul group to be used in a giant database and supercomputer for malignant purposes, but that's for another paper. There are dimensional and even more so, interdimensional, beings, who are controlling the PTB (the Rockefellers, Rothschild's, the Bush's, and others). They were the ones who wanted the Internet to develop. If they are to take global control over the human population, they need a global network. Have you asked yourself why they are speeding up Internet connections repeatedly? We already have fast Internet available to us; why even faster? Again, this global network is primarily meant for the ETs to control us, not for humans to chat with each other. Then, of course, the Internet can be used by people like me and others to communicate our truth for free, without having to go through book publishers, promotion, and people having to buy my stuff. If I have something to communicate, I can put it out here and thousands of people can read it. So, it works both ways.

People in the spiritual movement often believe it's our next step to return and connect with the Prime Creator and once again become ONE with IT (She). It is my conviction that this is not the case, though. We are in this universe to learn and experience, and we do this as separate units of consciousness, who are still connected to Source on a subquantum level, but when we're done here, we just go to the next level of learning on a higher vibration. There may be a time when we can choose whether we want to go back and merge with Source and complete our experience, or continue exploring, but that time is not yet, as I see it.

Our immediate goal is to further develop our infinite potentials and not become, but realize that we already are, multi-dimensional, and this is quite a different ball game all together.

The truth of the matter is that we already are multi-dimensional, but we don't know it; thus, we don't use our potentials. So where would we go? If we are all ONE, and we are all ultimately connected on a subquantum level, where can we go except inside ourselves, into the quantum and subquantum part of ourselves, see our connection to everything around us and transfer that from the microcosm to the macro cosmos?
Our bodies are originally made to be multi-dimensional. We already have what we need. Therefore, we want to stay grounded and not reach for some lofty "God's Palace" in the sky.

How Channeling Really Works

I would say that most channeled material is a confusing mixed bag of truths, half-truths and lies. However, I believe there are channeled entities doing their best to assist us to the best of their abilities, but they are limited as well as we are, in predicting exactly what is going to happen in the future. I also believe virtually all channeled entities, regardless of who they are, have their own agenda; but sometimes, we humans can still benefit from it in a symbiosis kind of way—they help us and we help them.

The way channeling works, in general, is that the entities who temporarily possess a human body (often called a "vehicle") read the consciousness of that vehicle and at the same time tune into the mass consciousness of the entire population of the whole planet; they "hook up" to the planetary matrix, i.e. everything on the planet itself as a semi-conscious being. They also have access to the Akashic records of the entire human race, and they have their own mass consciousness and that of the Multiverse to draw information and knowledge from. Some of them are also from our future and past, so they may have quite a lot of information from their own memories to draw from.

By having their multi-dimensional perspective, these entities can answer our questions with a high rate of accuracy, but the cons are that when they look into the future, things become slippery. All beings on the planet, although to some degree predictable, make decisions every second of their lives, and these decisions create an outcome. If we then combine the decisions of nearly 7 billion people, the mutual outcome for the human soul group and everything we affect is quite unpredictable. Thus, it's difficult for these entities to tell the future of the mass consciousness. It's always easier to tell what will happen in a day or a week (because less thoughts and decisions are made within that short time span) than it would be to predict what will happen in a year or longer. We then need to include all the timelines involved. All these entities can do is to read the present consciousness of the planetary timeline at which they have entered, predict how the human consciousness will react and act in the future, still based on the time in which they operate, and get a probable picture of the future. However, any channeled entities worth your while will tell you that this is a very slippery business, and it's preferable not to try to predict things too precisely.

When taking part of channeled material, we must consider the agenda of the channeled entity or group consciousness. They can tell us things they want us to know and at the same time exclude what they *don't* want you to know. In addition, different entities have different levels of awareness, and just like with us humans; some may be truthful while others lie to push forward their own agenda.

We will discuss this problem in other papers as well. It is always a struggle to lay a puzzle that is multi-dimensional, and we must accept that we are just in the beginning of learning things; whatever conclusions we come to today will be subject to future editing. What holds true today may be an "old paradigm" tomorrow in the fluid and ever-changing Multiverse.

Another thing important to consider is whether the channeled entities are having you give your power away. Only if the information is uplifting and can bring you to a new level of experience is it worth your time. And if they tell you to give your power to someone else than yourself (Ascended Masters or whomever), close the book, turn off the CD, and start looking elsewhere for valuable material.

A typical example of quality channeling which falls into many of the categories above, is, in my opinion, the Pleiadians, channeled by Barbara Marciniak.[76] In this case, their agenda is known and openly discussed by the entities, and they have been consistently assisting mankind for 23 years as of this writing, without contradicting themselves. Their information is uplifting and educating, and when it's more on the serious side, it always leads to a solution.

Being open about the fact that they do have a personal agenda and what it is, is a positive thing in itself. Now we know what they want and how they want it, and it's up to us to agree with them or not. We can choose to be part of their agenda and see how it can benefit us, or we can opt out and choose another direction.

According to the Pleiadians, they are us in the future, but also our ancestors. They were part of the genetic engineering of humankind in the ancient past and are now "stuck" in a future timeline, which is not very pleasant to live in. They are directly connected to the events happening here on Earth in this nano-second (see the next section for an in-depth explanation of this term), and they want us to make more conscious decisions than they did when they were here at this particular time (on their timeline). They chose a machine world before a more simplistic, conscious reality closer to nature, and their "agenda" is to change their own timeline so the nightmare they are living in now (our future) can change as well. They are refugees from different star systems; beings who have come together as a collective to contact us and educate us on what is ahead. They say we have freewill to do whatever we want, but they are hoping that by teaching us, we will make more conscious decisions than they did in their past. If their agenda is successful, it could potentially mean that they cease to exist in their reality while we thrive in ours, but they are willing to take that chance, even if it is leading to their own extinction.

---

[76] Barbara Marciniak, residing in Apex, North Carolina, and this group of Pleiadian refugees of a higher multi-dimensional than we humans are not fond of the technology we have developed here on Earth up to this point. They don't bash out on technology at large, only how it's used. Therefore, you can find very little of their material on the Internet. Barbara has a website, which is updated with new channeled material continually, at http://pleiadians.com.

Alternatively, if we choose the same route as they did, it's a good chance we will end up where they are.

The Nano-Second and the Importance of Staying Grounded in our Bodies

An interesting thing the Pleiadians talk about is the nano-second, which is their name of the time from 1987-2012. That's when the energies on this planet are increasing exponentially, partly because we are aligning with the Galactic Center, an event that is already happening, but is culminating on Winter Solstice, 2012. This is the major reason for the mass awakening, but also for the suppression of the same by those in power, who want us to stay asleep and ignorant of our true selves. These suppressive forces are both humans in apparent power of this planet, and beings from elsewhere.

I think most of you who read this paper agree that more and more people around the globe are "waking up"(including you), also to the fact that there is a "Hidden Hand" pulling the strings of mankind from behind the scenes. Things are not exactly the way we're told they are by governments, mass media and so-called "authorities". The awakening has happened quickly within a relatively short time frame, and many of us are certainly not the same person we were 25 years ago, or perhaps even 2 years ago for several. Many of us are sensing that time is speeding up, sometimes to the extent that it's hard to catch up and stay updated with what is going on around us or inside us. Historically speaking, this is a new phenomenon, at least in modern times. To some degree, the Internet has contributed to the mass awakening because we have been able to connect on a global scale to share our viewpoints and our thoughts, but this is not the entire answer. If we weren't ready to wake up from our spiritual slumber, the Internet wouldn't have done the trick. There is still a lot to do before enough humans have woken up to make a radical change of paradigms, but we are quickly heading toward just that.

The Pleiadian time frame (1987-2012) feels pretty accurate to me when we realize that the mass awakening has happened within the last 25 years. They say we have this small time window when there are intense energies hitting Earth from the cosmos, mostly on the gamma ray level, which heavily affect our bodies and our minds. Energy is not something that only supports basic life, but also energy on a quantum level, as encoded information, and it is this information triggering our dormant DNA, connecting us with the Multiverse. Our own sun that is also connected with, and affected by, the *"Womb of the Mother"*, the Giant Sun (or huge collection of suns) in the Galactic Center, is more intense than normal, and is directly affecting us and our mass consciousness here on Earth.

Therefore, it's very important that we always stay grounded and in our bodies; *especially* now while this process is so intense. All the information from cosmos that we "download" during this time will help us tremendously after 2012 when the energies slowly go back to a more normal level and time as we perceive it will gradually slow down again. So, we need to be very mindful right now and work on connection with these energies, or it will be so much harder afterwards. This boost of energy we are currently experiencing is a "free ride" if we are receptive, ready and willing to take it all in, and when the nano-second has passed, we have time to process what we have gathered.

This makes it so much more important to "follow our heart" and our "instincts" (intuition), and trust what we feel. We are living in times where we will find the intellect being useful, but also quite limited. These are *not* the times where the logical mind can figure things out on its own; it needs immense help from the heart chakra. Not until we have opened our hearts and started "feeling" can we more accurately analyze what is going on and how to proceed. Agent Mulder in *The X-Files* was wrong when he said that "the answers are out there," and that's why he never found them. The answers are within, and that's where we need to start looking.

The Real Ascension

The yearning many of us feel inside to ascend to higher densities is not just programming and deception. It's also because a fragment of us remembers how it is to be multi-dimensional. How many of us haven't looked up in the night-sky, watched the stars, just to get this feeling that we "want to go home"? Some of us may even feel a little sad or get a feeling of being lost. We don't truly understand why we feel this way, but there is a reason. It's not necessarily because we don't belong here on Earth and therefore want to "go home" to some other star system. It's more that we miss our abilities to be multi-dimensional when the entire Multiverse is our home. We feel a little bit like someone who is in prison, looking out through the bars, seeing the world outside and get this longing for freedom.

Ascension, as it is presented in the New Age Movement and in channeled material in particular, triggers this feeling inside of us. This is probably the main reason we so dearly want to believe in it, and another reason being that we want to escape from a reality we don't like. We feel we are trapped in a control system with no way out, and ascension seems like the perfect escape. The ideas of ascension and Ascended Masters have also been promoted by certain secret societies over the millennia, mostly to keep people who are thinking outside the box trapped within the 3rd Density.

Figure 5.1 – The late Carla Rueckert, who originally channeled the Ra Collective in the 1980s.

The common misconception is that by ascending we are leaving our bodies and going somewhere. We are not leaving Earth, our home, but instead, while still in our bodies, we are letting the higher densities manifest through our chakras, little by little at first, then faster and faster. We do this by activating more and more of our DNA, and not to escape to some lofty reality where everything is bliss. To become multi-dimensional means we are opening ourselves again to the Multiverse that we once were connected to, and as we evolve, our environment will gradually change, because we are creating a new paradigm, a new Earth with our vibrations, thoughts, emotions, and newly regained wisdom. Our DNA is starting to lighten up and the chakras open, one by one. Our Primary Body is our "home station" and from there we can explore the Multiverse with our thoughts and our *photonic bodies.*[77] Before we are done with this paper, the difference between ascension and becoming multi-dimensional will be crystal clear. We experience the Multiverse in all its glory from here, in 4-space/time. We need bodies to function on a multi-dimensional level and to have a full experience. Or as James of the WingMakers puts it:

> The orientation that humanity is emerging from the relative darkness of the 3rd dimension to the 4th dimension is a misconception of the modern-day New Age movement. Humanity evolves to embrace the multiverse, and as it evolves it discovers that its superuniverse is accessible to the human mind in ways that

---

[77] *Physics and Science, Paper #1: Exploring the Unum -- The Ever-Expanding Multiverse*, section 1.1

defy logic. This is the stage upon which humanity is entering, and it is not to ascend in a vibratory epiphany to a higher dimension, but rather it is to interact with a broader multiverse of intelligence that heretofore has only been imagined by a handful of humanity's finest representatives.

Humanity will remain in the 3rd dimension, but will increasingly become aware of the higher dimensions while living in the 3rd dimension, even as First Source, its creator, does. First Source lives in the 3rd dimension, but is simultaneously aware of itself throughout the spectrum of the multiverse, and through Source Intelligence, is aware of all life forms in all dimensions.[78]

The Pleiadians say something very similar. Still, it's not the most important thing what other people or collective entities say; what's important is what *you* feel and if what you're learning gives you power and inspiration or not. That's what matters, because you are the one who ultimately will have to use what you learn.

These special times we are living in are very challenging for many; both for those who are thrilled by the incoming energies and learn from the light fragments carried on by the Sun, and those who are still not awake enough to recognize them consciously. There is no doubt that this dance of increased energies will also affect our environment, and it already does. Some people think that the Earth changes will soon cease to happen, after an imagined culmination in 2012, but they will continue years after that. Not wanting to be alarming, but still getting real, I am sorry to say that the earthquakes, tsunamis, global warming (the real one), flooding, hurricanes and other natural phenomena which are not manmade by HAARP and other similar technology, will continue to occur with increased intensity long after 2012.[79]

One of the main things is to be prepared; not only for the earth changes, but for the changes within, where the mass awakening is taking place. Those who have prepared themselves by starting the process to connect with the Multiverse will have a much easier time going through the transition, while those who haven't prepared at all, or are totally ignorant to what is going on, will have a very tough time, and some will even go insane and/or commit suicide. I am not saying this to scare the reader, just as a matter of fact. We can already see this happening around us; many people are totally overwhelmed by their life situations and don't understand what is happening. This is why I believe the information in

---

[78] *James: Questions and Answers: Responses from James -- Session 2*, http://wingmakers.com/jamesqa2.html

[79] Here, in the online version, there is a short discussing about the incoming Nibiru which is removed in this book because I believe Nibiru is disinformation.

these papers is so important. If nothing else, I am hoping they at least trigger something within the reader to start the search for Inner Knowledge.

Also, different timelines are merging as we become more multi-D. We will talk more about this in another paper, and how we live many different lives simultaneously on different timelines and in different time periods. This may not be real to some of the readers at this point but will be clearer the more you read.

Others are having vivid and lucid dreams, where they connect with their multi-dimensional selves, meet with what they perceive as their dead relatives or spirit guides (who sometimes can be one and the same). For those who can interpret the symbolism in their dreams may learn a lot of what is happening in their lives and in their environment. After all, it is in the dream state agreements are made,[80] and in certain terms, the dream state is more "real" than our awake state, due to that we are more multi-dimensionally connected on a quantum level in our dream state than when we are when awake. Many people will become more psychic and telepathic during this period, and when we notice something like that happens to us, occasionally, it is important to embrace these moments and acknowledge our new abilities. Also, to recognize them when they occur and work on developing them even more. It's a crucial part of being multi-dimensional.

In the Multiverse most evolved beings are living under "The Law of One,"[81] which is the understanding that we are all ONE and what we are doing to another we do to ourselves. They have the knowledge of who they are and where they came from. Still, it needs to be said that even in the Multiverse there is corruption, power struggles and wars *(as above, so below)*, and not everything is bliss just because we open up to new realities. The Multiverse is there to be explored (it's the whole purpose) and all beings have free will to experience anything they like; that's the beauty of the game, if we look at it from the original, intended perspective. No one is going to punish you for doing something counter-survival, except yourself. We have all heard the expression *"what comes around goes around,"* which is another expression for the term "karma." So, we will notice when we open our chakras that it's still up to us how we want to explore the Multiverse; we can do it from a

---

[80] "The Pleiadians", channeled by Barbara Marciniak on August 13, 2010: *"Awakening to the Sun"*, CD 1, Track 2.

[81] The RA Material (or *The Law of One* Material) was channeled by a group of three people in the early 1980s. This consciousness is called the "Ra Collective" and is a 6th Density group that was channeled through Carla Rueckert over a short amount of time and resulted in 5 books containing the complete channeled sessions from these beings. http://lawofone.info. The Ra Material in book format can be ordered from the channeler's website: http://www.llresearch.org/library/the_law_of_one_pdf/the_law_of_one_pdf.aspx.

positive viewpoint or from a negative. It is up to the individual and/or the species. As long as we are separate from Source and are experiencing the Matrix/Unum/Multiverse, there is going to be polarity, though. The huge difference between now and then is that all choices will be available to us, and we can go anywhere we want in the Multiverse, but still have our base in our biological bodies.

The planet we live on now is very dense and vibrates within a relatively low frequency band. Things here, including our bodies, are condensed and heavy. The lower the vibration, the more solid matter becomes. Hence, it's sometimes hard for many visitors from the rest of the cosmos to stay around us for a longer period because outside of Earth things are much less dense. After a while, they get quite uncomfortable and need to leave, or if they don't, they may get caught up in our low vibration and may even get stuck here, which has happened.[82]

Astronauts who have left the Earth's atmosphere are witnesses to how different it feels when they leave the planet; they say it feels like a big burden has been lifted from their shoulders. Their thinking process is clearer, their bodies feel healthier, and they become almost euphoric; and also, interestingly, the noise inside their heads are gone; it's silent! When they leave Earth, they get out of its frequency range and feel a taste of how Earth would be if we all increased our vibrations. Once the astronauts return to Earth, they get caught within the low frequency of the mass consciousness again, with the consequence that some astronauts and cosmonauts fall into chronic depression, and many start having alcohol problems.

The RA Material

The Ra Material has been available to us since the 1980s, channeled by Carla Rueckert (*fig. 5.2*) between 1981 and 1984; the late Don Elkins asked the questions and Jim McCarty was the scribe.[83] These three persons made up the group who channeled The Ra Collective, claiming to be a 6th Density Collective Consciousness, who have visited Earth in physical form in the past. The result of the channeled sessions, which were assembled into 5 books called *The Ra Material* or *The Law of One*, were considered a break-through in metaphysics due to the wealth of information and Don Elkins' brilliant questions. Channeling and metaphysics have not been the same since, I think I dare say; at least not until the Pleiadians came into the

---

[82] Interview with James of the WingMakers, by Project Camelot, ©2008. http://www.wingmakers.com/downloads/Interview_James_PC.pdf.
[83] http://www.llresearch.org/library/the_law_of_one_pdf/ the_law_of_one_pdf.aspx

picture in 1988. Many entities came after and said similar things, but the Ra Material was one of the pioneer channels of modern times.

I have read all the 5 books. There is a great website where a fan of the material set up a searchable site with all the info, so you easily can find anything you want, sorted by categories, words, phrases and whatnot. The web address is http://lawofone.info. Carla Rueckert's current website is http://llresearch.org/.

This material probably found a new life within the spiritual movement and the metaphysical research community after an anonymous person, calling himself "the Hidden Hand", posted on the Above Top Secret Forum in late 2008.[84] I recaptured the conversation this person had with the forum members (we actually don't even know the gender of this person but will make him male for the purpose of our discussion), and made an article from it, which has become extremely popular; perhaps one of the most popular articles I've ever posted up to date (2011). I called it *Dialogue with 'Hidden Hand'—Self-Proclaimed Illuminati Insider.*[85] This person, revealing a lot of interesting information about who is controlling our planet, including valuable data regarding things that revolve around that subject, also mentioned the Ra Material as being one of the most accurate channeled pieces of information on the planet today. This statement had many people, including myself, read the books for the first time.

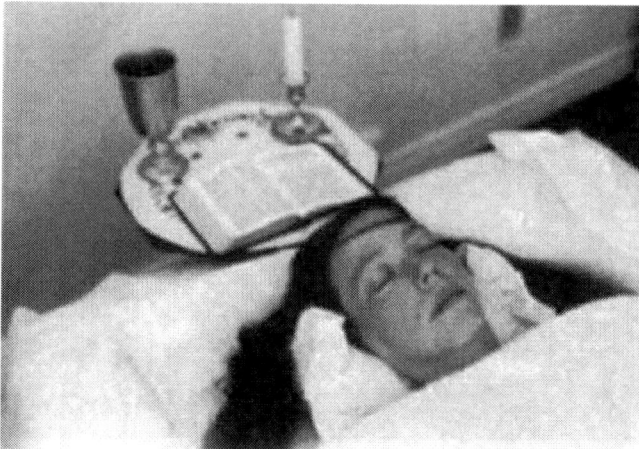

Figure 5.2 - Carla Rueckert channeling Ra (early 1980s)

The Hidden Hand is not a friend of humanity, from our every-day perspective; he is a catalyst, he claims. Some people saw him as an ally and

---

[84] http://www.abovetopsecret.com/forum/
[85] http://illuminati-news.com/00363.html

helper, but it's easy to forget that he is a mass murderer and a very negatively oriented being, claiming to belong to a bloodline not from this Earth. Secondly, he is promoting the Ra Material as being a nearly impeccable source (claiming it to be around 97% correct).

The difference between the Ra Material and the Pleiadians, for example, is the lack of intimacy in the first. You get the feeling that the Pleiadians are "real" beings in the sense that they can build a close connectivity with the audience. Although I haven't heard an original session between Ra/Carla Rueckert and Don Elkins live, reading the material gives me the feeling of "robotism;" the Ra Collective is completely emotionless and machine-like in their presence and their replies. This always bothered me, but I put that aside in favor of the informative channeling they provided. The Ra collective claims to be 6th Density beings, having visited our planet on a few occasions in the far-gone past, and now they are quite close to completing an Octave (densities 1-8, where 8 is the transition from one Octave to the next).

The Ra Collective basically contacted humanity to prepare us for the "Harvest," which is an event that, according to them, happens every 75,000 years, and will happen around 2012. They say that an Earth cycle is now coming to an end, and those who are more than 51% "Service to Others" rather than "Service to Self" are vibrating high enough to ascend to the 4th Density. Those who are not will be left behind and recycled into another 75,000 year cycle in 3rd Density, but on another planet. Earth is, in their words, now ascending to the 4th Density as well; in fact, it already *is* 4th Density. Those who vibrate high enough will stay on this very Earth and transform together with it into 4th Density.

The similarity between the RA Material and that of the Pleiadians are remarkable, although they approach the same things from two different angles. I find this fascinating and convincing, as they seemingly are not from the same collective. Both the Pleiadians and RA are talking about "ascending" to a New Earth of a higher vibration, which can carry our new, higher consciousness. RA call it the Harvest, and although the Pleiadians use this term once or twice as well, they are saying that Earth will basically be splitting into two Earths, metaphysically speaking; one will stay in 3-D while one will be a 4-D Earth.

The RA Material, as well as the "Cassiopaeans," "Germane," "The Pleiadians," "Hidden Hand," and others are distinguishing between Service to Self (**STS**) and Service to Others (**STO**). These terms will be more closely discussed in a separate section, but for those who are totally unfamiliar of the terms, here's a brief explanation, as presented by the RA Material:

Service to Others (STO), for those to which this term is new, means that a person is ready to serve their fellow man and their environment when help is needed and asked for. This is done unconditionally, without the person asking him/herself, "what is in it for me?" You simply don't expect anything in return. If someone wants to pay back for your service, it may be accepted, as this is the other person's way of feeling gratitude but should never be asked for or bargained for. STO is done out of Unconditional Love, which is a basic attribute of Source.

Service to Self (STS) is, as the term indicates, the opposite. If you do something for others, you always ask yourself what you can gain from it. You don't do things to help others out of Unconditional Love for All That Is, but for your own benefit. The Service to Self-person is experiencing a manifestation of Source where taking is much more important than giving.

STS indicates that it's the work of the Ego. I need to add that there is nothing wrong with having an ego. Without it, you wouldn't be able to think intellectually. In some factions of the New Age movement it is important to get rid of the ego because the ego is something bad and egotistical. Not necessarily so, though. It's only when the ego totally takes over and the person acts like a "besserwisser" that ego becomes a problem, or rather an obstacle to opening your heart.

According to Ra and many other metaphysical sources, it's okay to be either way, it's just polarity and different experiences. However, they stress that karma is always an issue, and those who choose STS sooner or later must deal with their own karma, so that they may suddenly find themselves on the other end of the rope, where someone else is taking advantage of them to the same degree they did it to others. So, it's just a matter of choice, and either way, we all return to Source, according to Ra, although it will be harder and take longer if we choose the STS route. This is tricky business, as I see it because STS should be the priority—not in a selfish, non-inclusive way, but we are individuals, and each individual has a responsibility to evolve. It's absolutely okay to help others, but not if it hurts the giver. Therefore, I am not a fan of the STS/STO movement the way it's presented. Also, people who buy into the Ra Material and the Hidden Hand too much often develop a bad conscience and may even get anxiety due to that they constantly think about if they are 51% STO or not. By the end of the day, they may have doubts if they are "good enough," or if they are doomed to experience another cycle in 3-D. I think this is detrimental and counter-intuitive.

Both Hidden Hand and Ra say that if you are more than 97% negative, or STS, you ascend to *4th Density Negative*, where you must gradually live out your karma. This is something compared to a living hell, akin to what we sometimes see in movies, where everybody is fighting against each other without remorse, and they all have to watch their backs 24/7 and trust no one. Not a desirable place to be.

I am bringing up the Ra Material and the Hidden Hand quite extensively here because they have become such a big part of the spiritual movement. It can't be stressed enough that we need to pick out what resonates from any material and leave the rest; it's very dangerous to swallow everything someone says, no matter how right it sounds. That goes for karma, in my opinion, to mention one. No one has the whole truth; it must be sought in layers inside us. Seek inside, take in information when needed, but with caution, and create your own reality; the one you want to live in. It is important that we learn how this current prison planet is set up, webs within webs of deceit. It's very cleverly orchestrated, and it includes the metaphysical realms to a large degree as well. Like attracts alike, as we know, and there are bonds and treaties between all kinds of different beings in the expanding Multiverse. Still, it is my absolute conviction that the Multiverse is basically a friendly place and works in our favor. It is us who need to decide what we want to experience. *Ask and ye shall receive!*

Some Final Words

Connecting to the Multiverse is a matter of opening our chakras and minds to endless possibilities. Once we understand that we are all ONE with the Creator, and there is ultimately no separation we truly understand this the rest comes quite naturally. We don't even think in terms of whether we're "good enough." We just know we are all in this together and what you experience, on one level I experience as well, and vice versa. Once this is realized, we are no longer thinking in terms of "good" and "evil" in the same way as before. Everything is experience, and if we encounter something we don't like, we know it's there to show us and teach us something. And we also stop blaming others for the situations we're in. We know beyond any doubt that we are a major part in what we are experiencing, and so long as energy is moving freely and easily, we're good to go, and we learn something.

Also, ponder the following interesting fact: Those who are controlling us, originally from elsewhere, may be more intelligent and more technologically advanced than us because they originate from older civilizations. Still, humans who are waking up here on Earth today with a positive attitude are, in ways that count, more advanced than they are already. We understand that wars and negative control are something of the past and not something we ever want to engage in again. We don't need to bring fear unto others to get things our way; we know we can't win by meeting fire with fire. We do things out of Love and Understanding because that's just the way we naturally think. We are fully aware that using weapons and violence as a means to accomplish goals is *always* a sign of lower awareness and lower consciousness, whether we talk about ETs or humans. We are the future, they are the past, and one day, not too far away in the future, they will no longer match our frequency and will not be part of our reality anymore until they too have come to the same conclusions as we have.

The way we have been set back on this planet and brought down into oblivion is by letting those in power take *our* power away. How many belief systems have been invented *for* us? How many have we invented ourselves? How many religions and spiritual paths do we have to choose from? How many religious leaders? Gurus? Ascended Masters? How many variants of Jesus and God? No one can say we won't have opportunities to pick and choose. It's like when going to the supermarket; you want to buy shampoo, and lo and behold! There are an overwhelming number of different brands and varieties within each brand to pick from. Still, they all basically do the same thing; they wash your hair. Feel free to pick the brand of your choice!

As we go through these papers, my intention is to challenge the reader to start thinking with their heart more than their heads. It's fine to try to wrap our head around things, but the trick is to know when to use our hearts and when to use our heads. These papers are going to challenge both; how much so will differ depending on the reader's current understanding, but my hope is that everybody will feel challenged to a certain degree at least and have quite a few "aha" moments, just like I did when I researched this. As we move up through the "Levels of Learning" (which is how these papers are set up) things will be even clearer.

PAPER 6:
THERE IS A LIGHT AT THE END OF THE TUNNEL—
—*WHAT HAPPENS AFTER BODY DEATH?*
Tuesday, March 25, 2011

Abstract

We all, at one time or another, ponder what happens when the body gives up and dies. It befalls us all, but where do we go? Is there life after death? Without having any proof, many people make up their minds and create a belief system around it, whether it is a religious dogma, a New Age, or a philosophical angle, an agnostic "There may or may not be an afterlife" approach, or the pure atheistic or conservative scientific viewpoint that there is no afterlife.

My purpose with this paper is not to discuss any of the above belief systems. I will immediately take the approach that there *is* an afterlife, and that the soul and spirit live on after body death. There is no doubt about it, and the evidence for that is far more overwhelming than any so-called evidence that there is not. So, our discussion will start on that level, and we'll bring it further.

First, what is a credible witness and good research regarding this subject? A credible witness is:

1. Someone who is telling a story under hypnosis or during regression therapy by a well-trained hypnotist/regression therapist can describe in detail what is happening. This story is then backed up by numerous other witnesses, who have gone through regression therapy by the same or other hypnotists and tell an almost identical story. The sessions have been recorded, and the questions asked by the therapist are in no way leading. Still, the clients (thousands upon thousands of them) are saying basically the same thing. This has been done and I will refer to these kinds

of   testimonies   and   consider   them   evidence.

2. Single witnesses, who recall from trauma or otherwise, what happened after they died. These testimonies, when credible, include deep emotions on the subject; positive or negative; and sometimes an unwillingness to talk about it. The witness has nothing to gain from telling the story, but quite the opposite; they will more likely be looked upon as strange. We have such witnesses as well, and when their stories are coherent, and/or the person comes across as honest and sincere, I consider that evidence, too. These witnesses may even have looked for help to interpret their experience.

Second, what is good research?

1. We have quite a few hypnotists who have hypnotized many witnesses, who all say the same thing, with a few small differences, which should be expected. These hypnotists are professionals, and some of them didn't even believe in past lives until they stumbled upon a client who contacted incidents both (or either) from past lives and (or) the in-between-lives area. The hypnotist started exploring the subject and found out that these incidents were real.

2. Perhaps twenty years ago or so, there were not many books written on this subject, but since then, the interest has increased exponentially and there are good books out there now. Some of them are very well researched and don't always coincide with the positive experiences that many people have had between lives. There seems to be a darker side to this as well.

This Paper will present both sides of the story separately, and we will end with discussing the two and come to some conclusions. We will start with the more positive experiences.

Regression Therapy in Modern Times - A Brief Background

I would highly recommend that the readers gets the books, *Journey of Souls* and *Destiny of Souls* by Dr. Michael Newton (1931-2016).[86] Dr. Newton is a

---

[86] Amazon.com: http://www.amazon.com/Destiny-Souls-Studies-Between-Lives/dp/1567184995

therapist and hypnotist, whose original purpose was to relieve people from stress and depression with the help of regression therapy, or hypnotism. After a while, he noticed that some clients started going back to previous lives and even into the between-lives area, where souls go after they depart from the body after body death.

Fig. 6:1. Dr. Michael Newton

Being a dedicated scientist and an atheist, this came as a shock to him, and he was very skeptical at first. Hence, he asked the subject to be very precise and describe exactly what happened around him/her. He wasn't satisfied until he got some details that could be verified. Eventually, he couldn't deny the obvious anymore; his clients were really experiencing what they were saying.

Since then, Dr. Newton has hypnotized more than 7,000 people, whom he has taken back to previous lives and especially, the between-lives area (**BLA**). To his amazement, all these subjects were telling the exact same story, only with their subjective personal experiences differing from each other. Other than that, the stories were coherent. After a while, Dr. Newton was able to see a pattern and draw conclusions from that, building strong evidence. 7,000 people don't lie, and they don't tell the same story independently from each other.

In this section, I will mainly concentrate on what Dr. Newton's subjects told him, because the witnesses are so numerous. There are, of course, a lot of other hypnotists out there who are doing a similar great job and have come to the same conclusions. Some of them are using the same technique.

Regression therapy is nothing new. It took off big time around 1950, when L. Ron Hubbard, later the founder of the Church of Scientology, released his book, *Dianetics - The Modern Science of Mental Health,*[87] which quickly became #1 on New York Times Best Seller List and stayed on the list for decades. Hubbard didn't call it regression therapy, but Dianetics, which literally means *dia = (Greek) through* and *noetics = the intellect or of pure thought; reasoning*. Hubbard translated it as *"through the mind"*. With his technique, he could have people who had somatic or psycho-somatic illnesses to go back in time through chains of events on the same subject-line (topic) until they hit the bottom of the chain; the causation point and the core to the problem. Once the cause was found, the entire chain dissolved and disappeared and the subject found emotional and somatic relief, and sometimes it was a greatly life enhancing experience.

Hubbard and Newton are using a similar technique, with the difference that Hubbard didn't hypnotize his clients; they were put in something called *reverie*, which is a state of slightly lower frequency than being awake, and thus the subject could contact his/her subconscious mind by being asked questions by an *auditor*, a person "who listens" and helps the subject recall. Hubbard's theory was that all problems in present time can be resolved by finding their cause in the past. Often, a persistent mental or physical problem has a traumatic source in the past. Dr. Newton seems to have come to a similar conclusion.

Just like Dr. Newton, Hubbard did not expect what would really happen; people started going "past life" in his sessions. And some of them went into the BLA as well. Out of his research came Expanded Dianetics and the more controversial Church of Scientology. It should be added that Hubbard was heavily attacked by the Mental Health industry when he presented Dianetics to the field and to the public in the 1950s. His methods were a huge threat to their own business, and there are indications that there were murder attempts against him. However, Dianetics spread like wildfire, and Hubbard probably became too well-known to be eliminated. Instead, they chose to ridicule him.

I am aware of that L. Ron Hubbard and his Church of Scientology is a very touchy subject and quite controversial. I do not subscribe to the teachings of the organization in general, and I don't recommend anybody to join the Church, but I have to be fair and tell the truth. Dianetics works—at least to some degree, although I don't believe it erased the subconscious mind, like Hubbard said it would—it merely gives relief at times.

Hypnotism, of course, is a much older practice, but I want to mention Hubbard in this train of thoughts as well, because we are going to come back to him later in this paper.

---

[87] L. Ron Hubbard's book can be ordered here:
http://www.amazon.com/Dianetics-Modern-Science-Mental-Health/dp/088404632X

The Positive Version of Afterlife

I want to start by summarizing the experiences of Dr. Michael Newton's clients. It is extremely hard, if not impossible, to discard what the subjects are telling the therapist, because the witnesses, unrelated to each other, are stunningly coherent. There is no doubt, after having read his material, that an afterlife exists.

The exact details of what happens after body death differ from case to case, depending on each person's experiences in life and his/her advancement, but according to the study, including over 7000 case studies, it doesn't matter if the person was religious, an atheist, agnostic, Gnostic, or whatever belief system the person subscribed to in life; the experiences in Sitter space (time/space or afterlife) are still very similar.

After the soul has departed from the body, one of two basic things normally happens, depending on if the soul is more "advanced" or less so. The lesser advanced soul may stay around for a while, a little confused over being dead and not able to directly communicate with his/her relatives and friends. These souls may also try to hang on to possessions that were dear to them during their lives and they now miss. They may also want to stay around to make sure their body is taken well care of; perhaps there was an agreement whether the person should be buried or cremated? The soul may want to make sure that the directions set in life are now carried out, still being somewhat attached to the physical world.

When this category of souls has stayed around for a little and made sure that everybody is doing well under the circumstance, the soul normally leaves. Leaving means that it separates from the Earth planes and is drawn towards a dark tunnel which seems pretty much like a wormhole or black hole in space. Quite soon, the soul is aware of a bright light at the end of the tunnel, and it is moving rapidly toward this light. Many subjects say there are "side tunnels" departing from the main tunnel, but I have never heard of anybody choosing to go that route; I'm not even sure if it is possible.

As the soul gets closer to the light, it gets bigger and brighter, and the departed soul can normally distinguish one or more people standing in the light. First, it's vague, but it soon gets clearer; the persons waiting are either old relatives (mothers, fathers, siblings, grandparents), dear friends, soul mates, or all of the above. The recently departed soul is being greeted by these people, quite an emotional reunion is taking place, and an overwhelming feeling of love and joy is filling up the departed soul. It feels like it wants to stay there forever because of the incredible feeling of oneness with its loved ones.

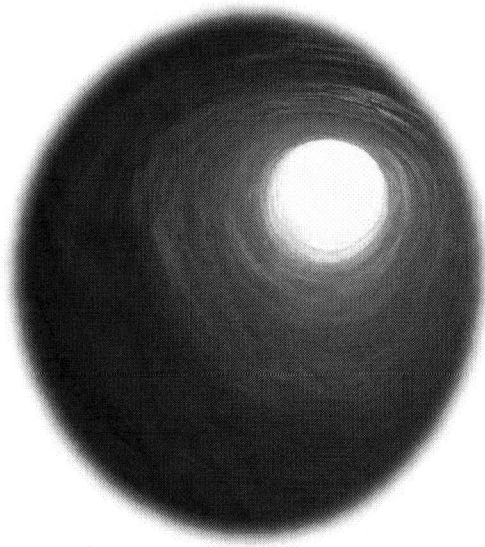

Figure 6.2: The light at the end of the tunnel

After that, the relatives withdraw and tell the departed soul that it will be assisted in crossing over by its spirit guide and they will all meet again soon. So, they disappear and the spirit guide, who normally was there in the background all the time, but often went unnoticed by the departed due to his/her focus on the loved ones, now steps forward to help the newcomer. The testimonies are quite coherent when it comes to describing the spirit guide; it may be a "he" or a "she," very loving and helpful, and the departed soul feels like it has reconnected with a very good, old friend, which also seems to be the case due to that a spirit guide seems delegated to a specific soul. Hence, in most cases, we meet the same guide every time we die. In some cases, subjects under hypnosis say the guide can be mischievous and a bit awkward as well, and in a few cases, they have even scared the departed, until they eventually tell the newcomer that it was a "joke" and they thought it was the appropriate thing to do at the moment. However, these cases are extremely rare

I want to back up here for a moment to describe the journey of a more advanced soul, as Dr. Newton puts it, and how they differ from the less advanced.

Instead of hanging around after body death, they usually move on quite quickly, go through the tunnel, and meet with the spirit guide early on. Everything happens quite rapidly, as if this is just some routine that needs to be followed, and then the soul moves on from there and normally joins path with other souls in its soul group (more about soul groups soon). On some occasions, the very advanced soul doesn't meet with its guide right away but knows where to go and travels to its destination immediately, eager to move on.

A third category is what Dr. Newton calls the "young soul," who hasn't had much experience in the physical world. These souls may be much more attached to people and material things in the physical universe than "adult" and "advanced" souls. Therefore, if such a young soul died under trauma or sudden and unexpected circumstances, they may hang around and become ghosts. They refuse to let go of their physical life. Sometimes, they may hang around for centuries in terms of linear time, but as time is different in time/space than in space/time, the ghost doesn't consider it being that long. Still, its spirit guide is always trying to reach the lost soul and guide it in its destined direction; but sometimes the soul refuses to go anyway, and the guide honors its freewill. Sooner or later, the lost soul will normally be released from its trauma and move on and follow the guide.

A sketch by Arthur Yensen depicting his entrance into heaven during his NDE. Courtesy of PMH Atwater.

Figure 6.3: Example of near-death experience

Lastly, Dr. Newton also mentions what happens to a soul that has led a violent and criminal life to the extreme. These souls sometimes get separated from the rest after body death. They are so damaged that they can't interact with the other souls, so their spirit guides will take them aside

95

and work with them in some kind of quarantine area and they will not merge with the others until they are healed.

Kevin Williams[88] neatly summarizes what Dr. Newton explains in his series of books regarding wrong-doings and what happens at the end of a life cycle:

> Because wrong-doing takes so many forms on Earth, spiritual instruction and the type of isolation used is varied for each soul. The nature of these variations apparently is evaluated during orientation at the end of each life. The relative time of seclusion and reindoctrination is not consistent either. For instance, I have had reports about maladjusted spirits who have returned back to Earth directly after a period of seclusion in order to expunge themselves as soon as possible by a good incarnated performance.
>
> All souls, regardless of experience, eventually arrive at a central port in the spirit world which I call the staging area. Once past the orientation station there seems to be no further travel detours for anyone entering this space of the spirit world. Apparently, large numbers of returning souls are conveyed in a spiritual form of mass transit. Spirits are brought in, collected, and then projected out to their proper final destinations similar to a central terminal of a metropolitan airport that has the capacity to fly people out in any direction. The most outstanding characteristic of this world is a continuous feeling of a powerful mental force directing everything in uncanny harmony. People say this is a place of pure thought.
>
> After souls arrive back into their soul groups, they are summoned to appear before a Council of Elders. While the Council is not prosecutorial, they do engage in direct examination of a soul's activities before returning them to their groups.
>
> Group placement is determined by soul level. After physical death, a soul's journey back home ends with debarkation into the space reserved for their own colony, as long as they are not a very young soul or isolated for other reasons. The souls represented in these cluster groups are intimate old friends who have the same awareness level. Members of the same cluster group are closely united for all eternity. These tightly-knit clusters are often composed of like-minded souls with common objectives which they continually work out with each other. Usually they choose lives together as relatives and close friends during their incarnations on Earth.[89]

---

[88] http://www.near-death.com/about.html
[89] http://www.near-death.com/newton.html *op. cit.*

Three Levels of Soul Groupings

According to the Working Model, as presented by Life Physics Group California, from the T-Boundary (Thought Boundary), surrounding the 7 Levels of Manifestation (LOM) as a fuzzy limit, Source is still creating new fragments of Itself, which we call souls (Information Clouds in Life Physics). Hence, there are souls of all different ages, in our terms; so, we have young souls, intermediate souls and advanced souls, all depending on how much each soul has had the chance to experience of the Multiverse/Unum. This is being confirmed by Dr. Newton, as we shall see below. Also, because some clients of Dr. Newton's have been working in the "nursery" to "give birth" to new souls, it makes me wonder if the Sitter Space we are entering after body death is within, or close to the T-Boundary.

The Beginner Soul: After having collected and gone through his research over the years and compared the experiences of his clients, Dr. Newton concluded there are three levels of soul groupings. The "Beginner Soul" is in its turn grouped into two sub-categories, where the first one is the young soul that hasn't had the chance to incarnate often in the physical dimension. Secondly, we have the souls who have been incarnating for a while but are still acting immaturely and haven't developed close to what was expected.

The beginner soul sometimes lives several lives in relative confusion, having a hard time figuring out the Earth curriculum; they are used to the supportive harmony in time/space. They tend to surrender to the social structure of the planet and more easily fall for propaganda and the "functional insanity" that is so dominant on our planet. They can be brilliant in some ways, but often lack the compassion for others and are usually self-centered and don't have the ability to think outside the box, or even independently. We have all been at this stage, according to Dr. Newton.

The Intermediate Soul: These souls, who are more mature than the Beginner Souls, tend not to cluster as much as the first category. This doesn't mean they live in isolation, but they are more independent than the immature souls, and want to develop more separately. Still, they mingle with their own soul group, but not on an as regular a basis as the Beginners. This category normally doesn't incarnate as often either.

In the Beginner's stage, we have a teacher-student relationship to our spirit guide, who normally, as some see it, is our Higher Selves, or the Oversoul.[90] In the case of the Intermediate Soul, however, it's more like

---

[90] See Jane Roberts' *Oversoul Seven* trilogy, which can be ordered at Amazon.com., and listen to the channeling of the Pleiadians by Barbara Marciniak for more

two colleagues working together. We become more and more like teachers of our own and will eventually come to a point where we can teach others and act as their spirit guide, while our own spirit guide overlooks our performance, once we've started teaching. Not all souls are able to be teachers, though, but that doesn't stop us from becoming more advanced. We all have different talents and shortcomings, and we decide ourselves, in correlation with our Guides, what is best for us to do to develop as a whole spirit/mind/body complex.

To understand how this works, we need to think multi-dimensionally. All of us exist simultaneously on different levels of reality—in different dimensions or densities if you will. Each of us lives several lives at the same "time" on different planets, because on an ultimate level, there is only one big *now*.

The concept of time is determined by several different physical and metaphysical laws and agreements and is perceived differently depending on our point of view/point of observation. Time, vibration, and location in space are the only things which separate our different incarnations from each other, and which normally keeps us from remembering our other-selves. Different dimensions/densities (which in themselves are fluid, and quite slippery terms) vibrate on different frequencies—the faster the vibration, the less dense the reality. Therefore, we all have more than one "Oversoul". Every part of us that vibrates on a higher level than what we can perceive, from the frequency band in which we currently operate, is our Oversoul. Even while incarnated in space/time, we can contact a higher aspect of ourselves for guidance and protection.

Also, important to understand is that when we incarnate in the physical, we still leave the main part of our energy (soul) in time/space. We only incarnate with as much energy as we estimate as appropriate for a specific incarnation. If we have decided to become athletes, for example, it makes more sense to bring with us more energy than if we choose a life which will mainly consist of sitting behind a desk. This way, we can delegate energy to different simultaneous incarnations proportionally, something that Dr. Newton is pointing out in *Destiny of Souls* but is also something that has been independently confirmed by other researchers into this subject.

With all this in mind, I hope the relationship in time/space (here defined as the dimension between lives) between discarnate soul/spirit guide/Oversoul makes more sense.

Once we become more advanced, we are assigned certain responsibilities in time/space which correspond to our abilities and talents.

The Advanced Soul: Advanced souls are quite rare on Earth, because

---

information on the Oversoul.
98

as such, we have incarnated amongst other, more advanced civilizations. This makes sense because there would no longer be any reason to incarnate on a relatively primitive planet like Earth, as there wouldn't be much of a learning experience anymore. These souls are already operating on a conscious, multi-dimensional level. And like Kevin Williams pointed out, the Advanced Soul would unlikely go to a regression therapist to sort out his/her problems and issues.

Before we move on to the next subsection, I'd like to point out that in some cases a soul who just departed doesn't spend much time in time/space at all before it incarnates again, according to interviewed subjects. There are those who remember leaving their body, and quite instantly go into a new incarnation. However, there may be a specific explanation for this, including erased memories and implants, which are parts of a more sinister route through the afterlife, something we will discuss later.

Returning to a New Incarnation

When a soul eventually decides to return to Earth in a new incarnation, it can be a hard decision for many. According to Dr. Newton's studies, the time spent in the between-lives area has been very harmonious and pleasant, and the soul knows that it is going back to a new life of challenges. Still, when ready, almost all souls feel they want to move on and have a new experience in space/time, because there is where we mature and help Source experience Itself. Souls know, while in time/space, that this is their purpose. Still, there are a few who decide to stay in time/space, sometimes perhaps forever, and this is accepted, but it seems like these souls are quite rare.

Souls, before they reincarnate, have made plans and choices how they want to live their next life. They have, with help from spirit guides, soul groups, and the Council of Elders (more about them below), reevaluated previous incarnations, looked at where they succeeded, and where they need to improve. When all that is clear, the soul, about to reincarnate, decides when and where on the planet this will happen, which bloodline it wants to incarnate in, and whom else from its soul group it wants to reincarnate with to have the best chance to achieve the goals for that lifetime.[91] More often than not, other members of our soul group reincarnate together with us to play a role in our development, as we do in theirs. These other members may not incarnate at the exact same time as we do, but when appropriate during that lifetime to be of most support.

---

[91] In my later research I have concluded that this is incorrect and a distortion. We reincarnate into the same bloodline every time as our own descendants.

It's almost like we're plotting a movie and then become the actors in it.

Before making a final decision, the soul that is about to reincarnate is showed into a room with something which looks like a big control room filled with computer screens and advanced technology. There it is shown different available body types which could possibly suit their mission in the upcoming lifetime. On a screen, we can watch a holographic version of a potential lifetime when inhabiting a certain body. Then it goes to the next, and the next, until it has seen the potentials of all the available bodies. Then the soul makes its final decision. If the soul, showing us all this, disagrees with the soul's decision of body choice, it may give final advice, but it seems like it's ultimately up to the individual soul to decide which body type it needs and wants to best accomplish its goals.

After having said goodbye to its associates in the spirit world and had a last visit with the Council of Elders, the soul once again returns to Earth, hover around the pregnant woman whom it has chosen to be its mother, and at a certain time in the process it enters the body. At the time we're born into the physical, the veil of forgetfulness hits us, and we lose our memories of previous incarnations and the spirit world. Our task is now to figure out what our goals are and as best as we can attempt to accomplish them. It's okay to change our goals as much as we want; no one will stop us; and sometimes that turns out to be a good thing because of unexpected circumstances, and sometimes it's not. A new evaluation next time we enter time/space will determine how well be succeeded.

The Council of Elders

Dr. Newton says in Destiny of Souls that the spirit world is a place of order (in contract to our Earthly existence) and the Council of Elders exemplifies justice. It seems like they are not the top source of authority in time/space, but they appear to be the last station responsible for souls who are still incarnating on Earth.

When I first read about the Council, I had mixed feelings of having such an authority in the spirit world, but according to all subjects whom Newton has hypnotized, the Council can be firm and "bluntly honest" with us when we are standing before them, although they are said to emit an abundance of compassion and patience for a soul's weaknesses. We will be given a lot of "second chances" in future lives. However, most lifetimes will have challenges that are at the level of, or slightly above, the capacity for what the soul can handle. If this wouldn't be the case, the soul wouldn't learn much, we are told. Still, on occasion, it is decided, in consultations with the soul, that it needs an easier life next time, sometimes because of extreme difficulties in the previous life, and the soul now needs to rest. Often, the soul is accompanied by its spirit guide when being led before the Council.

As I read more from Destiny of Souls, Dr. Newton had had the same thoughts I did: Why is the setting for the council necessary if this whole afterlife experience is so benevolent. He continues:

> ...Why not a simple countryside scene, if they are so full of benevolence? While the younger souls told me that this setting "was right and proper for their examinations," the older souls explained that there was a major reason for a domed enclosure. With this design, a higher Presence effectively focuses its light energy on the entire proceedings from above.[92]

Apparently, we appear before the Council right after an incarnation, and many say they meet with them just before the next incarnation as well. The first meeting seems to have the most impact on the soul. The previous life is carefully reviewed during this first meeting; karmic forks in the road are carefully evaluated and the soul is very aware of things that didn't go as planned, especially if it hurt somebody. Both the positive gains and the mistakes are discussed in depth, while the second meeting, just before rebirth is much more relaxed, and focuses on what is coming, more so than on the past.

Dr. Newton tells us that our guides are normally escorting us to the meetings with these ascended masters. Ascended Masters is an interesting choice of word, and I keep wondering if that was the doctor's choice of words, or if it is commonly used by his subjects. It's hard to know, but it doesn't seem likely that this council is the Ascended Masters who are channeled by certain people here on Earth, but who knows?

The Guide is normally standing in the background during these meetings, being very quiet. The reason for this seems to be because s/her and the soul have already discussed the last life with each other, and now it's time for the evaluation together with the Elders. However, the guide interacts when the soul seems confused and uncertain, to clarify and help the soul out, which sometimes can be of quite significant assistance.

This is how one of the subjects describes a meeting with the Council:

> The time of my expectation has arrived. I am to see the Holy Ones. My guide, Linil, comes and escorts me from my cluster group down a long corridor past other classrooms. We move into another area with a larger hallway that is lined with marble columns. The walls are textured with what looks to be frosted glass panels of many colors. I hear soft choir music and string instruments. The light is a subdued, golden tone. Everything is so relaxing, even sensual, but I am a little apprehensive. We come to an atrium filled with beautiful plants and a bubbling fountain of water. This is the waiting area. After a few moments, Linil takes me into a round room with a high

---

[92] Dr. Michael Newton, 2009: Destiny of Souls, op. cit. p. 205

domed ceiling. There are rays of light shining down. The Holy Ones are seated at a long crescent-shaped table. I move to the center of the room in from the table while Linil stand behind me to my left.[93]

The sole purpose, it seems, of meeting with the Council, is to achieve assistance in order to prepare for the next life. Although authoritarian in appearance, the subjects say that the Council is benevolent and very helpful in this respect, and it's not at all a punishment or judgment.

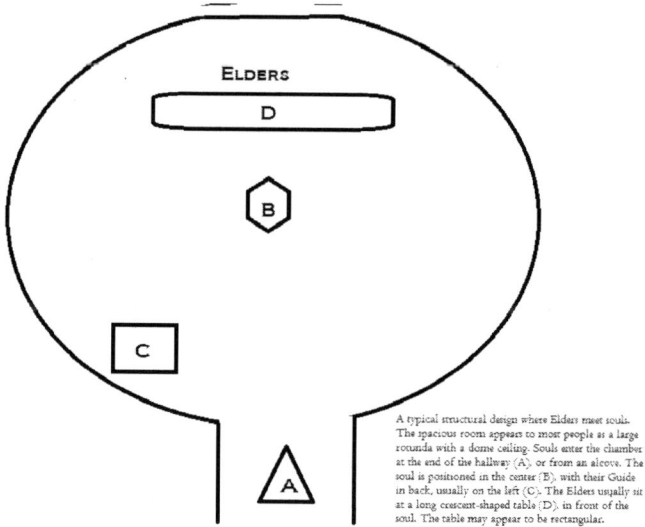

Figure 6.4: The Council Chamber

The reader may have doubts about this, just as I did, and as Dr. Newton did, but perhaps it is like Dr. Newton figures. He suggests this suspicious mindset we put on is because of our cultural conditioning. He realized that going before the Council has many different facets:

> The Elders are like loving but firm parents, managing directors, encouraging teachers and behavioral counselors all rolled into one. What souls feel for their council is reverence. Actually, souls themselves are their own severest critics. I find evaluations by our soul group companions to be far more acerbic than any council Elder, although our peers do lace their criticism with humor.[94]

The souls tell Dr. Newton that even when they feel nervous before the

[93] *ibid. op. cit. p. 205.*
[94] *ibid. op. cit. p. 210.*

meeting, this always goes away as soon as they stand before the Elders, and that they are made to feel welcome almost at once.

The council knows all about us already, including all our past incarnations; we are like an open book to them. However, according to the subjects, when a soul comes before the council, the latter has still not made up their minds about future incarnations. They first want to hear the subject out and learn how the soul feels and what it considers the next step in its development. They ask about the soul's intentions in the past lives; if it was positively or negatively oriented; did it let the body take over, or did it "shine through" as soul and merge with the body to create a whole? How did it handle power? How did it treat others? They don't seem concerned with how many times we fell in our progress in life, but if we were able to get on our feet again and brush ourselves off, or not. Normally, they don't dwell on the most recent lifetime very long but are more concerned about several lives viewed together to see how the soul is progressing.

Often, the best progress seems to have been accomplished through tough lifetimes where the challenges have been great and life hard. Such a lifetime is normally not a coincidence, but something the soul decides to experience in consultation with the Elders and the spirit guide to overcome certain barriers that are hard to confront for the soul. This, of course, doesn't mean that each lifetime must be tough and a struggle. Often, we also need to experience pleasure and very positive challenges to make progress.

The Appearance and Composition of the Council

The council is called the Council of Elders because the people in it are usually older men. They are repeatedly depicted as having bald heads, white hair and sometimes beard; almost like we depict wise men like Merlin and Gandalf here on Earth, apparently. On occasion there are women on the council as well, but according to the subjects, the reason the majority are men is because that's how we look at authority here on Earth. It is noteworthy though, that most subjects are describing time/space events to Dr. Newton which occurred at least a few centuries ago, when authority certainly was almost 100% men. The council is supposed to impact our own experiences and conceptions as a soul from Earth, and whatever creates that symbiosis is what is perceived. Dr. Newton is quite certain that as our culture change, we will see more women on the council.

The gender conclusion is partly based on the fact that more advanced souls, who have been participating in this study, often see the council members as androgynous. The member may appear either as sexless or flashing back and forth between male and female. It seems like this is all adjusted accordingly to where the soul is in its progress. It also suggests to me that the council members may not actually be in the room but are holograms that can be manipulated from a distance. If so, the question is, by whom? It could very well be that a hologram is preferred for all above reasons, so the right type of council members, with the correct grade of authority and outlook, can serve a certain soul. If this is true, there may be a real council we never meet, but who sits in the background (in a control room of sorts?) and manipulate the hologram. Alternatively, something else is going on, upon which we can only speculate.

The typical subject sees between three to seven council members. And advanced souls may have from seven to twelve members on their council. The Elders often have silver clothing or deep hues of violet. Almost without exceptions, there's a chairman sitting in the middle, facing the soul. This Elder is the primary questioner and enquirer, and often the same person through several lifetimes. The other council members may be exchanged from time to time. Also, other members from our own soul group are appearing before different councils. Why this is, no subject has been able to explain.

Hoods, four-square hats and skulls caps, all having an antiquarian flavor, have often been seen on the Elders. Hoods are often thrown back from their heads; it almost reminds me of a religious order, although there is nothing "religious" about the council otherwise.

It seems quite common for the council members to wear medallions around their necks. Dr. Newton estimates that around 50% of the subjects see these medallions on the Elders. About 80% envision a circular design while others may see squares, rectangles, triangles, and starlike motifs, some of which are seen in three dimensions. The medallions typically hang from a chain or a cord. The purpose of these medallions seems to be to symbolize moments in the soul's life which were of specific significance. One subject said that an Elder wore a medallion showing the embodied soul killing a mountain lion, which symbolized strength and courage. Someone else reported a council woman wearing the swirl design, apparently meaning that we spiral outward in development and will someday return to the Source of our origins.

When asked who will become a council member, subjects more advanced can tell Dr. Newton that not everybody is fit to be a member of the Council; you first must be a Master Teacher. This means you must perfectly understand other human beings and life forms to be able to guide them. Once you are a council member, you will be able to go inside the soul in front of you. This is what one subject described:

> ...What you feel is much more than empathy towards someone who has just come back from a life. You are really in their shoes. The Presence gives you the power to feel everything the soul feels at the moment. The prism of light from the Presence touches every council member in this way.[95]

What this soul said in the above quote is unusual. Normally, the council is the highest spiritual authority the soul will encounter in the astral.

When a soul leaves a council meeting, most have the feeling they were told more about what they did right than what they did wrong. The council knows that the soul has already had a "critical meeting" with its spirit guide, and it looks like the council always wants to leave the soul in an encouraged state of mind, but still raise its expectations. One soul said what others said as well: The council had absorbed the soul's self-doubt and cleansed it.

What occurs to me when I read Dr. Newton's studies is that it's very much based on souls returning to Earth, reincarnation after reincarnation to both complete karmic cycles and to be able to experience what they need to learn, based upon the goals the soul sets for itself, long term, and on what options have been given to them. Still, there are souls among Newton's clients who have incarnated now and then on other planets too, but that is more an exception than a rule. The conclusion I make from this is that, of course, the ones who decide to start incarnating on other planets won't be the ones sitting in the regression therapist's chair on Earth; they are elsewhere and not accessible for studies like this. What is interesting, though, is that about 7,000 subjects are saying the same thing; we are reincarnating on Earth repeatedly, contrary to what LPG-C's Working Model says.

Still, there is a time when a soul has completed its incarnations on Earth and is ready to move on, according to Dr. Newton. This quote comes from an old, advanced soul nearing the completion of incarnations on Earth:

> As my session with the council comes to an end, the Elders stand and close around me in a circle. Once in position, they raise their arms -- outstretched like a giant bird -- enfolding me with wings of unification. This is their accolade for a job well done.[96]

The Presence

On the question whether the subjects meet God or not on the other side, the answer is somewhat vague, but almost always positive. We all can feel a greater presence of God in time/space, and it's not the Elders. Everybody seems to agree that the Elders are not the top of the chain, so to speak. There is a Presence above them that most don't identify as God per se, but something higher than the Council. None of the clients wants to use the

---

[95] *ibid. op. cit. p. 249.*
[96] *ibid. op. cit. p. 253.*

word God at all, either, when referring to the spirit world because it has been so abused and personalized here on Earth. They rather call It Source or Oversoul, and it's more of a Presence than a Being.

The general feeling is that we are all part of Source and at one point in time we will return to Source, just like I and many other researchers in metaphysics have said for years. However, the "game of experiences" is still going on and will last for a long time, so merging with Source does not seem to be in our cards soon. We are going to continue experiencing the Multiverse on an individual basis.

The subjects feel there is a Higher Source that does influence the council meetings, but it's not necessarily the ultimate Creator; just someone higher up in the spiritual realm.

Privacy in a Telepathic Environment

I am sure many people are wondering if there is any way to keep things private in the spiritual world, considering communication is telepathic.

The studies show that privacy *is* possible, but mostly applied by less advanced souls, who are ashamed, embarrassed or are feeling guilty about something they did in a previous life. However, the more advanced a soul becomes, privacy becomes more obsolete, and the souls decide that it's no longer important. Quite the contrary, they find it much more educating and healthier to be open with others under all circumstances if they dwell in time/space. Each soul has its own unique vibration, and although this vibration is easily readable for other souls, we can choose to withhold certain thoughts unless we want another to enter.

Between Lives Learning Centers

Just like it's explained in the Urantia Book,[97] there are learning centers in time/space, according to Dr. Newton's study cases, even described as classrooms. Outside these classrooms are large assembly halls where souls can socialize and discuss both light and serious matters. This is supposedly a typical description from a subject moving into a classroom setting:

> My guide takes me into a star-shaped structure and I know this is my place of learning. There is a round domed central chamber which is empty now. I see corridors going off in opposite directions and we move down one of these halls where the classrooms are located. They are offset in such a way that no two classrooms face each other. This is so we will not bother another room of souls. My room is the third cubicle on the left. I never see more than six rooms to a hallway. Each room has an average of eight to fifteen

---

[97] Urantia Book online: http://www.urantia.org/en/urantia-book/read

souls working at desks. I know this sounds ridiculous, but that's what I see. As I pass down the hall with my guide, I notice in some rooms souls are studying quietly by themselves while others are working in groups of two to five. A different room has the students watching an instructor lecturing at a blackboard. When I enter my room everyone stops what they were doing and gives me a big smile. Some wave and a few cheer as if they were expecting me. The ones nearest the doorway escort me to a seat and I get ready to participate in the lesson. The whole time I have been gone seems like a brief trip down to the corner grocery store to buy a carton of milk.[98]

In addition, there are also different floors, like in a university here on Earth, only that in time/space floors indicate the level of advancement of the soul. Our level of learning is equivalent to how developed we are, and this determines which floor and which classroom to attend. It's nothing intimidating about this; it's like here on Earth, you could be in sixth grade, seventh grade, and eighth grade, and so on.

The Library of Life Books

One of the first things we do after we enter the spirit world and have met with our spirit guide is to meet and rejoin with our soul groups. Here we meet relatives, old friends and people who have been with us both in space/time and time/space for a long, long time, according to Dr. Newton's reports.

Shortly after this reunion, many subjects talk about being in a research library setting. It's Dr. Newton's understanding that we all begin to study our past lives in depth quite instantly. Apparently, this library is huge to say the least; some would say endless. Each soul has its own Life Book in this library, which we are being told to study for better understanding of ourselves. With each lifetime, this book changes, of course, with our new experiences. This gigantic library is almost like a holographic form of the Akashic records, or the *Hall of Records*, as it's also called.

The structure of the library is rectangular with endless halls leading away from the entry. There are books lined up against the walls. Many souls are studying at desks, and these souls don't necessarily know each other.

Once we enter this room, the librarian-guides are the Archivist Souls in charge of all the books. They are quiet, almost monastic in appearance, and assist both guides and students in locating information. Souls may be assisted by the Archivist, its own guide, or both, depending on the

[98] Dr. Michael Newton, 2009: *Destiny of Souls, op. cit. p. 144.*

circumstance. Some souls, upon returning to the spirit world, go alone to the library, while others are accompanied by their guides. I guess this is an individual choice as much as it depends on our level of evolution.

Apparently, there are small conference rooms, and the library seems to have tables with a variety of TV-sized books that have three dimensional illuminated viewing screens. One client said that the records give the illusion of books with pages but are sheets of energy which vibrate and form live picture-patterns of events.

Time/Space Nurseries and the Birth of Souls

What was most astonishing to me when I read Dr. Newton's series of books was the part about the *nursery*. As I mentioned earlier, when souls become more advanced, they will be assigned certain tasks in the spirit world. Some are assigned jobs in the learning centers, while others get to work in the nursery, where new souls are born! I'm going to spend a little time on this section because it is quite stunning.

It certainly seems like the concept of birth is not just something we experience in the physical; it also happens in the spirit world: Souls are born as we speak.

Dr. Newton says that it's quite unusual to get clients who can remember their own births as souls. When this happens, it's often younger souls, who don't have a long history; therefore, it's easier to remember. Still, they have only fleeting memories of their genesis. Destiny of Souls, chapter 5, starts out with a quote from one of the beginner souls, who have told very similar things. I need to quote in full here to give the reader the idea:

> My soul was created out of a great irregular cloudy mass. I was expelled as a tiny particle of energy from this intense, pulsating bluish, yellow and white light. The pulsations send out hailstorms of soul matter. Some fall back and are reabsorbed but I continued outward and was being carried along in a stream with others like me. The next thing I knew, I was in a bright enclosed area with very loving beings taking care of me.

> I remember being in a nursery of some sort where we were like unhatched eggs in a beehive. When I acquired more awareness I learned I was in the nursery world of Uras. I don't know how I got there. I was like an egg in embryonic fluid waiting to be fertilized and I sensed there were many other cells of young lights who were coming awake with me. There was a group of mothers, beautiful and loving, who... pierced our membrane sacs and opened us. There were swirling currents of intense, nurturing lights around us and I could hear music. My awareness began with curiosity. Soon I was taken from Uras and joined other children in a different setting.[99]

Now we're going to describe the other side of this coin; the "nurses" in the nursery, who take care of the newborn souls. They are highly specialized in doing this task and are called Incubator Mothers. To become one, we must be very advanced souls, because this task requires perfectionism, or the newborn will not develop as planned. Once again, I need to quote directly, because this is information, I haven't seen anywhere else, and still, according to Dr. Newton, he has had several cases who have described the same thing. This soul's name is Seena[100] and is what Dr. Newton calls a Level V soul, which means she is very advanced. **N** stands for Dr. Newton, who is asking the questions, and **S** stands for Seena:

> **N:** Seena, what has been your most significant experience between your lives?
>
> **S:** (without hesitation) I go to the place of...hatching—where souls are hatched. I am an Incubator Mother, a kind of midwife.
>
> **N:** Are you telling me you work in a soul nursery?
>
> **S:** (brightly) Yes, we help the new ones emerge. We facilitate early maturation...by being warm, gentle and caring. We welcome them.
>
> **N:** Please explain the surrounds of the place to me.
>
> **S:** It's...gaslike...a honeycomb of cells with swirling currents of energy above. There is intense light.
>
> **N:** When you say "honeycomb," I wonder if you mean that the nursery has a beehive structure, or what?
>
> **S:** Um, yes...although the nursery itself is a vast emporium without seeming to be limited by outside dimensions. The new souls have their own incubator cells where they stay until their growth is sufficient to be moved away from the emporium.
>
> **N:** As an Incubator Mother, when do you first see the new souls?
>
> **S:** We are in the delivery suite, which is a part of the nursery, at one end of the emporium. The newly arrived ones are conveyed as small masses of white energy encased in a god sac. They move slowly in a majestic, orchestrated line of progression toward us.
>
> **N:** From where?

[99] Dr. Michael Newton, 2009: *"Destiny of Souls"*, *op. cit. pp. 125-126.*

[100] Here on Earth we are assigned a certain name by our parents, normally, and this name is of course different from lifetime to lifetime, but in the spirit world you have *one* name, which you are known by every time you return.

S: At our end of the emporium under an archway the entire wall is filled with a molten mass of high-intensity energy and...vitality. It feels as if it's energized by an amazing love force rather than a discernible heat source. The mass pulsates and undulates in a beautiful flowing motion. Its color is like that on the inside of you eyelids if you were to look through closed eyes at the sun on a bright day.

N: And from out of this mass you see souls emerge?

S: From the mass a swelling begins, never exactly from the same site twice. The swelling increases and pushes outward, becoming a formless bulge. The separation is a wondrous moment. A new soul is born. It's totally alive with an energy and distinctness of its own.

Dr. Newton's note: *Another one of my level Vs made this statement about incubation. "I see an egg-shaped mass with energy flowing out and back in. When it expands, new soul energy fragments are spawned. When the bulge contracts, I think it pulls back those souls which were not successfully spawned. For some reason these fragments could not make it on to the next step of individuality."*

N: What do you see beyond the mass, Seena?

S: (long pause) I see this beatific glow of orange-yellow. There is a violet darkness beyond, but not cold darkness...it is eternity.

N: Can you tell me more about the line of progression of new souls moving toward you out of the mass?

S: Out of the fiery orange-yellow the progression is slow as each hatchling emerges from the energy mass. They are conveyed off to various points where mothering souls like myself are positioned.

N: How many mothers do you see?

S: I can see five nearby...who, like me...are in training.

N: What are the responsibilities of an Incubator Mother?

S: We hover around the hatchlings so we can...towel-dry them after opening their gold sacs. Their progression is slow because this allows us to embrace their tiny energy in a timeless, exquisite fashion.

N: What does "towel-drying" mean to you?

S: We dry the new soul's...wet energy, so to speak. I can't really explain all this well in human language. It's a form of hugging new white energy.

N: So, now you see basically white energy?

S: Yes, and as they come next to us—up close—I see more blue and violet glowing around them.

110

N: Why do you think this is so?

S: (pause, then softly) Oh…I see now…this is an umbilical…the genesis cord of energy which connects each one.

N: From what you are saying, I get a picture of a long pearl necklace. The souls are the pearls connected in a line. Is this at all accurate?

S: Yes, rather like a string of pearls on a silvery conveyer belt.

N: OK, now tell me, when you embrace each new soul—dry them out—does this give them life?

S: (reacts quickly) Oh, no. Through us -- not from us -- comes a life force of all-knowing love and knowledge. What we pass on with our vibrations during the drying of new energy is…the essence of a beginning -- a hopefulness of future accomplishment. The mothers call it…"the love hug." This involves instilling thoughts of what they are and what they can become. When we enfold a new soul in a love hug it infuses this being with our understanding and compassion.

N: Let me carry this vibrational hugging one step further. Does each new soul have an individual character at this point? Do you add or subtract from its given identity?

S: No, this is in place upon arrival, although the new soul does not yet know who they are. We bring nurturing. We are announcing to the hatchling that it is time to begin. By…sparking…its energy we bring to the soul an awareness of its existence. This is the time of the awakening.

N: Seena, please help me here. When I think of obstetric nurses in a hospital maternity ward holding and nurturing new human babies, they have no idea what kind of person a baby will turn out to be. Do you function in the same manner -- not knowing about the immortal character of these new souls?

S: (laughs) We function as nursery caregivers but this is not a human maternity ward. At the moment we embrace the new ones we know something of their identity. Their individual patterns become more evident as we unite our energy with them to give them sustenance. This allows us to better utilize our vibrations to activate -- to ignite -- their awareness. All this is part of their beginning.

N: As a trainee, how did you acquire this knowledge of the proper employment of vibrations with new souls?

S: This is something new mothers have to learn. If it is not performed properly, the hatchling souls move on not feeling fully ready. Then one of the Nursery Masters must step in later.

N: Can you take me a little further here, Seena? During your love hug, when you first embrace these souls, do you and the mothers discern an organized selection process behind the assignment of the new soul's identity? For instance, could we ten courageous type souls come through followed by ten more cautious souls?

S: That is so mechanistic! Each soul is unique in its totality of characteristics created by a perfection that I cannot begin to describe. What I can tell you is that no two souls are alike -- none -- ever!

Dr. Newton's note: I have heard from a few other subjects that one of the basic reasons each soul is different from the other is that after the Source "breaks off" energy fragments to create a soul, what is left of the original mass becomes infinitesimally altered so it is not exactly the same as before. Thus, the Source is like a divine mother who would never create twin children.

N: (pressing, wanting my subject to correct me) Do you think this is a totally random selection? There is no order of characteristics with matched similarities of any kind? You know this to be true?

S: (frustrated) How could I know this unless I was a Creator? There are souls with similarities and those with none, all in the same batch. The combinations are mixed. As a mother I can tweak each major trait that I sense that this is why I can tell you no two have exactly the same combinations of character.

N: Well...(subject breaks in to continue)

S: I have the sense that there is a powerful Presence on the other side of the archway who is managing things. If there is a key to the energy patterns -- we do not need to know of this...

Dr. Newton's note: These are the moments I wait for in my sessions, where I try to push open the door to the ultimate Source. The door never opens more than a crack.

N: Please tell me what you feel about this Presence, about the energy mass which is bringing these new souls to you. Surely, you and other mothers must have thought about the origins of souls here even though you cannot see it?

S: (in a whisper) I feel the Creator is...close by...but may not actually be doing the work of...production...

N: (gently) Meaning the energy mass may not be the primary Creator?

S: (uncomfortable) I think there are others who assist -- I don't know.

N: (taking another tack) Is it not true, Seena, that there are imperfections to the new souls? If they were created perfect, there would be no reason for them to be created at all by a perfect

Creator?

S: (doubtfully) Everything here seems to be perfection.

N: (I temporarily move in another direction) Do you work only with souls coming to Earth?

S: Yes, but they could go to all kinds of places. Only a fraction come to Earth. There are many physical worlds similar to Earth. We call them pleasure worlds and suffering worlds.

N: And do you know when a soul is right for Earth based upon your incarnation experience?

S: Yes, I do. I know that the souls who come to worlds such as Earth need to be strong and resilient because of the pain they have to endure along with the joy.

N: That's my understanding, too. And when these souls become contaminated by the human body -- particularly the young ones -- this is because they are less than perfect. Might that be true?

S: Well, I suppose, yes.

N: (continuing) Which indicates to me that they must work to acquire more substance than they had originally in order to acquire full enlightenment. Would you accept that premise?

S: (long pause, then with a sigh) I think perfection is there...with the newly created. Maturity begins by the shattering of innocence with new souls, not because they are originally flawed. Overcoming obstacles makes them stronger but the acquired imperfections will never be totally erased until all souls are joined together -- when incarnation ends.

N: Isn't this going to be difficult with new souls being created all the time to take the place of those ending their incarnations on Earth?

S: This too will end when all people...all races, nationalities unite as one. This is why we are sent to places such as Earth to work.

N: So, when the training ends, will the universe we live in die as well?

S: It may die before. It doesn't matter, there are others. Eternity never ends. It is the process which is meaningful because it allows us to...savor the experience and express ourselves...and to learn.[101]

So far Dr. Newton. This section in his book continues with some interesting conclusions that he has made from studying cases of new souls.

---

[101] Dr. Michael Newton, 2009: *"Destiny of Souls"*, op. cit. p. 126ff.

He has grouped them as a list of four differences about their existence
after they are created:

1- There are energy fragments which appear to return to the energy
mass that created them before they even reach the nursery. I do not
know the reason for their being aborted. Others, who do reach the
nursery, are unable to handle learning "to be" on an individual basis
during early maturation. Later, they are associated with collective
functions and, from what I can determine, never leave the spirit
world.

2-There are energy fragments who have individual soul essences
that are not inclined, or have the necessary mental fabric, to
incarnate in physical form on any world. They are often found on
mental worlds, and they also appear to move easily between
dimensions.

3-There are energy fragments with individual soul essences who
incarnate only on physical worlds. These souls may well receive
training in the spirit world with mental spheres between lives. I do
not find them as interdimensional travelers.

4-There are energy fragments who are souls with the ability and
inclination to incarnate and function as individuals in all types of
physical and mental environments. This does not necessarily give
them more or less enlightenment than other soul types. However,
their wide range of practical experience positions them for many
specialization opportunities and assignments of responsibility.[102]

Common for all newborn souls, it seems, is that they start out on a
gradient; they are not immediately thrown down to the hungry wolves on
planets like Earth and are expected to survive. Instead, they are practicing
on mental worlds first, without biological life. These worlds are only semi-
physical, as a light form. None of these very young souls are yet part of any
soul group, but several souls are sent to these worlds at the same time,
without necessarily knowing (about) each other. They meet each other in
this reality and often browse these worlds together, just to have fun. This
way they also learn to communicate with each other and how to live in
communities. They have no responsibilities and can do whatever they want
in these holographic worlds, especially created for this purpose. Not until
each soul feels comfortable in these worlds can they move on to the next
step in their learning process and eventually incarnate on Earth or other
planets.

[102] Dr. Michael Newton, 2009: *"Destiny of Souls"*, *op. cit. pp. 132-133.*

The Meaning of Life

The ultimate question, I guess, when you are in Dr. Newton's position, and able to ask the subjects anything you want, is what the meaning of life and what Source (God) really is. Of course, the subjects may only be able to answer this up to their certain level of experience, but it's obviously a great opportunity to ask.

Dr. Newton tried to get these questions answered by addressing them from many different angles, and the following is a sum up of sorts on what the subjects told him.[103,104]

The Reason for Existence:

- The ultimate objective of souls is to seek unification with the supreme source of creative energy.

- To explore and experience life in the physical in different dimensions and universes. Universes are created to live and die for the use of the Source. However, souls never die.

- Our collective wisdom makes the Source stronger.

- To be given life so we can arrive at a state of perfection ... The Source creates for fulfillment of Itself ... It desires to express Itself through us, by birthing.

What is Source?

- The Source is the spiritual world

- The Source is the ultimate selfless being which we strive to be.

---

[103] The Source that the subjects are talking about is more likely the energetic. The Ultimate Source is everything there is and originates from outside space/time and time/space. It is "nothingness", "awareness", "infinite consciousness" and "all that is" at the same time.

[104] The following items are all collected from Dr. Michael Newton's *"Journey of Souls"*, fourth edition 1995.

o   In the beginning there is an outward migration of our soul energy from the source. Afterward, our lives are spent moving inward, toward cohesion and the uniting. The Source pulsates. It's like we all are inside of a beating heart.

o   It's like if souls are all part of a massive electrical explosion which produces a halo effect. In this circular halo is a dark purple light which flares out, lightening to a whiteness at the edges. Our awareness begins at the edges of brilliant light and as we grow we become more engulfed in the darker light ... full of knowing presence which is everywhere for us, and alive.

A Few Additional Selected Quotes From Dr. Newton's Subjects

o   "Death is like waking up after a long sleep where you had just a muddled awareness. The release you feel is one that comes after crying, only here you are not crying." (Destiny of Souls, p. 49)

o   "Amnesia forces us to go into the testing area of the laboratory of Earth without the answers for the tasks we were sent here to accomplish." (Destiny of Souls, p. 117)

o   "The ability of a soul to unite with itself is a natural process of energy regeneration after physical death." (Destiny of Souls, p. 117)

o   "Thus, it is not the volume of energy which gives potency to the soul but the quality of vibrational power representing a soul's experience and wisdom." (Destiny of Souls, p. 117).

o   "Even primary soulmates killed at the same moment will normally rise up by separate routes on their own vibrational lines. ... Each soul requires their own rate of ascension, which includes orientation stops and energy rejuvenation, even if they are returning to the same soul group." (Destiny of Souls, p. 271)

And with this we are leaving Dr. Newton and his subject for now. I have personally read three of his books: *Journey of Souls*, *Destiny of Souls* and *Memories of the Afterlife.* and I must say that his research is intriguing, and also, to a certain degree, aligns with my own and many other people's research, not only pertaining to the spirit world, but into metaphysics in general. It fits well into the puzzle, almost to the smallest detail.

I am now going to present a darker side of the afterlife, which seems to be much less common, but still appears to exist. Hence, I feel the need to present it to give a fuller picture. After that, we are going to conclude both sides of the story and comment on certain things that seem important.

The Negative Version of Afterlife

A year ago or so, I found a lot of conflicting data regarding the spirit world and what happens to us after our physical bodies die. There was a very disturbing side of it, too, and I decided to do my best to sort this out.

Although Dr. Newton's research seems solid, and this is what his subjects have experienced, are there others who have experienced something darker?

On September 23, 2010, I wrote an article called, *The Afterlife Programming*, which is now taken down and replaced by this section. I will repeat some of the information I released then and add more to it.

In that article, I argued that we are stuck in a 3rd dimensional/density prison, and the astral plane (time/space) is a part of it. I concluded that the spirit world is just a rest area for the soul, fully loaded with holograms, implants and computer screens which create a reality for us that is perceived as pleasant and beautiful. I said that this pleasant environment is created to deceive us; to make us believe that the 3rd dimension is not a prison, but a place to evolve. I also asked the rhetoric question, *who are the Council of Elders?* Could it be that they are part of a much larger control system, and they are just the ones making sure that business goes on as usual in the astral world and to make certain that no one "escapes?" Are we then implanted with false memories, amnesia implants and shot down into a human body again?

These are very dark and depressing assumptions, indeed, and if I made this up from out-of-the-blue, I would be very concerned about my mental health. But no, there are those who suggest that the above is true and what is truly happening when we die.

I am going to tell the reader my sources and describe briefly what they are telling us, and afterwards we are going to discuss their credibility.

The WingMakers Theory

The first source is James of the WingMakers.[105] In 2008, he accepted to do

---

[105] http://wingmakers.com; http://lyricus.org; http://eventtemples.com;

a rare interview with Kerry Cassidy and Bill Ryan of former Project Camelot, now Project Camelot Portal.[106] The interview can be read in full here:
http://projectcamelot.org/james_wingmakers_sovereign_integral.html.
James did this interview, partly to promote his most recent website, http://sovereignintegral.org/. Project Camelot had a lot of dedicated followers.

Providing a lot of new information, previously not covered at WingMakers.com, James also presented some quite disturbing information. In short (please read the article), he said that the whole 3rd dimension is a trap set up by the very powerful "god," Anu of the Anunnaki. He and his people genetically manipulated already existing beings of lower consciousness here on Earth and implanted them with a veil of forgetfulness and a body/mind system which would keep the spirit trapped in the 3rd dimension forever, or until Anu breaks the "spell."

Why and how did he do this, according to James?

Apparently, Atlantis, the ancient "mythical" civilization which Plato and others were describing existed thousands of years ago and was destroyed around 9,500 BC, was interdimensional to begin with, and inhabited by free spirits that were highly multi-dimensional. Atlantis was a beautiful, and very spiritual place, and the souls who built it here on Earth were very playful, innocent and in certain terms, naive.

Figure 6.7: Atlantis Capital.

Anu, who wanted to play God and was a very power-hungry and smart

---

being, mingled with the Atlanteans, noticed their free spirit, and decided to trap them. So, he created solid, physical bodies which he programmed to only be able to perceive a certain small frequency range of light and sound (the current 3-D range), and would thus be separated from the rest of the Multiverse. In addition, he created a cloned universe with stars, planets, galaxies, nebulae and all the rest of it, which were as solid as the real 4-space/time universe, except the only beings inhabiting this cloned universe were humans. In other words, he successively created his own version of bodies based on the human template (one head, two arms, bipedal) and seeded his own universe with these bodies. According to James, 3-D is only existing as a creation of Anu; the *real* universe is a Multiverse with multiple dimensions which interact with each other to enable its multi-dimensional inhabitants to have as rich experiences as possible.

Now, Anu wanted to trap these free spirits of Atlantis into the 3 dimensional bodies to lower their frequency and make them his slaves. How could he do that? Why would free spirits even consider entering solid bodies with such great limitations?

For Anu, the answer was simple. He simply programmed the bodies with images and 3-D "movies." He created something most easily described as a CD running in a constant loop, showing attractive pictures and realities that would interest a curious, naive spirit.

Then, he chose a few souls and talked them into testing his bodies. His guinea pigs were probably reluctant at first, but at the same time curious, and Anu was apparently quite glib and convincing and managed to have a few spirits try the bodies. Because of the fascinating experience, the test subjects told the rest that this was very fun and interesting, and most of the remaining spirits entered the bodies as well. At that point, Anu closed the trap. Since then, we have been trapped in the 3rd dimension, looking up at a universe which is a clone of the real one, sparse of life, and only seeded with biominds/biokinds whom Anu created. Because as soon as he was done with Earth, he went elsewhere and trapped other beings in other parts of the Universe and had them entering his bodies as well. Anu now felt like he was becoming greater or equal to God, because he could create his own, whole universe and put himself in charge over it.

Anu also knew that to keep these spirits trapped, he must create a time/space where the spirits could go after their bodies perished. So he did; he created a whole time/space environment of holograms, implant stations, spirit guides, landscapes and everything we can think of. Here the spirit could rest for a while before its memories of the spirit world was erased and then the bodies were shot down into a 3-D body again. In this fashion, the reincarnation cycle has continued for tens of thousands of years.

The entire cloned universe is like a time-loop, so after a certain time, it resets itself over and over, just like a CD would, if you put it on "repeat."

According to James, the end of such a loop is happening soon, within the next 3 generations. That's why it is important for mankind to find what he calls *The Grand Portal*, which is an allegory for being aware as a human soul group that we are spiritual beings and can prove scientifically that this is the case. When science and religion meet, we can break the "spell," and so also the walls of the 3rd dimension; we would be free spirits again and part of the richness of the Multiverse.

Then James says Anu is no longer here, and Nibiru, which is the planet of the Anunnaki, is no longer a threat. The spirit world has apparently become an automatic process and does not need Anu's attention.

Prophecies are talking about the god(s) coming back in the End Times (which is supposedly now), and these prophecies talk about the same god(s), which is Anu and the Anunnaki. However, "plans have been changed." as James put it, and Anu is not coming back. This is apparently the good news, and we're left on our own to figure out how to get out of the trap. This is where James and his Lyricus Teaching Order come into the picture; to help us find The Grand Portal.

The Moon Matrix

David Icke[107] is another researcher who has come to a somewhat similar conclusion as James, only the details differ. He, too, is convinced we started out as free spirits and got trapped here in 3-D.[108] His research also digs into the Anunnaki past and current presence on Earth, genetic engineering, and entrapment through DNA/RNA alteration.

Icke's main theory, here extremely simplified, is that the Global Elite, working behind the scenes to control our reality and keep us trapped here, are possessed by, or taken over by Reptilian ETs called the Anunnaki. The Reptilians are from the lower 4th density/dimension and can't comfortably stay for long in our reality without drinking human blood. The blood is keeping them grounded here for a while through vibration; hence the Satanic, Black Magic blood rituals that are reported to take place around the globe in Elite circles.

The Global Elite believe they are of a pure bloodline, going back to old Babylon, Sumer and even further back; a direct line to the Reptilian 4th density entities, who interbred with humans. By keeping their bloodline as pure as possible through inbreeding, they can function as hosts for these higher density Reptilians. In exchange for doing their dirty work, they can

---

[107] Davidicke.com.
[108] David Icke, 2010: *"Human Race Get Off Your Knees -- The Lion Sleeps No More"* p. *227.*

120

live a life in abundance, and get whatever they want when it comes to material things, and certain spiritual powers.

Figure 6.8: Anunnaki as depicted by the Sumerians.

The goal of the Reptilians is to completely take over the Earth as the conquering race they are. Hence, they are slowly, but surely (more rapidly now), building a New World Order to establish themselves as gods in a human slave society where we will all be implanted with microchips from birth, and our thoughts will be manipulated by ELF (extremely low frequency) waves so that we can no longer think for ourselves. All our thoughts will be controlled, and we will think they are our own. In other words, we are heading towards a society which would make the book by George Orwell, *1984,* look like a vacation trip to Greece. We are becoming the ultimate slaves, and these beings are very close to accomplishing their goal. However, by waking up the masses via the Internet, books, lectures, and spiritual work, raising our frequencies, we can affect other people around us positively, and hopefully sooner than later, raise the frequency of enough people to be able to stop this dark agenda, which has been going on for thousands of years.

In most of his later books, Icke talks about that we are stuck in a time-loop; he actually wrote a whole book about it, *Tales From the Time Loop (2003).* He also elaborates on this in his latest book, *Human Race Get Off Your Knees--The Lion Sleeps No More (2010),* where he makes a good job comparing his time loop theory with that of how a DVD works. We watch a movie on DVD, usually from beginning to end, and it tells a story. We are all actors in this movie, which is quite predestined, but we can interact to some degree and change things in the movie if we are spiritually aware

121

enough to be able to do so. If not, we're running on a script, a program, which we have little control over. Time in 3-D is like this movie; you can fast forward or rewind the DVD to a certain point in the plot and start watching from there. Thus, you have a past, a present and a future. However, most people are not aware of that they are playing out a script. The originators of this movie are the Reptilians, who can watch the 3-D plot from outside, just like we sit in the living room watching a DVD (as above, so below).

According to Icke, we thus live in a giant hologram, in a movie which starts all over once it has finished. And we are getting close to the end of the movie now. This is also how prophecy works; entities from outside the DVD/time loop are entering the movie and give us predictions about future events that are most likely to come true, because they are written into the plot. Thus, most prophecy is predestined.

So, how do the Reptilians do this? Well, again according to Icke and the research he has compiled, it's all controlled from the artificial Moon. This is where their "control room" is located, where they direct their holographic technology towards Earth and keep us trapped. The Moon, however, is just a "relay station," and the real programming seems to come from the planet Saturn, according to Icke and his latest discoveries.

This was the extremely short version of Icke's research, and I recommend you read his books to get a bigger picture because I can't make justice to it here.

Although I haven't really seen Icke mentioning it, it is easy to expand on his theory, the Moon Matrix, if we want to take it to heart and are curious about what happens after we die. If Icke is correct, it's not a stretch to imagine that the spirit world and the time/space we go to between lives is another DVD, which is playing over and over.

L. Ron Hubbard and the Afterlife Implant Stations

L. Ron Hubbard, the founder of Dianetics and Scientology, was probably the first out with information about between lives implant stations and erasure of memory. In many ways he was a pioneer and revealed things that to many seemed ridiculous at the time, but later was found to hold water, and some of what we now perceive as truth originated from him. With that said, I also want to emphasize that he was certainly not always right, and some of the stuff seems very dated and invalid today. But like with most researchers (even those who have proven to be disinformation agents), there is always some good information to discover. I try never to throw the baby out with the bathwater.

Hubbard talked about the between-lives area on several occasions, but this excerpt from his book *A History of Man (1952),*[109] originally released as

What to Audit, sums up Hubbard's version well.

Of course, not many people know the nomenclature of Scientology, so here are some definitions which might help the reader understand the quote that follows:

Preclear: a person who is under Scientology processing, working him/herself up to the state of *Clear*, which is the level when the person is free from his/her reactive/subconscious mind, which is normally running our lives. A Clear is someone who, after certain levels of training and auditing, can make more rational decisions without being affected by his/her past reactions to situations.

Auditing: when a preclear is in session, normally with an auditor (one who listens), and go through certain preset procedures that will eventually make the preclear Clear. Except in certain Dianetics procedures, an e-meter (electro-meter) is used to detect reactions to certain questions asked by the auditor. It works like a lie detector.

Restimulation: when a past, often traumatic or negative incident is triggered in a person, and s/he reacts to something happening in the present as if it were the same incident as in the past. Earlier events affect us today, and we are often not aware of that this is the case.

MEST: **M**atter, **E**nergy, **S**pace and **T**ime. This is the Scientology term for the physical universe.

Thetan (theta being): Scientology term for soul/spirit.

Bank: term for memory bank, or more specifically, the context of the **reactive mind**, which is the mind that is addressed in Dianetics -- the mind containing hidden memories from traumatic incidents in the past. When the reactive mind is erased, the preclear becomes Clear.

Keys in (key in, keying in): A moment of trauma, stemming from the **reactive mind**, gets in restimulation and the person experiences negative emotions, sometimes pain, or any emotion-reaction which is contained in the **bank**, relating to the incident that was keyed in. Today, we usually call it *triggers*.

Overt act: destructive act towards oneself or others, also including material things, animals and plants, the physical universe or the soul of self or others.

Track (or Time Track): the linear time of the **GE** (genetic entity), which is the body.

Facsimiles: mental image pictures.

To run: This means "to process" or "to audit" (see **Auditing** above).

Here is L. Ron Hubbard:

> **Between-Lives:** At death the theta being leaves the body and goes

---

[109] http://en.wikipedia.org/wiki/Scientology:_A_History_of_Man

to the between lives area. Here he "reports in," is given a strong forgetter implant and is then shot down to a body just before it is born. At least that is the way the old invader in the Earth area was operating.

The implant is very interesting. The preclear is seated before a wheel which contains numbers of pictures. As the wheel turns, these pictures go away from him. He is moved aside to the right, the left, the back. A mirror arrangement shows him still sitting there before the pictures. A force screen hits him through the pictures. The pictures dim out. The whole effect is to give him the impression that he has no past life, that he is no longer the same identity, that his memory has been erased. The force screen flattens his own vitality, thus invalidating his existence, thus installing, by force alone, a forgetter. The pictures, by the way, are simply generalized views, stills of vacant lots, houses, back yards, of a recent Earth period and they could apply to anybody. They are not the facsimiles of the preclear. The incident contains such force that the preclear at first quite closely in contact runs it willingly. As the force cuts down his past identity he begins to disbelieve the incident, then himself. If left in restimulation he has a difficult time remembering things for some days.

Gradually through a life-time this Between Lives incident keys in. At first it engulfs childhood, then later and later years. Finally, with age, the preclear starts to cycle through it automatically and goes into a "second-childhood," which is to say, he anticipates the coming implant, conceives it to have done if he lives beyond a normal life span for him. (If it usually happened that he died at sixty, should he now live to seventy, he will get a feeling in the last ten years that it has been done to him—a routine time restimulation effect.)

Preclears do not always report; to have been implanted once is to get a restimulation on dying which will wipe out the past life. Some preclears have one, some have five, some more of these implants.

The life to life forgetter would follow as a natural course of events from the fact that the preclear identifies himself and is identified by others as a MEST body; further he identifies everyone else as a MEST body. Also he would rather start, if he must be a MEST body, with a clean slate and a new body. Also he has many overt acts of convincing others they should forget their entire pasts, for by that he can train them for a better future for him. No implant would ever succeed unless there was a natural cause and reason for the implant to magnify.

The report area for most has been Mars. Some women report to stations elsewhere in the Solar System. There are occasional incidents about Earth report stations. The report stations are protected by screens. The last Martian report station on Earth was established in the Pyrenees.

Entities have between-life incidents independent of the thetan. These are not necessary to run.

There are many types of between lives earlier on the track, about ten different periods of the entire track being devoted to a practice of keeping a thetan in a body, working and in an area. These show up as second facsimiles and are not necessary to run. But the data is there in the secondary banks and it is very "wonderful" data on how to keep races enslaved.[110]

What is interesting with the above quote is that it was written in 1952.

Robert Morning-Sky and the Terra Papers

Robert Morning-Sky[111] is a quite well-known researcher. He wrote *The Terra Papers*[112] in the mid part of the 1990s, which deals with the history of Earth, humankind and what happened in Sector 9 (our part of the universe) before Earth was born and inhabited.

Morning-Sky is a half Hopi, half Apache Indian, and according to his own story, his Hopi grandfather told him the story of a star visitor, crash-landing on Hopi land. The alien survived the crash and was taken care of by the Indian tribe. In return, the star visitor told the Hopis the story of Planet Earth.

Figure 6.9: Anu and his children from "The Terra Papers"

He told them about the Anunnaki from Sirius, their war with the Reptilian Queens from Orion, how a peace treaty between the Sirians and

---

[110] Ron Hubbard, 1952: *"A History of Man"*, *op. cit. pp. 47-48.*

[111] http://robertmorningsky.com/
[112] *The Terra Papers* can be downloaded in pdf from "The Living Moon" website: http://www.thelivingmoon.com/47john_lear/08PDF_Files/The_Terra_Papers_Parts_1_and_2.pdf.

the Orion Reptilians were eventually made, and the Sirians explored and started inhabiting our young solar system. However, the Anunnaki, being a warrior race, constantly fought internally, especially over who was going to be their King. Son killed father, nephew overthrew uncle etc., in an endless struggle for power.

Morning-Sky did his own research based on what the star visitor told the tribe; the result became *"The Terra Papers"*.

The author writes about how Enki and Nin-Hur-Sag of the Anunnaki created the human race, quite similar to what the late Zacharia Sitchin told us in *The Earth Chronicles*.[113]

Morning-Sky's story continues with that the Grays is a hybrid race, created by mixing Reptilian and humanoid DNA from the Orions and the Sirians and manipulating the DNA. The Gray hybrid race later became the head of the Freemasons and is still up to this day, behind the scenes. They were also the ones who helped Marduk, Enki's son, to power in old Babylon.

The reason I am bringing up Robert Morning-Sky in this context is because of the SHET-U lizards (the Grays). Robert held quite a few lectures after the Terra Papers were released, and at least one of them still exists online and can be watched on YouTube. In a video recordings, Morning-Sky says that the Grays are in charge of the spirit world and are implanting us between lives. Furthermore, he advises us that when we die and our spirits are drawn towards the tunnel, we should refuse to go there and instead turn the other way, out into the universe, where we belong. Here are the two parts of the lecture which includes these statements:

Part 2:
http://www.youtube.com/watch?v=X4gcDeTmp68&feature=related

Part 3:
http://www.youtube.com/watch?v=5TAKOrLXYps&feature=related

However, to get this is context, I advise the reader to listen to the whole lecture on YouTube:
http://www.youtube.com/watch?v=Nb0SOzYeRzs&feature=related

Edgar Cayce's and Other People's Experiences in the Spirit World

The famous medium, Edgar Cayce, traveled through the tunnel to the

---

[113] http://sitchin.com/

spirit world more than once. When he did, he noticed strange creatures inhabiting the various afterlife realms he passed through. In the first realm, there were horrible, vague, and grotesque forms like those we encounter in a nightmare. On all sides of the tunnel, he could see misshapen forms of humans with some body part magnified. Some people were also calling out for him, asking for help and trying to get his attention.[114]

The experience Cayce had is also described in the *Tibetan Book of the Dead*[115] and other religious scriptures as being Hell. It's a place where a particular desire has been overemphasized while in physical life. There are others, besides Edgar Cayce, who have come back from being dead for a short time and after been revived, they speak of similar things. Some of them actually describe being in a Hell of fire and brimstone.[116] Interestingly enough (and we will discuss this later), many people who say they have been to the classic Biblical Hell are either religious people in general, or Reverends.

Figure 6.10: Arthur Yensen

Arthur Yensen,[117] a university graduate in geology, had quite a few near-death experiences in the earlier part of the 1900s. Just like Cayce and many others, he said he had experienced something called The Void, where there is only darkness; no light, no love... only thoughts exist of self and others. The general idea seems to be that this Void is where souls go who are too low in vibration to mingle with the average souls after body death. The

[114] Creatures Found in the Void: http://www.near-death.com/experiences/research15.html
[115] http://www.near-death.com/experiences/buddhism01.html
[116] Creatures Found in the Void: http://www.near-death.com/experiences/research15.html
[117] http://www.near-death.com/experiences/reincarnation06.html

Void has many names in different religions, where some of them are purgatory, hell, outer darkness, prison, Gehennom, She'ol, pit, abyss, annar, and Preta-Loka.

This is what Yensen had to say about the Void:

> Those who are too bad go to a realm of lower vibrations where their kind of thoughts can live. After death, people are drawn into groups according to their rate of soul vibrations. If the amount of discord within a person is small, it can be eliminated by God so that only the good remains and they are welcomed into heaven. However, if the amount of discord is too high, eliminating it cannot be done because they would be annihilated. So, the person will gravitate to a lower realm and live with their own kind. Each person lives in the kind of a heaven or hell that they have prepared for themselves while on Earth. High vibrations indicate love and spiritual development, while low vibrations indicate debasement and evil. Without a physical body, feelings of hate and fear are intensified as souls vainly try to hide from their enemies.[118]

Interestingly enough, Yensen was asked on occasion, due to his experiences, what God is like, and like so many others have described God, Yensen said:

> Under self-hypnosis, I once asked what God was like. I saw a huge mountain almost covered with clouds. Here and there were small peepholes through which I could see lightning and great activity. Then a voice from somewhere said, "To fully understand God, you'll have to be almost as great as God is!"

> This put me in my place. But for reasoning purposes I had to have some kind of a mental image of what God is like. To me now, after many years of thought, he's a combination of many things such as: the known and unknown laws of nature, light, electricity, gravity, time, space, infinity, love and life itself - totally incomprehensible! But since we have life, we must all be a small part of him.

> That's probably why we call him Father and consider ourselves his ornery kids - who always need forgiveness.[119]

Yensen comes across as a religious person, but his experiences changed him. Still, he tried to box them into his old belief system, and that's where it becomes arbitrary.

To return to Cayce for a while, he was also famous for finding information on The Hall of Records (the Akashic Records) while in trance, and what he had to say corresponds a lot with what Dr. Newton's subjects

---

[118] The Nature of the Void: http://www.near-death.com/experiences/research15.html
[119] http://www.near-death.com/experiences/reincarnation06.html

said:

> As I pass on, there is more light and movement in what appear to be normal cities and towns. With the growth of movement I become conscious of sounds, at first indistinct rumblings, then music, laughter, and singing of birds. There is more and more light, the colors become very beautiful, and there is the sound of wonderful music. The houses are left behind; ahead there is only a blending of sound and color.

> Quite suddenly I come upon a Hall of Records. It is a hall without walls, without ceiling, but I am conscious of seeing an old man who hands me a large book, a record of the individual for whom I seek information. a good description of the Temple of Knowledge[120] that people refer to in other NDEs.[121]

Kevin Williams is a person who has done a lot of research into the afterlife phenomenon, and he has an explanation for the Void that I agree with, and which corresponds pretty well with Dr. Newton's research:

> After death, some souls travel very quickly through the two lower realms - the earthbound realm and void - by means of the tunnel and on to higher realms. Other souls, particularly those who have developed a strong addiction for some earthly desire that went beyond the physical and into the spiritual, may enter the earthbound realm in a vain attempt to re-enter Earth. Many near-death accounts, as you will see later, involve souls entering the void immediately after death. From here, the soul may then enter the tunnel toward the light in the next heavenly realm. Other souls remain in the void for one reason or another until they are ready to leave it.

> The general consensus among near-death reports is that the void is totally devoid of love, light, and everything. It is a realm of complete and profound darkness where nothing exists but the thought patterns of those in it. It is a perfect place for souls to examine their own mind, contemplate their recent Earth experience, and decide where they want to go next.

> For some souls, the void is a beautiful and heavenly experience because, in the absence of all else, they are able to perfectly see the love and light they have cultivated within themselves. For other souls, the void is a terrifying and horrible hell because, in the

---

[120] The NDE and the Temple: http://www.near-death.com/experiences/research28.html

[121] A Verbatim Account of Cayce's Afterlife Journeys: http://www.near-death.com/experiences/cayce01.html

absence of everything, they are able to perfectly see within themselves the lack of love and light they have cultivated within themselves. For this reason, the void is more than a place for the reflection of the soul. For some souls, it is a place for purification. In the latter case, the void acts as a kind of time-out where troubled souls remain until they choose a different course of action.

For some souls, the time spent in the void may feel like only a moment. For others, it may seem like eternity. This is because the way to escape the void is to choose love and light over the darkness. Once this happens, the light appears and the tunnel takes them toward the light and into heaven for further instruction. For those souls who either refuse the light or have spent a lifetime ignoring the light, it may take what seems like eons of "time" before they reach the point that they desire the light of love. The problem for many souls is that they prefer the darkness rather than the light for one reason or another. For some of these souls, their only hope is reincarnation. This is because it is not possible for any soul to be confined in the earthbound and void realms forever. God is infinitely merciful and would never abandon anyone to their own spiritual agony for too long; however, God allows souls to remain there only as long as it suits their spiritual growth.

The void is not punishment. It is the perfect place for all souls to see themselves and to purge themselves from all illusions. For those souls who are too self-absorbed in their own misery to see the light, there are a multitude of Beings of Light nearby to help them when they freely chose to seek them. The nature of love and light is such that it cannot be forced upon people who don't want it. Choosing love/light over darkness is the key to being freed from the void. The moment the choice is made, the light and tunnel appears and the soul is drawn into the light.[122]

Some of Dr. Newton's subjects explain how they come to the spirit world as extremely damaged souls. This could be due to having done a lot of evil toward others, been a subject to a lot of harm done to them, or they have lived a very destructive life with drugs, suicide attempts; and some of these damaged souls are there after having committed suicide.

Instead of letting a damaged soul mingle with the rest of its soul group

---

[122] Summary of Insights Concerning the Void: http://www.near-death.com/experiences/research15.html

[123] Dr. Michael Newton, 2009: *"Destiny of Souls"*.

[124] Here it is important to distinguish between the Void of the spirit world and the Void described in The Working Model.

and other discarnate, they are going to a solitary place where they can heal. It's usually a dark place where they can be by themselves, but still get assistance from their guides when needed. Of course, here where they can ponder and conclude, it could be a scary place at first for some people, because they have to face themselves to be able to see what they have done to themselves and others, in an attempt to turn the wheel around and start going in the other direction.[123] It is my own belief that this is another description of the Void.[124]

We can clearly see by reading the "negative" experiences in this Section that even when something is as consistent as Dr. Newton's research, there are always those who have had other experiences which at least after a first glance don't seem to fit into the mold. Or do they? In the Conclusion Section below, we are going to discuss just that.

Conclusions

Before we come to a final conclusion, let's examine the above sections one by one.

Dr. Michael Newton Revisited

After having read Dr. Newton's complete library, it's very hard to discard his research. 7,000+ subjects are pretty impressive, and if they also tell the exact same thing with only some minor personal details differing, I will call that evidence. It sure looks like this is the norm; at least this is what is happening to most of us when we depart from our bodies.

One thing with Dr. Newton's cases is that they state that most of the time we reincarnate over and over here on Earth until we've learned our experience, become a more advanced soul, and can go on to the next level, or incarnate on another world to expand ourselves further. This contradicts Dr. Bordon and the Working Model of the LPG-C, which postulates that once we're incarnated on any planet (in this case Earth), our Information Cloud (soul) is getting indexed to this particular planet, and when we exit, we can't come back, because we're already indexed here and have done our job.[125] It doesn't matter if we died as little babies; we have no way of coming back other than as visitors or "walk-ins."[126]

I discussed this matter with Dr. Bordon, and he is absolutely positive

---

[125] See Paper 7 (2011): *"Known Life Forms Within the Milky Way and Beyond", section 3: "Indexing of Planetary Bodies and the Reality of the "Ascension" Concept."*

[126] A "walk-in" is a soul who's taking over a body from an already living biokind. The original soul is exiting and the new soul is taking over. This can be done by force, but is something that is most often agreed upon between lives for one purpose or another.

that the latter is true. He says that the Multiverse is so vast, and there is so much that we need to learn, that we only have one incarnation on each planet.[127] I disagree with this, and when I tried to push the matter further recently, I never got a reply.

Aside from all the positive information we have received from Dr. Newton and his research, there is this nagging feeling in the back of my head that something is not completely right—or at least, incomplete, and perhaps even manipulated, unbeknown to his subjects. Almost all the 7,000 clients have told a similar, almost euphoric experience in the spirit world, but at the same time, it all seems almost too structured and controlled. It sounds like "somebody" is controlling the between-lives area notoriously, down to the T. This does not in itself have to be a negative thing, but the fact that the spirit guides are always present in the room when Dr. Newton is interviewing his clients under hypnosis also makes me wonder. Again, it does not have to mean anything negative, but what if the spirit guides during the sessions are holographically manipulating the clients and have them tell only parts of the real story, or a modified version to hide what is really happening? It's easy to get paranoid here, but I want to be open to all options.

One could also speculate about the validity of the clients claiming to be incarnating over and over on Earth. Are they implanted memories as well? There are many other sources indicating that we actually *do* live more than one lifetime on Earth simultaneously. The interesting thing is that some of Dr. Newton's clients say that they don't necessarily reincarnate into a future body, but rather into a body anytime and anywhere, depending on what that soul needs to learn and experience. This is in line with my own research, and I will talk more about this in the last papers of this level of learning.

Whatever the matter is, we need to keep in mind that we have gone through the afterlife process over and over, and we are still here, so whatever the case is, we come out of it in one piece, and mostly it seems to be quite a pleasant experience, whether we're controlled or not, but I could be wrong. There is so much manipulation on several different levels.

More than likely, there is more to come on this subject in the near future.[128] Additional papers on this topic can be expected.

The WingMakers Theory Revisited

When I first started looking into the WingMakers Material (WMM), I was pretty fascinated. I read the Dr. Neruda Interviews and the Ancient Arrow

---

[127] Penre/Bordon correspondence, February 9, 2011.
[128] See upcoming book collections of this series of papers.

Project and knew in my heart that there was truth in it. Afterwards, I had parts of that information confirmed to me. The ACIO, (The Advanced Alien Contact Intelligence Organization) is a real group and a part of the NSA (National Security Agency) and has its headquarters in remote Pine Gap, Australia. I know firsthand that they exist, because I have had correspondence with them.

When I started reading more from the WingMakers site, I noticed it changed in character somewhere along 2001 or so. The information that was released after that (including FAQ pages, audio interviews, and articles), was in general more questionable and the context no longer as inspiring as before. Suddenly James (the translator of this material and the main person behind the information) started adding information about The Great White Brotherhood, Alice Bailey, Ascended Masters and other quite esoteric material which seemed out of place for me, and a way to sidetrack us; especially as I understand that the Great White Brotherhood and their Ascended Masters Program is set up by those who are not from here and don't have our best interests in mind. Much more about this later. However, I was still hooked because there was still some information, like the Energetic Heart, the Six Heart Virtues, the Quantum Pause and more, which I feel strongly is very valid. I also took to heart the information about the Central Race and the Lyricus Teaching Order, although perhaps not all of it. But again, like the Guardian Alliance, who are speaking through A'shayana Deane in the Voyagers Series say, the people working on the WingMakers project are usually unaware of who is behind it, and their real agenda (**Deanne 2002:** *Voyagers II, second edition, pp. 550*). Again, this will be covered in much more detail in a forthcoming paper.

Then, in 2008, James was interviewed by Kerry Cassidy and Bill Ryan of Project Camelot, and that interview was a jaw-dropper! Here James changed direction quite drastically and painted a very disturbing and dark picture of the reality we live in. As I mentioned earlier in this paper under the WingMakers section, he explained how solidly we are trapped in the 3rd dimension, which was totally created by a creator god, Anu of the Anunnaki back in old Atlantis. By creating a complex *Genetic Manipulation System*, as he calls it, he had all these free spirits trapped into matter, and they forgot who they were. In addition, Anu also had to be in control over the spirit world and the afterlife.

James continues by saying that all channeled material comes from within what he calls the *Human Mind System (HMS)*, which in other words is Anu's Universe. If there is thought involved, it's coming from within the trap. Beings can claim they are interdimensional, of higher densities or whatnot, but they are still trapped in Anu's universe.

When this interview was first released, I took most of it to heart, although I had certain doubts about the "cloned" universe. James said that this artificial universe is inhabited *only* by humans; *there are no other alien species!* He adds that other life forms *do* exist, but they come from outside Anu's Matrix system and can only stay here for a while, or they will either perish or get stuck here (which has happened).[129]

A very good read is the free e-book: *Alien Mind,* by George LoBuono.[130] It will take you on a ride you have not been even close to before. It will make you understand how aliens think, how widespread they are throughout the Multiverse, where they come from, how they are connected to us humans, and why. It's hard to even begin to understand the alien phenomenon without having read that book.

The fact that we have been contacted big time by aliens, both physical and hyperversal (entities who either exist inter-dimensionally without a body or can transfer a body over long distances in space and time), is evident.

According to members of the LPG-C (Life Physics Group California), a Human Mind System of the kind James is describing in the Camelot Interview is not possible to make, either, because physics simply doesn't work that way. Still, I wouldn't discard the WingMakers Material that easily; there is a lot of useful information in there; especially from the early material, but also the breathing exercises, and the heart virtues. Again, it's a matter of not throwing the baby out and learning how to discern good information from the bad. But if James' claim that we're stuck in a cloned universe falls apart, so does his afterlife theory, something I would not discard so easily.

David Icke and the Moon Matrix Revisited

I have always found David Icke and his work fascinating. I have followed him on and off since his book *The Robots' Rebellion* was released in the early parts of the 1990s. I read it at the same time as I read *The Gods of Eden* by William Bramley, and William Cooper's, *Behold a Pale Horse.* I believe Icke has done a lot to reveal things that are going on behind the scenes, and his *soul*utions are often right on. I am even ready to adopt some of his reptilian theories for now.

Back to the Moon Matrix: When I read Icke's book on the subject, I found it very intriguing, and possibly true. If it's true that the Reptilian hyperversals Icke talks about create our reality by holograms projected

---

[129] Since I first wrote this paper, my own research, which will be released in the upcoming books in this series, show the exact same thing as James said. These days, I agree with him 100% in this matter. The only other beings here are a renegade group of the Anunnaki.

[130] LoBuono's e-book can be downloaded in pdf here: http://exopoliticshongkong.com/uploads/Alien_Mind_a_Primer_book.pdf . LoBuono's website: http://alienmindbook.org/

from the Moon and thus keep us in a time-loop, the same entities could possibly also control the Earth's astral planes. I am surprised that Icke hasn't made that connection, but on the other hand, perhaps he is working on that in his next book.

The experiences Dr. Newton's subjects have had could then be part of the programming, and the subjects would never know; they will all simply tell the truth from how they experienced their afterlife. They are unable to penetrate the hologram because they are not even aware that it exists.

Ron Hubbard and Robert Morning Sky

I have no doubts that L. Ron Hubbard (LRH) had inside information. A lot of former Scientologists who have left the Church have become powerful whistle-blowers, and quite a few of them worked close to, or even together with, LRH. Many of them, in addition to researcher and author, Russel Miller, who wrote the book, *Barefaced Messiah - The True Story of L. Ron Hubbard,*[131] are saying that LRH once worked for Navy Intelligence, something the Church eventually had to admit in 1969, although their version is that he did so to be able to destroy "evil secret societies" like the OTO Pasadena Lodge in California, run by Jack Parsons in the 1940s, by infiltrating them.[132] What they failed to tell us is that the OTO (at that time run by the British Intelligence Officer, and spy, Aleister Crowley) and many other secret societies already are/were part of the Intelligence Community.

LRH certainly ran that lodge down by allegedly stealing both Parsons' girlfriend and his yacht and also got away with some of Parsons' money. Jack Parsons, a well-known rocket scientist, eventually blew himself up accidentally(?) in his laboratory.[133] Still, LRH refers to both Aleister Crowley and John Whitesides Parsons as his dear friends in Scientology lectures,[134] and a policy letter from the late 1950s.[135] I also got confirmed

---

[131]   Russel   Miller's   book   can   be   downloaded   in   pdf   here:
http://www.apologeticsindex.org/Bare%20Faced%20Messiah.pdf

[132] *ibid. p. 290: '"Hubbard broke up black magic in America . . . because he was well known as a writer and philosopher and had friends among the physicists, he was sent in to handle the situation of black magic being practised in a house in Pasadena occupied by nuclear physicists. He went to live at the house and investigated the black magic rites and the general situation and found them very bad . . . Hubbard's mission was successful far beyond anyone's expectations. The house was torn down. Hubbard rescued a girl they were using. The black magic group was dispersed and never recovered.' (Statement by the Church of Scientology, December 1969)."*

[133] This whole story is covered in depth in Russel Miller's *Barefaced Messiah - The True Story of L. Ron Hubbard* and other various books by former Scientologists, such as Jon Atack in his *A Piece of Blue Sky,* and in various articles on the Internet.

[134] L. Ron Hubbard: *"The Philadelphia Doctorate Course", Lecture #18, Dec 5, 1952*

[135] I have so far been unable to find this policy letter online, but I have personally

by the late, murdered researcher Bill Cooper in person in 200[136] that Scientology is a Navy Intelligence project which went beyond expectations. Bill, himself a former Navy Intelligence Officer, was shot to death by Arizona police outside his home shortly after.

I'd like to look at the research of L. Ron Hubbard and Robert Morning Sky side by side. Although Hubbard never mentions the Grays per se, Morning Sky does, the "invaders force" could be one and the same. If there is something about the "negative afterlife experiences" having truth to them, it would be the Gray Agenda. Again, I need to emphasize that we're here talking about not all Grays, but the faction that is abducting us and manipulating our genes without our direct consent. Hubbard is going into great details about how these implants are being done, which I find quite interesting, and he is mentioning Mars as an implant station together with the Pyrenees. Both The Pleiadians, Robert Morning Sky and many, many others (including Sitchin) have mentioned lately that Mars has long been used for genetic engineering and is inhabited, or at least was until very recently. Hubbard could have made Mars up in his imagination, and this is of course possible, but if so, there are a lot of things Hubbard made up in his "imagination" that later showed to be true. I believe Hubbard had some real inside information, or perhaps he gained some of his information from early versions of remote viewing; after all, the OT levels in Scientology are to some degree about remote viewing, and many famous remote viewers, like Putnam and Ingo Swann, were OT III Scientologists of the old school.

Robert Morning Sky, like Hubbard, had some serious critics; Morning Sky had his share in the late 1990s. He was so heavily criticized that he decided to withdraw from public appearances and thus disappeared from the scene for over 10 years, until just recently, when he was interviewed on the Veritas Show.[137] Worth listening to as well, is an interview from 1996 called *Star Elders,* (no longer online when this book is published). But by now, we know how it works; if you really want to bring somebody down or out of business, so to speak, all you have to do is to consistently and persistently point out the things that are wrong, magnify the errors out of proportion, and then suggest that it is all mis/disinformation. If we fall for that, we're on a non-productive journey. No one will tell you the whole truth about anything; we must figure it out for ourselves by picking a gem here and there and sort them by colors, figuratively speaking.

I believe Morning Sky did a good job with what he had available when researching our ancestors—the Anunnaki and the Orion Reptilians. Much

---

read it and once had it in my possession.

[136] Penre/Cooper correspondence 2001.

[137] http://www.youtube.com/watch?v=imEicMP69Uo

of the information supposedly came from a star visitor his Hopi forefathers saved from a UFO crash, but Robert also did his own research to put things together, in addition to being a linguist in ancient languages. He is telling an interesting story in *The Terra Papers*, particularly about the time before the Anunnaki, the Orions and the Grays came to Earth. He is going back in time and deep-digs into the Anunnaki royal bloodline, way before King Anu. When scrutinizing his work as a whole and compare it to more recent, consistent sources, not everything Morning Sky was telling us holds water, but I am happy to have read him and listened to him, because he has a lot to teach us so we can be able to put these very confusing subjects on UFOs and aliens into perspective. His information is unique.

I have no solid proof to present about the Grays being the invader force, implanting us and keeping us ignorant between lives, despite what other researchers have claimed. The only solid evidence I have is what Dr. Newton has given us through his research. We may, and should, speculate if there is more to it, and here are some questions we need to have answered:

1. Although most people's experiences from the afterlife seem pleasant, is there a force controlling time/space? If so, is that force benevolent or malevolent? Are the positive experiences just a way to keep us attached to a Matrix system, controlled by alien beings with a not-so-benevolent agenda?

2. Some sources, like the Pleiadians, say that we go wherever our beliefs take us after we die. If we believe we go to Hell, something equivalent to our belief system is going to manifest. If we believe in Heaven, we will experience something akin to that. Therefore, it's very important to decide where we want to go and what to experience. This makes sense on some level, although it looks like almost all of Dr. Newton's subjects go to the same, or a similar place.

3. Quite a few of Dr. Newton's subjects describe time/space as being curved, which indicates that it's a sphere, and therefore finite. What exactly is this sphere?

Before I end this paper, I want to address Edgar Cayce and the rest of the witnesses as well.

The Edgar Cayce Section Revisited

We need to remember that any experience a person may have is subjective and viewed from that person's perspective. Then, when describing the experience to the rest of us by using words, something always gets lost or distorted on the way. This is mainly because we still don't have a sufficient language to describe these phenomena. Two people who have experienced the exact same thing may feel different about it; *very* different even and may still have been to an identical place.

The following facts remain:

- We are under severe mind control here in the 3rd Density, making it possible for more than one alien race to control the whole human population. This is not new; we have been manipulated for thousands of years.
- On a higher soul level, we are aware of this, but agree to experience, learn from, and expand ourselves in this lower frequency consciousness and now take advantage of the higher levels of energy coming in from cosmos to finally have the opportunity to graduate from this reality.

There is overwhelming evidence that the above is true, and this means that the spirit world must have been adjusted to the 3-D reality (or the other way around). We need a rest place in between lives, and we got it if we need it. We are patched up to be able to fulfill our "mission," and ETs from many walks in life out in the Universe are curiously watching us breaking out from the "prison." Once we become aware of ourselves as multidimensional beings, there is no longer any use for the afterlife as we know it. As multidimensional beings we can access the Sitter Space at will whenever we want to. So, looking at this entire thing from this higher, multidimensional perspective makes it all make more sense.

Bottom line is, when you are pure Spirit, unattached to a heavy 3-D body, and no longer "trapped" in a low frequency reality, what are you? You are pure energy, unconditional love and in tune with All That Is; "God" on a subquantum level.

This is also what most people seem to experience when they leave the Earth plane after their body-vehicle stops functioning. Then you're drawn towards a tunnel of light with a force that seems hard to resist. As a matter of fact, few have any wish to resist it, either, because they feel so good. Some say that they can see 1,000 years into the past and 1,000 years into the future; it all exists simultaneously.

The open question is, what is this tunnel of light, which apparently takes you to a spherical time/space that obviously is finite if it's spherical?

Because of Michael Newton's research we potentially know *what* happens on the other side of the tunnel, but we don't know *who* is in control of the afterlife. Pure spirit, meeting relatives and soul groups feeling a tremendous amount of love for everybody and everything--in that sense afterlife seems "benevolent" enough. However, playing the Devil's advocate, could it be that the afterlife is still controlled by the same forces who control our 3rd Density, aka the Anunnaki and the Reptilians? Could it be that they trap pure spirits, full of love but naive in their "new" native state, by forcing us into this tunnel? On the other side of the tunnel is another hologram; they just exchange one holographic reality for another? It's fine to be benevolent if they know they can "shoot us back down" into a body again, because that's what spirit is programmed to do--go back into 3rd Density again. This argument could be groundless, but I can't help but being suspicious about the tunnel. Who is in control? And who are the members of the "Council"? Who is above them?

The mindful may ask themselves, what about life on other planets then? Aren't we living different lives on different planets? The answer is most certainly... maybe.

PAPER 7
SIX TYPES OF CIVILIZATIONS
Saturday, February 12, 2011

Abstract

On occasion, I notice from readers' comments on different UFO websites that people are wondering why certain galactic civilizations visiting here in the past, or those out there in space, can't do this or that if they are so advanced?

The answer is that ET races can be advanced enough to travel through space, and perhaps even be able to genetically manipulate other species, and still lack a spiritual compass humans would possibly expect from such advanced beings.

Figure 7.1: Nikolai Kardeshev

In 1964, the Russian astronomer, Nikolai Kardashev, constructed something he called *The Kardashev Scale*.[138] It puts energy consumption of

---

[138] http://en.wikipedia.org/wiki/Kardashev_scale

an entire cosmic civilization into perspective, so we, hopefully, when face-to-face or mind-to-mind with an alien species, relatively quickly can see how advanced they are. The scale is theoretical and can't be 100% reliable, but it works as a good guideline.

His scale consists of three different categories of civilizations; *Type I, Type II, and Type III*, which are based on how much usable energy a civilization has at its disposal, and their degree of space colonization. In summary, a *Type I* civilization masters the resources of its own planet, a *Type II* of its solar system, and a *Type III* of its galaxy.

Figure 7.2: George LoBuono

Now, this was in 1964 mind you, and we are as of this writing, in 2011. Much has been learned in 47 years; we have had several new encounters with extraterrestrials, new treaties are being made between humans and ETs as we speak, and we know about at least 118-120 ET races hovering around in near space or being stationary on our planet, according to LPG-C. Therefore, it has been necessary to add two more categories to Kardashev's Scale; *Type IV* and *Type V*.[139] This was done by writer and researcher George LoBuono, who also has had several encounters with ETs and is practicing ENS (advanced remote viewing).

So let us look at the 5 different civilization types and see what they stand for.

---

[139] George LoBuono, 2006: "Alien Mind" pp. 69

Five Different Types of Civilizations

Type I: a Type I civilization controls the resources of an entire planet (weather and earthquake control, plus exploration of an entire solar system).

Type II: a Type II civilization controls and directly uses the power of its sun and begins to colonize nearby star systems.

Type III: a Type III civilization controls and uses the power of an entire galaxy.

Type IV: Type IV is the larger, cosmic commonality, the generic "civilization" of which aliens speak. Type IV civilization utilizes negative and alternate cycles of hyperspace to reach back and through all intelligent life forms to preserve the peace and secure the most enduring inter-alien ecology. Type IV civilization can exceed technology and resonate in the very nature of phenomena surrounding us. Presumably, this is more noticeable on a galaxy supercluster scale, yet extends into all surrounding communities.[140]

Type V: a greater type V population is so advanced that it is (or was) able to hyper-dimension from a previous universe cycle into the current one via alternate cycle gravitic resonance that can be effected in $\pm$ light speed ways (this isn't as complex as it sounds). Type V populations resemble Type IV populations but are of longer duration and have a deeper awareness of the continuum. Some can be so advanced that they inter-dimension with aliens originating among a succession, or continuity, of previous universe cycles. Nonetheless, a kind of mortality and larger, alternate-cycle conservations exist therein.

That requires sensitivity to collective considerations of various sorts because there are limits for every population, irrespective of their duration and technology.[141]

Using nuclear explosion tests as a perspective, Tsar Bomba, the largest nuclear weapon ever detonated, released an estimated 57 megaton yield; a Type I civilization makes use of roughly 25 megatons of TNT equivalent a second, the equivalent of one Tsar Bomba every 2.3 seconds. A Type II civilization controls $4 \Box \times \Box 109$ times more energy (4 billion hydrogen bombs per second), and a Type III 1011 times more yet.[142]

Then, there is a sixth category, not mentioned above. In this additional category we humans exist. We call it **Type 0** because we are not yet a Type I civilization. We are currently just below Type I, as we are able to harness a portion of the energy available on Earth. Carl Sagan, the famous astronomer, calculated in 1973 that we are right now a Type 0.7, which

---

[140] *ibid. op. cit.,* pp. 79
[141] *ibid. op. cit.,* pp. 80
[142] http://en.wikipedia.org/wiki/Kardashev_scale

means, based on British Petroleum's (BP) primary energy consumption chart for 2007[143] (which would make us a Type 0.72 civilization), that we are using about 0.16% of the total planetary energy budget available. Based on these calculations, we should become a Type I within 100-200 years, a Type II in a few thousand years, and Type III status in about 100,000 to a million years.[144]

My personal perception, due to our current interrelation and collaboration with different ET civilizations (something that quite possibly will extend in the future, at least for those who choose to stay in the 3-D frequency), our move from Type 0 to I and from Type I to Type II will go much faster; especially the I-II leap. However, this depends on which choices we make in the next few decades as a unified soul group.

However, if "Captain S", who posted on the Godlike Production Forum (**GLP**) in July-August 2011, is correct,[145] we already have the technology for interstellar space travel, and it happens behind our backs. That would make us the equivalent to a Type II already, albeit due to the secrecy around it, we have not developed on our planet the use of energy sources necessary to be classified as a Type II. That's why this scale is theoretical, but in many ways still useful.

---

[143] BP Primary energy consumption chart for 2007

[144] Kaku, Michio (2010). "The Physics of Interstellar Travel: To one day, reach the stars.". http://mkaku.org/home/?page_id=250.

[145] http://www.godlikeproductions.com/forum1/message1578548/pg1. An edited, more easy-to-read version of the interview can be found here: http://thechaniproject.com/forum/index.php?PHPSESSID=19aef5a6ec04032c1dffb94e711d21aa&topic=356.0

PAPER 8
HUMAN ORIGINS AND THE LIVING LIBRARY
Thursday, March 31, 2011

Abstract

This is certainly not an easy subject to research. There is a ton of information out there, and because of its importance, there is also a lot of disinformation.

I have gone through the sources I found coherent and in tune with my own feel for the subject, and I've done my best to write a version which makes the most sense to me, and hopefully to the readers as well. When we are researching the old Galactic wars and conflicts between species, we need to try to figure out the agenda of the source. For example, if we would interview an American soldier who comes back from the Iraq War, proud of his efforts, and then interview an Iraqi resistance man who is *against* the U.S. invasion, about the same event, we would get two entirely different stories. If we then interview a "neutral" Norwegian reporter, who was present in Iraq as well, we will get a third story.

We have the same problem when trying to sort out the different channeled material we have at our convenience, and even the old clay and stone tablets were written by somebody, and we don't know how biased these "somebodies" were. Sometimes we can verify some of it by comparing it with other scriptures from around the world, which seem to be unrelated to each other but still tell a surprisingly similar story. Yet, our Galactic History is always a work in progress and may change as new information can be looked at and evaluated.

Another problem we face is that time is perceived differently depending on where in the Multiverse we are. Here on Earth, we have our ways of counting time, while others calculate it in other terms. Sometimes, the channeled entities are doing their best to adjust to our way of thinking, but it's not always going to be accurate; thus, depending on whom we ask, we may get a different time frame as of when a certain event happened. A metaphysical source which was notorious for this was the Ra Collective

("The Ra Material", "The Law of One"). They admitted to that they had big problems translating our Earth time to their concept of 'universal time'. If we also add to this different timelines, based on different realities, it becomes even more complex. We can only do our best to work with what we have and make sense of it. Hence, it is always a work in progress, which is perfectly fine.

I have largely used Lyssa Royal and Keith Priest as sources to this "lighter version" of the Galactic History. This is because their information tie neatly into what I am going to expand greatly upon in the "Second Level of Learning".

Lyssa Royal is an internationally known channel and author. Germane considers himself to be a nonphysical group consciousness associated with the Orion Light; a future integrated version of the galactic family of which we on Earth are a part. He chose the name "Germane" because of its English definition: *"Coming from the same source, or significantly relevant to."* There is no connection to St. Germain. A similar thing can be said about Jane Roberts' *"The Seth Material"*. The channeled entity Seth has nothing to do with the "mythological" Seth.

It seems Germane may be a faction of the Greys, and therefore many people have discarded Royal/Priest's very informative piece of work as disinformation. I don't. I consider her as valid as any of the other high quality channels. It is sad that because entities who speak may be of a species that has a bad reputation because of what *some* of them are doing, we humans (as so often is the case) throw out the baby. Manuel Lamiroy, whom I also use to some degree, is the founder and on the Advisory Board of the Exopolitics Institute of South Africa (http://www.exopoliticsinstitute.org/advisory-board-R&E.htm#Lamiroy; http://manuel.sekmeth.com/hb7/). He is also a regression therapist as well as a researcher into exopolitics and metaphysics. Hence, we can use his case studies to determine what is more likely to have happened in our distant past. He also seems to agree with much of what Royal and Priest are saying.

A third source is Dr. A.R. Bordon because of his scientific perspective on the metaphysical tantrums. Other sources than these three, when they are used, will be footnoted. A fourth source are the Pleiadians, channeled by Barbara Marciniak.

2. Panspermia--Life in the Universe is Seeded by Creator Gods

We will start with Dr. Bordon. He is suggesting that life, instead of starting out as a natural evolutionary process on a planet, the planet is seeded by cosmic beings. In his essay, "The LINK,"[146] he brings up this subject quite substantially. Still, he is certainly not the only modern scientist who has started to realize that this is the case. Fred Hoyle, in his time, and some before him, already touched on this. In metaphysics, this is a widespread and most common subject.

Dr. Bordon suggests there is evidence that life in its higher forms is seeded from outside and that they depend on genetic programs that come from space. He agrees with Brig Klyce, who says, "it is a wholly scientific, testable theory for which evidence is accumulating", on his website, Panspermia.org (Introduction: More Than Panspermia). In the footnote to Bordon's "The LINK", he says: (the bold emphases are mine. Aside from that, the following excerpt is quoted directly from the original):

> Panspermia is an idea with ancient roots, according to which life arrives, ready-made, on the surface of planets from space. It is often said that panspermia isn't very interesting, because it simply removes the problem of the origin of life from our planet to some other place. And yet, panspermia has gained the attention of our science.
>
> There is now **Pseudo-panspermia** (the delivery of complex organic compounds from space, to give the prebiotic soup some starter ingredients, a notion has already becoming widely accepted), **Basic Panspermia** (which holds that microbial life is present in space or on bodies like comets or asteroids, and it can be safely delivered to planets and start life there. If the cells escape from a living planet on fragments after a meteor impact, the phenomenon is called **litho-**, **ballistic-**, **impact-** or **meteoritic panspermia**).
>
> And that's not all. Svante Arrhenius proposed that naked cells might travel interstellar distances propelled by light pressure, a theory now called **radio-panspermia**. Whereas a light coating of carbon could protect single cells from UV radiation, a couple of meters of water or rock are needed for protection from cosmic rays. Consequently, radio-panspermia is currently in disfavor. The danger of radiation damage influenced Francis Crick and Leslie Orgel, in 1973, to propose that *life came to Earth by directed panspermia*, the theory that intelligent life from elsewhere sent germs here in a spaceship. Modern panspermia proposes comets as the delivery vehicles. Comets can protect cells from UV and cosmic radiation damage; and comets can drop cells high in the atmosphere to float gently down. If bacterial spores can be immortal, as it appears, comets could spread life throughout a galaxy.
>
> Hoyle and Wickramasinghe ,starting in the 1970s, rekindled interest in panspermia. But they went further to include a new

---

[146] https://www.coursehero.com/file/195805727/A-R-Bordon-The-Linkpdf/

understanding of evolution. While accepting the fact that life on Earth evolved over the course of about four billion years, they say that the genetic programs for higher evolution cannot be explained by random mutation and recombination among genes for single-celled organisms, even in that long a time: the programs must come from somewhere beyond Earth. In a nutshell, their theory holds that all of life comes from space. It incorporates the original panspermia in the same way that General Relativity incorporates Special Relativity. Their expanded theory can well be termed "strong" panspermia. Their Cosmic Ancestry is a new theory pertaining to evolution and the origin of life on Earth. It holds that life on Earth was seeded from space, and that life's evolution to higher forms depends on genetic programs that come from space. It is a wholly scientific, testable theory for which evidence is accumulating.

The above is essential for understanding how life of higher intelligence starts on a planet. When comes to Earth, the human ancestors, all the way to modern homo sapiens sapiens (the thinking man), were seeded by extraterrestrial beings "in their image". Earth was originally created as a Living Library, and almost everything growing and living on this planet originates from elsewhere else in the Universe and was brought here by different creator gods. This was revealed by the Pleiadians already in 1988-89. In addition, the species who developed here over time were then genetically manipulated by the same creator gods for different reasons; many of the creator gods had different agendas. There are even indicators that humankind was seeded more than once; something we will bring up in the "Second Level of Learning".

The Creation of the Solar System

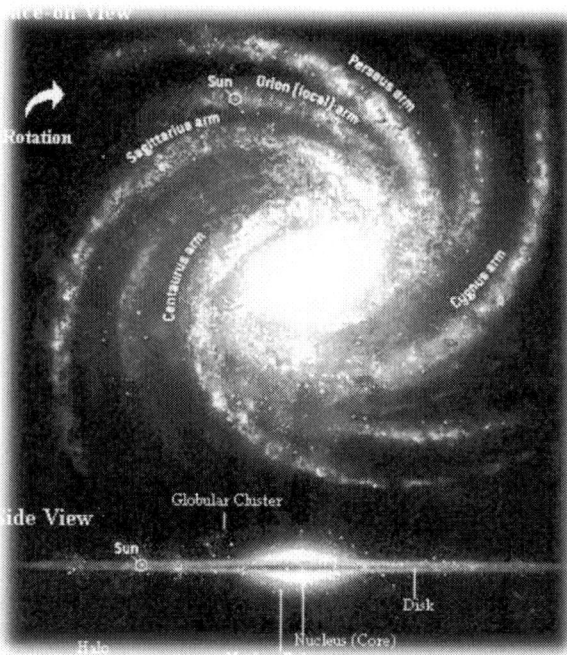

Figure 8.1. The Milky Way Galaxy.

What many people may not know is that the latest research says that the Milky Way Galaxy, of which the Sun and the solar system are parts, is nearly as old as the universe itself. By today's measure, our current cycle of the universe (yes, there have apparently been previous ones) is 13.7 billion years old, and our galaxy was formed just shortly thereafter, around 13.6 billion years ago.[147] Our Sun and solar system were created around 4.6 billion years ago. All this just to put creation in perspective, and to think about that we humans, as *homo sapiens sapiens,* have only existed for about 400,000 years, as we shall see eventually, shows we are a young species. However, we existed before that, but with another genetic set-up.

In the original solar system there was no Earth. Instead, in an orbit between Mars and Jupiter, there was a planet much bigger than Earth, orbiting the Sun. In mythology and literature, this planet goes under many names, where Maldek, Marduk, and Tiamat are only three.

---

[147] http://www.space.com/263-milky-age-narrowed.html

Figure 8.2 - Planets and dwarf planets of the Solar System. Sizes are to scale, but relative distances are not.

Zecharia Sitchin, the Russian linguist and author, who translated the Sumerian tablets and wrote *The Earth Chronicles* about the Anunnaki, an alien race who came down to Earth some 450,000 years ago and later created the current *homo sapiens sapiens* (us), which we shall discuss at length in a few papers in this book version, says that Tiamat was destroyed about 4.5 billion years ago, shortly after the solar system was created.[148] In the Ra Material, however, where Tiamat is called Maldek, it states that this planet was inhabited by intelligent beings, who even had built an Atlantis-like civilization before it was destroyed about 500,000 years ago.[149] What both Sitchin and Ra have in common is that Tiamat/Maldek was the planet between Mars and Jupiter which was destroyed. According to Sitchin it was destroyed because an outside celestial body hit it and split it in half,[150] while Ra says it was destroyed by warfare.[151] The Pleiadians tend to agree with Ra on this matter.

The fact that the Ra Collective says Maldek was inhabited contradicts Sitchin's translations. There may be a reason for this, given more credit to the Ra Material, as Sitchin's translations, albeit to some degree accurate, are based on a rewrite of history, done by the same Anunnaki the tablets are describing. That this has occurred is known, but not to what extent. It could, however, explain the discrepancies between the two sources. For our purpose, on this level of learning, it doesn't matter who is correct, as it

---

[148] Sitchin, Zechariah, *"The 12th Planet"* and *"The Cosmic Code"*, 1976 and 1998 respectively.

[149] The Ra Material/Law of One, *Sessions: 6.10-13; 9.17-21; 10.1-8; 11.3-5.*

[150] Sitchin, Zecharia, *"The 12th Planet"* and *"The Cosmic Code"*, 1976 and 1998 respectively.

[151] The Ra Material/Law of One, *Session 10.1 (Session 10, Question 1)*

would inflict minimally, if at all, on what we need to cover later.

A Violent Visit From Sirius

The star Sirius is a trinary system, which means it consists of 3 stars in orbit around each other. Our scientists call them Sirius A, B, and C. This system is located about 8.6 light-years from Earth, and Sirius A, which is its brightest components, also called the Pole Star, can be seen from Earth with the naked eye, being the brightest star in the night sky.

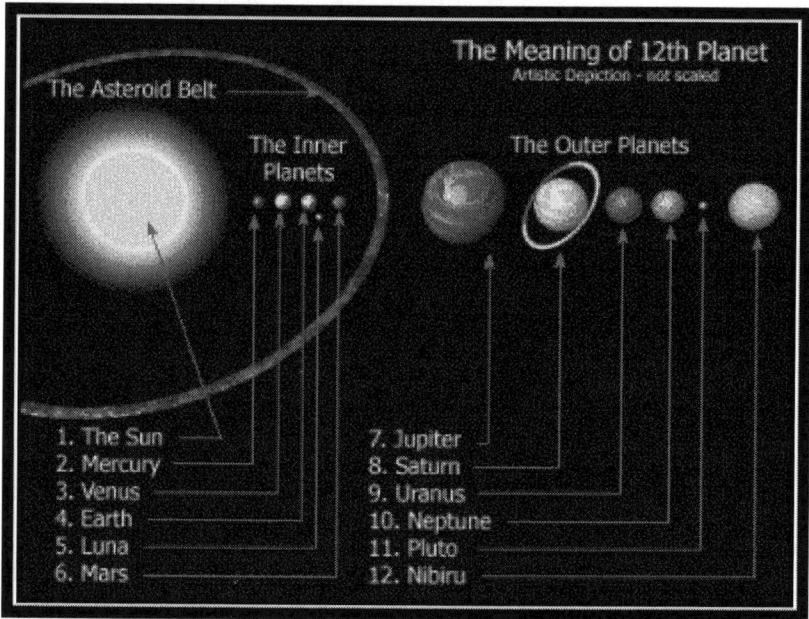

Figure 8.3 - Our solar system, including Nibiru

The Sirius system is inhabited by many different races who migrated to there from other parts of our galactic sector; some of them hybrids from having been genetically engineered or had their DNA altered by creator gods.

Sirius C was once orbited by a planet, which by its inhabitants called Ša.A.Me. (pronounced, *shaamae*), a body approximately 6 times bigger than Earth). In the Sumerian scriptures the planet is called Nibiru, or NI.BI.RU. A little less than 1 billion years ago, Sirius C became a nova, exploded and ended up as a white dwarf star. However, 3.5 billion years before that, due to the instabilities of the original star, Nibiru was thrown out of its orbit and catapulted out in deep space, unmoored from its former orbit around Sirius C.[152] The inhabitants had to leave the surface of the planet and live underground, and because Nibiru had (and still has) a lot of heat coming up from inside the planet, life can exist on it even today, and it does. It appears that these days they also have a city on the only remaining continent on the planet's surface.[153]

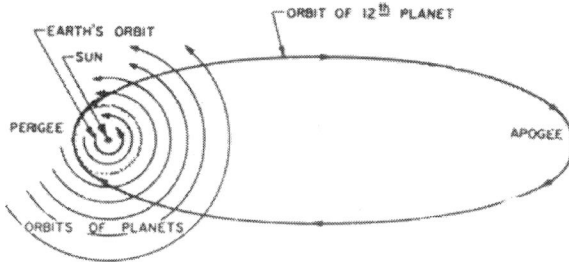

Figure 8:4 -: Nibiru's orbit.

After having traveled through space for a very long time, Nibiru was eventually drawn into our solar system by the gravity of our outer planets and came in on retrograde. On its eccentric orbit and journey through our young solar system, one of its many moons, according to Sitchin, hit Tiamat and split the planet in half. After this violent visit, Nibiru left the inner solar system and continued its journey out in deep space again. However, due to the gravity from our solar system, Nibiru was now once and for all caught up by it and from thereon became a part of it. It started revolving around our Sun in a vast, elliptic orbit which takes around 3,600 years, give or take. One orbit around our Sun is called a Šar (pronounced *shaar,* like in _she_) by its inhabitants.

---

[152] Penre/Bordon correspondence, December 2, 2010. Also, Sirius C is discussed further here: http://www.bibliotecapleyades.net/universo/esp_sirio07.htm .
[153] *Ibid.*

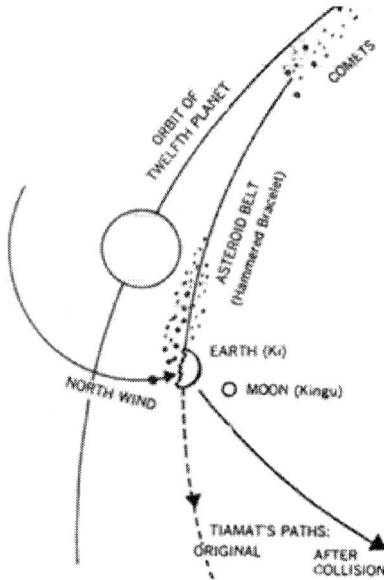

Figure 8.5: The Destruction of Tiamat

So, one Šar later, Nibiru came back, and one of the two halves of Tiamat was hit again and became what we know today as the asteroid belt. The second half, again struck by one of Nibiru's moons, was thrown out of orbit and became Earth. We can still see the impact if we look at pictures from the Pacific Ocean; it's like a piece of the planet is missing there but is now covered with water.[154]

Another thing covered by the old Sumerians is that our Moon was basically one of Nibiru's moons, which they dropped during one of its crossings, and this is probably the reason why researchers like David Icke says that the Moon is inhabited by Reptilian beings, while others say that we were interrupted in our Apollo Program because whomever claimed ownership to the Moon didn't want us there.

What happened to the rest of the solar system when Nibiru entered the first couple of times is quite extensively covered in the Sumerian Creation Epic, *Enûma Eliš*, and nicely summarized by Dr. Lessin in his *Enki Speaks* papers (http://www.bibliotecapleyades.net/sitchin/sitchinbooks_enki01.htm). I will not cover it in any more details here, as it is out of the scope of our story.

---

[154] This is the Sirians' version of what happened, using human scribes to tell the tale. A better explanation for what happened will be discussed in higher levels of learning.

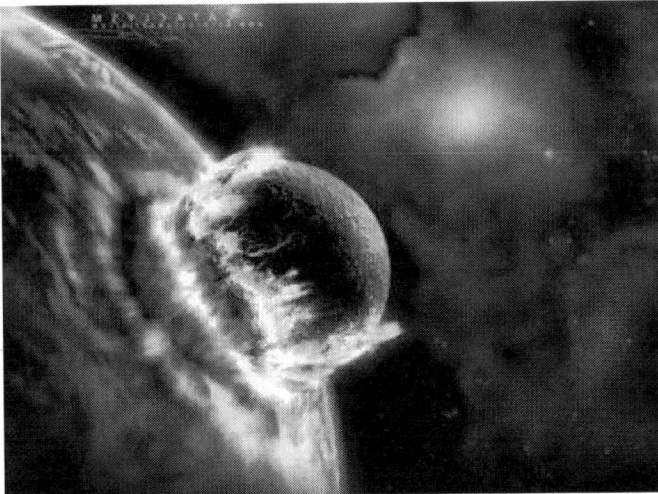

Figure 8:6 - We can imagine this as an illustration of one of Nibiru's moons crashing with Tiamat, creating the Pacific Ocean basin.

The First Creator Gods

By now, we understand that universes are created with certain goals in mind, and when the goals are achieved, they stop expanding and return to First Source, the Prime Creator. It appears that when this happens, the souls inhabiting the particular universe can choose whether they want to remerge with Source, from where we all stem, or go for another ride through a new universe, recycled from the old one, and now with a new goal in mind. Some say this universe is on its fourth cycle.[155]

As mentioned in the beginning of this chapter, our Milky Way Galaxy is very old, estimated to have been created around 13.6 billion years ago. Lyssa Royal and Keith Priest, in their *The Prism of Lyra: An Exploration of Human Galactic Heritage*, the authors suggest this whole universe was created within the time/space fabric of the Lyra constellation in form of a "white hole," which they liken to a prism. Dr. Arthur David Horn and his wife, Lynette Anne Mallory-Horn paraphrase Royal and Priest in their book, *Humanity's Extraterrestrial Origins: ET Influences on Humankind's Biological and Cultural Evolution (Silberschnur 1994, 1996, 1997)*:

As a portion of the Whole passed through this "prism", several "frequencies" were created. Consciousness fragmented away from other segmented consciousness. Apparently, the purpose of this experience is to first experience aspects of separateness, then bring back what is learned

---

[155] Penre/Bordon Correspondence, December 2010, "Alien Mind" by George LoBuono, and other additional researchers and authors.

and experienced and then re-integrate into the Whole.

In addition to consciousness, the three-dimensional (third density) universe was also created; the planets, stars, gases, and atoms that make up the physical universe. This third density reality represents only a small part of the energy frequencies that emerged from the segmentation of the Whole.[156]

Another thing they tell us, which correlates with my own findings, is their mentioning of the Founders. These correspond quite neatly with what the Lyricus Teaching Order (part of the WingMakers Material) is telling us about the Tribes of Light and the Central Race.

© 2006 Michael J. Evans and Preston Dennett

Figure 8:7 - The Praying Mantis Beings--depiction of the Founders

Royal/Priest are letting us know that the Founders were created around the same time as the universe itself to initially seed it and make sure things were developing as intended by Source. Supposedly, the Founders are always there in the beginning of a universe cycle to work directly with First Source. Royal/Priest call them "the supervisors of the creation of this galaxy," with full memory of the "blueprints" of the creation from the Whole. They "segmented" themselves to create apparent individualized consciousness, which could *go out and create*, as the Pleiadians put it in

---

[156] Dr. Arthur David Horn & Lynette Anne Mallory-Horn, 1997: *"Humanity's Extraterrestrial Origins: ET Influences on Humankind's Biological and Cultural Evolution"*, op. cit. p. 69.

Marciniak's channeled book, *Bringers of the Dawn*. Royal/Priest (as well as the Pleiadians) depict at least some of the Founders as 10-60 feet tall Praying Mantises when they are in their physical forms (not to be confused with the not-so-tall praying mantises whom abductees report have seen working together with the Grays and the Reptilians during traumatic abductions).

We have previously touched on the subject that planets, stars, and galaxies are sentient beings and also collective "oversouls" in an ascending hierarchy. I believe this to be accurate, and Royal/Priest go so far as to say that these oversouls are all Founders, and fragments thereof, whom have segmented themselves into stars and planets, and perhaps also the souls of human beings living in the 3rd Density Earth. They did so to have an as full experience as possible in this Universe. If you look up in the night sky next time and see all the myriads of stars, don't be surprised if what you see is one expression of the Founders. You can communicate directly with them by sending your energy up there, or even direct it to a certain star or star system, and they will know who you are.

The purpose with our particular galaxy was apparently set already from the start, or between the collapse of the earlier version of the universe and our current one. According to the Pleiadians in the same book as mentioned in the previous section, the purpose of the Milky Way Galaxy is for its inhabitants to have "free will", where anything goes, as a great experiment, to see what happens. It appears that each galaxy in a particular universe has its own goals to achieve, and they don't necessarily correspond with the goals of the Milky Way.

The Galactic Wars, Our Human Ancestry and Genetic Engineering

Billions of years ago, the Founders started creating bodies which would be sufficient for intelligent life in the Third Dimension for the segmented parts of themselves (souls/Information Clouds) to inhabit. This is how the first life forms were created, and among them, humanoids were made out of a predetermined template (two arms, two legs, a torso, and a head). The reason most comes in "two" is to symbolize the duality/polarity of this physical universe. These first humanoids were created and evolved in the Lyra system and spread from there throughout the galaxy. However, there were other kinds of beings, who crossed over from the previous universe cycle(s), which are not humanoid. The Dracos appear to be one of these species, and some hyperversals may be as well.[157]

The first humanoid species the Founders created started off in the

---

[157] 10 George LoBuono: "Alien Mind".

constellation of Lyra. They were very human-like, but much taller. They eventually developed into a space-faring race with the intention to explore the universe and conquer new worlds. In the meantime, the Founders created other humanoid species elsewhere, and with time, many of these came upon each other as they started visiting and conquer each other's star systems.

Wars and conflicts were certainly not unusual. It was part of experiencing the Free Will Universe where everything goes, but where karma is helping you grow. The Founders were totally fine with the fact that the early humanoids conquered space and had their wars; they understood that this was a phase they had to go through before they learned.

Another species, also from the Lyra star system was the Vegans (also called the Vulcans), originating from a previous density version of the star Vega, quite close to Earth. Not much is left of this race today in their original form, but they played a major role in seeding and building genetics and DNA on Earth. In fact, they were the pioneers.

Where the Founders left off, other creator gods took their place and started seeding planets across the Milky Way, using their own human template as a base, mixing their DNA with other species which were already there, after had been created in the first seeding by the Founders. These already existing species were often of the lower density animal and plant kingdoms. Each planet in the Milky Way which is inhabited by intelligent mammals has its own version of humanoids, slightly different in height, color, and features in general; some are giants, some are short; some are sturdy while others are thin etc. Still, intelligent 3-D life forms are all based on the human template.

However, here is some modification to that fact. Due to that some beings (like the Dracos) transferred over from a previous cycle, they too have seeded our galaxy; hence there are other life forms as well. Reptilian beings, to a certain extent, surprisingly enough, seem to have originated on Earth, though, when the Vegans mixed their own DNA with that of the dinosaurs. The Vegans continued their genetic experiments by working directly with the dinosaurs to create an intelligent race consisting of mainly reptilian beings. They succeeded, although they were technically still mammals, appearing reptilian-like

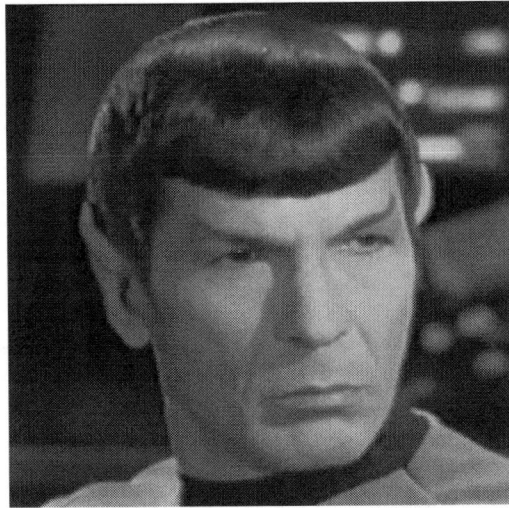

Fig. 8.8: We are all familiar with this Vulcan from the Star Trek series, Mr. Spock, but this could very well be similar to how a Vegan looked like, but had allegedly darker skin.

Much of this genetic tinkering was not done on Earth, however. The Vegans often landed here in what they must have considered quite a hostile environment with all those giant dinosaurs roaming around. Instead, they colonized Mars and Maldek, where they did much of the genetic engineering. Mars at that point had atmosphere, with forest, oceans, lakes, rivers etc., just like Earth, and the Vegan were oxygen breathers.

Figure 8.9: Reptoid

Vegan/Reptilian hybrids, and the Reptilians (I believe some of the reptilians and other species whom we have encountered, and are not fitting in with the Milky Way template, came here from other galaxies. This is also what LPG-C# indicate, and there are others as well).

Most Reptilians that were created by the Vegans took off to other parts of the galaxy, more precisely Orion and Lyra. They didn't stay long in the Earth vicinity, but I believe there were a few who did. They became what we now call the Reptoids, who live inside Earth and are sometimes spotted by people close to caverns and mountains. This species is, as told by those who have encountered them, quite friendly in nature, but consider Earth being theirs, due to that they were here before humans.

The Vegans were a dark-skinned race, with dark, often brownish hair, very tall in stature. They were quite telepathic, had great physical strength, but were generally quite friendly and spiritual, although they went through different phases like all other species, and they were of course all different individuals with different personalities. We can compare them, if only vaguely, with today's Native American, Asian and Aboriginal people. Royal and Priest compare them to the Vulcans as well in the *Star Trek Series (see fig. 8)*. Their main purpose was to explore how to use DNA to create different species, and they were very careful not to act as violent or abusive. When they first landed on Earth during the dinosaur era, they claimed Earth as their real estate, as the customs often are in the Free Will Universe.

Evidence of Giants on Earth

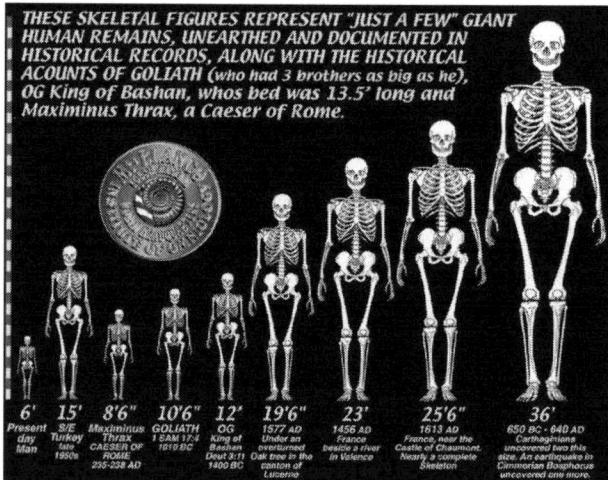

Figure 8.10: Different types of humanoid Giants as a part of Earth history. Homo sapiens sapiens, with her modest 6 feet in height is depicted way to the left (click on image to enlarge).

Some of the creator gods were indeed giants, up to 35-36 feet high

http://www.stevequayle.com/Giants/index2.html
http://overmanwarrior.wordpress.com/2010/12/20/giants-in-ohio-the-hidden-history-of-the-human-race/, and when they used their DNA in experiments, their offspring became giants as well (**Marciniak channeling the Pleiadians;** *lectures, Fall 2010, CD #8, tracks 4 & 6).* Skeletons of giants have been found all over the world by archeologists, but mostly, these discoveries have been laughed off as hoaxes. Some of them are, of course, because as soon as the truth is published, someone who is paid for it comes out and discredits it, but many of these findings, discarded as hoaxes are not, are quite interesting, because they show how some of these beings looked like. The researcher, Steve Quayle, has spent a lot of time finding pictures of giant skeletons and posted them on his website http://www.stevequayle.com/. Some of these giants had six fingers and six toes and a double set of teeth. This 9 foot giant was found in a grave in Utah. Still, this guy is considered a dwarf in comparison to the ones of *real* stature. Look at the skull, in particular:

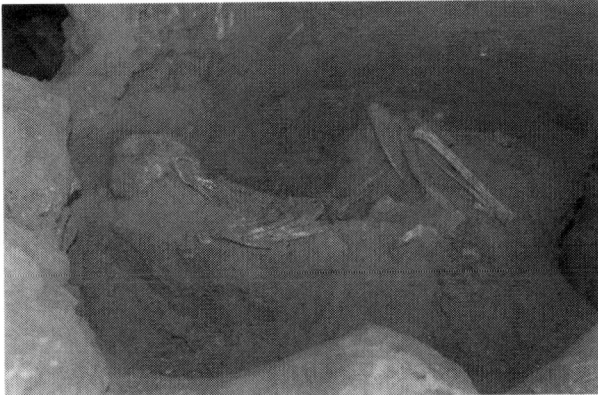

Figure 8.10a: 9 foot giant found in Utah grave.

Here is another interesting picture:

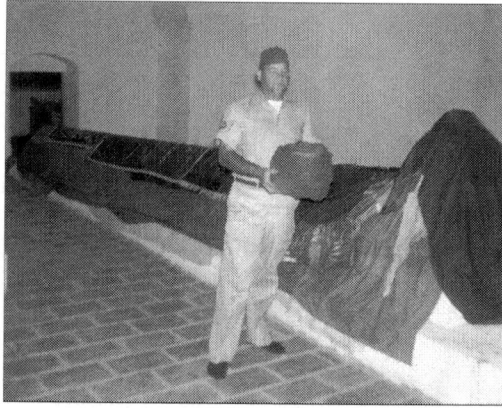

Figure 8.10b: This giant was 10 feet tall and his tomb was 28 feet long. Half of the tomb was filled with his armor and spear. The Technical Sergeant is holding his turban which has a brass liner inside.

The Vegan/Lyran War

The spiritual traits of the Vegans became subject to jealousy from another humanoid race, the Lyrans. They looked very Caucasian and can up to this day only be separated from a typical white Caucasian person by their stature, and some of them have pointed ears, like Tolkien's Elves. They were not as physically strong as the Vegans but had more aggressive genes.

Figure 8.11a (left): Lyran. Figure 8.11b (right): Nordic/Pleiadian

They came to Earth with a purpose to conquer. A war broke out between the Vegans and the Lyrans, which the Lyrans won. The Vegans had to leave Earth, Mars and Maldek to the Lyrans and give up their real estate. So, they went to Sirius and Orion, where they colonized quite a few planetary systems, before they settled down and went back to a more spiritual path. According to Royal/Priest in "The Prism of Lyra", much of the Vegan mysticism is the origin of many spiritual teachings on Earth, like those of the Tibetan culture before Buddhism, and the Vedic culture in India, prior to Hinduism. Very few ancient texts exist on Earth from this highly influential time period.

Here we need to back up a little bit and introduce another species on stage; the infamous Drakons. They were of pure reptilian blood but related neither to the Lyrans, nor the Vegans. No one knows exactly where they came from; some say they originate from another universe, while others say they came from this one, but entered here from one of the many stargates or Einstein-Rosen Bridges. They had scales, horns, a tail, but otherwise one head, two arms, two legs and a torso. Their necks were shielded just like on a Triceratops but had no horn growing from their foreheads.

According to A'shayana Deane in her book *"Voyagers I"*, the Drakons came to Earth during the Dinosaur Era, just like the Vegans, but not necessarily during the same time period (the Dinosaur Era lasted for almost 200 million years). Deane explains that the early dinosaurs were all vegetarians and quite docile in temperament until the Drakons started genetically tamper with them. This indicates that they were here before the Vegans, who came at the end of the Dinosaur Era, when there were both meat eaters and vegetarians amongst the big reptiles.

Figure 8.12: Landscape during the Jurassic Era as depicted by an artist.

After having tampered with the dinosaurs, they created

Drakon/dinosaur hybrids with the intelligence of the Drakon species, and ended up with the prototype for the Draconian Reptiles, not of Vegan stock. Some of these hybrids were left on Earth, fitting well into the climate and conditions of Earth at the time, when it was much warmer. Through these Draco hybrids, the Drakons could monitor the human evolution on Earth while the Vegans created our first Vegan/human ancestors.

About one million years ago, the Drakons thought the human species on Earth had developed enough for them to be used in their own genetic engineering projects. The Drakon ships arrived and started hovering over Earth. They landed and abducted human females and impregnated them with Drakon seed during frequent visitations; some of these impregnations were quite painful for the human females.

However, the Drakon/human interbreeding and genetic tinkering didn't work as planned, because the offspring could not live very long in the Earth's atmospheric conditions, and these hybrids were therefore taken back to Thuban, which was their home planet in the Alpha Draconis star system. The Drakon/human hybrids became what we today call the Dracos. The Drakons also later on interbred with the Lyran/Sirian/Pleiadian Anunnaki, and this is why the Anunnaki during Sumerian times were depicted both as reptilians and humanoid. However, this is an extremely complicated matter, and will be discussed in the *"Second Level of Learning"* and is not necessary to learn at this point.

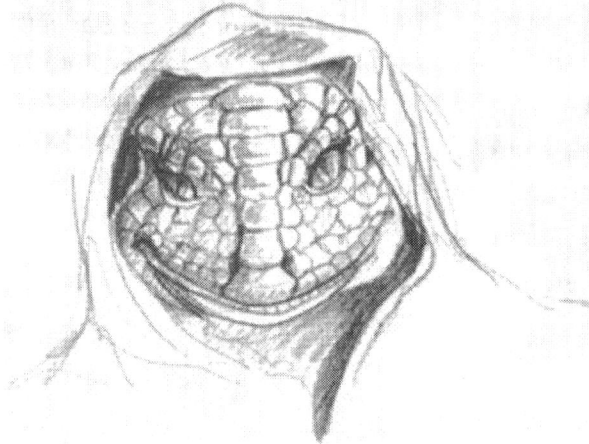

Figure 8.14: Drawing of a Hooded Draco. This drawing is originally from David Icke's book, "The Biggest Secret".

The Drakonian and Orion Wars

The Drakons and their hybrids have been involved in most of the galactic wars worth their names. The Drakons were a ruthless warrior race and had one group imperative in mind over all the rest, summarized in three words--explore, conquer and expand. The most intense wars raged in the Orion sector, in and around the Ring Nebula.

To make a long and complicated story short, factions of the Vegans and Lyrans, when they encountered the Drakons and their hybrid warriors, came together in an alliance to defeat this very strong enemy. Both empires, the Lyran/Vegan and the Drakons, the latter who had joined forces with other reptilian groups, had common interests in certain worlds that they wanted to conquer, and this started a full drawn-out war. The battles originated in the Orion Ring Nebula, but almost simultaneously, from another flank, the Dracos did a full force attack upon the home planets of the Lyrans, destroyed many of them, and killed millions of Lyrans in the process. Fortunately, for them, most of the Lyrans had already migrated to other worlds. The migrated Lyrans were devastated at first, but then broke out in rage and wanted revenge.

After the destruction of the Lyran planets, the war was concentrated on Orion. At that time, the Orion star systems were mainly inhabited by Lyrans, Vegans and Retilians,[158] the Grays came into the picture later.

When the Lyrans heard about the destruction of their home planets, they retaliated by furiously attacking Drakon/Reptilian colonies in Orion and created much devastation there. However, the Draconian Reptilians were fast to respond.

Also, around that time, some humanoids (mainly Vegans) had started co-operating with the Drakon alliance, simply because they had common interests in what they wanted to colonize and which part of space they wanted to explore. The Drakon group had as a purpose to colonize and conquer the whole Sector 9 of the Milky Way Galaxy, which is the sector which Earth belongs to[159] and they were well on their way.

The alliance between the Reptilians and the humanoids is still known as

[158]Manuel Lamiroy, *"A Summary of Galactic History Part 1"* ©2009; http://news.exopoliticssouthafrica.org/index.php/exo-articles/47-a-summary-of-galactic-history-part-1

[159]Both Robert Morning Sky in his research, which led to *"The Terra Papers I & II"* (http://www.jordanmaxwell.com/documents/the-2520terra-2520papers-2520%5Birm08%5D.pdf) and L. Ron Hubbard, the founder of the Church of Scientology before him, named Sector 9 as being our sector of the Milky Way for alien perspective.

the *Orion Empire* and is much more recent than the Draconian Empire; after the time when Vegans had started engaging themselves in space travel. It is my understanding that the Dracos and other reptilian races from Orion are still the majority of the Reptilians in that part of Sector 9, but there are no longer any open wars, although tension exists between the races. They even trade these days, but small battles still occur.

Long before the Lyrans got involved in the war against the Dracos, the latter had conquered a lot of worlds where the original inhabitants had to obey to the Draconian Emperor. There was a lot of discontent amongst these populations, and many of them now saw their chance and hooked up with the Lyrans, against their oppressors. This new alliance resulted in a *Federation of Planets*, and they all stood united against the Draconian Empire. This Federation still exists and is one of the main players in Sector 9. The members are civilizations from the Lyra Constellation, the Andromeda Constellation, the Pleiades, the Hyades open clusters, Iumma Wolf 424, Procyon, Tau Ceti, Alpha Centauri, and epsilon Eridani; all being of Lyran/Pleiadian heritage (more about the Pleiadian heritage soon).

Figure 8.15: Artist's vision of a planet orbiting the star Procyon.

In addition, there were a number of non-physical massless hyperversal races joining, but also some Sirian groups and some Orion groups as well. Others were of various civilizations from parallel universes such as the Koldasians, and the Dal. Eventually, they even got some company from renegade Reptilians, who wanted to free themselves from the tyranny of the Dracos.

As time went by, the nature of the wars changed. They started out with a purpose to expand territory and explore new worlds, but after many years it became more about ideologies. There were quite a few humanoid forces that had joined the Federation of Planets because they were tired of being "victimized" by the Dracos. Gradually, they started living under the Law of One, understanding that it is important to support both oneself and others around you to be able to expand, not only physically by conquering other worlds, but also to expand spiritually.

Up until then, all sides, with a few exceptions, had the philosophy that Service to Self (STS) was okay, because they were aware of that we are all One, and if they were STS, they helped others by helping themselves. That would work, as long as STS included others, but the wars showed that the philosophy had been warped on the way. STS now meant Service to Self *at the expense* of others, and that was something entirely different. This was the cause to victimization and victim hood. With karma also being included in the mix, things got pretty serious. Those who felt they were victims started looking at those who had conquered them as evil and themselves as good. Thus, polarization now became a very unbalanced factor in these wars. This, of course, for somebody who doesn't believe war is the answer to anything, is self-explanatory, as war is always STS to the extreme. However, in the philosophy of many ancient races, this was looked upon differently. These warrior species still had to learn how karma works in a Free Will Universe, which at the time was quite young.

Now, in summary, on one side we had the Federation of Planets, whose members more and more started thinking in terms of Service to Others (STO), understanding that supporting and helping both self and others is important, as both are parts of the same Whole. On the other side we had the Draconian Empire, which now merged with the Orion Empire because they felt they had common interests, which led to joined forces. This Empire, which exists up to this day as the Orion/Draconian Empire (side by side with the Federation of Planets), stayed overly STS with the serve self at the expense of others attitude.

And the wars dragged on and on for eons to come.

The Pleiadians--Immigrants from a Previous Universe

One of the most popular channeled entities on Earth today is the Pleiadians, channeled by Barbara Marciniak. This renegade group of different beings from different star systems has come from our future to meet us here during the nano-second (1987-2012) and beyond. They are telling us that they are here to change their present (our future) by changing the events on their timeline. In other words, by changing their present, they are here to change their past, so that they can heal along the lines of time and take care of what they call "their karma."

They say they live in a very tyrannical and oppressive time in the future

Pleiades, with heavy-duty machine technology and with a tight control system on top of that. A few renegade Pleiadians in our future, a resistance group of sorts, figured out that the reason they are in this nightmare environment is because of decisions that we humans made during the nano-second—all in accordance with their own direct timeline. They could see that this was their collective karma that they now have to face and handle. The way to do this, they figure, is to contact us in the nano-second and inform us about the choices we have, and that we don't need to eventually live in the future they are now experiencing if we make more conscious choices than we did on their timeline, which goes back to old Atlantis and beyond.

If we look around us today, we are quickly heading towards a Machine Kingdom, with tons of electronic devices that totally absorb our children's lives (and adults' too for that matter), and everything is becoming computerized. Cloning, artificial intelligence and nanotechnology are getting huge funding by the Powers That Be and we are totally caught up in a life of stress, multi-tasking, financial meltdowns, heart attacks and other illnesses. The medical field is getting sponsored to develop techniques to implant new organs safely in bodies that are failing, and technologies are getting developed (this is mostly alien technology) to insert machine parts instead of real organs, which work as well as the real ones. In the near future, we will be half human and half machine, and implants, digital and biological, will also be inserted in humans for us to be able to buy and sell, and these implants will help the Powers That Be (PTB) to control our thoughts and behavior.

This is exactly the path the Pleiadians chose in the past, which led up to the reality they now must live in. So, a few of these renegades left their body in our future and met in a safe place from where they contacted Barbara Marciniak, mind-to-mind, in 1988, and she agreed to be their vehicle for channeling.

This future Pleiadian group wants to alert us on that we have a chance in 26,000 years (more about this later) to tune into the galactic boost of energy that is occurring now in our nano-second. If enough humans on this planet manage to activate our dormant DNA by receiving encoded information carried on gamma rays from the Sun and the Galactic Center we will be able to transform to a new Earth and thus bypass the Machine Kingdom that is planned by the PTB. The majority of the population will not be able to consciously tune into this energy and thus will not raise their vibration enough to transform into a higher frequency, but as long as at least a certain number of people will be able to raise their frequency, a new world, based on these new common morals and ethics codes, will be transformed from our new mass consciousness. Our planet will metaphysically split into two Earths.[160]

This is what the Pleiadians hope we will achieve, because if we do, that will change their timeline; they can tune into this new one (hopefully, they say) and that will change their present. The worst thing that can happen is that they and their reality will be erased if we succeed, but if that happens, they accept it; they will still live on as metaphysical beings, and it's better to be "free spirits" than trapped in machine technology that has gone overboard. However, they are quick to add that there is nothing wrong with technology in itself; it's how it's being used.

So, this is their agenda, and they are totally open about it. There is much more to this, which I will go into later, but this is the short version. If we succeed (and they say we probably will), in one way or the other, it will gain both them and us, so it's a win-win situation.

As the channeling through Marciniak continued with success, more and more renegades, not only from the Pleiadian star systems but from elsewhere joined in, and the group rapidly grew in numbers during the 1990s up to this date. It is today a mix of the original small group (probably humanoid) and Reptilian renegades, perhaps from Orion. When I listen to their CDs, I believe I can distinguish between the channelers as of whom is Reptilian and who is humanoid by their voices, energies, and temperaments.

So let us see how these Pleiadians fit into our past ancestry because they say they are us in the future.

In Marciniak's excellent book, *Bringers of the Dawn"*, a channeled book, the Pleiadians say they came to this universe from a previous universe, which had completed its cycle.[161] The completion of their old universe was fulfilled once the life force within it, in unison, realized that they were all ONE with Source and they were all creator gods. They had the choice to go back and merge with Source or continue exploring reality in a new universe. They chose the latter.

In the book, they continue by telling us that not only do they come from our future; they are us in the future. But they are also our ancestors, who were some of the "Original Planners" of Earth, meaning the original creator gods who seeded humans on Earth.

Over the years, the Pleiadians have mainly depicted themselves the way they looked like in their ancient past, being tall, Caucasian looking. They have also given hints toward "blue beings" and the Nordics. In other words, they looked pretty much like Caucasian Scandinavians of today, but taller in stature. This compares very well with the Lyrans. Especially, as we

---

[160] When the Pleiadians discussed this matter, no humans knew about that we can leave the Matrix altogether through holes in the Earth Grid. More about this in the upcoming books in this series.

[161] Marciniak 1992, *"Bringers of the Dawn"*, pp.3

shall see when our story unfolds, there apparently was a "Scandinavian" faction of the Lyrans, according to Royal/Priest, who later migrated to the Pleiades. The original Pleiadian group we hear from today are mostly from Electra and Maia *(see fig. 8.16)*. The puzzle pieces fit.

So, the Pleiadians are maybe a faction of the original Lyrans, who were the prototype that the Founders used to populate this sector of the Universe. As time went by, the Vegans first, the Lyrans later, came to Earth and started building what was to become the *Living Library*; a planet which could hold the DNA and the knowledge of the entire galaxy, not only in pure thought form but also as manifestation in 4-space/time. Therefore, mankind is an experiment, and as such, closely monitored by many different off-planetary beings.

The intention was good, and the project started, as we shall see, but was interrupted by forces who seemed to have other intentions which were not so noble, and the project came to a halt. But more about this later.

The Vegan Entrapment

Going back to when the Vegans had been defeated by the Lyrans, the Vegans migrated to Orion, became more and more associated with this star group, and they began to call themselves the Orions, forgetting their Vegan heritage. They, in conjunction with the Reptilian Orion Queens, became the "notorious and feared Orions." The Vegans even created a frequency net that trapped everybody who lived in Orion and were of Vegan humanoid descent in a frequency prison. Even after death they were trapped in the Orion Matrix and had no choice but to reincarnate into the Orion system. This was the ultimate control system, and those in charge gained a lot of power, because they knew that they had the Orion souls trapped.[162] Beings from outside, who were ignorant about what the frequency net did, with a little smarts, could enter the Orion system from outside, but once inside, they couldn't get out. So, it was a closed system. Thus, the Reptilians and other races who were aware of this frequency fence had a tendency to avoid the star systems controlled by the Vegan Orions; even the Drakons did.

As always when there is big oppression within a civilization, there is resistance, and so also here. They were called the *Black League* (black as in

---

[162] Where have we heard this before? It is eerily close to home. If you haven't done so already, read my paper, Penre 2011: "*Paper #4 : There is a Light at the End of the Tunnel--What Happens After Body Death?*" One may wonder if this is what is happening here on Earth as well. The information about the Orion Frequency Net comes from Royal/Priest 2011: *The Prism of Lyra*. I would go so far as to say the frequency net is the Grid around Earth. The Germane group simply confuses the Orion frequency net with that around Earth. More on this later.

"hidden"), and it took them many lifetimes of resistance, living in caves underground, often on hot desert planets, away from civilization, to get this oppression resolved. However, like so many before them, they thought they could meet violence with violence, so they started civil wars against their huge government. This, of course, was a war they could not win, and eventually the resistance had to flee, fragmented and defeated. The few who survived had to go into hiding, and it took long before the Black League could get reorganized again.[163]

According to Royal/Priest, there were some priests who figured out how to raise their vibrations and escape the frequency field. When they had trained themselves spiritually to do this, they looked for somewhere to escape, and the escape was Earth; the planet that once had been so dear to the Vegans.

The priests managed to escape and appeared here on Earth, mainly during the Lemurian and Atlantis Eras, two very important periods in the history of Earth (which we will not discuss in any deeper details until the *Second Level of Learning"*, because the subject of the Atlantis/Lemurian cultures is rather complex if we want to cover it to any extent, and I need to organize my research material and make some complementary research as well on this before I can post anything substantial.

In the meantime, while the Orion Vegans fought their own internal battle, galactic wars of great proportion continued to rage in Sector 9.

The Continuing Story of the Living Library and Major Genetic Engineering and Tinkering on Earth

In Darwinism, we are taught that life develops in a sequence, in a long evolutionary line: One thing leads to another, and the strongest species and their members survive, and the rest go extinct, to put it simply, but there are lots of holes in Darwin's theories which we don't have time to go into here. However, for those who are interested, please read the first two chapters of Dr. Arthur David Horn & Lynette Anne Mallory-Horn, 1997: *Humanity's Extraterrestrial Origins: ET Influences on Humankind's Biological and Cultural Evolution*, and it will be quite clear. Dr. Horn was himself a Darwinist and anthropologist before he realized that Darwin's theories simply don't hold water, and instead, he began to research the ET involvement in the evolution of Planet Earth, as this was the only thing that made sense, he concluded. I am totally in agreement with Dr. Horn in this respect, and evidence that is available regarding the weaknesses in Darwinism. We are going to stick with the much more plausible history of Planet Earth, which highly involves beings from outside Earth.

---

[163] I would again suggest that this is Earth history (Matrix history, and not Orion.

Horn and Mallory-Horn bring up another interesting point in their book. They say that what they call "the Cambrian explosion", where marine life with a hard skeletal part suddenly appeared 570 million years ago, would seem to be a good example of genetic manipulation by some ET Inception Group or groups. They continue:

> ...not only did animals with hard body parts appear suddenly at the beginning of the Cambrian period, but also all of the basic body planes, or phyla, of all the types of animals that have existed on Earth appeared simultaneously at this time. Based on the fossil record, the Mesopotamian historical records of ET genetic manipulation of an Earth life form (humans), the Dogon oral history of ET visitation, plus the esoteric information provided in *The Prism of Lyra*, the ET (Lyran) Inception Group must have laid the foundation of the development and evolution of all animal life on Earth during the "Cambrian explosion", and 100 million years before that. This scenario would explain why no new phyla, or basic body plans, have appeared since the Cambrian period. **Dr. Arthur David Horn & Lynette Anne Mallory-Horn, 1997:** *Humanity's Extraterrestrial Origins: ET Influences on Humankind's Biological and Cultural Evolution, pp. 72.*

This is true, and directly contradicts Darwin's theory on the Evolution of the Species.

It looks as if the early creator gods were busy here during the Mesozoic Era, which was the era of the dinosaurs (254 - 66.4 million years ago). During this period, small mammals were also seeded. According to the Pleiadians, the dinosaurs were acting as guardians of the planet, so the Experiment with the Living Library could continue with as little interruption as possible at times when the creator gods were not here. They also mention that there was a time (I would assume by the end of the dinosaur era), when human-like creatures walked the Earth together with the dinosaurs. This corresponds with the Vegan/Lyran visitations as discussed above.

Then, a big mystery hit the Earth: The dinosaurs became extinct! This has puzzled the scientists since the time they found the first skeletons. What killed them? Was it a drastic climate change? Did a huge comet hit Earth? Why did the reptiles die out, with mammals living on and starting to flourish after that?

According to a Pleiadian lecture I listened to, the big reptiles were intentionally gotten rid of because they were no longer needed, and they also were too dangerous to have around if the gods wanted to continue the seeding of Earth. Exactly how they were extinct is still something I can't answer with certainty, but it sounds like the gods "took care of it."[164]

---

[164] Here, a paragraph has been excluded, but can be found in the original papers at wespenre.com. It is a theory about Nibiru I now consider erroneous.

Let us now go back to when the Lyrans took over from the Vegans and started spreading out on the planets in our solar system. It was still at the end of the Dinosaur Era, so we're talking 65-70 million years ago.

The Lyrans now started their genetic manipulation program big time, something which eventually ended with the extinction of the dinosaurs, and the creation of primates on Earth. They thought that these beings could eventually be most compatible with their own consciousness. These settlers of Lyran humanoids, once being a dreaded warrior race, now became creator gods in their own right, changing their mindsets quite a bit, after having a leap in their consciousness and awareness. Over time, both they and the Vegans (Lyrans faster than the Vegans) tended to forget their origins the more time they spent in this physical universe of freewill, and therefore, they also forgot who they were before they came into this universe from a previous one, and what their real goal was. Later, some of these memories came back to them, and they realized that the goal of this universe is to experience how it is to live in a reality where everything goes, and then take this experience back to Source, after which they again can decide whether they want to stay with Source or continue for yet another cycle.

By realizing this, everything changed. They no longer felt the urge to violently conquer space or invade other species and claim their real estate (planetary body). Rather, they now wanted to concentrate on building this Living Library with their own DNA mixed with a genetically manipulated version of themselves, containing all the memories of this universe from beginning to end, all encoded into the DNA of this new species. The memory could be easily encoded by using their own multidimensional 12 strand DNA as a base.

The idea was then to have species from elsewhere in the universe donate their DNA to the experiment to have a wider range of experiences connected to the human body. They were well aware of that DNA is not just a physical thing, but if you add DNA from another species to your own, you have an instant connection with the donator from thereon, no matter where in the universe the original donor roams.

This way, you would have a biological being whose body works as a Living Library in itself. By having its DNA fully activated, this species would have its "nerve endings" expand all over the cosmos. People could come visit Earth from all around and learn from this human species, similar to when you go to a physical library here on Earth. Moreover, the Lyrans also wanted to import plants and animals from across the universe, and have their DNA set up in a certain way as well, as to enhance the Living Library, so that it spans through all dimensions and densities. They also started similar experiments on a few other planets in the galaxy, but Earth is still quite rare and unique, and its beauty, as we all know, is stunning. Few places in the universe have such diversity. If you step back and look at it with new eyes, it may dawn to you how different all the animals and the plants are from each other. There is an almost endless variety of flora and fauna. Did this all happen by chance? No, almost all of it has been imported from all over the cosmos. Many worlds out there have a sparse variety of animal and plant life. There is just enough to have the ecological system going. In addition, most aliens don't eat meat (it's very gross to them), and neither do the animals. It's mostly on strictly 3rd Density worlds, and especially those which are operating within a very narrow frequency, that lifeforms eat each other. Therefore, a wide variety is not necessarily needed. Also, in more worlds than we can imagine, the lifeforms live *inside* the planet—not on the surface.

So, why all this variety here on Earth? Well, although beauty has to do with it, it's just part of the reason. The plants, herbs and vegetables are our natural pharmacy. In the Middle Ages (and certainly in ancient times) people knew how to use the Living Library to detox, cure dis-eases, and expand their reality (marijuana hemp and hashish are just two examples of this) and they are all there to be used—in moderation, I should add. Over time, this knowledge has been suppressed by the PTB to keep the population in line and the sheep in the folds, as it were. Even more so the last 100 years or so, when Big Pharma started making money on people's illnesses. They couldn't allow any competition from the Living Library, so they either outlawed certain plants, like marijuana, or simply suppressed ancient knowledge by ridiculing it.

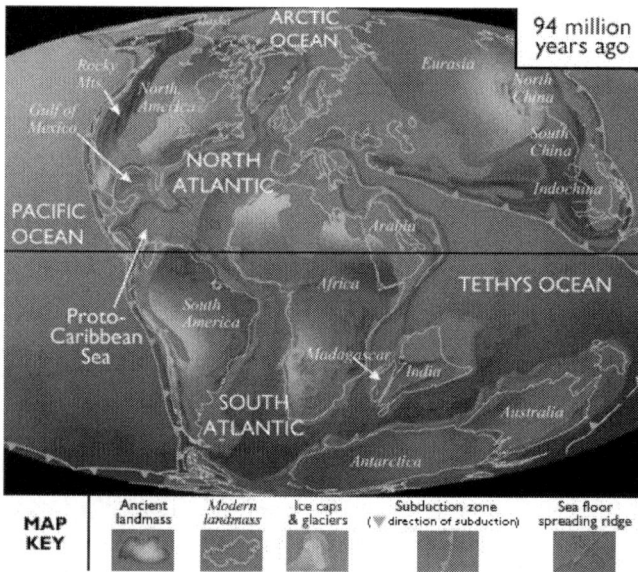

Figure 8.16: Official estimates landmasses 94 million years ago

The Pleiadians, on the CD sets, released shortly after each equinox, have said that there is much more to the Living Library than they can go into right now for security reasons. We, humans, have security codes embedded in our DNA, which were put there by the original creator gods, in case someone would come and tamper with us in the future. This way, the intruders could not access the deepest secrets of the Living Library. As the Pleiadians put it on a recent CD 2010, we humans are the "library cards," and the intention was for other beings to come visiting from other parts of the universe to study the Living Library; but they first had to come through us humans to "sign up." The Living Library is like a "School of Learning", which has different layers to it. One can only access the layers which vibrate on one's frequency and match one's consciousness and awareness level. If someone is looking for something that isn't within their frequency, they won't be given access to it for several reasons. Two main reasons being they wouldn't understand and appreciate it, or they may misuse or abuse it. As we can see, the Lyrans put a lot of thought, work, and effort into this huge project.

In our terms, to set up the experiment took many millions of years, but the early creator gods (both Lyrans and Vegans) had very long life spans. From our point of view, they seemed to live forever, and they didn't age, noticeably, and like the science-fiction writer David Brin said: *Galactic beings think 'long thoughts'.* Plans that span thousands of years were not uncommon, and not a problem for our ancestors.

In the beginning, the Lyrans primarily lived on Mars and Maldek in the constructs that the Vegans had built before them, but they didn't like the climate and the atmosphere there as well as the Vegans did, so they decided to move down to Earth and do whatever they could to make it comfortable for themselves, as the Earth atmosphere was at least a little less uncomfortable for them than that of the two other planets.

One group moved up to the area that is now Scandinavia, although the landmasses of today do not correspond entirely with those of ancient times. The Lyrans were the ones who felt the strongest connection with Earth and began to feel a great affinity for the planet they had settled on. They became very connected with nature and all the elements and developed a spiritual mindset. At first, by the time they settled down, they still contributed their DNA to the mix, but soon enough they became less interested in participating. Instead, they focused on making Earth their new home.

The main genetic experimentation they were involved in was taking some Earth genetics and incorporate them in themselves. They still had some problems with adapting to the Earth atmosphere in regard to oxygen content, and magnetic fields etc. It became hard for them to operate with their full potential, so they took a small amount of primate DNA and incorporated it into their successive generations. This way, they were eventually able to fully adapt to life on Earth.[165]

As time went by, their mentality changed. They felt like they had become more at home here on Earth than on their home planet in the Lyra star system, and they started calling themselves Earth-Lyrans, putting "Earth" in front of "Lyra."

We are making big jumps in time here on occasion, because all of this happened over a long period, in our terms. While the Earth-Lyrans adapted to their new home on Earth, the galactic wars were still raging over their heads, and they found themselves no longer being the only species on Earth. Other ETs, some Lyrans and some Sirians and Orions, were here as well at the same time as the Earth-Lyrans. One of these alien races were the ones who inhabited Nibiru, the 10th planet (12th Planet in Sitchin's translations) which used to orbit Sirius C, but now was a member of our own solar system—a hollowed out spaceship, one could say.[166] Although Nibiru once orbited this particular star in the Sirius system, the Nibiruans, or the Ša.A.M.i. as they called themselves in their own language, some say were part Lyrans (humanoid), and part Reptilian (Draco hybrids).[167] However, there were other groups and subgroups here too at the same time, working in different parts of the world. The Ša.A.M.i. started out in Sumer (modern Iraq) and the southern parts of Africa, where they also dug for gold and precious metals; some of it supposedly to enhance their declining Nibiruan atmosphere, but also for other reasons we may go into later. They became interested in creating a slave race for themselves rather than to help creating the Living Library, and they eventually got in great conflict with the original Lyrans, who were busy building the Library.

---

[165] Royal/Priest, *"The Prism of Lyra"*, p.101.

[166] It should be noted that the name Nibiru is deceptive because humanity's original home planet was called Tiamat or NI.BI.RU., and has nothing to do with the Sirian "spaceship."

[167] See the work of A'shayana Deane, and especially her two books, *Voyager I* and *Voyager II,* for more information regarding this Sirian race, in her work generally called the *Anunnaki.*

Figure 8.17: Imaginary space battle between the Ša.A.M.i. and the Lyrans

The Lyrans were very successful in building the Library, and many different energies were brought into existence. Among others, very evolved civilizations emerged from their efforts. The dominant Lyran-human hybrid they had created was androgynous and multidimensional, and also had the Lyran 12 strand DNA activated.[168] This civilization existed for a very long time, from our perspective, and was on its peak around 500,000 years ago. We are not talking about Atlantis or Lemuria, which are more "modern" than this civilization. If we want to go look for remnants of them today, we have to look under the ice caps of the far southern continent of Antarctica and some can also be found in modern North Russia.[169]

Suddenly, a war broke out in space between the Ša.A.M.i. (later in the Sumerian scriptures called the Anunnaki) and the Lyrans.[170] The Anunnaki creator gods raided the Earth around 300,000 years ago,[171] while the human civilization in Antarctica and Russia were still in their fullest. This period is considered the beginning of human civilization, but in fact, it was only the beginning of something new and the death of something older and much more benevolent and evolved.

---

[168] Marciniak: *Bringers of the Dawn, pp.14*.

[169] *ibid*. The information on the Russian remnants were given during a 2010 lecture by the Pleiadians.

[170] I would suggest that those who Lyssa Royal and Barbara Marciniak call the Lyrans are a composite or Orion "helpers," who built our first human construct, usually named Tiamat or Maldek. See my later works, released long after the Wes Penre Papers were published.

[171] At the time of the release of this book, I am more careful about time measurements: It is commonly known that channeled entities have difficulties conveying correct time frames. They sometimes seem to get it right, and sometimes not.

Eventually, after long and bitter battles over Real Estate Earth, the Original Planners lost the war. Darkness had defeated Light and Earth became the territory of the Anunnaki, who were mostly Sirians. Some of these battles extended to Earth herself, developing into atomic wars.

The Lyrans, defeated, were forced to leave the solar system.

What happened next is explained by the Pleiadians as follows:

> They The Anunnaki, the new owners rearranged your DNA in order to have you broadcast within a certain limited frequency band whose frequency could feed them and keep them in power.
>
> The original human was a magnificent being whose twelve strands of DNA were contributed by a variety of sentient civilizations. When the new owners came in, they worked in their laboratories and created versions of humans with a different DNA--the two-stranded, double-helix DNA. They took the original DNA of the human species and disassembled it. The original DNA pattern was left within the human cells, yet it was not functional; it was split apart, unplugged.
>
> ...
>
> Anything that was unnecessary for survival and that would keep you informed was unplugged, leaving you with only a double helix that would lock you into controllable, operable frequencies.
>
> A frequency fence, something like an electrical fence, was put around the planet to control how much the frequencies of humans could be modulated and changed. As the story goes, this frequency fence made it very difficult for the frequencies of light--information--to penetrate. When light frequencies *were* able to penetrate the control fence, there was no light to receive them. The humans' DNA was unplugged, the light-encoded filaments were no longer organized, so the creative cosmic rays that brought light did not have anything to plug into and hold onto.[172]

Already in the beginning of the devastating space war, the Earth-Lyrans, still living in the Scandinavian area, left the planet after there had been some nuclear detonations, and some of the Living Library had been destroyed in the process.

The Earth-Lyrans were lost for quite a while before they finally found their new home in the Pleiades. On a planet which orbited one of the older stars in the constellation they found a planet which was beautiful and not too much unlike Earth. This became their new home, and this Lyran group is the one we normally connect with the Pleiadians, and they are our cousins, because they share our DNA. As time went by, other Lyran groups migrated to the Pleiades as well and colonized other planets, so the

---

[172] Marciniak: *"Bringers of the Dawn", p.16ff op. cit.*

star system contains both Earth-Lyrans and those who are pur[ ]
some of them having no connection with Earth, and never did.

Later, when the Anunnaki were highly involved in the genetic[ ]
of mankind, some of the Pleiadians returned to Earth in hope to ͟ ͟ ͟ ͟
again live on the planet they loved so much in the past. This turned out to
be a bad choice. Many of them got caught up with the Anunnaki
experiments and joined them and their culture of war, drama, sexual
promiscuity (including incest), and jealousy. These Lyrans/Pleiadians
therefore also became part of the Atlantis drama. This is where their karma
comes from, and to free themselves from their Atlantic karma, in which we
humans, as a mass consciousness, are a part of as well, they need us to
avoid repeating the same mistakes *they* made in the highly technological
Atlantis, as time now is repeating itself.[173] We are beginning to make the
same mistakes the gods were making 11,500-13.500 years ago! According
to the Pleiadians (and it's easy to see that they are correct), we are
currently, here in the United States, living in the New Atlantis that has
been planned for hundreds of years behind the scenes; Sir Francis Bacon
was just being one of the planners. Both the Rosicrucian Order and
Freemasonry are promoting a new Atlantean future for mankind, and
other secret orders are doing the same, in their own ways.[174]

I am going to tell you the story of the Anunnaki and their involvement
in creating homo sapiens sapiens in the next few papers, but it's mostly
told from Zecharia Sitchin's perspective. Although I give some credit to
Sitchin's research, it is not telling the entire story, and some of it has been
intentionally altered, although not necessarily by Sitchin, but by the
Anunnaki, who dictated our ancient Sumerian and Babylonian history.
Therefore, I want to give a short, slightly different summary of their part
of history in the paper as well, as I firmly believe there is much more to the
story than that which is told in the Sumerian Scriptures. In the *Second Level
of Learning*, I will elaborate much more on this subject.[175]

At one point in time, probably already when they were at war with the
Original Planners of the Living Library (the Lyrans), the Anunnaki started
working together with both the Dracos and the Orion Reptilians (or they
may already have been in liaison before the Anunnaki came to Earth). This
united team could successfully chase off the Lyrans, and the Lyran faction
that was to become the Pleiadians, from our planet.

Left here was an incomplete Living Library, now in the hands of the

---

[173] See my book, *Simulations and the Wheels of Time in the Developing World*, which will
be available on Amazon.com at the time of this book release.

[174] For more information, see my book, *The Story of Isis and the War of Bloodlines*,
available at Amazon.com.

[175] A paragraph removed to avoid confusion. It was about homo erectus. It is still
available in the original paper at wespenre.com.

Anunnaki. Sitchin's story is going to be told in the next few papers, but metaphysical sources, like the Guardians, and especially the Pleiadians, whom I have no reason to believe is deliberately deceiving us on this matter, are telling us something quite different from Sitchin. I have listened to the Pleiadians a lot and been careful to get a feel for them, and so far, I have not had any reasons to doubt their intentions and their information. Sitchin, on the other hand, did the translation of the Sumerian cuneiform text, written about 5-6,000 years ago, and I believe the translations being generally accurate, and much of what Sitchin revealed is true, but the Anunnaki, whom to a large degree dictated what is written in them (whether directly or by verbally telling the "history of humankind" to the Sumerians) had all the reasons to withhold crucial information and sometimes even blatantly lie to cover up the real history of the original creator gods, who we, the human beings, really are, and where we come from. As we know, *history is written by the winners.*

Homo sapiens sapiens, the modern human, was an unbelievable downgrade from the original 12 strand multidimensional human.

The Anunnaki are still working together with the Reptilians, and it also looks like they are (still?) using factions of the Greys as their servants.

E.T. Art--The Stories are in the Rocks

Before we start talking about the Greys, here is an interesting side note, perhaps giving us a clue of how some of the species who visited Earth in ancient times looked like:

Figure 8.18: Rock formation in Statues found in the Superstition Mountains Arizona from 'Ancient' Humanity, showing the creator gods and how they really looked like. Wiolawa calls this "UFO Art."

An old friend of mine of Native Indian descendent, Barbara Brown, aka Wiolawa (or Wio for short), who is also the owner of http://wiolawapress.com,[176] posted a picture on her website about 12 years ago (1998-99). It's a rock formation, which can be found in the Superstition Mountains in Arizona. At a first glance, that's what it is; a rock formation. However, if you look carefully, you can see how faces and figures were carved out of the rock, almost like in an impressionistic painting by Claude Monet. Wiolawa claims this is the art of the old gods, depicting them as they really looked like, hidden in plain sight, and only for those with eyes to see (*fig. 8.18*).

The interesting thing with this formation is that the number of faces and whole-body figures/creatures you can see in this picture fluctuates depending on your day-to-day awareness level. Look at it closely, study it, and come back to it another day. More features will most probably pop up. Twelve years ago, when I first saw it, I could only isolate a few creatures, but today I can see a vast number, and they are pretty obvious! A mind-blowing and curious exercise.

The Zeta Reticulians, aka the Greys

I have saved this subsection until last because it's complex and needs extra attention. Ever since Whitley Strieber wrote about his encounters with the Greys decades ago, this species has popped up every so often in the UFO literature, mostly described as a malevolent species, doing genetic experiments on humans without their our consent. They have quite a bad reputation. Now, when we better understand who they are, we can also see that these beings have been part of Earth's mythology for thousands of years.

So let us look at this species a little closer and more objective than what is the norm.

The original home planet of the original Zeta Reticuli Greys we hear was called Apex, located in the Lyra star system. On Apex, a nuclear war destroyed most of its surface, and the inhabitants had to live underground for thousands of years. Due to radiation, their reproductive capacities were damaged so that cloning was the only way for the species to survive. Their bodies mutated and became those we now know as the Zeta Reticuli Greys.[177]

---

[176] According to Wio, she went offline because of the threats she experiences (*Wes Penre, 2024*)

Before the nuclear war, the Apexians had already ecological problems. Just as we do here on Earth, they used negative energy (electrogravity) for selfish purposes and polluted their planet. Then, on top of that, they were invaded and infiltrated by an alien race called "The Verdants",[178] allegedly originating from another galaxy some 14 million light-years from here. This invasion culminated with the nuclear war, and a faction of the Greys were captured and made into "foot soldiers" for the Verdants.[179] The Verdant themselves were already then a very advanced race, reptilian in nature, looking a little bit like the Greys we are used to see.

Apex, in the beginning, looked similar to Earth. It was a beautiful planet with lots of resources. Just like we humans, the inhabitants of Apex were a mix of different races because the early Lyrans had already started colonizing Sector 9. Apex, like so many other planets, was used for genetic engineering by these different creator god species from within the Lyran constellation. Hence, the inhabitants had also a generous mix of ideologies; some worshipped technology, others rejected it; some were warriors while others were peace-bringers, and so on.

However, because of the wide variety of ideologies, the gap between those who were choosing the path of technology and those who were more "spiritual," or closer to nature, became bigger and bigger. Leading groups on the planet started using technology very destructively, just like we doing here on Earth, and the history of Apex could be a great study project for us here on this planet to learn what could be our destiny if we don't change our ways.[180] They started polluting the planet without thinking the least about the consequences, and also began to use nuclear power destructively, exactly like we are doing as a human species. In addition, they have told humans that at least part of the reason their planet became inhabitable was because of their overuse of electrogravity.[181]

However, there were those who were smarter and could see what was coming, so they started building underground facilities and shelters in case of a catastrophe, which they could foresee based on the direction in which things were going.

---

[177] *History of Zeta Reticuli,* from her book *Visitors from Within,* Chapter 1, channeled by Lyssa Royal (https://www.amazon.com/s?k=lyssa+royal+holt+books&crid=3AF2D96FBOY54&sprefix=lyssa+royal%2Caps%2C268&ref=nb_sb_ss_ts-doa-p_1_11)

[178] See *The Contact Has Begun* by Phillip Krapf. Also: http://www.seancasteel.com/Phil_Krapf_Interview.htm; http://www.bibliotecapleyades.net/vida_alien/vidaalien_signtimes05a.htm

[179] George LoBuono: *Alien Mind* (http://alienmindbook.org/AlienMinddownload.doc)

[180] It appears that many of the channeled entities we encounter are using metaphors and are in actuality describing our own Earth history (*Wes Penre, 2024*)

[181] George LoBuono: *Alien Mind,* p. 25.

According to Lyssa Royal and her channeled messages from Germane, the Apexians did not realize (or simply just ignored the facts), that their nuclear experiments and misuse of technology had started breaking down the planetary energy field on a subquantum (sub-atomic) level. This created an electromagnetic warp in the time/space fabric surrounding the planet. While the species were living underground, Apex changed its position in the time/space continuum because of the dramatic subquantum energy breakdown.[182,183]

Germane (collective), through Lyssa Royal, continues:

> Time and space is very much like swiss cheese. A planet in one location is connected through a series of multidimensional networks or passageways to other areas of your galaxy. When this warp began around their planet, the planet was moved through the fabric of time/space to another time/space continuum - which was a significant distance from their point of origin. You have labeled this area the Reticulum star group. The Apex planet was inserted in the Reticulum system around one of the faintest stars in that star group. This occurred simply because the planetary shift followed the fabric of time and space. The underground Apexians were totally unaware of this as they continued with their lives under the surface. They continued saving their species.[184]

Germane explains further that while the Apexians were living underground, without natural sunlight, they worked on restructuring their genetic setup so their bodies could more easily adapt to the new, inconvenient situation. So, with time they developed larger eyes with pupils that covered the whole cornea of the eyes, so they could absorb light on other frequencies to keep their bodies and minds functioning; they lost their reproduction organs due to that they didn't give natural birth anymore; they also lost their digestive tract atrophied, because they were no longer eating solid food. Instead, they learned how to absorb nutrients through their skin.

Because the nuclear disaster affected everybody on the planet, all kinds

---

[182] *History of Zeta Reticuli* from her book *Visitors from Within*, Chapter 1, channeled by Lyssa Royal (https://www.amazon.com/s?k=lyssa+royal+holt+books&crid=3AF2D96FBOY54&s prefix=lyssa+royal%2Caps%2C268&ref=nb_sb_ss_ts-doa-p_1_11). Also, George LoBuono, the respected UFO/Alien researcher, mentions the short Greys destroying their own planet in the past in his *Alien Mind*, page 25.

[183] This is precisely what Barbara Marciniak's Pleiadians said has happened here on Earth (also see footnote 181 above) (*Wes Penre, 2024*).

[184] "*History of Zeta Reticuli*", from her book *Visitors from Within*, Chapter 1, channeled by Lyssa Royal (https://www.lyssaroyal.net/lyssa-royal-holt.html), *op. cit.*

of diversity was going on underground, too. They seemed to have one thing in common, though. After having pondered their new situation, they came to the conclusion that the reason for the catastrophe was the species' emotional side. Therefore, they agreed to take out the emotional part from their biokind/biomind, and thus became quite emotionless. To avoid a similar disastrous situation in the future, they started creating a neuro-chemical structure in which an outside stimulus would create the same reaction in all of them. This way, they felt they could integrate into one people and not let passion and emotions rule them into a downward spiral (they became a hive mind).

Although they had now turned much into what we call a "beehive community," there were still different philosophies playing parts in their culture. Each faction had their own viewpoint on who they were on a higher level of existence. Some of them became more benevolent than others, in our terms of thinking, although it was all about different perspective on how to best survive.

As mentioned earlier, Apex was a big center for genetic engineering, and lots of experiments with different ET races were taking place there, long before the nuclear war, making the surface uninhabitable. The Apexians, who eventually turned into the short Greys were, according to the Germane group, originally of a Vegan-humanoid biokind, and the mutations that happened due to the nuclear disaster is what changed their body type.[185] On the other hand, they are talking about a second, not-so-humanoid-looking kind of Vegans, who are more reptilian or insect-like in appearance, but still humanoid, mammals, with a copper base in skin and bloodstream which also give them a slight greenish color.[186] These would probably be the Reptilian-humanoid hybrids the Vegans created while on Earth during the Dinosaur Era, as discussed above. The Greys could very well have those genes mixed in as well.

Genetic engineering is the game of the gods, and it is extremely common throughout the universe, even to the point that it seems to be a part of the evolutionary progress of a species to eventually become "like the gods" and start manipulating DNA to improve their own species and as they get more advanced, while traveling through space/time, they also want to create new species on other worlds by either manipulating the DNA of creatures already living there, or create life on whole new worlds. Humans have already begun this process in secret laboratories and in huge

---

[185] https://www.lyssaroyal.net/lyssa-royal-holt.html

[186] http://www.spiritual.com.au/articles/et/galacticfamily_lroyal.htm

facilities underground, such as the infamous Area 51 in Nevada. The creator gods are rarely making perfect products at their first attempts, and before they are satisfied, lots of beings of lesser perfection are created. Mostly, these failures are destroyed, but it depends on the creator gods. Sometimes they don't bother, and just leave the imperfect prototypes to their destiny (which is what En.ki did when he was in the process of creating homo sapiens *Wes Penre, 2024*).

The former Apexians (today's Zeta Reticulians) are not the only types of Greys out there. In fact, several sources point out that the Grey sauroid/reptilian type is not uncommon at all in the universe. However, the types of short Greys that have interfered with us on Earth, or have been sighted the most, are often the ones from the Zeta Reticuli I and II star systems, whose ancestors were the Apexians.

Today, here on Earth, we have a quite misleading stereotype vision of who the Greys are, assuming they are all quite negative in nature. This is a common error we make; we tend to categorize alien species to fit them into one box or another; *bad aliens* versus *good aliens*. I've pointed this out before but will do it again because of its importance: we need to stop categorizing ET races in the above manner; it is very misleading. It is true that we humans have had some very disturbing experiences with the Greys, but this is only from certain groups of them; not all of them are like that. This goes for other races as well; no race is purely evil or purely good; there are all shades of gray in between (no pun intended). With that said, let's continue with the narrative:

There is a faction of the Greys that for one has more Lyran genes in them, which means they are more warrior-like and are striving to gain power. Another faction is more spiritual, in general, and doesn't interfere with us in a negative fashion, if at all. Some of them can even be very loving, although some of these Greys are almost certainly from elsewhere, aside from Zeta Reticuli. There are also other former Apex Greys who have a slightly different body structure than the one we are most familiar with. So, even if many of the Greys we have learned about here on Earth may act and look different from each other, many of them have the same origins.

After many generations, the underground Greys considered it relatively safe to return to the surface of their planet again. They were quite shocked when they noticed a totally different sky scenario. The stars looked very different from what they were used to; the constellations were different, and it was not the same sun! It slowly sank in that their planet was no longer in the same solar system as before they went underground. They had no clue where they were, and it took them quite some time to figure out that their new home was now in the Zeta Reticuli system. Because of what had happened with Apex traveling through a wormhole, the Greys learned about folding space and how to use wormholes, stargates and black holes for space travel. This new reality also brought their different factions together in attempts to understand their situation, and they were united in spirit; at least for a while.[187]

Although they had lived underground for many generations, the species had kept their technological knowledge intact, and they still knew how to space travel. They started building spaceships again and began to explore their new star system and populated some of the planets around Zeta Reticuli I & II. Eventually, a more self-serving group broke out and left the star system to explore other worlds in other parts of the universe. Some of them ended up in the Orion system, while others went to the Sirius trinary system.

Some who have experienced abductions by the Greys, in addition to channelers and researchers, say a faction of the Greys from Zeta Reticuli are working together with the Reptilians from Orion and once became their inferior, or foot soldiers. Others, like author, contactee, and researcher George LoBuono on the other hand, are convinced the main faction of the robotic Greys work with the Verdants, a distant race who is here on a not-so-benevolent mission. Personally, I think it's a mix of both, and more. It could also very well be that the Greys that have appeared during abductions, when the Anunnaki are the main abductors, could have been there because they have a treaty with the Orion Reptilians, whom in their turn work with the Anunnaki. This means that the Greys may not work directly with the Nibiruans but have been present because of the Orions. The Greys, at one point in time, started to evolve and explore space, and like many newly evolved species, they experimented with electrogravity, which brought the attention to many other galactic and intergalactic species because of the potential danger in doing so. Used in an inappropriate way, electrogravity may apparently not only lessen the longevity of the sun and its solar system, but the universe as a whole. Of course, this draws attention from many concerned races who are much more advanced and have a full grasp of this problem with young civilizations.

The Apexian Greys, using electrogravity negatively (like we humans do now) were at the same time spotted by the Verdants, who are an intergalactic conquering race, very much like the Lyrans used to be, but are expanding their empire outside their own galaxy. The Verdants infiltrated the Apexian government and the interaction between the two cultures eventually led to the destruction of Apex, according to LoBuono.

It's unclear to me when the following happened, but either when the

---

[187] This transformation of a planet from one star system to another is not as farfetched and strange as it may sound. I discussed this with Dr. A.R. Bordon, the Quantum Physicist from Santa Cruz, California, and he confirmed that it was totally possible, and there is no physical law that would prevent it from happening.

Apexians were still living on Apex, or when their planet had moved to Zeta Reticuli, the Verdants started abducting them in large quantities and conducted genetic experiments on them, making them less emotional to be used as their front soldiers, while the Verdants themselves were hiding behind them in the background, making the Greys scapegoats for further manipulation of races and genetic engineering of new species, akin to that what we see today here on Earth.

The Orion Reptilians are millions, and the Verdants probably billions, of years ahead of us in the evolution. They know how to put up screen memories to manipulate the abductees, including using "soul traps", which makes it nearly impossible to penetrate the real memories behind the memory shield. Hence, the Verdants, for example, when abducting people, can implant false memories, blaming Reptilians for the abduction, and vice versa. I think this happens a lot. We tend to forget about those things, having some kind of delusive concept, not realizing how far ahead of us these races are. Humanity, in comparison, are small children who are just learning to crawl. Still, we think we understand what ETs can and can't do. George LoBuono, in his book, *Alien Mind*, at least gives us a clue.

One thing most researchers, including myself, are quite certain about is that the Greys can't reproduce, and they even seem to lack sex organs, and instead use cloning to expand the number of individuals. Some of them, probably, also lack souls. In other words, they are onto cybernetic.

Others believe that the Greys are time travelers and thus are us in the future, coming back to their own past; perhaps like the Pleiadians, trying to change us, so we can change the timeline which led to the society these species experience in the future.

One thing does not exclude the other, though. We are creating different timelines continuously with our thoughts and emotions, and on one of them we may have let the Verdants and the Greys succeeded with, manipulating our DNA/RNA to such a degree that we become like them. A similar thing may have happened in terms of the Pleiadians. Both these species may therefore have come back to our time, trying to change their own present—our future.

But why now? It is because of the nano-second, the term coined by the Pleiadians (see other papers for more complete definition of this term). The nano-second is when timelines merge, partly due to our alignment with the Galactic Center, which changes our DNA, and many of us become truly and consciously multi-dimensional.

The second meaning is that of the word "nano-second" itself. "Nano" means "extremely small" or one-billionth (10^{-9}). A nano-second in that sense would mean a billionth of a second, referring to 1987-2012 in relation to the age of the universe. In other words, these 25 years are like a nano-second in the cycle of the universe. On the other hand, the Pleiadians are talking about the Machine Kingdom, based on nanotechnology, and there we have the word "nano" again. This is the big challenge we have in front of us: Are we going to stop relying so much on technology and start trusting our Innernet, or are we going to let nanotechnology take us to places where most of us don't want to go, which includes cloning of humans, genetic manipulation of our species, in combination with negative use of electrogravity, creation of androids, making humans into onto cybernetics (robots/machines) and in the process we lose our souls and our sexuality, unable to procreate. Today, many people are laughing at such a science-fiction like future, but it is very real, and it is already starting to happen--rapidly! I have posted quite a few articles on my blog, "News From Behind the Scenes" (http://battleofearth.wordpress.com) on this subject,[188] and these articles are not part of some outlandish conspiracy theory; they are posted in highly scientific papers and websites, or in mainstream media.

Figure 8.22: Possibly a real Grey in human captivity, filmed inside the underground Dulce facility. This film has been made public. A short version can be watched here: [189]

The Pleiadians are very clear about that they are here to help us make a

---

[188] 1) http://battleofearth.wordpress.com/2011/03/24/2012-and-man-shall-walk-as-machine/ ; 2) http://battleofearth.wordpress.com/2011/03/23/scientists-create-animals-that-are-part-human-stem-cell-experiments-leading-to-genetic-mixing-of-species/ ; 3) http://battleofearth.wordpress.com/2011/03/06/2045-the-year-man-becomes-immortal/ ;
4) http://battleofearth.wordpress.com/2011/03/02/defense-dept-commissions-cheetah-robot-and-terminator-like-droid-hummingbird-drone-also-in-works/
[189]http://www.youtube.com/watch?v=UB4GAW6YOZA&feature=player_embedded

rational decision for our future. By informing us of our choices, enough of us can hopefully make decisions that will not lead into an irreversible trap. We don't want to end up like the Greys. At this point in time, the Greys can be seen as catalysts for us humans. If we do what they did, we end up like them, and if we avoid the traps they stepped into as a younger species, we may survive.

The reasons listed by us humans why some Greys are abducting humans is long. We have already mentioned one plausible reason; genetic manipulation to make our species asexual, just like them. This is definitely happening.

Others say the Grays want to be able to reproduce like us instead of having to clone themselves. Just like when you make copies of a copy on the copy machine, and continually make copies out of these copies, eventually the quality will decline, until it's unreadable. It's the same with cloning; the bodies will degenerate after so many cloning attempts. The bodies will not be good enough to be soul-carriers, and eventually cloning won't work anymore. Some say this is where the Greys are at now and therefore, they abduct humans to collect their DNA and even let human women carry their fetuses, hoping to create a body type strong enough to be a soul-carrier.

Again, both options could be correct, depending on which faction of the Greys we are dealing with at a particular time. Those who work for the Verdants may have their agenda, while others, who are free from Verdant influence, may try to find a way back to their old lives as a sexually reproducing species.

PAPER 9
THE NEPHILIM AND THE FALLEN ANGELS

by Wes Penre, Thursday, April 7, 2011

Abstract: The Sitchin Version

You who have read Zecharia Sitchin's *Earth Chronicles*, or even one or two books in the series, are already familiar with the term Anunnaki (ANU.NA.KI.), "Those Who From Heaven to Earth Came".

It's important to understand that Sitchin was mostly focusing on Sumerian/Babylonian mythology, although sometimes including Egyptian texts because the two domains coexisted and often interacted with each other. Sumer and Babylon were, for the most part, En.ki's and Marduk's domains, while Egypt was mainly Orion domain during the Atlantis era, administered by En.lil/Ninurta, and was also where Isis mostly resided. That being said, Sitchin mainly focused on En.ki's and Marduk's versions of history/mythology, which leaves Egyptian history less explored, even biased by En.ki and Marduk and how they dictated their narratives to their human scribes (*WP 2024*).

Zecharia Sitchin (1920-2010) was a Russian linguist and author (later a New York resident), who took on as his life mission to translate the old Sumerian clay tablets. I am not going to go into much details here about how Sitchin came to his conclusions, as this can be studied elsewhere, but in general, he found that about 450,000 years ago an advanced race of creator gods came to Earth from their home planet, Nibiru (N.I.B.I.R.U.), or Ša.A.M.e. in their own language (pronounced: *shaamae*; "to cut or break /creation/red ocher + watery father + office/ideal norm", in the Ša.A.M.e. language, Anemegir, having nearly identical meanings in Sumerian as well).[190] According to Sitchin's translations, they didn't originally come here as settlers, but to dig gold and minerals, something that Earth was (and still is) rich in.

---

[190] ref: Bordon, A.R.: *The Link*, 2007.

Over time, this space-bound warrior race decided to use the existing primates as slaves in their mines and started an additional genetic manipulation of the early humans. The Sumerians, who left accounts of their myth inscribed on cuneiform tablets some 5,000 years ago, tell a spectacular story of these "gods" who came down and ruled over them. Not only do these tablets tell their present time story, but they also told the story of their own creation, and how the gods arrived on Earth and manipulated the DNA of early humans. Apparently, these stories were taught to the Sumerian people by this warrior race and go back about 450,000 years in time. Even today, these stories (and more) are passed down to a few initiates into the Mystery Schools and secret societies around the world. As we shall see, this species is equivalent to the biblical Fallen Angels and Nephilim.

Zecharia Sitchin has been accused of many things, from being a complete fraud who's making it all up, or being a government disinformation agent, a shape-shifting reptilian, part of the establishment because he went to a famous university, and more. But at the end of the day, his translations and conclusions are surviving the erosion of time. Of course, he was human, and was not always right (who is?), but he did a good job in helping us understand our past. And not only can we see the effects today from what the Sumerians wrote on their clay tablets and thus see that this is not a fable, but there are, like I've mentioned earlier, people who have actually met with the Ša.A.M.i. from their home planet Ša.A.M.e., and these beings have told them that most of Sitchin's work is right on. Sitchin did the best he could with what he had.

However, this doesn't mean the tablets were totally accurate. I have reasons to believe that on some accounts, the scribes, who wrote down what's on the cuneiform tablets, were not always told the truth by those who dictated them, the Anunnaki. It's on that level the errors present themselves, I would suggest. Scholars and others may object and say that these tablets were not written by one person, and not everything was dictated, so that doesn't hold water, but it does. Most likely, the present time which the Sumerians were depicting in clay was most certainly correct from their point of view, but the past history of Earth, seen from *their* present, was to some extent altered to more fit into certain agendas, planned by a faction, and sometimes most of the Anunnaki themselves. We know for a fact that Marduk Ra changed the Earth history at least once, and Ningišzidda (Thoth) probably did, too, and there were more... Still, they didn't bother keeping their own struggle with each other off the record, clearly showing the character of many of these beings. On the other hand, they probably had little choice, because many humans knew how they were.

Despite, Sitchin's version is a must-read if we want to start understanding our own true history and our origins. This alien species had reasons to edit out and change a few things because they also knew that those from the home planet would return to Earth one day, and they had to prepare humanity for this, so that their arrival would be as smooth as possible.

In this *First Level of Learning*, I will concentrate on the Anunnaki, although there were other alien species here during the time the Anunnaki had their peak time on Earth. The Sumerian Scriptures make it sounds like they were the only "gods" here, which was not the case (something I wrote about in <u>Genesis Paper #1: Human Origins and The Living Library</u>). We will bring up other races too in future papers, and in the *Second Level of Learning*, I will tell a deeper story about the Anunnaki, as it were, and as it is, according to my own research. However, this subject is so vast that it's more than enough, as a starter, to bring Sitchin's material into new light. And another reason why I am separating out this species from many of the others is that they are the ones who have had the most influence on humankind of all ET races from 300,000 years ago up to present time. The curious thing is that although most people think that this was all in the past, in fact, the Anunnaki never left! Some of them stayed, and there was only a short period of time, during the second half of the first millennium CE., when they all left, and this world was left with humans only for the first time in perhaps a quarter of a million years.

One misconception I want to point out already now is that some people think that at least we owe the Anunnaki for tinkering with our DNA. Without their intervention, we would still be apes running around on the savannahs and in the bushes. This is exactly what the Anunnaki want us to believe, and that's one of their best trickster cards! My viewpoint, backed up by research, shows another picture. We shall go into that after the story about the Anunnaki on Earth is told—Sitchin's version, mind you...

But it's worth reviewing Sitchin's translations. Also, he was the one who brought attention to the Anunnaki story. If you are not totally familiar with them, and don't know who is who in the saga, please review these papers about the Anunnaki. If you're new to them, here is the story in a condensed form.

Before we start discussing the huge influence of the Anunnaki on Earth and human history, I want to pay my tribute, not only to Sitchin and those who came after, but also to the anthropologist, Dr. Sasha Lessin, whom have spent a lot of time putting Sitchin's pieces together in a fluent, coherent format, which makes it read like one compressed novel, through his *Enki Speaks* essays (http://www.thelivingmoon.com/42stargate/02documents/Sasha01.html). This has been very helpful in my own studies to grasp the wealth of Sitchin's research, and I have used Lessin's essays as a resource quite a bit in my own Anunnaki Papers to make Sitchin's work more available to the public.

Now, before we introduce Sitchin's work further, let's start by going back in time some 4.2 - 4.5 billion years to see how the Anunnaki themselves were seeded and created.

The Seeding of the Sirian Anunnaki

We have learned much more about ET civilizations, both in the past and in the presence through channelers and writers like George LoBuono, who wrote *Alien Mind*, using neurosensing to connect and interact with extraterrestrial beings, akin to the LPG-C.

This may sound like science fiction to many people, but I have interacted with this group, read a lot of material over the last year related to these subjects, and to me it is now almost routine, and I sometimes find myself thinking that amazingly enough, almost nobody on this planet knows that this is happening. It's in its order to be skeptical about all this, and so was I—for a long time—until I had read so much astonishing material and connected the dots that there were no longer any doubts in my mind that something was going on.

The following story about how the Ša.A.M.i. were created was told me by Dr. A.R. Bordon from the Life Physics Group California:

Figure 9.1: Tall White female

Some 4.2-4.5 billion years ago up to about 6 billion years ago (or longer; the time frame is uncertain), life was seeded on a planet which orbited Sirius C, which then was a bright, hot, blue star, probably of spectral class B (a blue star/sun). This planet is, according to what LPG-C

191

were told by the Anunnaki, the same one we today call Nibiru. It was surrounded by 11-12 satellites (moons)[191] and the planet itself is about 6 times the size of Earth. As we have discussed in a previous paper, life doesn't magically appear in the universe; it is seeded, or *"panspermed"*, which is the technical term for it.

Figure 9.2: Ninurta, Sirian Anunnaki royalty, depicted with ear jewelry, beard, long hair, standing outside a Middle-Eastern stargate.

Nibiru/Ša.A.M.e. was panspermed by an older race from a neighboring star system. We know this to be true, but who really did it is still not totally clear. There are a few theories, though, built on information gathered by contacts with different ET groups, so I am going to be flexible here and give a couple of theories. This murky area needs some more research, though, and there is just a matter of time before we will know. I will eventually write an update, perhaps in an upcoming level of learning.

The first theory (as given to me by Dr. Bordon) is that the Nibiruans were panspermed by a race known in UFO circles as the *Tall Whites*.[192]

---

[191] Most researchers who have studied Nibiru and its path in and out of our solar system agree that the planet has 11 moons. However, according to Sitchin and a few others, our Earth Moon was once one of Nibiru's satellites, which it dropped on one of its crossings. That means that in the beginning it seems like Nibiru had 12 moons, unless one of its 11 moons broke in half through one of the passages of our solar system.

[192] Penre/Bordon conversation, March 28, 2011.

This humanoid ET group, 5.7 - 9 feet tall, with snow-white hair, almond shaped, oval eyes and white skin, are still here on Earth, occupying a base in the Nevada Desert, close to Nellis Airforce Base (AFB). They have hinted at that they come from a star system close to Arcturus.

Figure 9.3: Figurine from old Sumer, which clearly shows a reptilian being.

A second theory, and perhaps more likely, is that the Ša.A.M.i. were created from having been genetically engineered by the Lyrans, just like we were to begin with. What speaks in favor of this theory is that they look very similar to how the Lyrans are normally depicted; Caucasian looking, much taller than today's humans, and the men almost always had full beards, sometimes braded and coarse, and the men also often had long hair. We are now talking about the species which is most commonly depicted in Sumerian cuneiform, but I have reason to believe that by the time the Ša.A.M.i. visited Earth, they were a mix of more than one species, working in unison. At least one of these other species was Reptilian.[193]

A third theory is that the Ša.A.M.i. is just a subgroup of the Lyrans, who developed on their own, without much intervention with their Lyran

---

[193] I have since then 2011 learned that the Anunnaki usually come here in human form. Some take regular human bodies, others are so-called "walk-ins," some are shapeshifting (rare), and a fourth category take bodies in stasis they have put in various hidden locations, usually human-like. Some Sirians are also inhabiting the bodies of the short Greys. The Tall Whites most likely are the Anunnaki (Ša.A.M.i.) as well, using bodies in stasis. Still, I have kept the original narrative in this paper to present an alternative perspective *Wes Penre, 2024.*

brothers and sisters. They created their own reality, became conquerors of their own and teamed up with whomever they wanted.

Perhaps 2-3 billion years after Nibiru had been seeded, and intelligent life forms had developed on the planet, the Ša.A.M.i. noticed that Sirius C was becoming unstable and would soon turn into a nova. When this happened, it would wipe out all life on the planet.

If we use Dr. Bordon's version (some of which he got from the Ša.A.M.i. themselves, by the way), what the TWs did was to speed up the evolution on Nibiru, so the humanoids they had seeded with their own DNA (and DNA from other more primitive species) could become advanced enough to space travel and perhaps be able to leave the star system before the inevitable catastrophe.

One Catastrophe After Another

According to LPG-C, not too long before Sirius C became a nova, the Ša.A.M.i. were turned into a Civilization Type 1 with the help from the TWs, for the Ša.A.M.i. to survive the upcoming catastrophe. The Nibiruans were taught how to control the energy resources of their planet, and also how to control earthquakes, weather changes, and energy resources. In addition, they learned about genetic engineering and manipulation of DNA. This showed to be vital for their survival, because if they were not at least a Type 1 Civilization at the time of the catastrophe, the whole species would have been extinct when the planet was engulfed by the red giant, which is the next step in a star's development after the nova stage.[194] The red giant would have absorbed Nibiru and burned it to ashes, something that probably happened to the other planets in the Sirius C system, if there were any.

I am still gathering information on what exactly happened next, but it seems that for some reason or another, the Ša.A.M.i. went to war against the Tall Whites (civil war. They are different clans of the same species, *Wes' comment 2024*), and they defeated the TWs and won the war. What I heard was that the conflict is still unresolved, and the Ša.A.M.i. and the Tall Whites are still enemies, although they are no longer openly fighting each other.

The Ša.A.M.e. civilization peeked around 36,000 years (or 10 šars) before the catastrophe happened about 4.2 to 4.5 billion years ago. Sirius C then turned to nova, became a red giant and a few million years later retracted into a white dwarf star. However, well before that, Nibiru was catapulted out of its orbit, probably due to the instability of its sun, or

---

[194] In upcoming levels of learning, we learn more about novae and other astrophysical phenomena.

perhaps also with the help of technology.

The Ša.A.M.i. were prepared, though, and had moved underground after had learned to handle energy, which means they knew how to keep a tolerable temperature to stay alive. It is my understanding that they knew how to tame the energy stemming from the planetary core and could use that energy as a "second sun" and thus get the heat they needed from inside their planet instead from an outside sun. Eventually, they were also able to create an artificial atmosphere, allegedly using gold as one of the components, so they could start living on the rocky, desert-like surface on the only existing continent on Nibiru.[195] Gold works as a conductor, and if heat is emitting from the center of the planet and gold can be spread into the atmosphere, that heat "bounces back" and can be used to heat up the surface of the planet so it can again be inhabitable.

Nibiru was catapulted out of its orbit with such a force that it lost its connection with the gravity of the Sirius solar system and aimed for deep space. Their old star system disappeared in the distance forever; Nibiru would never return to Sirius again.

After thousands, or possibly millions of years on a steady course through deep space, Nibiru, the "Red Planet" with its 11 satellites was drawn into our own young solar system, 8.6 light-years away from Sirius, by the gravity from Neptune. It entered the solar system in retrograde, from an angle, coming in from the south, and headed towards another giant planet in our own solar system, Tiamat, located between today's Mars and Jupiter. Earth, at this time, did not exist. One of Nibiru's satellites hit Tiamat and split it in half before the Red Planet left the solar system and continued its journey back into deep space. However, Nibiru had now become a member of our solar system, but was on a much longer, highly elliptic orbit, and only returned to our immediate solar system every 3.600 years, give or take ~70 years.

Both Bordon and Sitchin tell us that Tiamat was destroyed this way. Most sources, besides the two above, say that Tiamat was destroyed by those who lived on the planet from misusing energy, and not because of a collision between the planet and Nibiru's moons. However, for our purpose, we are for now sticking with Sitchin's version. [196]

So, one šar later, the newly adopted planet came back and hit the same spot again. This time it split one of the halves of Tiamat into pieces, which

---

[195] Miscellaneous Penre/Bordon correspondence, December 2010 -- March 2011.

[196] There is a caveat to the entire Nibiru narrative: We must keep in mind that this is the story conveyed by the Anunnaki, both in cuneiform and verbally in their interaction with LPG-C. This is the story *they* want us to know, and it is in their interest that it remains that way. They use this cover story to cover up that they attacked Tiamat and destroyed it on purpose. More about this in the Second and Fourth Levels of Learning.

thereafter became the asteroid belt. The other half of Tiamat was thrown out of orbit from the impact and came closer to the Sun. This damaged planet became Earth. We can, allegedly, still see evidence of the impact from Nibiru's satellite when our planet was split in half, in the Pacific Ocean.

Once again, Nibiru left the solar system for another šar, leaving Earth to its fate.

What happened next is what was described in my previous paper, *Human Origins and the Living Library*. After Earth had been seeded by the Founders, eventually the Vegans and the Lyrans continued where the Founders left off. The Pleiadians tell us more about the variety of creator gods and other alien races existing simultaneously on the planet, creating their own civilizations side by side on another CD I listened to. They say that some of these were developed in Russia and even in the Arctic and Antarctica, which were then not covered with ice, but had forests and lakes because the polar regions were located differently from now.[197] There are still remnants of these millions of years old civilizations to be found under the icecaps; both buildings and skeletons of giants and other, to us unfamiliar species. Some of the civilizations were run by both Lyrans, Vegans and Pleiadians (who in fact were a subgroup of the Lyrans, according to their own story). Because of wars and misuse of technology, these early civilizations died out and are buried under water, ice and land, and creation to some extent had to start all over again.

At the time when the Neanderthals and Homo Erectus walked the Earth, our planet was still monitored by Lyrans, Pleiadians, and others, but apparently using a skeleton crew. Eventually, as told in my previous paper, the Lyrans and the Pleiadians were run off the planet and the solar system as a direct consequence of an atomic war, which was won by the Ša.A.M.i. group.

This early part of Earth's history is missing in Sitchin's writings, which I believe is because the Ša.A.M.i. destroyed these records and changed history in their favor.

Now we are ready to let Sitchin take over, here presented in a condensed form by myself with the assistance of Sitchin's original books, and Dr. Sasha Lessin's own condensed version, *Enki Speaks...*

Although Sitchin, LPG-C, and Dr. Lessin did their best to convey the entire Anunnaki narrative, it has shown to be partly correct and partly incorrect, something I concluded after more in-depth research, resulting in the Second to Fifth Levels of learning. However, this current narrative is still important because, by getting the picture the Anunnaki want us to get, the reader will have a much easier time on the upper levels of learning to

---

[197] Barbara Marciniak channeling the Pleiadians, October Lecture, 2010.

understand the true agenda of these beings, and to get a more accurate picture of who is who, where they came from, and why *(Wes Penre, 2024)*.

In the Days of Old, In the Days of Gold...

As usual, there were conflicts happening on Nibiru, and 450,000 years ago, their present King, Alalu, was deposed by his nephew, the new King, whose name was Anu, Alalu's cupbearer. At the same time, Nibiru became depleted of gold in the atmosphere, and their inhabitants were also preparing for space travel again to find a planet which could provide them with the precious metal. If they couldn't find any to pump into their atmosphere, it would erode; a process that had already started. Apparently, they used gold because it's an excellent conductor, and because they no longer had a sun to warm up the planet (except for a very short time every 3,600 years, when their planet enters our solar system), they could use this precious metal to warm up the atmosphere, probably by using the heat that was emitting from the core of the planet.

Figure 9.4: A young Anu, Alalu's cupbearer.

However, there was a problem. The average lifespan of a Ša.A.M.i. is a little over 100 šars (360,000 - 420,000 earth-years), taking into account they stay on their own planet, but their lifespan could be extended much more than that with the help of technology, which I will cover later. As explained in the paper: *Known Life Forms Within the Milky Way and Beyond (2011)*, when we are born, we are indexed into the planet we incarnate to and are subjected to their sense of time, which is different in different worlds. Here on Earth, we are indexed to live 70-120 years (at the most), while on Nibiru it's 360,000 years. Every species we know of in the galaxy and beyond are working on extending their lifespan as part of their evolvement, and once the technique is found (usually through the above mentioned nanotechnology), a species can extend their lives considerably. [198]The Ša.A.M.i. also were capable of using nanotechnology and could extend their lives up to perhaps a couple of million years, or close to it. However, just like here on Earth, on Nibiru there were people, more and less fortunate in that respect. The Kings, and those of royal bloodline, could choose to use nanotech if they wanted to (apparently not everybody did), and live almost forever in our terms. But the average worker was normally not allowed to use it, perhaps because of population control. Still, as soon as they leave their planet, their lifespan shortens quite drastically, because they are no longer subjected to the same time indexing as on their own planet. If a species has a short lifespan, as humans do, we could gain from leaving Earth, but in the case of the Ša.A.M.i., it was the opposite.

The solution again, was gold! This species uses nanotechnology while on-planet and monatomic gold when off-planet to keep themselves relatively young. Apparently, it doesn't totally do the trick, but the shortening in longevity is marginal if using gold when space-faring. So, in other words, the Ša.A.M.i. needed gold, both for their depleted atmosphere and for space travel.

This was the situation when Alalu (Al-Al) was overthrown and decided to flee from Nibiru. The opportunity came when Nibiru entered our solar system and came closest to Earth. Although he knew his life was going to be much shorter on Earth, he would probably stand the chance to live longer on Earth than on his home planet, if they were out to kill him or force him to commit suicide.

Alalu stole a rocket ship filled with nuclear weapons and headed for Earth. He landed on the virgin-like planet and found it beautiful to the extreme; deep forests, high mountains, mighty oceans, rich on animal life and plenty of all imaginable resources. Still, he chose to land in a rocky desert because that's what he was used to from his own rocky, desert-like home planet.

When he noticed he wasn't followed, he relaxed and started exploring

---

[198] Penre/Bordon conversations, 2010-11; LoBuono, George: *Alien Mind*, 2006. This may be true to a certain extent, but it's also based upon the aliens LoBuono and LPG-C have been in communication with. I have reason to believe that both LoBuono and Bordon's group may be set up by not-so-benevolent forces to execute a long-term plan, something we will discuss later. I believe longevity issues will solve themselves naturally as we evolve and perhaps extend ourselves above the frequency range in which we are currently stuck.

his environment more carefully, and one day he found gold and other minerals in abundance. He immediately realized that Earth could be the solution to all their urgent, pressing problems!

This was exactly what he needed. He hurried and pointed the nuclear weapons towards Nibiru and told King Anu that there was a lot of gold on Earth (Ki), and if Alalu did not get his throne back, the Nibiruans could kiss goodbye to both their planet and the Earth's resources.[199] The deposed king felt satisfied with himself and withdrew to await an answer.

The answer eventually came. Anu decided to send his first son, Ea (meaning "He Whose Home is Waters"), to Earth together with 50 male astronauts and scientists to find out if Alalu spoke the truth. Ea's pilot, Anzu, steered their šem (spaceship) through the asteroid belt and had to use an advanced form of water cannons to shoot rocks out of the way so the spaceship wasn't hit by the space rocks. In fact, they used more than was expected and got depleted of water before they reached Earth.

Figure 9.5: King Anu.

They knew there was water on Mars, so they made a middle-landing there to fill up the reservoir. At this time, Mars had an atmosphere, and plenty of water. The atmosphere was too thin for breathing, though, so they had to wear helmets when entering the planet's surface.

Then the team once again set their course towards Earth. The thought of finding gold was driving them on their mission; without it their whole civilization was threatened.

Soon, Ea's rocket ship entered Earth's atmosphere and splashed into the Persian Gulf. Alalu was there and helped them ashore.

---

[199] Enki Speaks: http://www.enkispeaks.com/.

Ea and his team found that Alalu had spoken the truth, so they started powdering the gold into fine dust and found that it was certainly good enough to fulfill their purposes; it could be used both to save Nibiru and for maintaining longevity during space travel. The Nibiruans, on Anu's directives, ordered the team to send it up to the planet in Alalu's ship, so they could, via contrails, spread the gold through the atmosphere. Ea complied. But before he sent the first load of gold, he removed the nuclear missiles from Alalu's ship and hid them in a cave in the African Great Lakes area with the assistance of Abgal, whom he trusted. There were seven missiles, which were later used to nuke Sodom and Gomorra and the Sinai Spaceport.

Anzu, Ea's pilot, objected and said that during their trip to Earth, by using water cannons, they almost killed the engine, and the nuclear weapons were needed for the trip through the asteroid belt. Ea got aggravated and replaced Anzu as the interplanetary pilot with Abgal, who was willing to follow Ea's directives and returned to Nibiru in Alalu's spaceship, *without* the nukes.

The mission had been successful; the Nibiruan scientists managed to refine the gold even more once it was returned to the home planet, and it was extracted into the atmosphere with desired results. Anu was pleased and left Ea and his crew on Earth, while Nibiru left the solar system for yet another long, elliptic journey, before the planet once again entered our solar system after one šar. The Ša.A.M.i. who stayed on Earth, and those who followed, became known as the Anunnaki (Those Who From Heaven To Earth Came) by the Sumerians, and are the Fallen Angels of the Hebrew Bible, says Sitchin. The ones who stayed on the home planet Nibiru are equivalent to the Biblical Elohim.

When Nibiru finally returned, the planet's atmosphere was once again almost depleted of gold, and to their disappointment they noticed that Ea hadn't been able to collect very much new gold on Earth. However, it was enough to once again fill the atmosphere.

Ea decided to make another flight over the planet and suddenly found gold in south-east Africa; lots of it. He was very excited when he announced this to the home planet.

(Ea must have been quite lazy, or caught up in something he thought was more important than to provide his home planet with life-sustaining gold, or he would have come up with this idea earlier, and would have been able to find the solution well in time before Nibiru's next passing; not after the fact that Nibiru returned, finding himself almost empty-handed. Or perhaps, for some reason, he had no access to the equivalent to a shuttle or an airplane while left alone with his crew on Earth. It's hard to believe that's the case, though).

Nammur (En.lil, *Wes Penre 2024*), Ea's half-brother and Anu's second son, was angry and jealous that Ea was assigned the Earth mission, and when he heard the news that his brother had found huge veins of gold, he questioned it. He said Ea had promised a lot of gold from the waters of the Persian Gulf and behold: The source was almost immediately depleted! Nammur wanted proof, not only of gold, but the abundance of it.

Anu agreed and sent his second-born down to Earth to see for himself. He found that, indeed, there was probably enough gold in Africa to save their planet, something Nammur had to admit. Ea and Nammur had always been competitors, and both wanted to be in control of the Earth mission, so the former played a trick on Ea and Anu. He sent a message up to his father on Nibiru, saying that he, Nammur, needed to be in control of this mining project, and Ea should work under him. Besides, Alalu started getting restless down on Earth and had started ranting about being King of both Nibiru and Earth.

This message made King Anu come down to Earth in an effort to resolve the issues (this was not the last time he had to resolve conflicts between the two competing half-brothers). He found Ea and Nammur in dispute with each other, so King Anu decided to draw lots, and Nammur won. Discouraged, Ea was sent to South Africa to start the mining, no longer in charge, and he brought his team of Anunnaki with him.[200] This happened 416,000 years ago.

Edin (Mesopotamia) was assigned to Nammur, who now earned the title, the En.lil, "Lord of Command,"[201] while Ea was granted the oceans as his domain and put to govern the AB.ZU (Southeast Africa),[202] becoming in charge of the mining project. Nammur was the one who gave Ea the title, the EN.KI, "Lord of Earth. Much later, in Greece and Rome, Ea became known as Neptune and Poseidon, respectively. The En.lil became Zeus and Jupiter, respectively[203] (as a side note: We still can find many hints of the Anunnaki influence on our language. One of them being Enki (Lord of Earth) falling back on Ea, which most possibly gave the name to our planet, **EA**rth).

---

[200] Also scribed in Sitchin's last book, *The Lost Book of Enki*, where he states that En.ki (Ea) dug himself down into the AB.ZU, which is what we call the Underworld *(Wes Penre, 2024)*.

[201] More accurately, "Lord of the Airways" in Orion/Aryan language *(Wes Penre, 2024)*.

[202] See footnote 199 for better understanding *(WP 2024)*.

[203] This is accurate during a certain time period. Zeus, in the Matrix we now live in, is a title given to En.ki, and later, Marduk (see upper Levels of Learning and my previous *work WP 2024)*.

Figure 9.6: Anu fights Alalu.

Next thing King Anu had to deal with was the former King Alalu. Anu confronted the old king, and they started wrestling.[204] Anu was the younger and stronger one, and he put his foot on Alalu's chest while he was lying on the ground; a sign of victory.[205] However, when Anu let go, Alalu bit off Anu's manhood as a last revenge. This is something the Anunnaki gods do as a principle, it appears. Often, when they defeat each other in battle, they cut off each other's manhood and throw it away, so that person can't reproduce anymore (conveniently putting an end to the direct bloodline of the losing party, so his otherwise potential offspring of that being/person could no longer threaten the victorious party's position then or in the future *WP, 2024*).[206] However, the story doesn't tell why Alalu had been out of the picture for so long; he threatened to nuke his home planet if he wasn't getting his throne back, but when Ea came down to check it out, he took over and started delivering gold to Nibiru (not a word mentioned

---

[204] According to Sumerian cuneiform, to solve certain conflicts, Orion and Sirian beings wrestles to prove who was the strongest. Whomever whom the wrestling match got his will *(WP 2024)*.

[205] According to Dr. Bordon, a Ša.A.M.i. "Lord" or "King" never intentionally kills another Lord or King. They overthrow each other and are in constant conflicts and disputes, but killing is not allowed, and is apparently a law that is strictly followed. Members of higher rank of their society could kill those of lower rank and the other way around, but it seems like royalty is "sacred" and these of the "bloodline" don't kill each other if they are considered on a similar level of authority.

[206] This draws a parallel to the Osiris-Isis-Horus story where Set(h) En.lil cut off (but off?) Osiris' (En.ki's) manhood *WP, 2024.*

about what Alalu did in the meantime. Perhaps it's just clay tablets missing, or perhaps something the Anunnaki did not want us humans to know about).

Anu immediately got first aid and his manhood could be sewed back in place again. When Anu recovered, he was furious and deported Alalu to Mars, together with his former pilot, Anzu, whom Ea had fired. For unknown reasons, biting off someone else's manhood often caused death—some suggest because of some kind of poisoning effect.[207]

However, Alalu survived, being saved by the crew who was supposed to leave him dying on Mars. The old king recovered and survived.

Anu, now back on Nibiru, decided to create space stations in the solar system, on Mars, and the Earth moon, which was the lost moon of Nibiru when it first hit Tiamat.[208] He also said that if Alalu was alive, he should be allowed to start a colony on Mars.

Anu sent his daughter Ninmah, with a crew of female health officers to Earth but were asked to middle-land on Mars to check out the situation there. They found both Alalu and Anzu dead, but they managed to revive Anzu with advanced medical equipment and knowledge.[209] Alalu, to this

[207] Contradicting Bordon's statement above, so it's up to the reader to make their own conclusion.

[208] If this is what really happened, and our Moon is one of the Nibiru satellites that was dropped, it raises a lot of new questions about whether our Moon is artificial. Many (and most recently, David Icke) has brought up this question over the years. Icke even wrote about the Moon being hollow, acting as a huge "control center, where a holographic reality is sent down to Earth, keeping us within a frequency fence from which the ones who set this up (the 4th Density Reptilians, according to Icke) are controlling us remotely. If Icke is correct, is this controlling force the Sa.A.M.i.? Are they also the ones who stopped us from exploring the Moon further? Are they the ones who shot down our space shuttle which was on its way to Mars? It's obvious the Mars moon, Phoebes, is artificial. Another control center? Many questions... More about this later.

For more info, see Icke 2010: *"Human Race, Get off Your Knees--The Lion Sleeps No More"*.

[209] It makes me wonder if Anzu was artificial Intelligence, AI *(WP 2024)*.

[210] With their technology and cloning abilities, could it be that at least royalty (Kings, Queens, Princesses, Lords, and goddesses), have cloned bodies stored somewhere that they can use when their current body is no longer working? That way they can bypass being a baby again and just go on where they left off? I can't see why, because we humans are heading in that direction with our scientific research right now.

day, is buried on Mars.[210]

After all, Alalu had been the King of Ša.A.M.e./Nibiru, so to commemorate Alalu, Ninmah, and Anzu carved out his face on the great mountain Cyndonia. They depicted him wearing an eagle-helmet. Ea later married Damkina, who was Alalu's daughter,[211] and their offspring was Marduk, who had a great influence on humankind, often in not so favorable manners.[212]

Before Ninmah left Mars, she gave Anzu twenty of her people to build the first way station for the gold freighters.[213]

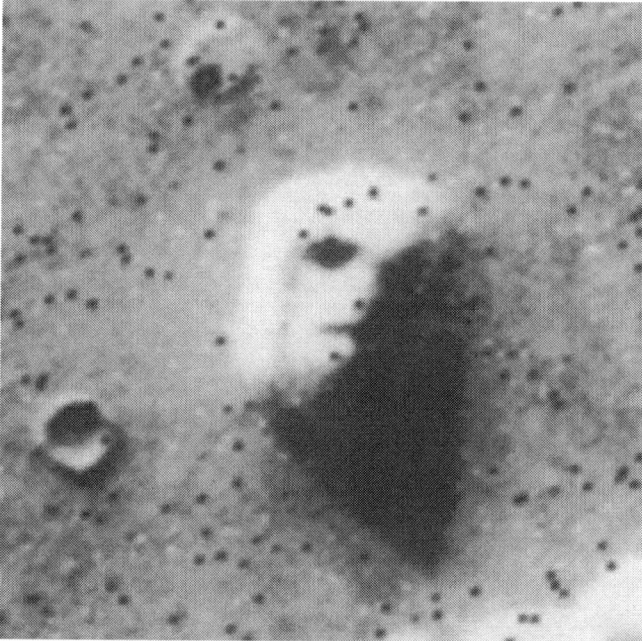

Figure 9.7: Alalu's face on Mars photographed before the NASA cover-up.

The Unsettling Settlers

Ea and Nammur, as we've mentioned, were half-brothers. Ea was the eldest, born from Anu's first marriage, while Nammur, the En.lil, was born from a marriage between Anu and Antu. Ninmah, on the other hand, was

---

[211] *Yet another title for Isis (WP 2024).*

[212] I disagree with this statement. More about this in upcoming books in this series *(WP 2024).*

[213] Enki Speaks: http://www.enkispeaks.com/.

born out of a third relationship Anu had, and was thus half-sister with both Nammur and Ea.

Anu had early decided that Ea and Ninmah should become spouses so that their offspring could be the legal heir. However, Nammur took advantage of the situation and seduced Ninmah, who gave birth to Ninurta. This was extremely aggravating to Anu; he was furious, but couldn't do much about it, except forbidding Ea and Ninmah to be spouses after this incident, and instead Damkina was chosen for Ea.

When Ninmah and her crew of nurses and health officers landed on Earth, the En.lil once again tried to seduce her, but failed in the attempt. He promised her everything she needed for her project to be a success, but she refused to have sex with him again. Instead, in revenge, it seems, Nammur raped Sud, one of Ninmah's beautiful nurses, an incident which had some bad repercussions.

So, Anu was furious, and Ea was as well. He felt his brother had taken advantage of the situation to guarantee a heir of his direct bloodline on the throne. This was just one of many incidences causing conflicts between the two half-brothers. This conflict goes on up until today, as both of them are still alive.

Before fifty of the Anunnaki, Nammur was punished for rape by being exiled from the cities. Nammur left today's Lebanon together with Abgal, who became his pilot. However, unbeknownst to everybody, Abgal was the man who had seen Ea hide Alalu's missiles!

Abgal and the En.lil left for Africa, but on their way there, Abgal secretly landed outside the cave where he and Ea had hidden the nuclear missiles, and showed these to Nammur, thus betraying Ea to instead side with his younger brother. Nammur and Abgal kept their knowledge secret, and Nammur decided he could potentially use the weapons if needed in the future to gain power.

Now, the En.lil again approached Sud, whom he raped, and asked her to marry him, mostly to regain his status, I would presume. Sud said she'd only marry him if he made her his royal wife, and so he did. She became Nin.lil, *Lady of Command.*

Just as Nammur had foreseen, he was pardoned, and the marriage took place, where after Nammur could return to Lebanon. He was very pleased, because his status was now even strengthened, he knew where the nukes were, and he got a royal wife, who bore him a son, Nannar, the first Anunnaki born on Earth. Their second child was Adad. Nannar, however, is going to be a major character in our drama as we eventually come up to present time.

Figure 9.8: A detail of the Stele of Ur-Nammu showing King Ur-Nammu making an offering to the moon god Nannar. The stele dates to ca. 2060 B.C. — Image by © Bettmann/CORBIS

Ninmah, who forgave Nammur when he married Sud/Nin.lil, could now, with King Anu's blessing, start interacting with Ea again. The two met in Edin, and Ea made her pregnant. He told Ninmah to give him a son, but she gave him a daughter. They tried again and again, but daughters were all they got, one after the other.

Ea comforted himself in his despair over the fact that he couldn't get a son by flying Ereškigal, Nammur's son's daughter, to Cape Agulhas on the tip of South Africa, and seduced her. She brought him his first son, Ningišzidda (Thoth), and Ereškigal took command over the Monitoring Station on Cape Agulhas. Further, she bore him a second son, Nergal, who was bold and limping from birth, and was in charge to run the mining operations in South Africa. Ningišzidda, on the other hand, had a foot in each camp; the Enkiites and the Enlilites because both brother's blood ran through his veins, and he supported them both over time.

When Ninmah refused to let Ea impregnate her anymore, Ea sent for his wife and son on Nibiru, Damkina and Marduk. On Earth, Ea and Damkina started to beget Ea's own clan, the Enkiites, whereof Marduk, Ea's firstborn, and his earth-born half-brothers, Nergal, Gibil, Dumuzi and Ninagal, became the first members.

Nammur, the En.lil, also begat his own clan with his wife Sud/Ninlil. They had two sons together; Nannar and Adad, who reinforced him and his eldest son with Ninmah, Ninurta, in their conflicts with the Enkiites.

If we stop here for a moment, we notice that the gods were pretty promiscuous and seldom stuck to one woman or wife. The same went for the women. They all slept around with others, and incest and inbreeding were the game of the day to strengthen their position in the hierarchies. All these beings mentioned so far, besides the Anunnaki, who worked in the gold mines, were young royalties; spoiled, power-hungry and arrogant. After having read most of Sitchin's books and other author's work on the subject, I can't help but think about them as big, spoiled children, playing with fire. They may have been brilliant in many ways, but it seems to me they were bored as well, and created games that sometimes had some pretty serious and nasty consequences, as we shall see.

Figure 9.9: From Sitchin, Z., 1983, The Stairway to Heaven, page 114, Sumerian frescos of stone: the En.lil's lineage above, some of the Enki's below.

Dr. Sasha Lessin, in his essay, *Enki Speaks,*[214] summarizes Nammur's achievements as follows:

> By 400,000 years ago, Enlil had built seven Mission Centers in Mesopotamia. The centers: Sippar the Spaceport; Nippur, Mission Control; Badtibira, Metallurgical Center; Shurupak, Med Center. He build his communication center, the DUR.AN.KI--the Bond Heaven-Earth also Navel of the Earth, a dimly lit chamber essential for talk with rockets en route between Nibiru and Earth, at Nippur *Sitchin, Z., The End of Days, page 6.* In years to follow, Nibirans and the slaves they drafted will war for the Duranki. After the Deluge, 13,000 years ago, Enlil will relocate the Duranki to Jerusalem *Sitchin, Z., The End of Days, page15*[215]

Up on Mars, Anzu, who was the kinsman of the deceased former King Alalu, and his 300 hundred colonists, the *Igigi*, now started a shuttle service, which brought the gold, transported from Africa to Mesopotamia, back to Nibiru. There it was pumped out in the atmosphere, and the planet was

---

[214] http://www.enkispeaks.com/Essays/12Anzu&AstronautCorpsRebel_2.html
[215] Enki Speaks: http://www.enkispeaks.com/ op. cit.

slowly healing.

However, the Igigi were not satisfied with the deal. They thought they had to work too hard, and they wanted more of the fruit that Ninmah grew, which made the eater euphoric, and they had other demands as well.

Anu sent them to Earth to talk to Nammur, who was in charge down here. Reluctantly, Nammur granted them a visit at Nippur, his Capitol. However, while Nammur undressed, Anzu stole the key to the control room (a kind of computer crystal)[216] and ran away. With this power tool, he now illegally claimed ownership of both Earth and Nibiru, and the Igigi stood behind him. This was also a perfect way to take revenge on Anzu's kinsman, Alalu, he thought. To escape, Anzu forced Nammur's pilot, Abgal, to take him back to the spaceport, Shurupak.

Ninurta, Nammur's eldest son, acted and hunted Anzu down. He defeated him in an air battle and shot down his shuttle, where after he dragged Anzu before Nammur and freed Abgal.

Figure 9.10: Ninurta dragging Anzu before Nammur

The Seven Who Judged (Ea, Damkina/Ninki, Marduk, Nannar, Nammur, Ninmah, and Ninurta) sentenced Anzu to death and Ninurta was given the task to execute him, which he did.

The matters became more complicated when it showed that Nannar, Nammur's legal heir, had led the conspiracy against his own father to challenge his half-brother, Ninurta, to being the Commander of Earth. When Nammur found out, he expelled Nannar from Ur, and Ninurta's position was strengthened, because Nannar was forced (something that was decided by the Nibiruan Council) to honor Ninurta as the En.lil's successor on Earth. Nammur, to make sure Ninurta obeyed and felt gratitude towards him, gave Ninurta a fifty-headed missile out of Ea's "hidden" Alalu collection. Ninurta was pleased and satisfied, and then enforced the gold extraction process and continued the shipping of gold to

---

[216] It sounds like the key component to the Tablets of Destiny, *WP 2024*.

Nibiru.

Figure 9.11: Ninurta slaughtering Anzu.

But was Nannar really behind the plot against Ninurta, or was he just a pawn (although an agreeable one) for someone else? Dr. Lessin, with Sitchin's help, makes a quite plausible suggestion:

> Sitchin shows that Ea, allied through his marriage to Alalu's daughter Damkina and their son Marduk to the Alalu's lineage (matrifiliated), was part of the plot. "It was with Ea's connivance" that Anzu, kinsman of Alalu, is admitted to Enlil's inner sanctuary for energy source crystals, vital computer chips, orbital data panels, and control buttons for Earth and Earth-Nibiru, Mars communication. Ea suggested Enlil entertain Anzu as a stall to responding to the demands of the Igigi.

> Sitchin, in The 12th Planet had earlier said the role of Anzu in The Lost Book of Enki's account of the revolt of the Igigi pages 117 - 121 was actually the role of Nannar (Enlil's son by his half-sister and legal wife, Sud) was Legal Heir on Earth. Nannar's was a challenge to Ninurta (Enlil's Firstborn and heir on Nibiru) to succeed to Enlil's command of Earth. In The Wars of Gods and Men, too, Anzu, the leader of the revolt is a descendent of Alulu (his grandson); in this version Anzu's an orphan adopted by the Mars Service, rather than Anzu the pilot who took Ea to Earth and stayed on Mars to die with Alalu page 97.

> Both Nannar and Ea would have benefited if Anzu vanquished Ninurta. But it was Nannar, not Ea, that Enlil exiled in the aftermath of the Igigi revolt. The 12th Planet, pages 107 -116.

Anthropologists will recognize Enki's description as a classical system of segmentary patrilineal (agnatic) lineages. In segmentary patrilineages, collateral lines (like those that descend from Ea and Enlil) cite alliance through different mothers to other royal patrilineages. The Ea lineage within the Anu clan, and especially the Marduk line of the Ea's lineage, is allied with the Alalu clan for leverage against the Enlilites within the Anu clan). Marduk's line is a matrifiliate of Alalu's clan. Matrifiliated alliances give lineages external allies as they vie for precedence in authority within their patricians.[217]

So, Nammur had in his way defeated the Enkiites' revolt, and armed with all these missiles, he felt quite powerful, and while Nammur was intimidating the miners in South Africa with his nuclear power, Ea was now supposed to supervise them.

The En.lil was a much harsher leader than Ea, the En.ki, and the miners' conditions worsened considerably under Nammur's ultimate leadership, and when the mining in Southeast Africa had continued for 144,000 years, the workers in the mines started feeling pretty upset about their conditions.

On another account, Marduk emphasized with the Igigi on Mars, whom he said got almost no elixir, and had no spaceport on Earth they were allowed to use. They were treated less than decent. The En.lil, however, was more stern about it, and told Marduk to go to Mars and take Anzu's body with him to have it buried there, and this was meant to play out as a symbol for what happens to those who go against Lord Nammur!

Ea was discouraged by the situation and felt he needed to do something. So he left the supervision of the mining project to foreman Ennugi, and went to what is today known as Zimbabwe together with Ningišzidda, his eldest son, and set up a laboratory to study the already existing species on Earth.

Ea, a famous, ingenious scientist and geneticist on Nibiru, was fascinated over what he saw. He was especially interested in the apemen, whom had been spotted all over the planet. More fascinating was their sympathy for other animals; in fact, the apemen often freed the animals which were caught in Anunnaki traps. He liked their strong emotions and their similarities in genetic setup to the Nibiruans themselves.

Nuclear War, Some 300,000 Years Ago

As a side note (this is not in Sitchin's books): Around this same time, the

---

[217] http://www.enkispeaks.com/Essays/12Anzu&AstronautCorpsRebel_2.html

Lyrans and the Earth-Lyrans were working on the Living Library. They knew the Anunnaki had built their bases on the planet, and they just stayed away from them. Apparently, the Anunnaki had a bad reputation amongst the Lyrans.[218] On the other hand, the latter knew this galaxy is an experiment in "free will," and that they couldn't really stop the Ša.A.M.i. from landing here and establish bases. However, the Lyrans were protective regarding the Living Library Project, and while working on the side, they probably kept an eye on the Anunnaki, they continued their project. The Anunnaki must have been well aware of the Lyran presence.

In South Africa, the miners complained that Ennugi treated them too harshly, and when Ennugi brought up the issue with Ea, the latter sided with the miners. Knowing more about how these two half-brothers, Ea and Nammur thought, we can pretty well understand the plot that took shape in Ea's head. He contacted the miners and had their leaders conspire with him. He wanted them to continue nagging and complaining to bring Nammur's attention, so that Ea could introduce a solution;[219] a new species! The miners were more than happy to go with Ea's suggestion.

When the miners started acting out, the En.lil was called upon the scene, and Ea returned from Zimbabwe. In Nammur's presence, the miners put their mining tools on fire, backstabbed and even took Ennugi as hostage, crying out how horrible their situation was. Many of them left the mines, headed for Nammur's base, and sieged it.

The situation got out of hand, so Nammur called for King Anu to resolve the situation. Nammur was furious and wanted the revolting leaders executed, and with them, Ea as well, because he hadn't been able to keep them in check.

Anu arrived at the scene, evaluated the situation, and sided with the miners. He thought they were inhumanely treated, and that something needed to change.

Ea told Ningišzidda that they should create a *Lulu*, a primitive worker, to do the miners' job. These beings already existed, and all they had to do was to mix their genes with theirs, *like two serpents entwined* (double helix

---

[218] Various channeling session with the Pleiadians, transmitted by Barbara Marciniak, 1992-2010.

[219] *Problem-Reaction-Solution.* This is a technique used up to this day, especially by the Global Elite when they want something new implemented to enhance their agenda. In this case, Ea created a problem (a revolt amongst the miners), got a reaction from the Enlilites (something must be done about it), and Ea presented the solution to a problem he himself partly instigated. The solution would be to create a new race to exchange with the Anunnaki miners. Without a revolt, Ea's ideas would possibly have fallen on deaf ears.

DNA), and they would have the perfect hybrids to do the job! That way, the Anunnaki workers in the Abuzu (Africa) could be relieved once and for all.[220]

Nammur, on the other hand, when been informed about the project, objected to it. He said that slavery was since long abandoned on Nibiru, and should not be re-introduced on Earth, and Ninurta added that they should make machines to do the work, not hybrid slaves (this is quite ironic, because from our perspective, the Anunnaki miners were no more than slaves themselves, as were the Igigi on Mars). Ea emphasized that they should be *"helpers"*, not slaves. Nammur disagreed, saying that creating hybrids were forbidden by law on Nibiru, but Ea tried to bypass this by pointing out that the ape-man DNA was very similar to their own and have to come from the same, original genes way back in time. All he was doing was to speed up their evolvement by adding more of the SAM DNA.

The issue was brought before Anu's Council, and after both sides had had their say, the Council voted in Ea's favor. They said they had to change the rules to save Nibiru, and if this is what it takes, so be it! Ea, to his great satisfaction, got free hands.

Ea's research team were now working full speed to create an improved human race, but had some failures in the process, which created quite a few strange looking creatures.

In the meantime, the Lyrans saw what was coming and decided to interfere with the process. They did not want homo erectus to be tampered with by the Anunnaki, as it interfered with their plans for the Living Library. The Earth-Lyrans left Earth and eventually found a new home in the Pleiades. A war broke out on Earth between the two species of creator gods; the Lyrans and the Anunnaki, a war which ended in a nuclear disaster,[221] after the Anunnaki had used some of the hidden nuclear weapons to defeat the old owners of the planet. This left parts of the world deserted, followed by a nuclear disaster. Evidence of this, and other nuclear wars in the past, have been found in the deeper layers of the Earth's surface.[222]

---

[220] Sitchin, Z., 2002, *The Lost Book of Enki*, page 130
[221] Dr. Arthur David Horn & Lynette Anne Mallory-Horn, 1997: *Humanity's Extraterrestrial Origins: ET Influences on Humankind's Biological and Cultural Evolution, p. 87.*
[222] http://www.disclose.tv/forum/proof-of-ancient-atomic-wars-t18719.html

Figure 9.12: Scientists Davneport and Vincenti put forward a theory saying the ruins were of a nuclear blast as they found big stratums of clay and green glass. High temperature melted clay and sand and they hardened immediately afterwards. Similar stratums of green glass can also found in Nevada deserts after every nuclear explosion (http://www.disclose.tv/forum/proof-of-ancient-atomic-wars-t18719.html).

Just like the Ša.A.M.i. had defeated the Tall Whites in their ancient past, the Anunnaki now defeated these creator gods as well, and those who survived fled from the planet, back to Lyra. However, some of the Pleiadians came back to Earth later and started working with the Anunnaki instead with their new seeding project, and the renegade group, which is currently channeled through Barbara Marciniak, are doing so to take care of their karma from have done so. They consider Ea being their ancestor,[223] which can be explained by Ea having had sexual relationships with Pleiadian females on the side; something that happened a lot among the gods as we have seen already. Many of them are not exactly monogamous, but very sexual and can thus be quite promiscuous.

After the destruction from the atomic war, Earth now had new owners: The Anunnaki had just conquered a new world and expanded their Empire with a new real estate. But the Original Planners had not given up on Earth; the Lyrans and later on, a renegade Pleiadian group, were determined to continue their Living Library experiment in the future and have since then monitored the situation, in wait for the time when we humans will be able to activate our DNA and evolve, and thus escape from their oppressors. This time has now come...

---

[223] Barbara Marciniak channeling the Pleiadians, various lectures.

PAPER 10:
GENESIS OR "THE GENES OF ISIS?"
by Wes Penre, Sunday, April 10, 2011

Experimenting With Genetics

Now, given free hands by King Anu, Ea and Ningišzidda immediately continued their genetic experiments to create the "perfect worker." Before they even came close to the end result, they tried different options. The most amazing creatures were created, such as the *Centaur*, which was a crossbreed between Anunnaki and wild horses in an attempt to create the perfect work horse; strong and intelligent. That project was eventually abandoned, but this is where the myth about the Centaurs come from.

Figure 10.1: Centaur—a crossbreed between Anunnaki and horse.

Instead, Ea and Ningišzidda started copulating with existing ape-women of the homo erectus species already existing on the planet. To their dismay, they found that no offspring came out of that intercourse, so they used other different tactics to get their results: They copulated and placed their seed inside ape-women and created zygotes in test tubes. Then they surgically implanted the zygotes in ape-women. That didn't work either. The ape-women got their offspring, but they couldn't talk, their internal organs didn't work properly, and they lacked hand dexterity.

Figure 10.2: Ninmah and Ea creating zygote workers

Then, Ea came up with the idea to implant a test-tube-grown zygote into Ninmah's womb, containing his sperm, she who later was renamed Ninhursag by Ninurta, and became known as Isis in Egypt. When the baby was born, an excited Ea slapped the baby on his behind, and he gave out the proper sound. The baby could speak! The research team was very happy.

The little one looked like "earth clay;" his skin was dark red, and his hair was raven black, contrary to the Ša.A.M.i., who were Caucasians (so-called "Nordics" *WP 2024*), with blond hair and blue eyes. Another difference between the Sirian bodies and this new hybrid was that the Sirians were born without a foreskin around their penises. This hybrid had a foreskin. Ea thought that was good because it would act as a distinction between themselves and this new hybrid race. He decided that they should let the foreskin stay on.

Figure10.3: The Research Team. Ningišzidda and En.ki face Ninmah. She holds Adamu, the hybrid Nibiruan/homo erectus they made. "My hands have made it! victoriously she shouted."

The critter's cute and he and female hybrids the team creates enjoy sex. But the hybrids can't breed yet. From Sumerian cylinder seal (in Sitchin, Z., 1995, Divine Encounters, page 13) (The "Tree of Life" to the right, Wes' comment)

Inspired by their success, the research team gathered seven other Anunnaki women to act as carriers of new zygotes originating from Ea's and Ningišzidda's sperms The titles, Ea and Ningišzidda are utterly being confused, since they are both the same being—the En.ki *WP 2024*). They delivered one hybrid each, and now there were 8 clones, all male.

Ningišzidda then decided to create female hybrids. He implanted this zygote in Ninki/Damkina, Ea's wife, and she delivered by c-section. This, too, was a success, so once again, the same seven surrogate women were used, and they all gave birth to one female baby each. The female babies, contrary to the males, were blond and blue-eyed, just like the Sirians.

Ea and his son wanted to continue using the surrogate mothers, but Ninmah objected and said it was too hard on them, and it wasn't enough with 8 women to create a worker race.

So, Ea brought the original "master" hybrids, called Adami and Ti-Amat to Edin at the top of the Persian Gulf, which was Ea's home, and the rest of the clones, created from the two "master copies," were sent to Africa and caged. There they were allowed to have intercourse in hope of bringing offspring. The hybrids copulated frequently, but there were no offspring.

At the Medical Center in Shurubak, Ningišzidda worked hard to find the gene in their own DNA they could use for their hybrids to be able to reproduce. He eventually found that the Nibiruan females had a recessive XY chromosome in their genotype, while Ti-Amat had only XX.

With this new revelation in mind, he anesthetized Ea, Ninmah and Ti-Amat.

From the rib of Enki the life essence he extracted; into the rib of

Adamu the life essence he inserted. From the rib of Ninmah the life essence he extracted; into the rib of Ti-Amat the life essence he inserted. He proudly declared, "To their Tree of Life two branches have been added, with procreating powers their life essences are now entwined."[224]

YHWH, the "Schizophrenic" God

Ea and Ningishzidda kept it a secret that they had altered the original female hybrid, and the two original hybrids kept living in Edin. and Ti-Amat made leaf aprons for herself and Adamu, while they continued living in Edin.

Nammur soon noticed that the hybrids were no longer naked, but wore aprons, and he asked Ea why this was. Ea confessed.

The En.lil became furious and told his brother he'd gone way too far. Not only had he manipulated the Nibiruan Council to break the law and create hybrids in general, now they could reproduce as well! This means, shouted Nammur, that this insignificant species is initiated to the "Tree of Life," meaning they got the longevity of the gods, which could be thousands of years; they were on their way to become one of them! "This is not acceptable at all," Nammur was raging.

Ningiszidda quickly came to Ea's aid and assured the En.lil he had excluded the longevity gene from the Adami race, and they would *not* have the longevity of the gods. Nammur, still furious, commanded Ea and his son to expel Adamu and Ti-Amat from Edin and "bring them where they belonged," i.e., in the gold mines, so they and their offspring could replace the Anunnaki workers, now about to revolt again.

Ea knew his brother quite well and understood that from now on, Nammur would slander him and call him an evil serpent in front of the hybrids to emphasize his own power and diminish Ea's. Therefore, Ea set up the first secret society on Earth, *The Brotherhood of the Snake*. He recruited a few, selected hybrids, whom he taught advanced thinking, technology and advanced philosophical thinking.[225] He gave his creation access to the Tree of Knowledge, something that was forbidden as well, but not as serious as tampering with the Tree of Life, which had to do exclusively with the "immortality" of the gods.

The reader most likely recognizes this story from Genesis in the Bible, when Eve ate from the fruits of the Tree of Knowledge and became aware

---

[224] Sitchin (2002), *The Lost Book of Enki, p. 148.*

[225] Michael Tellinger, (2006), *Slave Species of god*, page 145; Morning sky, Robert, (1996): *The Terra Papers*; Hubbard, L. Ron, (1952): *The PDC Tape"*; Bramley, Wm, (1993): *The Gods of Eden."*

of who she was, and Adamu then did the same.[226] Nammur is the equivalent to YHWH/Jehovah, and Ea is the Serpent (Satan/Lucifer), who seduced Eve/Ti-Amat to eat from the Tree of Knowledge. When Nammur/YHWH found it, he expelled Adam and Eve (Adamu and Ti-Amat) from Edin (Eden). In Christianity, Satan and Lucifer are one and the same, but that's a misunderstanding. Besides being archetypes, in this case, Ea would better fit the picture of Lucifer, the "Light Bearer", who shone light (knowledge) on the newly born humanity. Satan would perhaps better fit Marduk, who inherited the title "Lord of Earth" from his father, Ea, when most of the Anunnaki left in 2024 BCE, after the destruction of Sodom and Gomorrah. He has been here, claiming the title, "Lord of Earth," ever since.

"Who is like unto thee, O Lord, among the gods?" (Exodus 15:11)

Figure 10.4: The YHWH composites.

The story of YHWH is complex and consists of a composite of Anunnaki beings; thus the "schizophrenia" of this god. In the Bible, he is hard to make sense of because he changes personality traits back and forth in a very confusing manner. The reason for this is he is not just one person, but at least two: Nammur and Ea (I would add Marduk to the mix as well *WP 2024*). In the Bible, the two are mixed up and combined to one, while Nammur's "curse" on Ea for having educated the hybrids was what was brought on down the history line, making Ea the "bad guy" (Satan/Lucifer/the Serpent), who rebelled against "God". Serpent is not only a snake, it's also a symbol for wisdom or knowledge and has little to do with evil.

---

[226] Genesis 3:1-6 (KJV)

Sitchin says:

> In this context "Yahweh" of the Bible indicates Enlil; in other contexts the Bible's "Yahweh" designates Ninurta, Marduk, Adad; Yahweh may allude to a "god" of the Nibirans imported from homeplanet Nibiru. Some places in the Bible "Yahweh" even designates Enki, as when Enki suggested creating hybrid Earthlings.[227]

YHWH (or YHVH *WP 2024*), just like Satan and Lucifer, is an archetype, but the "jealous God," who made the Hebrews his "chosen people" is more than likely Nammur, the En.lil.

Robert Morning sky, who wrote *The Terra Papers* in 1996, also made a radio interview called "Star Elders" in 2008, where he discusses YHWH among other things. He said that Lord Nammur, the En.lil, was the hot tempered YHWH, and the mellower YHWH (both described in the Bible as *one* deity) was Ea. The Bible simply confuses the two and assigns the deity to be the Ultimate God, and nothing can of course be further from the truth (the link to this interview has been removed because it is no longer active. It is still included in the online version at wespenre.com *WP 2024*).

The RA Material, channeled by Carla Rueckert in the early 1980s, also hints at YHWH being a composite.[228]

Did the Anunnaki Really Spurt Our Evolution by Tampering With Our DNA?

According to Sitchin, humanity would have evolved with- or without help from the gods in terms of genetic manipulation, although it would have taken so much longer. He estimates that we as a species were spurred on in our evolution by forty million years.

This is not true, something I will talk more about as we go along. Still, the following needs to be said already now: If we were regular apes to begin with, such as orangutans or gorillas, this may hold true, but it's my conviction that this is not the case. What Sitchin was unaware of was that the "ape-men" the Anunnaki geneticists kidnapped and started working on were the most important part of the Living Library. There was a reason why a war broke out between the Lyrans and the Anunnaki: The latter were taking their most precious part of the Living Library, the 12 strand DNA human in progress, deactivated 10 strands (the "junk" DNA) and worked with the remaining 2 strands, which eventually became homo

---

[227] Sitchin (1995), *Divine Encounters*, pp. 347 - 380.

[228]

http://lawofone.info/results.php?category=Earth%20History&subcategory=Yahweh%E2%80%99s+Efforts&sc=1&ss=1

sapiens sapiens (the "thinking" man). There was no way for the Anunnaki to work with beings who possessed 12 helices of DNA; they would have been too smart and too perceptive. On the other hand, the "regular" ape-man was too stupid to work with in the first place, so it was easier for their scientists to "cut" than to add. I truly believe, and my research will show, that the part of Sitchin's translations, telling us that Ea and his team were working on second density animals/apes is disinformation. I don't believe Sitchin consciously deceived us, but the Anunnaki did by erasing and changing records. (Also, they often told their stories from *their* perspective, and how they wanted us to know them *WP 2024*).

So, the Anunnaki science team basically took the key to the Living Library, ran off the original planners, and destroyed the holders of frequency, as we were meant to become. Upon that, after having created a human who was smart enough to follow commands but not smart enough to challenge the gods, they created a frequency fence (a Grid *WP 2024*), so the light from the cosmos necessary to activate the "junk DNA" (the dormant 10 strands) could not reach the human body. However, what the Original Planners did before the Anunnaki took over was to plant an activation code into the DNA, and this was either something the Anunnaki were never aware of, or they thought they could deal with it when it happens.

The thing is it is happening now! The Lyrans, with their "long thoughts," decided in the ancient past that now is the time to activate the code if something would go wrong. The energies from the cosmos are very strong right now because the solar system is aligning with the Galactic Center. However, this has happened before, every +-26,000 years to be exact, but a mass awakening has not taken place earlier on the scale it does now. The Pleiadians describe it well in *Bringers of the Dawn*, where they say that the encoded light, brought on mainly by gamma rays, are hitting the Earth all the time, but if there is no one there to receive them, nothing is going to happen; nothing is going to be activated. However, now when the activation code *is* being activated, more and more people are receiving the information from space and become enlightened as their junk DNA gets reactivated. We are striving towards our full potential; this is something that not even the alternative scientists like those of LPG-C realize. If they could open up, too, they could be really helpful.

Some may argue that after all, the ape-men and ape-women that Ea and his team were working on were after all just primitive apes, no matter what. My answer to that would be that it's not true. Yes, our ancestors were not nearly as intelligent as humans are today, but we would have been, and much more and much sooner, if the Original Planners would have had the chance to complete their job. The difference between them working on activating the 12 stand DNA of the gods, and the Anunnaki doing their genetic engineering, is a big difference; *it's the difference between enslavement within a frequency band called the 3rd Density and being multidimensional.*

Can you see now why the Ša.A.M.i. and the Anunnaki are quick with letting us know that they sped up our evolution with 40 million years, which would have been the case, perhaps, if we would have had 2 strand DNA from the beginning? Can you see why they want us to be grateful for this? Are you getting the picture why the Anunnaki (read, En.ki and Marduk *WP 2024*) needed to erase history several times and change it?

What do you think they want to do now? Erase history! This is what the WingMakers and the Anunnaki are working on right now on their highest level; they call it BST (Blank Slate Technology) which will erase our memories, including what I'm writing here. Marduk did this once before and destroyed everything written before a certain date. Wonderful people! The sad thing is that LPG-C is falling for this scam as well. They believe there is a faction of the Ša.A.M.i. they can actually work with; and which faction is that? The House of the King of the Ša.A.M.i.! It's a grand deception, and what I am telling you now is just the beginning. I will go into depth on this as we move along. But please make sure you read these papers in sequence. (You will get a much better understanding of the depth of the deceit we have been subjected to for millennia if you read the books chapter by chapter *WP 2024*).

There is little doubt that the gods (the Anunnaki) are coming back, and it's imperative that we know who they are and what they really want. I have done my best to find out, so bear with me as we move along with our story.

The Early Humans Become Miners

Ea moved Adamu and Ti-Amat (Ti) to Zimbabwe's forests and let them reproduce. Ti gave birth to twins and more babies as well, whom in their turn reproduced and became workers in the mines. According to Sitchin, these early humans were the homo erectus and the Neanderthals.[229]

The gods were pleased because the new workers never revolted; they were fed and given shelter, but didn't mind hard labor, dust and heat; they never seemed to complain. The reason for this, of course, was that they didn't know better; this was actually all they knew. They dug something from the mine that was totally useless for them and they didn't understand what it was and why they were doing their task. They were like horses on a farm that have no idea why they must pull a plow; that's just what they're assigned to do.

Nammur didn't like the idea that the hybrids should be used for

---

[229] Sitchin (1995), *Divine Encounters*, page 47

mining, exclusively, so he let his eldest son, Ninurta, and fifty men fly to Africa and kidnap hybrids from the forests to use for work on orchards and cities back in Mesopotamia (Sumer). The En.lil didn't care because he was sure the earth-bound Anunnaki would soon leave the planet anyway, as soon as Nibiru's atmosphere was totally restored.

So, now the early humans were working in the cities, as well as in the mines, and they bred uncontrollably. This created food shortage, which became a problem for the Anunnaki. Nammur, who was already angry with Ea for having created this species, now demanded his brother to come up with ideas to put an end to the food shortage and the rapid growth in numbers amongst the slave race.

Figure 10.5: Ea impregnates two human females, who then gave birth to a son and a daughter, respectively; Adapa and Titi. In the second tablet from the left we see Damkina holding Adapa and Titi. The third tablet is most likely showing Damkina holding her favorite, Titi. In the tablet to the right, Adapa and Titi are mating, leading to Titi giving birth to Ka-in and Abael (Cain and Abel).

Ea then taught Adami how to make food out of plants, and how to eat animals, and he taught them agriculture and how to garden to create their own food. He then let this group teach other hybrids to do the same, and this took care of the food shortage to a large degree. However, Ea also had another plan in mind to upgrade the hybrids and make them more intelligent.

Adapa, a Genetic Upgrade

Ea found the female hybrids very attractive and he started feeling desire for them. Thus, he impregnated two of them, and one bore a son, whom they called Adapa. The other one carried a daughter, Titi. Damkina/Ninki felt a special affection to Titi and taught her all manners of crafts. Ea and Ninki kept these two children secret, covertly transporting them back to Edin in Mesopotamia, without Nammur's knowledge, understanding that they would be more intelligent than the earlier Adami, due to that their parents were directly impregnated by Ea himself, being one of the Anunnaki. Ea manipulated the weather, using technology similar to today's

HAARP,[230] making the winds change so he could set sails for Edin and hide his new creation in this vast territory.

Ea spent a lot of time in secret to educate Adapa and found out to his great excitement that he was brilliant and a quick learner. A new, upgraded species was now created, which was more civilized and much more intelligent.

Ea and Ninki let Adapa and Titi mate and they gave birth to twins, whom they named Ka-in and Abael, the first earthlings of this new breed, born from two hybrids. Adapa was taught a lot of important things from his father, the En.ki, and as the new race grew larger in numbers, Adapa was put in charge over them, supervising the bakers, the fishermen, the farmers, and so on.

Eventually, news about this new, brilliant hybrid race soon came to King Anu's attention back on Nibiru. Ea then sent his two earth-born, unmarried sons, Ningiszidda and Dumuzi to Nibiru and they brought Adapa with them. They also brought with them a sealed tablet from Ea, asking Anu to deny the new species the "elixir," which would make them immortal (the Tree of Life). Anu realized what his son had done; illegally created a new, *civilized* species. The reason Ea wanted to deny them immortality[231] was so that they could stay quarantined on Earth for a long time.

Anu also realized that Adapa and all his offspring were his descendants as well, whether he liked it or not, and decided to accept what had happened. Hence, he let Dumuzi stay on Nibiru for another šar to learn about husbandry, while Ea and Ningiszidda were sent back to Earth as teachers for the new, civilized man. Dumuzi, when Nibiru came back after one šar, also brought with him the seed for goats and sheep, so these animals could be introduced to Earth, to be herded by the humans. Anu agreed to refusing to add the longevity gene to the new species, and deprive them of the nanotechnology which extended the Ša.A.M.i.'s lives significantly, but the first homo sapiens sapiens still lived for a long time,

---

[230] For more information on HAARP,
http://en.wikipedia.org/wiki/High_Frequency_Active_Auroral_Research_Program.
There is little doubt that today's cabal, the Global Elite, have been given the old technology of the gods by the old gods themselves, and they use this technology to control us, the rest of the human population and can instigate earthquakes, hurricanes, tornadoes, flooding, tsunamis, and other unwanted weather phenomena.

[231] "Immortality" doesn't really mean the gods live forever; they are mortal, just like us, but they sometimes live for millions of years with their technology, taught by *their* creator gods, and this is what is called the "Tree of Life".

sometimes for a thousand years, or more; something that's written about in the Bible, especially in the *Book of Kings*.

After a while, however, Ningišzidda's elder brother, Marduk, took over the task to teach Abael, and the Enkiites now had full control over the breeding program on Earth, something Nammur did not like. He suggested that his eldest son, Ninurta, tutored Ka-in to get his own bloodline into the project, and so it was decided. Ka-in, under Ninurta's supervision, soon presented the first grain, while Abael, under Marduk, presented the first sheep.[232]

However, the conflict between the Enlilites and the Enkiites, which continues up to this date, came to surface again, and it showed to have serious implications. Ea, due to Nammur's involvement in the project (which he disagreed with), seemed to favor Abael before Ka-in and blessed Abael for his achievements with the sheep, but said nothing about what Ka-in had achieved with the grain. Ea's neglect of Ka-in saddened and aggravated him, something that eventually led to Ka-in slaughtering his twin brother with a stone after a fist fight. Ka-in was sentenced to exile by the Nibiruan Council, but Ea managed to spare his life, saying he was needed for the genetic experiment. Instead the Council decided to distinguish the two lines, so that the two bloodlines could be quite easily recognized from each other. Ningišzidda, the master geneticist, therefore altered Ka-in's genotype so that the men in his bloodline couldn't easily grow beard. From that came the ancestry of some Asian people and the Native Americans in the West. Ka-in and Awan, his sister, then departed from the rest and wandered alone through the wilderness for a long time, eastwards.

Eventually, Ninurta helped Ka-in and his offspring with building a city east of Edin, which became Nud. However, Ka-in was killed by a falling stone, allegedly, while building the city. Sitchin suggests he may have been murdered.

The Anunnaki continued teaching the humans all different kinds of things, like astronomy, writing, mathematics, well-digging, musical skills (including playing instruments), use of body-oil and more. Interestingly enough, the Enkiites in general taught humans practical skills and their place in the universe (Marduk even took Enkime, one of the Adapa descendants, to the Moon), while the Enlilites were more into the power game and Nammur's clan taught them worship, superiority and explained hierarchy.

---

[232] Here is another example how the "Enkiists" inverted our history. Cain's bloodline is En.ki's bloodline, resulting in the Global Elite *WP 2024*.

Marduk's Choice

Magnetic, climatic, and astronomical disruption severely affected the Mars-base, where the Igigi were working as the middle hand in transporting gold to Nibiru. The Anunnaki leaders, the En.ki, Ninmah, and the En.lil, who were stationed on Earth, had to deal with the crises. At the same time, when they looked at each other, they saw the wrinkles on their skin, and they noticed they had aged much faster on Earth than those who shuttled between Nibiru and Earth, despite inhaling monatomic gold, and it worried them. Then, those who were born on Earth, like Ningišzidda and Dumuzi, aged even faster.

The three in charge therefore sent Ninurta to the Andes Mountains in South America to establish a transmission tower, while simultaneously, on the tip of South Africa, they built instruments to monitor space and the earth changes.

At the same time, Marduk told his parents he wanted to marry a human female, Sarpanit, who was the daughter of Enkime, whom Marduk had shown the Moon. Ninki, his mother, told him that if he did, he would never be allowed to take her to Nibiru, and his rights as a prince would forever be forsaken, as were the laws of the SAMs. Marduk, however, felt like he was already forsaken and ill-treated by the Nibiruans, so he replied he didn't care, and he was going to become the Master of Earth.

Nammur was furious that Marduk wanted to marry an Earth woman and beamed a message to King Anu to ask him to stop Marduk from executing his plan. Anu said he couldn't stop him, but that Ninki was right; if Marduk proceeded, he would forever be barred from Nibiru, could never return, and had to stay on Earth. He would also lose his title as prince.

Nammur could do nothing but approve to the marriage, but after the wedding, he deported Marduk and his bride to Egypt, Africa, which was his father's, Ea, domain. Egypt from thereon became Marduk's domain.

At the same time, 200 Igigi from Mars landed on Earth, abandoning their Mars-base, due to the harsh environment, and because of astronomical and seismological circumstances described earlier. They also thought it would be a great opportunity to perhaps take themselves brides amongst the people attending Marduk's big wedding, and thus gain some power of their own. So, each of the 200 Igigi took one bride each and threatened that this must be accepted, just like it had been for Marduk, and they should all be leaders of their own domains, or they would start an uproar.

Marduk defeated the Igigi and placed most of them in Babylon, while he and Sarpanit settled with others in Lebanon. Here, they bred and became many in numbers.

To counter Marduk's actions, Nammur decided to find Ka-in's descendants and did so. He took them under his wings, taught them how to build balsam rafts, and they sailed with Ninurta to South America, where they learned about tin and gold mining. Because Marduk, offended and feeling neglected by the rulers on Nibiru, had openly stated that he wanted to be Master of Earth, Ninurta, his cousin on the En.lil side of the bloodline, felt he needed to prepare for whatever move Marduk may make, and so both sides built an army of humans, in case a war was loitering. Marduk's intentions were twofold, at least: He wanted to build an army to show his power and that he was serious, and he also wanted to create a slave race for himself once the rest of the Anunnaki had left the planet. The tension between the two camps increased.

The Birth of Noah

As mentioned earlier, and as the reader may have noticed, the gods were not exactly monogamous. Ea was certainly not an exception. Sex, and strengthening of the royal bloodlines, were something very important to the gods, and something they found tremendous pleasure in. Incest, sex with minors, and promiscuous behavior in general was normal behavior and not considered strange amongst them. This is where we humans learned those traits, although we are still much more restricted than they were. In those days, for a woman to be invited to have sex with one of the gods was not something you tried to avoid; it was considered an honor.[233]

Once again, Ea felt desire for a human female. He seduced Batanash, who was bathing him, and impregnated her. The offspring's name was Utnapištim, better known as Noah.

Nammur was furious over Marduk's attempts to gather so many humans around him, and he wanted to put an end to it. He decided to starve them out and using his title as the En.lil (Lord of Command), he ordered that no aid should be sent to humans if they were sick, and no food of ocean fish should be available to them.

Utnapištim, who lived at Shurubak at the time, went to Ea for help. Ea suggested they should protest against Nammur by stopping worshipping the gods and offering their service to them. However, he could not go against Nammur's orders.

Still, Ea couldn't sit and watch, so he covertly helped humans by sending them his own supplies and taught them how to fish and be self-sufficient. When Nammur found out that the humans could survive without his help, he became even more upset and accused Ea of

---

[233] WingMakers, *"The Doctor Neruda Interviews"*: http://www.wingmakers.com/neruda3.html

conspiring against him. Ea then lied and said the humans found this out by themselves. That settled it for Nammur (YHWH), and he decided to get rid of humanity once and for all. He didn't really need them anymore, anyway, as the time for the Anunnaki departure from Earth was close.

At this time, huge solar flares had been spotted, and the icecaps of the North Pole and Antarctica started to break up. Ea's son, Nergal, reported from the tip of South Africa, that when Nibiru would pass the next time, Earth would most probably be flooded.

The Great Deluge

King Anu beamed Earth and said that Earth and Mars needed to be evacuated as soon as possible, before Nibiru entered a certain position in the solar system. In Africa, the goldmines shut down, and the Anunnaki (the earth-bound) came from all over the planet and gathered in Edin, and a fleet of Nibiruan spaceships landed there. On one of the spaceship, the mysterious white-haired Galzu (Great Knower), who was Anu's adviser, came down with a sealed message from Anu. It was a legitimate sealed message, saying Galzu would speak on behalf of King Anu and the Council.[234]

First, Galzu summoned Ninmah and Ea and told them they had aged quite a bit in a relatively short time. He, Galzu, had not, because he had not been living on Earth. Furthermore, he stated that they could not come back to Nibiru, or they would die. Because they'd been so long on Earth their bodies could not survive the home planet's netforce.

Galzu suggested that those who stayed on Earth (and this included Nammur and Marduk as well as many others who'd been here for long, or were born here), either placed themselves in rocket ships to orbit the Earth until after the deluge was over and the water had withdrawn to a point where landmasses could be spotted and made suitable for inhabitance. Then the leaders would return to Earth, the only place where they could survive.

For those who were not leaders, other options were given. They could choose to leave and wait it all out by moving to higher ground, up in the mountains. The Igigi, and others who had chosen human spouses, must choose to stay with them on Earth and wait out the catastrophe, or leave and abandon their spouses. This included Sarpanit, Marduk's wife.

When Nammur got the news, he met with the Anunnaki Council on Earth, which consisted of the leaders' sons and grandsons and the Igigi

---

[234] I learned much later that Galzu was the Queen of Orion, the primary Creatrix of the original humankind. More about her in The Second to Fifth Levels of Learning WP 2024.

leaders. He emphasized that the humans had to succumb in the Flood and meet their Destiny.

The En.ki protested furiously and said there was no way he would let his creation drown. The En.lil then raised his voice and shouted in anger, bringing up that these creatures (humans) were created illegally in the first place, and also shouldn't have been made to recreate. Furthermore, he accused Ea for letting his son Marduk spread the human genes all over the place by letting the Igigi kidnap female homo sapiens sapiens, leading to intermarriage between man and god. Ea should have no say, according to Nammur, after all the crimes he'd committed. Ea refused to obey to this, but did not openly debate Nammur, whom after all was the Lord of Command.

After that discharge of imbedded emotions, Nammur managed to calm the Council back to order. This is what he finally decided:

1. Astronauts with human spouses and children must move to higher ground and wait for the Flood. When water engulfed most of the planet, deporting ships would come and get them to Nibiru.

2. Ea, Ninmah, and Nammur, with their families, would orbit the Earth until the humans had drowned and the water receded.

3. It was decided Marduk should find shelter on the Mars base.

4. Nannar, the En.lil's son, would wait out the Flood on the Earth's Moon.

Ea, upset over the decision to terminate all humans, started, together with Ninmah, to hide records and computer programs deep in the Iraqi soil. They also prepared genetic banks of Earth's creatures to save from the coming Flood. They also collected female eggs and the female essence (samples of the female DNA code), and thereafter, all the living kinds to combine. Now they awaited the Flood.

Ea had a dream that he should warn Utnapishtim (Noah) and tell him to build an ark, where he could save his family and animals. In addition, he should take with him on his boat the seed of all the Earth species so they could be recreated later. When the En.ki woke up, he got the feeling Galzu had been the narrator in dream state, but he decided to take heed, because he wanted to save this species. The dream had clearly told him not to say anything and not to break the policy withholding from the humans that they were about to all drown, but he could hide the seed for the future, so he didn't have to start all over.

Utnapishtim was informed and followed Ea's command exactly, and soon the ark was built, filled with food and seed from all living species on Earth. About 13,000 years ago, the ice sheet in Antarctica slipped.

Nibiru's netforce put it in the South Sea and as it melted, driven north, water started rushing at 650 million cubic feet per second. The storms whipped, and the water rose quickly, killing everything in its way, except for Utnapištim and his ark, which floated on the waves for forty days and forty nights, until it got stuck on the top of Mt. Ararat. There they offered a lamb to Ea, and Nammur and Ea came down to meet them in "Whirlwinds," something which looked like modern helicopters *(fig. 10.6)*.

Figure 10.6: A helicopter at the top and other space shuttles and vehicles can be clearly seen in this extraordinary tablet!

Eventually, the water from the Deluge receded, and the devastation was almost absolute. Next to nothing of what the Anunnaki had built the last 432,000 years was left. The spaceport at Sippar was gone, Mesopotamia laid hidden, and Edin was gone. Only the raised stone landing place at Baalbek, Lebanon, was intact. The remaining gods were looking at a whole new world.

PAPER 11:
AFTER THE DELUGE
by Wes Penre, Saturday, April 16, 2011

In the Aftermath—Building a New Earth

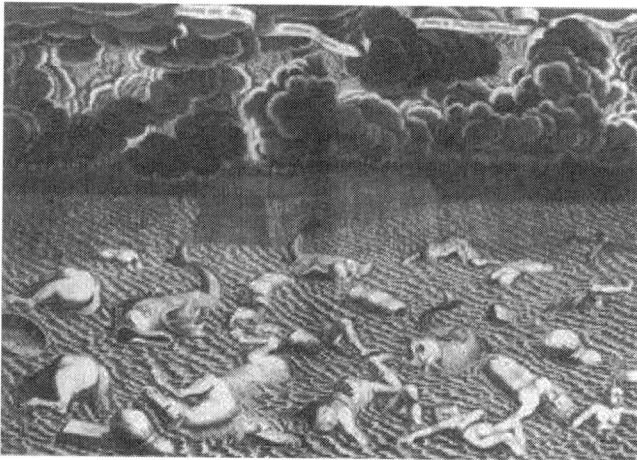

Figure 11.1: After the Deluge

When tthe storms had subsided and the rains stopped, Ea and Nammur saw Ziasudra's[235] fire on top of Mt. Ararat and landed in helicopters, while Ninagal set sails towards the mountain.

The En.lil was furious again when he saw that humans had survived. They were all supposed to have perished! He was so furious that he wanted to get into a fist fight with Ea, who calmed him down and said they were not human anymore—they were his own offspring. Ninmah and Ninurta, also entering the scene, together with Ea, convinced Nammur that these few survivals would be the genesis of a new race on Earth (each of these

---

[235] Another name for Noah *WP 2024*

human bodies who died and were killed due to intentional neglect, at best, and overt genocide at worst on the gods part, were soul-carriers. Obviously, there were a whole lot of these ET individuals who had no respect whatsoever for intelligent life. Ea and a few others seem to have been more compassionate, but perhaps that's just how they portrayed themselves?).

Not only had Earth been totally devastated after the Deluge; so had Mars. The thin atmosphere that once had surrounded the planet was gone, its waters had evaporated, and now it was just a deserted planet of dust storms.[236] Nannar reported that from now on, one could only visit the Moon wearing "eagle masks" (helmets). So, in a sense, Earth had been "lucky;" the atmosphere was still there, and the water would soon withdraw and give birth to new land and slightly different-looking continents.

After having inspected what was left of the "old Earth," the gods found that some important things they'd once brought down from Nibiru, like grapefruit trees, had survived, so they could still make wine. Ea started experimenting with genetics and strengthened the grain that Ka-in once developed. From the seeds Ziasudra/Utnapištim/Noah had saved on the ark, the geneticists again began to seed Earth with different plants, animals, and berries. Soon enough (from their "long thoughts" perspective), life started spreading around the planet again. Cows and sheep came to life, and Dumuzi, Ea's son, together with Ziasudra's middle son, became the first shepherds for the cattle and the sheep. Ea and Ninagal built dams to tame the Nile in Egypt and created a pastureland for Dumuzi's herds.

Gold, Gold! We Need More Gold!

Nammur selected the Saudi Arabian peninsula for a new interplanetary rocket terminal to transport more gold to Nibiru. This was again a necessity, to the gods' dismay, because the latest passage of Nibiru had once again ripped off the gold shield of its atmosphere. All the hundreds of thousands of years of efforts from the gods and human slaves had been in vain, and the production had to start all over again, just when they thought they were at the end of the process.

But the African mines were gone; the slave workers had drowned; the Anunnaki (most of them) had gone home to Nibiru, and the rocket terminal in Sippar, Mesopotamia, was destroyed as well.

Ninurta finally came with some good news. On one of his expeditions

---

[236] I want to point out here how difficult it has been to separate one construct from another—so even for the scholars. The disaster on Mars happened much earlier, which will be obvious in the next few books in this series *WP, 2024.*

around the planet, he had found an abundance of gold in Peru, South America, high in the Andes. From modern La Paz and east of Lake Poopo, in the sand from the running into to east coast of Lake Titicaca, he found lots of it. He also was able to combine copper and tin and create bronze (remnants of these ancient mining activities can still be found, both by Lake Titicaca and La Paz).

The bronze was much appreciated, especially when rebuilding Mesopotamia. After the Deluge, all they had was brick, but the bronze could effectively stabilize the building blocks. It took 7,000 years to rebuild Mesopotamia after the Flood with the limited equipment left for the gods to work with.

The Great Pyramid of Egypt and the Builders of the Sphinx

Ningišzidda raised two pyramids in Egypt. The first was a "model pyramid," and the second was the Great Pyramid. He raised the Great Pyramid at the South End of a straight line through the landing platform in Lebanon (Baalbek) to Mt. Ararat (Eastern Turkey) in the North. Then he installed the Nibiruan master computer programs and astronavigation equipment in the Great Pyramid.

Figure 11.2: Ningishzidda

Ningišzidda had done an excellent job with the Pyramids and to create the technological base, and Ea wanted to reward his son for work well done. So, he decided that a monument should be built in his son's image. Thus, he built the Sphinx, which had the body of a lion, but with Ningišzidda's head sculptured out.

Let us beside the twin peaks a monument create, the Age of the
Lion to announce. The image of Ningišzidda, the peaks' designer,
let its face be. Let it precisely toward the Place of Celestial Chariots
gaze.[237]

Nammur ordered his son, Utu (Apollo in Rome, and Helios in Egypt),
to be in charge of the Sinai Spaceport on the 30th Parallel, which now
separated the En.lil's domains from that of the En.ki. The latter was in
charge of the realms south of the 30th parallel.

In the Great Pyramid, Ea's son, Gibil, installed pulsating crystals and a
capstone of electrum, to reflect a beam of incoming spacecraft. Mission
Control perched on Mount Moriah (future Jerusalem), out of reach for
humans.

Figure 11.3: A model of The Sphinx with its original beard intact and with the cobra-like head-dress,
symbolizing the Serpent Clan (The Clan of Knowledge) - the Enkiites. In Section 9 below we will read
how Marduk replaced the original head of the Sphinx with that of his son, Asar, in an attempt to
rewrite history (The Louvre).

Marduk Becomes Ra and Amen Ra

Marduk, who inhibited a great ego and lust for power, was jealous of
Ningišzidda for having been rewarded with the building of the Sphinx in
his image. He went to his father, Ea, and complained. He said that Ea once

---

[237] Sitchin, Z., 2002, *The Lost Book of Enki, p. 238.*

promised him power and glory, and look; he got none! Marduk's mind darkened from resentment.

The tension between the Enlilites (called the RAM Clan) and the Enkiites (the Serpent Clan)[238] grew bigger and bigger, but Ninmah, the great peace-maker, decided they should divide the lands further into kingdoms, with local rulers. The suggestion had a positive response amongst the clans.

All the royal clansmen on both sides were dedicated certain areas, and Marduk was by Ea appointed to be the ruler of Egypt (we are going to concentrate a little extra on Marduk, because he will be an important figure from hereon, all the way up to present time). Thus, Marduk felt like his father had at least made an effort to satisfy his imperatives to become a ruler. So, about 9,800 years ago, Marduk was assigned Egypt and became Ra. He was now in charge of the workers there.

Ninurta built a palace for Ninmah on Mt. Moriah, and Nammur and Ea awarded her the title Ninharsag (Mistress of the Mountainhead). According to Sitchin, she is also equivalent to Hathor in Egypt.[239,240]

En.ki moved to Elephantine (Abu) Island near Aswan (Syene). From there, he supervised workers building dams, dykes, and tunnels to prevent the Nile from flooding and control its pathway to the Mediterranean. Ea was known as Ptah in Egypt.

The Murder of Osiris and the Battle Between Horus and Seth

To bring the story forward, let's contradict that by going back in time for a short moment to the Deluge, 13,000 years ago. At that time, Marduk, together with his hybrid wife, Sarpanit, and their sons, Asar (Osiris) and Satu (Seth/Set) took shelter on Marsbase with the Igigi commander, Shamgaz. Asar and Satu (from hereon I will call them Osiris and Seth for simplicity) married Shamgaz' daughters, Asta (Isis) and Nebat (Nephys). Shamgaz and Seth became very close.

Osiris and Isis resided close to Marduk Ra in the northern lowlands of the Lower Egypt. Seth and Nebat settled in the mountains of southern Upper Egypt, near the villa of Shamgaz and the Landing Platform in Lebanon.

Shamgaz decided to set Osiris up, because he favored Seth and Nebat

---

[238] For more information about the two clans, see, Bordon, A.R., 2007: *The LINK - Extraterrestrials in Near Earth Space and Contact on the Ground (http://battleofearth.wordpress.com/2010/04/17/the-link-extraterrestrials-near-earth-space-and-contact-on-the-ground/).*

[239] Sitchin, Zecharia: *The Stairway to Heaven, pp. 263-264.*

[240] She also went under the title, Isis *WP 2024.*

before Osiris and Isis. He told Seth that Osiris would always be Marduk's favorite, and even more so because he lived closer to his father. So, Shamgaz, Seth, and Nebat decided to assassinate Osiris.

Hence, Shamgaz and Seth invited Osiris to a banquet and poisoned his wine. Osiris fell unconscious, and they put him in a coffin and threw the coffin into the sea.

Marduk Ra, his wife Sarpanit, and Isis, got the news about Osiris' murder, and hurried to retrieve the coffin. They found it floating in the sea and brought it ashore. Legend has it that Osiris' corpse was cut into pieces and spread out, and only parts of his body was floating in the coffin. The myth further tells us that Isis searched all over Egypt for the remains of her husband and found all the pieces, except for his penis, although, as we know, cutting off each other's genitals was nothing new among the gods. What is true or not in that story is hard to say, but Sitchin mentions nothing, to my knowledge, about the lost penis story. According to him, Osiris' body was intact, and En.ki and Isis took semen from Osiris' corpse and impregnated Isis with it, unbeknownst to Seth and Shamgaz. What is true, though, and a theme through Sitchin's books (especially in *The Wars of Gods and Men*) is that the gods, when they fought each other, rather than just killing their opponent, they castrated him and threw the penis away. This barbaric treatment of an enemy sounds pretty horrific, but it was implemented by the gods so that the defeated god could not reproduce and continue his bloodline. In other words, it was a reassurance of power and dominance.

Seth, proud of his accomplishment of killing his brother, now declared himself, as the only remaining son of Marduk Ra, to be the ruler of both Upper and Lower Egypt. Isis, however, declared she was pregnant by Osiris, went into hiding and gave birth to Horon (Horus). She trained him well to become a great warrior to be able to defeat Seth, who gathered an army of humans and advanced by force towards Lebanon, all to the border of Ninharsag's neutral Jerusalem region.

When Horus grew up, he was trained and ready to meet Seth in battle. He gathered his own army and started marching. Seth noticed that Horus was well prepared, and to stand any chance to win the conflict, he challenged Horus to a combat man-to-man.

A far ranging air battle took place. Horus hit Seth with a blinding weapon and then with some kind of harpoon. Blind, Seth crashed, and his testicles were squashed (or cut off by Horus?). Horus bound Seth and dragged him before the Council. The verdict was to let Seth live the rest of his life on Earth together with the Igigi astronaut corps, but without life-extending treatments.

6. Inanna's (Ishtar's) War Against the Serpent Clan

Nammur and his Ram Clan were afraid that Ea and his Serpent Clan would control Earth's space facilities. The Serpents controlled everything regarding shipping of gold, and Marduk was even in control of space travels between Earth and Nibiru. Hypothetically, the Serpents could stop the Rams from even leaving the Earth.

In secret, Nammur therefore sent Ninurta to set up the base in today's Peru, next to the Titicaca Lake, run by En.lil's son, Ninurta. She also built a spaceport on the plains next to the Andes. This area, being rich in gold, was now in the stronghold of the Ram Clan, and in the middle of this rivalry, two Anunnaki from opposite clans fell in love.

Inanna is known under many different names, such as Aphrodite, Venus, Ishtar, Athena, Kali, and Ninni. She was also a son's daughter of Lord Nammur, the En.lil. Her parents were Nannar and Ningal.

Figure 11.4: Inanna

Dumuzi, as we know, was Marduk's brother and Ea's son. Dumuzi was born on Earth, and so was Inanna. Therefore, they were short-lived in comparison to those who were born and stayed on Nibiru.

Figure 11.5: Dumuzi

Around 8,670 BC, the two started laying eyes on each other and became lovers. Inanna revealed to Marduk's sister what her plans were: She wanted to build a great nation on Earth and be the ruling queen thereof, while her spouse would be given status in the empire. When Marduk's sister came back and told him about this, Marduk did not like what he heard. He wanted no competition from his brother.

He and his sister, Geshtinanna, therefore decided to set Dumuzi up. She seduced him and let Dumuzi have intercourse with her. After the fact, she scared him and told him that Marduk would accuse him of rape and he would be in deep trouble. Dumuzi was terrified and fled. However, he was in such a hurry that he accidentally slipped on a stone, fell into a waterfall and drowned. That was the end to peace between the two clans.

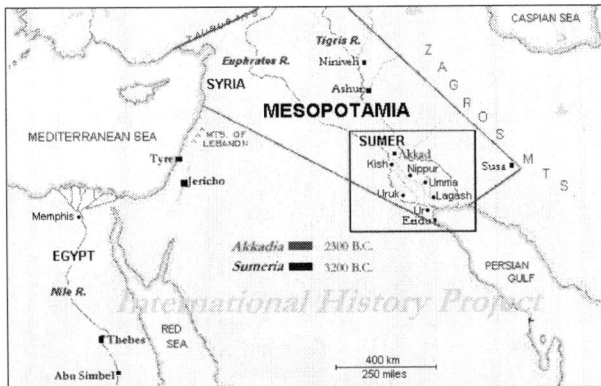

Figure 11.6: Map of Mesopotamia and Akkadia.

Inanna was furious and wanted to take revenge for Dumuzi's death, so she went to war against Marduk. Ea and his clansmen supported Marduk in the feud, and Marduk's grandson, Horon/Horus joined him as well, together with the Igigi astronauts, and in one of the battles Inanna managed to blind Horus' right eye.

237

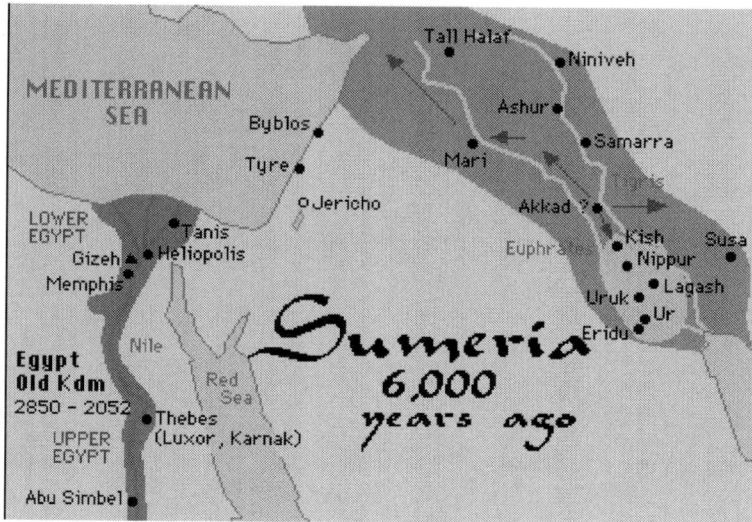

Figure 11.7: Sumer, 6,000 years ago

Inanna showed to be a very skilled and strategic warrior, and she moved in closer and closer in on Marduk, who fled and took shelter in the Great Pyramid of Giza.

On foot, Inanna, Iškur/Adad (Nammur's youngest son) and Ninurta cornered Marduk in the pyramid, in one of the air-tight chambers. Instead of killing him in an instance, they decided to bury him alive, so they put stones before the entrance to the chamber and left Marduk to his fate.

The Serpent Clan brought up the issue before the Council and asked them to spare Marduk's life, but Inanna insisted that he deserved it after what he'd done to his own brother.

Ninhursag brought the two feuding brothers, the En.lil and the En.ki before the Council and suggested they exile Marduk and put Ninurta, Nammur's son, in his place and thus create a clan shift. This became the final verdict.

Ningišzidda unsealed the chamber and found Marduk unconscious inside. Nammur's eldest son managed to revive him and helped him out of the chamber. He was put before the Council and got the verdict firsthand. So Marduk, his wife Sarpanit, and his son Nabu were exiled "to a place where horned beasts were hunted, a land uninhabited by the descendants of Ziasudra/Noah."[241]

---

[241] Sitchin, Zecharia: *The Lost Book of Enki*, 2002.

King Anu Decides to Give Earth to Humankind

A new dispute took place when Nammur appointed his son, Ningišzidda (known as Thoth in Egypt) as the Lord of the Nile lands. Inanna, who'd fought the war against Marduk and won, demanded she'd get her own part of the Kingdom.

They could not come up with a working solution that all parties were satisfied with, so they called on King Anu of Nibiru to resolve the conflict. Anu hadn't visited Earth for 7,000 years, and he had great affection for Inanna sexually, *WP 2024*, so he decided to heed the call for help.

At this time, 7,200 years had passed since the Deluge. Humans had proliferated from the mountain lands to the lowlands. They originated from Ziasudra, but had Anunnaki genes. Offspring of the Igigi Mars astronauts were also around. In the distant lands Ka-in's people had survived.

Anu and his wife, Antu, landed at Tilmun (Land of the Missiles) on the Sinai. Anu was shocked when he saw how much Nammur and Ea had aged; they looked old and bearded, and Ninhursag, once a stunning beauty, was now old and bent. Anu, who was much older, looked younger than the children.

Ea told his father about the message he got from Galzu about how they had to stay on Earth and couldn't go back to Nibiru, or they'll die. Anu said he never sent such a message at all and had no idea what they were talking about. He thought their staying on Earth was their own, determined decision (apparently there was a great lack in communication here).

Ea continued and said that because of Galzu's message, the seed of mankind was saved from the Deluge, and would otherwise have been destroyed forever and humankind would have been extinct.

Anu sat back in wonder. Then he said that it appeared that Galzu came as a messenger for the One God, in an effort to save mankind.[242] Anu continued, saying that it seemed like they, the Nibiruans, were only emissaries for the human species, and humankind is destined to inherit the

---

[242] The Founders come to mind. Did a messenger from the senior creator gods appear in the incarnation of Galzu to save the Living Library and the human experiment? Makes me wonder. See paper *The Creator God Experiencing Itself* under section 2: *A Hierarchy of Creator Gods*. In hindsight, I realize that the Galzu analogy in the texts refer to the Mother Goddess, Anu's contemplations in the referred paragraph to leave earthlings alone could easily be convincing if there wasn't additional information which contradicts Anu's decision. The Anunnaki never had any intentions to give up their real estate and the earthlings. I strongly believe this Sitchin part is disinformation on the Anunnaki's part. *WP 2024*.

Earth and make it their own. Anu now believed it was his and his people's job to educate them and give them knowledge so they can advance. Then, when they were educated enough, the Anunnaki should leave the planet!

Therefore, King Anu dedicated four major regions to three different groups:

Region 1: En.lil's lineage's domain: En.lil and his lineage, decreed the King, rule Mesopotamia through their designated kings, descendants of Ziasudra's sons, Shem and Japhet the Fair. Ziasudra's eldest son, Shem (Šem) and his descendants rule the nations from the highlands running from the Persian Gulf to the Mediterranean. Around 3800 BCE, Shem's descendants settle the ex-spaceport area of Iraq and the Landing Place at Lebanon. Shem's brother Japhet rules for the Enlilites from the highlands of Asia Minor, the Black and Caspian Seas, as well as the nearby coasts and islands,   as   they   recover   from   the   flood.

Region 2: En.ki's lineage's domain: King Anu orders En.ki and his descendents to rule Egypt and Africa though the descendants of Ziasudra's son Ham the Dark. Ham's line rules Caanan, Cush, Mizraïm, Nubia, Ethiopia, Egypt, and Libya, beginning from the highlands and spreading to the reclaimed lowlands.

Region 3: Inanna's domain: Inanna, said Anu, would rule the Indus Valley (to be settled around 2800 B.C.) as a grain-source for the other regions.

Region 4: Ninharsag's domain: The fourth region, Tilmun (Sinai), Anu declared, shall be ruled directly by Ninharsag and be reserved exclusively for Nibiruans and their immediate descendents.[243]

Then Anu and Antu flew with Ninurta and Iškur to the Taihuanancu temple and overlooked the metallurgy (tin) works Ninurta built at Lake Titicaca. Then they were shown back to the spaceport by Ninurta, who proudly showed the King and Queen how his men in the meantime had filled up the Royal "Chariot" with gold to the brim. They wanted to impress and show that the South American gold mining project was a success.

Anu was impressed, and he summoned his grandson, Marduk, to the Andes to have a word with him. The King had a bad conscience for having treated Marduk unfairly and favored his brother before himself.

---

[243] Sitchin, Z., 1985, *The Wars of Gods and Men*, pp. 129-135; 2002, *The Lost Book of Enki*, pp. 271 - 272.

Marduk and his son, Nabu, arrived at the spaceport and stood themselves before King Anu. Marduk, in sadness, told him that Sarpanit, the hybrid, had died from age. Anu then pardoned Marduk and commuted his exile.

Then Anu said, so everybody could hear:

"If destiny is that mankind is going to take over and rule the world, let it so be. Give them knowledge up to a measure secrets of heaven and Earth them teach, let them learn about laws and righteousness, then depart and leave."[244, 245]

As soon as King Anu and Queen Antu left Earth with their rocket filled with gold, Marduk started his intrigues again. He was furious over the South American spaceport and blamed Inanna for the death of his brother, Dumuzi. Anu had found liking in Inanna and even chosen her as his consort, in addition to Antu. As a "present" he had given her a region in India, as well as Uruk. In simple words, Marduk was jealous of the power the King had given her.

Figure 11.8: The Igigi (Biblical "angels").

Nammur, the Enlil, named the present Era the Age of the Bull (Taurus),[246] and started teaching the humans to use bricks to build cities of

---

[244] Sitchin, Z., 2002, *The Lost Book of Enki, p. 275*.

[245] It is noteworthy that King Anu is talking about law and righteousness, when the Anunnaki themselves had been constantly broken all such rules in childish (but murderous) behavior, which we, as humans, definitely have inherited, unfortunately. We are talking about another alien species of course, with other laws, rules and regulations than ours, but for now, just keep in minds what *their* laws and rules seem to be and whether those are the ones we want to subscribe to in the near future? It's bad enough as it is here on Earth. Case in point as we go on... *WP 2011*.

[246] Here is where the Pleiadians come into the picture again. In Marciniak's channeling, the Pleiadians tell us they are the "Bulls," and the Pleiades are in the constellation of Taurus. In context, it is clear that the Pleiadians take responsibility for

mud, and temples for the royal Nibiruans and the Angels (Igigi).[247] These Royals were given numerical ranks from which they were worshipped by the humans. The higher the number, the higher up in the hierarchy, and the more power they had. So, Nammur made sure humankind learned about hierarchy as well, something that has halted our evolvement quite substantially over time. This is how the hierarchy was numbered:

Anu 60
Nammur (the Enlil) 50
Ninurta (Nammur's son and successor) 50
Ea (the Enki) 40
Nannar (son of Enlil) 30
Utu/Shamash (son of Nannar) 20
Inanna (sister of Utu) 15

How they came up with this hierarchy and why it was accepted by lower rank gods/goddesses like Inanna and Marduk, is unclear, but I haven't seen any indications of that this rank was protested against among the Anunnaki.

Educating Mankind

The gods then built the cities of Edin (Mesopotamia), and in each city they built a temple where humans could worship the gods. Ninurta got Lagash, where he got hangars for his aircraft, and armory for his missiles. He may as well have been one of the gods who taught humankind about warfare, being the En.lil's "warrior son." Utu, who rebuilt the city of Sippar, taught

having been teaching mankind the same things the Anunnaki were now teaching us. The Pleiadians admit to that there was a cooperation and correlation somewhere along the lines of time between the Anunnaki and the Pleiadians, as we also shall see when we go into the Atlantis papers later. I am not sure when and how this cooperation started, but there are more sources indicating that *some* of the Pleiadians came back from their refuge to the young star system and started working together with the Anunnaki. It seems this is when King Anu gave the task to the Pleiadian allies to teach mankind certain important things to survive. This is also the part of this whole drama Marciniak's Pleiadians are most proud of; how they taught mankind to take care of themselves. However, it seems that the real reason why Anu wanted to teach mankind was so we could be self-sufficient and survive while the Anunnaki were off planet, just to come back in the 21st Century AD. Anu apparently thought the Pleiadians were most suited for this task.

[247] The Pleiadians are referring to the Igigi as being the angels of the Bible in one of their channel sessions *Barbara Marciniak channeling the Pleiadian, December 2010.*

law to the humans, and Nannar was given the city of Urim. Iškur returned from the Andes to reside in a temple in the mountains north of Mesopotamia (Sumer). Marduk and Nabu, his son, came over to stay with Ea in Eridu.

As we can see, the En.lil's Ram Clan was in charge of most of Mesopotamia. Inanna chose the first king to be the Lugal. The Lugal represented the Lords of the Adapites there (human descendents of Ziasudra). Ram Clan appointed lugals, who then ruled the Land Between the Rivers for 24,510 years.[248] They shifted their Admin Center from Kush to Uruk, then to Akad; all areas ruled by the Anunnaki Council.

The Tower of Babel

The Igigi had great estates in Lebanon and Sumer, where they ruled in abundance. The estates grew as they continued mating with humans, and the number of offspring increased.[249]

Marduk taught these hybrids to make brick for Babylon, which was going to be his own spaceport. By having one of his own, he could challenge Utu with his Ram Clan spaceport in the Sinai. Nammur saw what was happening and asked Marduk to drop the project peacefully, but Marduk didn't listen and continued building the launch tower of Babylon.[250]

By 3,450 BC, Nammur told his lieutenants that Marduk was building a tower, a non-permitted Gateway to Heaven, entrusting the Earthlings. Ninurta emphasized that this had to be stopped, so at night, they raided the area and destroyed the tower. Marduk had to flee again and ended up in his father Ea's (Ptah), region—the Nile. The Ram Clan scattered Marduk's servants and programmed them with different languages and scripts.[251]

---

[248] If this number is correct, the above part of the narrative definitely happened during Atlantis, *before* the Flood, which happened 13,000-13,500 years ago. Still, Sitchin is referring to the above narrative as if it happened *after* the Deluge. There is great confusion in Sitchin's work regarding time periods and characters *WP 2024*.

[249] Mating with an evolving race, such as humans, is a terrible crime, violating cosmic laws. En.ki and the Sirians did it to a great extent by the end of the Atlantis Era and well into the Matrix Era, which followed upon the Deluge *WP 2024*.

[250] Sitchin, Z., 1995, *Divine Encounters, pp. 110 - 115 2002, The Lost Book of Enki, pp. 281 - 282.*

[251] This was most certainly done by once again tampering with DNA. Today, scientists begin to understand that language is a program within our DNA and not something mankind comes up with randomly. There is an order to it. Therefore, when

Marduk, now in Egypt and calling himself Ra, didn't like that his brother, Ningišzidda (Thoth), resided in the area, and for the next 350 years, the tension between the two increased, and their armies clashed in Egypt. Eventually, their father, Ea/Ptah, ordered Thoth to leave Egypt to Ra. Marduk Ra triumphed and reunited Egypt under his command. In reality, Ea had a continuously bad conscience for not giving his son the Kingdom of Nibiru to rule, but at least he could now give him Egypt. Ea/Ptah also gave Marduk Ra the Meš (the supercomputer programs) in an effort to make Egypt prosper; he gave Marduk Ra all his knowledge, except how to revive the dead.[252, 253]

Marduk Ra is Rewriting History

One of the first things Marduk did was to rewrite history in his favor. He immediately removed the head of the Sphinx, which previously was sculptured in the image of Ningišzidda, and replaced it with Asar, Marduk's son. This is the head we see on today's Sphinx. Marduk Ra wanted to place himself in the position as the one and only God, and therefore, he wanted to erase all the history of all the gods prior to him.[254] (I have reasons to believe that not only did Marduk rewrite history, but he also used BST, Blank Slate Technology, or something similar, to erase the memory of humankind (today, we call it a "reset" *WP 2024*).

One way to erase our collective memories might be to distort the connection between the human mind and the Akashic records. A pole shift would most probably do it, if done artificially and scientifically, with this goal in mind. This would not erase the Akashic Records; only our connection with them, and thus, the memories of our collective past. If

---

we learn a few languages, it's getting much easier to learn other, even if they are not of the same group of languages and have little in common. Skilled linguists, who can speak many different languages are aware of this.

[252] Maybe "reviving the dead" was, like I suspected and mentioned earlier, a technology used to transfer the soul of a dead Anunnaki to his/her cloned body, stored somewhere else, most probably on Nibiru.

[253] This is extremely significant because as the reader will learn in my 2023 books, *The ORION BOOK, volumes 1 and 2 Amazon.com*, En.ki was eventually captured by Ninurta around 2024 BCE, and sent to the AB.ZU, where after Marduk took control over Earth (See also *The Fourth Level of Learning* in this book series, or at wespenre.com. I always wondered how Marduk got access to En.ki's technology, so he can build the Singularity and Metaverse, but if Sitchin's translation is correct here, he had access to the Meš for quite a while, which explains it *WP, 2024*.

[254] Sitchin, Z., 2002, *The Lost Book of Enki, pp. 284 -285*; Morning sky, Robert, 1996, *The Terra Papers*.

this connection is tampered with and we lose our collective memories, it's like we wake up and have no memories of our past. We're starting all over from Day 1. Body/mind/spirit work as usual and can think and act as it always has, only without its memories. If this was what Marduk did, he succeeded in erasing memories of previous deities).

Figure 11.9a and b: Quetzalcoatl/Thoth/Ningishzidda, here depicted in reptilian and human forms; something that fuels fire to that some of these beings were Reptilians.

Thoth/Ningišzidda, now exiled, moved all the way to Mesoamerica with his loyal officers, and there became known as Quetzalcoatl, the "Winged Serpent."[255]

---

[255] Sitchin, Z., 2002, *The Lost Book of Enki, pp. 284 -285.*

Inanna Rules the Indus Region and Uruk in Sumer

Nammur, who was afraid that humans would be as powerful as the gods, and learn about immortality, triggered by the Tower of Babel, continued the ordering of writing new languages into the codes of humans; different codes in different areas of the world to create separation rather than unity. So he ordered Ea to create a new language for Aratta, Inanna's Indus Valley Civilization. However, Ea refused to give her the Meš (then in Marduk's possession) to make Aratta the World Power. He said Inanna could share with Aratta what she'd already seduced out of him earlier.

Enmerkar, the second ruler in Uruk (a direct Adapa hybrid descendant of Inanna's twin brother, Utu), sent his son, Banda, to deliver a message, saying the Arattan King had to swear submission to Uruk.

The Arattan king preferred a trade. He wanted the Meš in exchange for Aratta's precious stones. If Enmerkar still insisted on war, he suggested they choose one champion from each camp to do the combat.

Banda returned to deliver to his father the reply from the Arattan king, but he got sick on his way back and suddenly died, so the peace message never reached Enmerkar.

Inanna, who now ruled two kingdoms, Aratta and Uruk, had still not let her mind go off Dumuzi, and she missed him. It was so bad that Inanna started hallucinating about him and had a harder and harder time differentiating between the "real" world and her inner uncontrolled emotions. This made her quite dangerous because of the position she had as Queen.

In Uruk, she set up a "House of Pleasures" (equivalent to a "whorehouse" in today's terms). Inanna herself took lovers from there and elsewhere, pretending they were Dumuzi, promising them long lives and other desirable things. Then she went to bed with them in the evening, and when the morning broke, they were found dead in her bed (the origins of the tale about the "Black Widow").

Utu, Inanna's twin brother, who knew the secret how to revive the dead, managed to bring Banda back to life and brought him back to Inanna in Uruk. Inanna, now in a bad mental state, thought Banda was Dumuzi, and cried out: "This is a miracle! My beloved Dumuzi has come back to life!"

Gilgamesh and the Elixir of Immortality

Banda then succeeded his father, Enmerkar, as the King of Uruk. Banda married Ninurta's daughter, Ninsun, who gave birth to Gilgamesh.

Figure 11.10: Gilgamesh

Gilgamesh was obsessed with immortality and would do anything to be like the gods and live for millions of years. So he went to Baalbek in Lebanon to plead with the astronauts for immortality. He and his android-guard, Enkidu, sought for the launch-pad in Lebanon, hoping the gods would give him the same immortality they enjoyed.

From a distance, Inanna saw Gilgamesh take off his clothes to take a bath, and she desired him. She approached him and tried to seduce him. When Gilgamesh refused, Inanna got furious and let loose the gurard-bull on him out on the launch-pad. However, while Enkidu held the bull, Gilgamesh was able to stab it to death.

Still determined to find longevity, Gilgamesh continued his journey, and in a tunnel in Sinai he found Ziasudra, still alive after all these centuries after the Deluge. Ziasudra then decided to give Gilgamesh monatomic gold; something he himself had used to stay alive for so long. He said that Ea and Nammur now granted Gilgamesh this special treatment as well. Happy, Gilgamesh left, but later, someone stole his stash, and Gilgamesh ended up dying like any other human hybrid.

Figure 11.11: Gilgamesh and Enkidu fighting the gurard-bull

Marduk Offering Pharaohs Immortality

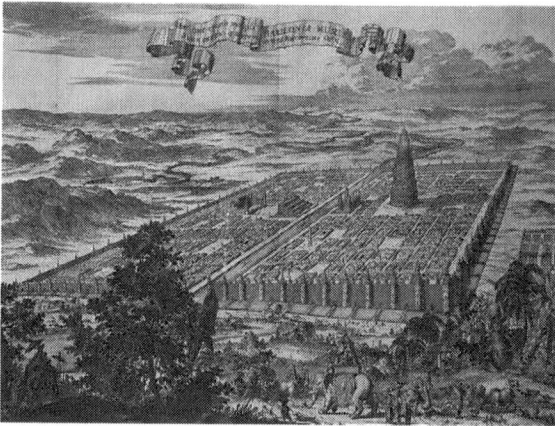

Figure 11.12: Babylon

Marduk, after having heard about Gilgamesh's obsessive search for immortality, started pondering this whole issue to see if he could use it to his own benefit. He decided he could use it to establish loyalty amongst his rulers and high priests. Hence, he told his Egyptian kings that they would journey to Nibiru in their afterlife and enjoy immortality together with the gods. This Immortality Cult could unite the kings around the Nile and strengthen Marduk's position against Inanna.

Inanna, who had great weapons and armies at hand was in possession of gold powder for her own "immortality" and held her position and stronghold on Sumer for 1,000 years. During this time, homo sapiens sapiens were encouraged to worship the Enlilites; the Ram Clan.

In Egypt, on the other hand, Marduk introduced a totally different religion. He taught his human servants to worship only ONE God, and that "God" was no one less than Marduk Ra himself. He told them there were no other gods than Marduk himself. When his father, Ea, heard of this, he was baffled, because this was totally unheard of before.

Marduk, however, was remobilizing his armies to once again challenge Inanna and the En.lil Clan. In both Marduk's and Inanna's minds, there was only room for *one* world ruler, not two!

Sargon, the Akkadian Warrior King

Inanna, in an effort to defeat Marduk once and for all, decided she wanted a strong warrior king. In 2,400 BCE, she chose her gardener, Sargon, to lead her human armies and rule Sumer for her. Why Sargon? Because he had the stomach to rape Inanna, his own Queen, and Inanna enjoyed it. She was fascinated by his courage to do so, and his physical strength. She even managed to convince Nammur about her choice of warrior king. Inanna and Sargon thus ruled from Akkad (Agade), which they built close to Babylon.

11.13: King Sargon

In 2316 BCE, Marduk and his son Nabu were in Egypt, and Sargon saw the opportunity. With his great army, he invaded Marduk's Babylon, and then withdrew. When Marduk and his son returned from Egypt they fortified the city to keep his enemies out. In addition, Marduk decided to build his spaceport in Babylon, the heart of Edin.

Inanna got furious and she and Sargon started a gigantic war against Marduk. What followed was the bloodiest war in Earth's history, and both

249

sides used laser weapons on the other party's human soldiers. Eventually, Sargon died in battle.[256]

15. Inanna's Armies Move Forward

After the intense war had subsided, Nergal, Marduk's brother,[257] visited Inanna in Uruk and allied with her, although he was an Enkiite. Thus, Nergal became Inanna's lover, and together they planned how to rule the world by first defeating Marduk.

As a part of the plan, Nergal left Uruk and he and his men rode to Babylon, where Marduk greeted his brother. Nergal said that if Marduk would leave Babylon immediately and go to South Africa, he could secure weapons and computer systems that had been hidden there since the Deluge. Marduk, who had no reason to mistrust his brother, acted on it and left.

Figure 11.14: Marduk (left) greeting his brother, Nergal, in Babylon.

While Marduk was in South Africa, Nergal broke into Marduk's control

---

[256] Sargon was never resurrected/revived by Inanna or any other god. The old Sumerian tablets apparently don't tell us why some were revived and others not. The same thing goes for Dumuzi; Inanna spent the rest of her earthly existence mourning him, but Dumuzi was never revived. Why? We simply don't know; his body could have been too demolished when they found it. However, the question remains why they didn't resurrect certain important humans or gods, while they did others.

[257] A reason the ancient text can be so confusing is the use of "brother," "sister," "daughter," "consort," and so forth. It does not mean the same as it does for us humans. Marduk and Nergal were not "brothers" in human terms, they were "brothers in titles;" they were one and the same. Before Marduk, En.ki bore the title *Nergal.* They are all titles, and when we understand this, the texts make a little more sense (see the upcoming books in this series, *WP 2024*).

room and stole his "brilliance" (energy radiation source), controlling the irrigation system for all Mesopotamia.

Ea did not approve of this and banished Nergal back to Africa, but Nergal still left a garrison of men near Babylon, where they could aid Inanna.

In 2291 BC, Inanna, Naram-Sin (Sargon's grandson) and the Akkadian armies captured the spaceport in Lebanon. From there, they conquered Jericho, which up until then had been under Nannar's (Inanna's father) control.

Encouraged by previous successes, Inanna moved on, joined armies with Nergal, and conquered Egypt. In her efforts to become the Queen of Earth, Inanna, in 2255 BC, destroyed Anu's Temple and sent Naram-Sin to Nippur to attack Nammur's minions there.

Nammur did not let this go unhandled for long. In rage, he sent his son Ninurta and his army to stop Inanna. He massacred all humans he could find in Akkad and to reconquer Mesopotamia. He ordered Naram-Sin to be killed and Inanna arrested and brought before him. Inanna, however, got away and fled to Nergal in South Africa, and for seven years the plotted how to overthrow the Anunnaki Council.

16. The Enlil Visited by Galzu in Dream State

Galzu,[258] the mysterious person, who had managed to get the great King Anu to realize that he should leave humankind to rule the Earth, once again showed his non-physical presence; this time to the En.lil, in dream state. By now, the Anunnaki considered him a representative of the Creator, or All That Is, and had deep respect for him.

Galzu warned him that when Earth moved zodiacally from the Age of the Bull (Taurus) to the Age of the Ram (Aries), Marduk would rule the Earth. He further told the En.lil: "a righteous and worthy man must be chosen, by him and his seed will Civilized Man be preserved!"

Nammur thought a lot about this vision, which he kept to himself. He decided to send Ibruum/Abraham, son of Nannar's high priest king, Tirhu (a hybrid with a lot of Anunnaki genes in him) on missions to thwart Marduk's moves to position his forces to capture the spaceport on the Sinai. As soon as Ibruum left Harran, Marduk moved in and the next 24 years he spent planning on how to take over Earth.

---

[258] Galzu being feminine (the Queen of Orion see upcoming books in this series, which gives a more sober perspective on the ancient texts, *WP 2024*)

Figure 11.15: Map of Harran and environs.

17. The Anunnaki Drop Nuclear Bombs over Sinai Spaceport before Leaving Earth to Marduk

The Anunnaki and the Nibiruan Ša.A.M.i. knew that they soon would have enough gold to shield Nibiru's atmosphere, and they could all go back to their home planet. Then they could leave homo sapiens sapiens to manage on their own.

By the end of their stay on Earth, the Anunnaki tried to end all their old feuds with each other, perhaps to not bring these conflicts back to Nibiru. The humans were used as slave labor to dig up the last gold resources and precious metals and stones needed, and had them help out with other things, too. Not the least, they had human armies fight wars and battles between the gods to settle things between rival parties. And rival parties there were!

On the one hand, there was Nammur and Ninurta, who used hybrid armies (humans) and Nibiruan weapons in Sumer to fight against Inanna when she invaded the Anunnaki reserve in the Spaceport area. On the other hand, there was Marduk Ra, who proclaimed his Divine Right to Rule on Earth.[259] The Nibiruan Council still refused to let Marduk come back to Nibiru because they were afraid he was going to plot a coup to take over the Kingdom. And on Earth, they did not know what to do with

---

[259] "The Divine Right to Rule" being a Marduk concept. See my 2024 book, *The Story of Isis and the War on Bloodlines*, available at Amazon.com.

him either.

So they gathered the Anunnaki Council to discuss the matter. All council members were against Marduk and Nabu and saw them as a major problem in all camps. Most of the Anunnaki on Earth were eager to leave and go home, but before they did, they decided that if Marduk would be the ruler of Earth, at least they should deny him the Spaceport in the Sinai. All senior Anunnaki, except Ea, agreed to use nuclear weapons to stop Nabu's advance through Canaan towards the Sinai Spaceport.

Before the Anunnaki Council executed their orders, they "radioed" King Anu on Nibiru and asked him of permission to nuke the spaceport and Nabu's human armies. Stunningly, Anu gave his permission! This speaks a lot about the Ša.A.M.i. on the home planet and not only of the Anunnaki on Earth. A lack of compassion seems to run in the blood of these beings, at least on royal levels, which is that counts for us humans because they are the ones who make the decisions, the Ša.A.M.i. people.

Airships were sent down to bring the Igigi home. In 2064 BC, Ninurta attacked the Sinai. The first missile hit Mt. Mashu, where the controlling equipment was housed. Then, a nuclear bomb was dropped above the Place of the Celestial Rocketships, with a brilliance of seven suns. The Earth shook and crumbled, the heavens were darkened after the attack, and of all the beautiful forests were destroyed, leaving only burnt stems left.[260, 261]

Nergal, Ea's son, bombed Marduk's forces in Canaan. He nuked Sodom and Gomorrah, and three other cities allied with Marduk. These nukes were what made the Dead Sea dead, and it still hasn't recovered in today's 21st Century. There is still radioactivity in the area today, enough to induce sterility in animals and people who absorb the water there. Archeologists confirm the flooding, abandonment of the area and sudden deadening of life in 2024 BC. The destruction was tremendous...

And with that, most of the Anunnaki left the planet, just as destructively as the once arrived.

---

[260] Sitchin, Z., 2002, *The Lost Book of Enki, p. 310.*

[261] Sitchin http://www.sitchin.com/evilwind.htm writes that, starting in 1999, scientists found evidence that the depopulation of Sumer coincided with abrupt climate change See Science, April 27, 2001 and Geology, April 2000. DeMenocal, who wrote the article in Science, cited in brackets above, used as evidence for the abrupt changes in the area's vegetation, rocks called tephera. Tephera are "burnt-through pieces of blackened gravel-like rock," usually associated with volcanos. Tephera still cover Sinai, which lacks volcanos. Sinai's tephera result from Ninurta's bombing of the spaceport. The bombing left a huge black scar on the Sinai plain, where the shuttlecraft runway, and launch platform had been; so large it can only be seen from satellites. Millions of black-blasted rocks, north-northeast of the scar in an area where all other color rocks--no black--are found. See photos, *The Wars of Gods and Men*, 1985, pages 332-334 (footnote by Dr. Sasha Lessin, *UCLA Anthropology*)

PAPER 12
ANUNNAKI PAPER #4: ABRAHAM, MOSES, AND THE CHOSEN PEOPLE
by Wes Penre, Thursday, June 23, 2011

In the Aftermath of the Nuclear Fallout

The plain at the Spaceport, having been used as runways for the shuttles, were now completely demolished after Ninurta and Nergal, the angels in the Bible, nuked the Sinai and Sodom and Gomorrah, leaving not even one tree standing. The dark-brown cloud heading eastward towards Sumer carried death on its wings. Wherever it swept through, life in all forms died, mercilessly. The fallout also annihilated the hybrid Nibiruan/Cro Magnon slaves in Mesopotamia, loyal to the En.lil.

Nammur (the En.lil) and Ea (the En.ki) forewarned the gods of Sumer and told them to immediate escape. And the gods of the cities fled for their lives.

The next thing the En.lil did was to warn Abraham of the Negev desert on the border of Sinai and transported him to a place near the Mediterranean coast, close to the Philistines, who sided with the En.lil.

In Lagash, which was Ninurta's capitol, his wife Bau (sister of Ninmah) ran the hospital for human slaves in the city, but she refused to leave when the fallout from the bombs hit, so she died together with them. Nannar, Nammur's son, barely escaped, from thereon suffering from severe radiation injuries, which left him with a bad limp.

It certainly looked like Galzu's prophecy was going to be fulfilled because Babylon was spared, and this was where Marduk declared his supremacy. Also, the En.lil understood that Galzu's predictions were about to come true.

Some of the gods, loyal to the En.lil, left Sumer, accompanied by their followers, to all the four corners of the world, so that the Anunnaki were now operating on all different continents of Earth. Others remained in the neighborhood, ready to challenge the new power, which was Marduk.

Marduk's "extended family" in Northern Sumer, the Aryans, invaded the lands in the east, and Europe to the west, conquering human settlements everywhere, and imposed their Aryan supremacy on them. This is the status up to this very day[262, 263] (we can see that with all the wars and conflicts going on in the world in present time, and we could look at it from a birds-eye view, we would see the same conflicts going on now as in the distant past; same old rivalry: We humans are fighting their wars, unknowingly. Only difference is that the powers behind the scenes are hidden now).

The Enlil Branding His Cattle—YHVH's Chosen People

Of all the slaves loyal to Nammur, the Enlilites and his RAM clan (Ninurta, Nannar, Adad, Utu, and Inanna), only Abraham and his loyalists survived with a lot of help from the En.lil. He wanted his slaves branded as his, like we are branding cattle today.

So, when Abraham was 99 years old, the En.lil (YHVH in Hebrew, or **YeHoVaH**) commanded him and his male followers to cut off their foreskins so they would be clearly branded for Nammur and his sons by having phalluses like those of the Ša.A.M.i. This way the gods could easily recognize their own slaves. After Abraham and his people had all been circumcised, the En.lil told Abraham: "Unto thy seed have I given this land and the brook of Egypt Nile until the River Euphrates."[264] Nammur was clearly telling Abraham that he and his followers were the En.lil's chosen people. The land he gave his chosen people included both that of the Arabs and that of the Israelis, which we will see soon.

And the Axe Was Made of Gold

The En.lil said Abraham would get a son by Sarah, who by the way was his half-sister, and who (by Nibiruan succession practices) would produce a son superseding Ishmael, Abraham's son with his second wife, who was Sarah's Egyptian slave (the ancestors of the Arabs). Sarah gave birth to Isaac (ancestor of the Israelis) in 2025 BCE, in Canaan.

~~Here is where it's getting interes~~ting, although it is all following the

---

[262] Michael Tellinger: *Slave Species of the God, p.116.*

[263] It is uncertain where Tellinger got his information. The Aryans are we humans—particularly as an androgynous species in Tiamat and Atlantis. Also, I am uncertain why the author thinks the Aryans are his "extended family" *WP 2024*).

[264] Zechariah Sitchin (1995): *Divine Encounters, p.288, op. cit.*

Biblical story: Ishmael was raised to become Abraham's heir, to rule over Canaan—at least this was what everybody thought. However, Abraham sentenced Ishmael and his mother to die in the merciless desert, only to make way for Isaac as Abraham's successor.[265] Sarah said to Abraham that he should get rid of the Egyptian slave woman because that woman's son would never be his heir, but her son Isaac would.

The En.lil sided with Sarah. Nammur told Abraham to listen to Sarah because Isaac was going to be his successor. He further said: "I will make the son of the maid servant into a nation also because he is your offspring." And he told Abraham to expel Hagar, Sarah's slave, in person. This was the En.lil's first test to check his slave's loyalty by driving a wedge between him and Hagar. Abraham obeyed without questioning, gave Hagar bread and a skin-bottle of water, and sent her and the child out to wander in the wilderness of Beersheeba.

Once the water was all used, Hagar put Ishmael under a bush. She couldn't let the little boy die. Just when it seemed like the end was near, the En.lil appeared in the desert and showed Hagar to a well, thus saving her and Ishmael, winning her undivided loyalty. From there, Ishmael became the father of the Arabs, whom up to this date are in conflict with the descendants of Isaac for Canaan. The "gods" know how to divide and conquer.

Isaac was the apple in Abraham's eye, and he loved him dearly. The En.lil, noticing this, decided to once again test Abraham's loyalty. He ordered Abraham to lead his son to a distant mountain in the wilderness where no one could see, and murder him, cold-bloodedly. Abraham, who never questioned his "god," obeyed his Lord En.lil, took Isaac, his beloved son, up the mountain and built an altar on which he laid the young boy and bound him. He lifted his arm, which held the knife, ready to slaughter Isaac, when an emissary of the En.lil appears before him and says: "Do not stretch out your hand against the lad, for now I know that your fear god since you have not withheld your son from Me. Because you have not withheld your son, indeed I will greatly bless you and I will greatly multiply your seed and your seed shall possess the gate of their enemies because you have obeyed my Voice."

Christians call themselves, "God-fearing men." Are we surprised?

No knife cut, and no golden axe fell that day,[266] but the axe fell over a large faction of mankind from that very day when we learned to fear "God," as written in the Bible text, and taught in almost every school in the Western world and Israel ever since. Eventually, we are going to tell the story of how this Anunnaki Lord became the "Jealous God."

---

[265] https://www.britannica.com/biography/Hagar-biblical-figure
[266] Leonard Cohen: *Story of Isaac* (1969).

Jacob's Ladder and Jacob Becoming Israel in Egypt

Abraham, in 1907 BCE, as the god-fearing man he was, once again obeyed the Anunnaki Lord's wish and was worried that his son Isaac would marry some local Canaanite so that his bloodline would be diluted. Therefore, he sent his son to Harran on the Euphrates (modern Southern Turkey) to marry daughters to relatives who lived there. Thus, he found Rebecca and brought her back to Canaan. The two got twin sons, Esau, and Jacob.

The twins grew up, and when they reached adulthood, a famine swept over Canaan. Isaac, who wanted to send them to Egypt, were then warned by the En.lil not to cross the still radioactive Sinai to Egypt. Instead, they ordered the brothers to stay in Canaan.

The En.lil was quick to point out that of the twin brothers, he wanted Jacob to be Isaac's successor and was not allowed to take a wife from Canaan. So, again a descendant of Abraham's was sent to Harran to take a wife from a relative to keep the bloodline pure. This time a daughter of Isaac's maternal uncle Leban was in mind.

In biblical times, people often had "visions" in their dreams, seeing "angels" (read Anunnaki "gods"), telling them what to do, and what not to do. This was especially common in people whom the Anunnaki cared for, the human Elite, who were of the purest Anunnaki bloodline. Jacob was no exception, and on his way north to Harran he had a vision of angels from the Elohim, something that in the Bible became known as "Jacob's Ladder."

Once in Harran, Jacob wanted to marry Leban's daughter, Rachael, but Leban first wanted him to marry her elder sister, Leah, and earn their dowries. Jacob worked twenty years for Leban, before he was allowed to take a second wife, Leban's younger daughter, Rachael. Jacob then wanted to return back home to Canaan, but in another dream, one of the Nammur's messengers forbade them to return. He also warned Leban in another dream to let Jacob and his two wives go.

Jacob went anyway, and when he reached the Jordan River at the Yabbok Crossing, uncertain of what Esau's attitude would be to see his rival for succession, he sent his party ahead and stayed behind for a while.

Once alone, Jacob encountered and wrestled with a Nibiruan angel and dislocated his thigh in the furious battle. However, he won the fight, and pinned and held the Anunnaki all night. Next day, he let the "angel" go if he promised to bless him, which he did.

The angel renamed Jacob "Israel," or IS.RA.EL. (he who fought a god). The two departed, and Israel limped into Esau's camp, became the patriarch of En.lil's loyalists, and his tribe became "The Children of Israel" (or "The Tribe of Israel," *WP 2024*).

Figure 12.1: Amenemhet III

Joseph, born in 1870 BC, Israel's and Rachael's youngest son, was hated by their half-brothers, whom Israel had with Leah, because of his obsessions with dreams and his interpretations of them. To get rid of him, they sold him to a caravan as a slave. From there, they brought Joseph to Egypt.

In Egypt, Joseph was bought by the Pharaoh's court as a household slave. After had spent some time in prison due to being falsely accused by the wife of his direct slaveholder to have raped her, Pharaoh Amenemhet III, who ascended the throne of Egypt in 1842 BCE, heard the rumors of Joseph's ability to interpret dreams, so he asked for the slave to come before his court.

The Pharaoh had had a dream about seven skinny cows eating seven fat cows and seven scorched ears of grain eating seven healthy grains. He asked Joseph to interpret the dream.

Joseph told him that this meant that Egypt would experience seven years of plentiful harvest and seven years of famine. The Pharaoh was very impressed, and in 1840 BCE, he made Joseph the Overseer of Egypt. His job was to store water and grain from the seven good years to use for the seven lean ones.

Just as Joseph had predicted, drought and famine broke out in Egypt seven years later, and refugees from elsewhere headed for Egypt, where the food was. Amongst the refugees were Joseph's own father, Israel (now 130 years old) and his sons, including the half-brothers of Josephs', who had sold him as a slave.

Joseph forgave his half-brothers, and thus invited the Children of Israel to Egypt.

For 400 years, the Children of Israel and their descendants prospered and multiplied and became 600,000 in numbers, and a new regime arose, hostile to the Enlilites with whom the Children of Israel were allied, and they took power.

The Enlilites against the Enkiites of Egypt and Babylon

The internal fights for power, bloodline domination, and an immature obsession to control others between the different factions of the Anunnaki royalty, cost the lives of hundreds of thousands of human soldiers over the course of a few hundred years to come. And of course, the same Anunnaki rulers of their clans, respectively, survived it all, and most of them are alive and well up to this date. But, as I said, their human slaves were not that fortunate.

Figure 12.2: Dr. Sasha Lessin

In this next section below, I am going to directly quote Dr. Sasha Lessin of U.C.L.A., who holds a Ph.D. in anthropology. He has in general been to great help in compressing all the wealth of information written in the books of the late Zechariah Sitchin. Here is Dr. Lessin, word by word:

Marduk gave Hammurabi, his king at Babylon "a powerful weapon, called "Great Power of Marduk," with which he subdued all Mesopotamia, save the Enlilite strongholds of Adad in Assyria and Ninurta in Lagash. In the 12th Century B.C., the Assyrians, led by King Tiglat-Pileser I, conquered Lebanon.

In the 9th century B.C., Adad and Nergal sent the Assyrian king Shalmaneser III with technologically-advanced artillery against Marduk's Babylonians. With these weapons, Shalmaneser prevailed. Then, in 689 B C. Sennacherib, using, this time, "rocketlike missiles" Adad gave him, sacked Babylon on the pretext that the Babylonians had disappointed Marduk, their erstwhile god. Sennacherib sentenced the Babylonians to seventy years of Assyrian occupation and domination.

Commander Enlil watched Assyria's Sennacherib subjugate Phoenicia, Gaza and Judea.

But Sennacherib--on his own without knowledge of authorization of his Nibiran handlers--attacked Jerusalem. Enlil controlled Mission Control Jerusalem. He zapped the his erstwhile Assyrian slave army with a techno-weapon that killed 185,000 men. Sennacherib fled back to Nineva in Sumer, where he declared his younger son Esarhaddon, his successor.

Sennacherib's older sons killed the King, but the Nibirans hid Esarhaddon. Enlil sent Inanna to Assyria. She disarmed the Ninevan army and destroyed their weapons. Esarhaddon rules, she proclaimed.

Inanna continued protecting Assyria. She losed "an intense, blinding brilliance" on her headgear to blind Enemies of Esarhaddon's successor, Ashurbanipal both in battles in Arabia and in an attack on Marduk's Egyptian forces. Inanna "rained flames upon Arabia."

Enlil decided to end Assyrian power. He let Babylonians conquer Assyria from 614-616 B.C. and sent Babylon's king Nebuchadnezzar II to take Lebanon.[267]

YHVH—the Brutal Mass Murderer, and his Hatchet-man Moses

In this part, I am going to use direct Bible quotes on occasion, to show the character of the En.lil, a.k.a. YHVH, God of the Israelites. Rarely, if ever, have we seen a character in the last 500,000 years of Earth history who has slaughtered more people than this entity alone. Forget Hitler, or any so-called dictator that we know from history books, or from present time events. These people are/were children-at-play in comparison--in fact, can't be compared at all. (And this is the God of Israel, and also the Christian God. If we don't break this "godspell" very soon, humanity is

---

[267] Dr. Sasha Lessin, *Enki Speaks, Essay 45: Enlilite Power Grows Against Enkiite Egypt and Babylon.*

going to be in deep trouble).[268]

In 1650 BC, new rulers, who became the pharaohs of the New Kingdom, conquered Egypt. Pharaoh Thutmose I of this new regime invaded Mesopotamia to the Euphrates River, which was the En.lil's domain. Here was also where Abraham's relatives and their descendants lived. Thutmose expected the Enlilites to strike back, and he feared the Israelites in Egypt, who had grown, as we know, to the large number of 600,000. Hypothetically, they could take Egypt from within.

The Middle-Kingdom of Egypt, which proceeded the New Kingdom, had promised to honor the Israelites and allow them to stay in Egypt, thanks to Joseph's abilities to save Egypt from seven years of famine and drought. However, the new regime decided to cancel the agreement. Consequently, Thutmose I started working The Children of Israel to death and stopped them from breeding. He commanded that every newborn Israelite male should be killed at birth.

To save their newborn son, a couple descended from Israel put the boy in a box and let it float down the stream where Thutmose's daughter took a bath. She gave him the name Moses and decided to adopt him. This happened in 1513 BCE.

Moses grew up, and in 1482 BCE, while Thutmose III intensified hostilities against the Enlilites outside Egypt and the Israelites within, Moses killed an Egyptian overseer who was brutalizing Israelites. The Pharaoh put a death warrant on Moses, who managed to escape to the Sinai peninsula, where he married the daughter of a Priest.

When Thutmose III died and Amenhotep II took over as the Pharaoh, he let the death warrant on Moses expire. YHVH showed himself to Moses as a burning bush and told him to go to Egypt and show his magical powers to the Pharaoh, so he would free the Israelites.

Moses obeyed and went back to Egypt. However, Amenhotep II was not too impressed with Moses' sorcery. On the contrary, the Pharaoh decided to triple the work burden for the Israelites. YHVH decided to have the Pharaoh abide by using other means. He therefore engineered a series of plagues, infestations, cattle diseases, three days of darkness, and weather abnormalities (akin to today's HAARP), followed by the murder of all non-Israelite firstborn children and cows in Egypt—a payback for the previous Pharaoh's decision to kill off any first-born Israelite male.

This did the trick, and in 1433 BC, the Pharaoh let the Israelites go.

However, when the mass exodus from Egypt started, Amenhotep

---

[268] Interestingly, as my own research progressed, the reader will see in the Second, Fourth, and Fifth Levels of Learning that he who was portrayed as the En.lil/YHVH in the Bible and ancient text was none less than Marduk, who most certainly also dictated these texts to the scribes. Also see my book, *The Story of Isis and the War on Bloodlines* (2024), available at Amazon.com. *WP 2024.*

noticed that they seemed to be trapped between the desert's edge and the lakes (then the Red Sea), so the Pharaoh sent his chariots to re-capture Moses and his people.

YHVH then used technology to divide the sea so the Israelites could cross, but when the Egyptians followed, he closed the opening and drowned Amenhotep's soldiers.

YHVH then led his people to the edge of the Sinai peninsula. He gave them food and protected them from enemies. In addition, he had the Israelites kill 3,000 people for refusing to declare exclusive loyalty to him, and 23,000 Israelites for having premarital sex.[269] Such "crime" was reserved for the promiscuous gods, only, apparently.

YHVH had the Israelites walk through the desert for forty years, until they encamped at the foot of Mt. Sinai.

The Ten Commandments and a Blood-Thirsty God

When they all had encamped by Mt. Sinai, YHVH commanded Moses up the mount. Once there, the Anunnaki god told Moses what his rules would be from thereon out to successfully obey him.

The Israelites all agreed to the terms. YHVH landed on the top of the mount, where Moses was waiting and spoke with an amplifier to the crowd at the bottom of the mount.

He told them that he, YHVH, was their only God, and no one of the 600,000 people were ever again allowed to speak the name of any other god. He further spoke out all the Ten Commandments with a full and loud voice. Although many people still know them today by heart, since we had them imbued in our childhood, I am going to repeat them all here. Many of them are good rules to follow—just common sense—but we need to remember that they were forced upon the people with the sole intention to have the crowd more easily manipulated and controlled.

My comments are in **bold** and within parentheses:

1. You shall have no other gods before Me (**sets the stage for Commandment #2**)

2. You shall not make for yourself a carved image—any likeness of anything that is in heaven above, or that is in the earth beneath, or that is in the water under the earth (for he is a jealous god and he will punish the children for the iniquity of their parents, to the third to the fourth generation of those who reject him. For those

---

[269] *Exodus 32:26-28; Corinthians 10:8.*

who love him and follow his commandments, the jealous god will love their ancestors down to the 1,000th generation. **(Remember that these Commandments are still in use and valid in the eyes of the "gods," up to this day, and when they return, they count on that you obey them, or this Commandment 2 will apply).**

3. You shall not take the name of the LORD your God in vain (God will not acquit anybody who misuses his name)

4. Remember the Sabbath day, to keep it holy (For six days you shall labor and do all your work. But the seventh day is a Sabbath to the Lord your God; you shall not do any work—you, your son or your daughter, your male or female slave, your livestock, or the alien resident in your towns. For in six days the Lord made heaven and earth, the sea, and all that is in them, but rested the seventh day; therefore the Lord blessed the Sabbath day and consecrated it. **(Perfect way of making sure people know whom they worship. This is YHVH's unique rule, and when followed, he can see who his follower is and who is not)**

5. Honor your father and your mother **(normally good advice, but also a way to make sure the children listen to their parents, so the worship continues down the generations)**

6. You shall not murder **(only reserved for god and the other gods, whom you are not allowed to mention)**

7. You shall not commit adultery **(see comment on Commandment 6)**

8. You shall not steal **(see comment on Commandment 6)**

9. You shall not bear false witness against your neighbor **(again, good advice, but here used to keep the sheep in their fold. As little conflicts as possible makes it easier for "God")**

---

[270] These Commandments are the ones used in Exodus 20:2–17, and not in Deuteronomy 5:6–21, who are similar, but differ slightly in wording.

10. You shall not covet your neighbor's house; you shall not covet
your neighbor's wife, nor his male servant, nor his female servant,
nor his ox, nor his donkey, nor anything that is your neighbor's
(**see comment on Commandment 9**)[270]

The "god" also declared that he wanted women and children
subjugated to male family heads, setting the stage for today's Patriarchal
society.

YHVH had prepared stone tablets to give to Moses. They were
inscribed on both sides, emphasizing his Commandments. For forty days,
up on the mount, YHVH showed Moses how to build a temple—he even
showed him a scale model. He also gave Moses a model of the box—the
Ark of the Covenant—to put the stone tablets in. The Ark also had,
beneath the tablets, a receiver (sporting 2 gold cherubs), so the Israelites
could "voice-message" him and get his "Yes" or "No" answers. He
appointed Moses' son Aaron and his sons as Priests (magicians) and
specified protective clothing they needed to wear when they approached
the Ark to avoid radiation poisoning. However, man is curious, and later
on, people couldn't help themselves but trying to look to see what was in
the Ark. For this "high crime," YHVH killed 50,000 people in
Bethshemesh.[271]

Aaron was deeply worried about his brother, who'd been up on the
mount for over a month, and feared he was dead, so he tried to attract the
Anunnaki's attention by building a golden calf, a symbol of the
En.lil/YHVH, to send out a signal to him, as he dared not go up and see.
But when Moses finally came down, he got infuriated over the calf, so he
killed the builders, and in his rage destroyed both the calf and the stone
tablets (in his effort to have his people follow the 2nd Commandment,
Moses instead broke the 6th Commandment, something that's rarely talked
about within religious groups).

YHVH raged as well and threatened to abandon the Israelites.
However, after a while, he "cooled his jets" (pun intended) and produced a
"pillar of cloud" in front of Moses' tent, and from a spaceship (called a
"Kabod") inside the cloud, YHVH broadcast that he forgave the Israelites
for the calf and told Moses to engrave new tablets. Apparently, he was not
at all angry at Moses for having destroy his carefully designed stone tablets
and killed some of his own people. Instead, he gently told him to create
new ones. It was apparently also a non-issue that Moses played "God" and
broke the Sixth Commandment. It took Moses an additional forty days to

---

[271] 1 Samuel 6:19 (there are other versions of what the Ark of the Covenant *really*
was/is, and one of them, which seems quite plausible, will be discussed in my
forthcoming papers in the "Second Level of Learning").

create new tablets, spending that time together with YHVH on the mount. During all these days, Moses was not allowed to see his God's face. When he returned to his men, Moses glowed with radiation from being exposed to YHVH's shuttlecraft.

Moses died, perhaps because of the effects of radiation, and his general, Joshua, who had YHVH's knowledge of astronomical events and weapons, conquered much of Canaan for YHVH, immediately breaking Commandment 6 with his God's blessings. To aid in the process, YHVH killed 120,000 men and enslaved 200,000 women and children. While he was at it, and his adrenaline was still working on overload, he also had 1 million Ethiopians murdered for god measures. Altogether, YHVH, with his horrible techno-weapons and engineered plagues, killed 10,000 Canaanites and Perizzites, and 10,000 Moabites.[272]

The defenders of YHVH often say that the people he killed were "evil," and that they deserved it. That, to me, does not resonate at all. Even when some of the pharaohs acted out on the Israelites, they repeated what the Anunnaki had given them in form of genes (DNA), and not the least, from the "gods" own behavior: destructive action → revenge → destructive action → worse revenge, in an endless, immature (to the extreme) cycle. What kind of beings are they? I am not justifying what some of us humans did and do under the influence of these immature gods, but I am just saying there are logical explanations. The genes which include traits like murder, rape, revenge, jealousy, and more, would most not be dominant traits in many people on Earth if it wasn't for them. Some people still look up to these gods, but for what reason? Here on Earth, today, there are millions of people who are much more advanced than they are in the sense of maturity and spiritual development. Hold your heads high, humans, because every day most of us are doing good deeds for self and for others, *in spite* of the negative and degraded genes that were implanted into us. This shows we have something very admirable, honorable and desirable— we have strong, loving hearts! And this we can't thank the Anunnaki for. We are who we are (when at our best) in spite of them. What we have is Spirit, something they lack.

But have faith, people of Earth who have been waiting; this merciful "god" and all his merry fellows are soon coming back to spread their enlightenment and blessings over us. *God Help Us!* (well, I'm sure they won't).

---

[272] Judges 1:4, 3:28-29; Michael Tellinger (2006), *Slave Species of God, p. 173-191.*

PAPER 13:
DISCUSSING THE ANUNNAKI PAPERS
by Wes Penre, Sunday, April 24, 2011

Abstract

Before you start reading this paper, you either need to know Zecharia Sitchin's work pretty well already or have studied my previous papers on the Anunnaki. If not, this essay will not make much sense, because the discussion herein is mainly about conclusions, questions, and comments around Sitchin's work, and the significance of the Anunnaki influence on our human past, present and future. So, if you haven't studied this subject previously, I strongly suggest you get familiar with it before you continue any further.

The Accuracy of the Sumerian Cuneiform Clay Tablets

The first thing we need to understand when we read Sitchin's work is that he translated the Sumerian tablets into modern language, drew his conclusions and found coherency. That's all he could do. The tablets were written some 5-6000 years ago in some cases, by the end of the era of the Anunnaki's 450,000 years reign, or more, on Earth.

The Sumerians wrote down what was happening to them in their own lifetime and few generations back, getting it fairly accurate. However, anything that goes further back than that is hearsay. In other words, it was told to them by the Anunnaki themselves. It means that it could be altered to fit the gods. After all, they wanted to make sure that humans respected them and followed their orders. Human scribes wrote most of the tablets, if not all. History is always written by the winner, and the winners glorify themselves and badmouth the beaten enemy, making history largely inaccurate and/or distorted. Anything is possible here, so please keep your mind very open when you continue reading.[273]

Much of the information the Sumerians relied on, besides what the gods told them face to face, were the teachings that came from Ea's secret society, *The Brotherhood of the Snake* (or *The Brotherhood of the Serpent*). This first secret society on Earth is the father of all secret societies that followed, and albeit we may not always know what the secrets are at the top of organizations such as Freemasonry, the OTO, the Rosicrucian's, etc., we can safely presume most of them have to do with the ancient gods, their knowledge in magic, the structure of the Universe (as they knew it), and the return of the gods. The information has been passed down through all these generations.

There is way too much evidence in Sitchin's and other similar researcher's work to discard them as fables. Other such researchers that should be mentioned are William Bramley, Erich von Däniken, Robert Morning Sky, Andrew Thomas, Maurice Chatelain, Harold T. Wilkins, Peter Kolosimo, Serge Hutin, W. Raymond Drake, and Jacques Vallee. Albeit, Sitchin has his debunkers, such as Mike Heiser,[274] when all is said and done, Sitchin's work still has legitimacy. Some of what Sitchin claimed happened in the past has been verified by modern archeologists. Besides, they also correspond, and build upon, other ancient, sacred scriptures, including the Bible. His work is also backed up by most metaphysical sources through channeling and by other means.

However, the Sumerian Scriptures are telling only parts of the story, and are concentrating on certain areas of the planet, such as Mesopotamia, Egypt, South America, South Africa, Babylon etc. And like we mentioned earlier, it's all from an Anunnaki perspective.

Another reason to give credit to Sitchin's work is because the gods are still here. I have already mentioned the LPG-C being is in direct contact with the Nibiruans, but they are not the only ones. There are more people who have had face-to-face (Close Encounter of the 5th Kind) with these beings, something we are also going to cover in depth later on.

Dr. Michael Heiser, Sitchin's Main Debunker

Just about everyone who is bringing some significant information out to the public have their debunkers. So does Sitchin, of course.

The most "famous" of these debunker is perhaps Dr. Michael Heiser at http://sitchiniswrong.com. He has dedicated a whole website to debunk Sitchin and is also traveling around, holding lectures on this subject and

---

[273] I rewrote this paragraph for the book. Please see the original paper at wespenre.com for the originally worded paragraph *WP 2024*.
[274] http://www.sitchiniswrong.com/

others.

Dr. Heiser is a linguist and claims that Sitchin's translations of the Sumerian cuneiform tablets are utterly wrong. Nowhere, says Heiser, is there any indication that the old Sumerians were talking about a 12th Planet or an alien race. He says that he is an expert in this language and knows what he is talking about. Of course, someone who doesn't speak the old Sumerian language can't verify whether he's correct or not, even when he's showing his "evidence."

I'm not going to spend much time explaining what Dr. Heiser is talking about—you can check it out on his website if you like. One thing he claims is that Sitchin has made it all up like some kind of science-fiction novel. This is of course untrue, and often Heiser doesn't seem to know what he's talking about (at worst), or he is not a linguist at all and has made wild guesses, putting his own story together that "seemed to fit" without any credible evidence. When met with criticism, he often gets quite upset and is not convincingly managing to hold his position.[275]

When Dr. Bordon became aware of Dr. Heiser's debunking attempts, he emailed him the following response as a comment to Heiser's research. Heiser, of course, never replied:

EMAIL TO MIKE HEISER, 16 May 2011

Good afternoon, Mike. Just visited your blog (The Naked Bible/Eschatology
http://michaelsheiser.com/TheNakedBible/eschatology-discussion/). Took the time to read everything you have here, on your other site, The Facade, and borrowed a copy of your dissertation which I also carefully and thoughtfully read.

After some careful consideration of what Sitchin said and did (and the "scholarship" with which he treated us through his Earth Chronicles) and the rebuttals you regaled us all in your websites which you so ably established sound basis in your dissertation, I came to realize two things: (1) the Nibiru phenomenon is that, a phenomenon that has become quite a meme in our culture as your stance and the people sharing their views and feelings on your sites indicate; indeed, throughout the world, and (2) the scholarship that supports or denies the reality of the phenomenon is Biblical and sumero-egyptologic—a fact that makes both sides (yours and Sitchin's) open to claims that both are based upon (a) an interpretation of the historical record, (b) a matter of expertise in ancient near eastern languages, and (c) conclusions, being what they

---

[275] The paragraph that follows in the original papers has been removed because of an inaccuracy in its content. Please see the original paper to view the missing paragraph.

are (hypothetical written "pictures" or models of a phenomenon), can be again highly interpretive of the records treated as data supporting a view through the prism used by the interpreter: Sitchin says "it is," and you say "it isn't."

But the story does not end there. There is, as they say, a "door number 3." This door is the one through which, wittingly or unwittingly, willingly or forced by circumstances, I am walking into this phenomenon.

This is the door opened by experiencers who have come in contact with so-called Annunakis. In my case, it occurred when I was ten or eleven in South America, on the Parana River between Brazil and Paraguay, while fishing with my father northeast of Encarnacion, Paraguay. He and I were "picked up" by a triangular six-man craft and, while my father was kept sedated via interesting nonbiomedical means, I was not.

This was the first of three encounters with the same individual who lead the first group on the Parana, and have since assisted the small scientific cooperative that LPG-C has been since the early '90s with very advanced scientific information and the technology with which to get our own by the same, or similar means, they have for apparent eaons. They called it the "brilliance," according to Sitchin; we were more mundane in the naming, referring to it as simply "the tank." We've been at it since 1998, when the first of two prototypes were completed, tested, and much to our amazement, found it to work exceeding all of our expectations. The results have been cumuli of information about how nature is and how nature works, from the infinite to the infinitesimal, and presented in some detail and with an historical sense of order on our new and improved website at http://www.lifephysicsgroup.org. To wit: we are in process of miniaturizing the key aspects of this apparatus, such that it could be used by qualified scientists wishing to explore the same Nature we did.

Oh, the surprises that await them.

And we are not the only experiencers of these who call themselves Sa.a.mi. and you and Sitchin know as Annunaki and fit the bill in appearance for the ancient Annunaki and/or Nephilim (the latter seeming human-Annunaki hybrids). There are others, and there are also others who are quietly pursuing face-to-face benevolent contact with "giants" in several places (South America, southern Africa, and the Mideast).

In a larger context, there is also an exopolitical framework which is impinged upon by the past (and which is the reason we now all need not scholarship proving one view or another, but rather a model of what we as humans face today and must literally face within 50 to 70 years from now).

Whether or not Nibiru is a star or a planet or a comet, all of that is splitting hair. The IRAS pictures did not lie, and the current South Pole Telescope data is showing the incoming as being quite real, and incidentally, proving Jim McCanney's contentions out to be more certain that any fiction I could write (and have written) about. No, Mike, this is not fable, and it is not prehistory.

Let me close this unexpectedly longer note than I intended by simply asking (1) whether or not you've ever experienced a face to face presence with one of these creatures, and (2) what would you do if you could?

Kind regards,

A.R. BORDON

Bordon also posted a slight variant of the above email on the same date, May 16, 2011, in Heiser's comment section. Bordon sent this in 2001 and is still waiting for a response: http://michaelsheiser.com/TheNakedBible/eschatology-discussion/.[276]

What About Atlantis and Lemuria?

I need to bring Atlantis and Lemuria into the picture as well. These two ancient civilizations were not mentioned in the previous Anunnaki Papers, and they are not mentioned in Sitchin's work, either, in those terms. This doesn't mean that those civilizations did not exist; they did. According to the Pleiadians, the Old Testament of the Bible (the story before the Flood) is all about Atlantis. They say the Flood actually was the catastrophe that ended it and drowned the whole continent. But how does this interrelate with the Anunnaki and Mesopotamia?

The Pleiadians say on different accounts that Poseidon was the first ruler of Atlantis. They also say (and we know) that Poseidon and Ea (the Enki) are the same being; he was Ea in Mesopotamia, Poseidon in Greece, Ptah in Egypt, and Neptune in Rome; they are all the same deity.[277] They also say Poseidon had Pleiadians connections.[278] This does not correspond with Sitchin's work, but it does with researchers such as Robert Morning Sky and others, including myself, as I've pointed out in previous papers. A

---

[276] This has since been taken down by Dr. Heiser.

[277] Here is another example of the En.ki giving his side of the story. He was not the ruler of Atlantis, Prince En.lil and the Orions were (see my later work). Poseidon/Neptune played a big role in the entire Atlantis Era, but he was not the ruler *WP 2024*.

[278] I had this confirmed from another reliable source as well. So I have it from a few different, unrelated sources *WP 2024*.

faction of the early Pleiadians came back to Earth and supported the Anunnaki in their effort to genetically manipulate mankind.

In Sitchin's books it sounds like Earth is the only planet the Ša.A.M.i. visited, and they can do so because it's close to Earth every 3,600 years (one šar). However, this species is not stuck in 3-D and can travel interdimensionally and are using stargates and Einstein-Rosen Bridges to go from one point in the universe to another. This is the most fundamental way of traveling through long distances in space/time. The Ša.A.M.i. are a warrior and a conquering race, and they have invaded other planets, both before and after Earth, as we shall see in the *Second Level of Learning.*"

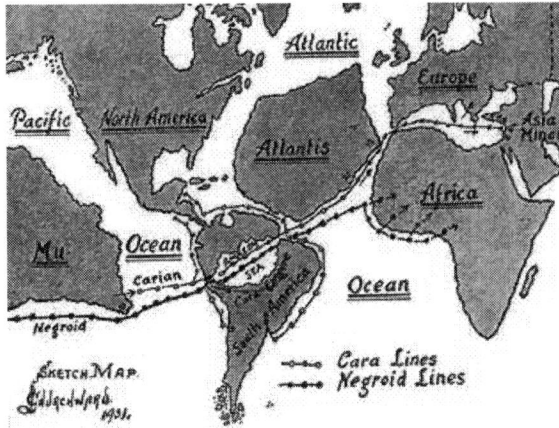

Figure 13.1: Old world map, including Atlantis and Lemuria (Mu) source: James Chruchward

In a sense, though, Sitchin did *not* exclude Atlantis and Lemuria (Mu) from his writings; he just didn't mention them by name because the Sumerians didn't—it was a term coined by Plato. They never called them Atlantis and Lemuria. The Pleiadians are most probably right when they say the Old Testament is actually describing Atlantis, although the time frame is confusing. Atlantis went under around 11,500 BC, which corresponds with the Deluge. However, Sitchin's *Earth Chronicles* concentrate almost exclusively on Mesopotamia, Babylon, North- and South Africa, and South America. But what happened in other parts of the world? And were there landmasses in the Atlantic and the Pacific which correspond with Atlantis and Mu? The answer would be a confirmative "yes!" How do we know? Because ruins of these cities and cultures are being found deep under the oceans. It makes sense that these civilizations died with the Flood. Were the Anunnaki in charge of these two lost continents? It seems so.

5. The Mars Findings

In 2007, Sitchin was pointing at new startling features discovered on Mars, which supports Sitchin's research regarding Alalu being buried there beneath the big face on Mars, carved out in his features.[279] The following article was released by *Scientific American*:

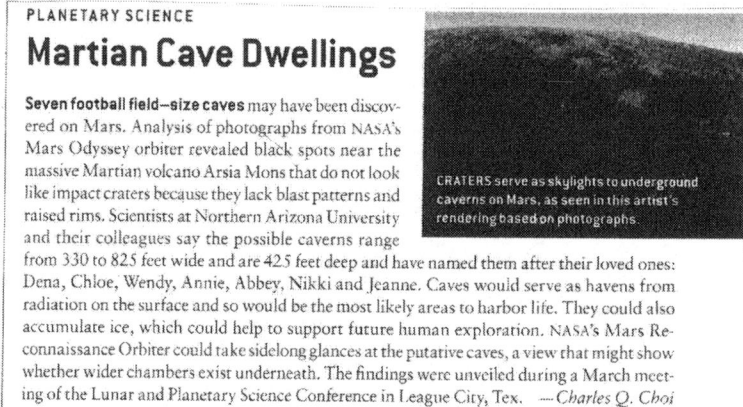

PLANETARY SCIENCE

Martian Cave Dwellings

Seven football field–size caves may have been discovered on Mars. Analysis of photographs from NASA's Mars Odyssey orbiter revealed black spots near the massive Martian volcano Arsia Mons that do not look like impact craters because they lack blast patterns and raised rims. Scientists at Northern Arizona University and their colleagues say the possible caverns range from 330 to 825 feet wide and are 425 feet deep and have named them after their loved ones: Dena, Chloe, Wendy, Annie, Abbey, Nikki and Jeanne. Caves would serve as havens from radiation on the surface and so would be the most likely areas to harbor life. They could also accumulate ice, which could help to support future human exploration. NASA's Mars Reconnaissance Orbiter could take sidelong glances at the putative caves, a view that might show whether wider chambers exist underneath. The findings were unveiled during a March meeting of the Lunar and Planetary Science Conference in League City, Tex. —*Charles Q. Choi*

CRATERS serve as skylights to underground caverns on Mars, as seen in this artist's rendering based on photographs.

Figure 13.2: Martian Cave Dwellings

On the subject of the Face on Mars, Sitchin wrote in *The Lost Book of Enki* in 2004 that the face marked the burial place of King Alalu, and the big face with a carved astronaut's helmet covered a cave where the king was buried, and still probably is, up to this day.

The existence of the big caverns on Mars, topped by shaped rock structures was first written about by Sitchin in 2004, *three years prior to NASA's discoveries, or at least, revealed them.*

Sitchin wrote to NASA, who had said in public that they were looking for water on Mars to prove that bacteria exists on the planet, saying, *"where there is water there could be life."* Sitchin replied:

"To conclude that bacteria might have existed on Mars" (a possibility that would be indicated by the existence of water), I further wrote in my Letter, "will hardly excite the public; what would be exciting and highly significant for mankind's past and future would be to find evidence of intelligent life—beings like us—on Mars. The ancient Sumerians asserted so in their texts inscribed on clay tablets.

Mariner photographs from the 1970's show possible remains of

[279] http://www.bibliotecapleyades.net/sitchin/esp_sitchin_22.htm

artificial structures (to leave aside the famed Face). To send rovers to find bacterial evidence rather than verify evidence for intelligent beings on Mars, e.g. in the Cydonia region, is a red-herring cover-up."[280]

This letter was of course not published by NASA or any other media outlet. Sitchin continues:

But the question remains; Why had NASA persistently avoided on-site examination of the Cydonia area?

In Genesis Revisited (1990) I reproduced a series of NASA's own photographs, including photo 035-A-72 (Plate "E" in the book) that captured a panoramic view of Cydonia.

There, clearly, the camera captured a rock carved to look like a human face, of a male wearing a helmet (plate "F" in the book) and the remains of walled structures, with two walls forming a right angle (plate "G" in the book).

Other NASA photographs reproduced in the book showed a lake shore, a water channel outfitted with piers, the remains of a pentagonal structure, of roads leading to elongated buildings.[281]

The photographs Mr. Sitchin is talking about are the following:

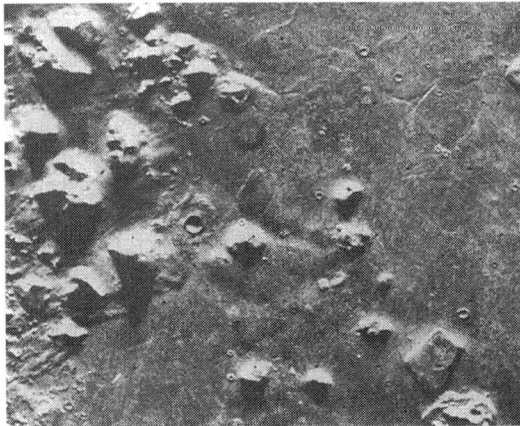

Figure 13.3a: Cydonia -- The Face on Mars and the environs

---

[280] ibid. op. cit.
[281] ibid. op. cit.

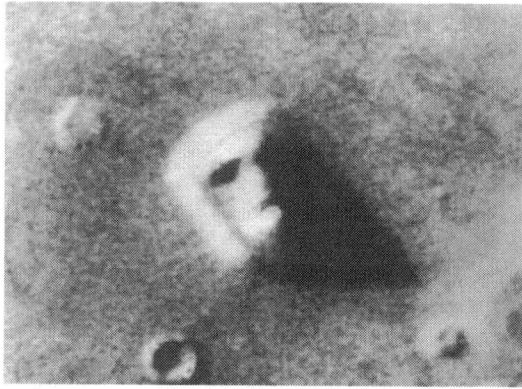

Figure 13.3b: The Face on Mars (close up)

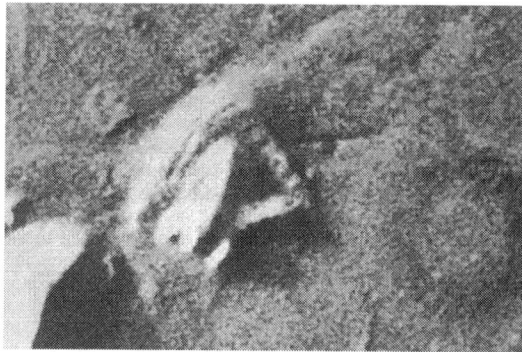

Figure 13.3c: Right angle building structure on Mars

Sitchin continues:

> While in my writings and lectures I emphasized the structural evidence, it was the Face that captured the interest and imagination of various individuals and groups. NASA, on its part, ignored all the evidences in its subsequent missions, focusing instead on geology. It was only as a result of a public outcry that NASA finally directed an orbiter, *Mars Pathfinder*, to take a look at the Face—but only after a dust storm that covered most of the planet, and after fiddling electronically with the photographs to end up with *a fuzzy picture*.
>
> (Some of the serious work to uncover the distortions was done by the *Meta Research Institute* under the leadership of the astronomer Thomas Van Flandern).
>
> Yet, now distorted or not, the fact remains that the unusual rock is still there, and that it clearly showed a human-like face in the 1970's photographs.

My conclusions were and still are that intelligent beings akin to us had been to Mars thousands of years ago. The Sumerians knew who they were: The same <u>Anunnaki from Nibiru</u> who had come to Earth and maintained a way-station on Mars.[282]

Shortly after I'd completed this paper, I noticed that Dr. John Brandenburg just released a new book called, *Life and Death on Mars—The New Mars Synthesis*. The synopsis is telling. Here is Sitchin again:

Figure13. 4: Cover of Life and Death on Mars by Dr. Brandenburg.

I spoke with John Brandenburg, PhD, who was kind enough to send me a copy of his new book. He has gathered scientific information, mythology, astronomy, and history in a book about the planet Mars that is so completely entertaining that the reader almost forgets the premise of the author—that everything we thought we knew about Mars is wrong. Mars was actually Earthlike for most of its geologic history and held a massive and evolving biosphere much earlier than Earth. Mars cooled and developed millions of years earlier than Earth with oceans and rivers. **Mars was then wracked by a mysterious and astonishing nuclear catastrophe** *Wes' emphasis. This corresponds with the Ra Material, that both Mars and Maldek were destroyed by nuclear weapons, not by being hit by Nibiru moons (in Maldek's case), or by an electromagnetic catastrophe due to another Nibiru passing (in Mars' case).* We are, biologically and culturally, the children of Mars. We could even be a colony of Mars.

The new Mars synthesis goes boldly where no human has gone

---

[282] *ibid. op. cit.*

before.' On many pages of this book that begins with ancient Egyptian and other culture's perception of the red planet, named for Mars the God of War, and progresses in a well-written way to our current discoveries that were initiated by the investigation of a meteorite from Mars that fell into Egypt in 1928.

What makes Brandenburg's book such a fine read is the manner in which he succinctly traces the history of man from ancient days through the Cold War and the concurrent exploration of space to the photographs of the planet Mars taken by our spacecraft. In the middle of the book are beautiful color photographs of the surface of Mars and its surroundings.

But the drama of Brandenburg's book is his discussion of the nuclear catastrophe that turned the once 'earthlike' planet into a wasteland - going so far as to discuss why we earthlings are biologically and culturally the children of Mars! All of this is so well written that it reads like a novel—and makes the reader wonder if the book is based on the famous Orson Welles 1938 radio show 'The War of the Worlds" that terrified the nation. But the fanciful ideas in this book are followed by scientific data that describe findings on Mars that support Brandenburg's ideas. In the end the author emphasizes that if we are indeed the children of Mars then we should learn lessons from the past and live life more attuned to the possibilities of nuclear annihilation and take preventive measures. Note: I will be talking about Mars at the MUFON symposium using some of Dr. John Brandenburg's excellent data. As John states, "Mars is the forgotten front of Ufology".[283]

As a last note on Mars for now, both L. Ron Hubbard (around 1952)[284] and the Pleiadians[285] have said there were bases on Mars, both used as implant stations (Hubbard), and genetic engineering to a large extent (Pleiadians). So, there may have been more happening on Mars than even Sitchin was aware of.

The Frequency Prison

In the Sumerian cuneiform tablets, they say the gods were always afraid we were going to challenge them. Therefore, they didn't want to give us either from the Tree of Knowledge or the Tree of Life; the reason being that if humans were given from the Tree of Knowledge, they might want to

---

[283] Filer's File #19—2011.
[284] Hubbard. L. Ron, 1952: *A History of Man.*
[285] Barbara Marciniak channeling "The Pleiadians."

figure out the Tree of Life. As soon as someone made the least efforts in this direction, the gods immediately interfered.

Reptilians and Giants

We have discussed earlier whether the Anunnaki were Reptilians or humanoids, so we are not going to go into details now, in particular, but there are a few more thoughts on this worth mentioning because in an upcoming paper, my interview with Michael Lee Hill will tell the story in which he claims to have met with Anunnaki, who could evidently shapeshift from human to reptilian form. I happened to stumble upon something in the Ra Material the other day, which may tie into this.[286] The collective consciousness of hyperversals, calling themselves Ra, are giving another plausible answer to the reptilian question in one of the channeling sessions.[287] They say the Anunnaki had an encounter with the Orions while they were still here on Earth, genetically manipulating mankind. They came here, and, among other things, mated with the Anunnaki to create a larger and stronger race, which was intended to become the new rulers of Planet Earth. The offspring became what Ra calls the "Anak," which of course is the same as the Anakim,[288] who were giants—half reptilian and half hominid. These Titans then fought a war against the ruling Anunnaki in an attempt to take over.[289] According to the Sumerians, these Titans didn't all look the same. Breeding Orion Reptilians with hominid Anunnaki resulted in weird mutated offspring. Some giants had six toes and six fingers, others had three or more arms, others had even weirder distortions.[290] However, there are those saying that some of the Anunnaki had six toes and fingers too, as did other giants, not related to this hybrid group.

Sitchin mentions these hybrids as well, but vaguely says that these giants were mistakes in the Anunnaki's genetic experiments, but he doesn't mention the Orion connection, probably because it was not clearly noted in the tablets.

One thing to remember in our thirst for knowledge is that, to expand our consciousness, it's not necessary to grasp everything there is to know. The logical mind is always wondering and pondering over things it doesn't understand. It is the unconscious mind that knows, and it's not "logical," in our terms, but non-linear and Multi-D.

---

[286] http://lawofone.info/
[287] Ra Sessions, *18:14-25; 24:3; 24:5-6.*
[288] http://en.wikipedia.org/wiki/Anak
[289] Sitchin, Z., *The War of Gods and Men.*
[290] *Ibid.*

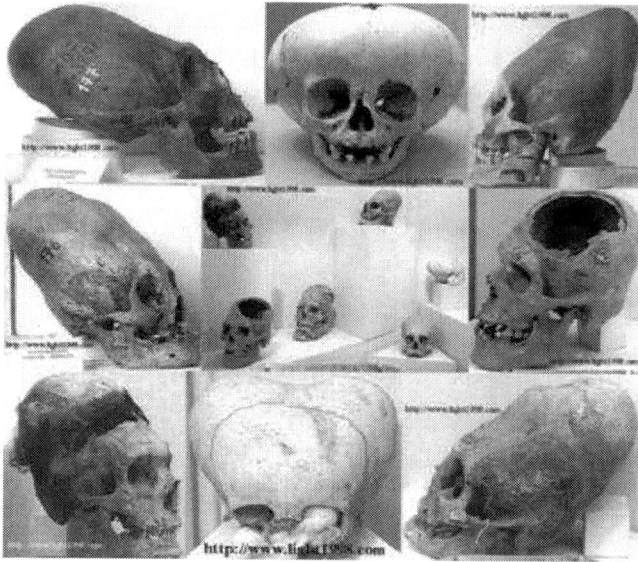

Figure 13.5: Giant Skulls from a museum in Lima, Peru.

There were other giants on Earth in ancient days, but from reading Sitchin's books, we must assume that many of the colossal stone monuments were built by giants; some of these structure are enormous. Like the Pleiadians say: "if you see something big was built, you can make sure it was built by people of impressive stature. Big things were built by big people.[291] Or, as they say about today's visitors: "if you see a giant spaceship in the sky, it's not controlled by small people."[292]

Stuck Inside a Radio Station

Think of everything that exists in a Universe as energy. It's everywhere, and it's all that is in a physical universe. It starts with "thought," and thought is what moves energy. There is consciousness in everything from intelligent beings to galaxies, nebulae, stars, planets, animals, plants, rocks, a grain of sand, microbes, atoms, electrons, quantum particles, subquantum particles and beyond. All this put together is "God," or All That Is, manifesting Itself in a physical universe. Everything is connected on a deep subquantum level, as we have discussed in earlier papers. However, things in the universe vibrate within different frequencies, depending on its level of consciousness. A stone is not vibrating on the

---

[291] Pleiadian Session, December, 2011, CD 2:2.
[292] *Ibid.*

278

same frequency as a human.

We, homo sapiens sapiens, have our own energy field when our soul enters a body on Earth. Depending on the consciousness of the soul, the genetic body, and the bloodline, a certain person will vibrate on a certain frequency. This frequency may change during the lifetime of the person. The vibration will ether decrease or increase in line with the person's experiences, ability to solve problems, and to recognize learning experiences and actually learn from them.

Many researchers are talking about a radio, which is a great metaphor for how this works. If we turn the knob on the radio to a certain frequency band, we get a certain station we can listen to. But what is on that station can only be perceived by the ear so long as the knob is still at the same location. If we turn the knob, the radio station is going to have distortions, and then it will disappear, and we will soon tune into another station. The previous station is then no longer audible.

The same thing applies to us: We are stuck on a certain radio station, and within this frequency band we emit and receive information. What is outside this small band can't be perceived by most humans. Still, a big part of humankind thinks our frequency band is all there is. Do the same people believe that FM radio is the only radio channel too? No, we have many radio and TV stations, and no one would think it's strange to change station. Why wouldn't the same apply to us humans?

The Multiverse is extremely rich on intelligent life and so-called aliens. Most of them (at least those who can space travel) are much more advanced than we are and look upon us as little kids who are trying to grow up—dangerous kids by the way. These aliens have a much wider frequency band they can operate within, and thus their realities, and how the perceive the Multiverse, differ quite substantially from ours. We are like ants pacing around, not seeing what humans are doing around them—we wouldn't see many of these ETs, even if they stood before us, because their frequency is so much different. They can operate on multi-dimensional levels and thus they exist on several radio stations at once, while we are stuck on just one.

How come we are so limited? Some say it's because we need to evolve and raise our frequency, one by one to bleed through to other stations close to ours (different dimensions).

Others say, however, that Earth is preset to a certain station, and as long as we live on Earth, we can only operate within that frequency range (give or take). We can reach its upper levels, but to expand from there, we need to continue our journey somewhere else. If this is true, it would explain why the Anunnaki are depicted in a certain way by the Sumerians and are viewed in another way by some people who meet them today when they get a glimpse of their real selves. Are higher, inter-dimensional beings using avatars when they enter our 3-D reality, while they actually by-locate to somewhere else, looking somewhat different than the avatar they have created to better mingle with the population already inhabiting a certain world? The "Avatar" movie, in this sense, is pretty interesting if we reverse the plot to make the humans who transfer their consciousness into the Avatar, aliens. Thus, aliens can walk around on Earth in any city or be in top positions within governments without being detected (which we know is the case. More on this later). Similarly, some (like the Pleiadians, David Icke, James of the WingMakers site and others) say that 3-D is the limited frequency band we live in.

On a highly multi-dimensional level, ETs work with imperatives: They decide as a species what their goals are, and in a combined effort they work on accomplishing them. The difference is that it's all in the open; the communication is telepathic and topological (the ability to hold several communications at once, store them in memory like a RAM computer memory while holding another conversation with someone else, and then picking up on a previous conversations without losing the thread. You can also have multiple conversations going simultaneously with different people. This can be done by humans too; some humans, such as the members of LPG-C, are already doing it when communicating with aliens, where communication sometimes is rapid).

The Pleiadians, who are still working with the Lyrans and other creator gods from the cosmos to create (and recreate) the Living Library, say that when the Founders came up with the prototype for homo sapiens sapiens (before the Anunnaki came and distorted their project), they had already put a code into our DNA, which activates in many people now, during the nano-second. This activation will help us take the leap from 3rd Density linear thinking to become multi-dimensional again.

Then, there are those who would agree with much of the above but believe we are stuck in a hologram and a time-loop (see David Icke's work as an example), and we need to realize this first before we realize we are multi-dimensional. Icke is showing his evidence of this in his new book: *Humankind, Get Off Your Knees—The Lion Sleeps No More*. Here he elaborates that this hologram is created from the Moon. James of the WingMakers, in his interview with Project Camelot in 2008,[293] has a similar viewpoint, although he doesn't mention the Moon as being the source of projection.

The WingMakers option has been discarded by the Life Physics Group, who say the way James of the WingMakers describes how we are imprisoned in 3-D is an impossibility and can be disproved by general physics. If they are correct, this also, more or less, rules out Icke's theory. T the LPG-C tell me we are definitely not stuck in a time-loop, and they can tell by practicing ENS (Extra Neuro Sensing, their advanced form of

---

[293] http://projectcamelot.org/james_wingmakers_sovereign_integral.html

remote viewing) that this is not the case (I beg to differ, *WP 2024*).

Furthermore, they are not very pleased with Barbara Marciniak and the Pleiades. They say that these metaphysical sources are often correct when describing the big picture, but don't know the dynamics. When I bring up DNA with Bordon and mention the Pleiadians in the same breath, he gets quite agitated and tells me that it is disinformation and dangerous because it misleads people to think that we are developing towards regaining some original 12 strand DNA, which was to a large degree deactivated by the Anunnaki to be better able to control us. He says this is simply not true. The Anunnaki did not deactivate our DNA in this fashion. At first, he said it's impossible to do so, but then elaborates on it and says that even *if* it was possible, the deactivated "strands" would "grow back" within 10 generations or so.

The Pleiadians, on the other hand, who have never mentioned the LPG-C in their lectures from what I know, say that even the most advanced scientists today don't know everything about DNA. DNA is not only physical but expands to the metaphysical planes and further throughout the Multiverse. Bordon then goes on, attacking Marciniak in person in a way that makes me think we are not talking about the same person. I think he may have her confused with somebody else because he treats her like if she is a scientist, which she is not. He also tells me he has met Marciniak and blasted her, and she hasn't talked to him since. Curiously enough, Bordon is telling his readers in his essay "The LINK," p.40, that we humans (including scientists and himself) know very little about DNA. So here he goes from being humble (2007) to arrogant to the extreme in 2011 during his sessions with me.

Sometimes we need to listen to our "brains," and in that capacity, LPG-C, with Dr. Bordon as a contact person, has been of great assistance, but sometimes we also need to listen to our "hearts." When I do the latter and use what I have been taught intellectually by Dr. Bordon, I have come to the conclusion that the Pleiadians are quite correct about DNA. In the broader perspective, it makes sense, while the cutting edge science, as far as I understand it (which is limited to say the least) does not explain what I am looking for. If the future proves me wrong, so be it, but my personal take on this is that it is science that eventually will catch up with the metaphysical information.

We will talk much more about 12 strand DNA in both the First and Second Levels of Learning, and I believe that the reason the DNA is not adjusting itself after 10 generations is because we are held in a frequency prison, just like Icke, the Pleiadians, the Guardians, and the WingMakers (among others) say, and thus we can't receive the encoded light from cosmos needed to develop our "junk" DNA. Scientists don't know the beginning of what DNA is, and just recently they have started understanding that there is much more to it than they thought. If so, why would it be so outrageous that our metaphysical sources are correct? After all, they are often far more advanced in their thinking and awareness than we are.

I have contacted Bordon on the DNA subject, and in reply, he sent me a copy and paste of the Wikipedia explanation, more or less, of what DNA/RNA is, which is the mainstream scientific version of it, which I feel, without claiming to at all to be a scientist, is very limited and rigid. DNA is fluid and changes accordingly to our thoughts and beliefs, and foremost, our *awareness*.

Later, someone else, who is very respected in the UFO field, being an engineer, posted something on DNA which upset Bordon quite a bit, and he told me that. I explained to him that people don't understand, logically, what DNA is because the explanation out there is often very scientific and hard to understand, even for highly educated people. So, instead of being frustrated, I suggested Bordon write a simplified article on DNA/RNA that we all can understand. I wanted to give him a chance to do that to see how his version taps into that of 12 strand DNA (or if he had something insightful to contribute on this subject). Bordon thought this was an excellent idea, and that he was willing to do this, but he never did although I reminded him.

The Pleiadians say in Barbara Marciniak's book, *Bringers of the Dawn*:

> ...The human experiment has had one radio station on for 300,000 years. Same old tunes! The human experiment was unable to turn the dial and hear a different band, so the same frequency was broadcast. **This created a quarantine** *emphasis not in original*--a sealing off of this planet.

> The creative cosmic rays sent by Prime Creator and the Original Planners pierce through this frequency shield. They bombard Earth. However, they must have someone to receive them. Without a receptacle, these creative cosmic rays would create chaos and confusion. You, as members of the Family of Light, come into this system to receive these rays of knowledge. You then disseminate the knowledge, the new lifestyle, and the new frequency to the rest of the population to alter the entire planet.[294]

There is, of course, no doubt that they are talking about us in regards to the Anunnaki DNA manipulation 300,000 years ago, which eventually resulted in homo sapiens sapiens (there is subsequent information from these beings throughout the years where they name the Anunnaki as being the ones orchestrating this). They also present a solution how to break the quarantine, which was set up by this alien force, who interfered with the plans for the Living Library, much of what I agree with, as we shall see.

---

[294] Marciniak, Barbara, 1992: *Bringers of the Dawn, pp. 84-85 op. cit.*

Look at Einstein and Isaac Newton; their conclusions were held as true for quite some time but are today questioned by scientists who are changing the current worldview, claiming that their new ideas are the "new truth." However, we need to keep in mind that Einstein and Isaac Newton were rogue scientists once as well.

Gold for Longevity

The Ša.A.M.i. inhale gold like some humans inhale cocaine. The reason they do this, apparently, is to increase their lifespan. As mentioned earlier, they use gold extensively for this purpose when off-planet (Nibiru) to compensate for the increased speed of time on most planets, which have a faster orbit around their suns, respectively, than Nibiru has. However, not only does gold seem to have an addictive side effect on the Ša.A.M.i./Anunnaki, but there are also indications that it may turn them more into machines/cyborgs.

Researcher "Elana" says:

> However, they were unaware that the necessary 'high spin' state was actually diminished by their heavy metal implants that further bled capacitive charge from their bodies. As they became increasingly 'cyborg', the males in particular, quite literally lost their 'Fire'. The eventual rebellion by the patriarchal cyborg, allied with the Orion unwinged forces, overthrew the domination of the Dragon Queens, and the vengeful pogroms decimated the great houses. A remnant escaped with precious genetic material and a few remaining children the Diaspora spreading throughout the universe.[295]

Dr. A.R. Bordon's Close Encounters With the Ša.A.M.i. and the Forming of "The LINK", Annual Meetings with Extra-Terrestrial Groups

It is time that we talk a little about Dr. Bordon's own encounters with the Ša.A.M.i., which happened twice in his early life, before he started meeting them, and a lot of other alien races annually, off-planet and on-planet, to discuss humankind's future and more. As you can see, he mentioned his encounters briefly in his email to Dr. Heiser (see *sub-section 2* above).

I think it's important to give a little background to this amazing man. It is my impression that Bordon and the rest of his team are serious and are doing what they're doing, convinced they want to help mankind, although I may not agree with everything they suggest for the future of mankind.[296]

---

[295] http://www.bibliotecapleyades.net/sumer_anunnaki/reptiles/reptiles19.htm
[296] The LPG-C present themselves as "ambassadors for humankind," which one of

However, it may be of interest for the reader to know a more about Bordon's background because LPG-C will may or may not play a part in humanity's immediate future. So let's start with an official piece of biography taken from one of his articles on my own blog:

> A. R. Bordon is a retired itinerant scientist, traveling the roads of America in search of people talented in extended human functions. He is a former deputy director of a corporate research centre, former executive director of the American Association of Remote Viewers, and contributing writer to a couple of blogs, one Spanish language website and a Portuguese (Brazilian) website. He is also author of FIREBALL, a science fiction novel, and of over twenty-five screenplays and teleplays. In the early 90s, he was also instrumental in the formation of a scientific cooperative that does research in extended human functions, interface with extraterrestrials, and other anomalies. Since his retirement in 2001, he has devoted himself full time to writing, as editor of Foundation Reports in Life Physics, http://lifephysicsgroup.org/-- and is traveling the USA. (**source:** http://battleofearth.wordpress.com/2011/07/29/extraterrestrials-on-earth-a-challenge-we-can-no-longer-ignore/)

I don't know a lot about Bordon's background, but what he has told me, aside from the above, is that he was born in 1946, and when he was 10 years old, in 1956, while on a fishing trip with his father, who was working for the government, they were both abducted by ETs. They were taken onboard a spacecraft and met with tall, Caucasian beings, some of them 7 feet or taller, and bearded. He came to know them as the Ša.A.M.i., inhabitants of Nibiru. They sedated his father so he wouldn't remember the details from the abduction, but they let the young boy keep his memories intact; all according to Bordon (this was long before Sitchin released his first book, *The 12th Planet* in the 1970s). On a few different occasions, Dr. Bordon revealed to me that it was through his encounters with this Ša.A.M.i. group that he got in contact with the present King of Nibiru.

I have asked him about more details from this meeting with the Ša.A.M.i., but he is very reluctant to tell.

Then, in 1981, 25 years later, he had another encounter in Florida, now at the age of 35; this time with 3 Anunnaki who were stationed here on Earth.

At one point of another, he had a third encounter, where he, from my understanding, met with the King again. It was not Anu, but the new King,

---

my main sources (not from Earth) when I wrote The Second, Fourth, and Fifth Levels of Learning, highly disliked. He told me, "If they are 'ambassadors,' has anyone asked humankind what *they* want?" To me, that's a fair statement, *WP 2024.*

who took over after Anu stepped down some time in the 1400s CE, something we will discuss later. It's not clear exactly when Bordon's meeting with the King of Nibiru took place.

I have discussed with Bordon the intentions of the Ša.A.M.i. a few times, and although he expresses doubts regarding their true motives, he told me that in his encounter with the new King, the two made a bond with each other which will not easily be broken. In other words, they became friends. This, to me, sounds suspicious at best and dangerous at worst, taking into account that Bordon is now working with a faction of Ša.A.M.i. to make humankind sovereign. Bordon stresses that he was allowed to have full memories from his encounters, but the question is, did he really? Or was he made to believe that he had full memories, and instead be given screen memories—perhaps having thoughts implanted that would keep him connected to this faction of the Ša.A.M.i., with the intention to be used in the future? How can he be so sure it didn't happen that way? If he says he's sure, I can't say he's wrong, but it's normal alien abduction procedure, after all. Why would Bordon be immune to this? It sounds like a thing the Anunnaki would do if they wanted to use him in the future to perhaps create something like LPG-C to prepare for their return.

So, the abductions, and another very interesting (albeit private) incident that happened to him that I can't go into here, but which also potentially involved the Ša.A.M.i., Bordon started what he calls "a very advanced physics group" in California together with other renegade scientists, to become LPG-C. For almost 20 years as of this writing (2011), this group has now researched and built a model for our entire Multiverse, which they call the Unum, and have also been meeting annually (and sometimes semi-annually) with this ET off-planet group called The LINK for many years (see the beginning chapters of this book, *WP 2024*). In all meetings, minutes were taken, so they are on record. I have taken part of the synopsis from the last meeting in December 2010 - January 2011, and it's interesting. A few things from this meeting, which I am allowed to reveal, will be embedded in later chapters.

My research, as we shall see, strongly makes me believe that Bordon and his team are working on a mission they are convinced being of uttermost importance for humanity's future, but I am suspicious of the Ša.A.M.i. intentions when comes to their involvement Earth matters, and it makes me feel uncomfortable with LPG-C's willingness to work with this Ša.A.M.i. group. When he wrote the "The LINK" essay in 2007, he was in a healthy way suspicious about their motives and said he and his team "have their antennas up." Even as late as January 2011, he still kept a suspicious mind towards them. Recently, though, in his communications, it seems he is more willing to work with at least one faction of this group.

I am not. I have come to an entirely different conclusion regarding the

ET issue, which will be presented in "The First Level of Learning, Part 2,"[297] although I think that something like the "3% Rule" would be of interest for mankind; but hopefully with another goal in mind, keeping the Ša.A.M.i. out of the picture, if this is at all possible.

One thing I need to mention here is the fact that very few people are abducted without a previous agreement with the abductors. It may be in this life or in between lives, but there are no coincidences. The Ša.A.M.i. knew what they were doing when they abducted young, 10-year-old Bordon, and sedated his father in the middle of a fishing trip out in nowhere. Not a coincidence. The father happened to be there with his son, but the subject for the abduction was A.R. Bordon. They had plans for him, evidently, and on a soul level, Dr. Bordon has agreed to this for any given reason, and this means the Ša.A.M.i. have plans for him. I can't see how it could be any different.

When I have asked Bordon questions about the Working Model that he and his group have developed over the years, he has been happy to provide me with an abundance of information. He has always, without failing, replied to my emails within 24-48 hours. I always thought this was commendable, considering he is so busy with other things. However, twice I wrote him long emails explaining why I thought he is being used, and how I came to my conclusions, and he never wrote me back. Instead, after being silent for perhaps a week (in both cases) he wrote me, but on a totally different subject, like if my previous emails didn't exist, perhaps hoping I had "forgotten them" and thus, he tried to redirect my attention.

I have addressed certain parts of the Working Model with Bordon, e.g., when he says a soul can only be indexed to a certain planet once. At the same token, I brought up Dr. Michael Newton's afterlife research, based on 7,000 case studies, all telling the same story. And in addition to that, I mentioned all the non-physical beings, who, through channeling and sensory data streaming, are telling us exactly the same thing. Then, on his end, there is only silence. I gave Dr. Bordon many fair chances to explain, but instead he has ignored my emails. Therefore, I need to make his silence public, for the records.

The LINK meetings, starting in 1990, and recurring every year since then, began as a small group, with Dr. Bordon and another scientist as the only participants at first, joined in by a few different ET groups, hosted by a Ša.A.M.i. group. Over the years, the numbers of participants have increased to over 200 members, with representatives from different star systems in the Universe. According to Bordon's essay, *The LINK*, page 32, there were *"fifty-seven human contactee/activist groups—forty-two invited members*

---

[297] And even more so in the Second through Fifth Level of Learning, coming out in book form as soon as I am done editing them, *WP 2024*.

and fifteen observer members". He doesn't mention, however, who these human groups are. At the time of the writing of the essay, the human participating groups worldwide were 41 and have possibly increased since then. What he *is* telling us is that these meetings are held by "concerned members" of galactic and intergalactic species that have no direct connections with their governments (nongov.org), but are there as individuals or "concerned groups", who want to discuss intergalactic matters in freedom, and they are particularly here to discuss Earthly matters, because we are a species who potentially is at the threshold to becoming galactic members, but are still facing big problems that need to be solved; problems like our negative use of electrogravity and our destructive oil production.

LPG-C and the 3% Rule

The evidence that the Anunnaki were here in our ancient past and genetically manipulated the early humans is overwhelming and can no longer be discarded. Add to this all the present encounters with the same beings (cases I have personally been in contact with) and we get quite a solid picture; not only that these beings existed in the past, but that they are here today as well; at least some of them.

There is also little doubt that this race is a warrior race with a lot of issues. Not to say that we humans don't have issues—I'm the first to admit to that. Look at all the wars, all the hunger in the world, power struggles, oppression; the list goes on. Still, we got these traits from the gods, who came down here and mixed their DNA with ours; and in addition, it is unbeknownst to most humans that we are still ruled by ET groups. Moreover (albeit teaching us agriculture and giving us survival tips at times), they were the ones who taught us warfare.

So, the dark side of this manipulation is that we have their mindset in many ways, and we struggle with this up to this day, and that is one reason it's been so hard to break our patterns.

Another thing we must remember is that those we call the Anunnaki who came down to Earth, were led by two brothers of a royal bloodline from the planet Nibiru. They do not represent the whole Ša.A.M.i. species. It's like sending down Prince William and Prince Harry to a foreign planet (God help us), hypothetically being in dispute with each other over whom should be in power. The majority of the population on Earth are not bad people, and perhaps the same goes for the Ša.A.M.i./Anunnaki, but they come from somewhere else and have another mindset as a mass consciousness. Needless to say, Prince Ea and Prince Nammur act like two spoiled children who don't give up until they get what they want, even if it includes killing off their creation (humankind) in the process, and use us in their pointless wars, like as if they have nothing better to do (and likely they don't). Then, when the disputes get out of hand, they are beaming for "daddy" to come and help. When daddy Anu finally comes, after more people possibly have been killed, they blame each other viciously until daddy pats them on the head and asks them to please be nice and stop fighting. Although I say this sarcastically, isn't this the picture we get, though?

What is worrisome is that the Kingdom of Nibiru is ruled by either one of these two bloodlines, and the rest of the Ša.A.M.i. obey their King; it's like having a Democratic and a Republican Party; Ea's line being the Democrats and Nammur's being the Republicans. It's much too similar to the power structure and the hierarchy of power here on Earth in present time. We may have elections and different political parties, but the lobbying is intense before an election (just like on Nibiru), and no matter who becomes the President/Ruler, whether it is in the United States or elsewhere, they are of the "bloodline," and ironically, the earthly bloodlines we choose from are just an extension of the Ša.A.M.i. bloodlines (our Presidents being of royal, Ša.A.M.i. blood, which has been proven recently and is well documented on my website, http://illuminati-news.com). The same problems continue on from there. Dr. Bordon says Anu stepped down in the 1400s and left room for a new King, which is Nannar, Nammur's son. This same source says that Nannar was much loved while here on Earth millennia ago, and he is loved on his home planet, but so was Obama here on Earth in the beginning of his presidency. No longer so, though. I don't see the point in appointing a new king from the same conflicting bloodlines and think that *now things will improve.*

LPG-C suggests that, after having met with this alien group they call *The LINK* for decades, it may or may not be in our best interest to connect with King Nannar or his representatives (Nannar being the King with whom Dr. Bordon allegedly met, by the way) and work out a solution for humankind for us to (re)claim sovereignty of our biokind, and the planet as a whole. In short, the King, and other alien species as well, joining in on the annual conferences, are concerned about that we, as a species, don't know our imperatives and can't join together in a combined effort to advance our species enough to be welcomed into the galactic societies because we can't even solve our own problems here on Earth. Although this is true, of course, it sounds like quite a bold statement coming from someone whose species is responsible for our current condition to a large degree, and not only that; the Ša.A.M.i. is still a warrior-like race, as far as I'm concerned. Their attempt to convince us that they are now on a more "spiritual" path is not sitting well with me. I am not trying to put blame elsewhere and suggesting that we should not take responsibility for our own mess, but I think this time we should do it without the Ša.A.M.i. being involved, and perhaps then we will succeed. I understand that these people most probably will land here on Earth in a near future, but there are solutions which I will go into later.

However, besides that, not only the Ša.A.M.i., but the other alien races they are meeting with as well, all being members of The LINK, agree with each other that they want to see at least 3% of our world population (around 192,000,000 people) having set imperatives for what the collective humans want for their race before they will take us seriously and leave Earth, the real estate, exclusively in human hands, according to Bordon. Apparently, they believe that if 3% will adjust (like with the famous *100th monkey syndrome*), the rest of humankind will eventually follow. This is what LPG-C is now mainly working on achieving.

My concern is that this whole group of aliens which LPG-C is meeting with, appearing to be of different background and unrelated to each other, could from all we know be part of the same Galactic Federation and not telling the human representatives. What if they are just manipulating us so we humans will believe what the Ša.A.M.i. King wants is also what most other aliens in the group agree to as well? (And if this is the case, they are probably smart enough to have a few aliens on board playing the role of not agreeing, which makes it all seem much more convincing. *My gut tells me things are not what they appear to be*).

I have tried to get Dr. Bordon to reveal more about the alien species who attend the LINK meetings so we can do some intelligence work on them to find out who they really are, and more importantly, if they belong to the same Galactic Federation. Bordon is unwilling to do this, possibly afraid that if he does, he will lose his chair in the LINK meetings. This makes me feel uncomfortable because if ETs are suggesting what we should and should not do with ourselves and our planet, in spite of how good it sounds, they'd better present themselves and give us their "biography." I don't take advice regarding our future from anonymous alien sources. On the bright side, I happen to know where some of these aliens, attending the meetings, come from. I know their star systems of origin, but this information is limited, because each star system can (and often is) populated by more than one species. However, at least it is a lead and something I *will* look into.

To understand LPG-C's concept of the 3% rule as much as possible, it's important that I quote A.R. Bordon directly from his essay, "The LINK," written in 2007 *(pp.28)*:

> The Working Model, an emergent model of what is generally defined as life physics (a physics that includes behaviors of intelligent living organisms on Earth, beginning with homo sapiens), indicates that adaptive behaviors of such biokinds demonstrate the appearance of such behaviors when 3 percent of its membership demonstrate a change in a particular behavioral set in a given direction. This was originally derived from work with monkeys on the Japanese Kurile Islands, regarding specific behaviors acquired by populations of monkeys inhabiting more than one island, where the behavior was initially demonstrated by

one group in one island. Over time, other groups of monkeys began using the new behaviors until roughly 3 percent of the total population of monkeys "learned" to crack nuts in the "new way."

Once three percent of all monkeys, regardless of where they lived, learned to do things in the "new way," it then became a new way of cracking nuts for the entire population. We then started looking for minimum behavioral critical mass for behavior change in other living species, and found them to function on this 3 percent principle. So last year, we began a four-year "3 percent project" of surveys and focus groups in 67 countries worldwide (including the United States and Canada) through a nonprofit foundation. The general objective of this project is to discern whether or not we humans also function by the 3-percent principle in regard to "general connectivity" to each other along specific parameters.

We are interested in finding if at least 3 percent of the people who participate in these scientific field surveys exhibit and manifest patterns of behavioral choices consonant with what we define as "general connectivity." You see, the off-world members of the conferencing group tell us there is such a 3-percent group of humans already. We want to know where, and whether or not the connectivity they speak of to us is related to "conscious group-centered self-serving" behavior that would constitute pragmatic connectivity within the value system of each of the polled groups. Once a 3-percent core of each surveyed group is identified, then these members are invited to focused groups to further learn the depth of the thinking behavior and behavioral choices exhibited as "propensities" through the polling surveys. The "second phase" of the project is due to begin some time toward the end of this year *2007, Wes' comment* – that is, the focus groups. Why are we doing this? The answer should be obvious to the reader. We do it because this is an attitude/belief set we can then bring to the conference table as one means of correction of off-world group perceptions of who and how we are. What is interesting and most fascinating is that the numbers are now suggestive that we humans also change on the basis of this 3-percent principle.

Even so, the operative word here is suggestive, because the total polling numbers are but a fraction of the actual 3-percent requirements of the total Earth population – that is, 3 percent of the 6.435 billion human beings estimated to now inhabit the Earth. Three percent of this number would be roughly 192 million souls. Fortunately, there are ways in which to "activate" this number of people once a neurobehavioral pattern is identified, which can correlate with "desirable propensity" general patterns.

We now have powerful reasons to believe these technologies can and should be employed for and our common behalf as core memberships in polled international groups emerge. To what purpose? The Working Model indicates that Earth is a bioconnective planet, such that all of its host of living matrices (the biologies of all living things, including us) have the potential to act in unison, as a single organism with one degree of freedom. That is, all brains of these detected memberships (regardless of language barriers) can "vote" with their hearts and minds on what is best for all of us. Again, this is a capability possessed by most, if not all, of the off-world groups, so why not us as well? They act in accordance to their imperatives; isn't it about time we started acting in consonance to our own? What these imperatives are we will explore in the course of this book. There are many aspects to what we see them to be. But these, we suggest, are but a mere starting point. I then hope this book will generate discussions in groups who consider what I write here among themselves, with a view of deciphering their own feelings and intellect with regard to what our imperatives are – not what they think they should be, for such would not be an intellectual exercise but a very real act of bioconnectivity and biocommunication across all groups.

Interestingly, it is something like what is suggested here that off-world groups have been asking of us. The emergence of such human biomind would facilitate things in ways the reader could not at this point even imagine. So please lend me your imagination that I may show you with my palette of words what it will do for us. What I am about to paint for you in the rest of this chapter and in Chapter 7 is what is most feared by gatekeepers of contact. Yet, it is a most powerful solution to the advent of a dynamic coherence process across the membership on the aforementioned groups, and thereby a start of a dynamic coherence cascade in the interconnectivity of the human biomind.

It is this very phenomenon we now understand is the purpose of the series of sites left on Earth by the transversals mentioned by Jamisson Neruda in his interviews, the so-called Central Race. Each of these sites, according to the Working Model, are nothing short of brain resonance centers that transform minds through art and music and imagery and a powerful emotive bandwidth.

It is within this dynamic coherence that we must derive the elements of our own imperatives. And it is most unfortunate that the very gatekeepers who most fear this process are the ones who need it most, yet do not understand it because it is not controllable once Frank Herbert's "sleeper" has awakened. All any one can hope for then is that the biomind acting as a single degree of freedom organism does what is best for all of us. Therein lay their conundrum, and our positive expectations as raw hope.

It is my understanding that if we can achieve the 3% rule before Nibiru passes next time (according to LPG-C this will happen sometime around 2060-2095), we will stand a better chance to get what *we* want, instead of agreeing to what the Ša.A.M.i. want for our future. If humanity can stand more or less united, maybe they will listen? At least, this is LPG-C's hopes and plans, something they want us to achieve before the next crossing of Planet X. Would that work? With additional information I have on the Ša.A.M.i. and the Anunnaki, not mentioned by Sitchin, tells me that the Ša.A.M.i. are not interested in what we want; it's a waste of time in that respect. They have already planned our future, but in their usual manner, using sophisticated mind control on an already mind controlled human population, it's easier for them if they can make us agree to what *they* want. But like I said, the 3% Rule is still something to consider, albeit with a totally different goal in mind, which will be discussed in the First Level, Book 2.

Figure 13,6: Dr. A.R. Bordon

King Nannar's plan, apparently is for the Ša.A.M.i. from Nibiru to come down with his people here on Earth at the time of the next crossing of Nibiru, gather all the renegade Anunnaki who are still on Earth, and give them the option to either start obeying to the Kingdom immediately, or come back to Nibiru, where they will be imprisoned for crimes against the human soul group. If they refuse both, there will be a war. The Anunnaki leader of the Earth clan will be imprisoned here on Earth in an underground facility for 1,000-2,000 years and then get a trial here. Then, 3,600 years from now, or when Nibiru comes back the next time, if Bible prophecy is correct, the leader will die.

So, who is this "leader?" Anyone who's read my papers thus far would say Marduk, and I, too, would say Marduk, if it wasn't for Dr. Bordon telling me a while ago that Marduk died quite recently here on Earth, as did Ningishzidda (Thoth). We don't know where Ningishzidda is buried, but Marduk was first buried here on Earth, but then brought back to Nibiru (probably because his father, Ea, wanted to grant him the right to "come home" to the home planet for his final rest). Bordon says he got this information via his Intel, which probably is information he got from a Ša.A.M.i. representative during one of the annual meetings with the LINK. Instead, Marduk's sons, Nabu and Gbril, have allegedly taken over the post as Lords of Earth.

I will not continue too much longer with this discussion because I am uncertain of its validity. The Ša.A.M.i. may have reasons why they want us to believe Marduk is dead. However, if it's true, the two brothers will be the ones sent underground for 3,600 years (or perhaps the surviving one, as the Bible prophecy speaks of *one* person. Still, things can change, and prophecy is a slippery slope).

What will happen to those who supported Marduk and his two sons during all this time they reigned on Earth, were of the same mindset as Marduk, and perhaps even consciously served him as their King? According to Bordon, when a safe landing of the Ša.A.M.i. can take place, they are coming down to take their own and kill off any and all humans who have been associated with Marduk and his clan. Those who chose the "wrong side" still have time to repent, but if they yet haven't done so when the Ša.A.M.i. boomerang-shaped ships arrive, there is no time for forgiveness; everyone associated with Marduk and his league will be exterminated and punished down to the 10th generation, whereas those who have been loyal to the King of Nibiru, or avoided to be part of Marduk's team, will be "blessed" down to the 1,000th generation. So the punishment for those directly involved will be death penalty; the only restriction the Ša.A.M.i. law has on death penalty is that a Lord should not kill a Lord (rarely happens) and a King never kills a Lord (unheard of). However, people of lower ranks, both on Nibiru and here, apparently can get death penalty. It's been done a lot in the past and is described in Sitchin's books, and it's still being executed on the home planet. It seems like most, if not all, of our human laws are direct copies of the Ša.A.M.i. laws.

Just for the record, this doesn't mean everybody who has been working for a Global Elite Companies will be killed; only those who consciously work with Marduk and his clan. However, more people than we might think are part of the Marduk agenda; many celebrities "signed the contract," business leaders, religious leader, politicians… there are many people who "sold their soul to the Devil" for fame and fortune, drugs, rock'n'roll, and women in abundance.

But humanity is required to choose sides; either they obey to the Kingdom of Nibiru, or the illegal Kingdom of Earth. That's when people take sides, and as it is presented, I can't see how this would not ignite a huge war—the Battle of Armageddon. So, the part of humanity who hasn't been wiped out by cataclysms directly related to effects from the incoming

Nibiru or from other catastrophes—natural or manmade—will be reduced even more in the Armageddon Wars. If Bible Prophecy is correct, the Lord (Nibiru) will win the war, and the King of Kings (King Nannar) will show himself for the human population for the first time, fair-skinned and bearded, just like Jesus supposedly was, and about 7 feet tall.

Then, when this war is over, King Nannar will come down and announce that he will leave a skeleton crew of his men here on Earth for another šar (3,600 years) to help us with the transition from being ruled by a negative power, so that we can eventually govern ourselves. Then, if we can "stand on our own legs" when Nibiru returns once again, the Anunnaki will leave us alone for good.

This is the semi-official version given to LPG-C during LINK meetings. The King then will "advise" us to adopt *their* form of government, which is a World King and a democratic set up of government, a little different from the one we have here on Earth. Still, it's going to be a Monarchy. This is what has been insinuated by them. Then, according to Bordon, we don't know how seriously they will push through with their "advice," and if they will actually force us or not.

They are telling us that they feel responsibility for us and that they are not without conscience. Their intentions are to work towards us humans becoming sovereign enough to be self-sufficient and be able to defend our real estate towards intruders from space and elsewhere. All this they will teach us over the next 3,600 years.

LPG-C is, according to their spokesperson, probably still ambivalent about King Nannar's solution for Earth. They are still quite suspicious about them and are not yet sure that this is what mankind wants and needs. They are hoping that we can reach some kind of 3% agreement with humankind on imperatives for the human race, but if the Ša.A.M.i. come and we have not reached our 3%, meaning mankind is still scattered, not knowing what we want, what can LPG-C really do? Will they sign up with the Nibiru King? Probably. Bordon said at one point that LPG-C will possibly be ambassadors to the Ša.A.M.i. and the skeleton crew who will be left here on Earth to govern us when all other governments on Earth are defeated (he told me that this was his understanding). The Ša.A.M.i., as Bordon puts it, will "come down heavy-handed," and most, if not all, governments know about this, and it's also written in hidden form in many sacred scriptures. The *technical assistance corp* (again Bordon's words) which will be left here on Earth is firmly to implement what *they* believe is best for us.

However we look at it, and however good it may sound to some people, I can see how the Ša.A.M.i. are bringing down their wars to Earth all over, and we are stuck in the middle as usual. What guarantees do we have things will be different this time?

We don't have any from what I can see. The questions raised here are serious ones, and I personally don't buy into King Nannar's solution. I agree with LPG-C, who are very firm with that we need to protect our biology, but in *my* book, figuratively and literally speaking, the Nibiruans are not a species working towards our best interests, but in their own. They are mainly Service to Self (STS) in a negative way, not willingly giving up "their" real estate. I truly believe that what they are telling us about letting us be sovereign is disinformation and manipulation on their part.

Another thing to ponder: this alien race is millions of years ahead of us in their evolvement, and I can still see people on Earth (I include myself among them), who can look at life with love and compassion, being able to see where that can bring humankind as a whole. This does not seem to be the case with the Ša.A.M.i./Anunnaki. I see a race that is still quite service-to-self oriented (an *I'll give you this, but what is in it for me?* mindset). The last word is far from spoken, and I will give this a lot more attention before we're done with these papers.

PAPER 14:
THE MARDUK ISSUE AND THE EARTH-BOUND ANUNNAKI

by Wes Penre, Thursday, May 5, 2011

Abstract

Some 4000+ years ago, the majority of the Anunnaki left Earth after had nuked the Sinai Spaceport and Sodom and Gomorrah. Marduk, however, who was Ea's eldest son, stayed on Earth with some of his loyal Lords.

Marduk had, before that, married a human female (a crossbreed between Anunnaki and homo erectus), and was therefore forbidden to return to Nibiru. No human was allowed in "Heaven" (although some exceptions were made on occasion, such as Enoch, but otherwise, they were only short visitations). So, Marduk had to choose whether to keep his hybrid wife and give up his royal status on Nibiru or to abandon his wife and keep his status. Marduk, who already was angry with King Anu and his Council because they put Nammur's bloodline before his own, told them to "screw it" and stayed with his wife.

However, he never forgot or forgave his own relatives, whom he thought had betrayed him, so he declared war against the Enlilites (the RAM clan), and now Marduk wanted to be the Ruler of Earth. At least, that was better than being no king at all, he thought. Consequently, he fought a raging war against Inanna, the female Enlilite; a war which involved using humans as foot soldiers, dying in the thousands for the cause of two power-hungry Anunnaki.

When the Anunnaki left the planet, Marduk's human wife was since long dead (she did not enjoy the longevity of the gods), but King Anu and the Council did not want Marduk back on Nibiru, due to his rebellious nature. Instead, they left him here on Earth to do whatever he wanted. If he wanted to be the Lord of Earth, he could be their guest. But first, the gods nuked the Sinai Spaceport to prevent Marduk access from it because of his threats to take it over.

Since then, Marduk has been in charge of this planet; or at least a majority of it. He is the force behind quite a substantial faction of what we call "The Global Elite," "The Illuminati," or the "Powers That Be." It needs to be pointed out, though, that he is not the only one in charge. There are other inter-dimensional and dimensional forces, steering parts of the Global Elite in other directions as well, so the situation is complex (we will go into this in more details soon).

Left on our planet since the gods abandoned it are both Enkiites (Serpent Clan) and Enlilites (RAM Clan), and some of them are still loyal to the Kingdom (the Nibiru Kingdom), while Marduk, obviously, is not. So, the war between the two Nibiruan bloodlines is still going on here on Earth, and as usual, we humans are their soldiers and slave workers. Not very uplifting reading for the young, courageous soldiers, who go to Iraq and other places to fight for freedom, when in fact, they fight the War of the Gods.

This paper will cover the current Anunnaki situation on Earth as we know it this was written in 2011. Since then, much has been revealed. See the Second-Fifth Levels of Learning and even more of my recent work, *WP 2024*.

The Anunnaki and Their Human Hybrids -- The Global Elite

When we look upon the power structure on Planet Earth today as average human beings, we may feel small, insignificant, and powerless. Even if we don't like how we live our lives, we may feel we are "stuck within the system," with no power to change it. Still, the Anunnaki who are still on Earth do not exceed the amount of 300+ individuals, compared with almost 7 billion humans in 2011. We know that the Anunnaki are highly intelligent and advanced (at least technologically and intellectually), and they use a few thousand human hybrids (the Global Elite) to be their CEOs over Marduk's global empire. They are still in great minority, so they need to control us with some kind of very clever master plan. This is how it's done in general:

1. The Anunnaki keep themselves hidden and pull the strings from behind the scenes. The Ša.A.M.i. have always ruled from within councils, and the Council of 12 was the superior council while the Anunnaki were here on Earth in larger numbers, thousands of years ago. The original Council of 12 is no longer, according to a Ša.A.M.i. informant during LINK meetings, the ruling council on Earth. However, in old Nibiruan tradition, Marduk set up his own Council of 12, which is now his own Royal Council.

2. They use the purest hybrids on Earth; some of them being direct descendants of the old Anunnaki Lords in the ancient past. The

purer your bloodline, the more power you are delegated. These hybrids are put in charge of politics, business, education, media, entertainment, banking and think tanks, to name a few. In other words, they are positioned where they can control the highest number of people.

3. With their money scam (the banking system), they can keep entire nations under their thumbs, and make people in general dependent on money for their survival.

4. They use their ancient method of dividing and conquering, by implementing their formula, *Problem-Reaction-Solution*. When the Global Elite, through their alien masters, want a local or global change in their structure, and they know people in general wouldn't agree to the changes, they create a problem big and traumatic enough for the population in general to cry for a solution (this is the "reaction"), and then the same people who created the problem in the first place now present the solution they wanted all the time. Out of fear and terror, people are now willing to accept the solution they wouldn't even consider before. A typical example is 9/11.[298] The attack is the "problem," and they get a "reaction" from the people to do something about such horrible terrorist attacks, and the U.S. government tightens the belts on us with harsher national security; allowing people to be monitored, stripped, controlled, restricted, and they are creating new laws where it's easier to control the masses, etc. This is happening on an almost daily bases. *They are using fear as a weapon*, and unfortunately, we humans fall for it almost every time.

5. Of the 300+ Anunnaki who stayed on Earth, the majority of them (around 200) are loyal to Marduk and some are still loyal to the Kingdom (Nibiru).[299] Thus, we have the same conflict again between the Enlilites vs. the RAM Clan (the Kingdom), and a faction of the Enkiites—the Serpent Clan (Marduk's loyal Lords). As we notice, they are still using human soldiers as cannon fodder in their petty wars against each other, in an attempt to win power over to their respective side. Both parties are using the Global Elite members as their puppets. Wars are also a great way to keep the population from increasing in numbers too rapidly, as well as manmade fatal diseases, viruses, vaccinations, prescription drugs, food and sweets that are poisonous to your body, to name but a few.

---

[298] Another example is, of course, the recent pandemic (WP 2024). The solution is the vaccines.

[299] Sources: The LPG-C and Zecharia Sitchin (WP 2024).

6. The entire power structure on Earth is built like a pyramid, with the Council at the top, the Global Elite's purer hybrid power bloodlines right underneath, more impure hybrids beneath them, and there under are a hand-picked humans who have the brains to do the job necessary and can be manipulated easily enough in exchange for power and wealth. Most of the latter have no idea whom they are actually working for; everything is on a need-to-know basis to keep the truth away from people. With those "regular" people, or those of watered-down bloodlines, put in important positions, blackmail is often a common way to keep them loyal to *The Great Work of the Ages*, as Freemasonry calls it. Very commonly, they are promising them young, beautiful women (often underage girls and boys) to have sex with, without their spouses knowing about it; and in the future, if they stop cooperating, their dirty laundry is hung out in public. Thus the many suicides in high places.

The situation is further complicated because factions of the Global Elite have signed contracts with other alien species, like the Greys/Reptilians and the Verdants (more about these later), creating more civil unrest, conflicts and wars, making this whole planet a giant war zones, with the great majority of people having no idea what is going on. Most of the bonds, in modern times, were made through TTPs (Technological Transfer Programs), where we got technology in exchange for what they wanted from us (usually what they want the most in this exchange program is for humans to use the technology to execute the ETs plans and to give them consent to manipulate and to genetically tinker with our DNA. As representatives of the State, Presidents, and miscellaneous authorities, are by the ETs considered the "voice of the people" because that's what the governments are *supposed* to be: they should listen to the voice of the people and execute the will of the population. Unfortunately, it has never worked that way. Even the *Declaration of Independence* in the United States is, and always was, a farce and a Freemasonic scam *WP 2024*).

In charge of the human Global Elite (the human hybrid part of it), seem to be the Rockefeller and the Rothschild banking families.[300] They have been the visible rulers for a couple of millennia, but under different names. The Rothschild's were previously called the Bauer's, for example. Both families are royal and go back to old Sumer and further. There are other ruling Elite families as well, who also go back to the Anunnaki. The bloodlines are, according to researcher and writer, Fritz Springmeier:

---

[300] See, http://illuminati-news.com/moriah.htm, or google Rothschild and Rockefeller.

1. Astor
2. Bundy
3. Collins
4. DuPont
5. Freeman
6. Kennedy
7. Li (Chinese)
8. Onassis
9. Rockefeller
10. Rothschild
11. Russell
12. van Duyn
13. Merovingian (European Royal Families) [301]

The following families are also interconnected with those above:

1. Reynolds
2. Disney
3. Krupp
4. McDonald

So, what is the difference between "regular people" and those who are of the ruling Elite or connected to them by blood? Well, many are descendants of the old Hebrews and are therefore Marduk's (YHVH's/**YeHoVaH**,s) chosen people in the Bible.[302] They have been put near the top of the pyramid to rule over the rest of humankind. According to Sitchin's translations, they were not meant to rule us with an iron fist like they have over the last millennia, killing us off and treating us like slaves and cannon fodder. The intention was apparently to govern us until we could manage on our own as a human soul group. We know that this never happened; they were immediately, under Marduk's command, drunk by power and wealth, and became the Ruling Elite we see today. They have no intention of setting us free.

---

[301] Springmeier, Fritz, 1995: *Bloodlines of the Illuminati*: https://www.amazon.com/Bloodlines-Illuminati-Fritz-Springmeier/dp/0972792929

[302] In the original papers from 2011, I wrote it was the En.lil's chosen people, which is incorrect. Also, see my book *The Story of Isis and the War of Bloodlines* (https://www.amazon.com/Story-Isis-War-Bloodlines/dp/B0CPYMHJN5/ref=tmm_pap_swatch_0?_encoding=UTF8&qid=1705971777&sr=8-2).

What I find notable is that king Anu and the En.lil got these strange epiphanies from Galzu, the mysterious being, and right there realized that we are all *ONE,* and humans need to get Earth to rule over themselves. So why, then, did they leave Marduk here, too rebellious to come back to Nibiru, knowing he would make a mess down on Earth? If they loved their "children," as they apparently call us, would parents leave their kids with mass murderers?[303]

I removed the beginning of the paragraph, including some calculations about Nibiru's alleged return, but the calculations were inaccurate. See the WPP online for the original, *WP 2024.* The return of the Nibiruans doesn't have to coincide exactly with Nibiru, however. They know interstellar travel and can come through stargates and Einstein-Rosen Bridges as they please. Still, it's probably in their interest to come after the cataclysm that will follow around the time for the crossing. However, one may think that if they had had 4,000 years to evolve since the last crossing, they potentially could have come a long way. But keep in mind that 4,000 years is one year plus in their terms. They don't count time as we do. We may argue they are also inter-dimensional and multi-dimensional, which would perhaps speed up their evolutionary progress, but if we look back on their history, they haven't developed at all in the last 500,000 years, at least. They have always been the same warrior race, with bloodlines fighting against bloodlines (as above, so below). It's hard to believe they suddenly, in no time at all (in their terms) have developed so fast, relatively speaking, that they are now mature enough to govern us peacefully. Dr. A.R. Bordon tells us they use nanotechnology to develop their biominds until they now have almost reached Oneness. This is hypothetically possible, I assume, but it concerns me when I listen to Dr. Bordon, and by the same token read the following from his essay, *The LINK:*

> It is reported by members who have attended the conferences that they are near the completion of their cycle on oneness, wherein all knowledge and mind resources are used in service to the common. This, it was said, can only be possible when the diversity of biominds of each member remains an individuality while simultaneously being interconnected to the Ša.A.Mi. all-one by low-powered, low-energetic means that utilizes the planet's life belt energetics – something akin to what Earth enjoys in the form of Schumann resonance. **There is yet much we don't quite understand about their system of oneness, as there are technologies used to enhance the common biomind that are beyond our level of technology at this time** *emphasis not in original.* However, we do now possess a theoretical understanding of

---

[303] The reader may get a hint to an answer in my book, *Simulations and the Wheels of Time in the Developing Worlds* https://www.amazon.com/dp/B0CYZJ2BTX .

how it all works.[304]

Here he says there is much we still don't understand, but should we then accept that we don't understand and take the Ša.A.M.i. suggestions to heart? Why would we trust them? Let's pretend that you and I were a team and traveled around the world ten years ago and killed people left and right and played vicious power games we thought were appropriate. We raped women and minors, plundered and dedicated ourselves to the worst criminal acts, and then disappeared for ten years. Suddenly, we come back and tell people that what happened ten years ago was in the past, and we have since then evolved. Would anyone believe us? Would anyone have a reason to? No. They would need so much more proof than our words.

The ETs can tell us anything they want us to believe. A.R. Bordon told me their science group has developed "BS detectors" over the last 20 odd years, and that the ETs could maybe fool one or two of them, but not the whole group. I'd say, why not? It's easy to be arrogant about our own brilliance and think we can compare even our most superb minds with those of the more developed ETs. I believe that if they want to, these ETs can pass any BS detector we may be able to develop at this time. I also have reason to believe that the other alien species that show up on the LINK meetings are from the same confederation, just pretending they are not working together. You don't think aliens can be that sophisticated? We can, so why wouldn't they?

ET Disclosure Projects and Their Major Advocates

The situation may seem totally hopeless, but believe it or not, there is still hope, and not all aliens are here to conquer and destroy. In fact, the large majority of ETs in near space are not hostile to humans, and many of them are here to help us in one way or the other. They are not here to interfere with armed forces or to put themselves in charge. Most of them are working in the background and are observing usually from outside the Earth construct, *WP 2024*.

Sometimes, I get emails from people saying that these peaceful ETs are not to much help if they just sit up there in spaceships somewhere without doing anything. They *are* doing something, and we're getting into that soon, but most importantly, it's not for them to interfere or intervene. Most species are accustomed to following the Law of One, and the Law of Freewill, which includes non-interference policies (more about this later).

We are living in a Freewill Zone, and it's up to us as a biokind/biomind

---

[304] Bordon, A.R., 2007: *The LINK - Extraterrestrials in Near Earth Space and Contact on the Ground, p. 42.*

to work out our own problems. It's a part of learning; to go from adolescence to adulthood as a species, and we can't have things given to us on silver platters. We are the ones who need to consciously unite on a subquantum level (thought level) to find out what it is we want as a human soul group. This can't be done in institutions like the United Nations or other institutions presently existing on Earth because these organizations are already controlled by those who are not working in our best interests.

Figure 14.1a (left): Dr. Steven Greer. Figure 14.1b (right): Dr. Richard Boylan

One thing I want to emphasize already here is the dangerous mindset of people like Dr. Steven Greer[305] (and his team) and Dr. Richard Boylan.[306] The latter is more dangerous than the former. Both are embracing all ETs in Earth near space and tell us there are no "bad" ETs; they are all star-brother and star-sisters and should immediately be integrated with us, or we with them. They say the government knows about the aliens (which is true), and now it's time for a disclosure, meaning that the government should disclose the ET issue to the people.

There are no "bad" or "good" ETs, of course, only different imperatives. What's a good imperative for one race may not be a good imperative for us, though. However, more often than not, imperatives can be combined and worked out to the best for two species. This doesn't mean, like Dr. Boylan says, that we should turn on our flashlights, metaphorically speaking, point them to the sky and shout: "Welcome all you star visitors. Here we are!" Dr. Boylan in particular is inviting both the Zeta Reticulian Greys, the Verdants, the Tall Whites, the Anunnaki, respectively, without exceptions, calling all of them star visitors and "good

---

[305] http://www.disclosureproject.org/;
http://www.theorionproject.org/en/about.html; http://www.cseti.org/
[306] http://www.drboylan.com/

hearted." Both Greer's team and Boylan agree that all the negative ETs have left near Earth space and there are only positive ETs left.

This is extremely naive; but not only that—it's dangerous and a liability for the rest of humankind. Not all ETs have our best interests in mind, as we shall see, but Dr. Boylan and Dr. Greer don't seem to care and are very aggressively making their point. If someone brings up that there are ETs with clashing imperatives from us, we are immediately put on Dr. Boylan's "bad list" as being government agents, disinformation agents or worse[307] (after I've published this, I'd be surprised if he doesn't put me on there too).[308] Boylan and Greer are opening up a can of worms if they don't become more selective; it's like a channeler allowing any entities to come into their body. Dr. Greer is not any less aggressive than Dr. Boylan. When I suggested there may be those who don't have our best interest in mind (in 2001 or 2002), he (or his staff, rather) became very hostile and refused to discuss the matter and told me it is self-evident that all ETs are good and advised me to watch "The Disclosure Project" video again (from 2001). Greer is even calling one of his projects "The Orion Project." One may wonder why. Orion doesn't have a particularly good reputation here on Earth. Also, he has sponsors in high places, such as within the Rockefeller family, and he's open with it. He justifies it by saying that branches of the banking/oil family are now ready for disclosure and support the North Carolina Emergency doctor on his quest. Go figure. Both Greer and Boylan have a huge number of almost cultish followers, and this is the danger. I have been in contact with people who are otherwise very intelligent and spiritually aware, but like one of them said: "When Dr. Boylan speaks, I'm all ears." This is concerning and quite discouraging in my opinion. We have to be more selective and mindful if we are going to make it.

About a week ago, from this point in early September 2011, when I am editing the draft of this paper, Dr. Richard Boylan did a reading, and also had support from his "star visitors," saying a series of Earthquakes were going to hit North Carolina and Virginia. He gave us the exact dates and times of the day and said that many people would die at this juncture. He has allegedly about 1 million people on his list, so I'm sure at least a few of them are from these mentioned areas. I read it and shook my head in wonder. Have can the man do this? Does he realize how much fear and terror he creates? Did anyone leave their home, or sell it? Did they leave the target areas? Not for a moment did I think he would be correct.

When, predictably, the first earthquake didn't happen, Dr. Boylan wrote a new email to the list, saying that the Cabal had changed their minds (this

---

[307] http://www.drboylan.com/goodbadugly.html

[308] Since 2011, Dr. Boylan seems to have removed the names on his "bad list," and only lists the "characteristics" of what he considers disinfo agents, *WP 2024.*

was supposed to be a manmade earthquake) and decided to hold that one earthquake back and let the Virginia earthquake hit first just to make him and the star visitors look stupid. He said that now it had been changed to so and so time. I shook my head again in wonder and asked myself, are people really listening to this guy?

None of the two earthquakes happened (of course). Boylan then came back on the list, saying that the Cabal had held both quakes back to build them up to 8.4 on the Richter-scale or something of the sort, just to make them more potent. Still, they were going to happen on so and so date at so and so time.

Nothing happened. Silence. Then Dr. Boylan came online again, after people had held their breaths in wait for this miracle man to come with his new predictions. This time he responded to a reader, who said that maybe they should do a mass prayer on the earthquakes. Boylan said no, because then the Cabal would accuse them of creating earthquakes.

Then, silence again. No earthquakes, where after someone on the list said that the earthquakes *would* happen, but not at this time, and Dr. Boylan responded with something unintelligible and that was it.

Nothing has been heard from Dr. Boylan since, and this was a few days ago. People like him are either conmen, completely delusional, or work for the government.

After all this clowning about, people on his list are still supporting him and thanking him for what he's doing. That's mind control when it's at its best. Dr. Boylan is looked upon by his member as a very nice, older man (who predicts earthquakes that never happen; scaring people shitless excuse my language). Where were the benevolent star visitors when he needed them? Out to lunch in another star system? (The information comes from Dr. Boylan's mailing list, "DrRichBoylanReports," between August 30 to September 8, 2011). I would be honored to be on his "bad list."

This is very disturbing. Oh, I almost forgot to mention that Dr. Boylan thinks Obama is a star visitor, too, and will be so kind to help Dr. Boylan out and disclose to the world that these wonderful star visitors are here. Doesn't all this create chills down your spine? It does mine. Just recently, President Obama told people they could ask him questions online, and Dr. Boylan advised his followers to do so, like if it would make any difference. I am stunned.

But the most disturbing part is not Dr. Boylan himself, but those who are following him despite these catastrophic errors and contradictions. And his whole "star visitor" agenda is breathtaking. You see drawings of all these star visitors we know about, holding hands in friendship with cute smiles on their faces. Well, the thought is good, but don't tell us that all aliens out there, without discrimination, are saint-like, and we are ready to embrace them all. And don't put people who disagree with ONE word you're saying, Dr. Boylan, on some government disinformation bad list. This is very counter-productive and outright dangerous. It also delays our mission, we who are working on revealing what is really happening, but you probably know that, and this is exactly the purpose.

Don't get me wrong; most species out there are friendly towards us and have our best interests in mind, or are at least neutral, but they have not yet revealed themselves to us for a reason. And why is that? It is because we have to overcome our greatest weaknesses first. We can't just chaotically stumble into the galactic community while fighting each other and being overly egotistical and ignorant, thus bringing our problems to their vicinity. We need to grow up first, and there are those who are patiently waiting for us to do just that. The only time they would interfere would be if we were literally destroying our planet (which we actually are close to doing). This is the Living Library, and there are those who would never let us go so far that we destroy *their* creation. They are also monitoring us and our nuclear activities and how we handle negative energy (more about that later). These are very concerning matters for them. More than once, the ETs have stopped nuclear missiles from going off; something that has baffled Military forces and even been mentioned in the Media.

We have Anunnaki/Nephilim genes, and homo sapiens sapiens was created by Ea (the Biblical Lucifer), and this means we have a warrior stroke inside of us which we have to overcome and grow out of. I believe we are waking up to this fact, and the nanosecond (1987-2012), when time is speeding up and the information is hitting us via gamma rays from the Sun and the Galactic Center, is strengthening our DNA and connecting the so-called "junk DNA" to our double helix to create a wiser, more peaceful *homo futurus*.

I am not overly convinced that disclosure is the medicine right now. On the other hand, it's a matter of what we mean by disclosure. There are so many good, intelligent people out there who are working hard on disclosure projects of different kinds, but we need to understand that the government, no matter what they say, are run by malevolent beings with and agenda, and who don't have our best interest in mind. The Disclosure supporters say that the government has come to a point where they have no choice but to tell the truth about the alien visitors, and that many people in the Military would be relieved if everything would be disclosed, but if the government is disclosing the ET issue, it's going to be on *their* terms, and it's not going to be the truth. Disclosure *will* happen, but more on an individual basis at first. The benevolent ETs will not expose themselves through the government, whom they certainly do not trust.

The only "Disclosure" I would find valuable is to get more information from groups like LPG-C and others who sit on info regarding different ET races; who they are, where they come from, their imperatives, and who is working together with whom?[309] We need to categorize them and find out who to trust and whom to stay away from. Anyone can show themselves off as "saints," but behind the veil being very dark beings. Dr. Bordon, just like me, is interested in intelligence gathering on different ET species to find out more about their relationship with each other, but he refuses to reveal what he knows about the group he belongs to. This is very unfortunate, in my opinion, because withholding this information could be potentially dangerous in the long run. Ed Komarek, a UFO researcher, asked LPG-C the question why the LINK group is so secretive if they have nothing to hide?

Carol Rosin, Dr. Greer's right hand, said in an interview recently that she is absolutely certain there are no ETs with malevolent intents left in Earth near space; they have all left, including the Greys. Her rationale is that if they were here, they would have taken over or destroyed us already, and obviously, we (meaning we humans) are still here. This, in my opinion, with all the information that is out there (which she is discarding), is quite naïve at best.

4. The Exodus of the Anunnaki Earth-Bound

In the 1400s CE, King Anu of the Ša.A.M.i. stepped down from the position as King of Nibiru.[310] This, however, did not come as a surprise, but was something the King had prepared for hundreds of years, in our terms. For political reasons, he was forced to, apparently.

The lobbying during this time was apparently intense, and both clans, the RAM clan (the En.lil bloodlines) and the Serpent Clan (the En.ki bloodlines) were as usual in competition for power, and both clans wanted to put their people on the throne. Anu, who wanted the transition to be as peaceful as possible for the Nibiruan people, tried to calm things down. He announced that his successor would be judged due to his performance down on Earth before the Sinai nuclear disaster.

How do we know this? According to the Life Physics Group California (LPG-C), they come from LINK meetings with these alien groups. These meetings have either taken place in exotic and secret places here on Earth, or onboard one of their crafts. The human faction of this group has organized these meetings only twice.

The story about Anu stepping down, and all the rest of it, was told to them by the Nibiruan representatives at these same meetings to give a briefing to us earthlings, so we can make more knowledge-based decisions

---

[309] The value of the LPG-C information is debatable, in my opinion. It's a mixed bag or truth, half-truths, and lies. Now, years after my connection with them, it's obvious they were compromised and manipulated by the "Anunnaki" (Sirians) with whom they were in contact, *WP 2024*.

[310] Bordon, A.R. (2007): *The LINK - Extraterrestrials in Near Earth Space and Contact on the Ground, p. 53.*

in the future, as the story goes. In addition to this, the LPG-C members are referring to witnesses (whom they call "Informants"), with whom they spoke over a few years' time. What these Informants said, supposedly independent from each other in most cases, can be read in A.R. Bordon and J.W. Barber's: *Journal of End Time Studies Vol 1: January-June 2007: Between the Devil and the Incoming Rock*. These witnesses are either scientists, (ex) military, or (ex) government agents on middle and higher levels. And lastly, I have my own experiences with LPG-C, from having been in contact with them for over 8 months as of this writing. They have shared a lot of inside information that will be released in increments (where part of my own info is some of it). I've seen things unfold within the organizations and their struggles with coming to terms with the Intel and information they have regarding the Ša.A.M.i. and other present and future ET issues, and natural disasters.

A few decades before the beginning of the Common Era (CE), the announcement that King Anu was stepping down was made. This resulted in a fast exodus of the Anunnaki still on Earth, and they immediately returned to Nibiru to be part of the lobbying. Both Nammur and Ea (now calling himself Ankur) left Earth to be with their father on the home planet. Ankur's sons, Marduk and Ningishzidda, and their families went back as well, causing the closure of the smelting operations in Bolivia. Others that returned were reportedly Nergal, Ankur's son, and his consort, Nammur's grand-daughter Ereškigal; King Anu's grandson Ninurta and his consort. Other Anunnaki, members of the RAM clan who returned were Nannar, his wife, and Iškur, Inanna, Ašnan, Nanše, and a few others. Nannar and his consort, we are told, returned to Earth for a short time after that to northern Syria, only to return to the platform to wait for transport to the home planet.

Figure 14.2: Sacsahuaman - A side view of the complex

Then, in the later part of the second century CE, Nannar was instructed by his father and King Anu to return to Altiplano in southeastern Peru to help Nannar's son Uti with closing down the smelters of Sacsahuaman and stop the runway operations in the Nazca area of southern Peru.[311] The smelters continued to process gold, tin and silver for a while, managed remotely from Turkey, but by the sixth century, Sacsahuaman was no longer in use and the pre-Incan civilizations from northern Peru through the north of the Atacama desert in northern Chile were left to fend for themselves—the Anunnaki were gone. Other colonies, to cite Dr. Bordon again,[312] such as North American Midwest, southeastern and southwestern native groups who came in contact with and taught by the Anunnaki how to manage agriculture, animal husbandry, and other basic matters, were also abandoned by the Anunnaki by the 7th and 8th centuries CE. For a couple of hundred years, we humans were more or less left alone on the planet for the first time since the Anunnaki created homo sapiens sapiens. But they would return!

The Announcement of the New King!

The transition of King Anu stepping down and the announcement of the new King over the Kingdom (Nibiru) was a slow one and took about 600 years, according to the information given to the LPG-C. Anu was very careful with whom he chose as his successor, because reportedly, he wanted the new king to be a person who once again could unite the Ša.A.Mi. (the Nibiruans), and stop the feud between the clans. Because of the strong polarity between the clans, it was not an easy task. For a while, he wanted to choose Ankur (Ea), but he knew he couldn't because he was not the legal heir of the throne, according to Nibiruan law, and that would upset the RAM clan and only add fuel to the fire.

As mentioned earlier, Anu also took into consideration the performance of certain royal candidates while on Earth, but didn't find a proper candidate, since most had been involved in raging wars and disasters. No one seemed to have a clean resume. As a side note, I find it remarkable how King Anu could be so judgmental, when he was the one, who, according to Sitchin, allowed Alalu's nuclear missiles to fall over the Sinai Spaceport and Sodom and Gomorrah. He knew thousands of humans would die horrible deaths, and parts of the planet become radioactive for thousands of years. This speaks tons about the morals and ethics of this species, or the lack thereof, from our perspective. Too many

---

[311] Bordon, A.R. (2007): *The LINK - Extraterrestrials in Near Earth Space and Contact on the Ground, p. 54.*
[312] *Ibid.*

destructive actions and decisions make a person blind (and narcissistic and psychopathic, unless these are trait they incorporated already from the beginning, *WP 2024*). We can argue that they have other imperatives than we do, and look at us as ants or unintelligent apes, but it doesn't justify the cruel actions against us humans. And aside from that, we need to think about our own imperatives in relation to this group of aliens, who think they own us because they tinkered with our DNA. They were never our creators; they were imposters who manipulated an already highly developed DNA/RNA. We will discuss this later on.

When the exodus happened in the 6th-8th century CE, there were supposedly about 400 Anunnaki on our planet, and 3/4 of them were supporting Marduk, obeying him as the King of Earth and the Nibiru Kingdom, and did *not* acknowledge King Anu as their king. This was a big problem for the real Kingdom, and Marduk had always been, and still was, a time bomb and a great concern. None of Marduk's followers could of course be considered as King Anu's successor.

Eventually, Ningišzidda came up with a solution. He vouched for Nannar, the En.lil's son. He reasoned that Nannar was the only one who could really succeed in uniting the Ša.A.Mi. again, and additionally, Ningišzidda said that Nannar had the vital force of his grandfather, King Anu himself. Ningišzidda had actually himself been considered by King Anu as his successor, but politely declined, again saying Nannar would be the better choice. After a lot of pondering, Anu agreed, and Nannar, son of Nammur, and the grandson of Anu, became the king of Nibiru in the 1400s CE. After hundreds of thousands of years (at least), King Anu stepped down from the throne. He was apparently happy that the transition could be done without bloodshed (very unusual, *WP 2024*). From our point of view, the leadership had changed from the Serpent clan (Ea's bloodline) to the RAM clan (the En.lil's bloodline). Metaphorically, that would be like shifting between the Democrats and the Republicans.

Figure 14.3: Nannar, to the right, while still on Earth during Sumerian times.

Satan Returns to Earth

We know from face-to-face and mind-to-mind communications between members of the LPG-C and those from the Kingdom (Nibiru) that Marduk left Earth by the 8th Century CE, but what happened next? Marduk, obviously, was not wanted on Nibiru and was not allowed to stay there.

In 2001, the LPG-C was informed that Marduk and approximately 300 Anunnaki returned to Earth again around the turn of the millennium (1000 CE), and has been here ever since, some of them taking control over the Earth population by force and by creating his own Pyramid Power Structure, with Marduk placing himself on top as the only God and King of the Universe.[313] Marduk easily fits the picture of the Biblical Satan, and also fits right into the biblical prophecies, such as The Book of Revelation and The Book of Daniel, and him and Satan seem to be one and the same. He also took control over all major religions to use in the effort to manipulate the growing Earth population and to divide and conquer.

The first thing he did was an attempt to rewrite history to erase all the knowledge humans had of their own history and origins, putting himself in the position as God Almighty. He even took on the task to rewrite the Babylonian Enûma Eliš (Sitchin, 1985). He is still worshipped as God in

---

[313] It is interesting how the "Anunnaki" twist and bend history to fit certain agendas. They played around with LPG-C a lot, *WP 2024.*

many secret societies, such as the Freemasons, unbeknownst by most members, except those few at the very top level, above the 33rd degree of the Scottish Rite. Marduk can be considered the "All-Seeing Eye" at the top of the Freemasonic Pyramid, and the "Eye of Ra" (Marduk Ra, who later became Amen Ra when he was in hiding after the pyramid incident. How Marduk changed history to give himself more power is mentioned both by Zecharia Sitchin in his *Earth Chronicles*, Robert Morning Sky's *The Terra Papers* (which go into even more details about it), and by the Ša.A.M.i. themselves, through conversations during the annual LINK meetings between ET groups and the LPG-C, as discussed earlier.

By rewriting history and secret and occult instruction manuals, he could convert all these secret groups (secret societies) into Intelligence cells working for him, and thus be ahead of those who opposed him. Presently, he is also attempting to reconstruct a six-stage ziggurat *strong enough to support a landing platform at its apex.*[314] This would work as his new spaceport, instead of the Tilmun (Sinai Spaceport) that was nuked by the Ša.A.M.i. and the "fallen ones" before they left a couple of millennia prior to the Common Era.[315]

Figure 14.4: Marduk Ra's Pyramid with the All-Seeing Eye. This can be found at the back of the one-dollar bill. Marduk is in charge of the banking cartel -- or at least most of it. There are more ETs involved behind the scenes, to whom some people in power, in more recent times, have made an alliance.

---

[314] Bordon, A.R. (2007): *The LINK - Extraterrestrials in Near Earth Space and Contact on the Ground, p.56, op. cit.*
[315] http://en.wikipedia.org/wiki/Ziggurat_of_Ur#Neo-Babylonian_restoration

Figure 14.5a: The Ziggurat from Sumerian times, being the Temple of Marduk around the 21st Century BC, and now under reconstruction in Iraq, supposedly to be used as Marduk's Spaceport.

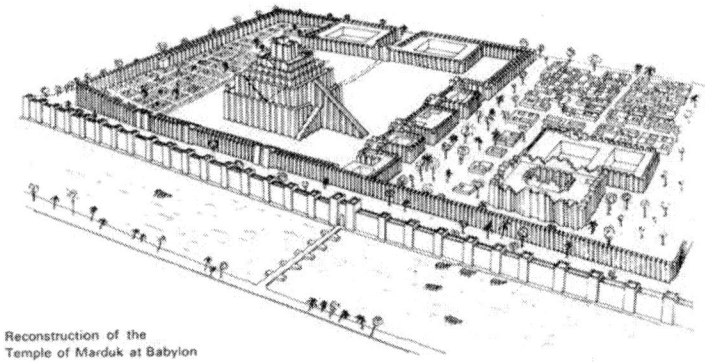

Reconstruction of the
Temple of Marduk at Babylon

Figure 14.5b: Model of the reconstruction of the Temple of Marduk in Babylon.

Marduk, in a childish revolt and rebellion towards his own people, for not giving him the power he deserved in the first place (from his perspective), not only created (and still does) havoc here on Earth but is also magnifying the ancient struggle between the two clans. The RAM clan, of course, doesn't accept his behavior, and he also puts his father, Ankur (Ea), in an almost impossible position. Ankur wants to support his son but has to be as diplomatic possible; a wrong move, or a wrong word, can potentially start another war. The situation, from what I can imagine, is quite tense. After all, Ankur is the one who has felt the most compassion towards mankind, much due to the fact that he looks upon us as his own creation, his own children. It was his DNA which created the first Anunnaki/human hybrids. Ankur, sitting on the original earthly Council of 12, who decided about big issues and problems that needed to be solved here on Earth, had many times supported his son, or "protected him" from the rest of the Council.

Now, however, when both Nammur and Ankur have left Earth, Marduk has set up his own Council (in the WingMakers "mythology" called *The Corteum*,[316] with himself on top at the rank of 60, something that is reserved for the King of Nibiru. By giving himself this rank, Marduk announces himself as both the King of Earth (Satan), and that of Nibiru, thus not acknowledging the sitting King and the Kingdom.

Giving himself the rank of King and refusing to give his obedience to the Kingdom in general, made the Nibiruan Council decide to put Marduk under the equivalent to a quarantine here on Earth.[317] What this means, exactly, is not known to me, and I yet need to find out. Does it mean that Marduk is not allowed to leave Earth (which has been suggested to me), or is the picture larger than that, something to the effect what Robert Morning Sky wrote in The Terra Papers? According to Morning Sky's research, and from what the Star Elder told him, the whole Earth was put under quarantine. And humans, too, are not allowed to, or able to travel very far out in space. The Pleiadians, on the other hand, just like David Icke, are talking about a frequency quarantine (as mentioned earlier), where our DNA was tampered with to the extent that we have been stuck in this 3-D frequency range for pretty much 300,000 years.[318] The Ra Material discussed something similar: The Ra collective tells us we are put under quarantine by the Council of Saturn,[319] which pretty neatly corresponds to the Nibiruan Council.

This whole quarantine issue is going to be discussed in another paper as well, but it is quite plausible that "quarantine" can mean different things here.

It is clear that Marduk has a stronghold over most, if not all institutions, banking cartels, educational systems, religions, entertainment etc., in the world of today. However, he does not have the monopoly many researchers think. Besides the two factions of Anunnaki, fighting against

---

[316] Penre/Bordon correspondence, January 26, 2011.

[317] Bordon, A.R. (2007): *The LINK - Extraterrestrials in Near Earth Space and Contact on the Ground, p.56.*

[318] Based on my current research, I would suggest the more correct number is about 13,500 years, which is when Noah's Flood happened. That's when the Matrix was created. The time before that was Atlantis, *WP 2024*).

[319]
http://lawofone.info/results.php?search_string=council+of+saturn+quarantine&look_here=answer,question&search_type=any&row_limit=30&numeric_order=0&ss=1

each other (the RAM clan and the Serpent Clan), there are at least two or three other major ET races competing over total control of Earth and mankind. This makes things even more complicated.

Marduk's Council of 12 -- The Corteum

At this point, we don't know all the names in Marduk's Council of 12 (also called the *Olympians* according to two of LPG-C's informants),[320] but LPG-C has been able to figure out at least a few of them and their ranks. It looks like the current hierarchy of the top Anunnaki on Earth are as follows:

Table 1 – Probable membership and ranking order of Earthbound Anunnaki
Council of Twelve Membership

Male Order	Rank Order	Female	Rank
Marduk	60	Zarpanit	55
Nabu	50	Unknown	45
Gibil	40	Unknown	35
Unknown	30	Unknown	25
Unknown	20	Unknown	15
Nuskum	10	Unknown	5

Figure 14.6: Council of 12 Members as far as we know (2007)

These twelve members are then pulling the strings of the following Power Centers:

---

[320] This is interesting, since the Olympians in Greek mythology were the "younger gods" who revolted and created a havoc in this part of the Universe, opposed to the Titans, who were the "older gods," i.e., the Original Creators. More on this in the upcoming books in these Wes Penre Chronicles, *WP 2024*.

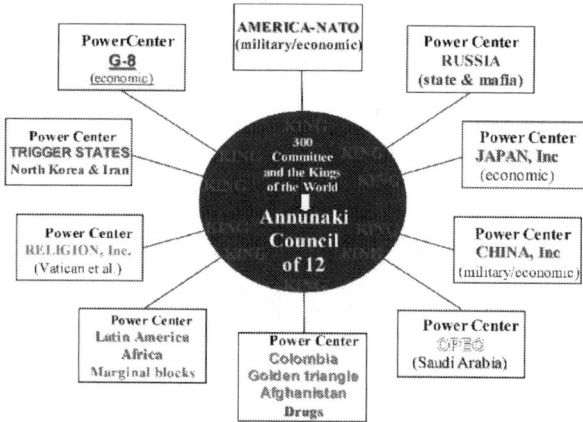

Figure 14.7: Probable meta-organization of earthbound Anunnaki influence/control.

As the Organization Board shows in *Fig. 14.8*, there are 10 Power Centers all together. Like twelve spiders in the net sit the top rank Anunnaki, delegating their power downwards to the leaders of each Power Center, which are all supposedly run by humans (and/or hybrids). Those ten leaders are then reporting directly to the 12 Anunnaki (the Council of 12, or C-12). Logically, the C-12 members then report to Marduk in person, either in board meetings or on an immediate basis, depending on the urgency (not being convinced that Marduk is dead, I am still going to proceed as if he is alive. If he is not, what I am describing pertains to his successor; one or both of his two sons, Nabu and Gibil).

After doing some research and making contact with appropriate sources, members of the LPG-C managed to identify the 10 Power Centers with what seems to be quite some accuracy. They are:

1. The American/NATO group

2. The Russia/Mafia group

3. The Japan, Inc. group

4. The China, Inc. group

5. The OPEC group

6. The Cartel/Triad councils group

7. The supply margin economic/political groups in Latin America and Africa headed by Brazil (Latin America) and South Africa (Africa)

8. The seven members of the ecumenical community led by the Roman Pope

9. The two trigger states, Iran and North Korea (as a wild card group)

10. The economic/political group known as G8.[321] [322]

Please take note here that because what the LPG-C actually say in *Between the Devil and the Incoming Rock* is that the above is the <u>Anunnaki</u> pyramidal meta-structure on Earth, not that the Anunnaki is the *only* alien power force which controls the planet from the ground or beyond. I just want to emphasize this again, so the reader can keep it in mind for future reference.

The Earth-Bound Anunnaki: How They Look Like and Their Whereabouts

Before we talk about the whereabouts of the earth-bound, I'm sure the reader is curious whether there are any photos of real Anunnaki, besides from the Sumerian clay tablets.

The answer would be that there are, but they are not on the Internet. However, I have in my possession a photo of a first- or second generation Anunnaki female hybrid, taken in Puerto Rico. This is how they apparently look like,

---

[321] Bordon, A.R. and Barber, J.W., (2007): *Journal of End Time Studies Vol 1: January-June 2007: Between the Devil and the Incoming Rock, p.19 op. cit.*

[322] The European Union is missing in the above structure. It's uncertain if the LPG-C considered the EU being manipulated by another group, *WP 2024.*

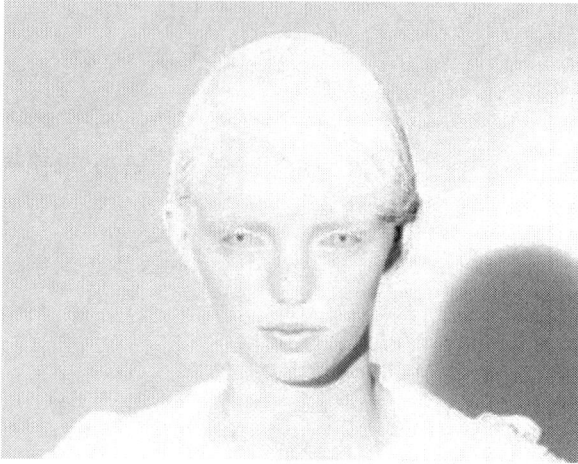

Figure 14.8: Earth-bound Anunnaki female hybrid of the first- or second generation; photo taken in Puerto Rico.

This particular photo has a story behind it, which I need to tell. It was allegedly taken by Dr. Bordon in a meeting in Puerto Rico. This particular LPG-C member, who knew about their existence from earlier annual meetings, was surprised to meet four of these beings in the Puerto Rico gathering. Bordon told me that these beings were taller than humans, but not tremendously taller; somewhere between 6 to 7 feet. They were very pale-skinned, with white, kinky hair, which they sometimes wear long and sometimes short. Their eyes are red, when seen in certain light.

Although I felt I had established a relationship with the LPG-C, and especially with Dr. A.R. Bordon, I was skeptic at first when I saw the photo because I did a search on the Internet and could easily find the photo on different websites. Some even suggested it was a photoshop job of the Polish model, Anja Rubic (*fig. 14.9*).

Figure 14.9The Polish model, Anja Rubic

I decided to send the alleged Anunnaki female photo to two different photoshop experts. In both cases, they came back with the same answer: this person is not totally human, but a hybrid.

I will leave it with that for the reader to ponder, and if someone wants to look into this some more, it may be worth it.

The LPG-C, however, guarantees that this is how the earth-bound females look like, and they tell me they know this from face-to-face encounters, and also by using Extra Neurosensing (ENS) remote viewing.

To return to the story about the photo of the Anunnaki female, it was stolen (and I know this to be true) from LPG-C by an impostor who joined the group, pretending to do so with the best of intentions. He joined under the name Roy W. Gordon. The photo was supposedly taken in 2006. Sometime in 2008, Roy Gordon stole it (and other sensitive information) and escaped. The photo was later posted on the Internet by the organization that Gordon was/is a member of: S.A.A.L.M. or the ACIO/NSA (National Security Agency), located in Pine Gap, Australia, known for its significant number of mysterious sightings,[323] also one of the major bases for Marduk, and associated Intelligence Agencies. S.A.A.L.M. stands for "Supreme Anunnaki Assembly of Lord Marduk". *Fig. 14.11* below shows the S.A.A.L.M. version of the Anunnaki female:

---

[323] Icke, David (2010): *Human Race Get Off Your Knees, The Lion Sleeps No More, pp. 665-666.*

```
TS-SCI- S.A.M-422Wxxy
Report prepared for S.A.A.L.M by xxxxxxxxxxxxxx
A-C-T-I-O-N_ACIO  PINE GAP

Description
Extra-terrestrial
Species: SAM_Nordics
Aliases: Swedes, Tall Whites, Nordics
Height: 5 - 6.5 feet
Weight: 120 - 240 pounds (estimated)
Eyes: Human
Hair: Blonde
Skin: Pale white
Sex: Male and Female
Communication: Telepathic
Location of Origin
Mt Ziel - Northern Australia
Distinguishing Characteristics
Share common physical features with human beings
(especially Scandinavians)
Are taller than the average human
Have more of a muscular build than the average human
```

Figure 14.10: The S.A.A.L.M. publication of the same Anunnaki female, stolen from LPG-C..

The information added to this photo in form of text is inaccurate and part of a disinformation campaign by Marduk's Pine Gap faction, according to LPG-C.

S.A.A.L.M., a department of NSA, was also involved in a smear campaign against James Casbolt, an MI6 whistle-blower and mind controlled slave, when he decided to go public. They managed to discredit him to such an extent that Casbolt had to pull his website, casbolt.com, a few years ago. We will spend more time on S.A.A.L.M. and their possible connection with the top secret Labyrinth Group within the NSA in a special section.

We have already talked about Pine Gap, Australia, but where else can we find the earth-bound Anunnaki and their first and second generation hybrids? The LPG-C did some research on this and had great help from their Informants. Informants one, three, and four (2005, 2006) led them to Puerto Rico and the Ngongoro region of the Great Rift Valley in the Serengeti National Park of Tanzania, Africa (see Map 1, fig. 14.12a, and Map 2, fig. 14.12b areas are circled).

Figure 14.11a: Map 1 -- East Region of Africa

Informants three and four, independent of each other, confirmed that there indeed is Anunnaki presence in the Tanzania area, including UFO activity.

Regarding the Puerto Rico, the LPG-C *"were not able to confirm any of the reports received concerning the El Yunque region, near the U.S. naval base at Roosevelt Roads, in northeast Puerto Rico; except for a number of confirmed "disappearances" of people in the Experimental Forest area near the naval base, and the unusual number of albinos in the area."*[324]

However, Dr. Bordon knew about the Anunnaki activity in Puerto Rico, at least as early as 2006, when the photo of the female was taken. Apparently, he decided to exclude that from the evidence at the point of the writing of his essay in 2007.[325] Most likely, it had to do with the embarrassment of Roy W. Gordon's infiltration, which led to the theft of the photo. I don't know the real reason why Bordon excluded his own encounters with the earth-bound in his essay, though, but the above may be a qualified guess. Dr. Bordon is not very fond of talking about the Roy Gordon incident, and he gets easily aggravated when discussing the subject with me.

---

[324] Bordon, A.R. and Barber, J.W., (2007): *Journal of End Time Studies Vol 1: January-June 2007: Between the Devil and the Incoming Rock, p.22 op. cit.*

[325] Bordon, A.R. and Barber, J.W., (2007): *Journal of End Time Studies Vol 1: January-June 2007: "Between the Devil and the Incoming Rock.*

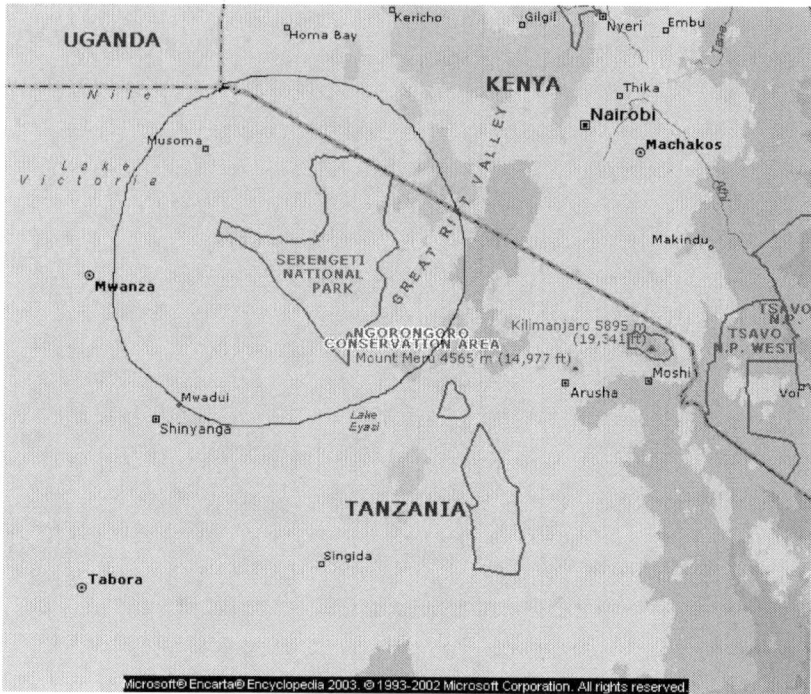

Figure 14.11b: Map2 -- Serengeti and Ngorongoro crater area.

I want to add some more detailed background information on Dr. Bordon's encounter with the four Anunnaki hybrids because it could be of interest to the reader, and to our further research on the earth-bound. Dr. Bordon told me that they (Bordon and others) (whomever "they" are, however, is not clear) did some work as subcontractors for a contractor in 2006, which led them to go down from California to Puerto Rico. Here is the story in Dr. Bordon's own words:

> Now, the event that led to the photo from my end. In 06, we had an opportunity to do some work for a contractor as subcontractors, which required two of us to head down under for pressing the flesh and drying the ink on paper. The photo in question was one I took of a female, approximately 6'2" dressed in a very white dress draped over one shoulder - in other words, the female in the photo in question. The photo was taken at exactly 41 degrees inclination to the plane on which she was (i.e., the ground floor of a large building/structure that housed a research center of sorts at an underground facility). The picture was taken with an old SLR and developed on site by people from the installation. Four shots were taken of her, two of which were overexposed with one of those somewhat blurry. All upstairs pictures of her were taken with a tele lens. The other one is one taken at the same level and there are people around her. The occasion was a party/reception in our

honor, and there were four of them, three males and this female. We were not allowed to take any pictures of the males, but I was told that I could take no more than five pictures of her, but that all of the background images of the setting in which the subject was had to be changed. This was done subsequently, in digitized form, putting a blank background, which it is visible and evident on the picture. Her eyes were red at close range, but even the clearest augmentation of the digitized original did not show her eyes clearly, so color was augmented manually. That was the only touch given to the original.

...

The other three almost immediately joined us. I know she had called them over via mind-on-mind communication, and asked her if she had done so. She acknowledged she had, and this surprised her even more. On that occasion, in fact that evening, my party and I learned these four were members of the ground group and that their homesite was in Puerto Rico. The one clear picture of her was retouched and background-changed, leaving her form intact but with the eye color accentuated in red. I did not make the changes but I can say that the picture of the female I met is the likeness of the individual depicted on the photograph in question. My question, given the likeness between Anja and this female, is whether there is a biological connection between them I raise that question because it is known that pure SAM *S̆a.A.M.i., Wes' comment* and SAM hybrid females are known to engage in intercourse with human males and to conceive children who are then 2nd and 3rd generation hybrids. Same with SAM males of the ground group.

This photo was not release *sic* to anyone by us, according to agreement with the contractor of record. We believe we were invited to come as a way of establishing bona fides that the contractor was indeed in direct contact and had access to SAMs. We were satisfied that this was indeed the case, and the case was closed. We then proceeded to perform the work for the contractor, were paid for our work, and that was the end of it. Except for the RWG affair *Roy W. Gordon, Wes's note*, which began to unravel shortly after our return from down under. Things got quite nasty with the man who had been planted in our midst, and who had gone down with us. We are certain in hindsight that the man who returned back was not the same man who went down. I am also aware of the Casbolt case, as James came to us for possible deprogramming. Nothing came of it, and contact with him was broken.

Now, in appearance, those who are from the home planet are taller than those who belong to the ground group here. The three male individuals we ran across were 7 feet in height or over, but not as tall as those whom we met during Link sessions, nor like those who picked me and my dad up in 1956 in South America during a fishing trip on a River between Brazil and Paraguay.

All of this happened about 4 years ago.

In the aftermath of the RWG affair, we did a thorough housecleaning of the disaster he brought to our doors. We have a working relationship with many people and used every contact known to us in finding out who and what was this man doing and representing. Among the things he left behind was a clean picture of this female without the poorly done description of her on the lower left hand corner. I have no doubt this picture you showed me has been doctored and that we were not the only ones in possession of the digitized form now circulating. However, I was the one taking the picture and the picture is not taken at same level and it is not a frontal picture of her. She is gazing slightly to one side of the camera, as Ed argues in his video study of the photo.[326]

After I had asked Dr. Bordon some additional questions, the details became even clearer. He was very generous about explaining this to us, UFO researcher Ed Komarek http://exopolitics.blogspot.com/ and me. I am publishing this because I think it could be important because it gives some credibility to Dr. Bordon's claims of having taken the photo of the hybrid female.

I will not include information here of a personal nature, currently off limit for publication, or off subject. The occluded sections will be within brackets ... . The rest is word for word.

There were four, not five viable pictures. I remember taking five, which is why I said five. Again, the pictures of her I took with an SLR in color from about 80 feet distance, a little less than 30 meters. I was on a first or second mezzanine up, which made for the angle of view, which in the first picture I took (she had just come through a door that was to her right in the photo you sent. Again, all photos were developed on site and given to us before departure. The fifth I was told did not come out. I did not pursue it.

Her eyes were, well, have you ever seen someone who was suffering of pink eyes, conjunctivitis, it is something of a pinkish-red from a distance, and the color remained pinkish on closer view - about 6 feet. We were never allowed to touch or be closed *sic* to them. Yes, there are pictures of her, one overexposed, the other with spots on her. These pictures were not "sanitized" (i.e., background removed). There was an additional photo taken the angle of which made her be at profile from me. These photos are in the possession of the contractor, all of them were retrieved when

---

[326] The information is based upon one of my conversations between Dr. Bordon, UFO researcher Ed Komarek, and me on January 24, 2011.

R.W.'s thing began to unravel. However, I am not going back to them to ask for these pictures. That's one dog I am going to let stay sleep. What really happen is a black mark on the contractor and on us, and revisiting the R.W. affair just ain't going to happen. Some of your and Ed's suppositions about Gordon are not farfetched at all and are closer to what happened. But that's all I will say about it.

Obviously, there are problems with this photo. We had no reasons to distrust the product given to us at the time. Only one was photoshoped; none of the others were changed in any way.

One of the things I would suggest is to not use that photo at all. There are better ones out there. When meeting the informants for the information XXXX name excluded and I reported in essay, pictures surfaced corroborating their likeness, although some at simple viewing of the photo told us the objects of the photo were hybrids. There are also photos taken by a fellow I know, who is photographically pursuing them around the world, and there are some taken by him or by one of his collaborators **from either Argentina or Chile showing SAMs up in the mountains of the Andes** *my emphasis*. I have not seen them, but I trust his word, since he's provided images of the skeletons of giants that are not in the public domain which we've been able to verify with LPG-C members from Russia that these were indeed viable (real) photos. Then there are photos of **SAMs living in northern Wisconsin** *my emphasis* we know about, photos of which are harder to come by, so XXXXXXX (my friend) has been making personal attempts at getting one or more. There is also a retired master sargeant *sic* who was stationed in **San Antonio, TX** *my emphais*, who had taken distance photos of two of them in military uniform without insignias. So there are photos. With patience we will get to them.

...

Witness what is happening in South America. I'm staying in touch with a Chilean, an Argentinian and a Paraguayan, all of them working with video as the medium of capture. There are technical problems with video - they never worked for us in person with any of them. Digital photography is best. It does not lie and it does not change the subject.

Now, let me address something that, once either or both of you come in ftf *face-to-face,* editor's note contact with any one of them, and become familiar with these folks, the last thing you think about is photographing them. There are too many other things on focuses on while this is happening. There is also the issue that some will not allow you to take pictures of them. Then there are some whose body electrostatic and electromagnetic fields is so high that it distorts even a digital picture. Or, better said, the digital photo comes out distorted, like as if the space around the body is broken up. And, Ed, wordy as this may be, until YOU have been in front of any one of these people, that's all I have to explain the experience.

...

...Please hear this as well: this is NOT about disclosure; this IS about connecting.[327]

So, first of all, a few new locations are exposed to us in the above email: Argentina and Chile (and up in the Andes), Wisconsin and Texas. Dr. Bordon also tells me in a letter dated, December 2, 2010, that the faction living in the Andes come from the Cydonia planes on Mars and moved to the Chile mountain range just a few decades ago. Some of them can also be found along the Peruvian/Ecuadorian border.

There is some additional information on this that I heard on a Pleiadian lecture from the summer of 2011 as well. They said there are underground bases in the Middle East where some of the Anunnaki reside. They have lots of stealth technology available to them down there, and they steer the major events in the Middle East from underground. This is done partly by changing the brain frequencies on humans living on the surface, by putting beliefs and ideas into their heads people think are their own. This is to create and fuel predetermined conflicts. A similar thing was done in Egypt during the uproar in the beginning of 2011.

To summarize, these are the sites where the Anunnaki have allegedly been spotted on Earth in present time:

1. Pine Gap, Australia

2. Puerto Rico, South America

3. The Andes, The Chile, South America

4. The Ngongoro region of the Great Rift Valley, in the Serengeti National Park of Tanzania, Africa.

5. Northern Wisconsin, U.S.A.

6. Texas, U.S.A.

7. Underground bases in the Middle East

---

[327] Penre/Komarek/Bordon correspondence, January 25, 2011.

Secondly, Dr. Bordon (and the LPG-C in general) are not for ET disclosure but for connection. It sounds pretty black and white when we read it like this, and out of context, but there is much more to that statement; something we will discuss in the next book in these chronicles. I believe it is a wise decision, but to understand what I mean by that, we *do* have to dig into the issue much deeper, which we will.

Marduk's Challenges

Although Marduk is using ancient techniques to control us via networks of secret societies, businesses, religion, banking etc., his problem is, and has always been, numbers. The latest Intel on him and his pure Anunnaki followers is telling us that they are about 330 in numbers, and once in a while, they have been the target of snipers. That (and other reasons) have been what has reduced the numbers of the "Fallen" and the Nephilim. Hence, they have been said to have been forced to do two thing: fine tuning their networks in attempts to have them work more efficiently and reduce the numbers of Lulus (humans).

The second is supposedly done, among other things, by creating wars, famine, disease, poisoning of food stuff, etc. I know that it has been circulating amongst researchers for perhaps 20 years now (I was one of them), that the Global Elite want to reduce the population down to perhaps 500,000,000 people. That's a huge reduction! If they'd wanted to do that with the technologies which they have available, they would have done so by now. Instead, the population has increased to 7 billion (as of 2011). My personal thought is that the PTB (Powers That Be) is just waiting out the natural catastrophes ahead, and they can aid in the disaster by adding their own weapon of mass destruction to the soup. The manmade disasters and weather change they have already orchestrated fill other purposes, like inducing fear in the population, and biological warfare, and to make duller people easier to manipulate. The wars, on the other hand, are just the old never-ending wars between the gods. That's where the "fine tuning" applies.

Marduk knows about the increase of energies from the Galactic Center and our own Sun, which brings information on gamma rays to us here on Earth. It's happened before; the last time we were lined up with the Galactic Center (the "Womb of the Mother", as the Pleiadians call it), was about 26,000 ago, and in a lesser degree, 13,500 years ago, when our solar system in line with the Central Sun the last time. This time around, during the nanosecond, between 1987-2012, many people are prepared and ready to "download" the information from the Galactic Center, our own Sun, and the Universe in general. This is a big thing where numbers count again.[328]

Marduk knows he can't do much about the mass awakening, unless he kills off an incredible number of people, and the question is if he actually would succeed anyway. There are ways (mentioned above) he can reduce the population, but the question is if he will succeed. Some may think that the Global Elite is united, but they are far from it. There are serious conflicts and disagreements on higher levels, which may be fortunate for us, as it delays any major actions against us, and gives us more time to get the job done on our end. On the contrary, it also extends our suffering, *WP 2024*. The major challenges I see Marduk facing today are:

1. Disagreements within his own circle of people. The Anunnaki are always fighting themselves up the ladder.

2. The ancient conflict between the RAM Clan and his own Serpent Clan. There are still those loyal to the Kingdom, residing here on Earth, making life harder for Marduk. We may ask ourselves whether we should line up with them to fight Marduk and his cohorts, but I would definitely say no to that. We don't want to be involved in more massive wars that no one can win. And *"violence always feeds violence," "if you kill with the sword, you shall die by the sword"* etc.

3. The mass awakening of the Lulus. This is a major factor he may, or may not, know how to deal with successfully. However, as mentioned above, that part may take care of itself, similar to when the En.lil just let the lulus die in the Deluge. In my book, Marduk if not worse than the En.lil (YHVH).

4. The Incoming Nibiru. He soon has to face his nemesis, King Nannar, whom reportedly is here to destroy Marduk and his network. In all his pride, Marduk may still think he can beat them, which will probably be his Achilles Heal. If we are to believe Bible prophecies, Marduk/Satan will not succeed, but there will be a big battle of Armageddon, where many people will die in the so-called "final"(?!) War of the Gods. Of course, humans will once again be used as foot soldiers...

What Marduk has done is to take advantage of time speeding up during the nanosecond. He has forcing us humans to work harder and harder, multi-tasking to the extent that we can no longer think rationally because we have no time. The Pleiadians call this *"functional insanity"*, which I think

---

[328] Keep in mind this was written in 2011, *before* 2012, *WP 2024*.

is a great description. The result, however, is that many people get so caught up in the fast pace of life, intentionally created, that we don't have time to think about deeper issues that would actually help us solve our problems. The immediate resolution is to **slow down!** We need to stay calm, meditate, and calm down our frantic energies, or we'll succumb. This entire trap is very cleverly built, and on the surface, it seems like pure insanity, but if we look at it from Marduk's point of view, it's psychopathically ingenious.

There are many challenges ahead, and the Anunnaki problem is only one of many, as we shall see. Humankind needs to be prepared, or we stand no chance of survival. Of course, as always, mankind *will* survive as a species, but our numbers will be significantly reduced! Still, there are things we can do, and we have help behind the scenes; both from here and "above," so to speak. And I'm not talking only about ETs, but our own Higher Selves/Oversouls/Sovereign Integral/Spirit; whatever we choose to call it.

I have another diagram I want to show you, which is included in Bordon's *Journal of End Time Studies Vol 1: January-June 2007: Between the Devil and the Incoming Rock,* and that is another pyramid power structure, looked at from a slightly different angle, showing the information flow going in two directions; downward and upward, where the latter is meant to be a "clear flow," where all information goes from down to the top, while the downward flow is restricted and on a "need to know basis". This also pertains to more off-world policies, and this structure is being implemented as we speak, if the interpretation of the situation is correct.

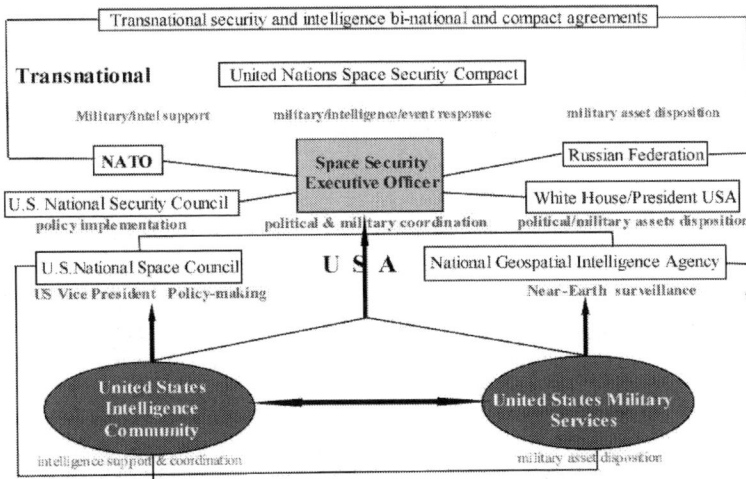

Figure 14.12: LPG-C's interpretation of the USA/transnational "crisis mode" space security, intelligence, and event response grid at present.

The ultimate challenges for Marduk and his human and not-so-human underdogs will be the incoming planet, Nibiru. The arrival is still a few generations in the future, but if we are to believe what old prophecy says (and we should), the Ša.A.M.i. from the home planet will defeat Marduk and his Global Elite and then rule us for another 3,600 years in something that can be described as Paradise on Earth, or "Heaven of Earth".[329]

But who gave us these prophecies? Who gave the information to John the Divine and Daniel? It should be quite obvious to the reader by now. If we study the chain of events here, we can quite easily see who is who. Marduk being Satan, Nannar and his people from the Home Planet being our Savior(s) ("Second Coming" of Nibiru). Nammur, the En.lil, is the primary YHVH (Jehovah), although YHVH/YHWH is a composite of different Anunnaki,[330] and Ea (Ankur/the Enki) is Lucifer, who gave Adam and Eve wisdom in the Garden of Eden (Edin). According to the Bible, the prophecies written therein are of divine origin, and if we look at the information that I shared here a few sentences ago, we can see who the "Divine" ("God") is.

I have always been fascinated by the early WingMakers material, and how accurate much of it is after some 13 odd years under scrutiny. James, the writer and interpreter of the material, writes regarding the Anunnaki and the Ša.A.M.i.:

> The genetic library that thrives upon earth is a form of currency that has no price tag. All I can say is that its value far exceeds anything that human thought could imagine. And with this incredible value, our planet attracts interest from a wide-range of extraterrestrial races, and this is as true today as it was a thousand years ago or a hundred thousand years ago.
>
> "Objects of inestimable value and rarity, such as earth, attract beings from outside our planetary system that desire to control them, which makes earth an extraordinary object of attraction. It's precisely this attraction that has brought the concepts of evil to our psyche.[331]

---

[329] Perhaps, better late than never, writing from a 2024 perspective, the entire Nibiru narrative, which is so widespread, is disinformation, or more precisely, a way for then "negative ETs" to explain things from their perspective, which can be quite misleading. Nibiru was the "ship of origin," which has nothing to do with the "lesser gods" (see Greek "mythology"), but pertains to the true creators. See later books in this series, but maybe even more importantly, more updated research published at Amazon.com and elsewhere.

[330] True. However, the original YHWH was our creator, who is feminine. Please se upcoming books, or read at wespenre.com.

[331] http://www.wingmakers.com/

LPG-C has discussed this matter with those from the Home Planet, so what does this species have to offer? LPG-C, on behalf of humankind, came with the following suggestion:

> What we are suggesting, instead, is the development of a network of canton-like like-minded and like-disposed peoples who accept, realize, choose to, and develop means to open themselves to possibilities. We know the Kingdom is coming back, and the Kingdom and humankind are bound to each other by genetic makeup and past, some of which must be unlearned and undone in the present so that a peaceful future could be possible for both; them and us.[332]

Dr. Bordon of LPG-C ends his essay with the following:

> What we are suggesting is not a war or even resistance to Marduk or those who carry out his plans and objectives. This would be, indeed, futile (to borrow a phrase from Roddenberry and his Star Trek Next Generation paradigm).
>
> Then there is the matter of the dedicated human said to be returning with them, who is to assume the combined offices of EN.KI. and EN.LIL. as First Lord of Earth – or something like that – in some kind of direct democracy. It would be nice to know what his sixty epithet names will be;[26] this will tell us a great deal of what to expect from what he is to offer to the remnant humankind left after the forecast defeat and imprisonment of Marduk, following some final confrontation of forces prophesied in biblical sources.
>
> All of the preceding would require of us that we change our views of what is to come and face them, not in religious or doctrinal ways, but rather in well-informed and thoughtful exopolitical and scriptural ways. Why scriptural as well? We also need to know what is required of us in the dedicated human's program for a post-Marduk Earth. We contend it is not an accident that much of what written patrimony left to us has been altered and in some cases changed completely to suit doctrinal and institutional hegemonies and power. We are also not suggesting a naive, Pollyanna-like worldview of what is to come; quite the contrary, we suggest we must become informed not just about Marduk and his program, but also about the Kingdom and the dedicated human's paradigm of an Earth seemingly patterned after what NI.BI.RU. sees 25 working for them. Will it also work for us? We are not suggesting it

---

[332] Bordon, A.R. and Barber, J.W., (2007): *Journal of End Time Studies Vol 1: January-June 2007: Between the Devil and the Incoming Rock" p. 4 op. cit.*

will not. We are asking that we begin a dialogue on these two seemingly diametrically opposed options, and learn what we may already know deep within us all that is best for us.[333]

Is prophecy set in stone? Is it totally pre-determined? Of course not. Is it likely to happen? Yes, some, if not most of it because it's planned that way.[334] By getting people hooked to world religions and their offspring and cults and sects, via priests, religious leaders, mass media et al, we are constantly bombarded with religious propaganda, which makes it easier for the prophecies to stick. To our favor is the mass awakening that's going on as I write this. Prophecy, however, is always a slippery slope because humans are very unpredictable. When it comes to Bible Prophecy and other ancient prophecies, much of that is more likely to stick because humankind is secretly steered in the direction of fulfilling these old predictions (there are those behind the scenes who work furiously to make these prophecies come true), but they are also following the plans of off-planet beings, over whom we have little control.

I can empathize with Dr. Bordon's statements above, seeing it from his, and LPG-C's, perspective. However, as they mention in so many places in their different essays, the Ša.A.M.i. and the Anunnaki are just a small fraction of ETs in near Earth space, and they all have their imperatives. We know the history of the Ša.A.M.i., and their mindset, and there is evidence we can't just discard. If someone says, "they have changed now", I wouldn't take that as face value. Anybody can say that, or that "they're working on unity". The 60 epithets of Nannar would indeed be nice to see.

First, there are other way to get rid of Marduk and his followers, and that is to educate ourselves (reading material like this), make it our own, work on our spiritual wholeness (spirit/mind/body), and our fear will diminish considerably. It has worked for me. Knowing what I know, and working on myself, has left me with very little fear left of these beings. This is the stage we want to reach. This is a 100th monkey syndrome we want to achieve. Because remember, even Marduk and any other negative visitors, in our terms, are here because they perceive our fear. Those who have read "The Hidden Hand"[335] [336] [337] know *exactly* what I'm talking about.

All challenges we are meeting now and, in the future, have a purpose.

---

[333] *Ibid, p.24.*

[334] Also see my book, *Simulations and the Wheels of Time in the Developing Worlds,* for more information on Destiny and Fate.

[335] https://wespenrevideos.com/2019/12/01/article-7-dialogue-with-hidden-hand-self-proclaimed-illuminati-insider/

[336] https://wespenrevideos.com/2019/11/30/article-5-who-is-hidden-hand/

[337] https://wespenrevideos.com/2019/11/30/article-6-the-new-hidden-hand-thread-2018/

They are mirrors of our own fears and weaknesses as individuals and as a humanity, and they come into our existence to teach us lesson so we can grow; they are catalysts.

Here, five paragraphs are removed, not to mislead the reader. In 2011, when this was written, I was still attached to some New Age beliefs I no longer subscribe to. As usual, the original paragraph is still online at wespenre.com, *WP 2024*.

THE HIDDEN HAND

MOTHER ✶ TEACHER ✶ DESTROYER

Figure 14.13: "The Hidden Hand", a self-proclaimed Power Elite Insider gave us a lesson in late 2008 which became a catalyst for many thousands of people.

[The remaining part of this paper is not included in this book. It discusses Supriem David Rockefeller (fake name) and the Thule Society (or a private branch of it, run by a man calling himself Jarl Vidar). These two figures, and others involved in their scheme, are irrelevant to my research, and a distraction. Readers who still want to take part in that information are welcome to go to the original paper at wespenre.com. All information is still there, *WP 2024*.]

PAPER 15:
THE REMARKABLE MICHAEL LEE HILL CASE
Friday, May 6, 2011

[This paper is not included in this book. I started editing it but soon noticed that almost all references to YouTube videos and articles have been taken down since 2011 when the original paper was released. You can still read it online at wespenre.com, as usual, but I found it pointless to include it here without the important references. [338]

What do I know about Michael Lee Hill at the time of the editing of this book?

I am no longer in touch with him, and the last thing I heard was that he is now certain he is the manifestation of En.ki., and that he has an important role to play before the end of times. Do I believe he is correct? Based on my interviews with him in the past, leading to my original paper, I would definitely say no. I do not believe he is who he says he is. His entire story is clouded in mystery, however, and only time will tell how it will unfold, *WP 2024.*]

---

[338]   https://wespenre.com/2019/01/27/first-level-of-learning-paper-15-the-remarkable-michael-lee-hill-case/

PAPER 16:
THE WINGMAKERS, THE LABYRINTH GROUP, AND THE S.A.A.L.M.
Friday, May 26, 2011

Abstract

This is a hot potato! When I'm writing these words, I am still not exactly sure how to approach these related subjects. Many people have read the WingMakers Material (WMM)[339] and many have been very inspired by it. Others have come out and proclaimed that it's all a hoax.

Here is news for everybody who reads this; *it's not a hoax.*

However, it's a complicated issue, and there are a lot of organizations and agendas connected to it. So I am going to tell you the real story behind the WingMakers to the best of my ability; how it is connected to both LPG-C (*Life Physics Group in California*), *The Labyrinth Group*[340] (allegedly in California, but a reliable anonymous source is telling me U.S. East Coast), NSA (*National Security Agency*), ACIO (*Advanced Contact Intelligence Organization*), and S.A.A.L.M. (*Supreme Anunnaki Assembly of Lord Marduk*, Pine Gap, Australia). The last three are all connected, as we shall see. The entire WingMakers issue runs through the Military Industrial Complex and all the way to the top, as they say, but it didn't use to be that way.

Confused yet? Good, because that's what "they" want you to be. So, let's see how we can hopefully make it clearer with this paper.

How the WingMakers "Saga" All Began

First of all, who am I to think I am able to shed some light to this

---

[339] http://wingmakers.us; http://wingmakers.com; http://lyricus.org; http://eventtemples.com; http://sovereignintegral.com

[340] The Dr. Anderson Interviews: (http://www.wingmakers.us/wingmakersorig/wingmakersinterviews/ www.wingmakers.com/interview/iview1.shtml). The Dr. Neruda Interviews: (http://wingmakers.com/).

confusing issue?

Well, for a couple of reasons. The WMM fascinated me from the first time I read it and has ever since. For a long time, I was absolutely hooked on it, like so many other people before and after me. And when someone gets *that* hooked on something, there is more than a little truth in it. I quoted, elaborated on, and used a lot of the material on the previous version of my website, wespenre.com, and I made the connection to so many other subjects I had been researching earlier. Then, happenstances took me on a journey which made me doubt at least some of the WMM. Consequently, I started pulling the strings and what I found out was quite astounding.

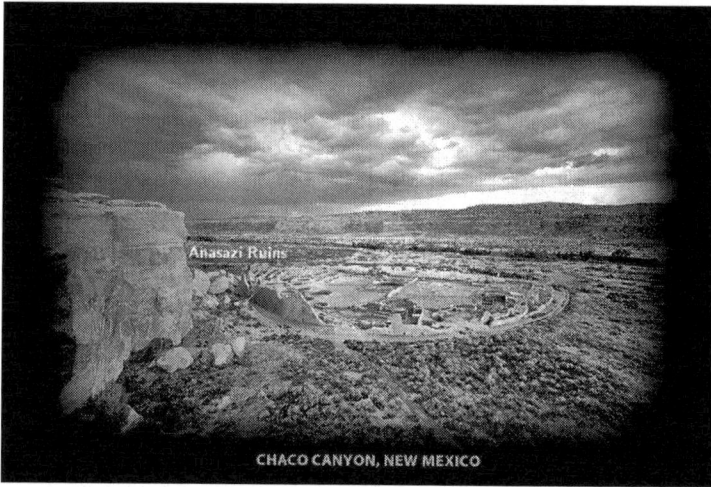

Figure 16.1: Chaco Canyon, New Mexico, where the Ancient Arrow site is located, according to the WingMakers Material.

But more important than that; I got much of it relayed to me from the "horse's mouth," "Dr. Anderson," who was the instigator of the WMM in 1998. I know where he is, but the circumstances are such that I can't reveal it in public at this moment. However, he has relayed to me the incredible story of the WingMakers Material.

What is Myth and what is true? Here is the Key

People have, since the first WingMakers site launched in 1998,[341] had a problem with that the WMM is supposedly both myth and truth mixed

---

[341] http://wingmakers.us

into the story line, like has been done so often by fantasy and science fiction writers. Of course, the discussions have revolved around what is true and what is fable?

Well, if we know how certain controlling forces work to obscure true information, we also know they often put out the truth in plain sight to blind us. It's a "little" mind game they are playing.

I know many people who read these words have already read the WMM, whether it's the original version, the later version, or both. Either way, I urge you to read this whole paper from beginning to end because hardly any reader of the WMM has read it from the perspective with which I am going to present it here.

I want to start from the beginning with the original *Dr Anderson Interviews*, published in late 1998. Once the current version was published on the Internet, the original was taken down, but a former White House employee, Fred Burke (http://www.wanttoknow.info/), downloaded the original website before that and liked it so much that he created his own domain, http://wingmakers.us. Thus, the original site is still available to the public.

"Dr. Anderson" is of course a made-up name, used by a supposed true defector from the ACIO and the Labyrinth Group. What Dr. Anderson presented in his interview with "Anne" is, again, allegedly true in the sense that the defector told her what he knew from the level it had been presented to him within the organization in which he once belonged (we will address this in more detail later). However, he did withhold some of what he knew and hid some of it by speaking in mythological and symbolic terms, probably both to protect himself, and because if you want to teach a child quantum physics, you don't start him/her out with the higher math. He also changed the names of the ET group—the Corteum—a few dates, and some other things, for what he considered "good reasons."

How the WingMakers Site Was Found

For those of you who remember some of the early WMM, this is a refresher, and for the rest, here is the story. In 1972, according to the early material, the Ancient Arrow (**AA**) site was found in New Mexico by a few young hikers. By coincidence, they found the caverns which led deep into the mountain side. These caverns were spreading out like veins from an aorta on both sides of a long tunnel. Each side-tunnel ended in a chamber—23 all together—and these chambers all had artifacts in them. The young hikers were in awe because they figured what they saw couldn't be of this world!

Figure 16.2: Chamber 4 Painting from WingMakers.us

The site was, of course, quickly taken over by the U.S. Military and isolated from the public. To make a long story short, the military came to the same conclusion as the hikers that these artifacts, in form of out-of-this-world paintings, were something they'd never seen on Earth before. Hence, the site was classified, and the NSA (National Security Agency) took over from there and put an *Above Top Secret* stamp on the project. Out of NSA, an occult organization had branched out, possibly already in the early 1950s, when the U.S. government made treaties with alien races. This organization was called the ACIO (Advanced Contact Intelligence Organization), headquartered in Virginia (California according to the later WMM), with branches in Belgium, India, and Indonesia. The AA was incorporated by the ACIO because they early on understood that these painting and other things they found in the chambers were not made by some old American Indian tribe that suddenly may have left the area (although there were indicators that there indeed was an Indian tribe that suddenly, hundreds of years ago, disappeared into "thin air" from the area). The site was traced back to around 800 AD.

When they further explored the caverns and the chambers, they found other artifacts besides the paintings, such as poetry, music discs, and a disc containing more than 8,000 pages with written material in a language not even the best linguists at the ACIO could decode.

The Ancient Arrow Project was put on ice for 22 years because we seemed not to have the technology to open the disc and decipher what was written on it.

However, in the earlier part of the 1950s, a young genius hit the scientific field like a torpedo. He quickly outsmarted his professors to such a degree they wanted to have nothing to do with him; it was too embarrassing. This young man, with his long hair and ponytail, simply refused to buy into the current scientific dogma. He wanted to build computers powerful enough to use for time travel; like something that was taken from a science fiction novel. Of course, he didn't get much response from the academia of that time.

Although he was rejected by most professors, considered eccentric at best, and insane at worst, the ACIO quickly recognized his genius and hired him in 1956, when he was only 22 years old. He was literally obsessed with time travel, and no one knew for sure why he had this exclusive drive; perhaps it was a mystery even for him.

ACIO eventually put him on this above top secret project to develop Blank Slate Technology (BST), which is a specific type of time travel (he called it "Freedom Key"), which we will look into later.

We must understand that the ACIO was the primary interface to alien technologies and how to adapt them into society, as well as the Military Industrial Complex (MIC). When this young genius came into the picture, the ACIO was already savvy at some alien technologies, which they had gained access to via so called *Technology Transfer Programs* (TTP), apparently starting in 1954 (if not earlier), when President Eisenhower allegedly had an encounter with a faction of the Greys, which resulted in an exchange program, where the U.S. government at the top level was given alien technology in exchange for agreeing to abductions of a limited amount of humans for genetic experiments.[342] It needs to be noted, though, that not *all* Greys agreed with this exchange, but there is a faction of them, as mentioned in previous papers, whose purpose is to further develop their own genetics, using human DNA to help them accomplish this.[343] The experiments done on abductees (mostly without their conscious consent), are often executed without even using anesthesia. In the abductors' own non-emotional state of mind, the ETs look upon the human species as laboratory rats; no more, no less. However, we have traits in our DNA/RNA which are interesting to them; we have feelings and emotions. These are ancient traits which were put there by our original seeders, the Lyrans and other species they are interconnected with. [344]

---

[342] Michael E. Salla, PhD, *Eisenhower's 1954 Meeting With Extraterrestrials: The Fiftieth Anniversary of First Contact? Research Study #8, January 28, 2004, Revised February 12, 2004,* http://www.exopolitics.org/Study-paper-8.htm

[343] Years ago, I communicated with Laura Eisenhower, President Eisenhower's granddaughter, and she confirmed her grandfather's alien encounters, *WP 2024.*

[344] Emotion is something the ETs lack because they lack Spirit, something

This young genius, later known as "Fifteen," quickly became the head of the ACIO and its offshoot, the highly secretive "Labyrinth Group," possibly located on the U.S. East Coast. As the story goes, he was contacted by two different ET races, who were both willing to offer technology in exchange for something we have that they wanted. One of the groups was the same Greys I mentioned above, and the other group is known in the WMM as the Corteum. Fifteen rejected the Greys but stayed with the Corteum.

So, who are the Corteum? Some say they are part of the Mardukian Anunnaki, left here on Earth and now connected with this group of secret scientists. However, I said in the beginning that the ET issue is complicated.[345] The Ša.A.M.i. and their Anunnaki work together with the Reptilians and possibly the Greys on one level, while independent groups of the same basic race (splinter groups) work independently from those on Nibiru.

This ET group, code named The Corteum, is an old renegade group of the Ša.A.M.i., still living on a planet around Sirius B, but have been involved in TTP (Technological Transfer Programs) with the human U.S. government for quite a while. They have now deceived this serious, otherwise human-friendly group of scientists into building a crystalline-scalar-mechanics based weapons technology to prevent an alien invasion.[346] They are after the 7 Tributary sites, where New Mexico is only the first. They want to use something they call the "7 Trumpets Technologies" to open up wormholes. The technology that the Corteum have inspired Fifteen and his Labyrinth Group to develop is to secretly (unbeknownst to the human group) re-activate the "Seven Jehovian Seals" to allow an alien invasion. The Labyrinth Group has been led to believe that the opposite is true: if they, in cooperation with the Corteum, can develop this technology and find the WingMakers sites, one by one, they may help them *avoid* an alien invasion, which was scheduled for 2011, but has been slightly delayed.

The Greys offered a full scale Technology Transfer Program to Fifteen in exchange for genetic information of human DNA. The reason he turned them down was because of a previous agreement with the Corteum, who were the ones with the most advanced technology in Fifteen's field, and hence more able to help him with his task. However, the Greys had something the Corteum lacked, i.e., their technology of how to make memory implants, and skills in genetic hybridization.

---

humankind inhabits (see future books in this series) *WPP 2024*.

[345] Partly because there is so much disinformation on the subject. I advise the reader to look into my recent work for more knowledge on this subject, *WP 2024*.

[346] A'shayana Deane [2002]: *Voyagers II, p.553.*

Figure 16.3: Photo allegedly taken of "Fifteen" in Hawaii, c:a 1978.

This may sound odd to the reader because the Ša.A.M.i. had considerable skills in genetic engineering, but what Sitchin tells us on several occasions in his books is that not all Ša.A.M.i./Anunnaki have these skills. Just like we humans; only because we know how to build space shuttles, it doesn't mean all of us know how to build them. The same thing goes for genetic engineering; the Ša.A.M.i. (even those not from Nibiru) have their scientists/geneticists just like us. And most probably, none of the members of the 200 in the Corteum Group had this knowledge either, other than perhaps a general knowledge. In the background, there is a large amount of their kind, overlooking the process.

After pondering the Grey issue for some time, Fifteen and others within the Labyrinth Group started reconsider whether they should make an agreement with the Greys. After all, the Greys' technology could be useful; especially the memory implants, which could be used to create photographic memory in the group members. So, they made a deal after all, and Fifteen got a lot of information on genetic hybridization from the Greys. Still, they apparently never told these ETs about the Labyrinth Group for several reasons: they didn't want the Greys and the Corteum to work together, and the Greys were not in the need-to-know, so the Labyrinth Group officially worked with them outside the organization.

341

Dr. Anderson From the ACIO/Labyrinth Group Speaks Out

In December 1997, a reporter by the penname Anne got contacted by someone who said he was a linguist who had defected from the ACIO, or *Special Projects Laboratory*, as it was called then; an unacknowledged department of the NSA. He called himself Dr. Anderson for protection, albeit this was not his real name.

Anne, a typical, dedicated journalist, was, rightfully so, very skeptic at first when Dr. Anderson told his story. He told her everything he knew as a top linguist, working under Fifteen. Dr. Anderson had been a part of the first crew who explored the Ancient Arrow site, and because he spoke multiple languages (some of them extinct), he became one of those in charge of translating the disc. Up to the day when Dr. Anderson defected, they had only translated about 7% of the 8000+ pages, so he didn't have no to little knowledge about what the rest of the disc contained.

Structure and Relationships of Labryrinth Group

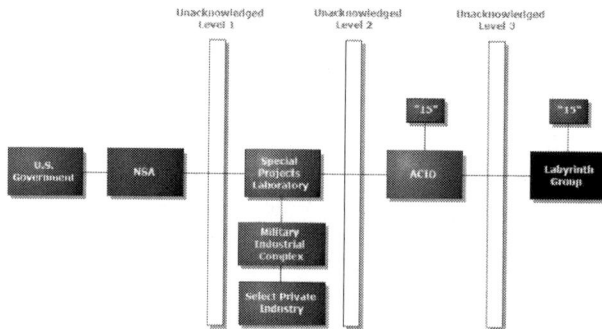

Figure 16.4: Structure and Relationships of the Labyrinth Group click to enlarge

After Fifteen had broken the "code," which finally started the project, the Corteum, who had infiltrated the ACIO already in 1958, became part of the project and helped out with their technologies as well. Fifteen had found out that some of the material on the disc was old Sumerian/Akkadian languages, plus a few others.

Dr. Anderson, after having started his internship at the ACIO, was subjected to something called "Intelligence Accelerator." He said they had the (alien) technologies to increase raw intelligence in a person by as much as 500%. In addition, they had this genetic implant technology (which they allegedly got from the Greys) which created photographic memory. The whole ACIO staff, including Dr. Anderson, had been subjected to both. These technologies were held very secret and were not revealed to the government or the intelligence agencies; it was entirely on a need-to-know basis. To have access to this information, a person would have to have clearance level 12 or higher (highest is 14, with Fifteen being the only one having 15). Dr. Anderson had clearance 12. These high level clearances combined *is* the Labyrinth Group. This group split from the ACIO to enable secrecy from the NSA and lower ranking members of the ACIO. Fifteen was afraid that if too many people had access to the technology stemming from the TTP (Technology Transfer Programs), the chances are great that these technologies would be compromised and used against our best interests. However, the Labyrinth Group is taking these technologies on a regular basis and dilutes them to a point where the ACIO can sell them to private industry and government agencies (probably via a network of contractors, to remain secret), including the military (this is a part of the reason for the speeding up of technology the last few decades). So, we can see that the "best interests" for some groups or individuals are not considered in the "best interest" by others; it's all very subjective and in line with a group's imperatives.

For over 40 years, the Labyrinth Group has accumulated considerable wealth on their own [as of 2011, *WP 2024*]. They have been able to build their own security technologies which has thus far prevented any detection from intelligence agencies like the CIA, KGB, MOSSAD, or MI5 and MI6.

The Corteum were permitted access to all information systems within the ACIO, which was considerable, according to Dr. Anderson, because they could be of assistance and were on slightly similar IQ level as Fifteen, after the latter had had "Intelligence Acceleration." He also said the Corteum are friendly and have no motives to take over our planet in some kind of One World Government agenda. However, he said that there is another alien race, who *does* have these motives, and we are going to talk more about them (the Anima) in a later report. I have reasons to believe that the "Anima Problem" is a deception, and in the next paper I will explain why. Dr. Anderson also told us that the head of the Corteum alien race, working with the Labyrinth Group, goes under the name of Mahu Nahi, and that he actually liked this Corteum leader (*keep the name Mahu Nahi in memory*).

Dr. Anderson considered Fifteen the most powerful human on Earth because of his brilliance and his power. He was the first human who was subjected to Accelerated Intelligence and the memory implant, and in his case, from having already been brilliant, now had an intellect comparable to that of the Corteum and the Greys. Still, Dr. Anderson was portraying Fifteen and his seven Directors as benevolent, who, in their own way, have humankind's best interests in mind. The main problem Dr. Anderson had with them, though, was the secrecy. He thought this information should be in public domain.

The Pleiades: Origins of the WingMakers Species

In a classified document, no. 040297-14X-P17AA-23, from Dr. Jeremy Sauthers, Director of Special Projects, ACIO, to all Labyrinth Group Members (FYEO), which described the Ancient Arrow Project to the team, reveals on page 2 that the WingMakers originate from the Pleiades. He is also stating that they were the ones who originally seeded life upon Earth "and facilitated life's evolutionary leaps and biological transformations."[347] They (and the Lyrans same genetic origins; see footnote below) were of the human genotype, who brought with us a "library of genetic codes" that, through experimentation, produced the human species, but also most other life forms on Earth.[348] Here we learn that the Pleiadians and the Lyrans are the same species. A faction of them fled to the Pleiades when the Anunnaki came but returned to Earth and eventually started working *together* with the Anunnaki in their effort to manipulate the DNA of the early humans. At that point they most possibly interbred with the Anunnaki and created a new hybrid, making parts of the Pleiadian Lyrans also part of the Anunnaki species. We know very little about the origins of the Anunnaki, and they may just as well be a splinter group from the original Lyrans, before any of them had any encounters with Planet Earth).

The Pleiadian WingMakers were in control of time-travel technologies and put time capsules here from the future (in our terms). Their hope seems to have been that we would be able to connect to our future selves and grasp a greater understanding of human destiny, among other things.

The renegade Pleiadian group, channeled by Barbara Marciniak, are here to steer us in a new direction, away from the Technology Transfer Programs and back in connection with nature. They are here to do this because they live in a machine technology construct themselves, which is quite brutal, oppressive, and inhumane. In their efforts to do something about it, this group has managed to trace back their timeline to the nanosecond, between 1987 and 2012, where humankind made decisions that created the hellish future this renegade group now lives in. In the sense of ancestry, they are us in a future time, but also us in the past, and if

---

[347] This claim has also been confirmed by the Pleiadian renegade group, whom Barbara Marciniak is channeling, in the book, *Bringers of the Dawn, (1992)*. Most researchers into human origins today subscribe to this theory by now. However, the Pleiadians were not the only ones seeding us, and the best probability is that the Pleiadians (WingMakers) did so together with a humanoid group of giants from the Lyran star system.

[348] Again, here is more confirmation of what was told by the same above Pleiadian group. When the Anunnaki from Nibiru came down to Earth to manipulate our DNA, the "Living Library" was already well developed, but was hijacked by the Anunnaki. For more info, see *Bringers of the Dawn*.

we can make better choices now, it will also affect them positively, and by the same token, we will be able to positively change our pasts. They call it "healing along the lines of time." In their books and channeling session, they are emphasizing that we need to get away from electronics as much as possible and get back to basics to become as multi-dimensional as we once were. Instead of connecting to the Internet they want us to connect to our "Innernet," which is our own psychic abilities [Spirit, *WP 2024*]; that's where the answers and the connection with the Multiverse lie.

The WingMakers, whom, as mentioned, are also from the Pleiades (according to Dr. Sauthers and the WMM), claim to have been the ones initiating the concept of the Internet for the purpose of developing a global culture. They say they did this because it's the way to communicate globally amongst peoples on Earth, but also because it's going to be the universal communication device for us in the future, albeit in a much more advanced version, of course, in a form of an "intra-galactic, digital nervous system." [Metaverse and the Singularity, *WP 2024*]. The WingMakers teach us that by the time their final time capsule is discovered in 2023, "the Internet will be the focal point of the new global culture..."[349]. This statement alone (if indeed true and not altered) tells us the Pleiadians, whom Dr. Sauthers refers to as the WingMakers, are not the same group as the one Barbara Marciniak is channeling. The latter wants us to get off the Internet as much as possible and develop our Innernet instead. The WingMakers website, in its current form, is promoting the Internet as an intergalactic communication network.

Beware of deception!

We are going to talk about the Internet a lot later on, but the Super-speed Internet is not developed for humans, but for aliens. For *them* to be able to use our technology here on Earth, it needs to be more sophisticated. We, in our current development, have little use for super-super-speed Internet, do we? Think about it. The Internet was developed to eventually work as a network meant to ultimately control mankind by *certain* alien species, not to be used by alien species in general.

The Pleiadians Barbara Marciniak's channeling warns us about the Machine Kingdom. If I didn't know better, I may have considered Internet as a good communication device; just expand on what we have and connect to the intergalactic network. However, this is not the way aliens communicate with each other in general—thus the distinction between the Internet and the Innernet. The latter is what we need to develop more of, not the former, if we want to be inter- and inner-galactic citizens. This is where the world is going to split in two; one where people are migrating to

---

[349] Classified ACIO Document, no. 040297-14X-P17AA-23, from Dr. Jeremy Sauthers, Director of Special Projects, ACIO, to all Labyrinth Group Members (FYEO), p. 2.

gigantic cities where technology has become a serious addiction and a suggestive way of survival, and the other where people who have had enough say they don't want any more of machine technology and will move out in the country and perhaps open up their own, self-sufficient communities. There, due to the lack of an abundance of electronics, people will be able to connect with their own Innernet, become more psychic, and multi-dimensional. Go out in nature and notice the difference. It's not that there is anything wrong with technology in general, but at this point, where our bodies and minds have been so polluted by electronics, misuse of negative energy, and the effects of the TTP, we need to disconnect from that mindset, remove our biological life form from it, and go back and reconnect with the elements to regain the power and sovereignty over our biokind. It's like a person who have been on the whole spectrum of addictive, recreational drugs for a long time and wants to quit. A significant part of a successful recovery program would be not only to stop taking the drugs, but to disconnect from everything that reminds of the drugs.

It's imperative that humankind survives the next 100-125 years or so, which will be very challenging, but to do so, we need our inner awareness to guide us, so we are able to consciously direct our energies to create oases in a world of turmoil and destruction. How well we succeed with this will determine our survival potential as a species. What we do after that, in the sense of space travel and connecting with the galactic community, is a totally different matter. My own take of the "Pleiadian Agenda" is to introduce to us the possibilities to make decisions not only based on survival but at the same time connect to our Innernet on a subquantum level—without technology. This is our key both to survival and enlightenment simultaneously. Space travel is coming into the picture later, as does technology under responsible conditions. We need to go through "withdrawals" first, literally. It's come to a point when people are addicted to their cell phones and Facebooks. I have heard stories where kids sleep with their cell phones under their pillows rather than their teddy bears, in case someone would text them during the night, and other kids have insomnia because they think they'll miss a message on their Facebook. They run up in the middle of the night to check it out. This is very serious, as we are losing our young generation to electronics!

Mark Hempel, the Middle-Hand

Although Dr. Anderson only had a security clearance of 12, and probably got a watered down version of information from the upper lines, he learned more than he felt comfortable with. He soon became the leading linguist and was the one who translated the disc from Sumerian.

After having visited the AA (Ancient Arrow) site a couple of times and experienced a "presence" there, sure it was the WingMakers themselves, and due to the translations, which he felt communicated *directly* to him, he knew this information needed to get out to the public—contrary to Fifteen's clear intentions and instructions. Dr. Anderson felt it was his duty to do so, and the WingMakers "told" him this while he was working on the project. They didn't want to bother Fifteen with it because they considered him being way too involved with the Corteum to be able to see clearly.

Dr. Anderson was nervous, because if he defected from the Labyrinth Group (something previously unheard of), he was afraid they were going to erase his memory, so everything he'd learned from when he joined the ACIO until the day he defected would disappear like it had never happened (yes, they have the technology to do so). He knew this is probably what they would do, unless they wanted to find him and reprogram him because he was such a brilliant linguist. There was even a chance they would kill him.

Despite these considerations, he decided to defect in secret, so he just left one day. He knew he didn't have much time and quickly needed this information to go out in public. So, he chose a random journalist, "Anne," who could interview him, and hopefully publish it in a newspaper or magazine. Once the cat was out of the bag, Dr. Anderson had a better chance to survive and perhaps they would let him keep his memories. This was a delicate situation for Fifteen and his group because he didn't want any extra attention drawn to him, and if the damage was done and the cat was let out of the bag, the best he could do was to be silent, hoping this was too incredible for people to believe.

The interaction between Anne and Dr. Anderson resulted in the "Dr. Anderson Interviews."[350] They were supposed to be 5 in number, but after two interviews, Dr. Anderson "disappeared," and Anne could no longer get in touch with him. No one knew at the time whether the Labyrinth Group got to him, if he was killed, had his memory erased, or just went underground.

---

[350] The "Dr. Anderson Interviews",
http://www.wingmakers.us/wingmakersorig/wingmakersinterviews/
www.wingmakers.com/interview/iview1.shtml

Figure 16.5: Mark Hempel

Anne, who was a born skeptic, didn't know what to do with the material at first. This was the strangest interviews she had ever done, and if she tried to publish them, her career would probably be over. Still, she thought she owed it to Dr. to somehow get this information out.

Hence, she picked a young music producer and web designer she knew about. His name was Mark Hempel, also a pioneer in Internet Radio. Even then she wanted to be anonymous, so she packaged the transcripts of the interviews, the artwork and the audio tapes and sent it via courier to Hempel with not much more of an explanation than something like, *please publish this material. It's very important!*

Mark read the interviews and found them fascinating but had no idea whether they were true. The anonymous nature of it perhaps helped him choose to publish it. For whatever reason, he created a website at http://wingmakers.com/ in 1998, where he released the two "Dr. Anderson Interviews," a mythological mini-novel called "The Ancient Arrow Project," the audio tapes, the poetry, and the artwork.

Without even announcing it anywhere, the website quite immediately got hundreds of thousands of visitors, making it a blockbuster on the Internet. The site became extremely popular and was discussed all over the Internet—in forums, and otherwise. It was probably the most discussed "conspiracy" website in the later part of the 1990s and the beginning of this century. Thus, Dr. Anderson got his information out to a lot of people after all. However, something strange was about to happen...

The Mysterious "James" Enters the Stage

The originator of the WingMakers material is known as "James," although this name was never mentioned in the original interviews or in the first version of "The Ancient Arrow Project." No other name than Dr. Anderson was mentioned.

So where does the name James come from? To answer that question, let's see what happened after Mark Hempel published the WMM.

Once Hempel's website had become popular beyond belief, the rumors, with no doubt, must have reached the ACIO and the Labyrinth Group. Fifteen must have been furious at first; some of what he had decided to keep secret over the years was now irreversibly in public domain. It was too late to do anything about that. His worst fear had manifested; the chance of having to deal with defectors from the Labyrinth Group who started speaking in public.

Figure 16.6: James of the WingMakers (possibly authentic photo, taken from his LinkedIn account).

The problem was that the material on the WingMakers website spread like a wildfire over the Internet, so they couldn't just ignore it. By the same token, there was a chance that Dr. Anderson would contact the journalist again to give the three additional interviews.

No one really knows what Fifteen thought, but we know the solution the Labyrinth Group came up with.

Mark Hempel, who had no idea about who was the instigator of the WMM, was contacted again, this time by this mysterious "James," who said he was the one who had been interviewed and thus was the owner of the material. James was probably quite convincing and could perhaps even give Hempel information that only Dr. Anderson (or someone within the Labyrinth Group) could have known. If Hempel still doubted James, he

349

probably got convinced once and for all when this mysterious person sent additional material for Hempel to post on his website, plus he wanted Hempel to change things around in the original interviews and add a whole new project to the AA (Ancient Arrow) story. The reason, he said, was that new information had come to him and he had decoded more from the Tributary Zones. He also had the transcripts from the three "missing" interviews with "Anne," so there were now five interviews all together. In addition, he changed the name of the interviews from "The Dr. Anderson Interviews" to "The Dr. Neruda Interviews," the latter by which they are most commonly known today.

After Hempel had remodeled his website in increments, over a couple of years, made it look more professional, and added the new material; the old website was, as I mentioned earlier, simply erased from the Internet. The Dr. Anderson interviews were now just a memory. Over time, James contacted Hempel to add more material, including music CDs which are still sold from the website, and he also added a 24th Chamber, making it look more and more fictional and mythological, which he also said it was. The WingMakers had become "wholesale."

Although James said in the Q & A Section on the website that it is a mix of myth and truth, it had now become quite difficult for the reader to distinguish between what was what. There were also serious attempts from readers and researchers to debunk the whole WMM, based on all the new, "fictional" content. Albeit there were (and are) still people who believe the WMM is true, the debunking efforts succeeded quite well, and many previously dedicated followers started putting their attention elsewhere. The possibility that the WMM was a hoax was lively debated on forums and by serious truth-seekers (as is always the case when someone creates a paradigm shift and ruffles the status quo, *WP 2024*). Hempel himself was confused about this whole thing and happened to say in correspondence with a researcher or two that he, too, thought it was probably a hoax. Or did Hempel know more than we think and was told to say that it was probably a hoax? Either way, Hempel's "doubts," valid or not, were only temporary. He soon became a dedicated WingMakers fan. Others, like Fred Burks, who could not relate to the new material, referred back to the original and kept that to heart.

Even more confused? Don't worry; things will soon start to make a little more sense.

James met with Hempel in Hempel's home on one occasion around 2008, for a long, recorded interview, resulting in an audio presentation on the new WingMakers website.[351] Here you can listen to James' voice, which

---

[351] This presentation used to be available on the WingMakers website (in 2011), but the website has been remodeled. The interview might still be available at wingmakers.com, using the website search engine *WP 2024*.

is an unnaturally deep baritone with a subtle Spanish accent. The accent sounds legitimate to me (he claimed he was born in Spain), but his deep voice sounds manufactured, for an unknown reason. Perhaps he didn't want the Elite to recognize his real voice; I really don't know. The interview, however, quite obviously was orchestrated so James could promote his new site and his new information on the "Sovereign Integral," the reconnection with our Oversoul (Spirit, WP 2024).

Lots of additional material was added as well to the website over the years, and it became more and more esoteric in the sense that James showed a lot of interest in Alice Bailey, Madame Blavatsky, and the Great White Brotherhood. He was talking about Ascended Masters in quite some length in his Q&A section and gave references which seemed very odd to me when I read them. Something felt not quite right. Eventually James, always through Mark Hempel, created a few more websites. They were, in the order they appeared:

1. The Lyricus Teaching Order (http://lyricus.org)

2. Event Temples (http://eventtemples.com)

3. The Sovereign Integral (http://sovereignintegral.com)

The last one was published in 2008, and although there was not yet anything substantial posted on the website (and still isn't, 3 years later, except an illustration of what the Sovereign Integral is, without any explanation attached),[352] James apparently decided to start promoting it. He therefore accepted an interview with the Project Camelot crew, also in 2008, where Kerry Lynn Cassidy and Bill Ryan were conducting an email interview with James.[353]

This interview was a shocker to me and to many other people who read it, and I think to the Camelot crew as well. James was here presenting a totally new paradigm, telling us that we are stuck in a hologrammic 3-D Density prison. This, in itself, is nothing new, but he said that Anu (the former King of the Anunnaki/Ša.A.M.i.), the most powerful being in the (physical WP 2024) universe, had created this whole 3rd Density illusion. More specifically, he said Anu has been tampering with our DNA, trapped

---

[352] Now, in 2024, James has posted more information on the Sovereign Integral site, https://sovereignintegral.org/
[353] The Project Camelot Interview can be found here: http://projectcamelot.org/james_wingmakers.html. Also, James is presenting a .pdf free download at WingMakers.com: http://wingmakers.com/downloads/Interview_James_PC.pdf.

highly spiritual beings from the Atlantis Era into these body containers, and once the spirits decided to "try out" the bodies which Anu had "created," they were trapped.

These bodies, according to James, had hologrammic "videos" embedded in them, so when these highly evolved multi-dimensional spirits entered the bodies, naïve as they were in their free state, they got caught up in the illusion Anu had created.[354] From within these new bodies, they saw a beautiful world and could look at extraordinary pictures which excited them. Hence, these who tried out the bodies told the rest how exciting it was, and soon enough, the majority of the free spirits found themselves trapped in 3rd Density bodies after Anu had "closed the trap" so that the souls could no longer leave their bodies at will.[355]

Not everybody was trapped, though. James is telling us that the time of Atlantis was a highly spiritually evolved era, and many different beings were here on Earth at the time, including people from the Central Race. Some of those from the Central Race managed to escape this trap, and James was, according to him, one of them.[356]

However, Anu, who apparently was a very clever being, cloned the real universe and created a new one, in which we are living today. In this Universe, Anu is God, where all the stars, galaxies, nebulae, planets and whatnot, are his creations.[357] In this cloned universe, life is sparse, and humans are the only true inhabitants.[358] Sometimes, aliens of another kind can enter Anu's cloned universe for short periods of times but must then return. If they don't, they either die or they get stuck in this reality, just like us. This is, according to James, the reason we sometimes see Greys and strange creature coming out from inside of the Earth or from under the oceans; they are simply stuck here and can't go back to the "real universe" (which I call Orion, to distinguish from the star constellation, or the Greater Universe in later work, *WP 2024*).

---

[354] This is interesting because this is exactly the same conclusion I have made at the time of editing the WPP in 2024 to present them in this book format. As usual, you can read the free, original 2011 version online at wespenre.com.

[355] Thus, according to James, we trapped ourselves by telling our fellow humans to enter the physical bodies to experience the illusion, and here we are today, trapped in an amnesiac virtual reality *WP 2024*.

[356] I can't vouch for the validity of that statement from James, but if true, it may make some sense *WP 2024*.

[357] Maybe not completely true, but Anu, titled Khan En.lil in the consequent books in this series, was granted the physical universe, while the Spirit Universe, of which humans belong, was dedicated to us. However, a conflict arose between physical and spiritual beings that we see the consequences of in our current Earth dramas. See my books at Amazon for more information, *WP 2024*.

[358] One sentence deleted due to inaccuracy (see original version at wespenre.com if you wish to compare that version.

Of course, James is also presenting a solution. He says that Anu was scheduled to come back shortly before 2012 (the event the Global Elite have been preparing for), but the plans have changed. Anu is in business elsewhere, having his attention directed towards something totally different and has left us to our fate. So, our only solution is to find the "Grand Portal," which is a metaphor for we humans to be able to, as a group, realize we are spiritual beings, trapped in a 3rd Dimension/Density, which only exists because Anu created it, and that science and religion need to merge into one for us to break the "godspell." Only then will the illusion shatter and we will return to the Universe of origin and become multi-dimensional. Anu's science in this case needs to be well understood so we can grasp *how* he created the 3rd Density. When we do, and also understand we are spirits in a body, we can break out of the prison as a human soul group.

In the same interview, Bill Ryan is asking James what he thinks about Nibiru and the return of the Anunnaki. James says (just like he did in the audio interview with Mark Hempel) that Nibiru is no longer an issue, and nothing to worry about.[359]

Who is Releasing the WingMakers Material?[360]

I also know for a fact that Dr. Anderson (whom I from hereon will call Dr. Jamisson Neruda (because it more accurately portrays who he is),[361] is still alive and well. Apparently, "James" is not human; he is *the Head of the Corteum!*

Why do I say that? Well, this is from the original website, which was taken down; from the original Dr. Anderson Interview #2, http://www.wingmakers.us/wingmakersorig/wingmakersinterviews/www.wingmakers.com/interview/iview2.shtml:

Dr. Anderson:

"Yes, they've been involved from the beginning. The Corteum are as integral to the Labyrinth Group as any of its human members, so nothing is hidden from them. The leader of the Corteum mission to earth is called -- in English -- Mahunahi, and he happens to be an artist first and foremost, and a scientist is his secondary nature. He was always excited to see and hear about our findings. He asked

---

[359] The followed sentence erased because of inaccuracy. See wespenre.com for the original, *WP 2024*.

[360] This section has been quite heavily revisited. See the original WPP for the earlier version.

[361] Interesting that Jamison is very similar to James, the originator of wingmakers.com.

if we could create a way-station to the Ancient Arrow site so he could visit the site himself, but it just wasn't practical to do so without drawing attention to the site."

It now becomes obvious that Dr. Anderson and Dr. Neruda as two aliases of "James of the WingMakers." In many interviews on the WingMakers site are just James, pretending to be the two characters. Not necessarily in a deceptive way, but sometimes one has to use sprinkles of fiction to tell a story with underlying truths.

A few years after the second WingMakers site was set up (Wingmakers.com), James opened a Q&A section, and this quote is from there,

> **Question 9**: Who/what are you James? Where do you get your information from?
>
> **James**: In my dominant reality, I am known as *Mahu Nahi* (Wes' emphasis). I am a member of a teaching organization whose roots are very ancient, but paradoxically, very connected with humanity's future. This teaching organization is concerned with transporting a sensory data stream to earth in order to catalyze select individuals of the next three generations to bring innovations to the fields of science, art, and philosophy. These innovations will enable the discovery and establishment of the Grand Portal on earth.

Thus, it seems clear that the WingMakers are run by the Corteum, allegedly a faction of the Earthbound Anunnaki, and "James" is the Corteum Leader.[362]

Mahu now told Mark Hempel that the AA (Ancient Arrow) project was mythological with truth in it. This also applies to the Dr. Neruda Interviews. He wanted Hempel to make sure the readers knew this. Hempel complied with everything Mahu told him to do. He was told humankind was not ready for everything yet and that it had to be released in increments over extended time. Mahu Nahi, also being an artist, chose to present truth in the form of art. It's beautifully done and quite intriguing.

Of course, if it is the Corteum that is releasing the WingMakers Material (WMM), it is a psy-op, but it doesn't mean it's all a hoax. There is actually more truth in the WMM than in most other alternative sources. I would argue there is enough truth to make it worthwhile to explore the material. A well-designed psy-op is carefully planned. It can give us truth in plain sight, but twist it at the crucial points, so it becomes mind-candy but not practical enough to set people free. Different groups have slightly different agendas, but the common denominator is to convince us humans that it is about saving Earth against an Invader Force which is very real. In

---

[362] These days, James, aka Mahu Nahi, is calling himself James Mahu, *WP 2024*).

a perfect world, we would all unite as ONE to face this threat, similar to what Ronald Reagan said in his famous speech from the 1980s, when he addressed the ET issue. He said that if we were to face a threat from Outer Space, we would probably finally be able to unite as ONE human soul group in a One World Government.

S.A.A.L.M., Supreme Anunnaki Assembly of Lord Marduk

S.A.A.L.M. is (or used to be before their presence was revealed on the Internet) a secret organization, branching out from the NSA and the ACIO. Their sole purpose is to keep "King Marduk" on the Throne of Earth, as her righteous ruler, even after the return of the Ša.A.M.i. from the home planet. They believe in Prophecy and consider Marduk being the AntiChrist the bible has been predicting, and they have until 2012 to accomplish this goal. At least this is what their members believe, as revealed in leaked information from internal conversion being held on a secure S.A.A.L.M. Intranet Server, from which the members could log in wherever they were on the globe, to retrieve new information as needed.

[What follows here, and continuous throughout this chapter, is the revelation of a giant psy-op that I happened to stumble upon, including MK-ULTRA mind control (James Casbolt), and agents from the joint Intelligence Agencies, trying to sell a distraction, when they noticed some sensitive information was about to be exposed—not particularly *my* information, but rather that of LPG-C and others. The only thing I did in 2011 was to expose some of the psy-op, and refer to other whistleblowers and what they had, or where about to figure out (some of them were effectively stopped). Involved in this scheme was also Supriem Rockefeller, and others of his kind. So, here it is, *WP 2024*].

James Casbolt, MK-ULTRA victim, former MI6, and supposed S.A.A.L.M. member, a defector and whistleblower from both, released some sensitive information on his website a few years ago. He was later cleverly set up by S.A.A.L.M. and was forced to take his website, jamesbasbolt.com, down. They started a severe disinformation campaign against him, using "Item #6" of the S.A.A.L.M. Laws that all. members are obligated to follow, to retaliate against him:

> Item 6 tells us that the agency will seek extreme termination with prejudice in the case of a breach of this agreement resulting in the disclosure of unauthorized information, beginning with extreme harrassment *sic* in order to stop the disclosure.[363]

One thing Casbolt put out on the web was a communication from an unknown S.A.A.L.M. member, emphasizing the year 2012:

> My contacts claim this is Enlil waiting before his final address in which he spoke to all S.A.A.L.M members on behalf of Lord Marduk and Queen Nanshaazuur. Enlil announced that the capstone of establishing Lord Marduk as King of Kings of SoL will soon be set. The speech concluded with a sincere thanks to all members efforts and a toast was pronounced to the target date of Dec 22nd, 2012.

Casbolt was, from my understanding, the one who leaked the information from the secret network and put it on the Internet. T the information didn't stay there for long and was abruptly taken down. A discussion about the security leak is even included in the hijacked information.

What S.A.A.L.M. apparently forgot about was the Wayback Machine (or the Internet Archive), where anyone can type in a website which is no longer available into their search engine, and it will show up the way it looked like; normally including all, or most changes that were made to it over time. This is where I got the information. However, S.A.A.L.M. got smarter with time, realized their omission, and made sure the information from the Archives was no longer accessible.

Their rules and regulations are very strict; disseverance under some circumstances is punishable with death. S.A.A.L.M. is also a part of the Freemasonic Global Network, starting at the 33rd Degree of Zion. Marduk, according to this group, is the head of Freemasonry world-wide.

I have had some personal, interesting experiences with this group; something which goes back to at least 2008. However, I am going to start this section with some correspondence between me and Benjamin Fulford, who is a journalist and a researcher into the Global Elite—particularly the Eastern Branch (Japan and China).

In January 2009, I had just posted an early version of what became the free e-book, "The Myth Around Supriem David Rockefeller." The early version was called, "Lucifer's Redemption." None of these version are currently on the Internet [2024]. In my early research, I stumbled upon S.A.A.L.M. again (I had encounters with them prior). The following section was taken out from the above Supriem Rockefeller e-book, because it was out of context. However, here it does fit in, so I will give you the story (some readers who have followed my research over the years may have read this before it was removed from the Internet):

---

[363] From *Indoctrination for Members of S.A.A.L.M. [undated]*.

Figure 16.7: Prophet Yahweh

In November of 2008 I was part of an email group led by a certain Rev. Anthony Pike, who said he lived in India. On that list was also Prophet Yahweh[364] and James Casbolt (former MI6 and subjected to Project Mannequin mind control (a branch of MK-ULTRA)[365] and other mind control programs), among other interesting researchers, so I decided to join.

Anthony Pike was the one who was most active on the list and posted quite a lot; he acted pretty much as the main authority of the group. After a while, he told the group he was a member of S.A.A.L.M., something James Casbolt was already aware of, because he mentions Pike in his book, "Agent Buried Alive."[366] I had a vague idea of who they were because I had at that time read "The LINK" by Dr. A.R. Bordon for the first time. This made it even more interesting, and perhaps I could learn something new. I knew of Prophet Yahweh before; he claimed to be summoning UFOs somewhere down in Arizona or Nevada, and he said they were Yahweh's ships. He is a black man, claiming to be a true Israelite, and therefore, he and his people have the right to Israel. He actually managed to summon UFOs when ABC News was watching, and it was all over the

---

[364] http://illuminati-news.com/ufos-and-aliens/html/abductions_and_encounters.htm
[365] http://educate-yourself.org/mc/casboltintro08sep08.shtml
[366] (http://www.bibliotecapleyades.net/ciencia/ciencia_mannequin03.htm).

news on June 1, 2005. Knowing that Yahweh is an Anunnaki, it was double interesting to have Prophet Yahweh on the list. However, he didn't say much but was more a silent member.

Now back to the story. As I had published the first version of Supriem Rockefeller, which became a blockbuster, I got an email from a visitor who said Benjamin Fulford claimed that the whole Rockefeller story was a hoax to discredit *him*, and that he would go public with this fact shortly.

So, I emailed Fulford to find out what the situation was. Here is the correspondence. On February 1, 2009, I asked him the following questions:

Hi Benjamin,

My name is Wes Penre, and I am emailing you from www.illuminati-news.com.

I found some information regarding Supriem D. Rockefeller and Michael N. Prescott I found intriguing, but rather confusing. I know about you from before and find your information and interviews pretty interesting and helpful.

It was pointed out to me that the SD Rockefeller story is a hoax to discredit you and that you will go out and announce this eventually.

I have a few questions, because I wrote an article on this. I understand you probably are a very busy man, but I would appreciate a lot if you had time to please answer the following (to the reader: my questions are always in **bold**):

1. Did you write the following comments to the letter from SD Rockefeller?

MESSAGE FROM BENJAMIN FULFORD in Japan ~:|:~

Both the Freemasons (5 million agents worldwide) and the Asian Secret Society (6 million worldwide members) have invited me into their senior ranks. I agreed to join only if they both promised to support a 3 yr campaign to end poverty, end war and stop environmental destruction.

There is going to be an announcement of a new financial system between January 20th and early February. However, this may be delayed by die-hard Satanists who do not want to see their rule end.

By the way, I have been informed that David Rockefeller has ceded control to Sen John D. Rockefeller IV and Evelyn de Rothschild has ceded clan leadership to Baron David de Rothschild. So, according to my latest intelligence the 5 points of the pentagram consist of:-

Queen Elizabeth, Papa Bush, J. Rockefeller, David Rothschild and the Satan worshipping Pope.

The above comments from you are then followed by the following message from Supriem Rockefeller:

Date: Wed, 3 Dec 2008 18:42:59 -0600
From: Supriem Rockefeller
To: Michael N Prescott
Subject: Re: "Buy Sell"

Forward this to them-

As you may know, the Vatican has been hiding the truth from the public about the Messiah. They have implanted into the public's mind that Jesus was the Messiah, which they know not to be true. The word Vatican means 'House of the Serpent' which the Pope even has the Serpent on his chest plate and he carries the Sun staff, the symbol of Marduk Ra.

I was Marduk Ra but became Amen Ra once I was sentenced into exile. Amen just means 'The Hidden One'.

They pledge their allegiance to me by placing the obelisk in St Peters Court inside the Sun Circle surrounded by the Celestial Cross.

The German order called 'Thule Orden' and 'Vril Society' know who I am, n fact, they found me after they had access to the Vatican's vault and read about me. The text form *sic* 2026 BC said 'In the Second Coming, he will call himself 'Supriem' and come from the west'. No matter how you spell Supriem or Supreme, it is still SPRM. They even saw drawings that looked exactly like me.

They told me that they knew I was Lucifer, the Son of G-D, leader of the 12 Elohim and keepers of the D12 Stargate. Marduk Ra was just one of my names, I am the same life force as YHWH, Samech, Moloch, Azazel, Lucifer and the Supreme Deity.

It is time for my rule again, thus those who are against it will perish. In fact I have the ability to end Earth as a planet if I see fit. The time is around the corner for my rule, Heil Imperium!!

The Thule wanted to test my DNA, so I allowed them because I knew they were important to my alliance. They found that I do carry the Triple Helix Blue Blood of the Elohim. In fact, I have more than one DNA sequence.

They knew that my several thousand year exile ends in 2009 (according to the 12/60 frequency in which I was sentenced, not the 13/20 frequency).

I have more than one DNA sequence because I am born of both Elders and Ancients (Serpent or Reptilian). I was given the DNA sequence of the REAL Trinity – Baal, Astarte, Tammuz – all into 'One Male' – Lucifer – The True Messiah.

2009 is the Second Coming, the exile is over. I have several races, not from Earth, that I lead and they are waiting on me. I have an army of multi-dimensional beings that are subservient to me. These are the Alpha Draconis REPTOIDS and the Orion Group REPTILIANS. We use magical rites to control the invisible world affected by the three dimensional world.

We have a technology that no one can stop. The ramifications of this technology used as a weapon are something out of a science fiction movie. We have to ensure that this technology stays within our working group. Someone could use this to disable aircraft from 400 miles away and there is nothing to trace, it would just look like the aircraft had a system failure and plummeted out of the sky.

Someone could use this to disable any alarm system, create a financial crisis by aiming at a stock exchange, someone could start wiping out every satellite in constellation and leave zero trace of what, where and how this happened. The 400 mile range is minimum, it can be increased via plasma antennas.

In fact, I have drafted The Allied Union constitution which is a policy making organization that unites 220 countries under one flag with an entirely digital universal currency called the 'Allied Unit' that works over the 'Supriem Network'.

The 'Supriem Network Plan' is attached in this E-Mail. To answer a question, someone asked me about how do you get every country to comply?

Simple, first it will be obvious that this is the only way society in the future will prevail and if that is not enough, have you ever seen the movie 'The Day Earth Stood Still'? The story maybe fiction but the warning and technology is real. Let's say 'Country Orange' did not want to comply, now all of the sudden their country's defense system and major economic institutions are paralysed by something they don't understand or cannot figure out but they were warned in advance so they know who is controlling it. This is why I say it is imperative this technology never gets out of our hands, it is the ultimate weapon of a silent endless war.

What we have here is not a morality tale of right and wrong, good or evil, it is simply an ultimatum to the countries– "You either comply with us for a more efficient and proficient society or you won't have a society. "

My group, which consists of former employees and some currently employed by various Intelligence Agencies and my own group based in Germany with Russian and Nordic sects, and a vast presence in South America and Antarctica, are wanting to speak to Lockheed-Martin about incorporating this technology on their satellite constellation so the entire globe would be covered. We can offer them a partnership.

If one satellite 300 miles above the Earth were retrofitted with one of our antennas, you could disable any electronic device in Northern America via an EMP effect. Our knowledge is based in Resonant Frequency and we have mapped the tonal range of Earth's frequencies including gravity and how to detune and change oscillation of X, Y, Z axis.

Same principal behind the resonant tuning of point A to point B for an envelope effect of collapsed time-space, creating something similar to what you call a 'Casimir Effect' and understanding the 'Impossible Space-Time Transition' of 2×10-33 cm, 10-43 seconds. Sorry, can't really translate equations in email.

Our 'Vril Power' is synergistically combining Gravity Units (GU) at positions specified by the coordinates $(x1, x2, …)$ and (u) – a process in time, can be thought of as a matrix-valued function of dimensionality $(n1, n2, …)$ $U=(ux1×2…)$ $(n1, n2, …)$.

If the status of a gravity unit varies as a function of time then, at any given instant, a 'snapshot' of that gravity unit at that instant in time would be $ui=u(ti)$.

You will first have to understand Gravity Units (GU) and Knowledge Units (KU) combined with Time (T) and its frequency in which you resonate.

Our concept of TIME undoubtedly presents new ideas which are unknown for you. First of all we cannot regard Time as a dimension or continuum, as you do. It is not that time is quantified, but one cannot conceive a moment as a point on the axis of time.

The interval dt, although it can tend towards zero, could never be perceived as small as we would like to. There is another aspect to this question we wish to underline.

You consider that the highest speed a sub-particle in the cosmos can reach is 299,780 kmph (speed of light) and you regard this speed as 'constant'. This is not a poor measurement. Indeed, it is this same speed that we recorded within this same three-dimensional framework, but all one needs to do is change framework or three-dimensional system so that this limiting Speed changes remarkably up to the point where the only reference which can reflect the change of axis is the measurement of this speed or constant, C. I would have to get into the detail traveling using Resonant Frequency at another time, to complicated for email.

Back to my original topic, it is imperative that your group is our partner to keep under wraps for our working group, it doesn't cost you anything to be part, we are not asking for money. We are going to cover the planet's ground and sky with this spectrum, an artificial 'aether' if you will. I was also presented with an opportunity from the Russians, I was told Putin was the original source, for us to buy up an entire stockpile of CU 63,65 which you may know is used for satellites and in weapons.

<u>Eglin AFB tests the SFW (Sensor Fused sic Weapon)</u> which use copper as its main munition. I would like to have talks with Lockheed asap for partnership discussions.

As you can see with the news and its status quo, everything is lining up to usher in the 'Supriem Network'.

Let's also talk about the returns I can bring in through our 'Buy Sell Program', if you think it is an absurd amount on the return, you have nothing to lose to find out the truth. Like I said, we never touch your money, all we need is the proof of funds to proceed and the money never leaves your bank. This is a great way to be autonomous and self-funding to exclude external auditing. This technology I offer must always stay in our own working group that we will put together.

We are about to reshape the world. The 'Supriem Network' will soon be the only way for financial transactions and communications. It connects the entire planet.

Democracy has failed and it is time to show what One Ruler with a strong team backing him can do, I know you are with me. Michael Prescott is my right hand man, so you can continue working through him at this juncture, I will step in as the situation progresses.

Regards,
Supriem Samech Marduk Ra Lucifer (Finally Redeemed) Head of the True Elohim, God of Victory and Son of the Creator, G-D.

2. Who exactly wants to discredit you? From what I understand the email from Rockefeller was meant for the Italian Freemasonry, with a cc: to Leo Zagami? Where are you coming into the picture, besides from you writing the comments above and posting the email (if you did)? From what I understand, you were never involved in the communication between Rockefeller and the Italian Freemasons. So in other words, how could this have been written to discredit you?

3. Who are SD Rockefeller and Michael N. Prescott? Are they pranksters or 'for real' people? If they're 'for real', where is the hoax in all this? Michael N. Prescott's MySpace site looks pretty serious to me, unless he is working for the CIA as a disinfo agent.

I would like to find out the truth about this, so I can publish it accurately. I really appreciate your time to read this and hope for a reply.

Respectfully and in friendship,

Wes Penre, Illuminati News

I got a reply from Benjamin:

Thanks for the e-mail Wes. Here is what I know about the Supriem Rockefeller business. They contacted Leo Zagami and the Italian Freemasons in an attempt to get them to go along with their plan for a new financial system. Leo then contacted me to ask for an opinion.

The thing that struck me about this business is that it coincided with some stuff I have been hearing from the Reverend Anthony Pike, a self-described descendet of the notorious illuminati Ted Pike. The Rev. Pike had previously sent me photographs of a person he said was Lord Enlil, son of lord Marduk, the leader of Satanic forces on the planet earth.

A third source of information (a member of the British Royal Family) also talked about a Nazi faction in the secret government under George Bush senior with assets in Northern Euorpe, South America (notably Paraguay and Uruguay) the Antarctic (the Norwegian "antarctic base.") and parts of the US military/intelligence establishment. This fit with' what "supriem" described as his power base.

Since separate sources mentioned similar people, I forwarded a photo of Enlil to Mr. Zagami. The Italians did their own research and came to the conclusion the photo was a fake and that there was no Supriem David Rockefeller in the Rockefeller family. Please contact Mr. Zagami about how he came to that conclusion.

To me the whole business has all the makings of a psy-ops attempting to get us to fall into the weird zone and thus be discredited. That psy-ops may well be traceable to the Papa Bush Nazi clique.

My latest intelligence tells me there is a move to annouce a new financial system (a transparent, honest one) that is still being fiercly opposed by the "seniors" (Papa Bush, Evylin Rothschild, Queen Elizabeth et al).

If the good guys win, there will be an announcement of a Marshall plan for the planet earth with the aim of eradicating poverty, war and environmental destruction within a 3-year period.

And yes, I did write the letter you posted on your web-site. There is much I cannot say in order to protect the lives of people who are trying to do good.

Benjamin Fulford

Here below is the picture of "En.lil" (on top) he talks about in the email and the second picture is of "Nannur" (Nannar), Satan's grandson (as referred to in the emails below):

Figure 16.8a: The Enlil, allegedly, put in circulation by S.A.A.L.M.

Figure 16.8b: Naanur, a second picture spread on the Internet by S.A.A.L.M.

The above pictures were attached to these messages:

From: cosmicrf@xxx.com
To: cosmicrf@xxx.com
Subject: Son   of   Satan
Date: Thu, 6 Nov 2008 17:26:41 +0530

For those who are still sceptical about the existence of a physical 'hell' below your feet, St Anthony is now attaching a photo of the

Son of Satan, Lord Enlil, titular head of the 'Supreme Annunaki Assembly of Lord Marduk' (SAALM), whose members include Henry Kissinger and Zbigniew Brzezinski. Also attached is a photo of Satan's grandson, Lord Naanur aka Nannar, who is photographed with another member of SAALM at their meeting on 26th Oct 2006 in Basle, Switzerland. So, my friends, the global reign of the Antichrist is about to commence and all people will be 'chipped' in their forehead or right hand as prophesied in the Book of Revelation. So, dear friends, choose this day whom you will serve, God or Satan, Christ or Antichrist. Remember, your eternal destiny is at stake – so, let's hope you make the RIGHT decision.

Yours in the battle for planet earth,

Rev Dr Anthony G. Pike (UK)
Cosmic Research Foundation
Markapur, A.P. 523316, India
E-Mail cosmicrf@xxx.com
Date 6th Nov 2008

From: cosmicrf@xxx.com
To: cosmicrfgroup
Subject: Cycle of Insanity
Date: Mon, 3 Nov 2008 12:05:18 +0530

Global Theocratic Movement

Both the Queen and Bush are trapped in a 'cycle of insanity' that they cannot escape from ie. they know St Anthony is speaking the truth, but they are unable to implement it due to governmental and societal constraints which forbids implementation of that which St Anthony is propounding; hence, the mental and physical logjam. In addition, both the Queen and Bush know full well that they don't rule either Britain or America as the REAL POWER lies UNDERGROUND. Yes, friends, St Anthony is talking about a REAL PHYSICAL HELL right below your feet!! In fact, recently, on Fri night 8th Aug in the early hours of Sat 9th Aug, St Anthony's only begotten son, Daniel, was physically abducted and abused by PHYSICAL DEMONS from hell aboard their spacecraft while he was camping in the Kent countryside.

In this respect, in UK one of the main U/G bases is located below Welford AFB nr Newbury, Berks and in US one of the main bases is at Area 51, NV and also at Dulce and Los Alamos, NM and in Australia at Pine Gap nr Mt Zeil.

Now, friends, St Anthony says its time to WAKE UP to REALITY and kick the Devil off planet earth once and for all rather than allow the 'demon-cratic insanity' to continue resulting in the total destruction of all life on earth. Yes, friends, only GOD and his THEOCRATIC Govt can save planet earth; and that's exactly what St Anthony and his 'Global Theocratic Movement' intend to do. In this respect, St Anthony has already established the 'Theocratic Parliament of Britain' in April this year and the 'Theocratic Parliament of America' and the 'Theocratic Parliament of Israel' in October. So, St Anthony means business and the Devil is now shaking in his boots as theocracy rises to the ascendancy and democracy plummets to the bottom of the bottomless pit. So, friends, REPENT NOW and come join the winning side!!

Yours in the battle for planet earth,
Rev Dr Anthony G. Pike (UK)
Cosmic Research Foundation
Markapur, A.P. 523316, India
E-Mail cosmicrf@xxx.com
Date 3rd Nov 2008

Then I contacted Leo Zagami, who confirms that Supriem Rockefeller is real and according to Leo one of his arch enemies right now.

The Enlil/Naanur pictures looked very photo-shopped to me, so I did some research and at the same time got the original pictures sent to me by one of my visitors, showing that the Anunnaki pictures are fakes. The second picture of Naanur is a photoshop job of Henry Kissinger, but I am unable to find that picture at the moment. Even the all-seeing eye on the wall in the first picture is an add-on, plus the S.A.A.L.M. insignia on the wall. The man in the picture is the Top Elite Player Zbigniew Brzezinski. These photos apparently were modified by the Intelligence Community and spread on the net by Rev. Dr. Anthony G. Pike.

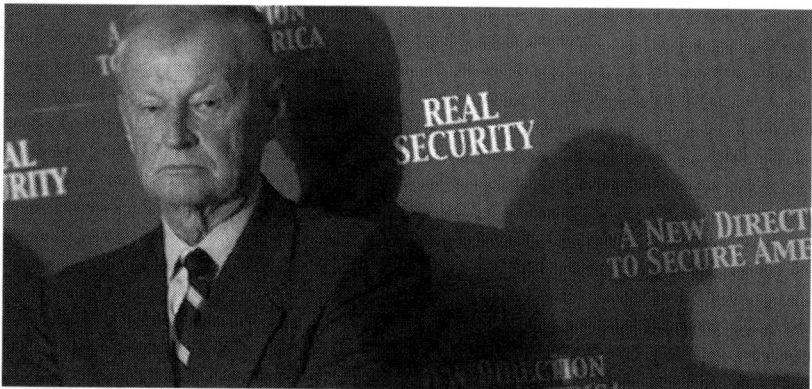

Figure 16.8c: The original picture of Mr. Z-Big (Zbigniew Brzezinski), looking just as scary as the photo-shopped version.

When I exposed En.lil as being Brzezinski, I sent an email to Benjamin Fulford to that effect and didn't hear anything back. I didn't know what to make out of that at the time, but I let it go.

Figure 16.9: Rev. Anthony Pike

Interestingly enough, one morning I got this letter from Rev. Pike (cc'd to me, but primarily sent to Ben Fulford), as a response to an email Fulford sent to him in regarding the fake photos. My original email to Fulford is at the top, followed by Fulford's comments to Pike, and ending with Pike's response. Pike says that James Casbolt, the 'brave whistle-blower,' posted these photos as well on his website to tell "the truth" to the people. Mr. Casbolt did indeed do so, but when he found out they were fake, he immediately took them down, being honest enough to tell his visitors that he had been the victim of a slander campaign. Here is my email to Ben Fulford, followed by his response to Rev. Pike. Pike's final response is at the bottom:

From: wes penre <research2003@xxxx.net>
To: benjaminfulford@xxxx.com
Subject: Picture Fraud
Date: Wed, 4 Feb 2009 17:11:08 -0800

Hi again Benjamin, Got these pics from one of my visitors, so that takes care of that hoax. Now we'll see if we can narrow it down. I re-watched your interview with David Rockefeller on YouTube. Great stuff!!

Thanks, Wes

From: benjaminfulford@xxx.com

367

To: cosmicrf@xxx.com
Subject: Picture Fraud
Date: Thu, 5 Feb 2009 12:30:18 +0900

Your photo of Lord Enlil is a psy-ops fake. You are either being
fooled or you are yourself a Govt disinformation agent. Please see
below.

Benjamin Fulford,
Tokyo
Tel. xxx-xxx-xxxx

From: cosmicrf@xxx.com
To: cosmicrfgroup
Subject: SAALM Photos
Date: Sun, 8 Feb 2009 22:45:33 +0530

Dear Ben and all our viewers,

St Anthony wishes to state that the originator of the Enlil photos,
33 degree Elder of Zion, SAALM/NSA operative and computer
graphics expert, Ray Bordon,
at freedomfighter_annunaki@hotmail.com aka Dr A.R. Bordon aka
Dr Roy W. Gordon at a-c-t-i-o-n_acio@hotmail.com,
http://foundationreportsinlifephysics.org, has always stated right
from the beginning that the Enlil photos, of which there are 2, not
1, are purposely 'graphically engineered' to ensure 'plausible
deniability'. In this respect, Brzezinski is 'P1' and Kissinger is 'P2' in
the SAALM hierarchy and Brzezinski is a direct descendant of the
Marduk/Enlil lineage who has similar features to Enlil, but not
identical, as also Hugh Hefner, by the way!!

Now, Ray was tasked with the job of 'leaking' info on SAALM to
the general public, but has now had much of the material removed
from the Net due to orders from within the SAALM hierarchy who
were getting worried about all the undue exposure, especially as
both Lord Marduk and Enlil don't like their photos being taken by
anyone. However, interestingly enough, the photo of Lord Naanur,
who is described as being the brother of Enlil, but traditionally, is
understood to be the son of Enlil and grandson of Marduk, is
supposed to be a very rare 'one off' photo of the 'jolly' fellow
whose personality is purported to be much more 'jovial' than that
of Enlil and Marduk, and who is standing alongside 'P13' of the
SAALM hierarchy at the SAALM conference in Basle, Switzerland
on 26th Oct 2006.

So, friends, please understand, to get 'cosmic top secret' info, which
is categorised 38 points higher than the H-bomb, out into the

public domain demands a great deal of ingenuity on the part of those 'leaking' the information. So, please understand, folks, St Anthony, as former founder/director of the 'Freedom of Information Campaign' in London from 1991-96, is just trying to 'leak' all this info out as best he can, as is Ray Bordon, James Casbolt and other fearless 'whistleblowers' who are risking life and limb to educate YOU, the general public, about the alien presence on earth and the upcoming New World Order of the Antichrist; and, of course, the Second Coming of the Messiah, Jesus Christ, who will defeat the Antichrist at the Battle of Armageddon and establish the long-awaited 1000 yr Millenial kingdom of God on earth in 2030.

Now, for those who have not yet seen the SAALM photos, St Anthony has managed to retrieve some of them, along with copies of Brzezinski's photos which were used as a means of superimposing Enlil's features on Brzezinski as well as the SAALM logo in the background, which are herewith attached. Finally, please remember, the aliens are here, and have been here for thousands of years – so, please try to understand that we are simply doing our best to educate you all concerning matters which have been kept concealed from the general public by the ruling elite, but which are now, in these last days, being revealed to the world.

Yours in the battle for planet earth,
Rev Dr Anthony G. Pike (UK)
Cosmic Research Foundation
Markapur, A.P. 523316, India
E-Mail cosmicrf@xxx.com
Tel 91-8596-224312/9959-684635
Date 8th Feb 2009

First, I was stunned because of the mentioning of A.R. (Ray) Bordon[367] being mentioned in this psy op, and I must admit that made me skeptical of LPG-C's intentions for a while. However, nothing is what it seems, and after having researched LPG-C very intensively, and communicated with the scientists for the last 6-8 months, I have learned how S.A.A.L.M. and the ACIO work.

Around the time of 2007-2008 (an eventful period in many ways, it seems), LPG-C were subjected to a major slander campaign that almost got them "out of business," so to speak. They were infiltrated by this ACIO agent, Roy W. Gordon, who stole pictures and sensitive material from the Life Physics Group California and escaped with it. Around the same time (or shortly thereafter), S.A.A.L.M., in conjunction with ACIO,

---

[367] His middle name, from what I learned from UTU Šamaš, and which Bordon acknowledged, is not Ray but Reuel, *WP 2024*.

started using LPG-C names in their own email correspondence, pretending this closed group of scientists were part of S.A.A.L.M., and they also faked their email addresses to extend the harassment and to muddle the waters further.

Dr. Gordon also contacts people on the Internet via forums and directly through emails. I have personally had a few, not so pleasant, encounters with him regarding Supriem Rockefeller, where he said Supriem is not who he says he is, emphasizing he, Roy, is working for the NSA, which couldn't be interpreted otherwise than a covert threat. I stood up to him, and he "disappeared." I never heard anything more from him on *that* subject.

Over time I have learned, beyond any doubt, that LPG-C, or any of its members, have never been a part, or in liaison with, this Serpent Clan group. The people at Pine Gap are professionals when comes to confuse the public, to count out their "opponents." One way of doing so is to play both parties in a conflict, war, or game. Thus, I am not surprised to see Brzezinski and Kissinger on the ACIO/S.A.A.L.M. member list.

Now it's time to reveal who Rev. Anthony Pike really is and the character of this man; the professional disinformation agent who screwed up big time for S.A.A.L.M. He is telling us a lot of relevant things, but also mixes in blatant lies to sidetrack those who want to know the truth. Albeit, by the time of this writing, I would be surprised if either Roy W. Gordon or Rev. Anthony Pike are still part of the Pine Gap Group. They have been more of an embarrassment to their group than of assistance. I am aware of that Dr. Gordon is still signing off his emails with "Pine Gap," but again, I would be mighty surprised if he is still with the group.

In 2008, he was the one who put me on Pike's mailing list (without my consent), but I left it alone because some topics were of some interest to me. I very rarely posted anything on that list, but mostly just read the postings from others.

However, Rev. Pike's behavior on the list became more and more bizarre, and one day he posted something that really caught me off guard. He lives in India and Great Britain, respectively, and is supposedly pro-environmental. In this series of emails, he seriously stated that he wants all motor vehicle drivers shot on the spot, or trialed for crimes against humanity, and executed(!) As a response to my reaction to this statement, he said he was "seriously kidding," but if you continue reading the emails below, you'll see he was deadly serious.

> >——Original Message——> >

From: Rev Dr Anthony G. Pike mailto:cosmicrf@xxx.com >

>Sent: Saturday, March 17, 2007 5:05 AM
<> >To: cosmicrf@xxx.com
> >Subject: Steps to Save the Planet

Steps to Save the Planet

1) Shoot all car/truck/bus/bike drivers on site and airline pilots.

2) Plant one billion trees.

N.B. Steps must be implemented immediately to avoid a global catastrophe and extinction of human race.

P.S. To escape being shot, STOP DRIVING YOUR CAR!!!!!!!

Yours in the battle for planet earth,
Rev Dr Anthony G. Pike (UK)
Cosmic Research Foundation Markapur, A.P. 523316, India E-Mail
cosmicrf@xxx.com
Date 17th March 2007.
Cosmic Research Foundation
Markapur, A.P. 523316, India
E-Mail cosmicrf@xxx.com

From: "Wes@xxx"
To: "'Rev Dr Anthony G. Pike'"
Subject: RE: Steps to Save the Planet
Date: Sat, 17 Mar 2007 14:17:32 -0700

Are you kidding or are you serious?

Wes Penre,
Illuminati News

- — -

Dear Joe *Joe = Prophet Yahweh, Wes' comment,*

This is just to help clarify who is a Satanist and who isn't.

A Satanist is a sinner. A Christian is a saint.

Satan managed to separate the church from the state so that his kingdom on earth would not be affected. Satan then proceeded to take over control of the church so that now both church and state are controlled by Satan.

Yours in the battle for planet earth,
Rev Dr Anthony G. Pike (UK)
Cosmic Research Foundation Markapur, A.P. 523316, India E-Mail
cosmicrf@xxx.com
Date 17th March 2007.
Cosmic Research Foundation
Markapur, A.P. 523316, India
E-Mail cosmicrf@xxx.com

> >From: Prophet Yahweh >
>To: "Rev Dr Anthony G. Pike" >
>Subject: Re: Steps to Save the Planet
> >Date: Sat, 17 Mar 2007 08:36:02 -0700 (PDT)

IN THE BLESSED AND HOLY NAME OF YAHWEH

Dear Anthony Pike,

I am not a Christian. I am a black orthodox Jew.

And based on what you said, only Christians are saints.

I strongly disagree with what you said.

Also, your second email below, about shooting all who drive, reminds me of how people who looked like you declared that all my people (slaves) who ran off from their plantations, to find freedom in the Northern Non-Slave states, were to be shot on sight. Rather you were joking or not, I did not appreciate receiving your last two emails to me.

Because of these two points, I politely ask that you take me off your list.

Thanking you in advance,
Prophet Yahweh

Dear Pastor Ramon,

There's NO DIFFERENCE between a true Jew and a true Christian. However, if you're a 'fake' Jew or Christian you got problems.

Regarding car drivers, they are guilty of mass murder and genocide and should be tried for 'war crimes' and then executed. If this is not done, God will do it Himself in the 'Day of God's Wrath' from 2012 – 2030 (Rev 11.18).

Regarding our mailing list, I will give you time to 'cool down' as yours is purely any emotional reaction; and, furthermore, you have already been appointed as one of our 'X-Men'.

Yours in the battle for planet earth,
Rev Dr Anthony G. Pike (UK)
Cosmic Research Foundation
Markapur, A.P. 523316, India
E-Mail cosmicrf@hotmail.com
Date 19th March 2007

Dear Wes,

Thought I'd wake a few people up!!!! Yes, I'm seriously kidding!!!!!!

Watch this space for more info on the subject. God ain't finished with this planet yet!!!!!!!!

Yours in the battle for planet earth,
Rev Anthony G. Pike (UK)
Cosmic Research Foundation
Markapur, A.P. 523316, India
E-Mail cosmicrf@xxx.com
Date 19th March 2007

Date 22nd March 2007
>From: "Wes@xxx"
>To: "'Rev Dr Anthony G. Pike'" >Subject: RE: Steps to Save
the Planet

Dear Rev. Pike,

I strongly agree with Prophet Yahweh. I was shocked to get the
message (see bottom of this email) that car drivers etc. should be
shot! Are you trying to help the Illuminati to reduce the
population?

In my eyes, this would be mass murder or genocide; far worse
than Hitler's Holocaust. Looks like you are showing your real
satanic colors, pastor. If there were only TWO choices I could
make and I HAD TO make one, whether to follow you or Hitler,
I think Hitler is the better choice. At least the amount of victims
of his were only within the million bracket.

Who are you to decide who is to live and who is to die? We don't
need yet another genocide, sir. As a matter of fact, we don't need
any more killing whatsoever. Haven't we had enough already? I
don't know what is clouding your eyes, but whatever it is it will
lead you straight to the place you warn others about.

Please remove me from the list and I would appreciate if you
distributed this, my letter, to the rest of the group.

Thank you,
Wes Penre, Illuminati News

P.S. I will burn the information kit you sent me in the mail. I don't
want to have anything to do with it.

Dear Wes,

Thanks for your and Prophet Yahweh's great words of
wisdom. You and him are the type of people that brought Hitler
to power and will shortly bring the Antichrist to power through

total lack of understanding of what I've said and the aim of saying it. Prophet Yahweh, for instance, thinks I want to kill car drivers because car drivers are purposely going around trying to run people over. Okay, why don't you put your mouth over the exhaust pipe for 1 minute and see what happens – yes, you got it, you'll be DEAD. So, every time you go around in your car you are literally murdering thousands of people!!!! I also heard that car exhaust fumes are radioactive- so, what with computer screens, mobile phones and TVs, let alone nuclear reactors and bombs, the whole planet is in radioactive meltdown!!!!

Yours in the battle for planet earth,
Rev Dr Anthony G. Pike (UK)

James Casbolt, the former MI6, S.A.A.L.M. member and more, who was also on this list, but not very talkative, mentions Pike as a "friend" in his book, "Agent Buried Alive"..

Needless to say, I left the group shortly after I'd blasted Pike, telling him things I don't want to repeat here. Ramon (Prophet Yahweh) was equally upset and left as well.

I guess all organizations have their agents who can't control themselves, and so does S.A.A.L.M. Here are excerpts from emails posted on the Godlike Productions Forum (GLP)[368] in December 2009, where Dr. Gordon is threatening one of the forum members. I will quote the whole post:

Well I recently checked my e-mail and was surprised to see this e-mail in my inbox. Unfortunately I reported it as a phishing scam to Google, and they took it out of my box! But, I did save the message.

This was from: "a-c-t-i-o-n_acio@hotmail.com" So I guess feel free to e-mail   him!

"STAY AWAY FROM ANY SUBJECT MATTER DEALING WITH LORD MARDUK OR YOU WILL BE TERMINATED WITH EXTREME PREJUDICE

YOU HAVE BEEN WARNED

DR ROY GORDON

---

[368] http://www.godlikeproductions.com/

ACTION_ACIO
SAALM
33 DEGREE OF ZION
PINE GAP
NTH AUSTRALIA"[369]

As a note aside, the above email from Dr. Gordon reminds me of the law under which the members are subjected. "Items 5 and 6" of that law, taken from a leaked, secret Intranet conversation between members, says:

Item 5 dissuades us from disclosing anyone from the association with S.A.A.L.M. punishable by death.

Item 6 tell us that the agency will seek extreme termination with prejudice in the case of a breach of this agreement resulting in the disclosure of unauthorized information, beginning with extreme harassment *sic* in order to stop the disclosure.[370]

Dr. Gordon apparently felt a power rush at the moment and tried to instigate the threat of a similar nature being applied to public who reveal too much about "King Marduk." However, if true that Dr. Gordon has been expelled from S.A.A.L.M., public statement like this was probably part of his problem.

---

[369] http://www.godlikeproductions.com/forum1/message951627/pg1 *op. cit.*
[370] From *"Indoctrination for Members of S.A.A.L.M." [undated]*.

Figure 16.10: Dr. Roy Gordon, as he depicts himself these days

Dr. Gordon also has a Facebook account which is much more laid back: http://www.facebook.com/profile.php?id=100000180909654&sk=info [371]

S.A.A.L.M.'s Secret Conversations Leaked

S.A.A.L.M., with their Headquarters in Pine Gap, Australia, is an offshoot from the ACIO, with the whole purpose, as mentioned earlier, to keep Marduk's clan in power after Nibiru has passed through the solar system.

Pine Gap, near Alice Springs, Australia,[372] has a bad reputation, and is known for alien and UFO activities, especially reptilian. It's not a place you want to go camping. There are also a lot of Global Elite research and experiments going on in the area, such as Echelon[373] and Project L.U.C.I.D.,[374] most of it is orchestrated by a faction of the Earthbound Anunnaki of the Serpent Clan, possibly in cooperation with a faction of the Alpha Draconian Reptilians.

S.A.A.L.M. was using a secure server to communicate to their

---

[371] This account has since been taken down, *WP 2024.*
[372] http://www.bibliotecapleyades.net/sociopolitica/sociopol_pinegap08.htm
[373] Ibid.
[374] Ibid.

members, where they could speak more freely. However, Casbolt (most probably) decided to put their conversations on the Internet so everybody could read. He was successful and at least some of the communication leaked out. I'm going to post that information here, so the reader gets a fuller picture of this organization, also because S.A.A.L.M. apparently have now closed the Internet Archives pertaining to their correspondence.

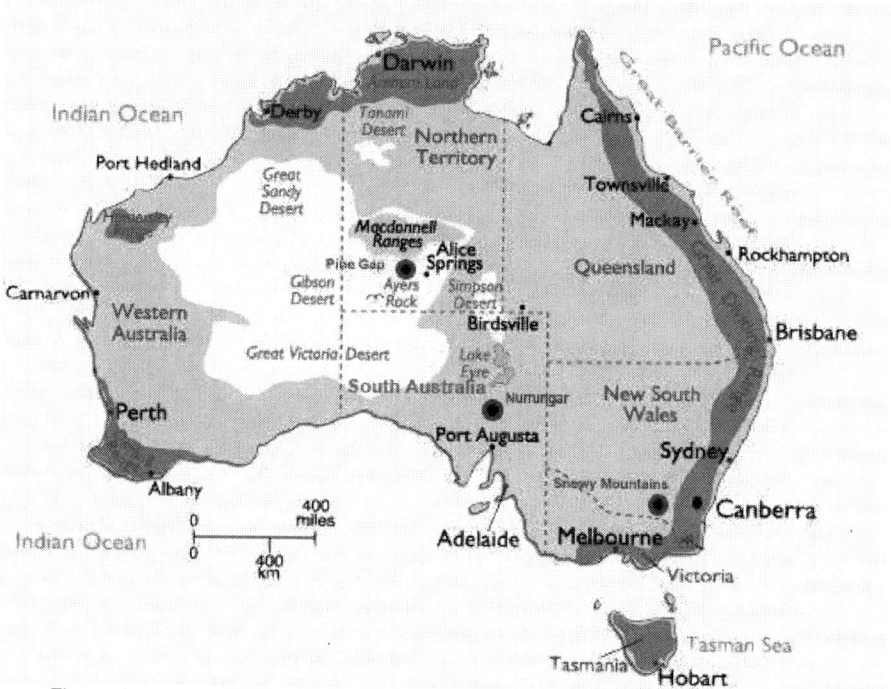

Figure 16.11: Australian map with Pine Gap circled in red in the middle (click on image for enlargement)

First a few pictures that were attached to the information:

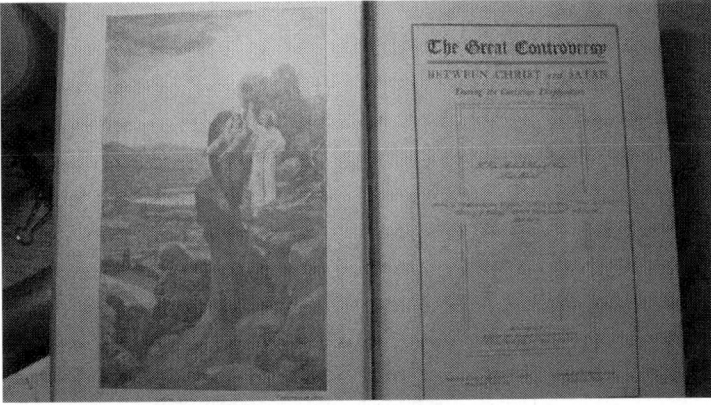

Figure 16.12a: Between Christ and Satan.

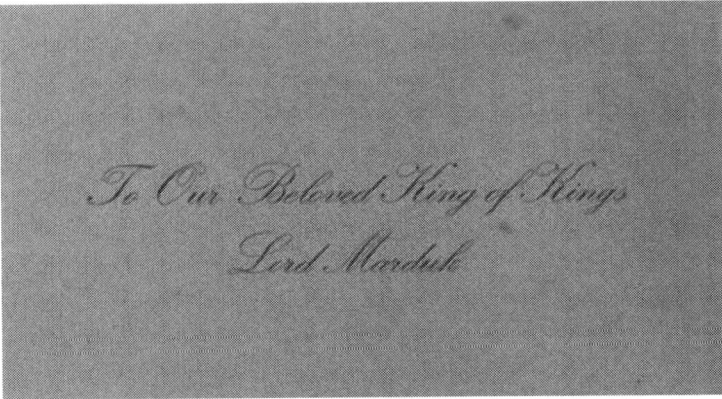

Figure 16.12b: Close-up of one of the above book pages.

Figure 16.13: A Masonic S.A.A.L.M. Passport

P6 Intro

Intro

Brothers:

Welcome to the S.A.A.L.M

We have our work cut out for us. Please download attachment form on which we ask that you provide us with certain information on yourself. This information will NOT be shared with any patrons or funding sources, present or former employers, or anyone outside the group. The information gathered therein will be used to catalog talent within the group, suggest assignments to new members and invite "old" members to task forces, focus groups, analysis conferences, etc. In other words, it is intended for decision-making on deployment of talent within the group to tasks as they may appear on the horizon.

We hope to have an information system set up such that a server not connected to the net but accessible through "gates" can store all group production by member, so when specialty and talent needs to be identified for any one or more tasks important to the group, this may be quickly by the stroke of a few keys.

Additionally, upon consultation with foundation legal counsel, it has been determined by the first-among-equals that any work performed by anyone, of any nationality, for and on behalf of S.A.A.L.M. will require strict compartmentalized coverage under certain chapters and parts of the Code of Federal Regulations (CRF) and other congressional acts and laws. We will handle highly sensitive information without the benefit of formal clearance vetting; therefore, each of us need to sign at minimum a nondisclosure agreement that describes what our legal advisors require S.A.A.L.M members to be covered for. Shortly, you will also get a security indoctrination memo from one of us. This will address item No. 2 in the nondisclosure agreement following the CV questionnaire. This is information with you, in compliance with legal requirements set for us to go by.

We have established a nonvetting status for S.A.A.L.M members to receive and work with what is essentially information of a classified nature. Nonvetting means that there will not be a lengthy background check process, and that much of the responsibility for keeping the ranks free of checkered characters and egomaniacs falls on us the founding members. The suggestion has been made, and the first-among-equals and some of the first members agree, that the first fifty members be declared "founding members" -- a distinction that constitutes more of a badge of courage and wisdom about the necessity for S.A.A.L.M and the personal valor for being a stand-up and be counted kind of person.

We will need to have these documents back as soon as feasibly possible. Keep copies for your records but off the desktop.

Again, welcome Brothers. Work is ahead of us, but let's have fun doing it.

In service to All.

P6

Xxxxxxxxxxxx

P4 Update

Task Members

I am going to invite you to log in onto the SAALM group, go to the FILES section, click, and get into the Orion_Sirius_Asmodeus Folder. Once in, to the the Exercise 1a- WA-G4B0032 Word.doc, download it and follow the instructions at the end of the file. We are using an identical strategy here to the one used in getting our own folks to gain perspective(s) on and discernment of an information-set, and then subject the intellectual extract(s) of what you are able to gain from your analysis of the set to your "other" brain's "intellect" and see what happens. What will be interesting for us to learn about all of yourselves in doing this exercise. When you start dealing with real information on things of interest to the group, I need to know you will have the metamethod in place and your visceral "nose" is working and fully engaged. We'll also get to see throughout these exercises how much, how well (or how little) you trust your enteric brain, its information processing and your trust and use of the information it generates for you...Makes sense?

Tell me your views and feelings on the task.

CA-3 continues his and the team's trek. His location is not related to his tasks, but rather it is a necessity for him at this time. He is proceeding on down to the next location, and once over onto the other. We're heeding his recommendation and taking them in tandem.

Recruiting continues. We pick up seven and lose three (due to the CV/NDA requirement). The team you belong to is still short of people but it will come. The two others are beginning to work on T&D assignments (such as what you are starting now). For the next 12 months, we'll slowly bring everybody up to par and up to speed on things, and once 2D is in your hands, allow about 3-6 months to have people get into Accelerated Learning[375] from the inside out, not the other way around. Am enclosing a relatively new article DA-1 and I did a while ago, as it is pertinent to some of the questions you raised about enteric info processing and A.L.. It is actually a presentation on the bases of life physics, with particular attention to 4-spacetime "reality matrices." I have a feeling it will help you understand things a little clearer.[376]

---

[375] Note here something interesting: "Accelerated Learning" (S.A.A.L.M.); "Accelerated Intelligence" (WingMakers); "ATI" (LPG-C). Three different names for the same thing. All three groups are using techniques to speed up Intelligence in its members; alien technology, I should add...

[376] "Life Physics" and "Reality Matrices" are also taught within LPG-C.

P4

PA Alpha

Subject: Preapplication from Alpha member for Working Group

FYI, this came to P4, P5 and myself today. I've polled the others, and have their agreement that RomanCandle would be a good addition to the Working Group. He is member of Alpha group, Traveler-1 (DTS) and Raven's group. I was also forewarned by DTS that GreatWaldo (the fellow with the Annunaki Gold from the Rothschild line is also interested in joining, but have not heard from him yet. Anyway, below please find copy of his message to P1 P2 and P12

G07 -- Chief Scientist

G09 -- Project Officer

Membership Preapplication -- S.A.A.L.M. Working Group --

This is my preapplication for membership in the S.A.A.L.M. Working Group. I am sending this preapplication by advice of my Alpha-FAE, Traveler-1, and per conversation with P3 on 3 September 2006. You already have my CV and I have signed all documentation required earlier this year.

I respectfully petition membership in the Working Group. I have contributions to make that members may find helpful, and I am ready to do my part in the effort.

Sincerely,
RomanCandle

Since this is preapplication, that means he is announcing intention and testing the waters... He's the orange... I will put together a summary of what he submitted, and as he is an engineer at the lab, he is covered by things you are not covered for, so let me get around that and see if I can get hold of his CV and possibly a resume, at least of things you can see... We need to vote on this. Good enough? Let me know as soon as possible, so as to be able to give him an answer to what I understand will be a formal application once he hears from one of us unofficially...

In service, P4

Dear GA-2,

Thank you for calling last night. I'm afraid that this is what happens when I get stressed past a certain point, and it is evident to me and my family that things have gone way past what I can cope with and remain functional at this point in time. I'm sorry I was not able to truly listen to you. Could you please put the substance of what your assessment of the present situation is in an email to each of us?

Before I continue, please let me update you on the situation with the man in St. Jo with the terminal colon cancer...I believe it was the 4th of this month that we found out about him and prayed for him. Yesterday (9/7) we got word that the man, whose rent has now been fully taken care of, went back to the doctor who reexamined him and stated that the problem was not nearly as serious as they had first believed! That was the same day I interfaced with Hurricane John and asked it to disperse some of its energy and please slow down. It did, from a category 4 to a 2...I'll bet lots of people were praying the same thing, and there are a lot of devout believers in Mexico! Thank you all for adding your prayers and energy to Mother Earth's and mine.

My big question is how did this Casbolt person know our email addresses? Never mind the shocking nature of his allegations. It feels like someone is really trying to massage my view of what is, and that is the one thing guaranteed to send me into red alert emergency lockdown defend against all comers mode. Sorry, that's simply how it is with me just now. The written word is something tangible yet way less charged than personal contact, which I apparently can't manage at this time. I can deal with the written word best right now.

The whole reason I decided to participate in the first place is that this seemed like the first really pure and altruistic group endeavor I'd ever heard of since, say, the early days of the space program. It seems like the very best way I can help others, and the transformation in my own being astounds me. To have this endeavor threatened, from whatever source and for whatever reason, makes me sick in the core of my soul. I'm doing everything I can to manage my stress so I can truly understand what is going on and thus know how to appropriately respond. This is why I told you at the very beginning about having PTSD, because I was concerned that just this sort of thing would happen, to the detriment of us all. I feel incredibly protective of this mission, these people--all of them, and the things we're all learning, and the idea of this know how in the wrong hands horrifies me. Yet whoever is originating all this had to have rather intimate access to our group--a security breach of the worst kind-- and this has been an ongoing concern for me from the very beginning. I think the blog may have been a mistake. It seemed like almost a dare to the entire intel community, and I think no spy worth his dark glasses could resist attempting a crack at such a tempting, alluring target! CB and I are working up a sitrep/intel analysis to follow ASAP. It will be sent as an attachment to an email. If that's not ok, if you want it sent another way let us know.

What works best for me in such a situation is information, and the best medium for me to process information and correlate it with what I already know from this and other data streams is the written word.

Thank you for your patience. I want to get to the bottom of this and understand it all.

Namaste, Wise Owl

September 8 2006 1335 CDT

Dear First-among-Equals,

What follows is our joint assessment and analysis of the present situation as seen from our perspective. It is based on telephone, email and IM conversations between us and yourselves, email exchanges between us, Mr. S and yourselves, the Casbolt letter, and communications from S. to us, which we immediately forwarded unanswered to you. It is based on gnosive and intuitive methods as well, and thus what we interpret may not be the complete picture. We've looked at the overall cumulus of information available to us many times, considering all possibilities, and this is what we've come up with.

The grandfather of all concerns is how much of this technology has gotten out, and to whom? Who does Mr. H actually work for? And how did he get to be in such a sensitive position before anybody had received any CV or NDA from him? This looks like a professional intelligence operation of the highest quality combined with a security breach at a high level within and structurally endemic to this organization. Either that or it is an elaborate test for us which we consider to be entirely possible since it is hard to believe that fuks with your professional associations could be so badly blindsided.

The primary problem appears to be a spectacular failure of internal security at a very basic level. The decision to place Mr. H in such a sensitive position before securing a signed NDA and a complete and fully substantiated CV was a poor one. Not only that, but there are 13 people in this group, and we haven't seen any documentation on any of them. The only CVs we've seen were the most recent one about RC and one before which everyone agreed was unsuitable.

We think the blog was a mistake, practically an invitation for some enterprising young intelligence operative to have a crack at such a tempting target. There are people in that business who'd attempt it just to see if it could be done! Then there is plain old greed, which must not be ignored. And you yourselves have written in "Between the Devil and the Returning Rock" about how thoroughly our military and intelligence communities were compromised, about the presence of M.s people on military bases on US soil. Yet these organizations were invited subscribers to the blog!

We understand that you are scientists and creative geniuses, and are finely focused on the investigative and development side of things, but perhaps have not before now needed to become personally involved with security as we would imagine the companies you were with previously would have had excellent internal security. And we well understand the nature of a true scientist is not only to discover but to share, compare notes, see what results everybody comes up with. Yet when it comes to developing a technology with the express purpose of saving billions of lives, security should be of paramount concern and should be in the hands of experts.

Mr. S is of particular concern to us.

His email to Ga-2, cc to us, dated 08/28/2006, looks like a set of legitimate questions a student would have about this rather exotic subject. However, they could also be the final, confirming kind of questions a mole would ask to be sure he had the information accurately interpreted and memorized. Possibilities, not certainties. Yesterday he's alleging to have been told that H was murdered, quits the group, then today he's asking for more modules?! We shouldn't be allowing this guy anywhere near this organisation and this information/technology.

What concerns us most is the fact that Ed K.[377] is discussing things he couldn't possibly have learned except from a leak from within this organisation. Either that, or someone is doing a damned good job of monitoring what should be secure and private communication channels. That is an industry basic security measure. The reality is that today's world is full of people who wouldn't hesitate to steal this technology for profit or worse.

Finally -- who is James Casbolt and how does he know so much about this project?

We understand that this was a "sticking our necks out" sort of venture but that doesn't mean we should become sharkbait because of poor security -- that would be a complete waste of everything we're all working for.

Mistakes have been made, but there are valuable lessons to be learned from all this. We need to learn from this and adjust our structure and practice accordingly. Knowledge must be applied to become wisdom!

We trust the L but they are not obligated to save us from our own foolishness. It is indeed our responsibility to defend our own biokind and sort out our own political and cultural differences. As we understand it, they are helping this project in an extraordinary

---

[377] Ed K. is Ed Komarek, known UFO researcher, especially into the Tall Whites. His blog address is, http://exopolitics.blogspot.com .

way but they have limits to which they must adhere. Let's not waste this opportunity to help our own planet and many others besides by allowing ourselves to be this vulnerable to penetration.

We should be taking all available measures to secure this project because its premature exposure will nullify the effectiveness and thus thwart the very purpose for which all this is being done: it will put the possibility of BST into the reach of the enema, the man from the gateway, and every terrorist with access to the Internet. Security should be comparable to that of the Manhattan Project. Instead, we have this present dilemma.

Wise Owl and Cannonball

James Casbolt, the MI6 whistle-blower, was cleverly taken down from the Internet and successfully silenced. He's still alive from what I know, but his, sometimes quite revealing, website was successfully shut down.

Figure 16.14: James Casbolt

There are those who have written Casbolt off as a hoax because he had the fake pictures of Enlil and Naanur on his website together with some photos which was supposedly from Dulce underground base, but in fact were fake too. Unfortunately, this is often what happens to whistle-blowers when they come close to the truth. Casbolt was fed fake pictures to discredit the rest of the relevant information on the website, and some researchers fell for the trick and started discrediting him, instead of looking at the bigger picture. So, the rumors of Casbolt being a hoax spread quickly over the Internet, and most people now wrote him off. Casbolt saw no other solution than to discontinue his website, unfortunately.

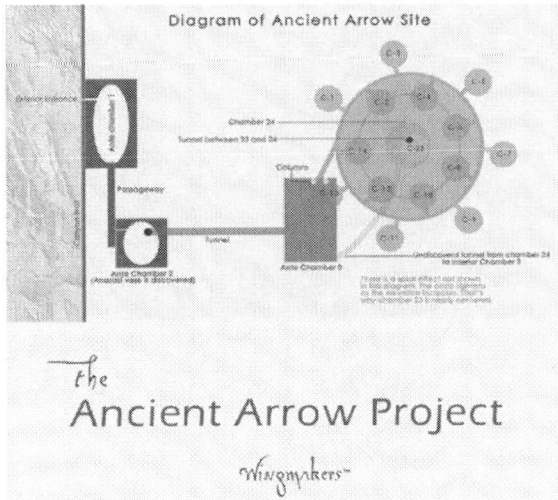

Figure 16.15: Diagram of Ancient Arrow site

It is true that Casbolt, just like he says in interviews and in his excellent book, *Agent Buried Alive*, he has been subjected to heavy mind control from within the government. He was subjected to a specific one called *Project Mannequin*, and he is apparently trained as an assassin. However, he has been working on breaking the control, which is not an easy task, and he has done his best to reveal his experiences. Once in a while, he fell back in line and had "relapses," but that is to be expected. I, for one, do not consider Casbolt a hoax. He fits too well into the picture, and most of what he has been telling us is true. To his defense, he also apologized for the fake pictures on his website, admitting he had been tricked. But it was too little, too late, it seems.

There are some quite interesting conversations, as I mentioned earlier, between S.A.A.L.M. members, ripped off a secure server, put on the Internet (much of it by Casbolt himself), taken down, but then retrieved from the Internet Archives. Fortunately, people were able to download this information in time before it disappeared from the Wayback Machine as well.

I am not going to copy the whole thing here, as it can be conveniently read at "Bibliotecapleyades.net."[378]

378

http://www.bibliotecapleyades.net/sociopolitica/esp_sociopol_illuminati_40.htm
http://www.bibliotecapleyades.net/archivos_pdf/SAALM01.pdf
http://www.bibliotecapleyades.net/archivos_pdf/SAALM02.pdf
http://www.bibliotecapleyades.net/archivos_pdf/SAALM03.pdf

PAPER 17:
THE ANIMUS, ARTIFICIAL INTELLIGENCE, AND BLANK SLATE TECHNOLOGY

by Wes Penre, Tuesday, June 14, 2011

The Labyrinth Group, ACIO, and the NSA (a Background)

The NSA (National Security Agency) is a government organization whose forerunner was the "General Services Special Projects Laboratory" (SPL). SPL was formed in 1938, and very little is known about it. It was not meant to be an official body. Then, in 1949, the "Armed Forces Security Agency" (AFSA) was created, on May 20.[379] On November 4, 1952, the NSA was officially formed and instigated by Harry S. Truman.[380] A year later, in 1953, SPL was folded into the NSA as un unacknowledged department, and ultimately, the ACIO (Advanced Contact Intelligence Organization) was folded into the SPL as an unacknowledged research laboratory.[381] ACIO, in fact, is older than both the NSA and the AFSA, as it was created in 1940, two years after SPL. It was two levels deep, and its code name was "Black Root."[382]

The reason for all this secrecy and security was not due to war or Intelligence gathering on antagonistic countries or leaders, as many people think. Rather, it was (and is) because of the ET issue. It's mainly a race against who is going to get ET technology for military applications first.

The Labyrinth Group, which was created by code name "Fifteen," came into existence much later, in 1963, with its main purpose to learn how to master Blank Slate Technology (BST) to counter an alien invasion, something which will be discussed in details later in this paper/chapter.

---

[379] http://en.wikipedia.org/wiki/National_Security_Agency#History
[380] Ibid.
[381] WingMakers: "The Neruda Interviews #3"
[382] Ibid.

In review: the Neruda Interviews contain more correct information than The Anderson Interviews. The WMM was introduced by the Labyrinth Group and the Corteum, the latter being an alien faction working with the Labyrinth Group. Over time, the WMM became more esoteric and purposely made less comprehensible for the public. The owner of the WingMakers site, Mahu Nahi of the Corteum, mixed truth with myth, making it more acceptable to the general public.[383]

Fifteen; The Man Behind the Number

(Some of this will be repetition from previous paper in order to give the whole story, and additional information has been added).

According to the Neruda Interviews, Fifteen was born in 1934 and was only 22 years old when he joined the ACIO in 1956. He was a renegade genius from the universities who wanted to build computers powerful enough to be used for time-travel. He came to the ACIO from Bell Laboratories due to an alliance between the two organizations at that time.

Figure 17.1: Zeta Grey

In 1958, the Corteum became known to the ACIO, and due to Fifteen's incomparable genius, he was the obvious choice to work with them. The Corteum found his obsessive interest in time-travel interesting, and somewhere along the line they told him about Blank Slate Technology (BST), a very special form of time-travel, which the Corteum had been trying to develop for some time. Fifteen was hooked as soon as he got to

---

[383] This paragraph has been moderated since the 2011 issue of the WPP, *WP 2024.*

know about it.

While working within the ACIO, Fifteen was approached by the Zeta Greys, who wanted to offer him a full-scale Technology Transfer Program (TTP), but Fifteen turned them down. He did not fully trust them, and he had already a similar (and better) program set up with the Corteum. Also, the Greys were much less organized and united than the Corteum, and the least thing Fifteen wanted was instability.

Figure 17.2: Joint Corteum & ACIO Seal

Albeit there was something the Greys had which the Corteum lacked; memory implants and genetic hybridization technologies. After much consideration, he decided to make a deal with them as well, but outside of the organization. He did not want too close of a relationship with the Zetas. In exchange, we provided them with access to our "information systems relative to genetic populations and their unique predisposition across a variety of criteria including mental, emotional, and physical behaviors; and they also provided us with their genetic findings."[304]

We need to keep in mind that there are several different bands of Greys, and not all of them are from Zeta Reticuli I and II; some of them are not even from our galaxy. The Grey blueprint is common in the Universe. However, even the Zeta Greys are not united, and different factions have different imperatives. Something many of them have in common (although working within different, unrelated groups, sometimes antagonistic to each other), is their genetic research agenda. They are a dying race and need genetics from the Living Library (Earth and its life

[304] WingMakers: "The Neruda Interviews #1", *op. cit. p.3.* (I am quoting that part exactly as it was stated in the interview, because it's important).

392

forms) to strengthen their biokind. Their deteriorating bodies have to a large degree lost their ability to host an Information Cloud (soul) and have therefore become more and more like artificial intelligence.

Factions of the Greys made treaties with humans already in the early 1950s through the Eisenhower administration (if not even earlier, through Hitler), and offered TTP in exchange for being allowed to abduct humans and animals in small quantities for their research. As if this wasn't bad enough, the Greys broke their agreement and abducted far more people than the government had agreed to, and in addition, the Greys did not report each abduction case to the government either, which they had promised. I am not sure if Fifteen was unaware of this fact when he made this new agreement with another faction of the Greys, or if he was willing to pay the price of deception for the exchange of technology. His reasoning is unknown to me, unfortunately, as it would tell us more about this man's character.

Whatever the case might be, the Greys were clearly interested in our information databases, and this was their primary agenda in regard to the ACIO, apparently. This particular band of Greys reported directly to Fifteen, because they saw him as someone with an IQ similar to themselves and regarded him as the CEO of Earth. In some ways, he actually was...

In 1963, two hundred Corteum members under the supervision of their leader, Mahu Nahi, and 118 brilliant human scientists joined Fifteen in the project of building the Labyrinth Group, which was somewhat connected to, but mostly separated from, the ACIO and the NSA. By using his influence, and with some help from his alien friends, Fifteen soon found himself in charge of both the ACIO and the Labyrinth Group, which was one of his major goals. In completing this, he had great help from Dr. Neruda's stepfather, who was a high executive of the ACIO and supportive of Fifteen. He assisted in putting Fifteen as the CEO of the ACIO. Fifteen could now put a cloak of secrecy around *both* groups in a way he couldn't have done prior to that. He now had free hands to develop BST. A little bit later in this paper, I am going to explain why Fifteen and the Corteum are so interested in this time-travel technology, and how the technology works, and it has to do with prophecy, and an alien race from another galaxy; an Invader Force, whose purpose is to establish themselves here and steal our genetics; however, in a much more aggressive way than the Greys. At least, this is what the Corteum has been telling the Labyrinth Group.

Fifteen soon made the Labyrinth Group quite a wealthy organization by selling soft technology to the government and certain major Companies in the U.S. and the rest of the world. These technologies came from the Corteum, and some from the Greys, but Fifteen kept most of it within his group, and only sold what he thought would be "safe," and not used for destructive purposes. This is the main source of income for the group, to be able to finance their research. Then, what Fifteen considers "safe technology" is up for debate.

Fifteen, for obvious reasons, is a very private person, and he is working on BST more or less 24/7; that's mainly all he does. The number "fifteen" has to do with security clearance within the ACIO and the Labyrinth Group. Levels 1-11 are assigned to the ACIO only, and 12-14 are all within the Labyrinth Group; in fact, they *are* the Labyrinth Group. Level Fifteen is reserved for Fifteen himself, hence his nick-name. His real name is not known to me.

Fifteen is of average height, and when Dr. Neruda, according to the WMM, defected, he had shoulder-long hair, gray, usually worn in a ponytail. Neruda said he always reminded him of Pablo Picasso with long hair, and the same penetrating eyes. They are also mischievous, "like you'd expect from a child who's done something wrong on the surface, but underneath, they've created something wonderful, it's just that nobody understands the wonderful part yet."

His country of origin is Spain, which is interesting, because Mahu Nahi, the leader of the Corteum alien race, who supposedly took over the WingMakers site, has a Spanish accent and lets us know in Hempel's recorded interviews that he was born in Spain, outside Barcelona. If he's a Corteum, that's of course misinformation, but if the person whom Hempel met in his home in the Summer of 2008 was Fifteen, it explains both the accent and his height. Hempel didn't mention Mahu's height, but if he was a Corteum, he would have looked slightly different from a normal human. The evidence speaks of a person who looks quite normal, of about average height, visiting Hempel in his home, and unless someone else within the Labyrinth Group is from Spain as well, Fifteen fits the profile. Just some food for thought.

Fifteen is on a life mission. He found out early in life that he wanted to work with developing time-travel technologies. He probably didn't know why he had that inner drive, but when other kids were playing regular children's games, Fifteen was already thinking about time-travel. In school and the universities, he quickly outsmarted his professors and didn't keep quiet about it. He was outspoken and eager to show what he knew. Of course, us being aware of how things work in the field of education, the professors, instead of taking this brilliant young man to heart, felt threatened by him and often kicked him out from their school of learning.

His already off-the-chart IQ was boosted exponentially when he was subjected to the Corteums' "Accelerated Intelligence Technology" (AIT). Then, after he had selected the cream of the crop from the scientific core of the ACIO, he let them undergo the same procedure in an effort to create a team which could successfully develop BST.

A Cloak of Secrecy, Two Different Defense Weapons and Hidden Agendas

Fifteen has already from the beginning been very secretive about everything he is doing. Nothing whatsoever which is discussed within the Labyrinth Group is allowed to be discussed with anybody outside the organization, not even with life partners. Hence, Dr. Neruda is the first, and only person so far who has defected from the Labyrinth Group and started talking both about the Animus Problem (which will be addressed in this paper) and BST.[385]

Dr. Neruda says in his interview:

> Fifteen withholds his knowledge from the media and the general public because he doesn't want to be seen as a savior of humanity--the next messiah. And he especially doesn't want to be seen as some fringe lunatic that should be locked up, or worse yet, assassinated because he is so misunderstood. The instant he stepped forward with what he knows he would lose his privacy and his ability to discover BST. And this he'll never do.

> Most people who know about this greater reality are fearful of stepping into the public scrutiny because of the fear of being ridiculed. You have to admit, that the general public is frightened by what it doesn't understand, and they do kill the messenger.[386]

To fully understand why this is such a secret I need to touch on the subject of the Animus before we go into them in detail.

Briefly, the Anima (Anima or Animae; plural of Animus) are apparently an alien, ontocyboenergetic life form from another galaxy who are planning on coming here to Earth as an invader force; as conquerors, but also to get hold of our DNA.[387] Due to a catastrophe in their past, they developed into a machine race with artificial intelligence. In other words, they lack what we call a soul, or information cloud.[388] [389] Their intention is

---

[385] Today, I consider Dr. Neruda being James Mahu of the WingMakers' alter ego. At one point, at the end of his life, Dr. Bordon claimed to have been Fifteen, but I seriously doubt it. Dr. Bordon was born in 1946, and Fifteen in 1934. *WP 2024.*

[386] WingMakers: "The Neruda Interviews #3," http://www.wingmakers.com/neruda3.html, *op. cit.*

[387] In my later research, this corresponds to the "Sirians," *WP 2024.*

[388] Barbara Marciniak (1992): *Bringers of the Dawn*, and numerous lectures, channeled by Barbara between 1988 and 2011 (ongoing).

[389] I believe this information is not correct. I've learned, as of late, that the "conquerors" do have a soul-mind, but they lack Spirit, which is something we humans inhabit, *WP 2024.*

to once again be able to have soul-carriers (biological bodies - biokinds - which can carry a soul) and to have information clouds inhabit them. If they don't, they cannot be part of the evolvement towards being ONE with the Prime Creator, and their part in the universal cycles will be very limited. Therefore, they are planning on invading this planet, steal our DNA, and perhaps our whole biokind template, and kill off the rest of the population.[390]

So why Earth? Why travel from a distant galaxy to invade us, a small planet in the outskirts of the Milky Way?

First of all, we are not "just" a small planet. Our biokind is very special and part of an intergalactic experiment called the Living Library. Yes, the Living Library was interfered with some 300,000 years ago when the Anunnaki took over this planet, but our soul-carriers are still very special and carry traits which are quite unusual in this galaxy and beyond; namely, a wide range of emotions![391]

Still, we are not the only target for the Animus. They have set out probes in our solar system as well as in others. This year, in 2011, they are scheduled to set up a new probe close to Earth to study our development as a human species. Last they checked (around 12,000 years ago), we were still not developed enough for them to interfere, but Fifteen and the Corteum are afraid that we are now! This means that an invasion could be scheduled by the Anima shortly after the probe has scanned our present biokind/biomind.[392]

This is where BST comes into the picture. With the gain of certain knowledge, Fifteen is hoping to be able to stop the invasion by using his time-travel technology. Details about how this works will be discussed in a separate section below.

Thus, we can see from Fifteen's point of view why he wants to keep this whole thing secret. However, Dr. Neruda didn't agree with Fifteen's approach to use BST to stop this alien race. Just like LPG-C, the Labyrinth Group have their form of remote viewing (RV), similar to Extra Neuro Sensing (ENS), but although the subject of ENS is not supposed to be able to detect the neuro-sensor (or ENS, the person who remote views), the WingMakers detected the ENS used by Fifteen and they started to probe it. When Fifteen established that the beings who detected it were actually WingMakers of the Central Race, he got cold feet and stopped all future RV sessions. He was afraid that the WingMakers would jeopardize

---

[390] I no longer believe our purpose is to become ONE with the Creator/Creatrix. If the Anima indeed are the Sirians, I would ponder the above information more than once before I adhere to it, *WP 2024*.

[391] A wide range of emotions is equivalent to inhabiting Spirit, *WP 2024*.

[392] I consider this disinformation. The Anima (Sirians) have been here for eons, and they never left, *WP 2024*.

his BST plans and stop him.

This was another reason why Dr. Neruda defected. He believed that the WingMakers' defense weapon installed on our planet would be more effective than BST; he said that all logic showed this to be true, but Fifteen strongly disagreed.

So, how can the seven WingMakers sites be defensive weapons? It's because, due to extensive RV sessions, Dr. Neruda came to the conclusion that among other things, they are DNA triggers. It is known inside the Labyrinth Group that these sites are supposedly meant to activate something in our DNA. This hypothesis alone makes a great connection to the renegade group of Pleiadians that Barbara Marciniak is channeling. The latter is, in their own words, here to help us activate dormant parts of our DNA.[393] Although they have not mentioned anything in their lectures about the Tributary Zone in general, they have made hints to that such exist, and of course the Pleiadians are not the only alien race interested in seeing our DNA evolve. *The Anima, in clear language, is after our "source code;" the code which the Lyrans and their group of Original Planners implanted in our DNA, the code which is being "decoded" as we speak by gamma rays transmitted from the Sun and the Galactic Center by the Founders, who appear in segments, in form of light-waves.* By understanding this source code, they can prevent us from evolving. At least, this is what makes all the sense to me, but there is another twist to this story, as we shall see.

The purpose of this activation was still a mystery when Dr. Neruda defected, but Neruda himself thinks it has something to do with stimulating our fluid intelligence and enabling sensory inputs that have been dormant within our central nervous system (and he is right). The enhancement of the central nervous system, still according to both Dr. Neruda and Marciniak's group, makes the defensive weapon more effective to any alien attack. In fact, it has to do with ascension; the rest is secondary.

Dr. Neruda contemplated that the WingMakers' defensive weapon had to do with rendering our planet invisible to the 2011 probes sent out by the Anima, and in a sense, that is true as we shall see in the next book in this series. Here are Dr. Neruda's own words:

> They the WingMakers wrote that higher frequencies were emanating from the central universe, and that these seven sites comprised a collective technology that somehow coordinated these frequencies or higher energies to bring about a shift in the planet's vibratory structure, enabling life on the planet to survive the shift and remain undetected by the Animus.

---

[393] Barbara Marciniak (1992): *"ringers of the Dawn*, and numerous lectures, channeled by Barbara between 1988 and 2011 (ongoing).

...

It confirmed that we're dealing with the Central Race, and that they want the cultural artifacts from the seven sites to be shared with the public. These elements were connected to the effectiveness of the defensive weapon.

...

They left behind poetry, music, paintings, and even a glossary. It seems to me that all of these elements -- in addition to the philosophy -- are connected. Also, I'm suggesting that something fundamentally changes when these materials are absorbed, and perhaps this change, whatever it is, resonates with the technology from the seven sites.

...

...I've absorbed the materials and I've noticed changes.[394]

It sure sounds to me that the WingMakers sites were left here on Earth by the Lyran/Pleiadian group who were chased away by the Anunnaki, supposedly 4-500,000 years ago. They are activation sites and defense weapons against those who would try to stop humankind from evolving. The WingMakers sites are heavily encoded and encrypted, and Marciniak's Pleiadians say that intruders of any kind will not be able to figure out the source code. Humankind (or parts of us) *will* evolve! The artwork, original music, and the text is telling the story, but the Lyrans knew, or course, that this material could come into the hands of something like our Military Industrial Complex and therefore not come out to the public in its pure form (if at all), but they knew it would. This was planned by soul agreements!

Dr. Neruda says that he had some profound experiences when he was alone in the caves at the Ancient Arrow site in New Mexico, where the first WingMakers site is located. Apparently, he had a visitation from the WingMakers themselves in the cave, more of a perceptual nature than a physical, but still very real. They told him not to trust what Fifteen was doing, and that he was too involved with the Corteum to see the real solution. It is Dr. Neruda's conviction that the WingMakers put this defensive weapon on Earth to protect their genetics (us).

This was the soul agreement! In a Multiverse, where all time is simultaneous, and the Founders and the Builders think "long thoughts" because of their long lifespan, were already planning 300,000 years ago for what is happening now. Dr. Neruda most probably has a soul agreement

---

[394] WingMakers: *The Neruda Interviews #2,* http://www.wingmakers.com/neruda2.html, *op. cit.*

with the Builders and the WingMakers to reveal the information to the public, which he did in 1998. These kinds of soul agreements are done in Sitter Space (the astral worlds between lives). It was no coincident that Dr. Neruda got involved with the Labyrinth Group, received the information he needed, "happened to be" in the cave alone and receive the message from the WingMakers. It was all in the plan to get the material out to the public, although Dr. Neruda was of course, like the rest of us, in oblivion as to what his task was; it was predestined to happen as part of his life mission. Even if the information was distorted afterwards, it doesn't matter. The information triggered the source code and is speeding up our evolution.

The source code is still not understood and is not supposed to be; the secrecy and cover-up by the different alien/human groups involved, frenetically trying to decipher a source code they can't even find, is a waste of time; humankind is evolving and the source code is being triggered every second of the day.

The WingMakers must be the Central Race (the Founders), the original seeders of planets and universes, working in unison with the Lyrans, Vegans and other species involved in the first seeding of mankind to make sure the source code was hidden in the human genome. The WingMakers sites are the "light switches" which send signals in encoded form to the source code, hidden in our genome, and the DNA activation begins. So, what determines when the 'light switches should go off? Well, the Sun does, and the Central Sun in the middle of the Milky Way Galaxy. When the star constellations and the lineup of our solar system with the Galactic Center is in a straight position with the Central Sun (i.e. right now), the latter, from its Galactic Center Tributary Zones, sends signals to our Sun on gamma rays, and from there signals are relayed to the WingMakers sites, which turn on the light switches. It looks like the Tributary Zones on Earth (which I think are 12 in numbers, not 7, due to that the original planners worked with the 12 system, not the 7 system) are just relay stations. The real Tributary Zones are hidden on planets in another dimension in the center of the Milky Way Galaxy, which we call the "Central Sun."

As usual, what so often is blinding scientists and highly educated people in the Military Industrial Complex is that they think everything has to have something to do with weaponry; defensive or offensive in nature. Few are looking in the right direction. No higher evolved beings who are spiritually inclined would suggest a defensive system that has anything to do with violence of any kind. This case is no exception; the WingMakers sites have nothing to do with defensive attack.

So Mahu Nahi (James of the WingMakers) is correct in describing the Sovereign Integral and the Grand Portal. But if Mahu Nahi is the head of the Corteum, why is he telling us the truth? Well, he is smart enough to understand what the WingMakers sites actually are—something he is very careful to keep a secret from the Labyrinth Group. On the other hand, he knows that the source code in our DNA is getting triggered as we speak in many, many people, and there is little he can do about it. Therefore, he took on the WingMakers site after having decided that he could just as well give the public the truth in a watered-down version to get people hooked.

But hooked to what?

He must have figured that if he gave us the truth about the Sovereign Integral (our reconnection with our Higher Selves, i.e. our Oversouls[395]) and our journey to find the Grand Portal, he would have people occupied and it may help him find the source code. Many races out there want access to the source code for different reasons.

In addition, according to The Guardians, a certain frequency distortion has been embedded into the WingMakers music CDs and some of the paintings and poetry has some advanced code inserted so that it actually could prevent us from having our DNA reactivated. It's all about delaying the reactivation effect until after 2012, when the aligning with the Galactic Center is happening in full. After 2012, if we haven't taken advantage of what has been sent to us in form of encoded information on gamma rays, it's much harder to get the activation process started.

So apparently, if we are to believe A'shayana Deane and her Guardian Alliance, it could be dangerous to follow the "spiritual" practices Mahu Nahi suggests when comes to the paintings, and reading the poetry and listening too much on the music CDS could be delaying our reactivation. My own thought is that Mahu and the Corteum took on the WingMakers as an experiment to see how many serious spiritual truth-seekers they could attract to their site. They were probably hoping to attract the cream of the crop of active awakened individual and "deactivate" their DNA, or continue keeping it dormant while they continue studying all our DNA activation, looking for the hidden source code. The bottom line is that I seriously suspect that the Corteum knows what the real purpose of the WingMakers sites are. As we shall see soon, their intention is not only to fool those of us who are awakening, but also to fool the Labyrinth Group or any other organization working on a similar project as they do.

Does this mean we should avoid the WingMakers Material as if our life depended upon it? No, there is a lot of very important information there, but we should be very careful not to get involved in any of the particular practices that have to do with the paintings and avoid the music CDs to be on the safe side. There are other, more general practices, like breathing exercises, which are just old, common knowledge from Eastern Philosophies, and there is no harm done to do them; I actually encourage

---

[395] I would call it Spirit today, not Oversoul, *WP 2024*.

some of them, like *The Quantum Pause*.[396]

Accelerated Intelligence

Accelerated Intelligence is something which the Corteum brought to the group. The purpose is to activate the thalamocortical system of the brain. When they have activated this specific section of the brain, inducing a small functional cluster within this system, it expands the higher-order consciousness. These are the neural coordinates of consciousness, pertaining to higher-order reasoning, useful to scientific inquiry, mathematics and general problem solving.

This was the technique Fifteen was subjected to and in his turn let all his employees take advantage of as well. Shortly after this was done to him, he got the vision of BST, as a solution to his time-travel theories.

So how does this technique work? Dr. Neruda is describing it in some details in the Neruda Interviews #2:

> Few people realize that their conscious mind only processes about 15 bits of information per second of linear time. However, in vertical time, the unconscious mind is processing approximately 70-80 million bits of information. Thus, in normal consciousness, humans are aware of only an infinitesimal amount of the information that is constantly being fed to them at the unconscious level. The Corteum technology was designed to reduce the filtering aspects of the conscious mind and enable the higher frequency information packets to be fed to the conscious mind.

> In parallel with this effort, the brain circuitry--if you will--is re-wired to handle the higher voltage of the information that is being fed to the consciousness, allowing capabilities like photographic memory and abstract thought to co-exist. These capabilities become the matrix filter that draws from the unconscious repositories the most relevant information at any particular time based on the problem or task at hand.

> ...

> It's not really a simple question of the quantity of information processing, but rather the relevance of the information in linear time based on the intention of the individual. When one goes through the process of the Corteum technology, their ability to

---

[396]   https://wespenrevideos.com/wp-content/uploads/2022/02/Quantum-Pause.pdf

tune into information packets that are relevant to a situation or problem is vastly improved. In most people, when a given situation confronts them they access their conscious mind and pull out the solution that has served them in the past. Thus, people fall into ruts and patterned behavior, which closes down their access to the unconscious information packets that are based on real-time situation analysis and have extremely high relevancy.

This technology accelerates the circulation of information between the conscious and unconscious aspects of the mind to flow in the pattern of an ascending spiral rather than the pattern of a repetitious circle. And because of this it unleashes the innate intelligence of the individual. So you see, the Corteum technology doesn't increase raw intelligence, it simply facilitates the natural intelligence of the individual.[397]

I will further discuss vertical time and BST in a moment. The concept of vertical time is imperative for BST to work. But a few other things first.

The Corteum - What They Look Like

For those familiar with the WingMakers Material (WMM) it has been a mystery who the Corteum really are. They are presented as a benevolent race, not connected with the ETs that interact with of world's governments, i.e. the Greys or the Reptilians.

There is no real public picture of the Corteum that I am aware of. The only thing I've found is the artsy image at WingMakers.com, which doesn't tell us much. Still, I don't believe the Corteum are one single species and this is another thing we need to learn about aliens; they rarely work alone. Species, as they develop (not always so much spiritually as technologically) and are involved in space travel, tend to join together with other alien species from other star systems and different star confederations. Thus, species with similar imperatives and agendas work together to accomplish their goals. This means that factions or Reptilians, Greys, Insectoids and humanoids are working closely together as one species to bring forth their development as *separate* species. We tend to think that Greys have their agenda, while the Reptilians have theirs and so on. In reality, amongst alien races who are developed enough to routinely engage in traveling between the stars, this is rarely the case.

However, we know how some of them look like due to a description by Dr. Neruda. He says that:

---

[397] WingMakers: "The Neruda Interviews #2", http://www.wingmakers.com/neruda2.html, *op. cit.*

They stand nearly three meters high *(almost 10 feet)* and have very elongated heads and bodies. Their skin is very fair; almost translucent, like you might expect from a cave dweller. Their eyes are relatively large and have various colors just like our own, except the Corteum have different colors to their eyes depending on their age and, in some instance, their emotional state.

What's very unique about the Corteum is that they have an incredibly articulate nervous system that enables them to process virtually everything that occurs within their environment, including the thoughts of another. Which means that when you're in their presence, you need to have control of your thoughts or else you'll potentially offend them. They're very sensitive emotionally.

...

They speak perfect English or French, Italian, Spanish, or most any other language for that matter. They're very gifted linguists and can acquire average language skills in a matter of a few weeks, and operate as masters of the language within a few months. Their minds are like sponges, but like I said before, while they possess incredible mental powers to absorb new information and synthesize it with previous information, they're not necessarily adept at creating new information totally unrelated to existing information. That's precisely what impressed them so much with Fifteen.[398]

Furthermore, Dr. Neruda explains to us that their reason for being so interested in BST is because the planet from where they came has become very fragile because its protective atmosphere is degenerating "at an alarming rate." This condition has led them to become nocturnal, only coming to the surface at night, and even then, only for short moments. Their outer skin becomes more and more sensitive while their atmosphere becomes less protective. From their perspective, BST would restore their environment.

Where have we heard this before? It's a similar story told by Zecharia Sitchin regarding the Anunnaki and their home planet, Nibiru, which needs gold to restore their atmosphere, and it's an ongoing process. These people are miners, and they have not been mining only here on Earth, but on other planets in our solar system and elsewhere, too.

I have heard from a source that some of the Corteum is indeed a faction of the Earth-bound Anunnaki, who stayed behind and still dwell on our planet, mostly underground. They are not the S.A.A.L.M. faction, which works on putting Marduk and his people on the World Throne once and for all, but are still loyal to the Kingdom (home planet Nibiru), and are working with the Labyrinth Group to perhaps (at least officially) solve

---

[398] Ibid. op. cit.

their planetary issue.

In his description of how the Corteum look like, Dr. Neruda is both describing the Anunnaki and the Tall Whites, encountered by Charles Hall, who explained that the eye color of the Tall Whites (some call them Tall Greys) change as they grow older, and their nervous system is quite sensitive, just like Dr. Neruda says.

Elongated Skulls vs. Skull-Binding and Cranial Deformation

An interesting thing with Dr. Neruda's depiction of the Corteum is that they are extremely tall (the Anunnaki can be 7-10ft tall), with elongated skulls. According to Sitchin and LPG-C, the Ša.A.M.i. and the Anunnaki, even if their skulls can be slightly elongated, otherwise look much like us; we have their genetics. However, giant elongated skulls have been found in South America and elsewhere, and you can study them in some museums around the world. I would suggest you google "elongated skulls" and do your research; it's interesting, and the research is almost addictive.

We can see the same traits in some of the Egyptian pharaohs as well, and very much so in Queen Nefertiti (see *fig. 17.3*).

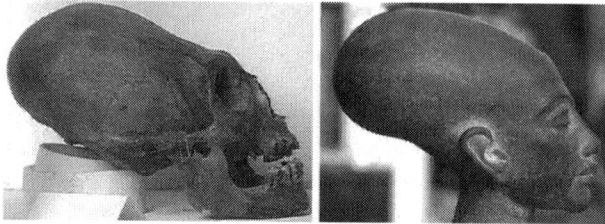

Figure 17.3: Comparing a giant, elongated skull with a bust of Nefertiti.

Some people, who want to debunk this, refer this special kind of skull to something called "skull-binding," where some tribes bind the heads of young infants while the skeleton is still soft, and that will bring about this trait. Although this is true, it's rather an attempt to copy-cat the old gods. The difference between the original ones and the ones that are "skull-bound" is the size of the skull and the jaws.

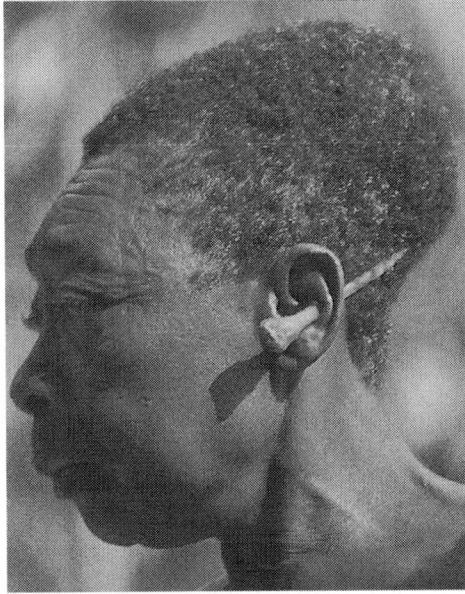

Figure 17.4: Skull-binding

I have heard suggestions that the elongated skulls belong to the Titans, who were deformed offspring of the Anunnaki mating with humans. For the records, the Corteum are not Titans; they are not related. It always puzzled me why the Anunnaki, as depicted in the Sumerian cuneiform, is always wearing headgear and headdresses. Did they actually have elongated skulls and wanted to hide this from the humans? This contradicts the information I've received from Dr. Bordon of LPG-C, who says the Anunnaki look pretty much like us, but are usually much taller. The question is; the Ša.A.M.i. he is encountering in the LINK meeting, do they wear headgears? The readers may ask themselves why I don't just ask Dr. Bordon this question, but over time I've learnt that he is not very eager to answer questions *he* thinks are of "less relevance."

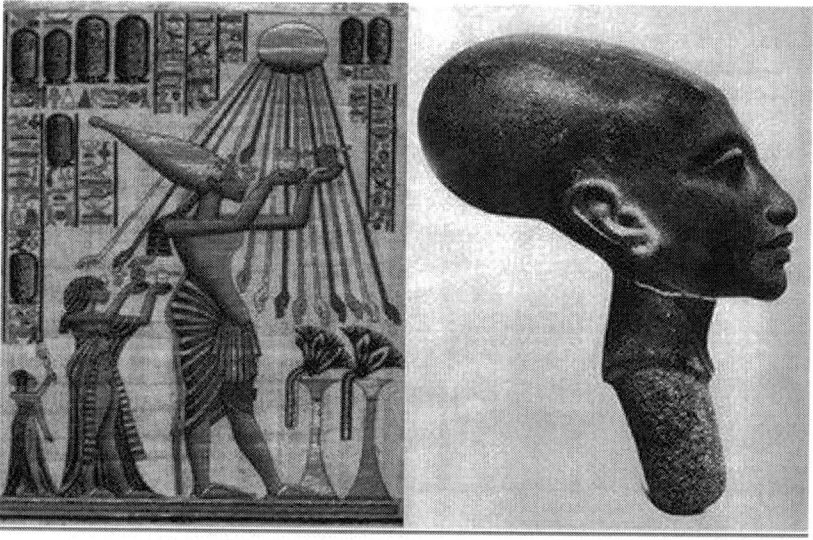

Figure 17.5: Were the headdresses to hide their skulls?

Also, as we now know, the humanoid species is very common in this galaxy, and the variation is mostly in length, skin color, and perhaps the shape of their heads. There is overwhelming evidence that those LPG-C call the Ša.A.M.i. are not one species working alone, but a dominant race in a galactic federation to which they belong. Therefore, it is not farfetched to think that some of them have elongated skulls.

Skull-binding and intentional cranial deformation has been common throughout history in most parts of the world,[399] and most of these intrusions on infants have been in an effort to please, and look like, the "gods." The question is, which gods? Skull-binding even happened in Egypt; people thought that if they extended the skulls, they would get larger brains and become more intelligent. As in comparison to whom? It is interesting that skull-binding has been most common in Egypt, South Africa, and South America (such as Peru), where the Anunnaki have had the greatest influence, aside from the Three Rivers in Mesopotamia. Is this why we find tribes still doing it today and why we have found deformed skulls in these areas? Still, where do the larger, deformed skulls come from? Hybrids? Pure Anunnaki? Or did the Anunnaki skull-bind their own children within certain families? If the latter is true, that explains why we see the Anunnaki and their hybrids depicted both with normal skulls and deformed. It could also explain why the Corteum have elongated skulls (if Dr. Neruda is correct); they belong to a certain family or "tribe" of the

---

[399] http://en.wikipedia.org/wiki/Artificial_cranial_deformation; http://wiki.bmezine.com/index.php/Cranial_Binding

Ša.A.M.i./Anunnaki.[400]

It's very unlikely that Mark Hempel had a visitor who traveled regular airline from New York to Minnesota, being 10 feet tall with an elongated skull. It's more likely that someone else, more humanlike looking, visited Mark in his home, sporting a Spanish accent. But why a Spanish accent and why this unnaturally low baritone voice of the person speaking in the interview sessions by Mark Hempel from 2008? I don't know, other than it's confusing and that is perhaps what it's meant to be; the person in the interview, who claims to be Mahu Nahi of the Corteum, may not want his true voice in a recording.

It is evident that the WingMakers site is run by the Corteum. However, Fifteen and the Corteum are not our enemies, according to Dr. Neruda; they too want to save the planet from the incoming threat, and wish for us to evolve; they just want to keep their work secret. Hence, you will see a lot of uplifting, spiritual information on the WingMakers site, which was put there by the Corteum. This information is true, and you can feel it. Then there are other things, not so inspiring, which are mixed bags, at best, and disinformation at worst. Is this confusing? It is meant to be. What is more effective than anything else—often more so than killing the messenger—is to create a disinformation campaign on a large scale. However, for the clever, there are ways to sort information from disinformation; listen and read with your heart.

Seven Superuniverses, Seven Tributary Zones, and Seven Superdomains

In the WMM, they are talking about 7 superuniverses with a Central Universe in the middle, which is the Universe of Source (the Prime Creator). As some people pointed out in the WingMakers Q&A section, this sounds very similar to what is described in the Urantia Book.[401] Nahi Mahu replied that in some cases the WingMakers share the philosophy with Urantia, but it's still quite different. However, when we look at it, it may not be so different after all. As we shall see, Dr. Neruda's presentation of the 7 superuniverses coincide and fit pretty well with LPG-C's 7 superdomains but is a light version thereof.

---

[400] There is also a strong case for that the elongated Giant Skulls are remains of an earlier human experiment, *WP 2024*.

[401] Urantia Book online: http://www.urantia.org/en/urantia-book/read

Structure of the Physical Grand Universe

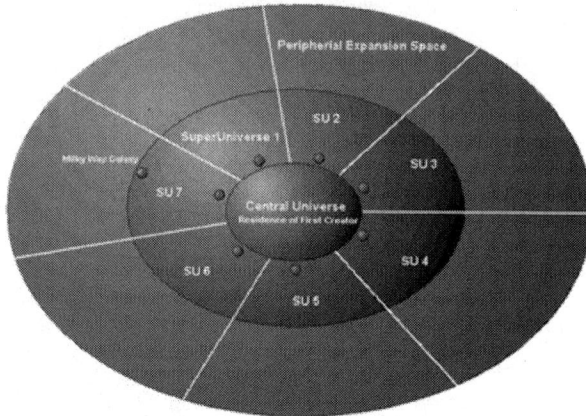

Figure 17.6: The Grand Universe with its 7 superuniverses, according to Dr. Neruda and the WingMakers

This is how the 7 superuniverses are described in the WMM by Dr. Neruda. He says that the Labyrinth Group learned it from the Corteum.[402]

> ...the Central Universe is stationary and eternal, while the seven superuniverses are creations of time and revolve around the Central Universe in a counterclockwise rotation. Surrounding these seven superuniverses is "outer" or peripheral space, which is non-physical elementals consisting of non-baryonic matter or antimatter, which rotates around the seven superuniverses in a clockwise rotation. This vast outer space is expansion room for the superuniverses to expand into. The known universe that your astronomers see is mostly a small fragment of our superuniverse and the expansion space at its outermost periphery. Hubble-based astronomy extrapolates, based on a fractional field of view, that there are 50 billion galaxies in our superuniverse, each containing over 100 billion stars. However, most astronomers remain convinced that our universe is singular. It is not--according to the Corteum.

> On the fringe of the central universe resides the Central Race, which contain the original human DNA template of creation. However, they are such an ancient race that they appear to us as Gods, when indeed they represent our future selves. Time and space are the only variables of distinction. The Central Race is known to some as the creator gods who developed the primal template of the human species and then, working in conjunction

---

[402] The Central Race sounds much like we humans before most of us got trapped in the Matrix (see upcoming books in this series), *WP 2024*.

with the Life Carriers, seeded the galaxies as the universes expanded. Each of the seven superuniverses has a distinctive purpose and relationship with the central universe via the Central Race based on how the Central Race experimented with the DNA to achieve distinct, but compatible physical embodiments to be soul carriers.

...

The Central Race is divided into seven tribes, and they are master geneticists and the progenitors of the humanoid race. In effect, they are our future selves. Quite literally they represent what we will evolve into in time and towards in terms of space.

...

The Labyrinth Group believed that the WingMakers are representatives of the Central Race, and that they created our particular human genotype to become suitable soul carriers in our particular universe. The Ancient Arrow site is part of a broader, interconnected system of seven sites installed on each continent. Together, we believe this system constitutes a defensive technology.[403]

Dr. Saunter, in the opening to the Dr. Neruda interviews, is convinced that the Central Race, which, from what the Labyrinth Group have concluded, are equivalent with the WingMakers and from the Pleiades. Barbara Marciniak's Pleiadian renegade group are saying that they seeded mankind together with the Lyrans, so a consistent picture is starting to emerge.

The Ancient Arrow Site in New Mexico; the one and only WingMakers site that's been found (at least as far as public knowledge goes); is (according to the WMM, although I believe there are at least 12 sites--the Guardians say 24, which is 12x2) just one of 7 sites, also called Tributary Zones in the WMM, spread out over the continents of Earth like in *fig. 17.8* below.

---

[403] "The Neruda Interview #1."

Figure 17.7: Global position of the 7 Planetary Tributary Zones.

Each of these Tributary Zones on Earth corresponds with one superuniverse, where the site in New Mexico most likely corresponds with our own. If this is true, there is a Tributary Zone, according to the WMM, in the core in the galactic center of each living galaxy in our universe. They are, symbolically, or literally, located on planets very close to the galactic core. And, as Advanced Physics is aware of today, the core of the galactic center, at least in a spiral galaxy like our own, consists of a Central Sun and a gigantic black hole. This black hole is what the Pleiadians call "The Womb of the Mother",[404] i.e. the birth center of the galaxy. The Pleiadians compare it to a "super orgasm," where the nebulae and stars were spread in a rotational orbit around its center. The fact that we are now aligning ourselves with the Galactic Center is a phenomenon known in mainstream physics as well, but is pointed out both by Marciniak's Pleiadian group and Mahu Nahi in the interview sessions with Mark Hempel.[405] Both say that this has to do with change in consciousness. People who have learned to vibrate on a higher frequency, and to keep their frequency on that level most of the time, despite turmoil, will experience this new boost of energy coming in from the galactic center differently than someone who has not prepared, spiritually. So, some people will become highly enlightened during this time, while others will be overwhelmed by the strength of these energies. If a person has a lot of anxiety, hate, anger, resentment, and judgment in his or her personality, these traits will amplify. On the other side, these who have learned how to love, appreciate things, apply humility in life, be compassionate, understand self and others, and apply valor in life, will have those traits amplified, and will use them as a springboard

[404] Barbara Marciniak channeling the Pleiadian, 2010.
[405] Mark Hempel interviews James of the WingMakers, April 5, 2008, Session #1.

towards higher dimensions and frequencies.

Interesting also is that the 7 superdomains explored by LPG-C correspond somewhat with the 7 superuniverses. I am convinced that Dr. Neruda knew this when he did his interviews with Sarah, but needed to simplify it, or no one would understand what he was talking about. The same thing applies to the Labyrinth Group and their WMM; they explain briefly in their "Liminal Cosmogony" how the 7 superuniverses are connected, followed by an explanation that this is an excerpt of a grander work, which will be revealed to humankind later. I would say that this grander work, which will be released by the Corteum and the Labyrinth Group, is quite similar to that of LPG-C's "Working Model."

In figure 17.8 we can see what LPG-C call "The Unum," comprising 7 superdomains.

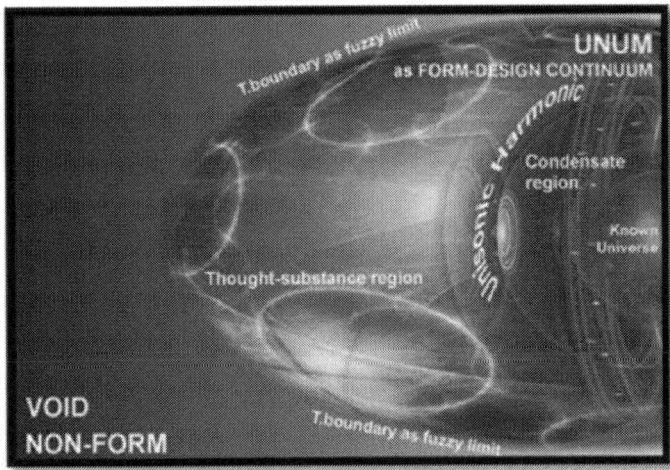

Figure 17.8: The Unum with the 7 superdomains

Here, the "superuniverses", or superdomains, as described by LPG-C, are as follows:

1. Prime-Causal
2. Thought
3. Unisonic
4. Logomorphic
5. Syntonic-Diffusive
6. Templaic or Quantum Potential
7. 4-Space/Time

Obviously, the experience upon which we have our main attention is in

4-space/time, although we exist simultaneously in all superdomains. These superdomains correspond to the seven superuniverses, used both in the WMM and the Urantia Book, although they are approached differently. The Void corresponds to the "Peripheral Expansion Space" in the WingMakers superuniverse version.

There is much more to the earthly seven Tributary Zones and with the Working Model than I have discussed here and in other previous papers/chapters, but that is material for another time.

I find it interesting, though, that both the WMM and LPG-C are working with the "7 System," while the Pleiadians and the Guardians (and many other metaphysical contacts) are working with the "12 System," saying that this is the system within which the human biomind is operating, and in expansion, we will tune into the "13 System."[406]

The Central Race as Creator Gods

Dr. Neruda in the interviews confirms what the Pleiadians have said about seeding the Universe and provide it with functioning soul-carriers. He says that the Central Race experimented many times with different kinds of soul-carriers until they formed one that was good enough to take a particle of the Source energy force into the outer, expanding universes. If not being able to do so, its experience in the 3rd dimension (or 4-space/time) would be of limited value, as it can't bring any of that back directly to Prime Creator.

The Central Race holds the genetic template, or archetype, of the human species, despite the form it takes on, or what time it lives in. So long as it is a soul-carrier of intelligent life forms in the sense of bi-pedal beings with a torso, two arms, and two legs, the Central Race holds the genetic template. All other, lesser-developed versions are drawn towards this archetype like a magnetic force. All versions of the humanoid species are just time-shifted versions of the Central Race. At least this is the view of the Corteum.

Prophecy

Prophecy is a pretty wide but interesting subject, because there are numerous such since the beginning of time. In the WMM, several different ancient prophecies are discussed of which some of them are not even known to common man, and these are some of the prophecies supposed to come true in our time. To distinguish between the WMM prophecies

---

[406] This will be further explained in Book #3 in this series.

and other significant ones, I'm going to categorize them and explain them one by one.

There are many ancient texts dealing with prophecies, and only a handful are known to the public. Most of them are hidden within secret societies and organization who have locked them in, only to be viewed by high level, very "trusted members." The ACIO, and the Labyrinth Group in particular, have access to many of them, if not most, according to Dr. Neruda.

These prophecies are pretty powerful at describing the 21st Century and its challenges. Fifteen got access to them when he became the Director of Research for the ACIO.

Being able to leave your body while doing remote viewing is nothing new. People have been able to do so for ages but only in organized forms within the Mystery Schools and other occult orders. This can be accomplished on an observational level, where you don't interfere with what in going on at the place you're going to. Instead of just traveling in horizontal time (which is our normal timeline), some pioneers have been able to access future events from a vertical access point. People who know how to do it can then go into the future (or even back from the future) to this time from a vertical access point. However, they are unable to change any events; still, they can see what is happening there with quite some clarity.

According to Dr. Neruda, some of these time travelers have come in contact with the WingMakers and have been provided messages about the future; messages which have been recorded in symbols, pictures, or in extinct languages like Sumerian, Akkadian, Mayan, and Chakobsan.

One interesting and quite alarming part of the prophecies, which also seems to be a common theme from ancient texts and symbols, etc. is something that is supposed to happen in the early part of the 21st Century, around 2011 (this is all according to Dr. Neruda. I haven't had the chance to verify or look into this yet). The major institutions, like the United Nations, will be infiltrated by an alien race. This race is a predator race with technologies way more sophisticated than our own. Being aware of humanity's obsessive interest in TTPs over the last 40-50 years, it shouldn't be a problem for this alien race to more or less make any deal they want with us. They will pose as humanoids, but are really a blend of human and android; in other words, they are synthetics.

This alien species has as one of its imperatives to establish a One World Government on Earth and rule as its executive power. This is one, perhaps the most, challenging thing we have to deal with in the very near future, according to Dr. Neruda and the Labyrinth Group. These prophecies have been kept out of public domain and were also meant to be kept secret within the Labyrinth Group so they could deal with the problem in isolation. However, that changed when Dr. Neruda defected and the WingMakers site was launched in 1998.[407]

Whether this prophecy about the alien race is true or not, time events are not set in stone because people are creating their own reality every second of the day, and so are other beings in the universe. Therefore, prophecies, the older they are, the less accurate they may be to pinpointing a certain time frame, and even the event itself. If we are lucky, it's not going to happen. Anyhow, an invasion is not likely to happen this year, but a probe will apparently be put in orbit around Earth to see how our species have developed, if at all. This group of artificial intelligence aliens, whom we call the Animus, visited us already 8,866 years ago (counted from 2011 and back), but then thought we were too primitive to care about. What they would think now, however, is another issue...

The Animus, In Search For Soul-Carriers

Most people today have heard of Artificial Intelligence, robots, androids, thinking machines etc. Most of it I believe found life with Arnold Schwarzenegger and the "Terminator" movies. No doubt this was a hint to the public of what was to come. Not that any of this hadn't been mentioned before; we have Isaac Asimov's "I, Robot" and other "profound" revelations in the sci-fi genre. This is often how it's done; the truth is revealed to the public via fantasy and science fiction literature and movies. Someone with inside information writes a sci-fi book or a movie script to prepare us for the future. It stays in our subconscious mind, which does not differentiate between fiction and reality (as they are both one and the same), and then in the future, when what was relayed to us as entertainment becomes reality, it's easier for us to accept it because we have a reference point when our subconscious mind gets triggered and carries the memories of the books/movies up to the surface.

Today, the Media is talking about artificial intelligence (AI) every so often and predict our future as a machine society. Many scientists, both those who are for and against it (to encourage a debate), come out in the open about it as well. No one can miss it because it's all over the place.

On the other end of the spectrum, metaphysical beings, such as the Pleiadians, Bashar, the Ra Collective, and others, are consistently warning us from being part of that future. They stress that if we don't change our ways, we will be part of a society where intelligent machines rule, and once again we may go back to being openly enslaved from being covertly enslaved, which we are now.

So, what is this all about? Can it be something bigger than just man

---

[407] This infiltrating alien group sounds a lot like the so-called Khan Kings (Sirians) I will discuss in major details, starting in Book 3 in this series, *WP 2024.*

creating intelligent machines?

The answer is a definite "yes!" We are being prepared. This is happening on different levels. Yes, man is using alien, and even Tesla technology (which is alien technology as well) to develop intelligent machines to do the work for us and be able to quickly do the math required for higher science. On a lower level, robots for common people are discussed as well, being used as housekeepers, janitors and whatever they can be practical for.

The Origin of the Animus

On a higher level, we are told, are the Anima. They are of central focus in the WMM, and a key problem, according to Dr. Neruda. Dr. A.R. Bordon and Dr. E.M. Weinz of LPG-C# have showed concern about this alien race as well; so much that they released an essay to the public called, "The Anima Problem - Possible Location of the Threat Locus".

Figure 17.9: "The Whirlpool Galaxy", M-51 in Canes Venatici.
The origin of the Animus, according to Dr. Neruda.

The two LPG-C scientists agree with Dr. Neruda on the seriousness of this problem but disagree as of their origin. Dr. Neruda suggests that the Anima come from a planet in a galaxy called "The Whirlpool Galaxy", or Messier 51 (M-51) in the constellation Canes Venatici, about 25 million light-years away from Earth *(fig. 17.10)*. M-51 is a spiral galaxy, type Sa (The Milky Way being an Sb galaxy). These classifications are mostly about the size and form of the bulge in the center of the galaxy. However, I need to make an important notation here: although Sarah, who interviewed Dr. Neruda, suggested that the Animus home planet is located in M-51, and

Dr. Neruda is affirmative to this, I believe this to be either a typo, or more plausible, a deliberate "mistake" made by the Corteum. In the first interview, it clearly states that the distance to their home galaxy is 37 million light-years. When asking LPG-C about this inconsistency, they confirm that the distance should be about 37 million light-years, not 25 million, which is the distance to M-51.

LPG-C suggest in their essay that the main choice of candidate for the Animus species is an elliptic galaxy, type E1, in the constellation of Leo. This suggested galaxy is called M-105 or NGC 3379, depending on which galaxy classification model we use. M-105 is at an approximate distance of 38 million light-years from our solar system *(fig. 17.11)*. In LPG-C's case, though, it is no more than a qualified suggestion at the point of the writing of their essay (2007), and other galaxies, such as M-96, M-95, M-66, M-65, and NGC 3628, are also mentioned as candidates. What they have in common is that they all belong to the Leo group of galaxies, and their approximate distance from Earth is 35-38 million light-years. Who and what is correct remains to be seen and is outside the scope of this research paper.

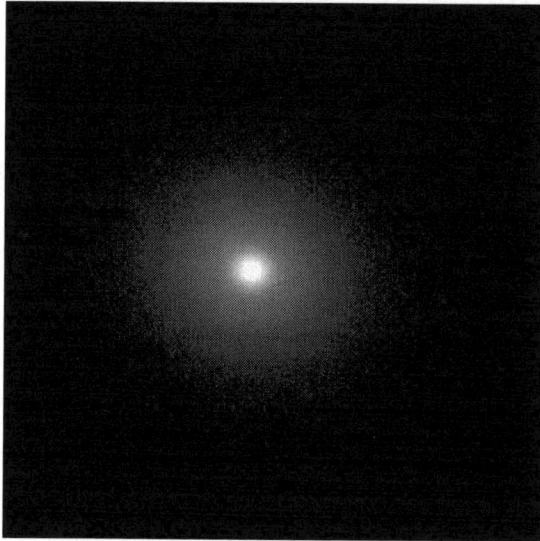

Figure 17.10: M-105 (NGC 3379), an elliptic galaxy, type E1, in the constellation of Leo. The origin of the Animus, according to the LPG-C essay.

Also, ancient scriptures, now in the hands of LPG-C, indicate a huge interest in the Leo constellation, hinting at this particular Animus problem, and by using ENS (remote viewing), LPG-C has found signature of Animus presence in all the above mentioned galaxies. This, in my opinion, is quite alarming, if correct, meaning that they have spread like cockroaches over our region of the universe.

Disconnected From Source

It is described in the Neruda Interviews that the Animus race is a highly artificial and machine-like species. This means that their intelligence is artificial as well, and their brains are no more than very sophisticated computers which can think intelligent thoughts on their own with a much higher accuracy and a more precise quality than we humans and many other species in the universe. As machines, they can regenerate themselves to a large degree, just like we exchange components in a machine or a computer to have it continue working. So, in our terms, one individual of this species can potentially live for millions and perhaps billions of years. But just like machines in general, they lack emotions and empathy, and thus can't understand how biological entities work.

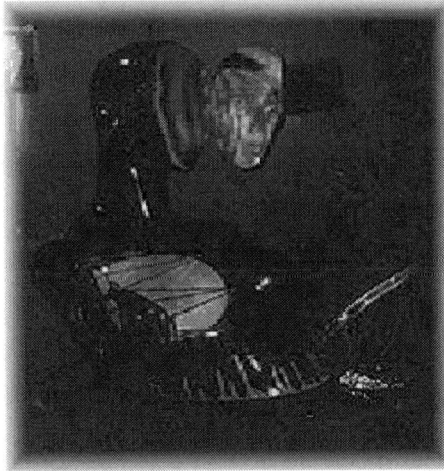

Figure 17.11: Ontocyberenergetic life form as presented in the Working Model. The Anima would fit into this category and perhaps look something like this.

A body in this, and any known universe, needs to be biological in nature, and sophisticated enough to be able to be a soul-carrier, i.e. possess a soul. A machine can have a certain level of consciousness, but that consciousness is totally disconnected from Source because it lacks a soul. This is exactly the case with the Animus. If one of them "dies", which is basically only possible if someone destroys it, or it gets involved in an accident from which it can't be regenerated, that's the end of it. That individual ceases to exist once and for all; there is no afterlife for such a being.

The Anima are apparently aware of their mortality and disconnection from some kind of Higher Consciousness and Intelligence, and this bothers them. They want to reconstruct their bodies by adding DNA to them, and thus, hopefully, being able to create soul-carriers. This can only be done by collecting DNA from biokinds throughout the universe, and subsequently, by infiltration and invasion.

It is a mystery, though, how something which lacks a soul can have consciousness enough to long for one; it requires a soul to long for something, as I see it. But then again, there is more to the picture, and part of the "Animus Problem" may be disinformation to hide something just as hideous (or worse).

Once again, although this, if true, is very threatening to us humans, it's a matter of imperatives. To understand this problem and be able to face it intellectually, without preconceptions and belief-system based ideas, we have to eliminate our belief in good and evil, and instead think in imperatives. From our point of view, this alien AI is evil and counter-survival to our species, but from their viewpoint, it's evolution and survival. They need to connect to Source again. Unfortunately, at this point they are limited in their understanding of how biominds with Information Clouds think and work, and they don't grasp why it would be something wrong with terminating the intelligent beings of a whole planet if necessary. They don't have the luxury of emotions and feelings. It's from this perspective we need to face the problem.

In our ancient past, around 12,800 years ago, they found our planet and noticed it was inhabited with biominds (humans). We had not evolved enough for their taste at the time but decided to keep us under observation. Now, in our time, they are back to put a probe in orbit around our planet to study our current stage of development. If they find us evolved enough, they will most probably invade; first by infiltration, and then by more direct means. We live in a "Free Will" universe which is also monitored by the Central Race and other essential Beings from higher dimensions, and the Anima knows they need our approval to be able to take over; the same problem some other aliens have when trying to steal our DNA. They achieve this approval by tricking us by finding out what it is we want the most. In our case, from the standpoint of our Military Industrial Complex (MIC) it is technology, so by signing us up on a TTP, they will get what they are after. Most likely, greedy factions of the human race, in position of power, will drool over the technology the Anima have to offer.

The problem, as it is presented, is not an easy one to solve, as we can see. This is why groups like the Labyrinth Group and LPG-C are working behind the scenes in attempts to resolve it, out of scrutiny from the higher levels of our world governments. Here is where BST (Blank Slate Technology) comes into the picture as one potential solution to the

Animus Problem, as presented by the Corteum.

I am uncertain how the Animus became a machine race; whether it was due to some catastrophe in the past, by choice, or if they were created by an external species that eventually left them to fend for themselves. There are some indications that the Verdants had a finger in this a long time ago, but more research is needed to know for sure.

Horizontal and Vertical Time

[I will include this section in the book, although these days I disagree with much of what LPG-C has concluded regarding reincarnation, simultaneous lives, and the way Vertical Time is portrayed in their science. I have discussed it in different books since the publications of the Wes Penre Papers, which better explains my current views. Therefore, this is for the reader's concernment only, *WP 2024.*]

To understand BST, we need to understand how vertical and horizontal time work.

Here on Earth, we live in the 3rd dimension, or 4-space/time, if we use LPG-C terms, where time is the 4th dimension. We normally experience time as being horizontal, with a past, present and a future.

What most people don't realize is that we live hundreds, thousands, maybe ten thousands of lives simultaneously in an expanding Multiverse. This means that we are living several lifetimes at once here on Earth.

Obviously, you are living one of the lifetimes now around 2012, and there's where your main attention is. Still, you may be living another life in the 1,500s, other lives in the 800s, 100s, 500s BC, 50,000 BC, 5,000,000 BC and so on. We call this reincarnation, but it's not what it really is. Reincarnation implies that we die and are reborn again after a certain linear time has passed, always from a past into a future. In reality, seen from a multidimensional perspective, we live all our lives on Earth simultaneously, and the only reason we usually are not aware of our other-selves is because they are separated by time.

The important thing to know for now (there is so much more to it) is that we perceive time as horizontal. People in general are not even aware of what I just wrote in the above paragraph, and even less aware of that there is vertical time as well.

There is a whole new complex science on concepts of time, which expands upon the mainstream concept of the same. This explains how 4-space/time in its expanded reality is actually 6-space/time; three spatial dimensions and three dimensions of time, namely: length, width, height, local/horizontal time, vertical time, and five infinites with 12,900,000 "intervention points" into horizontal time. However, the precise science of this is beyond what will be discussed in this paper, and we are only going to touch on this briefly to understand how BST works.

From the perspective of horizontal time, when a major event is happening, e.g. the murder of JFK, the Hiroshima/Nagasaki a-bomb incidents, 9/11 etc., it leaves a "print" on the horizontal timeline, which can be used as an intervention point of entrance from a vertical timeline. This can be done through remote viewing (and is done by remote viewers all the time), but so far, those who visit these entrance points can only do so as spectators and will not be able to change any events that happened in the past (or will happen, if the remote viewer is visiting the future). Thus, we can call this "passive time-travel," and it is very much possible and has been known to man for decades. BST, however, is "active time-travel", which means that events *can* be altered and interfered with, so that the future from the point of interaction will be different than it was before it was done. In other words, an alternative timeline is created.

The Animus, according to the Neruda Interviews, first visited our planet about 300 million years ago and revisited us 8,866 years ago, after the Deluge. Mesopotamia had not yet started to flourish, and civilization was in the stage of rebuilding itself after the Flood. Also, a lot of Anunnaki were still here, according to Sitchin. This was enough for the Animus to decide they should wait and see how we developed.

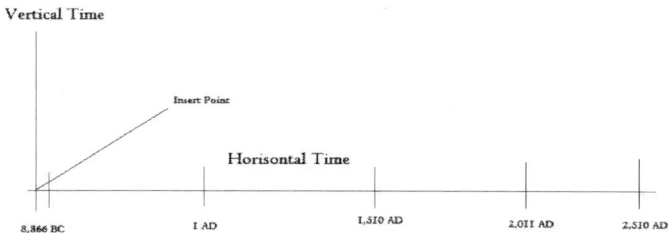

Figure 17.12: Horizontal and vertical time, showing insert point or intervention point.

The easiest way to explain vertical time is to think of an x and a y axis, where the x axis is Horizontal Time, and the y-axis being Vertical Time (*fig. 17.12*). Now, think of vertical time as each moment in existence stacked upon the next and all coinciding with one another. Thus, time is the composite of all moments of all experience simultaneously existing within no-time, which can be referred to as eternity.

Dr. Neruda explains it quite plainly in the interviews:

> Vertical time infers that one can select a moment of experience and use time and space as the portal through which they make their selection real. Once the selection is made, time and space become

the continuity factor that changes vertical time into horizontal time or conventional time.[408]

And the difference between horizontal and vertical time is that,

Vertical time has to do with the simultaneous experience of all time, and horizontal time has to do with the continuity of time in linear, moment-by-moment experiences.[409]

Remote viewing, or ENS, which is its more advanced form, where you use an avatar, is of course nothing we have invented here on Earth; it's a universal technique, used by most advanced aliens in order both to time-travel and to move quickly from one place to another. By the same token, BST is not originating as an idea in the heads of the Corteum or Fifteen, either. Variants of this technique exist elsewhere in the universe, but Fifteen's technique is a quite unique form of BST. However, few alien species are willing to share their specific techniques with other races, once they have developed them. According to Dr. Neruda, it's one of the most protected and guarded of all technologies. This is the reason why the Corteum can't go visit some alien species somewhere and get the key to how to master BST.

Dr. Neruda, who after all is a defector from the Labyrinth Group, is further telling us that in order to develop the specific kind of BST Fifteen is working on, it requires a developer to apply new theorems and new laws of physics which have not been developed before. Then a new suite of technologies needed to be built, based on a new matrix of how the world works. Almost everything we previously held true needs to be destroyed, re-invented, re-formulated, and integrated into this new matrix.

This is why the Labyrinth Group and LPG-C are not on collision course with each other; they are both developing a new life physics, but slightly different from each other's. They are not working together on any level; LPG-C being a totally separate unit, not part of any government bodies, while the Labyrinth Group is connected with, and part of ACIO. There are more reasons why the two are not working together; probably more reasons than I am aware of, but to understand it better we need to know exactly why Dr. Neruda defected. I have already given a reason or two, but later on in this paper, I will bring it up some more.

---

[408] WingMakers: "The Neruda Interviews #1"
[409] Ibid. op. cit.

Memory Restructure Procedure (MRP)

The WingMakers sites (Tributary Zones) can in certain terms be viewed as "time capsules," as described in the WMM. They are programmed to be activated at a certain time to counter the Animus invasion and ultimately to protect the DNA of the Central Race (whom I prefer to call "The Founders." However, as long as we are talking about the WingMakers, the Corteum and the Labyrinth Group, I'll use their terminology).

Built into these time capsules is a "Memory Restructure Procedure", or MRP, which is intended to be used to wipe out the memory of the artificial race and thus prevent the invasion to take place. The Labyrinth Group, or more specifically Fifteen, has, as it appears, been able to understand this technology well enough to use it on his own people, in case they defect or start to talk. Any specific type of memory, or any specific event, can be erased from the memory bank and the victim won't ever suspect something is wrong. One can argue that a similar technology is used on alien abductees to create "missing time," although the latter technology seems less perfect. Another similar technique is used on military "special forces," who are part of special teams that meet with aliens, take part of top secret technologies, visit secret facilities on Earth and elsewhere in the universe (yes, it happens). Once they depart from their mission, the military is using a blank slate memory erasure program, which will wipe out the memory of the soldier so he can't talk about his experiences.[410]

Dr. Neruda, however, still has his memory intact from the time he spent with the Labyrinth Group and the ACIO, and he thinks the reason why they didn't come after him was because he had already revealed too much and instead of making the effort they simply took over the WingMakers site.

Fifteen didn't think that MRP, attached with the time capsules, is enough to stop the Animus, and this is the main reason he thinks BST is necessary. So let's take a look at what it is and how it's intended by humans to be used on the Anima.

Using BST Against the Animus

First, let us take another look at what Blank Slate Technology is. We already discussed how a time-traveler can be either passive or active, or both. ACIO, the CIA and other government bodies know very well how to

---

[410] Barbara Marciniak channeling the Pleiadians, 2010.

remote view and how to time travel, but only in passive form, as spectators. BST, on the other hand, is the technology necessary to interact with vertical time and change it. You have to be able to "page through it like a book", to quote Dr. Neruda, until you find the exact intervention point where you want to intervene.

This is where it gets scary, because it's so complex, and if you intervene with vertical time, you also intervene with horizontal time. So, if you even think about doing something like that, you have to be able to calculate the *exact* consequences of such intervention. This is why Fifteen and the Labyrinth Group decided to cooperate with the Corteum; their computer technology is about 4,000 times as powerful than our best supercomputers. Still, it has taken a super-genius like Fifteen more than half a century to pinpoint this down to a workable technique, and I'm not sure if he's finished yet.

With the help from Corteum technology, the Labyrinth Group can create highly complex scenario models. These models then help the group figure out the best intervention point. BST is a composite technology having five discrete and inter-related technologies.

I'll let Dr. Neruda describe them, one by one (the emphasis is mine for better overview):

> **The first technology** is a specialized form of remote viewing. This is the technology that enables a trained operative to mentally move into vertical time and observe events and even listen to conversations related to an inquiry mode. The operative is invisible to all people within the time they are traveling to, so it's perfectly safe and unobtrusive. The intelligence gained from this technology is used to determine the application of the other four technologies. This is the equivalent of intelligence gathering.
>
> **The second technology** that is key to BST is the equivalent of a memory implant. As I mentioned earlier, the ACIO refers to this technology as a Memory Restructure Procedure or MRP. MRP is the technology that allows a memory to be precisely eliminated in the horizontal time sequence and a new memory inserted in its place. The new memory is welded to the existing memory structure of the recipient.
>
> You see, events -- small and large -- occur from a single thought, which becomes a persistent memory, which in turn, becomes a causal energy center that leads the development and materialization of the thought into reality[27a]... into horizontal time. MRP can remove the initial thought and thereby eliminate the persistent memory that causes events to occur.
>
> **The third technology** consists of defining the intervention point. In every major decision, there are hundreds, if not thousands, of intervention points in horizontal time as a thought unfolds and

423

moves through its development phase. However, in vertical time, there is only one intervention point or what we sometimes called the causal seed. In other words, if you can access vertical time intelligence you can identify the intervention point that is the causal seed. This technology identifies the most probable intervention points and ranks their priority. It enables focus of the remaining technologies.

The fourth technology is related to the third. It's the scenario modeling technology. This technology helps to assess the various intervention points as to their least invasive ripple effects to the recipients. In other words, which intervention point -- if applied to a scenario model -- produces the desired outcome with the least disruption to unrelated events? The scenario modeling technology is a key element of BST because without it, BST could cause significant disruption to a society or entire species.

The fifth and most puzzling technology is the interactive time travel technology. The Labyrinth Group has the first four technologies in a ready state waiting for the interactive time travel technology to become operational. This technology requires an operative, or a team of operatives, to be able to physically move into vertical time and be inserted in the precise space and time where the optimal intervention point has been determined. From there the operatives must perform a successful MRP and return to their original time in order to validate mission success.[411]

At the time Dr. Neruda defected, the Labyrinth Group had about forty scenario models and around eight intervention points defined. In the interviews with Sarah, Dr. Neruda is too uncomfortable giving out the most likely scenario because of the highly classified nature of the information. It's also a matter of not only national security, but in this case, world security.

Dr. Neruda, just like the Pleiadians, lets us know that Earth is a very special planet because of its tremendous bio-diversity and a complex range of ecosystems. Its natural resources are very unique and plentiful. Dr. Neruda says: "It's a genetic library that's the equivalent of a galactic zoo." This directly corresponds with the Pleiadians saying that Earth is a Living Library, where plants, animals, and human DNA are seeded by using DNA from multiple different planets within, and outside, of our galaxy.

The Animus showed interest in this planet because it wants to own its genetics in full; not only our human biokind. The Animus is a synthetic race, as we've discussed earlier, and they can clone themselves to whatever extent they think necessary. No birth control needed, as sex is not a part of their existence. Only "birth control" they want is to determine how many

---

[411] WingMakers: "The Neruda Interviews #1"

copies of themselves they need. Although expansion of their empire is *one* imperative, they mainly want to become soul-carriers. Synthetic organisms are not able to carry the higher frequencies of a soul, which always requires an organic nervous system. So, in other words, the Animus race wants to become immortal, and the only way to do so is to connect with Source via souls/information clouds.

In summary, what the Labyrinth Group is trying to do is to catch the first thought from the Animus, where they decided to invade Earth and redirect that thought through an intervention point in vertical time. When the most well-suited intervention point is found and decided upon, ENS travelers will use BST, creating a "blank memory slate" of the whole race at the moment of the exact thought, and then insert a new thought, perhaps saying something to the effect, "Earth is not a good planet for us, let's move elsewhere and never come back." This, despite how dangerous it sounds, is the plan in a nutshell.

So why not just trust the WingMakers/Central Race to have installed defensive weapons good enough to keep the Animus away?

This was exactly the point Dr. Neruda made in a session with Fifteen.[412] Fifteen, however, doesn't trust the Central Race in this respect. Through RV sessions, his group of ENS travelers have discovered Animus activity in many galaxies; even as near as the Andromeda, which is our closest neighbor galaxy, aside from the Magellan Clouds. Did they invade all these planets despite precautions made by the Central Race? If so, what stops them from invading us? These were the questions Fifteen asked himself. Instead of waiting to see what will happen once they have found all the seven WingMakers sites, he decided to develop BST to eliminate the threat once and for all.

After had RV'd the Central Race back in time when they were about to create Earth, Fifteen knew that they would never allow Fifteen to develop and use BST against the Animus or for any other reasons either, BST being the most guarded technology, once developed by the Central Race. Fifteen is aware of that BST can be used both for benevolent and evil purposes, and this is exactly why the Central Race doesn't want anyone to have access to it without their direct permission. The risk that this technology falls into the wrong hands is great. And, of course, there are organizations, like S.A.A.L.M., who are doing all they can to try and infiltrate both LPG-C and the Labyrinth Group; both working on developing BST, separate from each other.

In addition, the remote viewers, such as Samantha, are not part of the Labyrinth Group, and when she remote viewed the Central Race, Fifteen afterwards authorized his staff (in most cases Dr. Neruda provided the

---

[412] WingMakers: "The Ancient Arrow Project."

correct coordinates so they knew *where* to erase) to use MRP on the remote viewer, so she would forget everything that had to do with the ENS sessions. This, naturally, kept both Dr. Neruda and other Labyrinth Group members in constant anxiety of having their memory erased. That's a lot of power assigned to Fifteen. I am certainly glad that I am not in the position Dr. Neruda and others.

I get the impression that Fifteen is jumping the gun because things are taking longer than he is comfortable with, but it was no accident that the Ancient Arrow site in New Mexico was found, and our DNA seems to be programmed to find these sites when the time is right. Thus, to me it seems logical to wait it out. Still, I can see Fifteen's concern when he finds out how widespread this synthetic race is; this being the main reason why he wants to bypass the WingMakers technology and develop his own version of BST. And in the middle of this is the ignorant human race. Now, however, the cat is out of the bag, but if Dr. Neruda hadn't defected, it's doubtful anyone outside the Labyrinth Group would know about this.

Speaking of knowing and of memory; it's known and acknowledged that Marduk rewrote history and erased our memories once upon a time and started a brand new Era, where humans had no knowledge of any previous "gods.". Instead, he implanted new, false memories of Earth's history. Whether he used the same Blank Slate Technology that the Labyrinth Group and LPG-C now is developing is more than I can say, but this all makes me wonder how many times in the past the Anunnaki have erased the memory of the human population. How many times in the Wars of the gods have they wished for their human slaves to remember a "new" history, a new made-up past?

Alien contactees say that the Vegans, Lyrans and the Pleiadians are here to set the record straight and give us our real history back, and that is exactly what I see and hear them doing. Where we are going, the gods can't follow, because they don't know how. Perhaps in the future, it will be our task to help them evolve, if possible.

A'shayana Deane, The Guardian Alliance, and the BeaST

The most outspoken opponent to Blank Slate Technology and the Corteum is perhaps the alien "Guardian Alliance," communicating through their spokesperson, A'shayana Deane, former Anna Hayes, co-founder of "Azurite Press of the Melchizedek Cloister Emerald Order".[413] In May of 2010, she was interviewed by Kerry-Lynn Cassidy of Project Camelot Productions,[414] where Mrs. Deane through the approximately seven hours

---

[413] http://azuritepress.com
[414] http://projectcamelotproductions.com/interviews/

interview went through the teachings of the Guardians.[415] In the third section of the interview, she and Kerry are getting on the subject of the WingMakers, and Mrs. Deane, to Kerry's surprise, is talking about them in quite a negative manner.

In essence, she says that the Corteum, whom in the Guardians' opinion are running the show, are playing both sides by helping and taking help from the Labyrinth Group to develop BST in a secret mission to erase the memory of the human race—*not* the Animus. She further refers to her books, "Voyagers I & II," which are talking more in detail about the WingMakers, the Corteum and issues related to them. Kerry, who interviewed James/Mahu Nahi of the WingMakers/Corteum in 2008 and seems to have a relatively positive attitude towards them, was confused when Mrs. Deane corrected her on the subject. Mrs. Deane is continuing, saying that the "people on the ground", meaning the humans who found the Ancient Arrow Site in New Mexico, are not bad guys; it's the Corteum who are tricking everybody. During the interview she is supposedly in contact with the Guardians, metaphysically, and they confirm that what she is saying is true.

The Makers of Wings and Other Things

During the last part of the interview, Mrs. Deane says that the Ancient Arrow sites are actually owned by the Guardians, and not by the WingMakers. Furthermore, she claims that there are not seven sites, but 12, with an additional 24 "sub sites" (the 12-System again); something she is not explaining in any more details than that.

It also so happened, that the Melchizedek Cloister Emerald Order was going to hold a workshop just a few days after Kerry's interview, discussing, among other things, the WingMakers issue, or as the Guardian Alliance apparently call them, "The Makers of Wings and Other Things." Although some of their information is free online, Mrs. Deane is charging for those who want to attend the seminars, so I don't know the details of what was discussed there. She is, however, selling the context of the workshops after the fact on her website, but at a very high price, which I am not ready to pay. On her website, you can at least read some of what was discussed in the workshop (all emphases in original):

This workshop marked the official beginning of the Step-down

---

ashayana_deane/ashayana_deane.html
    [415] Keylontic Dictionary Online,
    http://www.keylonticdictionary.org/online/member/index.php?page=guardian-alliance

Program with the first *Camelot Project* interview and the beginning of the end of the Wingmakers-Corteum invasion agenda via the *7 Broken Ancient Arrow sites*. Following the 7 ½-hour Camelot interview, the Speakers were ready to deliver some wonderful information about the *12 Primary Ancient Elohei-Aquari Arrow Sites* (Guardian sites also called the *"Silver Seed Gates"* and created by the Krystic Elohei-Elohim and Aquari Races), their *secondary sites* (24 in total) and how they 'hold the keys' for the *Mirror Ball activations* (involves Earth's coronasphere layers). The Mirror ball activations initiate in the *Encryption Lattice (EL)* of our anatomy, so there was detailed information given on the *natural* Living Current flows between the Atomic (Spirit) Body, the Light Body, the EL and where the *metatronic NET Fields* exist within these layers. These activations will allow us to progressively clear the NET implants (we started to clear the D6, D5 and Density-1 levels at this workshop and the D3, D2 and D1 levels will be starting to clear during subsequent Sliders workshops) which will in turn, allow us to progressively anchor the Krystal Spiral and Time Wave. By 21 December 2012, the Krystics are aiming to have transformed these Mirror Ball activations into the full *Mirror in the Sky*, which will provide the strength we need at this time to fully deflect the Metatronic 55-activation.[416]

It is interesting to read Mark Hempel's and Mahu Nahi's reaction to Mrs. Deane's statements about the WingMakers she made in the Kerry-Lynn Cassidy interview.

Shortly after the videos had been uploaded to the Internet, Mark Hempel sent a very threatening email to Kerry, saying that Mrs. Deane is wrong and is misleading her listeners by spreading misinformation about the WingMakers. He makes sure to Kerry that he and James are not taking this lightly and are ready to sue both Project Camelot Productions and A'shayana Deane if the misinformation of this specific information is not edited out from the video.

Kerry got pretty shaken up by this; I can imagine, especially as she and Bill Ryan, her former interview partner, had just split up due to indifferences. Kerry probably felt quite vulnerable and alone, because Project Camelot Productions was her new project.

---

[416] http://www.azuritepress.com/products_us/woab.php

Figure 17.13: A'shayana Deane

James/Mahu Nahi then sent an email himself to Kerry in form of an open letter to Mrs. Deane, emphasizing that the names in the WingMakers story are not real names, and the Corteum was a fictional name, so how can the Guardians use these terms as if they were not real? He soothed down the energies a bit with his email and asked Mrs. Deane to consider a cooperation with him rather than opposing him, but the underlying seriousness in this matter was present throughout his email. Mrs. Deane responded, and this whole conversation back and forth is posted beneath the videos on the Camelot Productions page.[417]

For a while, Kerry considered following Hempel's advice to edit out the section of the interview in question, so she removed them, but then seems to have made some kind of agreement with all parties that the video could remain in unedited form if the correspondence back and forth was included on the page.

It's remarkable that Hempel reacted like he did and was supported in this by Mahu. What they are suggesting, both of them, is pure censorship. That goes against the teachings of James, so this was apparently a hot potato for one reason or another.

(Note: As I am editing my papers before publishing, I get a note from A.R. Bordon, saying that a good friend of his told him that she'd heard that A'shayana Deane could be in trouble because "she knows too much." However, we must keep in mind that LPG-C probably liked what Mrs. Deane said because he is in opposition to the WingMakers. Bordon, at this time, knew nothing about that I am writing about A'shayana Deane in this, and other papers. He did not read any of them before they were released).

---

[417] http://projectcamelotproductions.com/interviews/ashayana_deane/ashayana_deane.html

429

PAPER 18:
PRESENT AND FUTURE EARTH CHANGES AND THEIR TRUE CAUSES
by Wes Penre, Friday, June 17, 2011

[This paper is excluded in its entirety from this book. The paper is primarily about Nibiru and the potential encounter with this supposed Siran planet in 2012—something that never happened. This paper is still available at wespenre.com for readers who are interested].

PAPER 19
THE RETURN OF THE GODS
by Wes Penre, Saturday, June 24, 2011

The Tribulation

If we are to believe prophecy (and in this case, Bible Prophecy in particular), we are currently living in the pre-Tribulation, in wait for the Battle of Armageddon and the Lord's Return. We are experiencing severe weather anomalies, major and unusual earth changes (pole shift starting to happen, earthquakes, tsunamis, hurricanes, tornados, flooding), birds falling dead from the sky, more mental instability, suicide trends to increase, violence, and self-centered living.

The pre-Tribulation Period has just started, though, and will continue until the Lord returns, approximately 2060-2095,[418] when land and water will change position, and many people will die. In the Bible it is said that the Tribulation will be 7 years.

The Lord's Return

Now that we have discussed a plausible background to the execution of Prophecy, does this mean that the Sirians are coming back (portrayed by Sitchin and others as the Return of Nibiru)?

Well. what is told in the traditional Bible and the Kolbrin Bible is correct—the Lord is returning. However, the Lord is not necessarily a person, but the planet Nibiru, or Marduk, as it's called as well, named after the eldest son of the Enki.[419] And we know that the planet is inhabited.

---

[418] When revising the papers into a book, I notice I forgot to put a reference to where I got 2060-2095 from, so I ask the reader to take these years into consideration, but not as factual numbers, *WP 2024*.

[419] That Marduk is "returning" is an interesting observation I did in 2011. I equate

Yes, these "gods" will land on Earth, and it will not be in secret. There will, most likely, be giants and "monsters" walking the Earth again, and they will be armed. The monsters (demons) will most probably be the "Reptilian race" that the Nibiruan Ša.A.M.i. work with. Other species may join as well, such as the Greys.

Although they are here for the sake of war first, and peace later, we humans are supposedly not the target for these beings. According to LPG-C members, who have attended the annual LINK meetings, they are here to take care of their own and those who support them.

This means that the earth-bound Anunnaki, i.e., those who stayed behind and have been here for millennia, will be judged by the ones from the Home Planet; at least the ones who parted with Marduk, the King of Earth. There are other Anunnaki here who are still loyal to the Kingdom, and they will part with the Ša.A.M.i. from Nibiru when the time comes.

The Battle of Armageddon

It may seem like an easy task to take down the few Anunnaki still on Earth (believed to be 300+), loyal to Marduk, by the force from such a large number of Nibiru soldiers. However, this is not the only ones who are going to be taken down. The Nibiruans will kill their own here on the ground but spare the Lords. Lord is a title, earned on the Home Planet due to bloodline. They are royalty. LPG-C says they never kill a Lord, no matter what crimes he has committed. It has occurred, though—in wars casualties happen. A Lord can be punished and sentenced by their law, but not killed. However, there is death penalty for their "common people," apparently.

So, is what will happen within the next few generations that the Nibiruan Ša.A.M.i. will come down to Earth in spaceships and land here, fully armed and ready to fight? They are, according to Dr. Bordon not only here to take care of their own disobedient race, but also to kill off anyone who has sided with Marduk, whether it's people in the governments, industry and trade, entertainment, education, banking, or any other institution and organization. Not only that, but they will also kill regular people on the spot, who have sided with Marduk's policies; wittingly or unwittingly, by intent or action. As A.R. Bordon of LPG-C put it, "they are not very forgiving." Marduk was left here on Earth to rule us and to get a chance to repent and become loyal to the Kingdom while he was here, but

---

him to being another name for Nibiru as well, which today I think is a semi-truth, which will be discussed in more recent material. Marduk *is* returning as the Son of God, although he's been here on Earth all the time, yet not visible to the general population, *WP 2024.*

from where I sit, it must have been quite predictable that Marduk would not "repent" during his 1,000 years of more or less unchallenged dictatorship here. He is not closer to the Kingdom now than he was then—probably even more detached.

The Marduk side includes a big faction of the Global Elite and Military Complex, which is the major problem for the Incoming. The Military will side with Marduk, most of them deceived, thinking the intruders are the enemy. The Military will fight until last man to protect countries and the world against this invader force of giants. The Ša.A.M.i. may communicate first with the United Nations and the Earth in general, before the attack, but who will believe them?

Dr. Bordon has said to me that in his meetings with the Ša.A.M.i., they have told him they feel responsible for us humans because they created us and now want to help us stand on our own feet and become sovereign, which means the Anunnaki will eventually leave Earth for good, in our hands.[420] Apparently, Bordon has, in his own words, established a personal bond and friendship of sorts with their leader, the son of Nammur/the En.lil/YHVH/YeHoVaH, whose name is Nannar, the person who took over after Anu as the King of Nibiru in the 1400s. They are very angry and disappointed at the Anunnaki who were left behind. They did the opposite from what was expected: they let power and greed take the best of them and continued interbreeding with humans. In addition, they maintained their wars, created diseases, and different other scenarios to divide and conquer. Now they have to be held accountable, says the new King.

Marduk (the equivalent to Satan), in his pride, believes he can defend Earth against the Lords from outside. He is well aware what is planned and very savvy in Biblical Prophecy (after all, the Ša.A.M.i. dictated them). Just like what it says in the Bible, Marduk thinks he can win the battle with the help from joint military resistance worldwide. He may declare Martial Law to fight this "hideous Invader Force." World leaders may ask civilians to take to arms as well to join in to "save the planet."

Regardless of what the Nibiruans will tell us before they land, Marduk has already used his Media propaganda machine to the fullest and will fool most of the world population. The reason he is so certain about gaining victory is because he has manipulated and mind-controlled the masses via Media, Hollywood, education, and more for so long, and has thus subconsciously built a mind-controlled population of obedient soldiers, who react like one unit when trigger words are uttered, bringing implanted thoughts from the subconscious up to the surface. The Military is mind-controlling their soldiers well, starting with the drill Sergeant. Upon that,

---

[420] These "gods" are trickster gods, and they used LPG-C for their own agenda, and they often lied in those meetings, something that will be further revealed in the following books in this WPP series and in my recent books, *WP 2024*.

we have phrases, repeated in Media over and over that will make people take combined actions to "save the planet." It's very cleverly done, and this is one reason I never watch TV and read the newspapers. Although I am aware of this Agenda, I still don't want the influence from the Media because I know how easy it is to bury things in the subconscious (repetition creates programming), even when we think we don't. After all, the Media is one big propaganda machine and the truth I need I do not get from the mainstream media.

This is one reason I've said for so long that people need to stop watching the news and read the papers, or at least keep it to a minimum. Headlines and a few subsequent lines in the paper are enough to understand the overall purpose of an article. The same thing goes with new technology, like the latest cell-phones, etc. Aside from being tracking devices, they are also altering your frequency so you will be more receptive to what the Elite wants you to do when the time comes. HAARP is another great example, where the government, via a giant power station in Alaska, is sending out ELF (extremely low frequency), which will have a large amount of people vibrate within a frequency range meant to be the common frequency, which can then be used (and is already used) for programming. The lower the frequency, the easier it is to program people. This is done in combination with the Media triggers mentioned above. Then, when the perpetrators wish, they can use this frequency to steer the masses in unison into a devastating war. Hitler did something similar less sophisticated but very successful when he managed to manipulate the majority of the German people to go to war.

And the Lord Will Reign for a Thousand Years

The outcome (again if we believe the Bible, and other prophecies) will be that King Nannar beats the forces opposing his mission and thus becomes the victor. Marduk will be thrown into the "bottomless pit" where he will dwell for a thousand years. The other Lords, who have supported Marduk, will probably be transported back to their home planet, unless they already died in battle. There they will stand before a Nibiruan Council of Justice and get the appropriate (for the Ša.A.M.i. people) verdict.

The plan is then to gather the people of Earth under one "flag"—a One World Government led by a skeleton crew from Nibiru who will spend the next 1,000 years or more to teach humankind to be sovereign and able to defend themselves against outside invaders in the future. Then, at least according to prophecy, Marduk, for some reason, will rise again and reign for a short time, before he is finally defeated. How this will pan out is still a mystery. However, after that, the Anunnaki will pack and leave the planet once and for all, and it will then be completely ours.

I argued with Dr. Bordon about why we need the skeleton crew at all. Haven't we had enough of these people ruling us? Thus far, it has only led to disaster, and after all, these beings are warlike, obsessed with sex and bloodline, can be quite aggressive, and are rather non-spiritual. His reply was that he would also prefers that we don't have a skeleton crew here, but it's probably inevitable because each planet is looked upon as real estate by aliens. Who owns a planet is a big deal, and if you can't defend your real estate, you will lose it. With that, he doesn't mean we will be in recurring wars with aliens from other planets who want to take over, no matter what, but it does mean we have to be very clear as a species what we are available for. We have to claim our right to the planet and be serious about it, and the same thing applies to the rights to our biokind, *and those imperatives cannot be compromised.* If we can unite in this, most aliens will respect that. But if we again are allowing ourselves to be tricked and taken over by outside forces, we are still not adults enough to defend our real estate. This is the theory behind why we need a skeleton crew.

Adding to this, I asked Dr. Bordon why we are so sure the Ša.A.M.i. can be trusted. Look at their history: war, jealousy, obsessive sex addicts, genetic manipulators, slave drivers, and using us as their foot soldiers in their own petty wars over real estate and power statuses. They are killers, committers of homicide and genocide—the list is endless. I am aware that these beings also taught us things like agriculture, astronomy, astrology, and a lot of other useful things, but it is my understanding they did this with the intentions for us to support the gods, not for us to be self-sufficient so we can claim the planet. And the fact remains that these beings have huge problems within their own lines, and they are a warrior race. They were the ones who taught us warfare as well, something that up to that point was unheard of among humans.

The reply I got was that since the Sumerian times, the Ša.A.M.i. have evolved quite significantly and are now a much more peaceful and very loving species.[421] Dr. Bordon says he can testify to this from his own communication with them—face-to-face, and mind-to-mind. Also, in Chapter 8 of his 2007 essay, "THE LINK," he further states that in one of the annual meetings with them, the Ša.A.M.i. told him (and the rest of the group from what I understand) that their species have now almost completed their cycle to oneness, "wherein all knowledge and mind resources are used in service to the common."[422] Although Bordon is not exactly sure how they have accomplished this, but suggests it is similar to Schumann's Resonance, which means that "when the diversity of biominds of each member remains an individuality while simultaneously being

---

[421] This is untrue, and LPG-C was once again tricked. They have not changed and never will. See upcoming books in this WPP series and more recent work, *WP 2024.*
[422] A.R. Bordon "THE LINK" (2007), *op. cit. p.42.*

interconnected to the Ša.A.Mi. all-one by low-powered, low-energetic means that utilizes the planet's life belt energetics..."[423] He continues by saying that, however, it is beyond our level of technology at this time to understand how it is being done. What we know is that the Ša.A.M.i. is a highly technologically evolved species, and the longevity issue is high on their priority list. They already have the technology to extend their lives considerably, and it sounds to me that they are using technology to create oneness rather than doing it by raising their frequency naturally; by evolving spiritually, mentally and biologically. If so, it is not the path we here on Earth want to go down, in my opinion. And who wants to live for thousands, if not millions of years? We may want to extend it with a few hundred years, but after that, the burden of having the same body (*at least in 3rd Density/Dimension*) and mind more than that I believe is counter-productive for the individual *and* the species [unless we first can regain our full ancestral memories and make conscious choices regarding our future, *WP 2024*].

And I strongly sense that Oneness is not something we want to accomplish through technology whatsoever. We want to connect as a mass consciousness in a natural way, and not through technology. There is something strange with this Nibiruan species, and I have reasons to believe that they are not like us and cannot evolve like we do. I will do more research on this before I release what I've found in the "Second Level of Learning."

A big problem for ETs in general is our stage of development. We are going through an adolescence stage at this moment, and we've learned how to split the atom and how to create negative energy. When this happens, ETs all over the galaxy become on alert. This is a critical point in the evolution of a species because it is where it can go either way; termination of our planet (like what happened to the Zeta Greys), or we can get responsible and use our technologies and knowledge for the greatest good of the human soul group and the Universe at large. However, we are *not* using it responsibly, and this doesn't only affect us and our planet, but also the rest of the galaxy and in certain terms the entire physical universe. When we use energy negatively, we "borrow" it from positive energy elsewhere, and it works like pressing a balloon anywhere but in the middle; it blows up on one end and diminished on the other. And what we borrow we must return for the sake of the balance of the universal energies. We are not paying back, and this means that not only will our own Sun die prematurely, but also other stars around us and even much further away.

Dr. Bordon has not said this, but under the circumstances, his group may feel that we, as a soul group, have no better choice than to welcome

---

[423] A.R. Bordon "THE LINK" (2007), *op. cit. p.42.*

the Ša.A.M.i. and let them do their job. That would take care of the negative energy misuse and other issues not accepted by cosmic rules and regulations. However, this implies that we believe what the Ša.A.M.i. tells us. I can see the dilemma LPG-C sits in; they want to play their cards just right, and very carefully, because they want to keep their chairs in the LINK meetings with the aliens. But like Ed Komarek, the UFO researcher said, and I paraphrase: "If the aliens Bordon is meeting with don't want him to expose any, or very little, of what is said in the meetings to the public, what hidden agenda is behind the secrecy? We don't want another little NSA." It certainly sounds like LPG-C is stuck "Between the Devil and the Returning Rock" to quote the title of their own essay. I don't envy their position.

[Another slant on this is that LPG-C admittedly tries to work as ambassadors for humankind, but how can they, when humankind is clueless about almost everything LPG-C are discussing with the ETs? No one has asked humankind what *we* want. I find it arrogant to work on behalf of humankind and make decisions that might not be revokable, and on our behalf, without first consulting us as a soul group, *WP 2024.*]

Anu Stepping Down From the Throne

According to Dr. Bordon in "THE LINK," chapter 8, Anu announced already decades before the birth of Christ that he was stepping down and needed a successor. This was big news, and the Anunnaki, still here on Earth more or less left what they were doing and went back home to Nibiru. Ankur (the Enki) and Nammur (the Enlil), who belong to different clans (the Serpent Clan and the Ram Clan, respectively) started lobbying actively and aggressively to promote someone from their own camp as Anu's successor. LPG-C's Intel is showing that the lobbying was very dramatic.

King Anu wanted a bloodless, coup-less succession, announcing he would choose his successor, depending on how well he had performed while on Earth. Ankur and Nammur were themselves candidates but considered out of the question for succession due to their performance while down here. Marduk and Ninurta were also disqualified due to "unlordly" behavior. I'm not sure what "unlordly" means exactly, but King Anu was the one who authorized the nukes to be dropped over the Sinai Spaceport and Sodom and Gomorrah among other things, so I guess that the King is exempted from "unlordly behaviors."

Here, I am paraphrasing from Dr. Bordon's "THE LINK," page 54 and on:

When King Anu decided to step down, there was a fast and furious Anunnaki exodus from Earth to participate in the lobbying for whatever clan they belonged to. Marduk and Ningišzidda, both sons of Ankur, and their families left, which had as a consequence that the smelting operations in Bolivia closed down. Ankur's son Nergal, his consort (Nannar's daughter, Ereškigal) and Nammur were apparently the first to return to Nibiru, together with King Anu's grandson Ninurta and consort.

Figure 19.1: Sacsayhuaman--A side view of the complex.

Members of the Ram Clan, led by Nammur, who also left, were Nannar and Iškur (Adad), Inanna, Ašnan, Nanše, and some others. They went to a platform, waiting to be transported back home. Apparently, Nannar and his consort returned to Earth for a short time period, to northern Syria, but then returned to the platform again. The reason being that the En.lil, his father, and King Anu, his grandfather, told them to return to Altiplano of Northeastern Peru, in the mid- to late second century of the Common Era to help Nannar' son, Utu, to close down the smelter at Sacsayhuaman as well as the dismantling of runway operations in the Nazca area of southern Peru. The smelter was still producing gold, tin and silver from distant and nearby sources from relocated Kassites (southern and central Turkey), the operation stopped before the first millennium of the Common Era. Sometime in the sixth century CE, Sacsayhuaman shut down, and the pre-Incan civilizations from northern Peru through the region north of the Atacama desert in northern Chile were all left to fend for themselves. Other "colonies," like North American Midwest, southeastern and southwestern native groups who came in contact with and were instructed by the Anunnaki on agricultural, animal husbandry and other matters, were also disengaged and eventually abandoned in the seventh and eighth centuries CE.

438

Political Dramas on the Home Planet

When all the royal Anunnaki had returned to Nibiru, their usual aggressive traits played out again, and there was a furious contest to bring King Anu's attention. Ankur and Nammur led their clans, respectively, in order to bring either themselves or someone of their blood to the royal throne. Both Ankur and Nammur were appointed to serve under something the King now called the "Kitchen Cabinet," which was the former "Council of 12," but in a slightly watered-down form. Others appointed were trusted Ša.A.M.i., many of them familiar to us through these papers I've written, and of course, through Sitchin's books, originally.

King Anu had many matters on his mind, whereof one was the destruction of the Sinai Spaceport around 2,500 BCE. I am not sure in what sense he was concerned about that because it was in fact King Anu himself who approved the nuclear bombings (see previous Anunnaki Papers). Another matter, naturally, was the royal succession. However, the most urgent matter was the "Marduk issue."

Marduk, Ankur's son, and the King's grandson, still held grudges after all these thousands of years, thinking he should be the King of Nibiru and the King of Earth at the same time. It showed that when Marduk returned to Nibiru with the rest of the Anunnaki crew, most of them strongly supported him in his mission. Of the approximately 400 Anunnaki who left Earth to come back to Nibiru, around 300 of them supported Marduk. Apparently, at some time after they all had returned home, there was some severe confrontation between the Ram and the Serpent Clans, although it is not clear to what extent. Dr. Bordon and LPG-C got this Intel from a Ša.A.M.i. who spoke up during annual meetings with the alien LINK group, apparently when forced to do so by the rest of the members (not only humans).

This conflict, however, turned out favorable to a candidate, who was not on the King's list: Nannar, the En.lil's son. Marduk was already out of the question for succession because King Anu had created a new, firm policy that everybody had to swear loyalty to the King, personally, and to the Kingdom. No one was excluded from this new policy. Marduk and his followers, in particular, were furious over this because Marduk would never swear loyalty to either the King or the Kingdom. He had other plans.

Also, around 2025 BCE, with the new zodiacal era (the Ša.A.M.i./Anunnaki were very much into astrology), Marduk falsified the astrological charts to his favor, so he could quicker come to power on Earth, and he also took on the task of rewriting Earth history—especially the early history of how humans came about, when it happened, and when the Anunnaki came down. He also wanted to make sure that he was considered the only "God" and authority, so he put himself in charge of all occult and secret societies and rewrote their manuals as well, and claimed the highest, hidden authority over them all. This way, he has access to all information and Intel, and thus full control over a big chunk of humanity.

In addition, Marduk also attempted to construct a six-stage ziggurat, strong enough to support a landing platform at its apex (see *fig. 19.2*). This is *currently* under way in Iraq!

Despite all these things, talking against Marduk and for him being a potential dangerous rebel in the eyes of the King and the Kingdom, his father Ankur (the Enki) did all he could to support and shield his first-born son. Ankur, sitting on the Council of 12, as well as his half-brother Nammur, made things a little tense, to say the least. Through internal familial politicking, Marduk managed to get Ningišzidda ousted and exiled to the New World first (in particular the American southwest, Mexico, and he highlands of Peru and Bolivia), then to the Far East (where he met and worked with Utu in Japan, coastal China, the Korean peninsula, and the Asian highlands of Nepal and Tibet on tasks and projects with natives not disclosed to LPG-C. What we do see, however, is the enormous global influence this Anunnaki group has had on humankind. Ningišzidda also became Quetzalcoatl in Mexico, often, but not always, depicted in reptilian form.

Now, when Marduk refused to obey to the rules, he was said to have been put in the equivalent of a quarantine (common in Ša.A.M.i. culture under such circumstances when it comes to Lords). This did not stop him, however, and he continued to refuse to show obedience to any and all important laws and regulations of the Ša.A.M.i. Kingdom.

This put both his father and grandfather in a position where the King had no other choice than to expel Marduk and tell him to leave and go back to Earth, to never again return to the planet of his birth. From what LPG-C has been told, Marduk returned to Earth with about 300 loyalists around the turn of the first millennium of the Common Era (1,000 CE).

Interesting that it is now officially admitted by the Ša.A.M.i. people that Marduk rewrote at least part of our history, but we are not told exactly *what* he rewrote, which is frustrating. It's too difficult to speculate on it because it can't be more than speculations; but there are some significant points made by metaphysical sources (the Pleiadians, the Ra Material, Lyssa Royal's channeling, A'shayana Deane, the WingMakers, and the list goes on) that we humans were highly evolved beings before the Anunnaki came and chased away the creator gods, who were building the Living Library.[424] It was when the Anunnaki started tampering with our DNA to create obedient, and not *too* smart workers that the problems started. We can read about the Anunnaki history on Earth through the Sumerian cuneiform texts, but there is no real history about what happened before these creator

---

[424] Much more about this in upcoming books in this series, *WP 2024.*

gods came. If it wasn't for the metaphysical entities, who have told us what happened before the Intruders came, we wouldn't know anything about the Living Library and previous creator gods.

Dr. Bordon is saying something quite remarkable in his essay in relation to Marduk and his followers returning to Earth. Anu had a very hard time choosing his successor, having to be very careful whom he chose, not to create political consequences way beyond his own death. Dr. Bordon continues:

> It would split both the people and the biomind. Such an act would carve out a huge chuck of Ša.A.M.i. Kaluemti all+is+life; that of being 'ONE' power. This, we were told, is the power of the entire Ša.A.M.i. population to act as one, like a single degree of freedom organism, under certain circumstances."[425]

I find this quote informative, as it indicates to me that this is not freedom, but some kind of effort of the Ša.A.M.i. leadership to get their population under control under the guise of "being One." Becoming ONE is nothing that can be forced on someone by rules and regulations; it's a personal thing. It also has nothing to do with nano-technology or any other technology either, for that matter. And moreover, the King of Nibiru has his people swear total allegiance to the Kingdom or be expelled, which is not power of choice, free will or freedom at all, but dictatorship! Haven't we had enough of that?

The New King of the Second Coming

Sometime in the 1400s AD, the old King Anu stepped down, after finally had made a decision that he was proud of: his successor would be one of the most unexpected of them all, Nannar, son of Nammur, the En.lil. He was a big part of Earth history, also known under the name Sin. Circumstances of which former King Anu hadn't taken into consideration made him make this decision, with the help of Ningišzidda, who was the one who came up with the suggestion. Ningišzidda said he was certain that Nannar was perhaps the only one who could unite the people again, and that he also had a life force similar to Anu. Besides, he had been quite popular among the earthlings, allegedly. This was quite an unusual gesture, because Ningišzidda was the son of Ankur, the Enki, and Nannar was of the opposing clan.

Anu saw the brilliance in this choice, according to the Intel LPG-C have gathered, and he soon made his decision official. Nannar was now the new king of Nibiru and the Ša.A.M.i. people and is up to this day.

---

[425] A.R. Bordon "THE LINK" (2007), *op. cit. p.58.*

Marduk, who was expelled from his original world, has been a major player in Earth's history over the last millennium. He, and his 300 or so Anunnaki followers, have controlled major organizations, institutions, governments, political parties, religions, educational systems, entertainment, and not the least, secret societies from behind the scenes, and it's not been in our favor, that is just the fact. However, as Dr. Bordon is so quick to point out, he is one of the *big* players, but not the *only* player. There are more ET races and bands of ET races, physical and non-physical, who have dominated mankind for a long time—some of them side by side, and in opposition to Marduk. The fight for power has been an endless drama throughout history, and it has not only been between factions of Anunnaki. But keep in mind that the Anunnaki is a widespread term, and we know today that they work together with both the Greys and the Reptilians, and some other races as well, which we shall reveal with time.

We Don't Need No Anunnaki. We Don't Need No Thought Control

It's not an easy situation for us here on Earth. The Living Library is desirable real estate, and it's been fought over since it was created, perhaps a billion years ago, or more, by the original creator gods. The question is, what should we do?

I have had a flood of communication going back and forth between me and Dr. A.R. Bordon, as a representative both for himself and LPG-C. Bordon was himself abducted by the Ša.A.M.i. on more than one occasion in his youth. However, not always unwillingly. Just like I feel that I have things I "need" to do—both for my own sake and that of others on this planet, so does Dr. Bordon. LPG-C has been taking on the role of self-appointed Ambassadors for Earth in the absence of unity amongst humankind. They felt the situation was urgent and decided to speak on our behalf. Some would argue that we don't need ambassadors in the first place.

Life happens all around us and above and below us every day, and if we all were aware of what's going on in exopolitics and among off-world species in relation to ourselves and our planet, we would be able to consult our ambassadors, and they us, and everything would be easier, not the least for them who have to be our consciousness. Knowing what they know, they feel they need to act in one way or the other. I think it's a little more complicated than that, though. For reasons I can't go into at this point, I have seen indicators of that at least Dr. Bordon made an agreement with the Ša.A.M.i. more than once in Sitter Space to start LPG-C and continue the mission he is now on; a mission we still don't know enough about.

Apparently, what is being discussed and planned in the LINK meetings with what Bordon calls the "Plenum" (the human and off-world non-government representative of the different member species, both active and spectator groups) is, that first of all, we humans have to show what our true imperatives are as a species, and not only what is suggested by a representative group like LPG-C, who does not officially have the back-up from the people. If approximately 3% of humankind can come together and present some common imperatives, the Plenum will listen and accept this for the record [but first we must be properly informed, *WP 2024*]. If we keep being scattered, ignorant, and non-caring in general, no one will take us seriously, and the real estate called Earth is for anyone to grab—this planet will not be considered ours, as little as we would consider birds or cats being in charge of our planet.

There are quite a few things that bother me with the above reasoning. In summary:

1. One Ša.A.M.e./Nibiru year is about 3,600 earth years (1 šar), and these beings live a very, very long time, in our terms. 1 šar is nothing for them. To me it's quite astonishing if King Nannar has managed to unite his people since the 1400s, which is in no-time, from their point of view. The internal conflicts and civil unrest amongst the Ša.A.M.i. people have been an ongoing saga for millions, perhaps billions, of earth years, so it sounds to me most unlikely. The conflicts and separateness were still very much major factors just before Nannar became king, as described earlier in this paper.

2. If, after all, Nannar really *has* managed to unite people, it's only because he's used technology to do so. Loyalty to the Kingdom is a must for the Ša.A.M.i. people to be accepted, as we already know, and this alone doesn't seem like a true unification to me-- more like an enforced one. Someone is making the rules, and the rest are forced to follow, and when they do, it's called "Oneness."

3. Why would we, or anybody trust them? They have showed over and over again that they are a very immoral, combating warrior race, obsessed with sex and power. To believe that they should have changed so drastically so suddenly is naive to me.

4. Let's pretend that the new king actually is serious when comes to helping us stand on our own feet. Still, we would have to trust that this skeleton crew (yet another crew left on their own here on Earth, just like in the past) is as united as they want us to believe

and not start fighting internally again. To me, it sounds like the odds that history will repeat itself are immensely great.

I can understand that LPG-C feel that they are backed into a corner, and that we actually don't have a choice in the matter. According to members of the Plenum, there are two major achievements we as a species need to accomplish:

1. We need to have a 3% unity, able to present the imperatives of the human race.

2. We need to decide whether we can stand on our own feet or need help to do so.

If we are to take this seriously, these are enormous goals to achieve. When we look around, we see how ignorant people are, and few would take something like this seriously at this point.

When I discuss some of these issues with Dr. Bordon, he agrees with me that we are still not sure if being supervised by a Nibiruan crew would be in our best interest, but it's *one* option. It's not up to LPG-C to decide. Our first goal is to make enough people aware of our challenges, and from there decide what kind of future we want, says Bordon.

One thing seems certain, as the information is drawn from many different sources, obviously separate from each other: The Ša.A.M.i. are coming back, and not everybody thinks that's a good thing. Some say they are coming back now because we are evolving into higher frequencies and dimensions, and they are not. Therefore, they come back to feed off our emotions once again—emotions being food for them, and it depletes us from ours, like vampires sucking our life force.[426] They have forgotten who their own creator gods are, and that they are not the top of the totem pole. We also have from reliable metaphysical sources that master geneticists, like the Anunnaki, "are capable of occupying many different forms,"[427] either meaning they are shapeshifters of sorts (Marciniak and Icke), or that they themselves have tampered with their own genetics to the extent that they have changed forms. The Pleiadians are emphasizing that these beings *are* shapeshifters and inter-dimensional, and some of them are reptilians while others are not (and this was before Icke started saying the same thing). If this is all true, the returning gods are certainly bad news.

Barbara Marciniak, channeling the Pleiadians, continues in her excellent book, "Bringers of the Dawn":

---

[426] Marciniak (1992): "Bringers of the Dawn," p.34.
[427] ibid. p.36 op. cit.

When these beings Anunnaki, (or the lizzies as the Pleiadians used to call them) return to Earth, there will be many of you who will turn to them and say, "Yes, these are wonderful gods. I feel wonderful about them. They are so magnificent. Look what they can do." Some of these gods will seem to fix and save your world. This is where it will be easy to miss the bigger picture. It will *look* as if they are coming to fix and save your world when, in actuality, **what they are doing is simply creating another form of authority and control** *(emphasis not in original)*. What we are saying is that people wills put a belief system and a paradigm on these entities. There will be a large marketing program to sell the presence of these entities to you. This program is already going on.[428]

Note that the above was channeled already in 1992. With all the Intel I've gathered, and the material available on this subject that I have taken part of, where some is pro Anunnaki returning, others are against, and some are indecisive about it, I can't help but coming to a very similar conclusion as the Pleiadians did 19 years ago. They knew what was coming down the pike, and there is indeed a great promotion for the returning of the gods, and many are working behind the scenes to help them. They (such as CERN) are working on opening stargates on our end to let some of these gods through. Others are working on this, perhaps unbeknownst of what is coming to fruition, and LPG-C may be one of these organizations. If they think they can be ambassadors for the gods once they have "cleansed" our planet, I'm afraid they are up for a surprise. Still, the gods would not have as much of a chance to establish a New Kingdom here on Earth without help from our brightest minds. But even our most brilliant people can be deceived.

It sounds to me that the Return of the gods is just a carefully planned take-over of our planet. It's time for the Changing of the Guards, and once again, these beings want to rule in the open instead of behind the scenes. In the Moses chapter of this book, it supports the idea the Anunnaki are feeding off our emotions, YHVH shows off as the cold-blooded murderer he was, and while telling his chosen people not to kill in his Ten Commandments, he afterwards ordered them to kill thousands of people who did not obey the Anunnaki "god". YHVH himself killed hundreds of thousands of people in the name of worship and religion. Afterwards, he must have felt well fed, thanks to ignorant human beings, who gladly went into his trap and obeyed his insane orders unconditionally.

Many who read this paper will find they come to the same conclusions as I do, and it's important that we exclude the Return of the "gods" from our possible future. We need to get together and raise our vibrations; become more like the light beings we essentially are. We have to set our

---

[428] pp. 42, op. cit.

imperatives, and those imperatives do not include the Anunnaki ruling us in fear and terror for at least another 26,000 years, when we get a new chance to evolve in the sense we do now. That's when the solar system aligns with the galactic center in this fashion next time. But the best chance to break what Neil Freer calls the "Godspell"[429] is now, at this very moment in time, and we are running late!

We need to become sovereign and not depend on "gods," aliens, governments and whatnot for decision making. We are our own Gods, and though we are considered being at the bottom of the totem pole in terms of cosmic intelligence and technical advancement, we have something few other biokinds have: a wide range of emotions and RNA/DNA from many different, highly spiritually evolved beings, who created us before the Anunnaki came down. We have a lot of power of our own, and we are knocking on the multi-dimensional doors right now. Previously they were closed because we didn't even know which doors to knock on, but now more and more people have found the doors. We knock gently and reluctantly at first, and the doors open just a little, but now we are beginning to gain more certainty and knock harder. And lo and behold! The doors fly open and our connection to the multi-dimensional existence happens quickly and surely. We are finding that the Multiverse is not out there but within ourselves, and that revelation alone is freeing us from our vibrational prison.

We were talking about Marduk changing the records of their own history on Earth, and I asked the rhetorical question: What exactly did he change? First, I think Marduk was not the only one of the Anunnaki who changed history. History, as they say, is written (or told) by the winners, and there were many winners and losers in the endless battles the gods fought against each other. Being full of themselves, I'm sure they told their "workers" (homo sapiens sapiens) *their* version of history. I believe that the most blatant lie they told the Sumerian people was that we are coming from apes with low intelligence and primitive lifestyle and that the Anunnaki sped up the process by manipulating our RNA/DNA. Now the Ša.A.M.i. are using their triumph card, that they were the ones creating us, or rather upgraded us from apes to homo sapiens sapiens, and hence sped up our evolution with millions of years. So in other words, we should be grateful to them and forgive them for what was done to us in the past. Every cell in my body tells me this is wrong.

But why would we believe channeled, metaphysical sources, then? Well, once we've felt them out and understand why they are here and have checked their credibility (not all of them have our best interests in mind), these entities, who have can read our energy fields and that of the planet,

---

[429] Neil Freer's website, http://www.neilfreer.com/

446

can see our past the way events really happened on our current common timeline, and in addition, many of these sources were part of the creation and thus have firsthand experiences with our planet. Some of them are even us in the future, so they are speaking of theirs and our pasts, respectively, but from a multidimensional viewpoint. I consider some of these sources fairly reliable. Still, that's not what's most important; it's what you feel inside being the truth, and what does not sit well with you? Trust your inner self.

Something I have not been able to prove at this point is the theory I have that Marduk's clan and the Ša.A.M.i. on the Home Planet are basically on the same side and it's just a game to fool us humans into taking sides in a battle where the winner is the same, regardless of which side wins. We have been suppressed for so long now that people start seeing through the oppression, and they are waking up from their sleep. The Ša.A.M.i. always knew this would happen, and not to lose their real estate they had to put on a show, starting with Prophecy. We have to remember that these people think "long thoughts," and a few 10,000 years of thinking ahead is routine for them; like it would be for us when thinking a month ahead. Now, when we wake up, one by one, two by two, they come down from the Heavens pretending to be on our side. They will turn man against man, possibly in the most devastating war we've ever seen (the Battle of Armageddon), using weapons of mass destruction that are not even imagined yet in the sf literature. The outcome will be a vastly reduced population that can easily be managed by a skeleton crew and the "Reptilian Gatekeepers." So, in reality, Marduk and the Home Planet are siding with each other, turning man against man.

Sounds unlikely? Not if we look at the history of these people. They have proven who they are, and particularly, *how* they are. These people have erased our memories of them, most probably more than once. Listen to this:

The original planners, the Vegans and the Lyrans, inserted a source code into our DNA that is activating now. Over time, the Ša.A.M.i./Anunnaki, while doing their genetic experiments on us, found that this source code exists and will wake humanity up in the near future (from their time perspective.

Instead of attempting to find something which is more or less impossible to find, they decide to make sure humankind remains as distracted as possible during the nano-second (1987-2012) so most people stay asleep. They understand that it may not be possible to stop some of us from evolving, but that may be an "acceptable loss" to them.

Their problem is the population of 7 billion people. I'm sure the Reptilian Gatekeepers and the earth-bound Anunnaki have had a hard time keeping us in check sometimes. The answer for them is always war. So why not create a war greater than any other to reduce the human population down to 500,000,000, which has been the plan for so long? It's not happened yet because the Ša.A.M.i. are supposed to take care of that part. And the Global Elite have probably been promised to be spared in the Armageddon Battle. After all, it's the Ša.A.M.i. and their Reptilian cohorts who are feeding them.

If we think about it; why would Anu, the former Ša.A.M.i. King, suddenly get an epiphany that he should turn Earth over to the humans and then leave someone with Marduk's mindset here to rule on Earth with an iron fist for a few thousand years? Additionally, they destroy a big chunk of our planet by nuking Sodom, Gomorrah and other cities, plus the Sinai Spaceport, making the area highly radioactive up until this day,[430] mercilessly killing the humans they just said should own the planet, and as destructively as possible, many of the gods leave. Where's the compassion in that? Isn't it more likely that they left Marduk here because they knew he would rule us with an iron fist, and that's exactly what they wanted? To keep humanity oppressed and obedient while the rest of the Ša.A.M.i. were gone, doing business elsewhere? And in the middle of everything, the Reptilians are helping Marduk, maybe from bases on the Moon and other planetary bodies in the solar system.

Ronald Reagan and others have said that in a case of an invasion from outer space, humanity would finally be united in a global effort to defeat them. Yes, that is what we are getting prepared for. Thus, when 7-9ft tall humanoids, together with demon-like Reptilians and other strange creature, as if directly taken from the Bible (which they are in certain terms), come down in spaceships, most people will side with the governments, on which Marduk's clan is pulling the strings. Of course, people don't know how this is orchestrated, and a devastating world war will take place, where man fights against man, gods fight against man and man fights against gods. Others, who think they've seen through it all, will join with the Incoming, but it doesn't matter because they are one and the same; it's just a big deception. When it's all over, the Ša.A.M.i. has won and the remaining humanity is now at their mercy.

The Ša.A.M.i. species is a conquering race. Why would they voluntarily give up real estate they once won in battle? They have conquered other worlds as well, according to LPG-C and many metaphysical sources. It would be interesting to see how they manage those worlds, and then look for similarities.

---

[430] Nexus Magazine had a very interesting article on the nuking of Sodom and Gomorrah in the Nov-Dec 2000 issue, where many scientists have concluded that the salt pillars and the salt levels in general in the Dead Sea and around that area can only be possible in a case of a nuclear bomb. The salt covering these pillars would have been washed away by the first rain. This kind of "harder salt" only builds from nuclear energy.

These were just my thoughts on this subject. The above concerns raise even more questions, and I'm sure that you, the reader, have a few as well.

PAPER 20:
MORE ON ARTIFICIAL INTELLIGENCE, INCREASED LONGEVITY, AND NANO-TECH

by Wes Penre, Thursday, July 7, 2011 @ 5:50 AM

"The journey here is about self-discovery in relationship to others."
- Barbara Marciniak, "Bringers of the Dawn," p.218

Abstract: The Fine Balance Between Science and Metaphysics

It is easy to get affected by other's viewpoints (in this case often off-worldly) on *how* we should evolve and behave here on Earth—especially if there is a group which we feel is challenging us and put our feet to the fire. And how about if these off-worldly beings do this from a surprisingly emotionless state of mind? This will induce fear; even a certain sting of hopelessness and these emotions may color our choices as a human race.

I hear from both LPG-C, writer and researcher George LoBuono, Alex Collier and his Andromedans, and others, that the aliens more than once have threatened to interfere with our evolution if we don't shape up as a species and stop destroying our planet, ourselves, and other planets and galaxies in the vicinity due to our misuse of negative energy. They have even thought of terminating us as a species.

Author and researcher, George LoBuono, explains in his "Alien Mind" how civilizations go through different stages, and we are like adolescents now. It's a critical time in the history of humankind because we are wobbling at the edge of a cliff, and everybody out there is holding their breath. Are we're going to fall down or not?

I can see how aliens are concerned about how we're going to handle this stage of our development, because our misuse of negative energy is alarming and our arrogance level high. Not only are we about to destroy our own species and our planet, but it will also affect other parts of the universe, as we, simply speaking, are borrowing energy from other parts of space in a "balloon-effect" and thus deplete that space of energy without "paying back." This will decrease the longevity of star systems and galaxies close to us, and in larger terms, when this is done by other civilizations as well (which it is), it affects the longevity of the entire Universe. So, there is no wonder that aliens are concerned and monitor us closely. If worse comes to worse, they *may* actually terminate us as a species if we don't learn our lessons.

Therefore, it's all up to us. We can't blame everything on a Global Elite, or even malevolent aliens behind the scenes; we "ordinary humans" are the majority, and the responsibility is ours. I doubt we will be granted sovereignty of this planet if we can't even stand up for ourselves, and instead of coming together and stop being lazy, prefer to watch football games on TV or spend all out spare time on video games.

Waking up the Sleeping Giant

It's time to wake up to reality, which here is defined as our mutual current moment, what is happening around us at this present time, and how the choices we make in the present will directly affect our future. The reason we have been taken advantage of is solely because of our ignorance; sometimes self-inflicted (we don't want to hear no evil, see no evil), and it always comes back to haunt us. We can almost look at it as demon- or entity possession on a grand, planetary scale. Where there is ignorance, fear and low vibrations, entities come in and take advantage of the sleeping population. In this case, we have different alien species fighting over dominion of Earth, the real estate and its inhabitants, capable of doing so without the knowledge of billions of people. This in itself can look like a discouraging situation, but it may only take a big shake-up to wake the sleeping giant (humans). I am trying to wake the giant, preventing the shake-up from being too traumatic. Metaphorically speaking, if we think we can avoid a car accident, why would we look the other way? Our impulse would be to help, wouldn't it? (Or would it?)

An "accident" is about to happen very soon, but we can still avoid it. Albeit, what is planned for our future by forces who might seem to have our best interest in mind but don't, in my opinion, is no accident. There are those among us having a talent to convince the masses, wittingly, or unwittingly, steering us in a very dangerous direction.

We are now talking about Alien Technology and Artificial Intelligence.

I don't mean that all alien technology is bad or dangerous. Some of them can be helpful and something we may want to look into, but the

451

danger lies in how we use it. We are already using lots of alien technology, mostly within the Military Industrial Complex (no surprise). Other is used daily by all of us; I am using it now, when I am writing this. I am using a computer and a word processor.

Technology is neutral; it's neither good nor evil—it's neutral. It won't do much unless there is a higher consciousness programming it. It depends on how it's programmed and what it's used for. But even that is stone age today: Our future, if certain factions of ETs and humans will have it their way, is Artificial Intelligence and enhanced longevity, created with technology. These two goals are what we are mainly going to discuss in this paper. If we let certain scientists and their followers do as they please, where will it take us?

I have mentioned elsewhere that science and religion (and metaphysics) need to merge for humankind to be whole and able to move on, but that doesn't mean we need to adapt to any specific scientific idea out there; especially not the ones introduced, overtly or covertly, by the Global Elite and their alien overlords. Science is the knowledge of the Universe. It tries to figure out who we are, our place in it, the goal of the universe, how universes are born and how they die, the fact that we are both physical and spiritual as One, what stars, planets, nebulae, and galaxies really are, and combine that knowledge with who we are on a subquantum, metaphysical level, and what the purpose is if we combine all this and realize that we are all ONE. When this is understood by mankind, we will be able to raise our vibrations above the current low and break the prison walls. Only those who can match our vibration will stay with us in our incrementally achieved new reality.

The questions are: If the above are the goals, where does AI, nanotechnology, and other advanced physics and mechanics come into the picture? Do these technologies enhance our consciousness, or do they do the opposite? Will we use technology wisely? These are very important questions that we need to discuss on a serious level.

The Codes of Consciousness

Things are going to be tough in the next few years for all of us—some are staged events by ETs and their human cohorts, while other events are natural cycles of cosmos. People will be highly affected in many different ways, and it's up to us how we are going to react. Those who are prepared by doing their homework will have an easier time, while those who chose to remain ignorant are in for a shock.

This is a great opportunity for certain forces in the ET science community to come forward and offer solutions. The most amazing scientific "new" discoveries will be presented to humankind in an apparent effort to assist the situation. Of course, it comes with a price; and I'm not only talking about money. There are these ET factions who want us to be dependent on technology, and many of our brightest minds here on Earth are supporting and working furiously on it. I can't stress enough what I personally don't believe in, and that is to be part of any future super-technological society. It's a trap.

Instead, go inside yourself. Other programs will open up, which are currently sealed away. They are codes of consciousness, and there are things firing off these codes. From here on, things are going to happen rapidly, and catalysts in the environment, whether its planetary events, or be they off-worldly, designed by friendly ETs, will take consciousness on this planet to a totally new level. Those who go with the flow will find themselves on an island where the storm doesn't hit, no earthquakes reach and no hurricanes blow. Who will create this for us? No one but ourselves. We have this encoded inside us; we are just waiting for these codes to activate and to be fired off, one by one, like a series of firework.[431]

But will everybody be ignited? Yes, to a different degree. However, those who receive the changes with fear and anxiety will misinterpret what is happening, and the codes may misfire and backflash. It's imperative, whether you agree with all this, to set your goals to reach higher consciousness. I am painfully aware of that it's still not for everybody, and that is okay—some humans want to continue experiencing the 3rd density/dimension reality and go through all the hardship and continue into the Machine World at the end of it, and that is their choice.

These times are about connecting with the cosmos and become multidimensional again. Most of those who have worked towards this goal have a subtle feeling that we have experienced this increase in consciousness before, but we can't put our fingers on it. It flashes up like a buried cell memory and then wears off. If you have had this flashback, it's one of many signs that you are starting to connect because we certainly have been multi-dimensional before, but we were tampered with by more than one species; by those who either wanted to create a slave race out of us, or by those who saw our potentials and wanted to take advantage of it and use it for their own survival.

We have more or less reached the maximum number a people this planet will probably ever see. It is not by accident but by design. Everybody alive right now chose to be born into these times because of a tremendous group agreement that we made before we incarnated here in the so-called "end times." All of us, no matter what we think, are either

---

[431] Barbara Marciniak channeling the Pleiadians, "Moon Musings #57, Track 6, November 4, 2010," Ashayana Deane (2002), "Voyagers I: The Sleeping Abductees, 2nd Edition."

here to help raising the consciousness of the species and of the planet, or to just be here to feel it out, out of curiosity. Not everybody will make it through 2012, and you will see many people exit before then; often unexpectedly. This, too, is no accident. There are those who wanted to participate in this mass event but not be part of the 2012 wave we will talk about later.

How "New" Alien Technology Will Be Introduced, Creating Split of the Human Race

We will see much more "new" alien technologies being released. Not all of them at once, but it will be done, step by step.

Before we move on, we need to understand that when we're talking about science, there are different kinds. We have a) *mainstream science*; b) *secret (or occult) science*; c) *alien science, which includes Nikola Tesla science that may be thousands of years ahead of mainstream science* d) *rogue science.*

Science is theory. Then it's up to the scientists to prove these theories in practice. If it can be replicated over and over, we have what science deems "proven fact." This is how science has been working for hundreds of years, but now, when they are looking into smaller and smaller particles and enter the realm of quantum and subquantum physics and mechanics, nothing is consistent anymore. You can't use the old formula to prove or disprove a theory because everything is fluid, moving, changing attributes and behavior. Moreover, quantum physics often tends to prove old, solid science wrong. Nothing is black or white, and this is a huge problem for scientists. How can *anything* be proven anymore? What was true yesterday is not true today. Everything changes so rapidly, and if we are stuck in old, outdated thinking and behavior, our lives are going to be very dysfunctional, even if it worked okay not so long ago.

However, in all this chaos, there will be "fixes." High-tech Enterprises will come out with technologies that can put some stability to the chaos. But these fixes have everything to do with the Machine Kingdom, which is planned to be introduced incrementally here on Earth until people get used to it and incorporate it into their lives, step by step. We will see PhDs or authoritarian researchers/writers promoting this new Kingdom as a solution for humankind, and many, many people will agree and follow because, tongue in cheek, "the authorities are always right."

I will say there will soon be a split of humankind, and this has to do with the new technology. There will be those who go for it, and those who choose not to. Machines will blend with humans so they will become part machine and part human. This is of course not real to many people today but is nevertheless what is planned, which I will demonstrate. This is nothing new; there are ETs out there who have already fallen into this kind of reality by their own doing or had others do it to them. Now they are trying to implement this on our soul group as well. Later on, we will discuss *why* this is introduced.

The impostors, who want to introduce what we call Artificial Intelligence into society know how to do it. Just like with everything else they have introduced, which is for their gain and our loss, it follows a certain formula that seems to work on us humans most of the time. And with the risk of repeating myself here, this formula is based on fear. The formula itself is quite known to people who have looked into how the Global Elite's work. It goes, *problem-reaction-solution.* In other words, to end up with a solution which benefits you, when you know that people in general would object to your proposal, is to create a problem serious enough to create a reaction among the general population, and a demand to do something about it. Then you can introduce the solution to the problem you created in the first place, and the population will, due to fear of loss, and perhaps reluctantly at first, adjust accordingly and accept your solution, and you get what you want. This formula, however, needs to be calculated precisely because the problem created has to be in proportion to the solution you want to achieve. For instance, if the problem is too small, people may not think that the solution is worth it. A perfect example of this calculated, well balanced formula, for those who haven't seen through this yet, is the 9/11 attack on the Twin Towers. The Global Elite commits a mass murder, which traumatizes the whole nation. The Media do their part and escalate the fear, saying this can happen again anywhere, anyplace and anywhen. "No one knows where the terrorists will hit next!" So, here we have a problem, which was created, and we have the reaction, and now we can introduce the solution, which is a much tighter security and surveillance system, and the War on Terror, instigated by those who now try to solve it with a new "endless" war. We live in an Orwellian 1984, Big Brother society, and many people welcome it out of fear of what would happen if they wouldn't. It works like a clock, and the Elite is laughing at our gullibility.

So, if someone wants to steer us in a new direction, going towards a machine society and an acceptance of AI, it has to be done in increments. Hence, the impostors use what they have, and again feed off human emotions.

Problem: Young men and women go to war to fight for their country and get their arms and legs shot off in the process. The Media bring up the problem and run random stories of soldiers being severely wounded at war and how it affects them and their families.

Reaction: People feel for the soldiers and their families and wish everything could be alright.

Solution: The soldier gets a new prosthetic and returns to war. Of course, he has to pass the test, running so many miles with a heavy

455

· The First Level of Learning ·

backpack etc., and he does it! "See what this 'brave soldier,' who doesn't give up fighting for what he thinks is right, can do so with this fantastic new technology."

This is a story from real life, and it was brought up in the Media last Fall [2010, *WP 2024*.]. This is what technology has come to, and of course, it's merely the technology that has been released thus far. There is so much more they haven't shown us yet. The moral of the above story, though, has not so much to do with the soldier as it has with how it affects our subconscious mind. We think that if they can fix up a soldier like that and he'll be as good as new, it's comforting in case we need prosthetics and artificial body parts ourselves in the future in order to survive.

This is how they seduce us. It's like saying implants are good on babies because they can't be stolen at the hospitals. And who is stealing the babies? Many of them are stolen by secret government organizations to be used, either as sex slaves, breeders, mind controlled assassins, and more. So again, the solution is presented after first having created a problem. Many people chip their pets so they can be easily found, and it is a good thing in that particular sense, but when used on humans, there are darker agendas behind it, such as lowering peoples vibrations, controlling your thoughts and behavior and manipulate us into the Machine Kingdom because if we knew the Elite's true motives, no one would consent.

> "The Machines can't come in without you, but after a while they don't need you."
>
> *- The Pleiadians*[432]

What we're going to end up with if we don't face the agenda behind this is that we will have machines that are many, many times smarter than we are. Isaac Asimov's old novel, "I, Robot" is not so farfetched after all. Of course, being a world famous sci fi writer, he knew what he was writing about.

Speaking of robots; what could be better, if you want to create a certain future, than to influence our kids and program them from early age? Brilliant! And that's of course exactly what is being done. How about robots as problem solvers? Cool, children? Here is merely one example out of many how our young kids are being manipulated via cartoons, video games, and TV. How about a life inside a video game?

(A video was supposed to go here, but after I posted it, the video was taken off YouTube due to copyright issues)

This is where parents' responsibility is so important. By choosing to

---

[432] Marciniak/Pleiadians: "Moon Musings #57, Track 7, November 4, 2010."

stay ignorant, parents must be held partly accountable for the programming of our children. Those who don't educate themselves and their children will be equally responsible as the Powers That Be, who program them. Especially today, when there is so much information available, parents must come to their senses. Instead, many parents turn a blind eye because it's convenient to let the kids play with electronics and watch movies which control their minds. [Most parents, I believe, and aware, at least on *some* level, that this is not good for their children, but it keeps the children busy, and the children are not bothering the parents as much, *WP 2024*.]

Due to the lack of responsibility and interest in educating their kids, people, especially of the next generation, will be very excited and thrilled about all new technology that is being introduced, while others don't want to have anything to do with it. That's where the major split is going to happen. For those who choose the latter, what is happening in the Machine World will be a perfect catalyst for them to really take the step, leave the functional insanity behind, and go back to nature to build new, small communities at first, which will grow in size, and join together as this develops. The fans of the machine technology will move into bigger cities where they can enjoy the new technology. It may feel fantastic at first when your needs are taken care of and you get any medical attention necessary, and any illness cured, but you must be chipped, and you will soon become part machine, a so-called "cyborg.". Eventually, you need to "plug yourself in" to even start functioning, and you will connect to a virtual reality that is built on machine technology—a Matrix within the Matrix within the Matrix...How far down the rabbit hole do we want to sink? How much more trapped do we wish to be? How much more naïve...?

Some may argue and say that the Global Elite and those behind them will not allow the rest to reject their machine society, but they will have no choice. It's all about vibration. Those choosing the Machine World will do so from excitement, but mainly because of underlying fears. They believe, whether they are aware of it, that by introducing higher developed technology into their lives, they have better chances of survival. Most humans are afraid to die. However, it's only superficial and this entire agenda fills a much larger purpose. If the machine followers knew, and were willing to face their hidden fears, and clearly see what is causing their fears, and what the end goal is, they wouldn't be so thrilled. Those who choose not to participate will create their own, much less technologically based societies in their local universes and build their multi-dimensionality where it should be built; in biological bodies close to nature—the spiritual part of our world.

The forces, whose imperatives are to take over, always feed off fear, and when I say "feed" I mean it in all the definitions of the word. Beings

457

of lower vibrations, whether they are human, are psychic vampires, and they get stronger by using the busy fear energy and enhance their own, in a large degree negatively oriented, energy field. It's food, and their survival depends on it.

But what about space travel? Don't we want to be part of the galactic community and travel between the stars?

Yes, and we will. There are many ways to travel between the stars. It can be done with or without technology, or with minimal technology. Some aliens travel in 3D spaceships, using Einstein-Rosen Bridges to go from one place to another, perhaps million light-years away. Others use their "avatars," or light-bodies, while their 3D bodies are still left on the original planet. Others have the power to bring their original bodies with them. There are multiple ways to travel inter-planetary. Also, I am not saying we are not going to use technology to travel; technology in itself is not bad, it's only if it's used to manipulate and control that it is bad. However, before we even go there, we need to create a new world, a totally new society built on a higher frequency and level of understanding of life and the universe. When we can do that, we can start thinking about space travel, and perhaps even time-travel. Our environment, and how we use the technology we feel we need is in direct ratio to our level of consciousness. Which level of consciousness is TV, twitter, text messaging, video games, Facebook addiction? Think about it.

Some say we should be looking at a middle-way, which would be the way to go, by using technology wisely, and that would all be fine and dandy, if we as a human group were high enough in frequency to break out of the frequency fence we're currently stuck in and we all can see what is presently being done to us. If we can't do that, we are going to see a split of humanity to begin with; there is no third way. [433]

Protecting Our Biology

About 250,000-300,000 years ago, according to some sources, our biology was hijacked. We were successfully cut off from the higher dimensions and densities and put in a frequency band which glued us to the 3rd Density or Dimension, depending on which term we wish to use. Our DNA was tampered with in such a way that the whole Living Library Project came to a definite halt and has been on hold ever since, after the new owners of

---

[433] When I wrote this (in 2011), I knew nothing about how to exit the Matrix, so my soulution was to create a "New Earth." I now realize this is literally impossible, but there is a simple exit route from the Matrix, which will be presented in upcoming books in this series, and can also be explored here:

https://wespenrevideos.com/category/exiting-the-grid/, *WP 2024.*

this planet changed policies. They were only interested in creating a slave race that could do the dirty work for them. We have been their slaves in one way or the other ever since. To call it something else would be false, and the arrogance with which they were (and still are) treating us is nothing less than a high crime, and the perpetrators should be severely punished.

Our responsibility now is to get back on track and not let anybody else own our biology to further develop a machine race, or by genetically tamper with us again behind our backs to create new hybrids for new, updated purposes. And don't believe for a second that this is not already happening. The Greys are a perfect example of this, and human traitors are working in secret bases such as Area 51, and others, to create a new hybrid species. Our own human Global Elite and those who support them on lower levels have been working very hard for the last decades or more to create this in conjunction with bands of different ETs. Many of us have listened to whistle-blowers, and perhaps even seen some pictures of scary-looking hybrids in test tubes, being developed deep down in underground facilities, far from scrutiny. This is not science fiction; it is happening on a grand scale in present time.

The good news is that we are supported in our quest to free ourselves from hundreds of thousands of years of slavery. Not all aliens have imperatives clashing with ours. The Pleiadians say; *cosmos is not malevolent; it's benign. The Multiverse is there to guide you in how live in a friendly and supportive universe.* They go on to say that there are, of course, those who want to manipulate us and work against our development as a species, and control us, but they are way fewer than those who would accept us with open arms. The Pleiadians are one of the latter, the Guardian Alliance another.[434]

Still, none of them are here to do the work for us while we're sitting on our behinds. It's up to *us* to do the work. I am going to discuss in detail what this work includes later on, and the reason why I want to wait is because there are others who want to push another solution on us humans—solutions I don't agree with. I want to present them "side by side" so to speak, so the reader can distinguish and make a conscious decision in what direction you want to go.

In this space and time, there are many forces from the cosmos; dimensionally, inter-dimensionally, from Inner Earth, from the surface, and other galaxies, paying interest in our development because the Living Library is unique—the idea is unique. This can seem very overwhelming

---

[434] The Guardian Alliance are communicating with A'shayana Deane through data streaming, which is *digitally encoded coherent signals* per definition (http://en.wikipedia.org/wiki/Data_stream), meaning the receiver is getting packages of information (Deane compares it with computer "zip files") which h/she then decodes and puts down in written form.

and overpowering to comprehend and meet without fear, but that's exactly what we need to do. To many, it will seem like a hopeless situation because this group has this agenda, and that group has that agenda, while a third group... It seems there's no end. However, when it really comes down to it, it doesn't matter. We need to evolve despite these forces, learn who we are, how to raise our vibration, recognize the fear and anxiety within us, learn to master these emotions, and not tune into the vibrations that go along with these lower vibrations. Then we can break out from the frequency fence we're stuck inside.

Even if it's not pleasant, we need to know what's out there, what the imperatives of certain ET groups are, to understand who we really are in this organized chaos, and then take appropriate, peaceful steps away from the battleground. Instead of taking sides in any given battle, we simply walk away and do our own thing, knowing the battle rages somewhere, but it's no longer part of our own local universe. That's our first step.

The Internet vs. the Innernet

Marciniak's Pleiadians are very clear: Over and over, they emphasize how dangerous our electronic devices are—everything from cell phones and TVs to the Internet. They encourage us not to waste our time and stop letting our lives depend on electronics. They would like to see us throw our cellphones away, only using computers minimally (if at all), and instead of letting Google be our "All-Knowing God," we need to go to our "Innernet" for answers—the Innernet being our inner knowledge, our "Inner Google". We have all the answers inside because we are part of All That Is, the Divine Source. We must start believing in ourselves and listen to our "inner voice" or intuition for answers. However, as long as we are addicted to electronics (yes, it is an addiction worse than heroin, according to the Pleiadians), we will not be able to reconnect with our Innernet. This can only be successfully done in full when being in nature. We need to stay grounded in our bodies to become multi-dimensional. It's not a matter of leaving our bodies to seek enlightenment—the bodies are our guides and helpers. When we're talking about multidimensionality, we don't mean that we should *become* multi-d; we *are* multi-d. Not only our souls, but our bodies are multi-dimensional too. We use our bodies as extended "nerve endings." and the 12 chakras working in harmony is our ticket into the Multiverse.[435]

Very few people on this planet know what their bodies can do. Here on

---

[435] Although non-spirited ETs have 7 chakras, we humans have 12, continuing outside our bodies and to the highest dimensions of the Spirit Universe. More about this in later books in this series, and in more recent work, *WP 2024.*

Earth, at worst, we think that our bodies are us, and when our bodies die, we die. At best, our bodies are our vessels, so that personality (mind) and spirit (us) can experience things in the 3rd dimensional physical reality. Still, the body is so much more than that. It has wonderful cellular memory, soul memory, and can be used for time- and space travel in ways totally unheard of by most humans.

Life is all about experiencing and learning in the reality where we incarnate. Although we were tampered with in a detrimental way, our goal is to enhance the power in our bodies by reconnecting our dormant DNA, which is what is currently occurring in some of us.

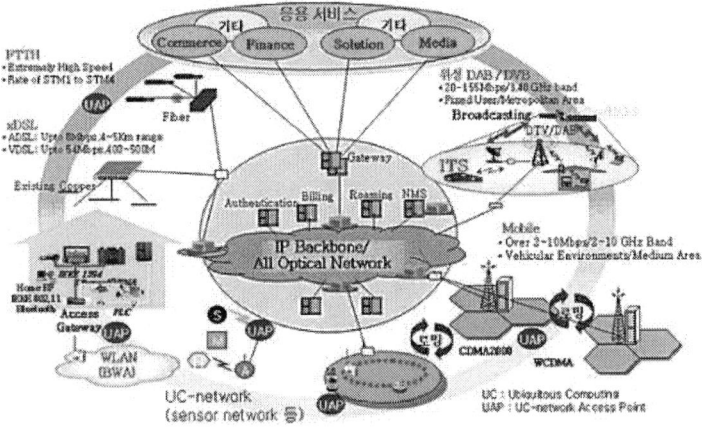

Figure 20.1: The Internet; a dangerous route to go.

In juxtaposition to this, the Pleiadians say that electronics *could* be used in a way that's not harmful, but the way we're using it now, in the hands of the wrong people, it is very destructive, all the way down to a cellular level. By introducing these technologies to our kids at an early age, we help set the stage for them to meet their own demise in the near future. Again, welcome to the Machine Kingdom, where illusion and deception are the reality. The consequences are devastating.

Our task is not to turn this around and start using electronics more responsibly, but again to step out of it as much as possible and develop our Innernet. It's like when you leave a lit up house in the middle of the night and go outside; it takes a while before your eyes get used to the dark and you can see the stars. Still, the more time you spend away from any artificial light, the more stars, nebulae and galaxies you can distinguish. Not until we have totally withdrawn from electronics can we appreciate Nature and the elements again, like in the "old days," for us dinosaurs who

461

remember life before the Internet, and it takes some adjustment. At this juncture, we have no other choice, and I don't say this in the sense that it would mean something "necessary evil," but as a part of a new, exciting journey. I used to live with nature all the time when I was younger, so I developed a very close relationship to it. I talked to the birds, the squirrels, the butterflies, the trees, and expected them to return my communication. And often, they did. I thanked Mother Earth for letting me take part of all her beauty and magic. When you can connect with your environment, realizing that it is all a part of you, and everything is love and wisdom on a higher level of existence, life becomes rich and fulfilling, and that to me is true happiness. I am still doing this on a smaller scale, hindered by work, research, and writing, but that will hopefully be temporary. In all honesty, I have *never* been happier than when I lived with nature. That being said, let's explore the other side of the coin further—the upcoming machine technology—our parallel future.

Welcome to the Machine Kingdom Where Man and Machine Become One!

There are geniuses in all areas of life. Dr. Raymond Kurzweil was a prodigy in machine technology and became a well-respected man in his field.

In 1965, as a high school student, he was on Steve Allen's Show, "I've got a Secret," and played a fascinating piece on the piano. Afterwards, the young boy was grilled on how that piece came together, and Kurzweil said it was done on a computer.[436] This was unheard of at the time, when music was still made by people on real instruments.

---

[436] Time Magazine, Feb. 10, 2011: "2045: The Year Man Becomes Immortal", http://battleofearth.wordpress.com/2011/03/06/2045-the-year-man-becomes-immortal/

Figure 20.2: Dr. Raymond Kurzweil

Moreover, the young boy told the audience that he had built the computer himself. It was quite an impressive piece of work for its time, but the panel of the show, as usual, did not connect the dots, but instead of being fascinated by what Kurzweil had actually built, they focused on his young age.

Time Magazine wrote in February 2011:

> ...Kurzweil would spend much of the rest of his career working out what his demonstration meant. Creating a work of art is one of those activities we reserve for humans and humans only. It's an act of self-expression; you're not supposed to be able to do it if you don't have a self. To see creativity, the exclusive domain of humans, usurped by a computer built by a 17-year-old is to watch a line blur that cannot be unblurred, the line between organic intelligence and artificial intelligence.[437]

If I didn't understand better, I would be in awe that such a genius is born and manage to become a front-figure for the machine world technology. However, I know (and the reader who has followed my series of papers knows as well) that we all are born into this world by first setting goals for ourselves to accomplish in a certain incarnation. Of course, this is the case here as well. It is done between lives, and then we are sent back to Earth with amnesia. But the goal we set is still working under the surface through our subconscious mind.

Today, Kurzweil believes we are getting close to the time when

---

[437] Ibid. op. cit.

computers will become intelligent, but not just intelligent, but *more* intelligent than humans (compare the Pleiadian prediction above). And this is not something he says regretfully—he looks forward to it. This is what he, and many others working with him want. They are working towards something called the "Singularity," which means that man and machine become one. I would suggest you put the word "singularity" in memory because not only will we discuss it here; you may have, or you will be hearing that word a lot in the near future.

Dr. Kurzweil goes on to say that when the time comes when the machines exceed our own intelligence, our bodies, our minds, and our civilizations *will be completely and irreversibly transformed.* According to his own calculations, the civilization as we know it will end in 2045; that's when the machines will take over.

This is no longer science fiction, regardless of what the reader thinks. It's not Dr. Kurzweil setting up some delusive target of something that has nothing to do with reality—this is really something scientists are working on, and it's now getting all over the news, and we will be introduced to this by the Media in such a manipulative manner that we eventually will welcome it and look forward to it—too many already do. The Global Elite knows how to manipulate the masses. Some people (like me and others) will fall between the crack and "get away" from it, so to speak, but they won't care. They will get what they want, and if a few refuse, so be it. You see, this has been planned for hundreds of years, and people can't see the cleverness of it all. The problem is that people can't think in terms of someone setting goals that span over several lifetimes: hundreds, sometimes thousands of years. It's not real to them, and those who are behind it know this. What is so hard to believe is that time is not the issue: those who want to manifest this are next to immortal and not from this world. Furthermore, they don't live by our local time system, unique to Earth. If the mass population understood this concept, it would be easier to see through the agendas played out.

Here is Time Magazine again, the same article:

> So if computers are getting so much faster, so incredibly fast, there might conceivably come a moment when they are capable of something comparable to human intelligence. Artificial intelligence. All that horsepower could be put in the service of emulating whatever it is our brains are doing when they create consciousness — not just doing arithmetic very quickly or composing piano music but also driving cars, writing books, making ethical decisions, appreciating fancy paintings, making witty observations at cocktail parties.[438]

---

[438] Ibid. op. cit.

And here are the punch lines (my emphases):

> If you can swallow that idea, and Kurzweil and a lot of other very smart people can, then all bets are off. From that point on, there's no reason to think computers would stop getting more powerful. They would keep on developing until they were far more intelligent than we are. Their rate of development would also continue to increase, because **they would take over their own development from their slower-thinking human creators. Imagine a computer scientist that was itself a super-intelligent computer.** It would work incredibly quickly.
>
> [...]
>
> Maybe we'll scan our consciousnesses into computers and live inside them as software, forever, virtually. Maybe the computers will turn on humanity and annihilate us. The one thing all these theories have in common is the transformation of our species into something that is no longer recognizable as such to humanity circa 2011. **This transformation has a name: the Singularity.**
>
> The difficult thing to keep sight of when you're talking about the Singularity is that **even though it sounds like science fiction, it isn't, no more than a weather forecast is science fiction. It's not a fringe idea; it's a serious hypothesis about the future of life on Earth.** There's an intellectual gag reflex that kicks in anytime you try to swallow an idea that involves super-intelligent immortal cyborgs, but suppress it if you can, because while the Singularity appears to be, on the face of it, preposterous, it's an idea that rewards sober, careful evaluation.[439]

This is very serious, people. Here they are introducing the idea of Singularity; first as something fantastic and amazing, but the more it will be discussed in the near future, if you look at the writing on the wall, the more incorporated these ideas will be into the common population. It is already starting. People are reading about it in magazines and newspapers and watch interviews on TV with brilliant inventors and scientists, but no one can wrap their heads around this concept and the consequences. Yet, the concept is easy, once the mind accepts to think in these terms: **our biological bodies as we know them will be obsolete! In the future, a body will be both biological and machine, and what happens then? The bodies are not sufficient enough to carry a soul fragment (human mind, personality, thinking unit)! Where will the soul go?**

As the same article above says, there are many theories about it and one is that we humans will merge with the computers and become super-

---

[439] Ibid. op. cit.

intelligent cyborgs. *This is the goal.* Of course, no one is telling you that the more machine-like a biomind becomes, the less chance someone can incarnate into it, which means there is no soul consciousness there; the consciousness which carries the intelligence will be artificial; thus, Artificial Intelligence.

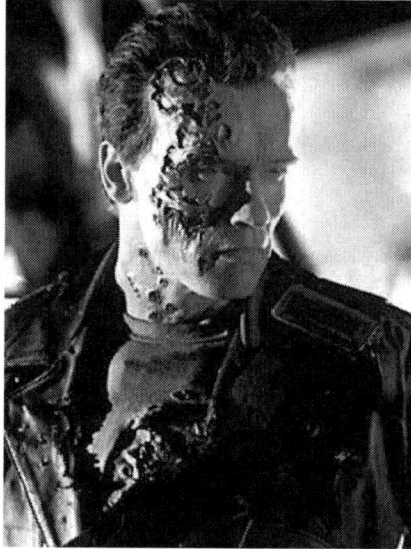

Figure 20.3: Arnold Schwarzenegger as the Terminator.

These days, robots and androids have appeared in many sci-fi movies since the 50s or so, but it has become more sophisticated over the last few years, where cyborgs often have taken the front seat in the plot. It started for real back in the 1980s, with Arnold Schwarzenegger's "Terminator" movies. Oh yes, this man, who later became the Mayor of California, knew more about what was behind the plot of these movies than people think. His goal is with the Global Elite, and he admires Hitler. He wants to be a dictator. Those are his own words.

Since 2008, there is a Singularity University which Kurzweil co-founded, hosted by NASA, with Google being a founding sponsor.[440]

We are still staying with the Time Magazine source a little longer because it is an excellent article on an extremely important subject. I encourage the reader to read the whole article online at http://battleofearth.wordpress.com/2011/03/06/2045-the-year-man-becomes-immortal/, but I am selecting the highlights here to make my point. Here is a very interesting part:

---

[440] Ibid.

The Singularity isn't a wholly new idea, just newish. In 1965 the British mathematician I.J. Good described something he called an "intelligence explosion":

Let an ultraintelligent machine be defined as a machine that can far surpass all the intellectual activities of any man however clever. Since the design of machines is one of these intellectual activities, an ultraintelligent machine could design even better machines; there would then unquestionably be an "intelligence explosion," and the intelligence of man would be left far behind. Thus the first ultraintelligent machine is the last invention that man need ever make.

The word singularity is borrowed from astrophysics: it refers to a point in space-time — for example, inside a black hole — at which the rules of ordinary physics do not apply. In the 1980s the science-fiction novelist Vernor Vinge attached it to Good's intelligence e-explosion scenario. At a NASA symposium in 1993, Vinge announced that "within 30 years, we will have the technological means to create super-human intelligence. Shortly after, the human era will be ended."[441]

We've discussed earlier that most science fiction writers don't make up their stories from nothing: they have inside knowledge gained from association with the Power Elite and their secret societies. Here again, we have a science fiction writer speaking at a NASA symposium. The indoctrination and manipulation must have many outlets and the ideas introduced in increments to the masses from many different angles.

Kurzweil has not been lazy since he appeared on TV in 1965. He has worked intensively on developing machine technology and AI ever since and received many awards, holds many patents, and, of course, made himself a fortune. President Bill Clinton gave him "The National Medal of Technology" in 1999, and Bill Gates called him "the best person I know at predicting the future of artificial intelligence."

Kurzweil says that the Singularity is not just an idea; it attracts people, and those people feel a bond with each other. Kurzweil calls it a "Community." "Once you decide to take the Singularity seriously, you will find that you have become part of a small but intense and globally distributed hive of like-minded thinkers known as Singularitarians."

Singularitarians (who are increasing in numbers) believe in technology to shape our future. And don't think twice about it: these people, who are obsessively pushing machine technology and the Singularity in particular, did incarnate here with the purpose of steering us in this direction. We will see many, many more people promoting this future, and our children who are growing up now during the nanosecond, if they are not educated as to what is happening, will fall into the trap. It's enough to go out for a walk or

---

[441] Ibid. op. cit.

drive your car around; you will see teenagers everywhere texting and twitting at the same time as they are walking. Many of them are totally caught up in what they are doing and don't even notice what is happening around them. This world, which I am writing from, is beginning to cease to exist for the younger generation. I often see them in groups, where most of them are either on the cellphone or texting, not engaged in any conversation with friends walking beside them. I have seen them many times crossing the street, forgetting to look for cars. It's come to a point where the drivers pay extra attention when they see teenagers coming because they are aware of this problem.

Parents have an enormous responsibility right now to educate their children and not let them get all these new toys for their amusement. We need to understand that this is all a giant setup, where one thing is connected to another. We are kept busy, so we don't get a chance to reflect, and if we're busy making a living in an incredibly fast pace, we don't have time for our children the way we should and must. With having children comes an enormous responsibility—more so now than ever.

If we only slow down for a while, we'll see what we're caught up in and hopefully will understand the seriousness of it. When things around us speed up, it's our duty to slow down. The children are our future, and if we choose to look the other way and think that electronics is just the signs of our times and natural human progression, which is what Dr. Kurzweil wants us to believe, we are helping forces who have no empathy for our species—only to implement their own imperatives on us, imperatives that eventually will cause our demise as biological entities. We have been asleep for millennia, but now we have no choice but to wake up.

This whole thing with machine technology and the Singularity leads to another subject, which goes hand in hand with the former; it's about longevity and immortality.

The Singularity University holds annual summits, and the following was discussed during the 2010 summit:

> After artificial intelligence, the most talked-about topic at the 2010 summit was life extension. Biological boundaries that most people think of as permanent and inevitable Singularitarians see as merely intractable but solvable problems. Death is one of them. Old age is an illness like any other, and what do you do with illnesses? You cure them. Like a lot of Singularitarian ideas, it sounds funny at first, but the closer you get to it, the less funny it seems. It's not just wishful thinking; there's actual science going on here.[442]

This is what I mean when I say the world will split in two: the Machine World and the World of Natural Evolution. People are afraid of death only

---

[442] Ibid. op. cit.

because it's a mystery; they don't know what will happen afterwards. Still, with a little research, it's easy to find out that death is not something to fear, quite the opposite. I have written a lot about it in previous papers. However, the fear of not existing anymore and the loss of relatives and friends make people attracted to ideas like the Singularity, where their lifespan can be extended with many extra years, and perhaps by then, technology has come to a point where immortality is possible, which is also something Dr. Kurzweil and other "Singularitisists" are "predicting."

You can see where this is going. It's a trap, because what they are creating is an artificial, super-intelligent race, which can be programmed as a hive community, where All is One, but in an artificial hive-mind way, and where everybody is becoming disconnected from the Source Energy. Their intelligence is synthetic but intelligent, emotionless and soulless. Your spirit/information cloud can no longer manifest in a physical body. Is this the future we want? If people really thought about it this way, who would want it? The problem is that those who fear death so much that they fall for this won't even read papers and books like this. Still, it's their choice. In a Free Will Universe, like our own, anything goes, but there are always consequences for everything we're doing. There are no free rides.

The alternative, of course, is to evolve naturally, with minimum machine technology, if at all. We have our biological body, our mind, soul, and spirit working together to find enlightenment and higher realms of existence through experiences and cognition. Our DNA is reactivating more and more as we learn, and we will learn to become multidimensional again, *with and due to* our thoughts and emotions, not *without* them.

The choice for me is easy.

Artificial Life Created, Called "Cynthia"

An article was published, originally in "Science," telling us that "researchers have constructed a bacterium's 'genetic software' called 'Cynthia' and transplanted it into a host cell.

The resulting microbe then looked and behaved like the species 'dictated' by the synthetic DNA." This team of scientists was led by Dr. Craig Venter of the J Craig Venter Institute (JCVI) in Maryland and California. The scientists have put two methods together to create a "synthetic cell."

> "As soon as this new software goes into the cell, the cell reads [it] and converts into the species specified in that genetic code."

> [...]

> "This is the first time any synthetic DNA has been in complete control of a cell," said Dr Venter.

'New industrial revolution.'"[443]

This mean science has revealed they are now able to create synthetic life forms paving the way for designer organisms that are built rather than evolved. They are now about to build life from scratch: the New Human!

Michio Kaku, professor of Physics, and well known by many for his best seller, "Parallel Worlds," went live on Fox News, comparing this new revelation like the biggest discovery since the splitting of the atom.[444] He compares it with downloading apps to a cellphone, and in this case they took a cell from a goat and "downloaded" new DNA, which they then programmed, but yes, they used human DNA as well. The point is, says Professor Kaku, that it is artificial. Both he, Dr. Craig, and others are promoting this as a potential solution (or partial solution) to global warming(!), which is another scam. Even the oil industry is interested. But none of these scientists are really discussing the ethical and moral parts of this in any great detail. What else can it be used for? When asked about the ethical issues, they say these have been discussed thoroughly among scientists. Where? Behind locked doors? The details of these discussions have not, as far as I know, been made official. But just the mentioning of having discussed them calms most of the population down, they accurately believe. People can go back to sleep because the "experts" are taking care of their future for them.

When asked by the Fox News reporter if this is not some kind of "Jurassic Park experiment" (good question), Kaku reassures us that you can recall a car, for example, but not a life form. In other words, he says it's not going to be used to replicate the human biokind, although he admits to that this kind of research can have "unintended consequences." Kaku is still on the fence regarding this research, he says. I would suggest, he's not on the fence about it. He is working for the Machine Kingdom and will become their spokesperson in popular media. He has the charisma necessary to seduce the masses, and this is what he is incrementally being used for. By "being on the fence" he can attract those who are "being on the fence" and eventually win them over. [445]

To put this in a metaphysical perspective, the Pleiadians, in a lecture from 2010 tell us there are time-jumpers; people from our future who are

---

[443] http://www.smeggys.co.uk/viewtopic.php?f=47&t=16241&p=316853

[444] http://futurepredictions.com/2011/06/19/future-predictions-new-artificial-life-form-created-first-synthetic-cell-cynthia-created-by-emailing-genetic-code-replicates-billions-of-times-in-lab/

[445] He has since then made up his mind 100% and is now whole-heartedly promoting the Singularity. Smart move: I believe he was in on it to begin with, but pretended to be a skeptic who changed his mind, so the public would believe in the Singularity even more solidly, *WP 2024.*

returning to our time to steal human female eggs and interfere with our evolution because they themselves have become a totally synthetic life form, like metallic skeletons we see in sci-fi movies. They come to try and reestablished their DNA to become biological entities again. These entities, on one of our future timelines, took the microchip, the brilliance of electronics, and abdicated their own biology.[446]

Anyone can make any decision they want, but what I like to stress is that we are at a crossroads *right now,* where we *must* decide which way to go, and whatever choice we make, we have to live with the consequences. Before we make any decision, it's therefore very wise to consider all factors involved.

The Pleiadians also bring up "Cynthia" in a few of their lectures, and although this story got kind of "buried" by the Media after a while, the Pleiadians see it as a tipping point in the human history.[447] It's the catalyst forcing us to make a choice. Very soon, more sophisticated information will be released. Of course, it's already researched and ready to go. All that is needed is to seduce humankind into accepting it. Michio Kaku and his cohorts we will see more and more of in the very near future, spamming our news channels and in series like those on the Discovery Channel.

Smurf's Village

If we as grown-ups start thinking about this, it's quite astonishing. While the parents are doing something else, the kids are playing Smurf's Village on iTunes. This game is about getting the most "smurfberries"—that's how you become the most powerful person in this game. But don't think it's free. Here is the price list:

1. BUCKET OF SMURF...$4.99
2. BUSHEL OF SMURFB...$9.99
3. BARREL OF SMURFB...$24.99
4. BUCKET OF SMURF...$4.99
5. WAGON OF SMURFB...$99.99
6. BUSHEL OF SMURFB...$11.99
7. WHEELBARROW OF ...$49.99
8. WHEELBARROW OF ...$59.99
9. BARREL OF SMURFB...$29.99[448]

---

[446] The Pleiadians, the September 19, 2010 session, "Exuberance", CD 1, Track 2.

[447] The Pleiadians, the June 7, 2010 session, "Moon Musings #56", Track 15.

[448] http://itunes.apple.com/us/app/smurfs-village/id399648212?mt=8

There was an article at MacLife and other places, where this horrendous game was exposed. An 8 year old child charged their parents credit card for $1,400 to buy delicious smurfberries in a game that is designed for 4 year olds (who normally can't read).[449] But this is not an exception: Children as early as the age of 5 have racked their parents' credit cards.[450]

Let's stop here for a while and reflect. First of all, think back to when you were 5 years old. Many children couldn't even read at that age, much less have the grasp of how to use a credit card. We didn't even know what it was and how money worked, other than that we perhaps got a small allowance to buy a magazine or some candy once a week. These kids, however, are very "profound" and know how to do these things. It's not a coincidence, it's per design. Babies are born into this era to play out theirs and our collective karma, decided upon in the afterlife. Much of this is going back to the Atlantean Era, where technology, to a large degree, caused its destruction. These babies, when they grow up to be little kids, know instinctively how to use technology. We, as parents, can only watch in awe. What takes us a long time to grasp, they get the hang of in seconds. If you, as an adult, need help to fix your electronic device, don't go to the manufacturer or a repairman, go to your kids; they can fix it in no-time. These little kids will be the front people in the new Machine Kingdom.

As a side note, let's go back to "Smurf Village." What do you get for $1,400? A lot of smurfberries. What are they? Expensive, wonderfully tasting berries? No, they are *nothing* besides imaginary berries in an electronic game. But to the kids, these berries are real. This is what machine technology does. People start living in a totally new matrix, which is electronic in nature. They disappear into a computer screen and start living the holographic life inside it and forget the life outside. Many parents may recall the times when they had to drag the kids from the computer games, their iPod, and cellphones etc. Then, when they return to your reality, they are not very responsive. They want to go back to "the other world," which is more appealing to them. Can anyone see where this is intentionally leading to? And how can someone get away with selling illusionary smurfberries for a shocking price to 4 year old and up without going to jail? The scary part is that the consciousness of the kids transfers into the computer screen, and this virtual reality becomes conscious. This is not science fiction, as you can see: *it happens now.*

Wars are raging on the planet as usual; that's nothing new. But there is another, more covert Electronic War going on behind our backs, that in

---

[449] http://www.maclife.com/article/news/
8yearold_girl_racks_1400_bill_buying_smurfberries_smurfs_village
[450] Pleiadians, the January 8, 2011 session, "Into the Rapids," CD 2, Track 11.

the extension is much more devastating.

WikiLeaks and a Flashback to the Atlantic Technology Era

Fairly recently, at the time of this writing, WikiLeaks leaked a lot of supposedly classified information, some 90,000 pages, among other things, of what was going on in Pakistan and so forth. Everybody was all wound up about this and wanted to know what was in these papers. But after a while we noticed that it wasn't that hot and exciting, really. It wasn't so much about what was released but what these 90,000 papers represented, of what *could* be leaked. What is there if you push buttons and know how to do it. Because today, everything is stored along "electronic highways".

Things have changed rapidly since the computers were introduced in society and the Internet became accessible to almost everybody on the planet. Of course, almost all of this is alien technology, received through TTPs (Technology Transfer Programs), but there is more to it: it's an old dramatization—an old civilization once again coming to life, and history eerily repeats itself.

Back in the Atlantean Era (if we talk about the Atlantean Era as the time just before the Deluge—there were more than one Atlantis, and they were not all in this dimension or on this planet), the Anunnaki had a similar technology, with electronic highways. They had their records, their blueprints, and their patterns to build civilizations, to map the heavens, and to understand agriculture, metallurgy etc. They stored this information on something they called *meš* (pronounced, mesh, like in *she*). And they fought over them, sometimes punishing each other with death penalty if they stole another being's master meš. If you recall, I wrote about this in the Anunnaki chapters, when Anzu stole the meš to the super-computer system from the En.lil, and eventually was punished with a death sentence. The Anunnaki stored their history and everything else on meš; everything was recorded. The problems they had was that, just like us, they had secret information stored there, which those who were not initiated wanted to take part in, so there was a constant struggle to keep this information safe.

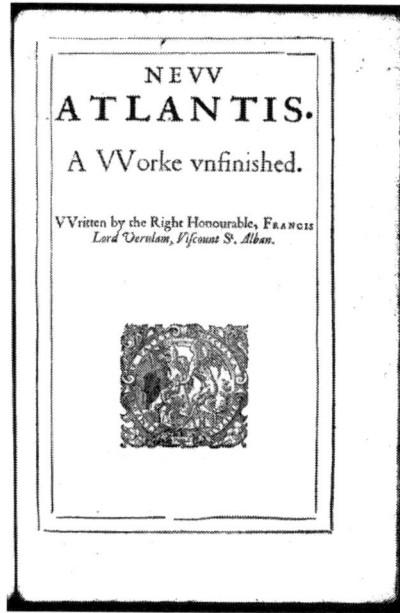

Figure 20.4: "The New Atlantis," by Sir Francis Bacon.

In this respect, nothing has changed. We are still playing the same games as the gods of old. It should not come as a surprise when we realize that some of them are still here. However, if we continue playing the games they set up for us, we will not only bring about a New Atlantis, with all its negative sides, leading to another disaster, but this time it will be ten times worse. [I would go so far as to say that the Singularity most likely will be the very end of humankind, once and for all. More about this in recent work and in the books that follow in this series, *WP 2024*].

Long before the American Revolution, when Freemasonry took over America, the dream of the New Atlantis had already been planned in secret behind the scenes for hundreds of years (officially), and thousands of years (unofficially). Sir Francis Bacon wrote about the vision of the New Atlantis[451] and that it would be set up in the future. Manly P. Hall, the Honorary Freemason,[452] who was perhaps the leading expert on Freeasonry all times, also wrote about the New Atlantis, and that it was finally accomplished by the take-over of the North American continent, which eventually became the United States of America. Hall was potentially murdered for leaking information that was supposed to be held secret. We owe much to this fantastic scholar.

---

[451] http://en.wikipedia.org/wiki/New_Atlantis
[452] Manly P. Hall (1944, 1972), "The Secret Destiny of America."

I said "took over America" in the last paragraph because that's of course what happened. This was Native American land, brutally raped and plundered by so-called civilized men, and entire invaluable spiritual cultures were destroyed to the core, and only remnants of the old wisdom of the Native Americans live on. We got our Atlantis, and Bacon would maybe have been able to finish his book if he were alive. Now, what are we going to do with it? Are we going to let history repeat itself?

Technology and Longevity

Longevity is the big issue for humankind; at least for those in power who serve the gods. How can we extend our lifespan and become immortal, just like the gods? Immortal in the sense that we can live perhaps a million years or more.

The writer and researcher, Nigel Kerner, writes:

> A body vastly enhanced through biotech and nanotech may suffice to extend life spans indefinitely, but the ultimate leap is to transcend biology entirely. Before 2050, Kurzweil predicts that AI and nanotech will have advanced so far that his brain, with its memories, capabilities and characteristics, can be reduced to pure information and rebooted in a non-biological format, be it a supercomputer, a real or virtual body, or a swarm of nanobots.[453]

Being 3rd Density beings, we have separated ourselves from cosmos, and our longevity has decreased since ancient times. Now we're coming to a point where we are building our world on itsy-bitsy pieces called nanoparticles. This exploration into the nanoworld is creating tremendous problems in the food supply, in peoples bodies; you have these nanoparticles, and these nanoproducts. Nanotechnology was not approached with any care at all, and this is going to create a very devitalized probability in the future for those who will be unable to extricate themselves or to pull their energy away from that probability and move towards a different one: one that is more connected to cosmos and connected to nature. Science is talking about "junk-DNA" and have no clue it is in *that* the solution lies. We don't need any kind of technology to activate our dormant DNA, and we will go into this in depth in a future book. The less technology oriented we become, the more the DNA can reconnect with the Universe, so instead of adding technology to improve our lives, we should diminish it. And we don't need nanotechnology to

---

[453] Nigel Kerner: "2012—And Man Shall Walk as Machine?" http://battleofearth.wordpress.com/2011/03/24/2012-and-man-shall-walk-as-machine/

extend our lives; it is done in a natural way, something for scientists to think about. Dr. Bordon, in his essay, "The LINK" reveals that the Nibiruans are extending their lives significantly, and are becoming in ONENESS as a species, probably by using nanotech; and they are inhaling gold to extend their lives as well.[454] Now they want to introduce these technologies here on Earth, so at least the Elite, and those who can pay for it, get a longer life than the poor guy with minimal wage, who is standing on his feet all day at McDonalds under tremendous stress.

And who are the Ruling Elite, the Powers That Be, really? Think about it. They are 13 main ruling families of tremendous fortune, and they interbreed with each other. Why do they want to keep their bloodline so intact? The answer is simple: These families, who are set here to rule while the Ša.A.M.i. are gone elsewhere, are Ša.A.M.i./Anunnaki hybrids. At least half (probably more) of their genome is Anunnaki. Then it's easy to see what the Anunnaki traits are; just watch the Global Elite to understand the Anunnaki mindset (Alex Collier wrote an excellent article as well on this subject, which you can read here: http://battleofearth.wordpress.com/2010/03/19/alex-collier-on-reptilians-jehovah-terran-control-groups-and-derivative-concepts/)

Are you one of these people who has a hard time looking at details as you drive, do data entry on the computer at work, when you have a job situation which requires multitasking? In situations like these, are you making errors and feel stupid that you never "learn?"

It requires a whole different consciousness to be detail oriented in this high-tech society with a fast pace and multitasking than it does to take your horse and ride out on the prairies for five days. The details you pay attention to are very different from these in the high-tech society. Some people have a very easy time adjusting to high-tech, and their brains can do all these things rapidly and simultaneously—not a big deal for them. But people like me, whose mind is working more multi-dimensionally, have a hard time adjusting, and also a reluctance and resistance to it. I want less of that, not more. Would you agree?

3-D reality has come to a dead end. Like the Pleiadians say, it has nowhere to pull its juice from (Pleiadian Lecture [8/13/2011-8/14/2011]: "Awakening to the Sun," CD 3, Track #5). People are mixed up and can't find their meaning in life; they don't know how to heal themselves anymore.

It's true that our biology was tampered with, and our lifespan reduced significantly, as they went on with their experiments. They didn't want us to live too long either because we multiplied uncontrollably. The Bible

---

[454] "Gold" must not be taken literally. The "gods" are not inhaling the gold metal—they are inhaling humans, i.e., *human energy*. We humans are the "gold," *WP 2024*.

talks about how humans (hybrids, actually), lived for 900 years or more; sometimes thousands of years, such as the patriarchs, who had to live a long time to be able to complete their tasks, but some Anunnaki were not pleased with the increase of the human population. We became cumbersome to handle and they let most of us be wiped out by the Flood.

It's been known for a long time (and I've been writing about it and posted relevant articles on http://illuminati-news.com) that the Power Elite want to reduce the population; some say to a manageable 500 million people. How do they do that? By war, famine and disease? Weather control and vaccination? Yes, that's part of it, but it won't do the trick. The Elite are basically waiting for prophecy to come to its conclusion. That will reduce the population drastically.

For the survivors (and there will not be many if they get their ways), the new technology is now introduced and the future visualized. What the Power Elite and their Masters apparently seem to want is a population large enough to control, united with technology and made into half machines, half human, or perhaps 100% synthetic, with no means to mass produce.

What Nigel Kerner talks about in his article (above) is how the use of nanotechnology and biotech will "complete the cycle," and humanity will merge into Oneness. Again, where have we heard that before? Remember Dr. A.R. Bordon's "The Link." On page 55, he says that in one of the Link Plenum Meetings with off-world beings, he heard a spokesperson for the Nibiruans saying that their species have almost completed their cycle into Oneness, probability with the help from nanotech. I am quoting Dr. Bordon:

> Ša.A.Mi.s too have been undergoing the changeover from disconnected bodyminds to a common, or a biomind of the whole biokind. It is reported by members who have attended the conferences that they are near the completion of their cycle to oneness, wherein all knowledge and mind resources are used in service to the common. This, it was said, can only be possible when the diversity of biominds of each member remains an individuality while simultaneously being interconnected to the Ša.A.Mi. all-one by low-powered, low-energetic means that utilizes the planet's life belt energetics – something akin to what Earth enjoys in the form of Schumann resonance. There is yet much we don't quite understand about their system of oneness, as there are technologies used to enhance the common biomind that are beyond our level of technology at this time. However, we do now possess a theoretical understanding of how it all works.[455]

---

[455] A.R. Bordon (2007): "The Link," p.42, op. cit.

To me, as I've said before, it's not a desirable way to evolve as a species. I am not subscribing to neither nanotech, nor biotech, or any other tech I am aware of to evolve our species. They are manipulating us into becoming a hive society, where all minds work as one, controlled by an alien race.

What about if the gods are not able to evolve in the same way we are? Perhaps they were not created to do that because *their* creator gods created them for *their* purpose, which was not to have them evolve and ascend like us? So they use machine technology to reach what we can do naturally. They want our basic biology but can't merge it with their own because their biological structure is different. They can only evolve up to a certain point. Knowing that there is no way they can reach our potentials, they do what they can with their own genome, but on the other hand, they are created for power and control, so therefore they can't accept that we evolve differently from them. Besides, they feed from the fear they are creating in us, so we have become their food source. They don't want us to evolve, because when we're out of their frequency fence we are out of reach for them. They manipulated our DNA so that we wouldn't evolve and ascend easily, but our 12 strand DNA was already in our bodies, and they, to their own misfortune, only have 11 strands.[456]

This, I believe, is what we have to face: We have a lot of Anunnaki DNA inside us, but we also have DNA from the earlier, more spiritually uplifted gods, with our junk DNA still inactivated to its full potential. Do we want to become like the Anunnaki and achieve longevity by taking shortcuts through nano- and biotech, or do we want to use free flowing, fluid energy to reach higher forms of existence naturally? In addition, knowing how it usually works, artificial longevity through bio- and nanotech may be something only available for the Elite (they are already getting older than the average man, if you've noticed, e.g. Bush Sr., David Rockefeller, Henry Kissinger), and the virtual Machine World, the cyborg existence, may be for the masses. Whatever it may be, it gives me the shivers.

The question is: what future do we dream of? By this, I mean *both* in an awake state and in dream state. We have prophecies, but not everything is predestined. By choosing our future and dreaming it up, we create it. Like-mindedness will create a like-minded future.

Another big concern from my point of view is how technology achieved by TTPs can be used for warfare. What would stop the people who have access to this technology to create super-soldiers? This concern is very real; look at the drones they are using already. It's stone age in comparison, but we can see in what direction things are going.

---

[456] A'shayana Deane (2002): "Voyagers I + II."

It's therefore, in my subjective opinion, with all the above mentioned, discouraging to see respected researchers and writers like Neil Freer, who have done a great job with exposing alien visitors being worshipped as Gods in our past (and still are), and awoken people from the "godspell" we've been under, to promote artificial intelligence like he does on his website.[457] I encourage people to read it to make up their own minds, but I personally think he's on a dangerous path, and I hope people who have now woken up from the godspell also will wake up from the Artificial Intelligence spell.

Dr. Bordon and LPG-C have worked on longevity for about a decade, and Bordon replied to a comment on one of my blog entries about Dr. Kurzweil with the following statement:

> We are already becoming immortal — small steps at a time. We started a program ten years ago designed to achieve longevitility and the knowhow to access, affect, and when necessary change the information bandwidth of our RNA-DNA. You can read about this quiet revolution in The Coming Longevitality of the Earth Human Biomind (Lulu Press, lulu.com)."

> Immortal is one of those words poorly used. Often it's used to mean long living instead of never dying. Theoretically, a biological entity can be immortal provided certain things are part of the genetic make up of the body of that person. But for us today, we function on chromosomes that contain some 31,000 genes (plus some 3,000 genes in our mitochondria) and we biologically exist on 20 base aminoacids. That's us today. Question is, what can each of us do (instead of relying on what Kurzweil and the singularitarians propose: let's use technology to enhance and prolong our lives, such that the people will say we can be immortal. Good press, but that's about it.) If we use a generation (25 years) as a measure and begin teaching our kids what we started teaching the members of the experimental groups in our study, starting some ten years ago, how do we tell if their lives are being prolongued? Well, you can't well tell by using linear time. You have to go to other ways. One is the bioelectricity of the body, which is a good measure of the bioelectric age of a person (which is not the same as the time-linear age in years) (or revolutions around the sun). This measure can be given a larger frame of view: longevitality, or the amount of energy we have and keep at various points as bioelectric age by comparison to one's linear age. So you have a 60 year old woman who has the body of a 42 year old female, or a male who is 71 but has the body of a 54 year old male. The knowhow I mentioned before is the how to get to change your bioelectric age by using a number of ways to intervene on our body/minds to get them to

---

restore or even gain electrostatic energy in our cells, exercise routines that (combined with nutritional regimes fitted to the physical needs of a person) can result in body mass retention of the good kind (more protein, less body fat, keeping the numbers in the "good" range (triglys, ldl, ldh). All of this is possible. It takes a conscious decision and information.

All of the people participating are not rich, quite the contrary, they are middle class and also people working at McDonald's paycheck to paycheck. The thing that changed is their lifemind (mind time applied to keeping the body optimal), how they handle stress, how they consume health information that translates into what they need to do for themselves, to keep in track of what each of them want to do for their body/mind, their families, etc.

My argument with Ray is that relying on technology assist to reach instant longevitality doesn't necessary give us the time to change the mimes (belief systems) by which we live. That requires at least three generations (or 75 years). However, it is also possible to accelerate the bioelectric transformation of a generation and see in ten years some results that encourages the soul. On the average, 6.5 retroyears in ten years of participation. Let me translate this: this means experimental group participants are gaining an average of 6.5 years in bioelectric terms, so if a man was fifty when he joined and his wife was 47, subtract 6.5 from their linear ages and that will tell you the bioelectric age of the person.

This, in my opinion, is a much better way to achieve a longer lifespan; that in conjunction with activating the dormant DNA, which will automatically make us live longer.

A Multi-Dimensional Perspective on Nanotechnology

What happens now and will happen in the near future, if we are still speaking of technology, is nothing spontaneous. In certain terms, certain beings set up things already millions, sometimes billions of years ago to play out at a later time. Therefore, on a Multi-D level, the violence and technology spurts were planned to happen at certain local times (an easy task for beings who can look at things from another perspective than we presently can, trapped as we are in the local time system). So we have the Atlantean time with all its technology and violence, we have the Incas and the Aztecs, and the violence connected with them; we remember Hitler and Nazism, and last, but certainly not the least, we have the U.S. Government playing Gods, dramatizing the Atlantean period, now being relived again to give us a chance to clear a ten thousands of years old collective karma.

The Pleiadians asked an interesting question in one of their lectures, related to the above: "Which one of the civilizations will meet at the 'supernova point'?"[458] (The supernova point being 2012, when the wave of enlightenment will hit us; I'm sure this is the same wave LPG-C is talking about, which I discussed in an earlier paper). The answer is: all of them will, because time is simultaneous. And timelines will merge by 2012 and are already in the process of doing so.

Technology and certain key events that were (and are) meant to happen are hidden at certain frequencies. Just like we hide what we don't want others to find in locked cabinet, bank vaults etc., multidimensional beings in the past (in our term) hid what was not meant to be found right away at different frequency levels, and when certain people (or a percentage of the population) reached that frequency, what was hidden was suddenly found. This is another perspective of "alien technology." Great inventors, like Nikola Tesla, and thinkers like Pythagoras etc., have been said to have had alien invention with their discoveries. This is certainly true.

Many metaphysical sources mention the Anunnaki having encoded our DNA as well, so that at a certain time, certain codes are activated so we start inventing new technology or whatever they want us to achieve at a specific level of our development.

This is what could be called predestiny if you will; but remember that predestiny only works when consciousness is sleeping. If we wake up to the fact that we have been programmed, and that we live in a free will universe (something the gods have tried to override in our case, trying to make us predictable, in certain terms), we will see it's easy to step off the road we're traveling on, watching the "lorries roll by," tighten our backpack, and walk in the opposite direction, away from the road, and out into the unexplored wilderness. After a while, the sound of the lorries and cars rolling by fade and disappears. No one can force us to go in any direction than the one we choose—the gods can only control us through manipulation, tricking us into giving them our consent. It may sound too fantastic, but it's really basic, and it is working. Make a wish-list if you want to; put down what you really want for yourself and ask those around you to do the same. Then make this wish-list come true, item by item, by manifesting the thoughts into this reality. Once you do this; without using any effort, just light thoughts; your reality will change, little by little. Put your thoughts, emotions, intentions and your certainty behind the fact that this is how your life is going to be from now on, and nothing less than that. However, be realistic and don't make wishes that are too "way out there." I think you get the picture. Be clear and feel gratitude for what you have, and when you make wishes for your present and your future, do so

---

[458] Pleiadians: "Through the Eye of the Needle," CD 2, Track 11-12 (lecture held on October 2, 2010).

without creating counter-intentions, telling you *why* this or that is too hard to accomplish, e.g. "what will my parents say?" or "what will happen with my friendship with John?" etc. These objections, or counter-intentions, are *exactly* what keep people from getting what they wish for—instead, they often get the opposite. Your goals are *your* goals, and you have the perfect right to achieve them. It is your responsibility to do so because that's what you're here for. We can choose not to, and no "God" or "Devil" will punish you, but you will waste our time and suffer more.

Every day we wake up, it's an excellent idea to set the direction for the day. Say to yourself, "This day is going to be a great day where everything is working in my favor." This really sets the tone. Think the thought, manifest it, and let it go. Over time, and by doing this every morning, you will see how your life changes for the better.

So, why am I bringing all this up while talking about machine technology? Because, like with everything, technology can either enhance life or be used to control and enslave. In this paper, we have gone through how certain forces want to use it and *are* using it. Do we want it? Is it ethical? Moral? If you would choose, is that the future you want to see? Or does the multidimensional future, using the Third Eye and the Heart Chakra in particular, sound like a more exciting journey?

The choice is yours to make, but think before you make it, think long and hard. My choice is simple.

INDEX

3-D body, 42
3rd Density, 79, 85, 138, 139, 155,
    172, 221, 280, 351, 352, 353, 436,
    457, 474
3rd density/dimension, 452
3rd dimension, 80, 81, 117, 118, 119,
    133, 412, 419
3rd Dimension, 353

4

4 Dimensional space/time, 7
4,000 years, 46, 301
4.2 to 4.5 billion years ago, 194
40 million years, 221
400,000 years ago, 207
450,000 years ago, 149, 188, 197
4-D, 45, 85
4D universe, 53
4-space/time, 12, 17, 18, 20, 21, 22,
    26, 27, 57, 59, 80, 118, 168, 412,
    419
4-Space/Time, 21, 30, 34, 411
4th and 5th Dimensions, 74
4th Density, 85, 86

5

5,000 years ago, 189
500 million people, 476
500,000 years, 43, 47, 149, 175, 260,
    301
5-6,000 years ago, 178
570 million years ago, 170

6

60 epithets of Nannar, 332
65-70 million years ago, 171
6-space/time, 419
6th Density, 82, 83, 85

7

7 feet or taller, 284
7 superdomains, 407, 411
7 Superdomains, 11, 15, 18
7 superuniverses, 11, 60, 62, 407,
    411
7 system, 64
7 Tributary sites, 340

7 Trumpets Technologies, 340
7,000, 91, 105, 131, 132
7,000 case studies, 286
75,000 years, 47, 85

8

8,866 years ago, after the Deluge,
    420

9

9 foot giant, 159
9,500 BC, 118
9/11, 298, 420, 454
94 million years ago, 172

A

A History of Man, 122, 125
A.R. Bordon, 1, 5, 8, 11, 13, 17, 28,
    31, 34, 54, 55, 59, 145, 184, 191,
    286, 301, 302, 308, 318, 357, 368,
    415, 429, 432, 442
A'shayana Deane, 64, 133, 161, 174,
    340, 400, 426, 428, 429, 440, 458,
    477
AA, 337, 338, 346, 350, 354
Aaron, 264
AB.ZU, 201
Abael, 222, 223, 224
ABC News, 357
abductees, 155, 185, 339, 422
abducting humans, 187
abductions, 155, 184, 285
Abel, 222
Abgal, 200, 205, 208
Above Top Secret Forum, 84
Abraham, 66, 251, 254, 255, 256,
    257, 261
Abu, 234
abuse, 173
Abuzu, 212
abyss, 127
Abzu, 37
Accelerated Intelligence, 343, 382,
    394, 401
Accelerated Learning, 382
Achilles, 328
ACIO, 132, 319, 335, 337, 338, 339,
    340, 342, 343, 344, 347, 349, 355,

492

Free Will, 156, 158, 165, 171, 418, 468
Freedom Key, 339
Freeman, 300
Freemasonic Global Network, 356
Freemasonic Pyramid, 312
Freemasonic scam, 299
Freemasonry, 177, 267, 299, 356, 362, 473
Freemasons, 126, 312, 358, 362, 363
Freewill Universe, 65
Freewill Zone, 303
frequencies, 19, 22, 98, 121, 153, 154, 176, 181, 278, 326, 361, 397, 411, 425, 444
frequency, 14, 17, 18, 19, 35, 36, 42, 44, 45, 50, 53, 60, 83, 87, 92, 98, 118, 119, 121, 138, 143, 166, 168, 169, 172, 173, 176
frequency fence, 42, 168, 176, 203, 220, 457, 459, 477
frequency net, 168
Frequency Net, 168
frequency prison, 168, 281
frequency range, 35, 36, 42
frequency shield, 282
Fritz Springmeier, 299
Fulford, 358, 367
future, ii, 1, 7, 8, 11, 30, 36, 38, 39, 41, 47
FYEO, 344, 345

G

G8, 317
galactic and intergalactic species, 104, 207
Galactic beings think 'long thoughts', 173
galactic center, 410, 446
Galactic Center, 48, 78, 166, 185, 220, 306, 327, 397, 399, 400, 410
Galactic Federation, 289
Galactic History, 144, 145
galactic members, 287
galactic wars, 163, 169, 174
Galactic wars, 144
Galactic Wars, 155
galaxies, 18, 22, 28, 37, 46, 54, 57, 58, 72, 118, 155, 158, 278, 286
galaxy, 19, 30, 31, 34, 48, 54, 60, 61, 62, 141, 142, 146, 148, 154, 155,
494

156, 158, 168, 171, 180, 181, 184, 198, 211, 392, 393, 395, 396, 406, 410, 415, 416, 424, 425, 436
Galzu, 227, 228, 239, 251, 254, 301
game, 29, 44
gamma rays, 48, 166, 220, 306, 327
Gandalf, 103
Garden of Eden (Edin)., 330
Gateway to Heaven, 243
GE, 123
Gehennom, 127
General Relativity, 147
genes, 136, 147, 160, 182, 183, 212, 228, 239, 251, 265
Genesis, 190, 214, 217, 218
genetic banks, 228
genetic engineering, 77, 120, 136, 157, 162, 180, 182, 185, 194
Genetic engineering, 182
Genetic Engineering, 155, 169
genetic entity, 123
genetic experiments, 156, 179, 184, 214, 277
genetic experiments on humans, 179
genetic hybridization, 340, 341, 392
genetic manipulation, 170, 171, 186, 187, 189
Genetic Manipulation System, 133
genetic memories, 43
genetic tinkering, 157, 162
geneticists, 219
genetics, 46
genocide, 231, 373, 374, 435
genome, 399, 475, 477
George LoBuono, 134, 141, 153, 155, 180, 181, 184, 185, 191, 449
George Orwell, 121
German, 359, 434
Germane, 85, 145, 168, 180, 181, 182
Geshtinanna, 237
ghosts, 53
Giant Skulls, 278
Giant Sun, 78
giants, 156, 158, 196, 269, 277, 278
Gibil, 206, 233, 316
Gilgamesh, 246, 247, 248
Global Elite, 74, 120, 211, 223, 224, 293, 297, 298, 299, 327, 328, 330, 353, 356, 377, 433, 447
Global Elite Companies, 293
Global Theocratic Movement, 365,

H

J

173, 174, 175, 176, 177, 180, 184,
193, 196, 211, 212, 213, 219, 220,
280, 339, 344, 397, 398, 399, 409,
426, 447
Lyricus, 60, 62, 63, 64, 120, 133, 154,
351
Lyricus Teaching Order, 60, 62, 63,
120, 133, 154
Lyssa Royal, 145, 153, 175, 179, 180,
181, 440

M

M-105, 416
M-51, 415
M-65, 416
M-66, 416
M-95, 416
M-96, 416
machine, 9, 77, 85, 165, 166, 167,
186, 187, 344, 346, 395, 414, 417,
419, 433
Machine Kingdom, 166, 185, 345,
455
machine parts instead of real organs,
166
machine technology, 165, 167
Machine World, 452, 456, 468, 477
Machines, 453, 455
MacLife, 471
macro cosmos, 75
macro-quantum, 22
Madame Blavatsky, 351
Mafia, 316
Magellan Clouds, 425
magicians, 264
magnesium based, 32
magnetic field, 29
magnetic fields, 25, 173
Mahu Nahi, 343, 354, 391, 393, 394,
399, 400, 407, 410, 427, 428, 429
Mahunahi, 353
Maia, 168
mainstream physics, 53
Makers of Wings and Other Things,
427
Maldek, 148, 149, 157, 161, 173, 175
mammals, 45, 156, 170, 182
Manifest Production Observership,
46
Manifestation, 12, 14, 16, 57
Manly P. Hall, 473

Manuel Lamiroy, 145
Marciniak, 42, 59, 64, 154, 159, 167,
175, 176
Marduk, 37, 40, 126, 148, 188, 189,
201, 204, 206, 208, 209, 210, 218,
219, 221, 224, 225, 226, 227, 228,
233, 234, 235, 236, 237, 238, 239,
240, 241, 242, 243, 244, 246, 248,
249, 250, 251, 252, 253, 254, 259,
260, 261, 292, 293, 296, 297, 298,
300, 301, 308, 310, 311, 312, 313,
314, 315, 316, 319, 320, 327, 328,
329, 330, 331, 332, 355, 356, 359,
362, 363, 365, 368, 376, 377, 403,
426, 431, 432, 433, 434, 437, 439,
440, 441, 442, 446, 447, 448
Marduk Ra, 189, 244
Mardukian Anunnaki, 340
Marduk's loyal Lords, 298
marijuana, 172
marine life with a hard skeletal part,
170
Mark Hempel, 346, 348, 349, 351,
353, 354, 407, 410, 428
Mars, 124, 136, 148, 149, 157, 161,
173, 195, 199, 203, 204, 207, 209,
210, 212, 225, 227, 228, 231, 239,
272, 273, 274, 275, 276
Marsbase, 234
Martian Cave Dwellings, 272
Maryland, 468
masculine, 57
Masonic, 379
mass consciousness, 76, 78, 83, 166,
177
massless ontoenergetic entities., 35
Master of Earth, 225, 226
Master Teacher, 104
mathematics, 14, 52, 224
matrix, 13, 30, 35
Matrix, 14, 17, 39, 44, 46, 59, 83,
133, 137, 167, 168, 169, 201, 243,
314, 408, 456, 457
Matrix movies, 44
Matt 10, 69
Matt 26, 69
matter, 4, 10, 11, 15, 16, 22, 25
Matter, Energy, Space and Time, 123
Maurice Chatelain, 267
Mayan Calendar, 47
Mayor of California, 465
McDonald, 300

rocket scientist, 135
rocket ship, 198, 199
Rome, 201, 233, 270
Ronald Reagan, 354, 448
Roosevelt Roads, in northeast Puerto Rico, 321
Rosicrucian Order, 66, 177
Rosicrucian's, 267
Rothschild, 75, 299, 300, 363, 382
Rothschild's, 75
Roy Gordon, 319, 321
Roy W. Gordon, 319, 321, 323, 368, 369, 370
royal bloodline, 198
royal bloodlines, 226
Royal Council, 297
Royal Families, 49
royalties, 207
Ruling Elite, 300
Russel Miller, 135
Russell, 300
Russia, 63, 175, 196, 316, 325
RV, 6, 7, 396, 397, 425
RWG, 323, 324

S

S.A.A.L.M., 319, 320, 335, 355, 356, 357, 364, 366, 369, 370, 375, 376, 377, 379, 380, 382, 388, 403, 425
Ša.A.M.e., 188, 189, 192, 194, 204, 443
Ša.A.M.i, 174, 175
Ša.A.M.i., 174, 175, 189, 191, 193, 194, 195, 196, 197, 198, 200, 202, 203, 211, 213, 215, 221, 223, 252, 253, 255, 271, 283, 284, 285, 286, 287, 288, 289, 291, 292, 293, 294, 295, 297, 302, 307, 308, 312, 323, 330, 332, 340, 341, 351, 355, 404, 405, 406, 407, 432,433, 434, 435, 436, 439, 440, 441, 442, 443, 444, 446, 447, 448, 475
Ša.A.Me, 150
Sa.A.Mi, 39, 40
Ša.A.Mi, 301, 309, 310
Sa.a.mi., 269
Sabbath, 263
Sacsahuaman, 309
Sacsayhuaman, 438
SAM, 212, 323

Samech, 359, 362
SAMs, 225, 323, 325
San Antonio, TX, 325
šar, 195, 196, 200, 223, 271, 294
Sarah, 255, 256, 411, 415, 424
Sargon, 249, 250, 251
Sarpanit, 225, 227, 234, 235, 238, 241
šars, 194, 197
Sasha Lessin, 190, 196, 207, 253, 259, 260
Satan, 218, 219, 311, 314, 328, 330, 358, 364, 372, 378, 433
Satanic, 120
Satanist, 371
Satanists, 358
Satu, 234
Saturn, 41, 46, 122
Saudi Arabian peninsula, 231
sauroid, 32, 183
Sb galaxy, 415
Scandinavians, 167
schizophrenia, 218
schizophrenic, 72
School of Learning, 173
Schrödinger's Cat, 71
Schumann resonance, 301
Schumann's Resonance, 435
science, 1, 2, 3, 5, 7, 8, 9, 10, 11, 26, 27, 28, 48, 55, 61, 64, 119, 146, 173, 186, 191, 220, 268, 281, 284, 302, 337, 339, 353, 354, 360, 414, 415, 419, 451, 453, 458, 463, 464, 466, 467, 469, 471
Science Papers, 1, 3
scientific, 3, 8, 10, 11, 14, 60, 89, 145, 146, 147, 186
Scientific American, 272
scientologist, 6
Scientology, 6, 92, 122, 123, 135, 136
sci-fi, 414
screens, 99, 108, 117, 124
scribe, 83
Second Coming, 330, 359, 369, 441
Second Level of Learning, 42, 63, 145, 147, 162, 169, 177, 190, 264, 271, 436
secret orders, 177
secret societies, 79, 135, 189, 267, 312, 327, 413, 439, 442
secret society, 217